P9-DMJ-376

CONTENTS

LISTINGS

INTRODUCTION

Eric Bradley

YOU'RE HOLDING the most complete visual reference to the world of fine art and collectibles available on the market today. Welcome to the latest *Antique Trader Antiques & Collectibles Price Guide*. As the No. 1 selling reference book of its kind, this big volume is overflowing with a broad range of items collected today – and each entry is illustrated with a full-color photograph to help you know what you're looking at.

Within this guide you will encounter some of the most important and sought-after collectibles to appear at auctions, shops, and shows during the last year. These pieces were selected from millions of items that have sold as part of the estimated $53.9 billion worldwide fine art and collectibles market. Some items will be very familiar – in fact, you may already own them – but there are others that are extraordinary and unique in their own right. These precious objects have been cared for and cherished and passed down for generations.

In addition to this annual guide, our staff produces *Antique Trader* magazine, which gives us a unique perspective on the market. A few trends surfaced during the past year, and we were surprised to see the number of categories being actively pursued by collectors that are on the move. From our vantage point, the collectibles hobby is certainly seeing an exciting resurgence of new buyers and those curious about what they already own or have inherited.

Here are our annual picks of some of the hottest areas in the hobby:

Petroliana (signs, cans, globes, ephemera)	Early American bottles	Regional U.S. paintings
Advertising signs in all conditions	Neoclassical furniture (urban markets)	Beatles memorabilia
Asian decorative arts	Scientific models and instruments	Sports memorabilia (with the exception of sports cards from 1974 and later)
Southern furniture	Abraham Lincoln collectibles	High-grade comic books across all eras
Silver "smalls"	U.S. coins	Jewelry (especially large colored diamonds and gemstones)
Toys (wind-ups, high-end adult figures, cast iron)	Curiosities or vintage objects that defy classification	
Vintage Colt pistols	Fine and contemporary art by well-known artists	
Americana		

You might notice this list is a bit longer than last year's list. These selections are influenced by a number of market conditions, but last year three important factors rose to the surface as the chief influence behind prices:

SINGLE-OWNER COLLECTIONS ARE HOT

Collectors love a chance to be the first to tap into a collection, even if the collection has been fabled in story and song for many decades. Privately held, single-owner collections are commanding strong prices. When these collections come to market, collectors acutely feel the double-edged sword. Although it's troubling to realize these massive, carefully curated collections may likely never be assembled again, it's gratifying to see other collectors enjoy rare objects for the first time in decades. Perhaps that's why prices realized for these collections are on the climb.

DISTINCTIVE IN DEMAND

You might be surprised to learn that vintage urban bus passes are a hot new collectible among the Millennial generation. Or that rock and roll concert t-shirts and posters are on the upswing. Unusual and unique collections appeal to new generations, and their fresh perspectives make all of us look at old things in a new light. The constant in any new market trend is *condition* – the No. 1 arbiter of value in today's market. Except, that is, for metal and porcelain advertising signs. These signs in even poor condition are finding buyers these days; however, a common collectible in near-mint to mint condition demands a higher price. Serious collectors have picked a side in the "quantity vs. quality" debate and quality wins.

CONDITION HAS REDEFINED MARKETS

The rare U.S. coin market is recording record sales, and these results can be mainly credited to the top of the market. With interest rates still low, buyers are happy to pay top dollar for rare coins that have the potential of appealing to collectors in the future. This "best or nothing" mentality at the top of the market has put new pressure on all buyers, but sellers must tread carefully as well. Serious collectors are saving their dollars to buy the very best. Collectors who are ready to sell should thoughtfully study prices realized across a variety of platforms when deciding which method is best to disperse a collection.

This doesn't mean you should never consider purchasing an item in excellent to very good condition. Just know that your resale price may be closer to what you paid the first time around rather than the windfalls you see on reality TV shows.

Top shelf collectors are willing to pay what it takes to own the prime examples and this mentality is something to keep in mind when you're ready to make big purchases: Buy the best you can afford. Some categories have seen price declines in recent years: 20th century wicker furniture, 20th century factory-produced ceramics and glass, carnival glass, Coca-Cola memorabilia, Mickey Mouse toys, comic books from the 1990s and later.

While all these factors influence what people collect, dealers, auctioneers, and shop owners are changing how people buy and sell. It's easier than ever to start a collection or sell what you've got, and this means a host of new services to help. Here are four major developments from the past year:

Sales of fine art and collectibles greater than $1,000 are increasingly taking place at public auction. Owners of general antiques stores say they rarely sell items valued at over $500. Dealers who specialize in one category (such as perfume bottles or Satsuma porcelain) sell higher-ticket items at shows, although they confess prices are substantially increased to help them afford the cost to appear at the show in the first place.

We continue to see dealers adapt social media sites to help reach collectors, and vice versa. Dealers are finding ways to supplement sales between shows, and collectors are increasingly comfortable placing "bids" on Facebook flash sales and auction format postings. Folk art dealers have

▶ Rare Deldare matchbox holder and tray combo with "The Fallowfield Hunt" of horses, riders and hunting dogs, backstamp 1909 logo reading "Made at Ye Buffalo Pottery, Deldare Ware, Underglaze," artist signed M. Boom, excellent condition, 3" x 6-1/4" l. **$250**

Courtesy of Mark Mussio, Humler & Nolan

united to form a group on Facebook called Sold! On Country, Early Country & Primitive Antique Auctions. More than 3,500 members now participate in such sales, with many happy results on both sides of the transaction. Items are generally bid up to prices less than $500. The same is happening among toy collectors, sign dealers, and even with fans of vintage typewriters, among others.

Young collectors are coming into the hobby, and they are entering it through flea markets. Flea managers say their gates have never been bigger. If you believe as I do that a rising tide lifts all boats, this should be welcome news to both sellers and collectors. Those who are new to the hobby are comfortable spending a few hundred dollars at a flea market. Maybe they are drawn by low prices, or perhaps it's the lure of amazing finds still left to be discovered at flea markets: In the last two years alone, a Fabergé egg valued at $33 million was discovered at a flea market in the Midwest, and an early $13,000 Coca-Cola bottle from the 1880s was found in a New Mexico flea for $4.

"$ (Quadrant)," Andy Warhol (American, 1928-1987), 1982, screenprint in colors, ed. 51/60 (each print unique), 40" x 32"..**$75,000**

Courtesy of Heritage Auctions

Only truly distinctive or one-of-a-kind furniture items are selling, but they are selling. Nice examples of Southern furniture are bringing good prices, as are neoclassical examples. But mid-20th century revival pieces are not. Shoppers and decorators want personality and character that cannot be obtained through the latest IKEA catalog.

If any of the categories in this book pique your interest, there are a few things to keep in mind before you start collecting:

Buy what you like: You never hear someone on "Antiques Roadshow" say, "I bought this 20 years ago instead of padding my 401(k)." Collect what fascinates you. The increase in value will come later as you evolve from being an accumulator to a true collector – someone who seeks items in the very best condition by upgrading what he/she already owns. It doesn't matter what you're interested in; the best of anything has proven to increase in value over the long term.

Invest in your education: Follow billionaire investor Warren Buffett's approach and "buy what you know." The first dollar you spend on building a collection should be on a reliable reference book. What better resource to help you avoid fakes, reproductions, and fantasy pieces? From Fenton art glass to Hot Wheels variations, thousands of topics are covered in hundreds of reference books. Take the time well before you start buying to build a strong reference library.

Join a collecting club: Collecting clubs provide a wealth of information. Members of the Antique Advertising Association of America (pasttimes.org) publish a highly educational newsletter filled with images and information on everything from signs to tins. Various clubs manage deep websites filled with practical information on fakes and reproductions as well as offer an instant marketplace for hard-to-find items.

Step away from the screen: Visit shops, shows, auctions, and flea markets and ask questions. Perhaps you'll learn, as I did recently, that decorators are searching for early 20th century

Antique Trader.

barnyard items for today's kitchens or that more people than ever are interested in magic collectibles. If you've outgrown a previous collection or would like to shift gears, learning tips like this at group shops and shows could help you sell for higher prices. Take the time to chat with the clerk behind the counter or the auctioneer behind the podium. Most everyone collects something, and you may be surprised at how gratifying it can be to learn something new about your interests.

And that's where this visual reference guide comes in. In this 32nd edition we've expanded and updated the most popular sections and added new ones, too. You'll notice special attention is drawn to the best items pursued by collectors as Top Lots. Special features show why some categories are irresistible to collectors. We've also been on the road – like many of you – meeting dealers, auctioneers, collectors, and show managers who gave us the scoop on what's really happening in the hobby. You'll see their smiling faces along with their top tips, opinions, and collecting advice in various chapters across this new edition under the header "Inside Intel." We hope this helps you get to know the people behind the prices.

A book of this size and scope is a team project and many thanks are owed to editorial director Paul Kennedy and editor Mary Sieber; Antoinette Rahn, editor and online editor and content manager of *Antique Trader* magazine; Karen Knapstein, print editor of *Antique Trader* magazine; designer Nicole MacMartin; and several specialists and contributors. Ever the professionals, they work year-round to make this book the best it can be. We also thank the numerous auction houses and their staffs for generously providing images. Their hard work and great ideas are always focused on one goal: selecting the topics, images, and features our readers will find the most fascinating. We hope you enjoy the results.

— Eric Bradley

Eric Bradley *is the author of the critically acclaimed* Mantiques: A Manly Guide to Cool Stuff, Picker's Pocket Guide: SIGNS, *and* Picker's Pocket Guide: TOYS. *A former editor of* Antique Trader *magazine and an award-winning investigative journalist with a degree in economics, he has appeared in* The Wall Street Journal, GQ, Four Seasons Magazine, Bottom Line/Personal *and* The Detroit News, *among others. He is a public relations associate at Heritage Auctions, HA.com, the world's largest collectibles auctioneer, and lives near Dallas with his wife and three children.*

ADVERTISING

ADVERTISING ITEMS, with the exception of glass and ceramics, is the most diverse collecting category in all of collectibles. Before the days of mass media, advertisers relied on colorful product labels, containers, store displays, signs, posters, and novelty items to help set their product or service apart from competitors.

In the United States, advertising became an art form during the boom years after World War II until well into the mid-1970s. The rise of the middle class and freely flowing dollars left us with a plethora of items to collect. These items represent the work of America's skilled and talented writers and commercial illustrators and give us an entertaining look into everyday life of the 19th and 20th centuries.

The arrival of large carefully curated collections at auctions and at specialty shows is also renewing interest in advertising items. Massive collections of tobacco tins, coffee tins, talcum powder containers, rarely seen syrup dispensers, and Coca-Cola memorabilia are being offered for sale. These large sales are increasingly offering grouped lots of up to 20 items, giving collectors the opportunity to purchase an interesting assortment of advertising items at one time.

The most popular pieces are sought after for one chief reason: eye appeal, according to William Morford, owner of William Morford Investment Grade Collectibles at Auction. Modern values "depend on the subject matter and the graphics – how powerful it is," he said. "The advanced collector who has the resources knows it's a smarter move to buy the best...and it's leaving all the lower end stuff behind."

Morford said another emerging trend is the popularity of male-centric items bringing higher than expected prices at auction.

"Hunting, fishing, oil, gas, and cars, gambling – pretty much all of them are popular now," he added.

The most heavily collected advertising pieces remain signs, especially those with porcelain graphics. Lately this segment also has become dominated by items in exceptional condition and by obscure examples. However, unlike other segments, some auctioneers are reporting interest in signs in poor condition, even if sale prices are low. It seems new collectors entering the hobby are seeking rusty, chipped examples made popular on television programs such as "American Pickers."

For more information, see *Picker's Pocket Guide: Signs* (Krause Publications, 2014).

Large embossed Dutch Boy Paint porcelain sign, oval with Dutch Boy with clogs and paintbrush, marked REG. U.S. PAT. OFF., very good condition, some chipping around edge, 27" x 44". $750

Courtesy of Morphy Auctions

Cream of Wheat advertising illustration, Mabel M. Buckmaster (American, 20th century), oil on canvas, signed lower right, good condition, surface grime, minor abrasions to corner and edges, 29" x 18". **$2,271**

Courtesy of Heritage Auctions

Rare 1930s Art Deco "Drink / Coca-Cola / Pause / Refresh" wooden lithographed hanging sign, back marked "Kay Displays Grand Rapids & New York," near mint condition, 14" x 10". **$2,500**

Courtesy of Morphy Auctions

1950s Willie Mays Chesterfield cigarettes cardboard sign, very good to excellent condition with small stain spots on top, broken easel on back, 21" x 22". **$1,135**

Courtesy of Heritage Auctions

H. H. Warner's Safe Kidney & Liver Cure lithograph sign, circa 1880, with U.S. President James A. Garfield being congratulated by group of constituents including his opponent, James G. Blaine, each political figure identified along bottom edge, capitol in background, "Copyright 1881 by Root and Tinker," some creases, folds and wrinkles. **$563**

Courtesy of Heritage Auctions

Robert's Lipton delivery truck, circa 1940s, pressed steel, yellow enclosed van body with opening rear doors, wood handlebars on roof, van side advertising decals, some loss to decal, overall excellent condition, 22" l. **$550**

Courtesy of Bertoia Auctions

Vintage Bagdad tobacco pocket tin, good condition, approximately 3-1/2" h. **$40**

Courtesy of Pioneer Auction Gallery

Large die-cut Wrigley's Double Mint store display showing woman in 1930s attire, five-section cardboard lithographed sign in frame, designed to be folded out so it is self-standing, very good condition, some tearing at seam and dirty spot in lower left, 36" x 71"..................................**$500**

Courtesy of Morphy Auctions

Young's Ocean Pier early tin lithographed tray of amusement park extending into Atlantic Ocean and various activities, with early postcard of pier, very good to excellent condition, 12" dia.............................. **$275**

Courtesy of Bertoia Auctions

Stork advertising figure for Castle Hall Twin Cigars, painted papier-mâché and wood, cardboard sign, rare larger size, very good condition with some paint loss, 44-1/2" h. **$400**

Courtesy of Rich Penn Auctions

Challenge coffee wooden store bin, paper label in front indent reads, "Challenge Roasted Coffee, Dubuque, Iowa," good condition, label with some pieces missing, advertising on wood behind it can be seen, top pull missing, 22-1/2" h. **$325**

Courtesy of Bertoia Auctions

1880s Tim Keefe *New York Sporting Times* sign with lithographed text reading, "N.Y. Sporting Times, 5c., For Sale Here," medium-weight tan card stock, water staining on upper left side of printing, foxing throughout, toned acidification on verso, 8-1/2" x 11".... **$2,271**

Courtesy of Heritage Auctions

◄ Joe DiMaggio Louisville Slugger baseball bats advertisement, 1940, thick cardboard sign in cartoon style refers to DiMaggio's 1939 batting title and that in 1940 there would be three DiMaggios in baseball, rare piece, 15-1/2" x 21", 18-1/2" x 23" framed.... **$956**

Courtesy of Heritage Auctions

top lot!

Tin display coffeepot advertising
T & K Coffee / F.P. Cook on one side,
T & K Tea / F.P. Cook on other, very
good-plus condition, red lettering with
yellow embellishments, typical wear
and fading, small nicks and scrapes,
31" h. $13,000

Joe Cannon cigar cutter,
metal framed, cigar box image
of "National Speaker" Joe
Cannon, push bar across top
activated to cut cigars, trap
at base opens to remove tips,
good to very good condition,
some light wear, 8" h. $275

Courtesy of Bertoia Auctions

Johnson's Peacemaker Coffee lithographed tin log cabin coffee bin, 1915 advertising calendar in doorway, very good condition, scuffing and surface scratches, 28" h. **$1,600**

Courtesy of Bertoia Auctions

Vanner & Prest's clock, embossed on tin, "Molliscorium Magnet & Pan" and "Polishes" on wood, good to very good condition, overall light wear, running condition, 31".........**$900**

Courtesy of Bertoia Auctions

Drink Blatz Beer neon sign, red, blue, and white cutout porcelain on white light box with "Blatz" neon marked Artkraft Milw, very good condition, wear to edges and near screws, 48" x 25-1/2"...........................**$2,500**

Courtesy of Morphy Auctions

Diamond Match Co. monumental matchbox art, circa 1948-1964, wood and heavyweight cardboard with striking panels to sides, containing 24 individual wooden matchsticks with realistically painted heads, likely countertop or window display, some wear and tear, 27" h. x 18-1/2" w. x 6-1/2" d. **$1,000**

Courtesy of Cowan's Auctions

◄ Early cast iron advertising boot, stamped with name J.R. Palmenberg and Sons, New York, very good condition, general paint wear, 8-1/2" h. **$200**

Courtesy of Morphy Auctions

Jewel Stoves tin advertising sign, rectangular form with convex curve, white and blue design and lettering against yellow ground, JEWEL / STOVES / AND / RANGES / DETROIT STOVE WORKS / LARGEST STOVE PLANT IN WORLD / B.S. Co., 52 State St., Chicago, manufacturer's label on reverse, sign mounted on wooden frame, areas of enamel loss, chips, areas of rust, 20" h. x 17-3/4" w. x 5-1/2" d. **$1,300**

Courtesy of Cowan's Auctions

◄ Goff's Braid Best Made spool thread oak cabinet/ countertop display case, four drawers, brass pull knobs and tin litho lettering inserts in drawers, advertising on back of case, very good to excellent condition, light wear, 15" h. **$300**

Courtesy of Bertoia Auctions

Whittier Milk porcelain sign, "Quaker Maid" with Quaker Maid girl logo, very good condition, 72" x 42-1/8". **$1,400**

Courtesy of Morphy Auctions

Porcelain Red Seal Dry Battery thermometer sign with slogans, "Guaranteed for all Open Circuit Work," "The Guarantee Protects You," circa 1918, marked "Pat. March 16 1918, Made by Beach Company of Coshocton O.," very good condition, slight chipping, 7" x 27" h. **$350**

Courtesy of Morphy Auctions

Double-sided Royal Crown Cola hanging sign, "Relax and Enjoy / Best By Taste-Test," marked AM 2-40, 1940, near mint condition, 16" x 24"...**$1,300**

Courtesy of Morphy Auctions

ICE CREAM
WRIGLEY'S
DOUBLEMINT

Porcelain die-cut double-sided ice cream sign with Wrigley's Double Mint advertising on front, Wrigley's Spearmint advertising on reverse, fair condition, some fading and chips, 9" x 30". **$600**

Courtesy of Morphy Auctions

Rare 1905 Dr. Pepper calendar, light cardboard embossed and die-cut, design by Tuck, three of six panel connectors are copies, everything else original, framed under glass, near mint condition, framed 17-1/4" x 11-1/2". **$1,300**

Courtesy of Morphy Auctions

▶ Mazda Lamps display with mascot and two light sockets with on/off switch, near mint condition, 35" x 37-1/2" on 6" x 10-1/2" base...................... **$950**

Courtesy of Morphy Auctions

MAZDA
LAMPS

1930s Formfit undergarment figure, hard rubber composition on wood base, excellent condition, 32" h. **$450**

Courtesy of Morphy Auctions

▼ Muller's Bread wooden box with handles, good condition, 28-3/4" x 15-3/4". **$125**

Courtesy of Morphy Auctions

Japp's Hair Rejuvenator tin countertop or wall-mount lithographed sign, circa 1910, new old stock, "Restores Gray Hair Instantly" with seven hair samples in different colors with cardboard easel on back, manufactured by J.G. Japp Toilet Requisite Co., Cincinnati, excellent condition, 9" x 13". **$475**

Courtesy of Morphy Auctions

◀ Stoneware rolling pin advertising Kelsey & Wegner, Adair, Iowa, orange bands, excellent condition with factory glaze missing in small circle, no chips or cracks, 15" l. **$475**

Courtesy of Rich Penn Auctions

Mayflower Shoe tin sign of woman with long hair, near mint condition, 26" x 18", **$1,400**

Courtesy of Morphy Auctions

Original watercolor art for sign advertising Meyer Rubbers, painted by Hans Dahl, framed under glass, excellent condition, 25-1/2" l. **$3,500**

Courtesy of Morphy Auctions

1956 P-F Flyers "Big League Baseball Stars on TV" sign with Brooklyn Dodgers center fielder Duke Snider, water stains and small tear at die-cut upper right corner, approximately 12" x 16". **$418**

Courtesy of Heritage Auctions

Advertising wagon, circa 1880s, all wood with angled dovetailed sides and wood spoke wheels, Cook & Brown Lime Co. / Solvay Coke / Tel. 59, advertising on one side in very good condition, other side in fair condition, overall very good condition, 21-1/2" h. x 18" w. x 28" l. **$650**

Courtesy of Rich Penn Auctions

Packard Six and Eight automobile advertising, circa 1920s, framed paper lithograph of U.S. Navy dirigible "Shenandoah," "Rainbow III" speedboat, PN-9 biplane, and Packard four-door phaeton, rare print in very good condition with spotting and fold break in upper left corner, 24-1/2" h. x 31" w. **$700**

Courtesy of Rich Penn Auctions

Continental Fire Insurance Co. of New York sign, circa 1900, lithographed on self-framed metal, very good condition with light-colored spots on bottom half, 30" h. x 20" w. **$800**

Courtesy of Rich Penn Auctions

Gainsborough Cabinet Store display cabinet for Gainsborough Hair Nets, wood with original advertising transfers on all sides, two lift doors on top and eight interior compartments for product, very good-plus original condition, 48" h. x 17-1/2" w. x 25" d. **$750**

Courtesy of Rich Penn Auctions

Red Wing blue and white stoneware pitcher with advertising for L.M. Mann's General Store, De Soto, Iowa, cherries and leaves design, excellent-plus condition with no chips or cracks, 9-1/2" h. **$1,000**

Courtesy of Rich Penn Auctions

Cigar lighter, H. Ehrlich & Son Mfg. Co., St. Joseph, Missouri, oak case with paper advertising panels on all sides, brass feet, excellent condition, 15" h. x 7-1/2" sq. **$850**

Courtesy of Rich Penn Auctions

Reliable Egg Carrier, wood with bale handle and egg crate interior, original stenciling advertising Stumpf & Langhoff department stores, overall very good condition, 13" x 11" x 12".............. **$1,400**

Courtesy of Showtime Auction Services

National Cigar Stand hanging leaded glass lamp advertising Black and White cigars, excellent working condition, crack in one of top red panels, 23" x 23" x 11" without fringe.............. **$2,600**

Courtesy of Showtime Auction Services

Native American fiber resin bust advertising Chippewa Boots, 14" h. **$375**

Courtesy of Morphy Las Vegas

Advertising sign for Clear Quill Flour from Union Mill Co., Waterloo, Iowa, circa 1910, colorful lithograph on self-framed metal by American Art Works, Coshocton, Ohio, excellent condition with original string hanger, minor wear on frame, 13" h. x 19" w.................**$7,500**

Courtesy of Rich Penn Auctions

Berry Brothers wagon for store display, dovetail wood with advertising on both sides for Berry Brothers Varnishes and Architectural Finishes, wood wheels with advertising, very good condition, 28" l. **$325**

Courtesy of Bertoia Auctions

ASIAN ART
& ARTIFACTS

ASIAN ART (AKA EASTERN ART) IS HIGHLY PRIZED BY COLLECTORS. They are attracted by its fine workmanship and exquisite attention to detail, plus the undeniable lure of the exotic.

Often lumped under the generic header "Oriental," Asian art actually embraces a wide variety of cultures. Among the many countries falling under the Asian/Eastern art umbrella: Bali, Bhutan, Cambodia, China, India, Indonesia, Japan, Korea, Laos, Thailand, Tibet, Vietnam, and the Pacific Islands. Also in the mix: art forms indigenous to the native cultures of Australia and New Zealand, and works of art celebrating the traditions of such Eastern-based religions as Buddhism and Hinduism.

The influence of Eastern art on Western art is strong. As Western artisans absorbed the cultural traditions of the East, stylistic similarities crept into their work, whether subconsciously or deliberately. (The soft matte glazes popularized by Van Briggle Pottery, for example, resulted from founder Artus Van Briggle's ongoing quest to replicate the "dead" glazes of the Chinese Ming Dynasty.)

Chinese porcelain was one of the first representations of Asian art to entice buyers in the United States; export of the ware began in the 1780s.

Japanese porcelain, originally billed as "Nippon," began to make its way to U.S. shores near the end of the 19th century. Early Chinese porcelain was often distinguished by a liberal use of blue and white; Japanese porcelain, by a similar reliance on floral and landscape motifs. Consumers found the products of both countries desirable, not only because of their delicacy, but also because pieces of comparable quality were not yet available domestically.

Porcelain was not the only outlet for Eastern creativity. Among the many other materials utilized: ivory, jade, bone, hardstone, marble, bronze, brass, gold, silver, wood, and fabric (primarily silk). Decorative

Asian carved coral figure of woman and child with three monkeys, 20th century, 9" h..................**$15,000**

Courtesy of Heritage Auctions

Two Chinese necklaces of hardstone and wooden beads, 20th century: one with water-drop-shaped jade pendant, six carved deep green hardstone beads, and more than 100 wooden beads; other with six hardstone beads and double-gourd-shaped centerpiece; to 28" l. **$1,968**

Courtesy of Skinner Inc.; www.skinnerinc.com

Four bronze alloy Buddha heads, Thailand, U Thong-style, each with band between hairline and forehead: one in gilt-bronze, wearing tiara with molded patterns; one with mother-of-pearl inlaid eyes; one with open eyes with incised pupils; and one with lotus bud-shape ushnisha; three heads mounted on modern wood stands, 2-1/2" h. to 5-5/8" h. **$677**

Courtesy of Skinner Inc.; www.skinnerinc.com

Chinese carved green nephrite bowl with French 18k gold openwork scrolling foliate handle mounted to rim, circa 1900, marks: boar's head, 3/4" h. x 3" w. **$1,875**

Courtesy of Heritage Auctions

Four Asian metal Buddhist hands: three in abhaya mudra, two in bronze and one in iron, Sukhothai-style, all mounted on various modern wood stands, to 5-1/2" l.; and cast iron hand with ornate bracelet on flowing fabric, mounted on modern metal stand, 5-3/8" h. x 4-1/4" w. **$1,169**

Courtesy of Skinner Inc.; www.skinnerinc.com

Two Asian carved coral figures of deities, 20th century, 6" h. **$5,938**

Courtesy of Heritage Auctions

Asian carved coral figures of scholar and god Hotei, 20th century, 3-1/2" h. **$4,375**

Courtesy of Heritage Auctions

treatments ranged from cloisonné (enamel sections in a pattern of metal strips) to intricate hand carving to the elaborate use of embroidery, gilt, and lacquer.

Asian art in any form offers a unique blend of the decorative and the functional. The richness of the materials and treatments utilized transforms even everyday objects into dazzling works of art. Among myriad items receiving this Cinderella treatment: bowls, vases, planters, chess sets, snuff bottles, rugs, robes, tapestries, tables, trays, jars, screens, incense burners, cabinets, and tea caddies. Even a simple item such as an oil lamp could be reborn through imaginative artistry: A Chinese version from the 1920s, its exterior worked in cloisonné, emerged as a colorful, ferocious dragon.

This multitude of products makes Asian art an ideal cross-collectible. Some may be interested only in the output of a specific country or region. Others may be drawn to a specific type of collectible (kimonos, snuff boxes, depictions of Buddha). There will even be those attracted solely to pieces created from a specific material, such as jade, ivory, or porcelain. Aficionados of any of these categories have a lifetime of collecting pleasure in store.

Chinese jade pendant, 19th and 20th century, carved into elliptical openwork shape with peaches and leaves, attached to chain with impressed mark "Italy" to clasp, chain 11-3/4" l., jade pendant 1-3/4" w. **$4,305**

Courtesy of Skinner Inc.; www.skinnerinc.com

The timeline of Asian art is a long one, with value often determined by antiquity. Due to age and rarity, minor flaws (jade nicks, porcelain cracks, and chips) are not generally a detriment to purchase. Any restoration should only be done by a professional, and only after careful analysis as to whether or not restoration will affect value.

Asian art continues to be produced and imported today at an overwhelming rate (and often of "souvenir-only" quality). Collectors seeking museum-quality pieces are strongly advised to purchase only from reputable dealers, and to insist on proof of provenance.

Chinese porcelain snuff bottle with painted river scene to either side, green hardstone stopper, marks: chop marks, 2-3/4" h......**$8,750**

Courtesy of Heritage Auctions

Chinese red/brown amber snuff bottle with dragons, 18th/19th century, oviform, resting on four animal-head feet, two loops at shoulder, well-hollowed, with two swirling dragons chasing flaming pearl amongst ruyi clouds in high relief, incised details, carved stopper with coiled dragon above ruyi clouds, translucent amber with spotty opaque yellow inclusions, 3-3/8" h..............................**$904**

Courtesy of Skinner Inc., www.skinnerinc.com

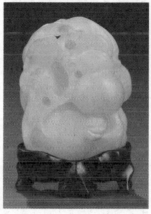

Chinese jade carving on stand, 19th century, peach-form jade with reticulation to upper branches, on fitted wood base, 2-1/2" h. **$750**

Courtesy of Heritage Auctions

Chinese porcelain phoenix, 20th century, standing fenghuang, with flowers and auspicious mushrooms, 23" h. **$431**

Courtesy of Skinner Inc.; www.skinnerinc.com

Chinese porcelain snuff bottle of traveling man, jadeite stopper, early 20th century, marks: chop marks, 3" h. **$500**

Courtesy of Heritage Auctions

Famille rose porcelain covered jar with wood base, 11-1/2" h. on stand. **$563**

Courtesy of Heritage Auctions

Southeast Asian watercolor panel on paper, 65" x 26-1/2"........ **$210**

Courtesy of Pook & Pook, Inc.

Two Chinese lacquered boxes, tea caddy and work box, 19th century, 6-5/8" x 12" x 9"... **$325**

Courtesy of Heritage Auctions

Asian patinated bronze figure of Buddha, 19th century, 23" x 16-1/2" x 12"................. **$2,125**

Courtesy of Heritage Auctions

Two Chinese cast iron lion attachments, possibly Tang dynasty, in form of crouching guardian lions supporting ring fixture, each modeled with individual features and expressions, on wood stands, 9" h. **$800**

Courtesy of Skinner Inc.; www.skinnerinc.com

Southeast Asian carved and painted panel, 37" x 17". ... **$148**

Courtesy of Pook & Pook, Inc.

Blooming hardstone and jade tree joined by silk-wrapped wires, in base with cloisonné narrative scenes to each panel, 20" x 17-1/2" x 12".........**$875**

.Courtesy of Heritage Auctions

top lot!

Skinner set a U.S. record in September 2014 when a monumental Fencai Imperial Qing Dynasty vase sold for $24.7 million.

The vase, which had a pre-sale estimate of $150,000-$250,000, was formerly in the collection of Ton-ying and Co. and is a tour-de-force of ceramic techniques employed by the Jingdezhen Imperial potters.

"This important vase was likely made for the Emperor so he could appreciate the technical achievements illustrated in the vase. It required multiple firings of the 15 different glazes and enamels that resulted in the exquisite floral and landscape designs," said Judith Dowling, director of Asian Works of Art.

The mark on the bottom of the vase.

The multi-tiered baluster form vase has two chilong-inspired gilt-bronze ears on the neck, with each tier having a different glaze, decoration, and technique. Each panel on the 12-lobed body depicts in fencai enamel six auspicious themes of sanyang kaitai (with sun), jiqing youyu (with boy), danfeng chaoyang (with phoenix), taipingyoujiang (with elephant), xianshangqiongge (with landscape), and bogu giuding (with nine pots) alternating with six floral scroll and auspicious knot designs with bats, ruyi, swastika, chilong, lingzhi, and huahui. The glazes are in blue and white, celadon, cobalt blue, turquoise, purple, pink, yellow, and white, and decorative techniques include fencai, molding, anhua, crackled ice, and gilt, red six-character Qianlong mark to turquoise enamel base.

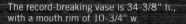

The record-breaking vase is 34-3/8" h., with a mouth rim of 10-3/4" w.

A close-up of one of the gilt-bronze ears on the neck.

A close-up of one of the panels.   Another close-up of one of the panels.

ASIAN ART & ARTIFACTS

"Jeune Fille," Vu Cao Dam (Vietnamese, 1908-2000), oil on canvas, 1969, signed and dated lower right: Vu Cao Dam 69, 11-3/4" x 9-3/4". **$5,000**

Courtesy of Heritage Auctions

Chinese Peking white and red glass snuff bottle with farmer and bull on one side and pond scene to other, marks to body: chop marks, 2-3/8" h.... **$5,000**

Courtesy of Heritage Auctions

Chinese painted porcelain bowl, 3-7/8" h. x 11-1/2" d. **$406**

Courtesy of Heritage Auctions

"Ariakero Teahouse, Imado, Japan," Kobayashi Kiyochika (1847-1915), color woodblock print, 1879, published by Fukuda Kumajiro, from series Pictures of Famous Places in Tokyo, signed on print, dated with publisher's seal on right margin, titled on bottom, oban yoko-e, 7-3/4" x 12-1/8". **$461**

Courtesy of Skinner Inc.; www.skinnerinc.com

"Snow Scene at Koume Hikibune-Dori, Japan," Kobayashi Kiyochika (1847-1915), color woodblock print, 1879, published by Fukuda Kumajiro, signed on print, dated with publisher's seal on right margin, titled on bottom, oban yoko-e, 7-3/4" x 12-1/8" **$1,046**

Courtesy of Skinner Inc.; www.skinnerinc.com

Japanese ivory netsuke, 20th century, man carrying staff with bird perched on stacks of firewood on his back, mark on base, 1-3/4" h....................**$185**

Courtesy of Skinner Inc.; www.skinnerinc.com

Japanese ivory netsuke of seated figure holding box, 19th century, 1-1/4" h...............**$215**

Courtesy of Skinner Inc.; www.skinnerinc.com

Japanese wood netsuke of two men, 19th century, seated samurai figure burdened with monk elbowing his right arm into samurai's back, signed "Masayuki" to base, 1-1/4" h. **$1,353**

Courtesy of Skinner Inc.; www.skinnerinc.com

◄ Japanese ivory netsuke of Oni, 19th century, standing in acrobatic pose with Japanese drum on his chest, carrying satchel on his back, lotus leaf branch near his feet, unsigned, 1-3/4" h. **$1,230**

Courtesy of Skinner Inc.; www.skinnerinc.com

Japanese wood netsuke of cicada, 18th century, resting with legs stretched out on leaf, signed "Tomotada" in incised rectangular cartouche to base, 7/8" h. x 1-3/4" d. **$7,380**

Courtesy of Skinner Inc.; www.skinnerinc.com

NETSUKES

Netsukes – the miniature buttonlike carvings used in Japan to suspend articles from the sash of a kimono and as ornamental fasteners on boxes – have been a high-end niche collectible in the United States for decades.

Japanese ivory netsuke of dancing demons, 19th century, playing musical instruments, dancing and surrounding seated priest, signed "Kogyoku" to base, 1-1/8" h. **$2,091**

Courtesy of Skinner Inc.; www.skinnerinc.com

Two carved netsukes: Shoulao with turtle, incised details in colors, signed to base; and boy reclined holding woman's mask, signed to base, 1-1/4" h. **$246**

Courtesy of Skinner Inc., www.skinnerinc.com

Japanese ivory netsuke of 12 zodiac animals entangled to form ball, 19th/20th century, incised details, unsigned, 1-1/8" d. **$123**

Courtesy of Skinner Inc.; www.skinnerinc.com

AUTOGRAPHS

IN *THE MEANING AND BEAUTY OF AUTOGRAPHS*, first published in 1935 and translated from the German by David H. Lowenherz of Lion Heart Autographs, Inc. in 1995, Stefan Zweig explained that to love a manuscript, we must first love the human being "whose characteristics are immortalized in them." When we do, then "a single page with a few lines can contain the highest expression of human happiness, and...the expression of deepest human sadness. To those who have eyes to look at such pages correctly, eyes not only in the head, but also in the soul, they will not receive less of an impression from these plain signs than from the obvious beauty of pictures and books."

John M. Reznikoff, founder and president of University Archives, has been a leading dealer and authority on historical letters and artifacts for 32 years. He described the current market for autographs as "very, very strong on many fronts. Possibly because of people being afraid to invest in the market and in real estate, we are seeing investment in autographs that seems to parallel gold and silver."

Reznikoff suspects that Civil War items peaked after Ken Burns' series but that Revolutionary War documents, included those by signers of the Declaration of Independence and the Constitution, are still undervalued and can be purchased for under $500.

Currrently, space is in high demand, especially Apollo 11. Pop culture, previously looked at as secondary by people who dealt in Washingtons and Lincolns, has come into its own. Reznikoff anticipates continued growth in memorabilia that includes music, television, movies, and sports. Babe Ruth, Lou Gehrig, Ty Cobb, and Tiger Woods are still good investments, but Reznikoff warns that authentication is much more of a concern in sports than in any other field.

The Internet allows for a lot of disinformation and this is a significant issue with autographs. There are two widely accepted authentication services: Professional Sports Authenticator (PSA/DNA) and James Spence Authentication (JSA). A dealer's reliability can be evaluated by seeing whether he is a member of one or more of the major organizations in the field: the Antique Booksellers Association of America, UACC Registered Dealers Program, and the National Professional Autograph Dealers Association (NPADA), which Reznikoff founded.

There is an additional caveat to remember and it is true for all collectibles: rarity. The value of an autograph is often determined less by the prominence of the signer than by the number of autographs he signed.

— Zac Bissonnette

Margaret Thatcher single-signed Rawlings
unofficial baseball, PSA/DNA. **$131**

Courtesy of Collect Auctions

The Beatles "Please Please Me" album with signatures of Paul McCartney, Ringo Starr, John Lennon, and George Harrison, circa 1963, PSA/DNA, Mint 9 condition..........**$28,888**

Courtesy of Iconic Auctions

John Bradley signed "Iwo Jima Flag Raising" First Day Cover, PSA/DNA. Bradley (1923-1994) was the last surviving member of the second flag raising, which is the more famous shot taken by Joe Rosenthal...**$89**

Courtesy of Collect Auctions

Christa McAuliffe signed commemorative cachet honoring "4th Flight Duration Cluster, 574 seconds," cover postmarked May 30, 1980, PSA/DNA. **$634**

Courtesy of Collect Auctions

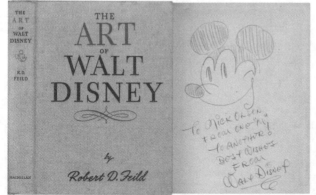

Scarce illustration of Mickey Mouse drawn and signed by Walt Disney inside first edition copy of *The Art of Walt Disney*, 8-1/2" x 11". **$15,125**

Courtesy of Nate D. Sanders

Photo of Clint Eastwood as "Dirty Harry," PSA/DNA, 11" x 14"..........................**$395**

Courtesy of Collect Auctions

Rare Abraham Lincoln signed carte-de-visite photograph taken by Alexander Gardner in 1861 and signed as president; John Hay, Lincoln's private secretary, authenticated signature on verso, 2-1/2" x 3-3/4"..$49,913

◀ Twenty-third President of the United States Benjamin Harrison's Fletcher National Bank personal check signed "Benjamin Harrison," dated June 15, 1900, made payable to Layman Carey Co. for $6.60, PSA/DNA, 7" x 2-3/4". **$238**

Courtesy of Collect Auctions

Nov. 19, 2007 issue of *Time Magazine* with signature of Hillary Clinton, "Hillary," in black Sharpie, PSA/DNA. **$109**

Courtesy of Collect Auctions

Coretta Scott King 1968 typewritten, signed letter on 8-1/2" x 11" sheet of "Mrs. Martin Luther King Jr." stationery, postmarked Nov. 1, 1968, JSA. **$359**

Courtesy of Legendary Auctions

Johnny Cash signed black and white promotional photo with letter signed by former longtime assistant Peggy Knight, JSA, 16" x 20". **$504**

Courtesy of Goldin Auctions

◀ Signed check by Carlo Gambino, notorious mob boss and head of Gambino organized crime family, 1963, PSA/DNA. **$484**

Courtesy of Goldin Auctions

AUTOGRAPHS

Abraham Lincoln signed card, dated Sept. 24, 1863, JSA, 2-1/8" x 3-1/2"............... **$3,795**

Courtesy of Hake's Americana

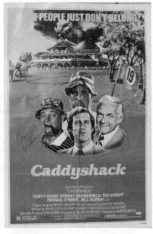

"Caddyshack" original movie poster signed by Chevy Chase, PSA/DNA, 27" x 40". **$238**

Courtesy of Iconic Auctions

Stan Lee signed rare original Spider-Man sketch, PSA/DNA, 8" x 10".......................... **$3,425**

Courtesy of Iconic Auctions

Signed black-and-white photo of Audrey Hepburn, PSA/DNA graded Gem Mint 10, 8" x 10"......... **$1,408**

Courtesy of Iconic Auctions

Albert Einstein signed album page from 1921, one of earliest known to surface, PSA/DNA, 2-1/2" x 4". **$3,504**

Courtesy of Iconic Auctions

Robert DeNiro signed Everlast boxing glove, likely in homage to his role as Jake LaMotta in "Raging Bull," PSA/DNA. **$300**

Courtesy of Iconic Auctions

Society of American Magicians President Harry Houdini signed membership card, PSA/DNA, 2-1/2" x 4". **$2,578**

Courtesy of Iconic Auctions

Contract signed by comedy legend W.C. Fields for 1935 film "Man on the Flying Trapeze," six-page contract, dated March 21, 1935, stapled inside white paper cover with Fields' signature on page 5. .... **$734**

Courtesy of Nate D. Sanders

Muhammad Ali signed Salvino Sports Legends figurine, white trunks version, limited edition no. 423 of 3,500, PSA/DNA, 9" h. **$436**

Courtesy of Collect Auctions

Neil Armstrong print signed and inscribed "Best Wishes / To Barry Kand / Neil Armstrong," JSA, 8-1/2" x 10". **$1,195**

Courtesy of Legendary Auctions

HBO poster of award-winning television series "The Sopranos" signed by James Gandolfini, actor who played Tony Soprano, PSA/DNA, 22" x 40". **$1,491**

Courtesy of Goldin Auctions

President Ronald Reagan signed vintage photo inscribed, "Best Regards Sara & Good Luck – Ronald Reagan," PSA/DNA, 8" x 10". **$432**

Courtesy of Collect Auctions

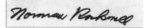

◄ Norman Rockwell signed print of his painting, "Hollywood Dreams," inscribed "My best wishes to Mrs. Natela Jones, sincerely Norman Rockwell," 10" x 13". **$500**

Courtesy of Nate D. Sanders

President George W. Bush signed campaign poster from 2000 election, PSA/DNA, 12-1/2" x 19". **$485**

Courtesy of Iconic Auctions

Original Maurice Sendak signed sketch of Max, main character from *Where the Wild Things Are*, charcoal drawing on white sketch paper, 6-1/4" x 9". **$2,813**

Courtesy of Nate D. Sanders

Jack Swigert's personally owned and signed "Apollo XIII" First Day Cover, postmarked April 11, 1970, 6-1/2" x 3-3/4". **$375**

Courtesy of Nate D. Sanders

Vintage photo of Natalie Wood signed in blue ink, PSA/DNA, 8" x 10". **$262**

Courtesy of Collect Auctions

July 1991 dated prayer slip signed by Mother Teresa, world famous Roman Catholic religious sister, missionary, and winner of 1979 Nobel Peace Prize, PSA/DNA. **$624**

Courtesy of SCP Auctions

Dr. Seuss graphite drawing on paper, circa 1950s, signed "Dr. Kamakazi Seuss," 8-1/2" x 11". **$2,813**

Courtesy of Nate D. Sanders

Photo of Titanic signed by Millvina Dean, famous last surviving passenger aboard legendary cruise liner, 8" x 10". **$188**

Courtesy of Nate D. Sanders

Signed original ink sketch of 28th president, Woodrow Wilson, by artist Bert Green, PSA/DNA, 16-1/2" x 23" framed and matted. **$640**

Courtesy of SCP Auctions

BANKS

MOST COLLECTIBLE BANKS are designed for one purpose: to encourage children to save money. How well the bank accomplished this task makes all the difference in making it collectible by later generations.

Manufactured from the late 1800s to the mid-1900s, mechanical, still, and register banks (which indicate the value of the coins deposited) are marvels of ingenuity made of tin, lead, or cast iron. Although banks come in all makes and functions, the most desirable banks employ a novelty or mechanical action when a coin is placed inside. Banks are sought after because they so efficiently represent the popular culture at the time they were made. This is evident in the wartime register banks sporting tin lithographic decorations of superheroes or animation characters or the cast iron figures that propagated racial stereotypes common from 1880 to 1930. Many early cast iron bank models have been reproduced during the years, especially in the 1950s and 1960s. A key indicator of a reproduction is fresh, glossy paint or dull details in the casting.

According to 10 years of sales data on LiveAuctioneers.com, most mechanical banks sell at auction for between $500 and $1,000. Morphy Auctions is the world leader in selling mechanical banks. The most important collection sold at auction so far is the Stephen and Marilyn Steckbeck Collection offered in October 2007. The top lot of the collection was an exceptional Jonah and the Whale mechanical bank, which realized $414,000. The $7.7 million collection still holds records for the most valuable banks ever sold, and they continue to dominate headlines whenever a piece from the Steckbeck Collection is resold. In September 2012, Morphy's auctioned an early Freedman's mechanical bank of a seated figure, measuring 10-1/2" high, with Steckbeck provenance, for $117,500.

A collection as fine and complete as the Steckbeck Collection hasn't come to auction since, but that doesn't mean fine examples are not coming to market. "There are a dozen or so collections that I know of that would bring over $1 million," said Dan Morphy, owner and founder of Morphy Auctions. "There are dozens of other bank collections that would fall in the six figure ranges."

However, it is apparent that collectors are holding out for those special examples. The number of fine banks offered at auction does not appear to be increasing. In fact, many auctioneers have taken to grouping banks together in order

Atlas Holding the World bank, Germany, circa 1915, scarce still bank in tin and lead, painted in silver overall, of god Atlas holding world money box on his back, key lock clasp, 5" h. **$550**

Courtesy of Bertoia Auctions

▲ Battleship Oregon still bank, J. & E. Stevens
Co., circa 1902, intricate casting, painted white
overall, red lifeboat interiors, green embossed base,
contains original base plate, 10-1/4" l. **$1,130**

Courtesy of Bertoia Auctions

◀ Man in Barrel still bank, J. & E. Stevens Co., circa
late 1800s, cast iron and japanned finish, whimsical
example with well-detailed casting effects, key lock
at chest for coin retrieval, 4" h............................**$690**

Courtesy of Bertoia Auctions

to push lot values over several hundred dollars, although this is only true with lesser quality
or common banks.

Morphy says condition – like all other categories of collecting – is king. "Banks in top
condition seem to be the trend these days," he said.

So, on the basis of affordability, now is the time to start a collection. "I always tell new
collectors that they should buy what they like," Morphy said. "Even if you pay a little more
than you should for a bank, the value in the enjoyment of owning it will more than offset the
high price one may pay."

A top on Morphy's list to offer at auction is a Darkey & the Watermelon mechanical bank.
Otherwise known as the Football Bank, it was designed and patented by Charles A. Bailey
on June 26, 1888. Known as the leader in mechanical bank design, Bailey's Darkey & the
Watermelon bank incorporated all of his imagination and design talents: When the right leg
of a figure is pulled back into position, a coin is then placed in a small football; a lever in the
figure's coattails is pressed and the football with coin is kicked over into a large watermelon.
Only one or two of these banks are known to exist.

"That would be my dream bank," Morphy said, "in that I would also want to buy it!"

Like their predecessors crafted nearly 150 years ago, contemporary banks blur the line
between tool and toy. Some modern banks that may make interesting collectibles in the
future include digital register banks that tabulate coin and paper money deposits or those
licensed by famous designers. But beware – antique banks are still being reproduced and can
be found very cheaply at lesser-quality flea markets or sold online.

For more information on banks, see *The Official Price Guide to Mechanical Banks* by Dan
Morphy, 2007, morphyauctions.com.

MECHANICAL BANKS

Circo Equestre tin mechanical bank, Spain, circa 1920s, lithographed tin, circus theme building bank with clown with tray in hand able to pivot and drop coin in slot by ticket collector window, 4" h. **$3,765**

Courtesy of Bertoia Auctions

Organ Grinder and Performing Bear mechanical bank, Kyser & Rex, Pennsylvania, patented 1882, cast iron and multicolored paint details, clockwork mechanism concealed in house, when activated, bear revolves as organ grinder and turns organ handle. **$6,902**

Courtesy of Bertoia Auctions

Reclining Chinaman mechanical bank, J. & E. Stevens Co., designed by James H. Bowen, Philadelphia, patented 1882, cast iron and hand painted, placing coin in his pocket and pressing lever allows him to show his four aces and salute depositor.......**$5,334**

Courtesy of Bertoia Auctions

World's Banker mechanical bank, scarce, Germany, lithographed tin depiction of John Bull, action created by pressing down hat, causing holder to rotate when releasing hat, globe rotating backward as coin is thrown into John Bull's chest, 7" h. **$4,706**

Courtesy of Bertoia Auctions

Owl Turning Head cast iron mechanical bank, J. & E. Stevens Co., 7-1/2" h. **$185**

Courtesy of Pook & Pook, Inc.

Football mechanical bank, John Harper & Co., Willenhall, England, patented 1895, cast iron, figure able to kick coin off platform and into net with coin slot when lever is pressed. **$3,765**

Courtesy of Bertoia Auctions

Preacher in the Pulpit mechanical bank, J. & E. Stevens Co., circa 1876, cast iron rarity, reportedly only three known examples; preacher standing at red-painted pulpit holds plate for coin placement, and as coin slides into bank, his head and arms lower and return to original pose; excellent condition. $263,550

COURTESY OF BERTOIA AUCTIONS

American sewing machine mechanical bank, manufacturer unknown, circa 1880s, rare cast iron bank, painted in black overall, reportedly given away by American Sewing Machine Co. but unconfirmed, coin slot appears on table, needle moves up and down, believed to be finest example known......**$32,630**

Courtesy of Bertoia Auctions

Horse mechanical bank, manufacturer unknown, circa 1890, only reported example, cast iron, saddle with blanket painted in red and yellow, coin deposit allows horse to paw ground.............. **$25,278**

Courtesy of Bertoia Auctions

Picture Gallery cast iron mechanical bank, Shepard Hardware Co., restoration to paint. **$5,324**

Courtesy of Pook & Pook, Inc.

Speaking Dog cast iron mechanical bank, Shepard Hardware Co., 7-1/2" h. **$861**

Courtesy of Pook & Pook, Inc.

Turtle mechanical bank, Kilgore Mfg., Ohio, designed by M. Elizabeth Cook, circa 1926, rare cast iron figural bank, inserting coin in slot on back causes turtle's neck to extend. **$43,925**

Courtesy of Bertoia Auctions

Red Riding Hood mechanical bank, manufacturer not confirmed, circa 1880, Red Riding Hood sits at foot of Grandma's bed and as lever is moved, Grandma's mask moves forward, exposing wolf's face and depositing coin. **$31,375**

Courtesy of Bertoia Auctions

Acrobat cast iron mechanical bank, J. & E. Stevens
Co., overall good condition. $3,888

Courtesy of Pook & Pook, Inc.

Lion and Two Monkeys cast iron mechanical
bank, Kyser & Rex, very good condition, small
monkey replaced.......................................$1,215

Courtesy of Pook & Pook, Inc.

Horse Race cast iron mechanical bank, J. & E.
Stevens Co., possible restoration. $1,580

Courtesy of Pook & Pook, Inc.

Boys Stealing Watermelon cast iron mechanical
bank, Kyser & Rex. $2,673

Courtesy of Pook & Pook, Inc.

Leap Frog cast iron mechanical bank, Shepard
Hardware Co., paint restoration to figures.........$850

Courtesy of Pook & Pook, Inc.

Boy Scout Camp cast iron mechanical bank, J. &
E. Stevens Co., overall good condition. $2,916

Courtesy of Pook & Pook, Inc.

Player Piano mechanical bank, E.M. Roche Novelty Co., excellent condition, 8" l. **$2,280**

Dentist cast iron mechanical bank, manufactured by J. & E. Stevens Co., gray base variation, tooth reattached, 9" l. **$11,400**

Clown, Harlequin, and Columbine mechanical bank, J. & E. Stevens Co., circa 1907, move trio to expose slot, position clown halfway around circle, place coin in slot, release lever and figures reverse themselves, causing Columbine to spin, 7" h. **$4,500**

Stump Speaker mechanical bank, Shepard Hardware Co., Buffalo, New York, patent June 8, 1886, press lever and speaker lowers coin into satchel. **$1,200**

Blind Man and Dog cast iron mechanical bank, (4460-A), yellow background, J. & E. Stevens Co., designed by William H. Lotz, patented Feb. 19, 1878, 6-3/4" l. **$49,200**

BARBIE

AT THE TIME of the Barbie doll's introduction in 1959, no one could have guessed that this statuesque doll would become a national phenomenon and eventually the most famous girl's plaything ever produced.

Over the years, Barbie and her growing range of family and friends have evolved with the times, serving as an excellent mirror of the fashion and social changes taking place in American society. Today, after 56 years of continuous production, Barbie's popularity remains unabated among both young girls and older collectors. Early and rare Barbie dolls can sell for remarkable prices, and it is every collector's hope to find a mint condition #1 Barbie.

▲ 1959 blonde No. 1 Ponytail Barbie in original labeled box with original swimsuit, earrings, and sunglasses, excellent condition, stand and shoes not original. **$2,500**

Courtesy of Theriault's Antique Doll Auctions

1959 brunette No. 2 Ponytail Barbie with V-shaped brows, red lips and solid feet, wearing swimsuit, hoop earrings, shoes and sunglasses, with first year ensemble #964, "Gay Parisienne," missing clutch purse, excellent condition. **$2,100**

Courtesy of Theriault's Antique Doll Auctions

◄ Circa 1959-1960 blonde No. 2 Ponytail Barbie with original black and white striped swimsuit, white sunglasses with blue lenses, black open-toe heels, fashion booklet, some hair has been cut. **$1,600**

Courtesy of Ivy Auctions

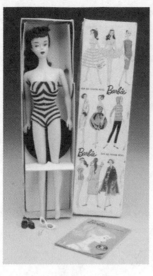

1960s titian No. 1 Bubblecut Barbie with original box, booklet, stand, and swimsuit. **$90**

Courtesy of Pioneer Auction Gallery

Brunette No. 3 Barbie with box, unusual blue eyeliner, earrings, shoes, sunglasses, two-piece stand, and box insert, doll in excellent condition, box in very good condition............**$500-$800**

Courtesy of Morphy Auctions

Blonde No. 3 Ponytail Barbie with box, swimsuit, sunglasses, earrings, and two-piece stand, very good-plus condition, small areas of greening around ear holes, lipstick slightly faded, box in very good condition, one corner split, and small area of loss to front.......................**$400**

Courtesy of Morphy Auctions

Blonde No. 5 Ponytail Barbie with box and red fingernails and lips, shoes, sunglasses, and stand, rare nipples, very good condition, minor paint loss to lips and nails, box in very good condition, lid with minor soiling, bottom with moderate damage and heavy tape repair............**$225**

Courtesy of Morphy Auctions

1960-1961 blonde No. 4 Ponytail Barbie in original swimsuit, excellent condition. **$350**

Courtesy of Theriault's Antique Doll Auctions

Brunette No. 5 Ponytail Barbie with box and red lips and fingernails, swimsuit, shoes, sunglasses, and stand, doll in excellent condition, box in very good-plus condition with two split corners on lid. **$175**

Courtesy of Morphy Auctions

top lot

1958 blonde No. 1 Ponytail Barbie
with original swimsuit, earrings, stand,
booklet and box, excellent condition,
minor loss to toenail paint, some staining
to feet from prolonged shoe wear, original
ponytail intact, original box with one split
corner. $5,000

COURTESY OF MORPHY AUCTIONS

1961 blonde No. 5 Ponytail Barbie with booklet and clothes. **$110**

Courtesy of Pioneer Auction Gallery

Circa 1962 redhead (titian) No. 6 Ponytail Barbie, #850, Japan, in red Helanca swimsuit with shoes and booklet, new in box with tag, excellent condition. **$650**

Courtesy of Morphy Auctions

Redhead No. 6 Ponytail Barbie with box and red lips and fingernails, swimsuit, shoes, sunglasses, catalog, and stand, very good-plus condition, nearly all red paint gone from lips, box in very good condition with split corners and tape repair. **$100**

Courtesy of Morphy Auctions

1962 blonde No. 7 Ponytail Barbie in red swimsuit, excellent condition. **$150**

Courtesy of Theriault's Antique Doll Auctions

Blonde Bubblecut Barbie with box and pink lipstick and fingernails, original red swimsuit, shoes, stand, and catalog, excellent condition, box (with insert) in excellent condition. **$125**

Courtesy of Morphy Auctions

Redhead Bubblecut Barbie in very good condition, no lip color, light soiling of legs. **$125**

Courtesy of Morphy Auctions

BARBIE

Two Bubblecut Barbies in original boxes, very good condition overall; brunette doll with heavy greening around ears and light soiling to legs, box with tape repair to one end flap; redhead doll with original stand and catalog, swimsuit, and shoes, heavy greening around ears, box in excellent condition. **$200**

Courtesy of Morphy Auctions

1962 brunette Bubblecut Barbie in original red swimsuit, excellent condition. **$100**

Courtesy of Theriault's Antique Doll Auctions

Brunette Ponytail Barbie in "Picnic" set, excellent condition, moderate loss to fingernail paint, minor soiling to legs. **$200**

Courtesy of Morphy Auctions

Blonde Barbie with original box.................................. **$110**

Strawser Auctions

◄ Blonde Twist 'n' Turn Barbie with box and original swimsuit, hair ribbon, and catalog, doll in very good-plus condition with light soiling, box in very good condition with light overall wear.............. **$175**

Courtesy of Morphy Auctions

Fashion Queen Barbie with swimsuit, head wrap, three wigs, and wig stand, excellent condition. **$100**

Courtesy of Morphy Auctions

Joshard Barbie with two outfits, near mint condition. $50

Courtesy of Morphy Auctions

1964 blonde Side-Swirl Ponytail Barbie with blue eyeliner and red Helanca swimsuit, in original labeled box with original red heels and booklet, excellent condition, slight green on ears.............$400

Courtesy of Theriault's Antique Doll Auctions

Circa 1960s blonde Side-Swirl Barbie with clothes. $65

Courtesy of Pioneer Auction Gallery

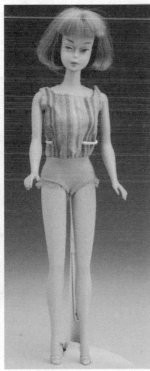

1965 redhead American Girl Barbie in vintage "Magnificence" #1646 outfit, gown with red satin bodice and pink chiffon skirt with pale pink flocking and crystal glitter, lined with pink taffeta, two attached red satin panels in back of skirt match panels attached to front of red satin jacket, collar of jacket with fur trim, single rhinestone accent at waist; one leg does not bend, small tear at knee, each breast of doll with pin prick, no shoes. $110

Courtesy of Ivy Auctions

1966 redhead Color Magic Barbie in original sealed box, #1150, with blue eyeliner, coral lips, bendable knees, original swimsuit, headband, and wrist tag in original sealed box (with remnants of Two Guys sticker on front), with original hair coloring and other accessories, excellent condition.................$1,000

Courtesy of Theriault's Antique Doll Auctions

American Girl Barbie with bathing suit and shoes, excellent condition, missing headband, one leg slightly loose. $425

Courtesy of Morphy Auctions

BASKETS

THE NATIVE AMERICANS were the first basket weavers on this continent and, of necessity, the early Colonial settlers and their descendants pursued this artistic handicraft to provide essential containers for berries, eggs, and endless other items to be carried or stored.

Rye straw, split willow and reeds are but a few of the wide variety of materials used. Nantucket baskets, plainly and sturdily constructed, along with those made by specialized groups, seem to draw the greatest attention to this area of collecting.

Abe Sanchez basket, Mission, 20th century, squat globular form with stair-stepped bands around body to flat shoulder and short neck, bottom with six paired birds and two single birds, excellent condition, 7" h., 11-3/4" dia....................... **$1,500**

Courtesy of Cowan's Auctions

Apache burden basket, circa 1900, woven with checkered bands painted with red pigment, reinforced with thick hide, fringe, expected wear, 13" h. without fringe, 14-1/4" dia. **$1,100**

Courtesy of Cowan's Auctions

Two Nootka lidded gift baskets in spruce wood and cedar bark, circa 1900, pink ducks and stripes, 3" h., 4-1/2" dia., and particolor ducks and stripes, central medallion, faded, 2-3/4" h., 4-1/4" dia..**$250**

Courtesy of Thomaston Place Auction Galleries

Miniature Makah basket, Neah Bay, Washington, late 19th century, round box in finely woven grass with red orange and black decoration, star on top, fitted lid, cloth-lined interior, faded, wear to lining, 2-1/8" h., 3-5/8" dia. **$100**

Courtesy of Thomaston Place Auction Galleries

Penobscot ash splint covered basket with tall bent oak crossed handles, late 19th century, overall porcupine quill decoration, marked in pencil calligraphy on bottom, "Mrs. Chas. H. Roberts, Biddeford, Maine," minor losses, soiling, 10-1/2" h. x 8-1/2" overall, 5-1/2" x 7-1/2" dia. basket body. **$225**

Courtesy of Thomaston Place Auction Galleries

Appalachian woven-splint gathering basket, fourth quarter 19th/first quarter 20th century, white oak and chestnut, deep circular form with X-wrapped rim, carved, notched, and arched chestnut handle, kick-up bottom, fine original dry surface with deep, mellow patina, 14" h. overall, 8-1/4" h. to rim, 13-1/2" dia. **$550**

Courtesy of Jeffrey S. Evans & Associates

Set of six graduated birch bark hanging baskets (three shown), late 19th century, probably Penobscot, found in Maine, each basket reinforced with bent willow, lashed with leather, hung from leather thong, 36" l. overall, 5" to 4" dia. **$250**

Courtesy of Thomaston Place Auction Galleries

◄ Pomo Degikup coiled basket, losses to rim stitches, 5" h., largest 10" dia............. **$3,500**

Courtesy of Michaan's Auctions

▲ Chinese woven baby basket and wood stand, 19th/early 20th century, with oval section basket fitted on stand carved with dragons, basket 38-1/2" w. **$425**

Courtesy of Clars Auction Gallery, www.clars.com

BASKETS

American woven-splint market or gathering basket, first half 20th century, white oak, rectangular form with canted sides, squared-arch handles on long sides, wooden bottom, original dry surface and mellow patina, 9-1/2" h. overall, 8-1/4" h. to rim, 18" w. overall.................. **$170**

Courtesy of Jeffrey S. Evans & Associates

Unusual American woven-splint hooded basket, fourth quarter 19th/first quarter 20th century, white oak, rectangular form with flared bottom, wrapped rims at openings, arched handle inscribed with initials "MEH" at top, fine old dry natural surface, 8-1/2" h. overall. **$750**

Courtesy of Jeffrey S. Evans & Associates

American woven-splint and stave basket, possibly North Carolina, mid-20th century, white oak, hickory, and pine, oblong oval form with X-wrapped rim, base, and handle, staves extend above rim, solid wooden bottom, original dry natural surface, 7-1/4" h. overall, 4-1/2" h. to rim, 15-1/2" w. overall. **$850**

Courtesy of Jeffrey S. Evans & Associates

Appalachian woven splint basket, late 19th/early 20th century, white oak, circular rim and square open-weave base, low arched handle with carved interior rim notches, original dry natural surface with excellent patina, 10" h. overall, 7" h. rim, 10" dia. rim. **$150**

Courtesy of Jeffrey S. Evans & Associates

Two New England woven splint baskets, 19th century, each in dry original surface: Rectangular form with wrapped rim and contrasting dyed splints, 8-1/2" h. x 16" l. x 12-1/2" w.; and circular form with arched swing handle, wrapped rim, and medial band with plaited weave, 9-1/2" h. rim, 13-1/2" dia. rim. **$80**

Courtesy of Jeffrey S. Evans & Associates

Painted rib-type woven splint basket, Shenandoah Valley of Virginia, late 19th/early 20th century, white oak, kidney form with double rim, arched handle with complex stepped supports, and fancy woven-over base rib, outstanding original dry blue-painted surface, 10" h. overall, 7" h. rim, 10" x 10-1/4" rim.......................................$1,200

Courtesy of Jeffrey S. Evans & Associates

New England splint woven swing handle gathering basket, probably Taghkanic, upstate New York, circa 1860, good condition with one splint loss area, 11" h., 17" dia. **$100**

Courtesy of A-1 Auction

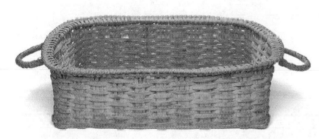

Woven splint gathering basket, Augusta County, Shenandoah Valley of Virginia, first quarter 20th century, white oak, with two wrapped handles and stepped, double-wrapped rim, and dry natural surface, 6-3/4" h. x 30-1/2" w. overall.. **$500**

Courtesy of Jeffrey S. Evans & Associates

Painted woven splint and stave basket, Rockingham County, Shenandoah Valley of Virginia, white oak with solid wooden bottom, flared sides, arched handle, staves extend above rim, original red-painted decoration, probably made in Brock's Gap area, circa 1930, 12-1/4" h. overall, 7-1/2" h. rim, 9-1/2" w. overall.......... **$350**

Courtesy of Jeffrey S. Evans & Associates

◄ Paint-decorated rib-type woven-splint basket, Virginia or West Virginia, late 19th/early 20th century, white oak, circular form with arched handle, tightly wrapped rim, and converging ribs, retains old paint-decorated surface in red, blue, green, and pink, 9-1/2" h. overall, 6" h. rim, 12" w. overall................$180

Courtesy of Jeffrey S. Evans & Associates

American woven-splint cheese basket, first half 20th century, white oak, circular wrapped rim and hexagonal open-weave body, excellent original dry natural surface, 5-3/4" h. overall, 10-1/4" dia. **$190**

Courtesy of Jeffrey S. Evans & Associates

Virginia painted rib-type woven-splint basket, fourth quarter 19th century, white oak, kidney form with converging ribs, double-wrapped rim, low arched handle, exceptional original worn dry blue-green painted surface, 6" h. overall, 4-3/4" h. to rim, 9" dia. overall. **$1,400**

Courtesy of Jeffrey S. Evans & Associates

Nantucket pocketbook basket with swing handle, circa 1950, signed by Jose Reyes. **$700**

Courtesy of Kaminski Auctions

▲ Pair of Maine potato baskets, splint ash with solid wooden handles, 18" h. x 16-1/2" dia. and 18" h. x 17" dia. **$50**

Courtesy of Thomaston Place Auction Galleries

Nantucket hand-crafted basket with swivel handle, mid-20th century, tagged on underside "Made by Ferdinand Sylvaro, 97 Orange St, Nantucket, Mass" with price of $3, fine condition, smudge of red paint on underside of handle, 6-1/4" x 9" dia. **$900**

Courtesy of Thomaston Place Auction Galleries

Nantucket lightship basket, bentwood handles, wicker circular body continuing to wood base, 15-1/2" h. **$700**

Courtesy of Clars Auction Gallery, www.clars.com

Shaker oval wood-carrying birch basket with bentwood handle, 19th century, finger-style cutouts held in place by copper rivets, some discoloration of patina on inside of base, 11" h. x 12" w. x 9" dia. **$50**

Courtesy of Louis J. Dianni, LLC Antiques Auctions

Nantucket swing-handled hickory lidded basket, early 20th century, unmarked, 11-1/2" x 10-1/2" **$1,000**

Courtesy of Rago Arts, www.ragoarts.com

Nantucket hickory swing-handled open basket by Ferdinand Sylvaro, early 20th century, original label, 14" x 12" **$1,300**

Courtesy of Rago Arts, www.ragoarts.com

Two Shaker oval lidded sewing baskets with handles and one basket with no handle, early 20th century, largest 3-1/2" x 8" x 6" **$425**

Courtesy of Rago Arts, www.ragoarts.com

Wicker fern stand, one-piece basket-woven stand with bulbous top and raised, rolled edge turned base, New England Wicker Co. label fragment, circa 1890, good condition, 36" x 16" dia. **$125**

Courtesy of Thomaston Place Auction Galleries

FAR LEFT American painted wicker plant stand in manner of Heywood Brothers & Wakefield Co., circa 1900, shaped rim, woven basket overlaid with cast floral garland, motif winds down support, some loss of paint and loosening of reed, 39-1/2" h., 14" dia. $54

Courtesy of Heritage Auctions

LEFT Rare Nantucket basket table/sewing stand, circa 1880-1890, open wicker basket at top set into turned and scribed top with inverted rim, lower wicker basket in typical form suspended from two loops, four-legged walnut frame, minor loss to rim of hanging basket, 32" h., 15-1/2" dia.........**$3,000-$4,000**

Courtesy of Thomaston Place Auction Galleries

Vintage Abercrombie & Fitch wicker picnic basket fitted with six plates, six cups and saucers, Thermos and canisters, and five canvas bags, case 16" h. x 21" w. x 7-1/2" d. $150

Courtesy of Neal Auction Co.

Micmac covered square picnic basket, circa 1900, checkerboard woven splint ash with rigid willow bale handle, very good condition, 10-1/2" h. x 12" x 10-1/2" overall, 5-1/4" x 10" x 10" body...............$100

Courtesy of Thomaston Place Auction Galleries

BOOKENDS

ONCE A STAPLE in many homes, bookends serve both functional and decorative purposes. They not only keep a person's books in order, they look good while they're doing it.

Bookends are commonly made of a variety of metals – bronze, brass, pewter, or silver plate – as well as marble, wood, ceramic, and other natural or manmade materials. The art they feature represents many subjects, with wildlife, domesticated animals and pets, sports figures or items, nautical themes, and fantasy themes as favorites.

The value of an antique bookend is determined by its age, the material it is made from, what it represents, the company that created it, and how scarce it is.

Four pairs of Lincoln-related cast metal bookends, one pair of seated Lincoln, one pair of Lincoln Memorial, one pair of Lincoln's cabin, and one pair of Bradley & Hubbard Lincoln bust, to 8" h. **$246**

Courtesy of Skinner, Inc., www.skinnerinc.com

Vestal virgin bust bookends, bronze, 19th century, with flower crowns atop veiled heads, unmarked, 4-3/4" h. **$450**

Courtesy of Skinner, Inc.; www.skinnerinc.com

Venus and Neptune bookends, Gleb W. Derujinsky (American, 1888-1975), 1922, bronze with brown patina, each inscribed along rear of base: © G. Derujinsky / 1922, each stamped along base: R.B.W., 7-1/4" h. and 7-3/4" h., each on 3/4" h. semi-circular marble base............................ **$2,375**

Courtesy of Heritage Auctions

top lot

Abraham Lincoln figural bookends, George Edwin Bissell (American, 1839-1920), circa 1916, bronze with brown patina, each stamped along base: Gorham Co Founders / Q449, scattered flecks of patina loss, 8" h.............$4,375

Bronze bookends after Michelangelo's "Tomb of Giuliano de Medici," late 19th century, minor chips to edges of marble bases, surface wear commensurate with age, 7-1/4" x 6" x 3"......... **$688**

Courtesy of Heritage Auctions

Bronze castings of dolphin-form bookends raised on molded gray marble bases, circa 1900, very good condition............. **$225**

Courtesy of Louis J. Dianni, LLC Antiques Auctions

◀ Bookends made from bronze taken from USS Constitution (Old Ironsides) during 1927 remodel of vessel, with portrait of ship and words "Launched 1797, 1804 Tripoli, 1812 Guerriere Java, 1815 Cyane, Levant," front bottom edges read "This Material Was Taken From US Frigate Constitution 1927," very good condition, light wear, toning, 6-3/4" h. x 5-3/4" w. x 1-1/4" d. These bookends helped raise funds to refurbish the ship that Bostonians built by conscription and launched in 1797.......... **$325**

Courtesy of Louis J. Dianni, LLC Antiques Auctions

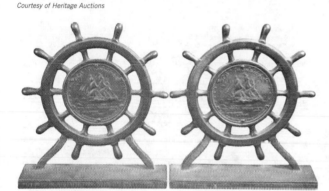

▲ Antique armor bronze Thai elephant bookends, P. Mori & Sons, 1920s, made with Galvano process, original felt bottoms, sticker of The G. M. McKelvey Co., Youngstown, Ohio under both elephants, very good or better condition, light wear. **$150**

Courtesy of PBA Galleries

Ben Seibel Jenfredware brass bookends, each with five wood diamond inlays, sticker on underside reading "Maison Gourmet a product of Jenfredware," 5-1/2" h. x 5-1/4" w. x 3" d. **$120**

Courtesy of Skinner, Inc.; www.skinnerinc.com

Art Nouveau solid brass adjustable bookends, early 20th century, very good condition, rubbing with patina to brass, folds flat, 4-1/4" h. x 8-1/2" w. (adjusts to 15") x 5-1/2" d................................... **$42**

Courtesy of Heritage Auctions

John Alden and Priscilla cast iron bookends, Bradley & Hubbard Manufacturing Co., Meriden, Connecticut, identified on front of base, maker's mark impressed on reverse, 5-7/8" h. x 3-3/4" w.**$48**

Courtesy of Skinner, Inc.; www.skinnerinc.com

Iron jacks bookends, larger 10" h. x 10" w....... **$125**

Courtesy of Uniques & Antiques, Inc.

Rodin's "The Thinker" bookends, stamped 1928 though probably later, very good condition, mild rubbing to finish, original felts bottoms, 7" h. x 2-3/4" w. x 4" d. ea.. $40

Courtesy of Heritage Auctions

Cast iron Federal Doorway polychrome painted bookends, Bradley & Hubbard Manufacturing Co., Meriden, Connecticut, early 20th century, impressed "B&H" marks on backs, partial paper label on one base, 5-3/4" h. x 4" w. $270

Courtesy of Skinner, Inc.; www.skinnerinc.com

Patinated cast iron figural bookends of Indian chief, unmarked, overall patina and light wear, 7" x 5-1/4" h. $110

Courtesy of Cordier Auctions

Horse head bookends, circa 1940s, original felt bottoms, very good condition, light rubbing and spotting to finish, 6" h. x 4" w. x 4-1/4" d. $36

Courtesy of Heritage Auctions

Spelter Art Nouveau bookends, seated female nude with draped cloth on legs, numbered 519 on back, slight paint loss, 6" h. x 3-1/2" w. x 7" d. **$190**

Courtesy of Stephenson's Auction

Art Deco chrome bookends with women in circles. **$110**

Courtesy of Strawser Auctions

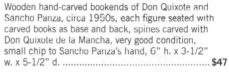

Wooden hand-carved bookends of Don Quixote and Sancho Panza, circa 1950s, each figure seated with carved books as base and back, spines carved with Don Quixote de la Mancha, very good condition, small chip to Sancho Panza's hand, 6" h. x 3-1/2" w. x 5-1/2" d. **$47**

Courtesy of Heritage Auctions

Fornasetti bookends, enameled metal, Milan, Italy, mid-20th century, red ground with black and white image of traditional musical instruments, one with felt to base marked Fornasetti Milano, Made in Italy in gilt, other with partial felt remaining, 6" h. **$480**

Courtesy of Skinner, Inc.; www.skinnerinc.com

Lucite snail bookends, P. Borras, metallic snail forms on Lucite base, signed, 4-3/4" h. x 7-3/4" w. x 3-1/4" d. **$225**

Courtesy of Uniques & Antiques, Inc.

Molded bookends of sailing ships painted to resemble carved wood, felt bottoms, very good condition, approximately 7" x 4" x 9" **$88**

Courtesy of Heritage Auctions

R. Lalique clear and frosted glass Tete d'Aigle bookends, circa 1928, molded R. LALIQUE, good condition, one mascot loose from base, 7-3/8". **$625**

Courtesy of Heritage Auctions

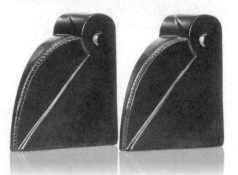

Pelican bookends, Cowan Pottery, A. Drexler Jacobson design, in black, silver, and bronze glaze, each impressed on back with circular Cowan logo, professional repair to back of each piece, 5-1/4" h. **$650**

Courtesy of Mark Mussio, Humler & Nolan

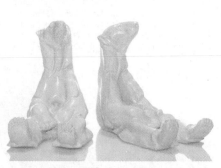

Rare polar bear bookends, Fulper Pottery, Flemington, New Jersey, in off-white matte glaze, shape 421, both marked on bottom with Fulper vertical "racetrack" ink stamp, professional repair to both pieces, one bear with minor crazing and glaze nick on foot, 7-1/2" h. x 8" l............... **$1,000**

Courtesy of Mark Mussio, Humler & Nolan

▶ Aztec mask bookends in Mission Verde glaze, Fulper Pottery, Flemington, New Jersey, 1910-1915, both ink-stamp marked, paper label to one, good condition, one with firing crack at front bottom, 5-1/2" x 5-3/4" x 3" ea. **$375**

Courtesy of Rago Arts, www.ragoarts.com

Jewel-tone Murano glass bookends with blue exterior and magenta interior, no defects, 7" h..................**$180**

Courtesy of Cordier Auctions

Golf-theme figural bookends, marble and white metal, circa 1930, 5-1/2" h. x 4" w. x 3.3" d. . **$125**

Courtesy of Louis J. Dianni, LLC Antiques Auctions

Roseville blue Magnolia pattern bookends, shape No. 13, excellent condition, 5-1/2" h. x 5" w. $50

Courtesy of Morphy Auctions

Ram bookends, Van Briggle, Colorado Springs, 1910s, marked AA, 4-3/4" x 5" x 3-3/4" ea. ... **$250**

Courtesy of Rago Arts, www.ragoarts.com

Art Deco women's heads ceramic bookends, excellent condition, crazing and minor paint chips, 8" h. **$125**

Courtesy of Morphy Auctions

Rare rooster bookends, Rookwood Pottery, Cincinnati, Arthur Conant design, 1933, with Coromandel glaze, marks: Rookwood logo, date and shape 6386, one piece with glaze nick at base, both with minor stilt pulls and faint crazing, 6-7/8" h. **$2,700**

Courtesy of Mark Mussio, Humler & Nolan

Elephant bookends by William McDonald, Rookwood Pottery, Cincinnati, 1918, with celadon glaze, Rookwood logo, date 1918, artist's initials and shape 2444, 4-1/2" h. **$325**

Courtesy of Cowan's Auctions

BOOKS

WITH IN EXCESS of 100 million books in existence, there are plenty of opportunities and avenues for bibliophiles to feed their enthusiasm and build a satisfying collection of noteworthy tomes without taking out a second mortgage or sacrificing their children's college funds. With so many to choose from, the true challenge is limiting a collection to a manageable size and scale, adding only volumes that meet the requirements of bringing the collector pleasure and holding their values.

What collectors are really searching for when they refer to "first editions" are the first printings of first editions. Every book has a first edition, each of which is special in its own right. As Matthew Budman points out in *Collecting Books* (House of Collectibles, 2004), "A first represents the launching of a work into the world, with or without fanfare, to have a great impact, or no impact, immediately or decades later. ... Holding a first edition puts you directly in contact with that moment of impact."

Devon Gray, director of Fine Books and Manuscripts at Skinner, Inc., www.skinnerinc.com, explains the fascination with collectible books: "Collectors are always interested in landmarks of human thought and culture, and important moments in the history of printing."

What makes a first edition special enough to be considered collectible is rarity and demand; the number of people who want a book has to be greater than the number of books available. So, even if there are relatively few in existence, there has to be a demand for any particular first edition to be monetarily valuable.

Author Richard Russell has been collecting and selling books since 1973; in his book, *Antique Trader Book Collector's Price Guide,* he explains that innovative (or perhaps even unpopular) books that are initially released in small printings "will eventually become some of the most sought after and expensive books in the collector's market." He gives as an example John Grisham's *A Time To Kill* (Wynwood Press, 1989), which had an initial print run of just 5,000 hardcover copies. The author bought 1,000 himself at wholesale with the plan to sell at retail and turn a bit of profit. When Grisham couldn't sell them at $10 apiece, he was giving them away out of his law office.[1] The book is valued at about $4,000 today.

Learning how to recognize first editions is a key to protecting yourself as a collector; you can't take it for granted that the person you are buying from (especially if he or she is not a professional bookseller) has identified the book properly. Entire volumes have been written on identifying first editions; different publishing houses use different means of identification, many utilizing differing methods and codes. However, according to the *Antique Trader Book Collector's Price Guide,* there are several details that will identify a first edition:

• The date on the title page matches the copyright date with no other printings listed on the copyright page (verso).

• "First Edition," "First Printing," "First Issue" or something similar is listed on the copyright page.

• A publisher's seal or logo (colophon) is printed on the title page, copyright page, or at the end of the text block.

• The printer's code on the copyright page shows a "1" or an "A" at one end or the other (example: "9

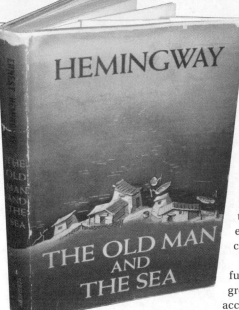

Ernest Hemingway, *The Old Man and the Sea*. First edition, signed and inscribed by author. **$3,220**
Courtesy of Philip Weiss Auctions

8 7 6 5 4 3 2 1" indicates first edition; "9 8 7 6 5 4 3 2" indicates second edition).

As is the case with so many collectibles, condition is paramount. If a book was published with a dust jacket, it must be present and in great condition to attain the book's maximum value. Gray uses an example to illustrate the importance of condition.

"A book with a very large value basically has further to fall before it loses it all," she says. "A great example is the first edition of the printed account of the Lewis and Clarke expedition. In bad condition its value is in the four-figure range; in better condition, it gets up to five figures; and in excellent condition, six figures.

"Another example: The 1920 first American edition of T.S. Eliot's Poems sells for around $300 in poor condition with no dust jacket; and $1,200 to $1,500 in good condition in a good dust jacket; the copy that Eliot gave to Virginia Woolf sold for 90,000 British pounds [approximately $136,000]; all the same edition."

A signature enhances a book's value because it often places the book in the author's hands. Cut signatures add slightly to a book's value because the author didn't actually sign the book – he or she may have never even held the book with the added cut signature. When the book itself is signed, even if with a brief inscription, it holds a slightly higher value. If the author is known for making regular appearances and accommodating all signature requests, the signature adds little to the value of the book because the supply for signed examples is plentiful.

"Real value potential comes into play with association material," Gray explains. "For example, a famous novelist's Nobel-winning story is based on a tumultuous affair he had with a famous starlet under his heiress-wife's nose, and you have the copy he presented to his wife, with her 'notes.'"

Even a title that has been labeled as "great," "important," or "essential" doesn't mean a particular edition – even a first edition – is collectible or monetarily valuable. After all, if a much-anticipated book is released with an initial print run of 350,000, chances are there will be hundreds of thousands of "firsts" to choose from – even decades after publication. Supply far outweighs demand, diminishing value.

The overly abundant supply of book club editions (which can be reprinted indefinitely) is just one of the reasons they're not valued by collectors. Some vintage book club editions were also made from inferior materials, such as high-acid paper using lower quality manufacturing processes.

Determining if a book is a book club edition is easier than determining if it is a first edition. Some of the giveaways that Matthew Budman lists in Collecting Books include:
- No price on dust jacket
- Blind stamp on back cover (small impression on the back board under the dust jacket); can be as small as a pinprick hole
- "Book Club Edition" (or similar notation) on dust jacket
- Books published by the Literary Guild after World War II are smaller format, thinner and

Shirley Hibberd, *Greenhouse Favourites, A Description of Choice Greenhouse Plants*, London: Groombridge & Sons, 1870. First edition, 36 chromolithographed plates, tissue guards, illustrations, contemporary dark green morocco, gilt, corners worn, rubbed, some foxing. **$475**

Courtesy of Dreweatts & Bloomsbury Auctions

Richard Lydekker, *A Trip to Pilawin*, London: R. Ward, 1908. First edition, scarce record of sport and preservation before World War I, original cloth with pictorial onlay, foxing to endpapers, spine slightly faded................................. **$416**

Courtesy of Dreweatts & Bloomsbury Auctions

Adam Smith, *An Inquiry into the Nature and Causes of the Wealth of Nations*, London: W. Strahan & T. Cadell, 1778. Second edition, one of 500 copies; 4to, contemporary speckled calf, gilt, spines gilt in compartments with red and green morocco labels, title slightly browned on vol. 1, with some spotting.................**$22,300**

Courtesy of Dreweatts & Bloomsbury Auctions

printed on cheap paper.

Fledgling book collectors should also be aware of companies that built a burgeoning business of publishing a copious number of "classic" and best-seller reprints; just a few of the long list are Grosset & Dunlap, Reader's Digest, Modern Library, A.L. Burt, Collier, Tower and Triangle. Many of these companies' editions are valued only as reading copies, not as collectibles worthy of investment.

Proper care should be implemented early on when building a collection to assure the books retain their condition and value. Books should be stored upright on shelves in a climate-controlled environment out of direct (or even bright indirect) sunlight. Too much humidity will warp covers; high temperatures will break down glues. Arrange them so similar-sized books are side-by-side for maximum support, and use bookends so the books don't lean, which will eventually cause the spines to shift and cause permanent damage.

A bookplate usually will reduce a book's value, so keep that in mind when you're thinking of adding a book with a bookplate to your collection, and avoid adding bookplates to your own volumes. Also, don't pack your volumes with high-acid paper such as newspaper clippings, and always be careful when placing or removing them from the shelf so you don't tear the spine.

Building a book collection – or any collection, for that matter – on a budget involves knowing more about the subject than the seller. Learning everything possible about proper identification of coveted books and significant authors involves diligence and dedication, but the reward is maximum enjoyment of collecting at any level.

— *Karen Knapstein* Print Editor, *Antique Trader*

1 John Grisham's Favorite Mistake: Giving Away First Editions, http://www.thedailybeast.com/newsweek/2012/04/01/john-grisham-s-favorite- mistake-giving-away-first-editions.html

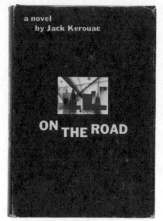

J.R.R. Tolkien, set of *The Lord of the Rings (The Fellowship of the Ring, The Two Towers, The Return of the King)*, London: George Allen & Unwin, 1954, 1954, and 1955, respectively. First edition, first impressions, all octavo with maps attached to rear flyleaf of each book, original dust jacket priced "21s net," custom-made full gray morocco, gilt clamshell cases...**$20,000**

Courtesy of Heritage Auctions

Jack Kerouac, *On the Road*, New York: The Viking Press, 1957. First edition, publisher's full black cloth, front board and spine lettered in white, jacket spine and rear panel toned, some rubbing and short tears to jacket, mild toning to text. **$2,500**

Courtesy of Heritage Auctions

Ray Bradbury, *Fahrenheit 451*, New York: Ballantine Books, 1953. First edition, number 213 of 200 copies, signed by Bradbury and signed in "an asbestos material with exceptional resistance to pyrolysis"; letter from Bradbury with copy of book that sold at earlier auction explained possible inclusion of additional copies than that indicated on frontispiece; octavo, housed in slipcase, rebacked, some rubbing and thumbsoiling to binding............................ **$4,375**

Courtesy of Heritage Auctions

Virginia Woolf, *Kew Gardens*, London: Hogarth Press. Third English edition, number 330 of 500 copies, signed by Woolf and illustrator Vanessa Bell on limitation page, original color block-printed paper boards, housed in blue cloth folding box; rebacked, boards and pastedowns repaired, corners bumped, some text toned. .. **$2,125**

Courtesy of Heritage Auctions

Charles Dickens, *A Tale of Two Cities*, London: Chapman and Hall, 1859. First edition, first issue, octavo, in seldom-seen original publisher's full red cloth, 16 inserted plates by "Phiz," including frontispiece and vignette title; spine browned and worn, tailcap strengthened, boards dull, rubbed and soiled, text shaken....... **$5,937**

Courtesy of Heritage Auctions

◄ Tolstoy (Lev Nikolayevich), *Anna Karenina*, Moscow: 1886. Sixth edition, three volumes in two, Russian booksellers' stamp on titles, Russian gift inscription on verso of Vol. 1 front flyleaf; 8vo, original brown cloth tooled in gilt and black with gilt vignette portrait of author... **$965**

Courtesy of Dreweatts & Bloomsbury Auctions

Stephen King, *Carrie*, Garden City: Doubleday & Co., Inc., 1974. First edition, presentation copy, inscribed by King on title page, "To David – / Best, / Stephen King / 2/27/81," publisher's full burgundy cloth, dust jacket, spine lettered in gilt; slight toning on spine, minor rubbing and thumbsoiling to jacket. **$2,125**

Courtesy of Heritage Auctions

Homer, *The Odyssey of Homer*, translated by T.E. Lawrence, London: Sir Emery Walker, Wilfred Merton and Bruce Rogers, 1932. Unpaginated, original full black Niger morocco, gilt-lettered spine with raided bands; minor rubbing to binding, occasional offsetting from roundels. .. **$2,000**

Courtesy of Heritage Auctions

Kate Chopin, *The Awakening*, Chicago & New York: Herbert S. Stone & Co., 1899. First edition, precursor to modern American feminist writing, condemned by reviewers and not treated to additional printings; publisher's green cloth, boards stamped in red and green, spine lettered in red; rebacked, binding heavily browned and soiled. **$1,250**

Courtesy of Heritage Auctions

C.S. Lewis, first American editions of *The Chronicles of Narnia (The Lion, The Witch and the Wardrobe; Prince Caspian; The Voyage of the Dawn Treader; The Magician's Nephew; The Horse and His Boy; The Silver Chair; The Last Battle)*, New York: The Macmillan Co., 1950-1956. Publisher's original harlequin cloth, dust jackets; jackets chipped and worn, toning and light soiling. **$1,875**

Courtesy of Heritage Auctions

John Steinbeck, *Of Mice and Men*, New York: Covici Friede, 1937. First edition, first issue, one of only 2,500 copies published, publisher's tan cloth with orange and black stamping, original pictorial dust jacket; minor shelf wear to boards, light edge wear on dust jacket. **$875**

Courtesy of Heritage Auctions

Andy Warhol, *Andy Warhol's Exposures*, New York: Andy Warhol Books/Grosset & Dunlap, 1979. First edition, signed twice with original sketch by Warhol, inscribed by Warhol on half-title, "to robyn / love / Andy" with accompanying sketch, recipient was assistant at factory and is featured in two photographs in book, photos by Warhol and text by Warhol and Bob Colacello; dust jacket; some rubbing and mild wear to jacket. **$750**

Courtesy of Heritage Auctions

J.D. Salinger, *Raise High the Roof Beam, Carpenters and Seymour an Introduction*, Boston: Little, Brown and Co., 1959. First edition, first issue, minus dedication page (added in second issue), dust jacket, publisher's full dark gray cloth, spine lettered in gilt; jacket pine sunned, some rubbing and light wear, one small tape repair. **$625**

Courtesy of Heritage Auctions

Ken Kesey, *One Flew Over the Cuckoo's Nest*, New York: The Viking Press, 1962. First edition, first state with required text about Red Cross, publisher's full green cloth, spine lettered in yellow, dust jacket with correct price ($4.95), Kerouac blurb on front flap; moderate toning and thumbsoiling to jacket, cloth spine sunned. **$2,375**

Courtesy of Heritage Auctions

Kurt Vonnegut, Jr., *Slaughterhouse-Five or The Children's Crusade*, New York: Delacorte Press, 1969. First edition, first printing, original pictorial dust jacket, with ownership signature of Pulitzer-Prize winning author Tad Mosel on first blank, later blue silk slipcase; jacket toned and lightly rubbed, faint stain on rear jacket panel. **$1,187**

Courtesy of Heritage Auctions

Alonzo Delano, *The Miner's Progress; or, Scenes in the Life of a California Miner*, Sacramento: Daily Union Office, 1853. First edition, seldom-seen original printed string-bound brown wrapper, satirical work about hardships of Gold Rush; some mild rubbing and foxing to wrappers, two vertical creases. **$2,000**

Courtesy of Heritage Auctions

Harriet Beecher Stowe, *Uncle Tom's Cabin; or Life Among the Lowly*, Vols. I and II, Boston: John P. Jewett & Company, 1852. Publisher's cloth with gilt titles and decorations on spine, some penciled annotations; leaning spine, rubbing and edge wear to extremities. **$812**

Courtesy of Heritage Auctions

Louise Sanders, *The Knave of Hearts*, with pictures by Maxfield Parrish, New York: Charles Scribner's Sons, 1925. First edition, color frontispiece with tissue guard, 15-page color illustrations by Parrish, original cloth and color pictorial label on front cover; minor wear to binding, fading and scuffing. **$937**

Courtesy of Heritage Auctions

Hal Clement, *Mission of Gravity*, New York: Doubleday & Co., 1954. First edition, publisher's yellow cloth in dust jacket; some edge wear on dust jacket. **$475**

Courtesy of Heritage Auctions

Edgar Rice Burroughs, *Escape on Venus*, Tarzana: Edgar Rice Burroughs, Inc., 1946. First edition, publisher's dark blue cloth in dust jacket, tipped-in notice of "this book [being] one of few survivors of a near disastrous fire" at Edgar Rice Burroughs, Inc.; light wear and soiling on dust jacket, some shelf ware. **$112**

Courtesy of Heritage Auctions

Ernest Hemingway, *A Farewell to Arms*, New York: Charles Scribner's Sons, 1929. First trade edition, first printing, sans legal disclaimer, dust jacket with "Katharine Barclay" misspelling on front flap, publisher's smooth black cloth with printed gold paper labels; shelf wear, corners lightly bumped and abraded. **$1,500**

Courtesy of Heritage Auctions

Erskine Caldwell, *Tobacco Road*, New York: Charles Scribner's Sons, 1932. First edition, dust jacket, publisher's full brown cloth, front board stamped in blind, front board and spine stamped in gilt; jacket toned, edge worn, chipped and rubbed. **$750**

Courtesy of Heritage Auctions

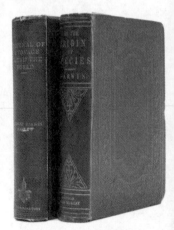

Charles Darwin, *On the Origin of Species by Means of Natural Selection*, London: John Murray, 1860. Second edition, publishers catalog dated January 1860 at end, pencil signature of John Mowat on front free endpaper; 8vo, original blind-stamped green cloth, gilt, inner hinges strengthened, corners bumped, slight foxing. **$3,270**

Courtesy of Dreweatts & Bloomsbury Auctions

CHILDREN'S BOOKS

Kate Douglas Wiggin, *Rebecca of Sunnybrook Farm*, Boston: Houghton, Mifflin, 1903. First edition, publisher's binding, chemised in quarter morocco slipcase. **$40**

Courtesy of Heritage Auctions

Janice May Udry, *The Moon Jumpers*, illustrated by Maurice Sendak, Harper & Row, 1959. Later edition, inscribed by Sendak, publlsher's binding and dust jacket.....................**$53**

Courtesy of Heritage Auctions

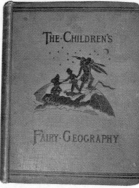

The Children's Fairy Geography, 1897, hardcover, illustrated. ..**$35**

Courtesy of Pioneer Auction Gallery

Garth Williams (1912-1996), illustrator, *The Tall Book of Make-Believe*, Harper & Row, 1950. Publisher's original pictorial boards and dust jacket. **$100**

Courtesy of Heritage Auctions

Pretty Pussies, 1942, softcover. **$10**

Courtesy of Pioneer Auction Gallery

Boys' & Girls' Bookshelf, 1915, hardcover, children's book of fact and fancy. **$8**

Courtesy of Pioneer Auction Gallery

Animal Pets, linen, 1913, illustrated, rare. **$14**

Courtesy of Pioneer Auction Gallery

10 Things You Didn't Know About Little Golden Books

1 The Little Golden Books line first premiered with 12 titles, all released at the same time – September 1942 – priced at 25 cents each. Today the average retail price of a Little Golden Book is $3.99.

Donald Duck's Adventure, signed by Walt Disney sold for $900 at auction.

2 The Little Golden Book *Donald Duck's Adventure,* circa 1950, signed by Walt Disney, with the words "BEST WISHES," realized $900 during a 2011 auction presented by Universal Live. The book had some age spotting on the cover, corner and some wearing along the spine, but the presence of a Walt Disney signature tipped the scales. It's not commonplace to find a children's book with Disney's signature on it.

3 The first 12 books to be released were: *Three Little Kittens, Bedtime Stories, The Alphabet A-Z, Mother Goose, Prayers for Children, The Little Red Hen, Nursery Songs, The Poky Little Puppy, The Golden Book of Fairy Tales, Baby's Book, The Animal of Farmer Jones,* and *This Little Piggy.*

4 Five months after the initial release, 1.5 million copies of the books had been printed. Forty-four years after the first 12 were published, the one billionth Little Golden Book, which incidentally was *The Poky Little Puppy,* was printed in the United States.

5 A first edition of *Smokey Bear and the Campers,* circa 1961, sold for $45 during a 2010 auction presented by Phoebus Auction Gallery.

6 A few notable authors and illustrators were responsible for bringing forth some classic Little Golden Books. Among those were Margaret Wise Brown, who also authored the timeless *Goodnight Moon;* Mercer Mayer, author of the "Little Monster" series; Richard Scarry, best known for his "Busytown" series of books; and iconic artist Garth Williams, whose illustrations brought to life the characters in *Stuart Little, Charlotte's Web,* and the "Little House" series penned by Laura Ingalls Wilder.

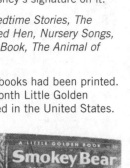

Smokey Bear and the Campers sold for $45 during an auction by Phoebus Auction Gallery.

7 Of all the hundreds of Little Golden Books published, one of the first 12 lays claim (so far) to the most copies sold – *The Poky Little Puppy.* At last count, more than 15 million copies have been sold. The book was banned in the Soviet Union for some time because of its capitalistic storyline.

8 The original Little Golden Books sparked a flurry of development in the 1950s, including an activity series of books (complete with learning wheels, paper dolls, and paints as some of the enhancements), development of Big Little Golden Books, and boxed puzzles featuring the cover of Little Golden Books.

9 Not unlike some popular toys, and even Depression glass, Little Golden Books were premiums included in products such as diapers and in children's meals at fast-food restaurants.

10 In 2013, Golden Books released *Everything I Need to Know I Learned from a Little Golden Book.* Written by Diane Muldrow, a prolific author of Little Golden Books, the book draws on more than 70 years of Little Golden Book wisdom to provide practical tips for adults.

– Compiled by Antoinette Rahn

Sources: LiveAuctioneers, Warman's Little Golden Books Identification and Price Guide, *www.little-golden-books.com, www.thesantis.com, www.randomhousekids.com.*

BOTTLES

INTEREST IN BOTTLE collecting, and high interest in extremely rare bottles, continues to grow, with new bottle clubs forming throughout the United States and Europe. More collectors are spending their free time digging through old dumps and foraging through ghost towns, digging out old outhouses (that's right), exploring abandoned mine shafts, and searching their favorite bottle or antique shows, swap meets, flea markets, and garage sales. In addition, the Internet has greatly expanded, offering collectors numerous opportunities and resources to buy and sell bottles with many new auction websites, without even leaving the house. Many bottle clubs now have websites providing even more information for the collector. These new technologies and resources have helped bottle collecting to continue to grow and gain interest.

Most collectors, however, still look beyond the type and value of a bottle to its origin and history. Researching the history of a bottle is almost as interesting as finding the bottle itself.

"The knowledge and experience of collectors in the hobby today is at a record pace," according to Jeff Wichmann, president of American Bottle Auctions. "It has not only brought a keener appreciation for the hobby, but apparently a bag full of money with it. Prices for the best of the best [have] never been greater, and as we continue to gain more experienced collectors, I see no limit in sight. It's still a very affordable hobby to pursue, but if the Tiffany of antique bottles is what you're looking for, you'd be advised to bring your checkbook and have a load of cash to cover it.

"It's not the addition of new offerings to the market as much as the limited availability of pieces that fit into that world of the very best," Wichmann said. "When a piece comes up, unlike even five years ago, it's now every [person] for himself. There has always been the average example and there always will be, but it's the one-known bitters or odd-colored historical flask that is finally getting its due respect."

For more information on bottles, see *Antique Trader Bottles Identification & Price Guide, 7th edition,* and *Picker's Pocket Guide: Bottles,* both by Michael Polak.

Fire grenade, "STAR" (inside five-pointed star) / "HARDEN HAND GRENADE – FIRE EXTINGUISHER," American, circa 1880-1900, turquoise blue, smooth base, rough sheared and ground lip, original contents, 6-3/4" h. **$60**

Courtesy of Glass Works Auctions

VISIT WWW.ANTIQUETRADER.COM

WWW.FACEBOOK.COM/ANTIQUETRADER

Sunburst scent bottle, probably Boston and Sandwich Glass Works, Sandwich, Massachusetts, 1820-1840, shield form with sunburst pattern, emerald green with profuse amethyst striations, ground mouth, pontil scar, rare color, 2-11/16" h. **$1,053**

Courtesy of Norman Heckler & Co.

Sandwich-type cologne bottle, American, circa 1850-1870, turquoise blue, thumbprint panels with herringbone corners, smooth base, sheared and tooled lip, 9" h. **$1,300**

Courtesy of Glass Works Auctions

Pattern molded decanter, probably early Pittsburgh district, Pittsburgh, Pennsylvania, 1840-1860, pillar molded inverted cone form with eight vertical ribs and heavy ring at mid body, amethyst, heavy tooled flared mouth, polished pontil scar, 11" h. **$702**

Courtesy of Norman Heckler & Co.

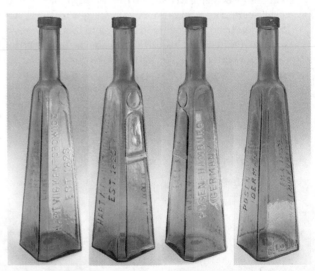

"DOYLES – HOP – BITTERS –1872" / (cluster of hops), New York, circa 1875-1885, yellow amber semi-cabin, "C & CO," on smooth base, applied double collar mouth, 98% original front and back labels, 9-5/8" h. **$500**

Courtesy of Glass Works Auctions

"HARTWIG KANTOROWICZ / EST. 1823 –POSEN-HAMBURG / (GERMANY) / C. 1/2 LTR," German, circa 1880-1900, medium yellowish green, tapered form, smooth base, applied mouth, 12" h. ... **$950**

Courtesy of Glass Works Auctions

Stiegel diamond daisy pattern flask, Stiegel Glass Works, Manheim, Pennsylvania, circa 1765-1775, deep purple amethyst, diamond daisy over flutes pattern, open pontil, sheared and tooled lip, 5-1/8" h. ... **$3,250**

Courtesy of Glass Works Auctions

◄ Umbrella ink, American, circa 1840-1860, light pink amethyst color, eight-sided, open pontil, sheared and tooled lip, 2" h. **$4,000**

Courtesy of Glass Works Auctions

Ink bottle, "ESTES'S / METROPOLITAN," American, circa 1840-1860, bluish aqua with hint of green, ribbed cone form, open pontil, crude applied tapered collar mouth, one of only two or three known examples, 7-1/2" h. **$2,200**

Courtesy of Glass Works Auctions

Nailsea flask, English, circa 1840-1870, clear glass with milk glass looping and internal cranberry flashing, teardrop form, pontil scarred base, sheared and tooled lip, 6-1/2" h. **$130**

Courtesy of Glass Works Auctions

"T.J. LUMMUS' / A.V. BITTERS – LYNN – MASS.," Massachusetts, circa 1840-1860, bluish aqua, open pontil, applied tapered collar mouth, 7-1/2" h. **$3,250**

Courtesy of Glass Works Auctions

"Dingens / Napoleon Cocktail Bitters" – "Dingen Brothers / Buffalo, N.Y." figural bitters bottle, America, 1845-1860, drum form, colorless with gray tint, applied sloping collared mouth, iron pontil mark, 10-1/4" h. **$6,435**

Courtesy of Norman Heckler & Co.

"H. A. FURMAN & CO. / ALBANY, N.Y. – THIS BOTTLE / NOT TO / BE SOLD," New York, circa 1875-1890, olive yellow tall beer, "VI N / K. HUTTER / N.Y." on smooth base, applied blob mouth, 9-1/2" h. **$230**

Courtesy of Glass Works Auctions

"A.M. BININGER & CO. / NO. 338 BROADWAY. – OLD LONDON DICK – GIN," New York, circa 1865-1875, yellowish grass green, smooth base, applied tapered collar mouth, 9-5/8" h. **$325**

Courtesy of Glass Works Auctions

"NAPA / SODA – NATURAL / MINERAL WATER / T.A.W.," California, circa 1860-1870, blue green, smooth base, applied blob mouth, 7-1/4" h.........**$375**

Courtesy of Glass Works Auctions

"DR. TEBBETTS' – PHYSIOLOGICAL / HAIR – REGENERATOR," American, circa 1865-1875, medium to deep pink amethyst color, smooth base, applied double collar mouth, 7-3/8" h. **$550**

Courtesy of Glass Works Auctions

"TITCOMB'S / INK CIN,"
Ohio, circa 1840-1860, aqua,
12-sided, open pontil, inward
rolled lip, 2-7/8" h. **$400**

Courtesy of Glass Works Auctions

Figural ear of corn bottle, American,
circa 1865-1875, yellowish amber,
smooth base, applied mouth,
probably label bitters or whiskey
bottle, 9-3/4" h. **$400**

Courtesy of Glass Works Auctions

"HANDYSIDE'S / CONSUMPTION,
CURE," English, circa 1880-
1895, deep olive amber, smooth
base, applied double collar mouth,
8-3/8" h.................................. **$210**

Courtesy of Glass Works Auctions

Triple cut glass inkwell, American, circa 1880 1900, clear cut and
polished stand with three recessed wells, red, clear, and turquoise faceted
glass lids attached to hinged brass mounts, 2-3/8" h., 5" x 2-1/2". **$800**

Courtesy of Glass Works Auctions

"SARATOGA / (five-pointed
star) / SPRING," New York,
circa 1865-1875, olive green
pint, smooth base, applied
double collar mouth. **$1,400**

Courtesy of Glass Works Auctions

◄"JOHN BULL – EXTRACT OF /
SARSAPARILLA – LOUISVILLE
KY," Louisville, Kentucky, circa
1845-1860, deep bluish aqua,
iron pontil, applied tapered
collar mouth, 8-5/8" h..........**$700**

Courtesy of Glass Works Auctions

Cathedral pickle jar, American, circa 1850-1865, bluish aqua, six-sided, pontil scarred base, applied ring mouth, 13" h. **$180**

Courtesy of Glass Works Auctions

Early pattern molded flask, diamond daisy pattern, Stiegel's American Flint Glass Manufactory, Manheim, Pennsylvania, 1763-1775, flattened bulbous form, amethyst, sheared mouth, pontil scar, 4-3/8" h. **$1,287**

Courtesy of Norman Heckler & Co.

Cornucopia/urn, Coventry Glass Works, Coventry, Connecticut, circa 1825-1835, medium olive yellow pint, open pontil, sheared and tooled lip......... **$240**

Courtesy of Glass Works Auctions

Blueberry preserve jar, Willington Glass Works, West Willington, Connecticut, 1860-1873, cylindrical with fluted shoulders and neck, medium blue green, applied double collared mouth, smooth base, 11-1/8" h. **$7,605**

Courtesy of Norman Heckler & Co.

"THE FATHER OF HIS COUNTRY" / BUST OF WASHINGTON – "A LITTLE MORE GRAPE CAPTAIN BRAGG" / BUST OF TAYLOR, Dyottville Glass Works, Philadelphia, circa 1848-1855, cobalt blue quart, open pontil, sheared and tooled lip. **$3,500**

Courtesy of Glass Works Auctions

U.S. Army officer/large sunburst, American, circa 1855-1865, bluish aqua calabash, iron pontil, applied tapered collar mouth...............................**$230**

Courtesy of Glass Works Auctions

"STRONG COBB & CO / WHOLESALE / DRUGGISTS / CLEVELAND, O.," Ohio, circa 1870-1880, cobalt blue, smooth base, applied mouth, 10-3/8" h. **$180**

Courtesy of Glass Works Auctions

"DR. LANGLEY'S / ROOT & HERB / BITTERS / 99 UNION ST. / BOSTON," Massachusetts, circa 1855-1865, yellow amber, smooth base, applied mouth, 7" h. **$1,100**

Courtesy of Glass Works Auctions

"BROWN'S / CELEBRATED / INDIAN HERB BITTERS – PATENTED / FEB 11 / 1868," Pennsylvania, circa 1868-1875, amber Indian princess, smooth base, sheared and partially inward rolled lip, 12-1/4" h....**$275**

Courtesy of Glass Works Auctions

"DR. JACOB'S / BITTERS – S.A. SPENCER. – NEW HAVEN, CT.," Connecticut, circa 1855-1865, bluish aqua, smooth base, applied tapered collar mouth, 10-1/4" h. **$450**

Courtesy of Glass Works Auctions

75

! top lot

"ZACHARY TAYLOR" / BUST OF TAYLOR / "ROUGH & READY" – "CORN FOR THE WORLD" / CORN STALK, Baltimore Glass Works, circa 1830-1840, light amethyst pint, open pontil, sheared and tooled lip. $26,000

COURTESY OF GLASS WORKS AUCTIONS

"BYRON ACID / SPRING WATER," New York, circa 1850-1965, blue green quart, iron pontil, applied double collar mouth.................... $9,000

Courtesy of Glass Works Auctions

Handled whiskey, "STAR WHISKEY / W.B. CROWELL JR. / NEW YORK," (on applied seal), New York, circa 1855-1870, yellow amber, cone form with vertical rib pattern, open pontil, applied mouth with hand-crimped pour spout, handle and seal, 8-1/4" h.................... $4,000

Courtesy of Glass Works Auctions

"L.Q.C. WISHART'S –PINE TREE / TAR CORDIAL / PHILA. –PATENT / (motif of pine tree) / 1859," Pennsylvania, circa 1870-1880, yellowish green, smooth base, applied tapered collar mouth, 9-1/2" h. **$350**

Courtesy of Glass Works Auctions

Unembossed fire grenade, American, circa 1880-1900, cobalt blue, horizontal rib pattern, smooth base, sheared and tooled lip, 6-3/8" h. **$190**

Courtesy of Glass Works Auctions

Target ball, "G.A. BASTMAN – STOCKHOLM," Swedish, circa 1880-1900, overall diamond pattern above and below embossed center band, yellow amber, rough sheared lip, 2-5/8" dia. **$1,500**

Courtesy of Glass Works Auctions

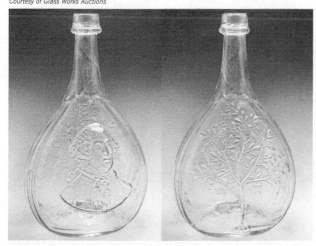

Bust of Washington/summer tree, American, circa 1855-1865, aqua calabash, open pontil, applied top hat mouth. **$475**

Courtesy of Glass Works Auctions

Medicine bottle, "I. Newton's / Panacea / Purifier / Of The / Blood / Norwich, VT.," probably Stoddard glasshouse, Stoddard, New Hampshire, 1846-1860, cylindrical with eight indented panels, medium yellow olive, applied sloping collared mouth, pontil scar, 7-1/8" h., rare. ... **$6,435**

Courtesy of Norman Heckler & Co.

BOXES

BOXES COME IN all shapes, sizes, and degree of antiquity – good news for the collector seeking a lifelong passion. Once early mankind reached the point where accumulation began, the next step was the introduction of containers designed especially to preserve those treasures.

Boxes have been created from every source material imaginable: wood, stone, precious metals, papier maché, porcelain, horn, and even shell. Among the most collectible:

Snuff boxes. These small, lidded boxes first came to favor in the 1700s. Although originally intended as "for use" items, snuff boxes are now prized for the elegant miniatures often painted on both the box exterior and interior.

Pillboxes. Like the snuffbox, these tiny boxes were as much in demand for their design as for their usefulness. Among the most desirable are 18th century pillboxes with enameled or repoussé (metal relief) decoration.

Match safes. In the days before safety matches, metal boxes with a striker on the base kept matches from inadvertently bursting into flame. Match safe material ranged from base metal to sterling silver. Although flat, hinged safes were the most common, novelty shapes, such as animal heads, also proved popular.

Lacquered boxes. Often classified as "Oriental" due to the 19th century fondness for decorating them with Asian motifs, lacquered boxes are actually found in almost every culture. Ranging anywhere from trinket- to trunk-sized, the common denominator is a highly polished, lacquered surface.

Folk art boxes. The diversity of available folk art boxes accounts for their modern collectibility. Folk art boxes were often the work of untrained artisans, created solely for their own needs from materials readily at hand. Among the many choices: wallpaper boxes, decoupage boxes, and "tramp art" boxes. Fueled by the imagination and ingenuity of their makers, the selection is both fascinating and limitless.

Three cut glass and gilt bronze table items with keys to two boxes, early 20th century: Large box resting on four clawed feet, medium-sized box, and cylindrical inkwell, marks to small cylinder: MADE IN FRANCE, light nicking to glass and rubbing to gilt mounts, surface wear commensurate with age, tallest 6-1/8" x 7-3/4" x 6"............$688

Courtesy of Heritage Auctions

Glass box with silver overlay with golf theme, golfer putting on green, circa 1920, 3-1/2" h. x 4-1/2" w. x 1-1/2" d.......**$90**

Courtesy of Louis J. Dianni, LLC Antiques Auctions

Velvet-lined box with original paint decoration of flowers, ribbons, and cornucopia on mahogany wood, circa 1870, 4-1/4" x 10" x 7".............. **$150**

Courtesy of Louis J. Dianni, LLC Antiques Auctions

Chinese export papier-mache game box with gilt decoration on black lacquer, circa 1860, flowers in landscape with bridges, domiciles, and water craft, games trays and box complete and original, 4" h. x 14" w. x 11-3/4" d............. **$325**

Courtesy of Louis J. Dianni, LLC Antiques Auctions

Vintage hand-painted crystal box with floral display in manner of Baccarat, circa mid-20th century, approximately 3" sq................................. **$250**

Courtesy of Elite Decorative Arts

Domed rectangular tortoiseshell-clad box, late 19th/early 20th century, cover centered by pierced foliate C-form handle over gilt bronze-framed white metal portrait medallion, portraits to each corner, fitted interior outfitted with nine compartments in three rows, seven with handled covers, within conformingly decorated exterior, overall good condition, 6" h. x 11-1/4" w. x 8-1/8" d. **$1,300**

Courtesy of John Moran Auctioneers

Mahogany knife box, circa 1770, converted to letter box in 20th century, exterior allover paint-decorated, top with couple in 18th century-style clothes playing musical instruments within landscape with flowers, urns, dolphins, ribbons, and quivers with arrows, paint surface may be 19th century, 15" h. x 9" w. x 12" d. **$325**

Courtesy of Louis J. Dianni, LLC Antiques Auctions

King George VI and Queen Elizabeth coronation musical cigarette box, images of king and queen to top and "God Save the King" to front, stamped to back "Rd No 813582, Crown Devon, Made in England," working condition, cigarette holder slightly askew, wood fitted piece for bottom not attached, 8-1/2" x 5" x 4"....**$160**

Courtesy of Cordier Auctions

top lot

North German Biedermeier temple-form fitted jewelry box, circa 1830, mahogany, Karelian birch, ebonized and painted wood, raised on three-stepped plinth, recessed walls with birch stringing to simulate ashlar blocks, double doors to front and back, full columnar arcade supporting entablature with pediment to front and back, mirrored lid with hidden box, hidden drawers, interior trays, minor losses to veneer at corners, one interior tray separated from its bottom, missing knobs to doors, general surface wear commensurate with age and use, 7-3/4" x 13-7/8" x 8-7/8"................ $3,750

Small Japanese wood box with 29 figural menuki, interior with 11 loose menuki, probably Meiji period, overall wear and patina, 6" x 4" x 2-1/2" h...**$100**

Courtesy of Cordier Auctions

Inlaid oak bible box, fourth quarter 18th century, hinged rectangular top with thumb-molded edge over case with scrolling vine and tulip inlaid decoration above plain molded base, turned ball feet, original hand-forged strap hinges, old surface, very good overall condition, replaced brass pulls and escutcheon, rear feet possibly replaced, 9 3/4" h. x 23" w. x 12-1/4" d. **$500**

Courtesy of Jeffrey S. Evans & Associates

School girl-decorated miniature sea chest-form pine box, 18th century, with folk paintings in oils of Colonial home and barn in New England woodland, front and sides delineating types of trees common to those forests, with brown framing, overhanging top, molded foot, and later ornate brass lock escutcheon, original iron strap hinges and lock, once had off-center partition, lined with lead foil as if used as tea caddy, edge wear, patina from use, 5-3/4" x 13-3/4" x 7-1/4"...**$850**

Courtesy of Thomaston Place Auction Galleries

New York Shaker sugar maple bandbox, 19th century, oval form bentwood, tapered "finger" lap joints secured with copper pins, varnished finish, very good condition with use wear, refinished, 5" h. x 12" w. x 8-1/2" d..........................**$190**

Courtesy of Conestoga Auction Co.

Anglo-Indian gentleman's travel box, 19th century, desk/dressing box in exotic hardwood with dovetailed case with overall floral and tombstone chip-carved decoration, set on molded bracket base, hinged lid with name inlaid: "N.Z. Azizullah Khan," interior of lid with hinged mirror flanked by red foil-backed reticulated panels concealing letter rack, body of case with blue velvet-bottomed compartments, central tray lifts out to reveal storage with green flannel bottom, front with pivot latches and lock (disabled), some fading to interior, 6" x 13-1/2" x 9 1/2". ....**$800-$1,200**

Courtesy of Thomaston Place Auction Galleries

American folk art inlaid walnut desk box, second half 19th century, pine secondary wood, double-sided example, possibly partner's desk, with stylized inlaid decorations of tree, birds, quarter fans, perched eagle with arc above, old surface with some sun-bleaching, very good condition, areas of bottom boards and base molding possibly restored, 6" h. x 24" l. x 16-1/4" d........................**$160**

Courtesy of Jeffrey S. Evans & Associates

◀ Chippewa quillwork dome-top birch bark box with lift-off lid, circa 1900, overall polychrome floral decoration, geometric border, minor losses, 3-3/4" x 6-1/4" x 4-3/4".....**$275**

Courtesy of Thomaston Place Auction Galleries

Pair of American paint-decorated pantry boxes, mid-19th century, lapped construction secured with copper tacks, original paint-decorated surface with white ground, star device to lid, scalloped band to lid and base, good condition overall with wear and minor staining to paint-decorated surfaces, 4-1/4" h. x 8-3/4" d. and 4-7/8" h. x 9-3/4" d. **$425**

Courtesy of Jeffrey S. Evans & Associates

Pair of George V silver and silver gilt pillboxes, Daniel Mfg. Co., Birmingham, England, circa 1915, engine turned ground to lids, silver gilt interiors, marks: (lion passant), (anchor), (date mark), D.M.C., MADE IN ENGLAND, rip to seam of one box, small dents to corners, surface scratches commensurate with age, 1-1/2" x 1-1/2" x 7/8" ea., 3.46 troy oz. **$83**

Courtesy of Heritage Auctions

Shaker oval red-stained pantry box, 19th century, shaped and lapped finger joints secured with iron tacks, good condition with minor wear and losses, 3-3/4" h. x 9-3/4" w. x 6" d. **$160**

Courtesy of Conestoga Auction Co.

Paint-decorated bentwood box of lapped construction, late 18th/early 19th century, with original painted decoration of tulips on lid, inscribed "Ephraim Gochenour / Shenandoah Co. / State of Virginia / 1833" in pencil to underside of lid, wear to paint-decorated surface, wear and damage to lid and lapped joints, 4-1/4" h. x 11" l. **$170**

Courtesy of Jeffrey S. Evans & Associates

◄ American silver-gilt pillbox, J.E. Caldwell, Philadelphia, early 20th century, circular body and hinged cover engraved overall with dense flowers and foliage against matted ground, marked on base "2 ozt 12 dwt," 3-3/8" dia. **$130**

Courtesy of Leslie Hindman Auctioneers

▲ Country paint-decorated pine dome-top box, first half 19th century, wooden-pin construction, lid attached with cotter-pin hinges, original dry painted surface with polychrome foliate decoration, found in Shenandoah Valley of Virginia, very good condition, light loss to rear base edge, typical wear to paint, 4-3/8" h. x 7-3/8" x 4-3/4"..................**$375**

Courtesy of Jeffrey S. Evans & Associates

Painted poplar tabletop storage box, second half 19th century, hinged lid concealing shallow well above three drawers, nailed construction, original red-washed surface, very good overall condition, small cracks to top at one end, normal wear, 7-1/2" h. x 35" x 8". $140

Courtesy of Jeffrey S. Evans & Associates

◀ Continental enameled pillbox, octagonal form decorated with courting couple, 1-1/2" w. $100

Courtesy of Leslie Hindman Auctioneers

Van Cleef & Arpels pillbox, 18k yellow gold, polished lid with central fluted dome accent, sides in crosshatch pattern, stamped: VCA 18K NY, 25.30 dwts. $2,600

Courtesy of Leslie Hindman Auctioneers

◀ American paint-decorated tole pillbox, 19th century, yellow ground with red edging and red, white, and black tulip, diminutive elongated form with hinged lid, excellent original oxidized surface, expected wear at edges and corners, 3/8" h. x 7/8" x 1-1/2"......................$325

Courtesy of Jeffrey S. Evans & Associates

Judith Leiber clear rhinestone pillbox with Swarovski crystals in shape of egg, 2" l., 35g.....$50

Courtesy of Elite Decorative Arts

◀ Silver and enamel snuff box with incise and punch decoration, circa 1890, likely French, enamel lid with cock and hen with bamboo leaves in Japanese traditional style, hallmarked E B surrounding lighthouse with letters FAB beneath. $150

Courtesy of Louis J. Dianni, LLC Antiques Auctions

CERAMICS

belleek

THE NAME BELLEEK refers to an industrious village in County Fermanagh, Northern Ireland, on the banks of the River Erne, and to the lustrous porcelain wares produced there.

In 1849, John Caldwell Bloomfield inherited a large estate near Belleek. Interested in ceramics and having discovered rich deposits of feldspar and kaolin (china clay) on his lands, he soon envisioned a pottery that would make use of these materials, local craftspeople and water power of the River Erne. He was also anxious to enhance Ireland's prestige with superior porcelain products.

Bloomfield had a chance meeting with Robert Williams Armstrong who had established a substantial architectural business building potteries. Keenly interested in the manufacturing process, he agreed to design, build, and manage the new factory for Bloomfield. The factory was to be located on Rose Isle on a bend in the River Erne.

Bloomfield and Armstrong then approached David McBirney, a highly successful merchant and director of railway companies, and enticed him to provide financing. Impressed by the plans, he agreed to raise funds for the enterprise. As agreed, the factory was named McBirney and Armstrong, then later D. McBirney and Co.

Although 1857 is given as the founding date of the pottery, it is recorded that the pottery's foundation stone was laid by Mrs. J.C. Bloomfield on Nov. 18, 1858. Although not completed until 1860, the pottery was producing earthenware from its inception.

▼ Prince of Wales centerpiece with shell-form dish above shell and foliate worked standard on mythical sea creature and shell-molded base, impressed Belleek Co. Fermanagh,13" h. **$1,625**

Courtesy of Leslie Hindman Auctioneers

Pair of nautilus shell compotes, 1863-1890, in pearlized white with pink interiors on pink coral branch standards, each on relief-molded circular base with shells and sand, first period black John Mortlock, Oxford Street, London stamp, impressed marks, 8-1/2" h., 6" dia. **$750**

Courtesy of Clars Auction Gallery, www.clars.com

With the arrival of ceramic experts from the (William Henry) Goss Pottery in England, principally William Bromley, Sr. and William Wood Gallimore, Parian ware was perfected and, by 1863, the wares we associate with Belleek today were in production.

With Belleek Pottery workers and others emigrating to the United States in the late 1800s and early 1900s, Belleek-style china manufacture, known as American Belleek, commenced at several American firms, including Ceramic Art Co., Colombian Art Pottery, Lenox Inc., Ott & Brewer, and Willets Manufacturing Co.

Throughout its Parian production, Belleek Pottery marked its items with an Irish harp and wolfhound and the Devenish Tower. Its second period began with the advent of the McKinley Tariff Act of 1891 and the (revised) British Merchandise Act as Belleek added the ribbon "Co. FERMANAGH IRELAND" beneath its mark in 1891. Both the first and second period marks were black, although they occasionally appeared in burnt orange, green, blue, or brown, especially on earthenware items. Its third period begin in 1926, when it added a Celtic emblem under the second period mark as well as the government trademark "Reg No 0857," which was granted in 1884. The Celtic emblem was registered by the Irish Industrial Development Association in 1906 and reads "Deanta in Eirinn," and means "Made in Ireland." The pottery is now utilizing its 13th mark, following a succession of three black marks, three green marks, a gold mark, two blue marks and three green. The final green mark was used only a single year, in 2007, to commemorate its 150th anniversary. In 2008, Belleek changed its mark to brown. Early earthenware was often marked in the same color as the majority of its surface decoration. Early basketware has Parian strips applied to its base with the impressed verbiage "BELLEEK" and later on, additionally "Co FERMANAGH" with or without "IRELAND." Current basketware carries the same mark as its Parian counterpart.

The item identification scheme (at right) is in the works by Richard K. Degenhardt: *Belleek The Complete Collector's Guide and Illustrated Reference* (both first and second editions). Additional information, as well as a thorough discussion of the early marks, is located in these works as well as on the Internet at Del E. Domke's website: http://home. comcast.net/~belleek_website.

MARKS

AMERICAN ART CHINA WORKS
R&E, 1891-1895

AAC (SUPERIMPOSED)
1891-1895

AMERICAN BELLEEK CO.
Company name, banner, and globe

CERAMIC ART CO.
CAC palette, 1889-1906

COLOMBIAN ART POTTERY
CAP, 1893-1902

COOK POTTERY
Three feathers with "CHC,"
1894-1904

COXON BELLEEK POTTERY
"Coxon Belleek" in shield,
1926-1930

GORDON BELLEEK
"Gordon Belleek,"
1920-1928

KNOWLES, TAYLOR & KNOWLES
"Lotusware" in circle with crown, 1891-1896

LENOX CHINA
Palette mark, 1906-1924

OTT & BREWER
Crown and shield,
1883-1893

PERLEE
"P" in wreath, 1925-1930

WILLETS MANUFACTURING CO.
Serpent mark, 1880-1909

Painted porcelain vase, signed on underside M. R. Robinson Apr. III 1905, 11" h. **$25**

Courtesy of Pook & Pook, Inc.

▲ Neptune teapot in yellow and cream glaze with seashell finial on seashell feet, 6" h. x 10" w. x 6-3/4" d. **$63**

Courtesy of Leslie Hindman Auctioneers

CERAMICS

bennington pottery

BENNINGTON WARES, WHICH ranged from stoneware to parian and porcelain, were made in Bennington, Vermont, primarily in two potteries, one in which Captain John Norton and his descendants were principals, and the other in which Christopher Webber Fenton (also once associated with the Nortons) was a principal. Various marks are found on the wares made in the two major potteries, including J. & E. Norton, E. & L. P. Norton, L. Norton & Co., Norton & Fenton, Edward Norton, Lyman Fenton & Co., Fenton's Works, United States Pottery Co., U.S.P. and others.

The popular pottery with the mottled brown on yellowware glaze was also produced in Bennington, but such wares should be referred to as "Rockingham" or "Bennington-type" unless they can be specifically attributed to a Bennington, Vermont factory.

Flint enamel pottery poodle, circa 1850, standing foursquare with lion-style "coleslaw" mane, 8-1/4" h., 9" dia... **$630**

Courtesy of Butterscotch Auction Gallery, LLC

Rare pottery standing lion with fruit basket in mouth, facing left, with textured ears, ruff and tail, in brown sponge glaze with blue fruit, fine condition, 8-3/4" h. x 9" l..**$1,652**

Courtesy of Thomaston Place Auction Galleries

Twenty-five brown and blue Bennington marbles and one large green painted clay marble, 15/16" to 1-1/2" dia............ **$90**

Courtesy of Dan Morphy Auctions

Two Rockingham dogs, early 19th century, one with chip to nose and base, other with chip to base, 11" h... **$175**

Courtesy of Cottone Auctions

VISIT WWW.ANTIQUETRADER.COM

WWW.FACEBOOK.COM/ANTIQUETRADER

CERAMICS

buffalo pottery

INCORPORATED IN 1901 as a wholly owned subsidiary of the Larkin Soap Co., founded by John D. Larkin of Buffalo, New York, in 1875, the Buffalo Pottery was a manufactory built to produce premium wares to be included with purchases of Larkin's chief product: soap.

In October 1903, the first kiln was fired and Buffalo Pottery became the only pottery in the world run entirely by electricity. In 1904 Larkin offered its first premium produced by the pottery. This concept of using premiums caused sales to skyrocket and, in 1905, the first Blue Willow pattern pottery made in the United States was introduced as a premium.

The Buffalo Pottery administrative building, built in 1904 to house 1,800 clerical workers, was the creation of a 32-year-old architect, Frank Lloyd Wright. The building was demolished in 1953.

By 1910 annual soap production peaked and the number of premiums offered in the catalogs exceeded 600. By 1915 this number had grown to 1,500. The first catalog of premiums was issued in 1893 and continued to appear through the late 1930s.

John D. Larkin died in 1926, and during the Great Depression the firm suffered severe losses, going into bankruptcy in 1940. After World War II, the pottery resumed production under new management, but its vitreous wares were generally limited to mass-produced china for the institutional market.

Among the pottery lines produced during Buffalo's heyday were Blue Willow (1905-1916), Gaudy Willow (1905-1916), Deldare Ware (1908-1909, 1923-1925), Abino Ware (1911-1913), historical and commemorative plates, and unique hand-painted jugs and pitchers. In the 1920s and 1930s the firm concentrated on personalized wares for commercial clients including hotels, clubs, railroads, and restaurants.

For more information on Buffalo Pottery, see *Antique Trader Pottery & Porcelain Ceramics Price Guide*, 7th edition.

— Phillip M. Sullivan

Emerald Deldare plate of Dr. Syntax in his sleeping quarters inscribed "Doctor Syntax Loses His Wig, The rats it seems had play'd the rig in tearing up the doctors wig," backstamp logo "1911, Buffalo Pottery Emerald Deldare Ware, Underglaze," artist signed M. Gerhardt, excellent condition, 9-1/4" dia. **$200**

Courtesy of Mark Mussio, Humler & Nolan

Deldare covered humidor of pegleg sailor and rhyming stanza, cupped lid painted with sailing ship and sailor portraits with pierced holes underneath, space for sponge, backstamp 1909 logo "Made at Ye Buffalo Pottery, Deldare Ware, Underglaze," artist signed H.E. Crooker, excellent condition. **$275**

Courtesy of Mark Mussio, Humler & Nolan

CERAMICS

cowan

R. GUY COWAN opened his first pottery studio in 1912 in Lakewood, Ohio. The pottery operated almost continuously, with the exception of a break during World War I, at various locations in the Cleveland area until it was forced to close in 1931 due to financial difficulties.

Many of the 20th century's finest artists began with Cowan and its associate, the Cleveland School of Art. This fine art pottery, particularly the designer pieces, is highly sought after by collectors.

Many people are unaware that it was due to R. Guy Cowan's perseverance and tireless work that art pottery is today considered an art form and found in many art museums.

For more information on Cowan pottery, see *Antique Trader Pottery & Porcelain Ceramics Price Guide*, 7th edition.

"Kneeling Nude" flower holder in Original Ivory glaze, unmarked, 6-1/2" h. **$350**

Courtesy of Mark Mussio, Humler & Nolan

"The Hunt" plaque by Viktor Schreckengost, first half 20th century, typical circular form with russet brown glaze, Cowan Pottery mark verso, 11-1/2" dia. **$750**

Courtesy of Garth's Auctions, Inc.

"Giulia" for Cowan Pottery, A. Drexler Jacobson (1895-1973), circa 1928, Rocky River, Ohio, black matte glaze, impressed logo on back of base, overall very good condition, minor surface scratches, 4" w. x 10" h.... **$1,586**

Courtesy of Treadway-Toomey Auctions

Hand-built glazed ceramic sculpture head of woman, 1912-1919, incised COWAN POTTERS with illegible artist signature, touch-ups to base, 11-1/2" x 7"....... **$2,600**

Courtesy of Rago Arts, www.ragoarts.com

CERAMICS

dedham

DEDHAM POTTERY WAS originally organized in 1866 by Alexander W. Robertson in Chelsea, Massachusetts, and became A.W. & H. Roberson in 1868. In 1872, the name was changed to Chelsea Keramic Art Works and in 1891 to Chelsea Pottery, U.S.A. About 1895, the pottery was moved to Dedham, Massachusetts, and was renamed Dedham Pottery. Production ceased in 1943. High-fired colored wares and crackleware were specialties. The rabbit is said to have been the most popular decoration in blue on crackleware.

Experimental vase, superior and early volcanic glaze, signed by Hugh Robertson, circa 1895, hand-thrown, excellent condition, 7-1/2" h. **$1,416**

Courtesy of A-1 Auction, http:a-1auction.net

Rare Fairbanks House pottery plate with rabbit border, 8-3/4" dia. ...**$984**

Courtesy of Carl W. Stinson, Inc., www.stinsonauctions.com

Poppy plate designed by J. Lindon Smith, 8-1/2" dia. ... **$984**

Courtesy of Carl W. Stinson, Inc., www.stinsonauctions.com

Plate with double moth design, 9-3/4" dia. **$2,091**

Courtesy of Carl W. Stinson, Inc., www.stinsonauctions.com

Plate with dolphin design with experimental sgraffito border, 8-1/2" dia...........................**$277**

Courtesy of Carl W. Stinson, Inc., www.stinsonauctions.com

CERAMICS

delft

IN THE EARLY 17TH CENTURY, Italian potters settled in Holland and began producing tin-glazed earthenwares, often decorated with pseudo-Oriental designs based on Chinese porcelain wares. The city of Delft became the center of this pottery production, and several firms produced the wares throughout the 17th and early 18th century. A majority of the pieces featured blue on white designs, but polychrome wares were also made. The Dutch Delftwares were also shipped to England, where eventually the English copied them at potteries in such cities as Bristol, Lambeth, and Liverpool. Although still produced today, Delft peaked in popularity by the mid-18th century.

For more information on Delft pottery, see *Antique Trader Porcelain & Pottery Ceramics Price Guide,* 7th edition.

Dutch Delft blue and white wall plaque, Holland, 19th century, oval form with shaped rim, coastal landscape above foliate cartouche, urn mark, scattered rim chips, 17-1/4" l. x 21" w.................**$554**

Courtesy of Skinner, Inc.; www.skinnerinc.com

▲ Pair of Delft blue and white vases with covers, Holland, late 19th century, each with octagonal foot and cover rim, ribbed bodies with birds amongst floral designs, Porceleyne Fles mark, 19" h........**$1,476**

Courtesy of Skinner, Inc.; www.skinnerinc.com

◄ Dutch Delft blue and white wall plaque, Holland, late 19th/early 20th century, shield shape with molded mask head to crest above floral border and central depiction of cavaliers in landscape after art by Wouwerman, painted Porceleyne Fles mark, 22-1/2" l. **$738**

Courtesy of Skinner, Inc.; www.skinnerinc.com

Pair of Dutch Delft polychrome decorated wall plaques, Holland, late 19th century, oval forms with shaped rims, coastal windmill landscapes above floral and scrolled foliate cartouche in blue, printed shield marks, 23-1/4" l. x 18-3/4" w........... **$1,230**

Courtesy of Skinner, Inc.; www.skinnerinc.com

Delft plaque of oval form with figures and ruins, 21-3/4" h. x 18-1/2" w... **$1,188**

Courtesy of Leslie Hindman Auctioneers

Delft blue and white potpourri vase and cover, Holland, 19th century, pierced cover and neck to rococo form with foliate framed panels alternating with windmill landscapes and country lovers, four scrolled foliate feet, finial off and reglued, base previously drilled as lamp, scattered glaze chips along edges, 22-1/2" h.. **$523**

Courtesy of Skinner, Inc.; www.skinnerinc.com

Thoost & Labouchere Delft blue and white plaque, Holland, late 19th century, roundel with cavaliers in landscape setting after art by Wouwerman, painted Porceleyne Fles and impressed marks, 18" dia............... **$554**

Courtesy of Skinner, Inc.; www.skinnerinc.com

Dutch Delft nautical tile picture, Holland, 19th century, 24 tiles decorated in blue and white with battle scene after art by Simon de Vlieger, printed Porceleyne Fles mark, each tile 6" x 6", framed. **$1,722**

Courtesy of Skinner, Inc.; www.skinnerinc.com

Pair of Dutch Delft lidded jars, 20th century, marks. LF, surface scratches commensurate with age, each with repairs to lip rims and one lid repaired at base of finial, 14" h.. **$2,375**

Courtesy of Heritage Auctions

Delft hand-painted 12-tile winter scene, 19th century, signed lower left L. Apol, some crazing, 24" x 18"......... **$1,089**

Courtesy of Cottone Auctions

Delft charger signed Louis Apol., nick to glaze, 2-1/2" h., 16" dia............... **$242**

Courtesy of Cottone Auctions

Royal Bonn Delft blue and white charger, Germany, late 19th century, wide fruit border surrounding central landscape with cows after art by Roelofs, impressed Franz Anton Mehlem mark, 19-3/4" dia. **$523**

Courtesy of Skinner, Inc.; www.skinnerinc.com

Delft blue and white tile panel of hunter and squire, Portuguese, probably 18th century, with possible attribution to Bartholomew Antunes, 42 tiles forming figural scene through elaborate Baroque surround, several tiles with breaks and repairs, edge chips and other typical flaws, set into later concrete ground, 34" x 35-1/2" x 1-1/4"............. **$1,178**

Courtesy of Brunk Auctions

CERAMICS

doulton & royal doulton

DOULTON & COMPANY, LTD., was founded in Lambeth, London, in about 1858. It operated there until 1956 and often incorporated the words "Doulton" and "Lambeth" in its marks. Pinder, Bourne & Co. Burslem was purchased by the Doultons in 1878 and in 1882 became Doulton & Co., Ltd. It added porcelain to its earthenware production in 1884. The "Royal Doulton" mark has been used since 1902 by this factory, which is still in operation.

John Doulton, the founder, was born in 1793. He became an apprentice at the age of 12 to a potter in south London. Five years later he was employed in another small pottery near Lambeth. His two sons, John and Henry, subsequently joined their father in 1830 in a partnership he had formed with the name of Doulton & Watts. Watts retired in 1864 and the partnership was dissolved. Henry formed a new company that traded as Doulton and Co.

In the early 1870s the proprietor of the Pinder Bourne Co., located in Burslem, Staffordshire, offered Henry a partnership. The Pinder Bourne Co. was purchased by Henry in 1878 and became part of Doulton & Co. in 1882.

With the passage of time, the demand for the Lambeth industrial and decorative stoneware declined whereas demand for the Burslem manufactured and decorated bone china wares increased.

Doulton & Co. was incorporated as a limited liability company in 1899. In 1901 the company was allowed to use the word "Royal" on its trademarks by Royal Charter. The well-known "lion on crown" logo came into use in 1902. In 2000 the logo was changed on the company's advertising literature to one showing a more stylized lion's head in profile.

Today Royal Doulton is one of the world's leading manufacturers and distributors of premium grade ceramic tabletop wares and collectibles. The Doulton Group comprises Minton, Royal Albert, Caithness Glass, Holland Studio Craft, and Royal Doulton. Royal Crown Derby was part of the group from 1971 until 2000, when it became an independent company. These companies market collectibles using their own brand names.

Teapot, covered, Bunnykins Series, wide short cylindrical body with angled spout and angled handle, Casino pattern, introduced in 1937. ....**$750**

Teapot, covered, faience, rounded cylindrical body with long serpentine spout, C-scroll handle and metal rim and hinged cover, stylized floral decoration, Doulton-Lambeth, circa 1900. .... **$1,000**

Teapot, covered, Old Leeds Spray pattern, squatty octagonal body, angled spout and squared handle, England, circa 1912. .... **$100**

Teapot, covered, Series Ware, low wide body decorated with Grecian figures, from Athens Series, introduced in 1910. .... **$600**

Teapot, covered, Cadogan-style pot, Crows pattern, circa 1907. .... **$2,000**

CERAMICS

Teapot, covered, Kingsware line, Witch pattern, introduced in 1902...........................**$500**

Teapot, covered, figural Old Charley model, designed by Charles Noke, introduced in 1939. ....**$2,000**

Teapot, covered, Marqueterie Ware, diamond lattice and swirl overall design, Doulton-Lambeth, circa 1890. .... **$4,000**

Teapot, covered, Kingsware line, self-pouring style, relief-molded half-length portraits on side, J.J. Royle's Patent design, circa 1900 .....**$2,000**

Vase, Sung Ware, bulbous ovoid body tapering to short cylindrical neck, Flambé glossy glaze in red mottled with dark green and gold, signatures of decorators Noke and Moore, early 20th century, base chip, 5-1/2" h. **$173**

Teapot, covered, Kingsware line, Dame pattern with motto around base, introduced in 1901...**$1,000**

Teapot, covered, Morrisian Ware, footed wide urn-shaped body with a squared handle and serpentine spout, design of dancing lady, circa 1900...........................$1,000

Vase, miniature, Titanian Ware, flat bottomed wide bulbous ovoid body tapering to wide flat mouth, overall shaded glossy green to dark blue glaze, Titanian backstamp, 3-3/8" h...........$173

Teapot, covered, Marqueterie Ware, low rectangular shape with straight spout and angled loop handle, large design reserve with scene of a child against swirled background, Doulton-Lambeth, painted by Ada Dennis, circa 1893. ....$5,000

Vase, Rouge Flambé, footed squatty bulbous body tapering to two-lobed upright rim, red ground and veining down through dark ground, marked with Flambé insignia, 4" h....$138

Teapot, covered, Titanian Ware, Bird of Paradise pattern, introduced in 1919... $800

Vase, Rouge Flambé, wide bulbous baluster form tapering to wide flat mouth, decorated with black-silhouetted Arabian landscape with men on camels, marked on bottom "Royal Doulton Flambé," early 20th century, 11-1/2" h. ....**$1,200-$1,800**

Vase, stoneware, round short pedestal foot supporting nearly spherical lower body below tall slender tapering neck with flared rim, lower body divided into large oval cobalt blue panels with ornate light green and white scrolls, another small blue band near top of neck, background in mottled brown and moss green, Doulton-Lambeth, No. 8413, 11-1/4" h. **$196**

Vase, Natural Foliage Ware, tall baluster-form body with short neck with cupped rim, mottled streaky yellowish tan and brown ground decorated with long branches of mottled dark blue and green leaves, Doulton-Lambeth, Shape No. 6768, 12-1/4" h ...**$230**

Washbowl and pitcher set, Aubrey pattern, deep wide rounded bowl and tall tapering cylindrical tankard pitcher with swelled rim and short rounded rim spout, long angled handle, light blue Art Nouveau design composed of stylized rounded blossoms and long undulating stems and leaves, geometric border bands, circa 1910, minor wear and tiny glaze nicks on rim of bowl, pitcher 12-3/4" h. **$460**

Vase, tall slender baluster-form with cylindrical neck and flat rim, Babes in the Wood Series, design of woman sheltering child in wintry landscape, 11-1/2" h **$750**

Vase, Rouge Flambé, footed ovoid body with the wide shoulder tapering to small, short rolled neck, black silhouetted desert landscape against crimson red ground, shallow scratch, stamped "ROYAL DOULTON - FLAMBE - MADE IN ENGLAND," 7" h. x 4-1/4" dia............**$250**

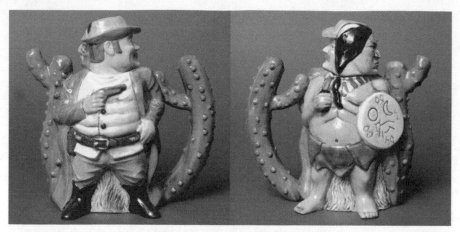

Teapot, covered, figural Cowboy and Indian model, designed by Anthony Cartlidge, limited edition of 1,500, introduced in 2002 .... **$300**

Teapot, covered, figural Falstaff model, 1989. ......**$175**

Teapot, covered, figural Long John Silver with parrot, 1989. ....**$225**

Teapot, covered, figural Policeman and Felon model, designed by Anthony Cartlidge, limited edition of 1,500, introduced in 2002. .... **$300**

CERAMICS

fiesta

THE HOMER LAUGHLIN CHINA CO. originated with a two-kiln pottery on the banks of the Ohio River in East Liverpool, Ohio. Built in 1873-'74 by Homer Laughlin and his brother, Shakespeare, the firm was first known as the Ohio Valley Pottery, and later Laughlin Bros. Pottery. It was one of the first whiteware plants in the country.

After a tentative beginning, the company was awarded a prize for having the best whiteware at the 1876 Centennial Exposition in Philadelphia.

Three years later, Shakespeare sold his interest in the business to Homer, who continued on until 1897. At that time, Homer sold his interest in the newly incorporated firm to a group of investors, including Charles, Louis, and Marcus Aaron and the company bookkeeper, William E. Wells.

Under new ownership in 1907, the headquarters and a new 30-kiln plant were built across the Ohio River in Newell, West Virginia, the present manufacturing and headquarters location.

In the 1920s, two additions to the Homer Laughlin staff set the stage for the company's greatest success: the Fiesta line. Dr. Albert V. Bleininger was hired in 1920. A scientist, author, and educator, he oversaw the conversion from bottle kilns to the more efficient tunnel kilns.

In 1927, the company hired designer Frederick Hurten Rhead, a member of a distinguished family of English ceramists. Having previously worked at Weller Pottery and Roseville Pottery, Rhead began to develop the artistic quality of the company's wares, and to experiment with shapes and glazes. In 1935, this work culminated in his designs for the Fiesta line.

For more information on Fiesta, see *Warman's Fiesta Identification and Price Guide* by Glen Victorey.

FIESTA COLORS

From 1936 to 1972, Fiesta was produced in 14 colors (other than special promotions). These colors are usually divided into the "original colors" of cobalt blue, light green, ivory, red, turquoise, and yellow; the "1950s colors" of chartreuse, forest green, gray, and rose (introduced in 1951); medium green (introduced in 1959); plus the later additions of Casuals, Amberstone, Fiesta Ironstone, and Casualstone (Coventry) in antique gold, mango red, and turf green; and the striped, decal, and Lustre pieces. No Fiesta was produced from 1973 to 1985. The colors that make up the "original" and "1950s" groups are sometimes referred to as "the standard 11."

In many pieces, medium green is the hardest to find and the most expensive Fiesta color.

FIESTA COLORS AND YEARS OF PRODUCTION TO 1972

Antique Gold	1969-1972
Chartreuse	1951-1959
Cobalt Blue	1936-1951
Forest Green	1951-1959
Gray	1951-1959
Green	1936-1951
(often called light green when comparing it to other green glazes; also called "original" green)	
Ivory	1936-1951
Mango Red (same as original red)	1970-1972
Medium Green	1959-1969
Red	1936-1944 and 1959-1972
Rose	1951-1959
Turf Green	1969-1972
Turquoise	1937-1969
Yellow	1936-1969

Ashtray, medium green........**$160**

Courtesy of Strawser Auctions

Ice lip pitcher, yellow. **$70**

Courtesy of Strawser Auctions

Onion soup bowl with lid,
cobalt................................ **$500**

Courtesy of Strawser Auctions

Footed salad bowl, red. **$275**

Courtesy of Strawser Auctions

Cream soup bowl, medium
green, rare. **$550**

Courtesy of Strawser Auctions

Onion soup bowl with lid, ivory. ... **$500**

Courtesy of Strawser Auctions

French casserole, yellow. **$100**
Courtesy of Strawser Auctions

Footed salad bowl, turquoise.**$225**
Courtesy of Strawser Auctions

No. 4 mixing bowl and lid,
cobalt lid only....................**$550**
Courtesy of Strawser Auctions

Rare green cake plate. **$550**
Courtesy of Strawser Auctions

Seven-piece nested mixing
bowl set, mixed colors, chips
and wear. **$150**
Courtesy of Strawser Auctions

BOTTOM MARKS

Bottom of 6" bread plate in turquoise, showing "Genuine Fiesta" stamp.

Bottom of a teacup saucer in turquoise, showing sagger pin marks and the "Genuine Fiesta" stamp.

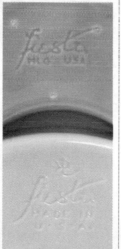

Two different impressed marks on the bottoms of relish tray inserts.

Note the different bottoms of two ashtrays. The top one has a set of rings with no room for a logo. The bottom one has rings along the outer edge. The red ashtray mark is an older example. The yellow ashtray with the logo can be dated to a time period after 1940.

An ink stamp on the bottom of a piece of Fiesta.

Bottom of No. 1 mixing bowl in green, showing sagger pin marks, the "Fiesta/HLCo. USA" impressed mark, and the faint "1" size indicator. The impressed size mark on the bottom of the No. 2 mixing bowl in yellow is too faint to be seen in this image.

Examples of impressed Fiesta bottom marks.

Fiesta pieces were glazed on the underside, so before being fired, each piece was placed on a stilt to keep it off the floor of the kiln. The stilt was made up of three sagger pins positioned an equal distance from each other to form three points of a triangle. If you inspect the underside of any piece of Fiesta, which has a completely glazed bottom, you will notice three small blemishes in a triangular pattern. Later in Fiesta's production run, the undersides of pieces were glazed and then wiped, creating a dry foot, before going into the kiln to be fired.

A 9" cobalt blue plate rests on a stilt with sagger pins to show the basic idea of how it worked. Please note that this stilt is not the exact one that would have been used by Homer Laughlin China Co., but rather an updated style in use today by many ceramic studios.

Bulb candleholders, red. **$65**

Courtesy of Strawser Auctions

Coffeepot, gray. **$275**

Courtesy of Strawser Auctions

Two-pint jug, chartreuse. **$110**

Courtesy of Strawser Auctions

Harlequin promotional casserole
in spruce green, rare. Provenance:
Turner Collection.....................**$100**

Courtesy of Strawser Auctions

Sweets compote, turquoise,
marked HLC.........................**$65**

Courtesy of Strawser Auctions

Rare cake plate, cobalt, very
minor wear. **$250**

Courtesy of Strawser Auctions

Post-'86 medium vase,
sapphire. $85

Courtesy of Strawser Auctions

Condiment set, ivory mustard
and salt and pepper shakers
with chrome holder. $475

Courtesy of Strawser Auctions

Eggcup, gray. $90

Courtesy of Strawser Auctions

Rare 6" dessert bowl,
medium green.................$275

Courtesy of Strawser Auctions

12" fruit compote, red. $150

Courtesy of Strawser Auctions

Two-pint jug, rose. $40

Courtesy of Strawser Auctions

Rare red striped ivory tripod candleholders, only pair known to exist. Provenance: Turner Collection. $11,500

Water set with yellow disk water pitcher and six original water tumblers. **$140**

Courtesy of Strawser Auctions

Eggcup, chartreuse. **$70**

Courtesy of Strawser Auctions

Kitchen Kraft utensil
group, red spoon
(nicks) and green
fork, ...**$45**

Courtesy of Strawser Auctions

Casserole, red........**$60**

Courtesy of Strawser Auctions

Chop plates, gray and rose,
13" dia..................................**$30**

Courtesy of Strawser Auctions

Deep plate, cobalt with
gold rim...............................**$80**

Courtesy of Strawser Auctions

CERAMICS

Medium teapot,
medium green,
minor spout nick................. **$225**

Courtesy of Strawser Auctions

Vase, cobalt, 12" high......... **$700**

Courtesy of Strawser Auctions

Mustard, cobalt. **$160**

Courtesy of Strawser Auctions

Syrup pitcher, red. **$190**

Courtesy of Strawser Auctions

Marmalade, green with chrome
holder. **$400**

Courtesy of Strawser Auctions

Relish tray, green tray, all six
colors. **$275**

Courtesy of Strawser Auctions

Juice set with yellow disk
pitcher with nick and six
original juice tumblers. **$75**

Courtesy of Strawser Auctions

Water carafe, turquoise. **$150**

Courtesy of Strawser Auctions

Promotional set, rare turquoise
figure-eight tray, red creamer,
yellow sugar, very minor glaze
nick to rim of creamer. **$450**

Courtesy of Strawser Auctions

World's Fair vase, cobalt,
7-1/4" h., rare. Provenance:
Turner Collection. **$425**

Courtesy of Strawser Auctions

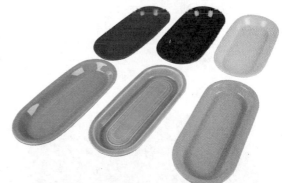

Utility tray group, all six
original colors.....................**$110**

Courtesy of Strawser Auctions

CERAMICS

Jubilee juice set with celedon green disk juice pitcher and four tumblers in rose, gray, beige, and shell pink...........**$200**

Courtesy of Strawser Auctions

Sweets compote, ivory, marked HLC. **$95**

Courtesy of Strawser Auctions

Disk juice pitcher, gray, vintage, rare.......................**$550**

Courtesy of Strawser Auctions

Platter, rose, minor wear..........**$5**

Courtesy of Strawser Auctions

Post-'86 pyramid candleholders in lilac, factory chip under glaze to one. **$450**

Courtesy of Strawser Auctions

World's Fair vase, yellow, 5-1/2" h., rare. Provenance: Turner Collection. **$400**

Courtesy of Strawser Auctions

Demitasse coffee pot, turquoise. **$250**

Courtesy of Strawser Auctions

Vase, turquoise, 12" high. **$750**

Courtesy of Strawser Auctions

Rare 4-3/4" fruit bowl, medium green................................. **$325**

Courtesy of Strawser Auctions

CERAMICS

CERAMICS

fulper pottery

FROM THE "GERM-PROOF FILTER" to enduring Arts & Crafts acclaim – that's the unlikely journey of Fulper Pottery, maker of the early 20th century uniquely glazed artware that's become a favorite with today's collectors.

Fulper began life in 1814 as the Samuel Hill Pottery, named after its founder, a New Jersey potter. In its early years, the pottery specialized in useful items such as storage crocks and drainpipes fashioned from the area's red clay. Abraham Fulper, a worker at the pottery, eventually became Hill's partner, purchasing the company in 1860. Renamed after its new owner, Fulper Pottery continued to produce a variety of utilitarian tile and crockery. By the turn of the 20th century, the firm, now led by Abraham's sons, introduced a line of fire-proof cookware and the hugely successful "Germ-Proof Filter." An ancestor of today's water cooler, the filter provided sanitary drinking water in less-than-sanitary public places, such as offices and railway stations.

In the early 1900s, Fulper's master potter, John Kunsman, began creating various solid-glaze vessels, such as jugs and vases, which were offered for sale outside the pottery. On a whim, William H. Fulper II (Abraham's grandson, who became the company's secretary/treasurer) took an assortment of these items for exhibit at the 1904 Louisiana Purchase Exposition – along with, of course, the Germ-Proof Filter. Kunsman's artware took home an honorable mention.

Since Chinese art pottery was then attracting national attention, Fulper saw an opening to produce similarly styled modern ware. Dr. Cullen Parmelee, who headed up the ceramics department at Rutgers, was recruited to create a contemporary series of glazes patterned after those of ancient China. The Fulper Vasekraft line of art pottery incorporating these glazes made its debut in 1909. Unfortunately, Parmelee's glazes did not lend themselves well to mass production; they did not result in reliable coloration. Even more to their detriment, they were expensive to produce.

In 1910, most of Parmelee's glazes disappeared from the line. A new ceramic engineer, Martin Stangl, was given the assignment of revitalizing Vasekraft. His most notable innovation: steering designs and glazes away from reinterpretations of ornate Chinese classics and toward the simplicity of the burgeoning Arts & Crafts movement. Among his many Vasekraft successes: candleholders, bookends, perfume lamps, desk accessories, tobacco jars, and even Vasekraft lamps. Here, both the lamp base and shade were of pottery; stained glass inserts in the shades allowed light to shine through.

Buttress vase in green crystalline over Famille Rose glazes, marked on bottom with Fulper vertical racetrack ink stamp, excellent original condition, 8-1/4" h............ **$225**

Courtesy of Mark Mussio, Humler & Nolan

◄ Twin-handled urn-shaped vase, shape number 489, in Mahogany glaze with Chinese Blue flambé dripped from rim, excellent original condition, attached original Panama Pacific International Exposition paper label, 8" h. ...**$400**

Courtesy of Mark Mussio, Humler & Nolan

Twin-handled vase in Copper Dust Crystalline glaze, marked on bottom with Fulper vertical racetrack ink stamp, excellent original condition, 7-1/2" h. ...**$150**

Courtesy of Mark Mussio, Humler & Nolan

Bum pup bulldog doorstop in blue flambé over tan, unmarked, shape number 492, fine overall crazing, 8-1/4" h. **$700**

Courtesy of Mark Mussio, Humler & Nolan

Always attuned to the mood of the times, William Fulper realized that by World War I the heavy Vasekraft stylings were fading in popularity. A new and lighter line of Fulper Pottery Artware, featuring Spanish Revival and English themes, was introduced. Among the most admired Fulper releases following the war were Fulper Porcelaines: dresser boxes, powder jars, ashtrays, lamps, and other accessories designed to complement the fashionable boudoir.

Fayence, the popular line of solid-color, open-stock dinnerware eventually known as Stangl Pottery, was introduced in the 1920s. In 1928, following William Fulper's death, Martin Stangl was named company president. The artware that continued into the 1930s embraced Art Deco as well as Classical and Primitive stylistic themes. From 1935 onward, Stangl Pottery became the sole Fulper output. In 1978, the Stangl assets came under the ownership of Pfaltzgraff.

Unlike wheel-thrown pottery, Fulper was made in molds; the true artistry came in the use of exceptionally rich, color-blended glazes. Each Fulper piece is one-of-a-kind. Because of glaze divergence, two Fulper objects from the same mold can show a great variance. While once a drawback for retailers seeking consistency, that uniqueness is now a boon to collectors: Each Fulper piece possesses its own singular visual appeal.

CERAMICS

Early vase with cast geometric design at rim, shape number 19, in Mahogany glaze with coating of green flambé applied to outside, clean drill hole through bottom and faint crazing, drill hole partially obscures early large rectangular Fulper ink stamp, 6-1/2" h., 9-1/2" dia. **$250**

Courtesy of Mark Mussio, Humler & Nolan

Original lamp in combination of Cat's Eye flambé and Flemington green to Cucumber Crystalline near base, all on large and uncommon form, shade with 36 individual pieces of glass, marked with rectangular ink stamp logo, Fulper Vasecraft ink stamp logo, number 20, and "Patent Pending U.S and Canada," original sockets and switch, needs rewiring, professional restoration to cracks in ceramic portion of shade, copper-wrapped glass in excellent condition, 20-1/2" h., shade 15-1/4" dia. **$5,000**

Courtesy of Mark Mussio, Humler & Nolan

Cream pitcher and lidded sugar in Mission Matte brown glaze, marked with early rectangular mark, mark on sugar covered with glaze and unreadable, excellent original condition, pitcher 4" h., bowl 4-5/8" h..**$130**

Courtesy of Mark Mussio, Humler & Nolan

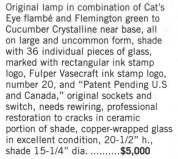

◄ Early experimental shouldered vase, shape number T35, in mustard mat glaze with light green flambé dripped from rim, marked on bottom with early Fulper rectangular ink stamp and stamped D, indicating trial piece, excellent original condition, 4" h., 6-1/4" dia. **$325**

Courtesy of Mark Mussio, Humler & Nolan

◄ Vase, shape number 483, in Mirror Black to Mahogany to ivory flambé glazes, marked on bottom with rectangular Fulper ink stamp, faint crazing visible in ivory glaze, 7-1/2" h. **$150**

Courtesy of Mark Mussio, Humler & Nolan

Twin-handled vase, shape
number 659, in Cucumber
Crystalline glaze, marked
on bottom with die-stamped
"incised" Fulper logo, excellent
original condition, 8-3/4" h. **$170**

Courtesy of Mark Mussio, Humler & Nolan

Pair of early Ramses II book blocks in Verte Antique glaze,
one marked with early Fulper squatty ink stamp and other
with original handwritten Vasekraft paper label, one piece
with chip to rear of plinth, other with smaller chip to stand
holding Ramses' book, 8-3/8"..**$250**

Courtesy of Mark Mussio, Humler & Nolan

Flower frog in form of castle with bridge
and road on craggy green landscape,
marked with larger rectangular Fulper ink
stamp, restoration to two rooftops, 4-3/4"
h. x 5-3/8" l. **$160**

Courtesy of Mark Mussio, Humler & Nolan

Vas-bowl, shape T17, in mustard mat
glaze and with green flambé applied
to inner portion of piece and dripped
from rim, marked on bottom with Fulper
rectangular ink stamp, excellent original
condition, 5" h. **$250**

Courtesy of Mark Mussio, Humler & Nolan

Vase in Chinese Blue flambé, shape
number 657, marked on bottom with
die-stamped "incised" Fulper mark with
original handwritten paper label, excellent
original condition, 5-3/4" h. x 9" dia. ...**$250**

Courtesy of Mark Mussio, Humler & Nolan

CERAMICS

gouda

GOUDA IS ONE of the decorative art world's strong and silent types, notwithstanding its bright colors and rich floral and abstract designs, considered by many to be its calling card. While its place in today's market is less robust than some of its contemporaries, its pairing of subtle strength of identity and eye-catching design is what attracts people to it and makes it a collectible to watch.

One of the indicators that Dutch pottery shouldn't be counted out is that higher-end pieces continue to attract attention, not unlike many other categories of antiques today.

"There appears to be a line in the sand with Gouda right now," said Stuart Slavid, vice president and director of Fine Ceramics, Fine Silver, European Furniture & Decorative Arts at Skinner, Inc. "Spectacular pieces are still doing well, but there is very little or no movement for lower-end pieces."

The reasons for that vary, but some contributing factors appear to be advanced collectors looking for advanced pieces rather than more basic items; and the way in which people collect overall has changed some, Slavid explained.

"It used to be more people would start with good pieces, move to better pieces and then to great. Now more people with available discretionary income are starting with the very best pieces," he said.

Riley Humler, auction director and art pottery expert at Humler & Nolan, echoed Slavid's sentiments, adding that high-end pieces in every collecting arena are doing far better than the rest.

"Serious collectors are looking for better pieces and avoiding lesser items," Humler said. "Quality has finally taken over for quantity. Part of that may be that serious collectors are generally older and have money. There are not enough young collectors to buy the more reasonable pieces, so one end of the market is doing fairly well and the other, not so well."

As with many situations, there are exceptions to the status quo, and that's also true in today's Gouda pottery market. While the most common Gouda pieces are seen in matte finishes, which are more modern and also more plentiful, early pieces, especially those with birds or butterflies under their gloss finishes, may be somewhat hard to find and tend to be more interesting, according to Humler.

Looking at the history of Gouda pottery, it's possible the founders of the earliest factories would be surprised to see what has become of their pottery, especially since many of the first companies to produce Gouda pottery did so to diversify their primary operation of clay pipe production. With an abundance of clay in the Gouda region of the Netherlands, it made good sense for the companies to expand into pottery; and the public demand confirmed it, according to information on the Museumgouda website, www.museumgouda.nl.

It was 1898 when Plateelbakkerij Zuid-Holland, often referred to as PZH or Zuid-Holland, produced its first piece of Gouda pottery. Named for the region in the Netherlands, Gouda encompasses the pottery produced by several factories located there. While the earliest examples of Gouda were not the same as

Pair of earthenware vessels, circa 1900, marks: MADE IN Z. HOLLAND, (indecipherable mark), 5014/287, wear commensurate with age, small chip to handle of one vessel, 9-1/2" h. **$375**

Courtesy of Heritage Auctions

Monumental candlestands with arched handles, each with partial "Zuid Holland Potter at the Wheel" paper sticker on sides, both marked "156, Purduli, Gouda, Made in Holland, 4254," with 1920s date symbol, house and RA monogram plus PZH paper sticker beneath, 19-7/8" h. x 6-1/4" w. across bases..........**$110**

Courtesy of Mark Mussio, Humler & Nolan

Arts & Crafts art pottery vase, shouldered form with wide neck, applied handles, tapering to circular foot, polychrome geometric bands, marked "985 Marion Z Holland," 11" h. x 7-1/2" w. **$250**

Courtesy of Clars Auction Gallery, www.clars.com

Charger painted by Henri Breetvelt, design by C.A. Prins, circa 1925, allover pattern in multiple colors, house logo hand-marked in blue slip, cipher of Prins, "Gouda, Made in Holland, decor: Breetvelt" and 392 in brown slip on back, small chip at edge of rim, 16-1/2" dia........................**$250**

Courtesy of Mark Mussio, Humler & Nolan

Charger painted by Jan Kool with flower stalk over colorful backdrop, circa 1899, black slip marked "Made in Zuid Holland" with artist's cipher and house logo, impressed "6BAW" and shield logo under glaze, excellent condition with faint crazing, 12" dia........**$200**

Courtesy of Mark Mussio, Humler & Nolan

the brightly colored, matte glaze pieces collected today, they were often sought after for the same reason as today: décor for the home.

However, like many types of pottery, it didn't necessarily start out that way, said Joe Altare, founder of the Regina Pottery Collectors site (www.reginapottery.com). "One of the key points to remember about these wares is that some were designed as giftware and others for day-to-day use," Altare said. "Both were marketed to the middle class, [which] finally had discretionary income to purchase decorative, rather than utilitarian wares."

People, then and now, are drawn in by the remarkable colors and designs.

Although many of the companies that produced Gouda pottery remained in operation through the mid-1960s and 1970s, many consider the heyday of Gouda to have lasted through the first three decades of the 20th century. In fact, in the 1920s, a quarter of the workforce in the Gouda region was employed in the pottery industry, according to Museumgouda.

While Gouda pieces may not be setting high-profile auction records today, it remains a strong and serious representative of the ingenuity of decorative pottery. Plus, as more people are shopping at places like IKEA and Crate & Barrel for modern décor and furnishings, decorative pottery like Gouda lends itself nicely to that scene.

With a history steeped in innovation primed by practicality and fans across the globe, a renewal and widespread rediscovery of Gouda pottery isn't out of the question.

— Antoinette Rahn, Editor, *Antique Trader*

CERAMICS

grueby

FINE ART POTTERY was produced by the Grueby Faience and Tile Co. established in Boston in 1891. Choice pieces were created with molded designs on a semi-porcelain body. The ware is marked and often bears the initials of the decorators. The pottery closed in 1907.

Fat vase with six tooled leaves by Ruth Erickson, impressed Grueby pottery circular logo and number 144, incised E.R. artist mark, restoration to rim and nicks to high points, 7-3/4" h. **$1,700**

Courtesy of Mark Mussio, Humler & Nolan

Tulip tile in deep green matte glaze with incised leaf and stem with yellow tulip, good condition, 6" sq. x 1". **$1,210**

Courtesy of Fontaine's Auction Gallery

Two ship tiles, one in cuerda seca and one in cuenca, circa 1910, one stamped 82 and signed RM, other with remnant of paper label and signed ET, small chip to corner of larger tile and small flakes to two corners of smaller tile, 8" sq., 9" sq. **$3,250**

Courtesy of Rago Arts, www.ragoarts.com

Lobed vase with yellow buds, circa 1905, circular pottery stamp, professional restoration to two chips at rim, small chips to high points, 8-1/4" x 4-1/2". **$1,600**

Courtesy of Rago Arts, www.ragoarts.com

Earthenware vase, circa 1900, leaf-decorated form with flared rim, base with two Grueby labels, area of glaze loss at base ring, possibly as made, 8" h. **$3,000**

Courtesy of Brunk Auctions

Cabinet vase, early 20th century, Faience-stamped, 3-1/2" x 3-1/2". **$704**

Courtesy of Rago Arts, www.ragoarts.com

CERAMICS

haeger

SLEEK, SINUOUS, COLORFUL and cutting edge, timeless, trim of line, and, above all, thoroughly modern. That's the hallmark of Haeger Potteries. Since its 1871 founding in Dundee, Illinois, the firm has successfully moved from the utilitarian to the decorative. Whether freshly minted or vintage, Haeger creations continue to provide what ads called "a galaxy of exquisite designs...visual achievements symbolizing expert craftsmanship and pottery-making knowledge."

Today's collectors are particularly captivated by the modernistic Haeger output of the 1940s and '50s – from "panther" TV lamps and figurines of exotic Oriental maidens to statuary of rearing wild horses and snorting bulls. But the Haeger story began long before then, with the Great Chicago Fire of 1871.

Founder David Haeger had recently purchased a budding brickyard on the banks of Dundee's Fox River. Following the fire, his firm produced bricks to replace decimated Chicagoland structures. For the next 30 years, industrial production remained the primary emphasis of the Haeger Brick and Tile Co. It wasn't until 1914 that the company, now under the guidance of Edmund Haeger, noted the growing popularity of the Arts & Crafts movement and turned its attention to artware.

From the beginning, Haeger was distinguished by its starry roster of designers. The first: J.

Royal Haeger chicken #R1726 USA, all original, excellent condition, 20" h.................... **$48**

Courtesy of Milestone Auctions, www.milestoneauctions.com

Royal Haeger Art Deco pottery vase with doe leaping over tall grass, marked on bottom, 15" h................................. **$111**

Courtesy of Capo Auctions, Ltd.

Four Haeger Helmut Bruchmann glazed vases: Marked 10" ribbed vase, number 4075; marked 8" stick vase, number 4001; unmarked Siamese trio, 12"; and unmarked 4-1/2" x 8" gourd vase; all with glossy autumnal drip glaze over matte black, excellent condition. **$140**

Courtesy of Mark Mussio, Humler & Nolan

CERAMICS

Martin Stangl, former glaze wizard for Fulper. The design emphasis of Stangl and his early Haeger successors was on classically simple, uncluttered Arts & Crafts stylings. Haeger's roster of pots, jugs, vases, bowls, and candleholders all proved big hits with buyers.

An early zenith was reached with a pavilion at the 1934 Chicago World's Fair. In addition to home environment settings accented with Haeger, there was an actual working factory. Once fair-goers had viewed the step-by-step pottery production process, they could purchase a piece of Haeger on the way out. The World's Fair brought Haeger to America's attention – but its grandest days of glory were still ahead.

The year 1938 saw the promotion of Edmund Haeger's forward-thinking son-in-law, Joseph Estes, to general manager, the arrival of equally forward-thinking designer Royal Arden Hickman, and the introduction of the popular "Royal Haeger" line.

The multi-talented Hickman, snapped up by Haeger after stays at J.H. Vernon, Kosta Crystal, and his own Ra Art, quickly made his mark. Earlier Haeger figurals were generally of animals and humans at rest. Under the guidance of Hickman and the soon-to-follow Eric Olsen, motion was key: leaping fish, birds taking wing, and a ubiquitous snarling black panther. The energetic air of underlying excitement in these designs was ideally suited to the action-packed atmosphere of World War II and the postwar new day that followed.

In 1944, Hickman left Haeger following a dispute over lamp production, returning only for occasional free-lance assignments. The 1947 arrival of his successor, Eric Olsen, coincided with the official celebration of Haeger's "Diamond Jubilee"; that's when much of the Olsen line made its debut. From towering abstract figural lamps to long-legged colts, self-absorbed stalking lions, and mystic pre-Columbian priests, his designs were ideal for the soon-to-be-ultra-current "1950s modern" décor.

Today, The Haeger Potteries continues as a family affair under the leadership of Joseph Estes' daughter, Alexandra Haeger Estes.

Royal Haeger "Toe Tapper Musicans Quintet" spirit decanters in brown textured mat glaze with glossy brown glaze, all marked "Royal Haeger, USA," factory sticker attached to one, excellent condition, 8" to 12" h. **$160**

Courtesy of Mark Mussio, Humler & Nolan

Two Royal Haeger rooster planters, all original, excellent condition, each 12" h. **$72**

Courtesy of Milestone Auctions, www.milestoneauctions.com

Pair of Haeger ceramic male and female figures forming circle, one black, one pink, good condition, each 14-1/2" w. x 14-1/2" h., 5" dia. **$123**

Courtesy of Roland Auctioneers & Valuers, www.rolandauctions.com

CERAMICS

hampshire pottery

HAMPSHIRE POTTERY WAS made in Keene, New Hampshire, where several potteries operated as far back as the late 18th century. The pottery now known as Hampshire Pottery was established by J.S. Taft shortly after 1870. Various types of wares, including art pottery, were produced through the years. Taft's brother-in-law, Cadmon Robertson, joined the firm in 1904 and was responsible for developing more than 900 glaze formulas while in charge of all manufacturing. His death in 1914 created problems for the firm, and Taft sold out to George Morton in 1916. Closed during part of World War I, the pottery was later reopened by Morton for a short time and manufactured white hotel china. From 1919 to 1921, mosaic floor tiles became the main production. All production ceased in 1923.

Tall factory lamp base with leaves and buds, 1900s, with electrified oil font, unmarked, vase 15" x 9", with fixture 27" h. **$1,800**

Courtesy of Rago Arts, www.ragoarts.com

Bowl with blue matte ground, good condition, 6" h. **$97**

Courtesy of Rachel Davis Fine Arts, www.racheldavisfinearts.com

Vase with surround of leaf blades alternating with buds covered in organic green Grueby-like glaze, incised "Hampshire Pottery" beneath, thinness of glaze to high areas, glaze nicks to edge of base, 6-3/4" h. **$325**

Courtesy of Mark Mussio, Humler & Nolan

Vase with field corn in husk, raised front and back, organic green glaze, impressed "S. Taft & Co., Keene, N.H.," excellent original condition, 5-7/8" h. **$250**

Courtesy of Mark Mussio, Humler & Nolan

Vase #124 with gray/blue glaze, signed, 9-1/2" h., 6-1/2" dia........... **$397**

Courtesy of Treadway Toomey Auctions

VISIT WWW.ANTIQUETRADER.COM

WWW.FACEBOOK.COM/ANTIQUETRADER

CERAMICS
CERAMICS

ironstone

DURABILITY: WHEN INTRODUCED in the early 1800s, that was ironstone china's major selling point. Durability also accounts for the still-ready availability of vintage ironstone china, literally centuries after it first captivated consumers. Unlike its fragile porcelain contemporaries, this utilitarian earthenware was intended to withstand the ravages of time – and it has.

Ironstone owes its innate sturdiness to a formula incorporating iron slag with the clay. Cobalt, added to the mix, eliminated the yellowish tinge that plagued earlier attempts at white china. The earliest form of this opaque dinnerware made its debut in 1800 England, patented by potters William and John Turner. However, by 1806 the Turner firm was bankrupt.

Ironstone achieved its first real popularity in 1813, when Charles Mason first offered for sale his "Patent Ironstone China." Mason's white ironstone was an immediate hit, offering vessels for a wide variety of household uses, from teapots and tureens to washbowls and pitchers.

Although the inexpensive simplicity of white ironstone proved popular with frugal householders, by the 1830s in-mold and transfer patterns were providing a dose of visual variety. Among the decorative favorites: Oriental motifs and homey images such as grains, fruits, and flowers.

Mason's patented formula for white ironstone lasted 14 years. Upon its expiration, numerous other potteries jumped into the fray. By the 1840s, white ironstone found its way across the ocean, enjoying the same success in the United States and Canada as it had in England. By the 1880s, however, the appeal of whiteware began to fade. Its successor, soon overtaking the original, was ironstone's most enduring incarnation, Tea Leaf, which was popular into the early 1900s.

Mason's ironstone china washbowl and pitcher, England, mid-19th century, Asian-style transfer design with hand-coloring, peacocks, one black mark, one green, pitcher with serpent handle, 7-1/2" h., paneled bowl 11" dia. **$188**

Courtesy of Garth's Auctions, Inc.

Pair of Mason's ironstone pitchers, England, mid-19th century, red house design on blue ground with gilding, dragon handles, wear on handles, gilding, and edges of panels, one handle with firing separation in crest, other pitcher with ground down chip on rim near handle, 7-1/2" h. **$420**

Courtesy of Garth's Auctions, Inc.

▶ Mason's Imari pattern lidded ironstone tureen and underplate, polychrome and gilt floral design, shellwork handles and finial, each marked, 14" h. x 14-1/2" l...................... **$1,000**

Courtesy of Neal Auction Co.

Four Gaudy Blackberry pattern plates, impressed "Paris White Ironstone China, Walley," very good condition, 8-1/2"........ **$333**

Courtesy of Conestoga Auction Co.

Oversize Mason's ironstone teapot, England, mid-19th century, Chinese-style transfer with hand-coloring, pewter lid with dove finial, 14" h. **$1,080**

Courtesy of Garth's Auctions, Inc.

Mason's ironstone covered vase, mid-19th century, Asian-style transfers with hand-coloring, double dolphin finial and handles, black mark, top of finial repaired, 21" h. **$420**

Courtesy of Garth's Auctions, Inc.

Pair of Mason's ironstone vases, England, second quarter 19th century, Imari pattern with dragon handles and gold trim, good condition, paint flakes along handles, 11-1/2" h......................... **$750**

Courtesy of Garth's Auctions, Inc.

CERAMICS

kpm

KPM PLAQUES ARE highly glazed, enamel paintings on porcelain bases that were produced by Konigliche Porzellan Manufaktur (KPM), the King's Porcelain Factory, in Berlin, Germany, between 1880 and 1901.

Their secret, according to Afshine Emrani, dealer and appraiser at www.some-of-my-favorite-things.com, is KPM's highly superior, smooth, hard paste porcelain, which could be fired at very high temperatures.

"The magic of a KPM plaque is that it will look as crisp and beautiful 100 years from now as it does today," he said. Even when they were introduced, these plaques proved highly collectible, with art lovers, collectors, tourists, and the wealthy acquiring them for extravagant sums.

KPM rarely marketed painted porcelain plaques itself, however. Instead, it usually supplied white, undecorated ones to independent artists who specialized in this genre. Not all artists signed their KPM paintings, however.

While most KPM plaques were copies of famous paintings, some, commissioned by wealthy Americans and Europeans in the 1920s, bear images of actual people in contemporary clothing. These least collectible of KPM plaques command between $500 and $1,500 each, depending on the attractiveness of their subjects.

Gilded, hand-painted plaques featuring Middle Eastern or female Gypsy subjects and bearing round red "Made in Germany" stamps were produced just before and after World War I for export. They command between $500 and $2,000 each. Plaques portraying religious subjects, such as the Virgin Mary or the Flight into Egypt, command higher prices but are less popular.

Popular scenes of hunters, merrymakers, musicians, etc., generally fetch less than $10,000 apiece because they have been reproduced time and again. Rarer, more elaborate scenes, however, like "The Dance Lesson" and "Turkish Card Players" may be worth many times more.

Highly stylized portraits copied from famous paintings – especially those of attractive children or décolleté women – allowed art lovers to own their own "masterpieces." These are currently worth between $2,000 and $20,000 each. Romanticized portrayals of cupids and women in the nude, the most desirable KPMs subjects of all, currently sell for up to $40,000 each. Portraits of men, it must be noted, are not only less popular, but also less expensive.

Size also matters. A 4" x 6" plaque, whose subject has been repeatedly reproduced, may sell for a few thousand dollars. Larger ones that portray the same subject will fetch proportionately more. A "Sistine Madonna" plaque, fashioned after the original work by Rafael and measuring 10" x 7-1/2", might cost $4,200. One featuring the identical subject, but measuring 15" x 11", might cost $7,800. A larger plaque, measuring 22" x 16", might command twice that price.

The largest KPM plaques, measuring 22" x 26", for example, often burst during production. Although no formula exists for determining prices of those that have survived, Afshine Emrani said that each may sell for as much as $250,000. Rare plaques like these are often found in museums.

The condition of a KPM plaque also affects its price. Most, since they were highly glazed and customarily hung instead of handled, have survived in perfect condition. Thus those that have sustained even minor damage, like scratches, cracks, or chips, fetch considerably lower prices. Those suffering major damage are worthless.

Porcelain table service: Two serving trays, 12 large bowls, 9-1/2"dia., and 12 shallow bowls, partial gilt border with garland swags on white ground with cobalt blue accents, centering polychrome floral decoration, each signed with underglaze blue scepter mark.......................**$3,500**

Courtesy of Clars Auction Gallery, www.clars.com

Vase with stylized Art Nouveau poppies, circa 1900, Theodore Schmutz-Baudiss, 15" h., 5" dia............................ **$2,299**

Courtesy of Cottone Auctions

Plaque, "The Penitent Magdalene," 19th century, Magdalene reads book resting on skull, 12" x 15". **$2,541**

Courtesy of Cottone Auctions

KPM painted plaques arouse so much interest and command such high prices that, over the last couple of years, unscrupulous dealers have entered the market. According to dealer Balazs Benedek, KPM plaques are "the mother of all fakes. About 90 percent of KPM plaques are mid- to late-20th century reproductions. And about 70 percent are not hand painted."

Collectors should be aware that genuine KPM paintings always boast rich, shiny, glazes that preserve their colors, and though subject matter may vary, they typically feature nude scenes, indoor portraits of women, or group gatherings in lush settings. Anything wildly different should raise suspicion.

Genuine KPMs, on their backs or edges, feature small icons of scepters deeply set in the porcelain, over the letters KPM. These marks are sometimes accompanied by an "H" or some other letter, which may indicate their production date or size. Some are imprinted with the size of the plaque as well, which facilitated sorting or shipping. Shallow or crooked imprints may reveal a fake.

— Melody Amsel-Arieli

CERAMICS

Hand-painted rectangular porcelain plaque of Mary Magdalene, Berlin, late 19th/early 20th century, after Pietro Antonio Rotari (Italian, 1707-1762), penitent Magdalene in blue drapes with eyes cast towards heaven, unsigned, with impressed scepter and monogram mark, framed, sight size 20" x 14", 37-1/2" x 29-1/2" total........**$3,690**

Courtesy of Skinner, Inc.; www.skinnerinc.com

Porcelain plaque, circa 1900, after "Épanouissement" by Angelo Asti (Italian/French 1847-1903), inscribed "R. Dietrich I" lower left, titled with impressed factory marks on reverse, 10" x 7-1/2" in gilt frame. **$6,563**

Courtesy of Neal Auction Co.

Oval porcelain portrait plaque of young Arab woman, marked KPM, 8-3/4" x 6-1/2", in 20" x 18" gilt wood frame. **$1,003**

Courtesy of Woody Auctions, LLC

▲ Dessert set, 24 pieces total: Eight plates, 8" dia.; eight fruit saucers, 5-1/4" dia.; and eight cups, 2" h.; hand-decorated with floral sprigs and garden bouquets, bordered by raised gold scrollwork, gold trim inside each cup with handle in gold; each piece with red mark of KPM and Imperial Orb as well as flow blue scepter with diagonal bar under glaze, other marks: Maltese Cross in flow blue or ink black on four cups and three saucers, other impressed or hand-applied factory marks, two plates with hand-painted butterflies on back; excellent condition. **$1,300**

Courtesy of Mark Mussio, Humler & Nolan

Plaque of Ruth, 19th century, signed lower right E. Volk, 16" x 10". **$3,630**

Courtesy of Cottone Auctions

Plaque of Three Fates, scepter mark on reverse, artist signed lower left, illegible, 13" x 7-3/4". **$4,356**

Courtesy of Cottone Auctions

Rectangular porcelain plaque of woman with two young children during winter, late 19th/20th century, impressed K.P.M., sceptre mark, and x, 15-1/4" x 12". **$1,968**

Courtesy of A.B. Levy's Auctions

Rectangular plaque with full-length portrait of Queen Louise von Mecklenburg-Strelitz of Prussia, after German artist Gustav Richter (1823-1884), late 19th/early 20th century, impressed "KPM" and scepter marks, further impressed "K.P.M / Sz / W" and inscribed "330.900," marked in pencil "a 814 / 28011," discretely signed lower right, "Keller," in pierced giltwood frame, plaque 12-3/4" h. x 7-3/4" w. **$9,000**

Courtesy of John Moran Auctioneers, Inc.

Plaque of woman and child fleeing into rocky landscape, woman with rifle slung over her left shoulder, late 19th/early 20th century, impressed KPM scepter mark and monogram, further impressed "H" and "L" and incised "12 7/8 - 7-5/8," paper label affixed to verso "Flight of the Brigand's Wife / after Schmidt / by Griener" with further Cyrillic text, signed lower left "A. Finye (?)," in white foliate frame, plaque 12-7/8" h. x 7-7/8" w. **$4,000**

Courtesy of John Moran Auctioneers, Inc.

◄ Hand-painted porcelain portrait plate after work by Frederick Auguste Kaulbach (1850-1920), impressed "KPM" below scepter mark in green, portrait of woman in elaborate dress, black hat with white flowers, silk blouse with gold necklaces and brown cape, good condition overall, 7-3/4", within cast bronze reticulated frame, 11". ... **$806**

Courtesy of Brunk Auctions

Plaque of woman holding dagger, 19th century, 9" x 6-1/4". **$1,029**

Courtesy of Cottone Auctions

Porcelain plaque of woman holding cat, circa 1900, with impressed mark, 7-3/4" x 5-1/2" framed. **$4,375**

Courtesy of Neal Auction Co.

Plaque of courting couple with man playing violin, marked KPM on reverse, 10-1/4" x 7-3/4". **$3,509**

Courtesy of Cottone Auctions

CERAMICS

limoges

"LIMOGES" HAS BECOME the generic identifier for porcelain produced in Limoges, France, and the surrounding vicinity. Over 40 manufacturers in the area have, at some point, used the term as a descriptor of their work, and there are at least 400 different Limoges identification marks. The common denominator is the product itself: fine hard paste porcelain created from the necessary components found in abundance in the Limoges region: kaolin and feldspar.

Until the 1700s, porcelain was exclusively a product of China, introduced to the Western world by Marco Polo, and imported at great expense. In 1765, the discovery of kaolin in St. Yrieixin, a small town near Limoges, made French production of porcelain possible. (The chemist's wife credited with the kaolin discovery thought at first that it would prove useful in making soap.)

Limoges entrepreneurs quickly capitalized on the find. Adding to the area's allure: expansive forests, providing fuel for wood-burning kilns; the nearby Vienne River, with water for working clay; and a workforce eager to trade farming for a (hopefully) more lucrative pursuit. Additionally, as the companies would be operating outside metropolitan Paris, labor and production costs would be significantly less.

By the early 1770s, numerous porcelain manufacturers were at work in Limoges and its environs. Demand for the porcelain was high because it was both useful and decorative. To meet that demand, firms employed trained, as well as untrained, artisans for the detailed hand painting required. (Although nearly every type of Limoges has its fans, the most sought-after and valuable are those pieces decorated by a company's professional artists.) At its industrial peak in 1900, Limoges factories employed over 8,000 workers in some aspect of porcelain production.

Myriad products classified as Limoges flooded the marketplace from the late 1700s onward. Among them were tableware pieces, such as tea and punch sets, trays, pitchers, compotes, bowls, and plates. Also popular were vases and flower baskets, dresser sets, trinket boxes, ash receivers, figural busts, and decorative plaques.

Although produced in France, Limoges porcelain was soon destined for export overseas; eventually over 80 percent of Limoges porcelain was exported. The United States proved a particularly reliable customer. Notable among the importers was the Haviland China Co.; until the 1940s, its superior, exquisitely decorated china was produced in Limoges and then distributed in the United States.

By the early 20th century, many exporters in the United States were purchasing porcelain blanks from the Limoges factories for decoration stateside. The base product was authentically made in France, but production costs were significantly lower: Thousands of untrained porcelain painters put their skills to work for a

◄ Enamel pillbox, 19th century, octagonal form, hinged lid, with scene of Neptune in shell chariot driven by seahorses, brass mounts, 2-1/4" h. x 2-3/8" w. x 1-3/8" d. **$375**

Courtesy of Neal Auction Co.

▲ Fish set with hand-painted fish and gold leaf trim, platter, 12 plates, and sauceboat, artist-signed Dubuis, Limoges S & C, France, platter 23-1/2" w. x 9" d. **$1,452**

Courtesy of Cottone Auctions

Large hand-painted porcelain box, early 20th century, Celeste blue ground and hinged and domed cover with 18th century-style figures in landscape, sides painted with views of landscape garden, interior with polychrome flower sprays to white ground, gilt-metal mounts and spurious Sèvres mark, 14-3/4" l. **$400**

Courtesy of Skinner, Inc.; www.skinnerinc.com

Gilt and polychrome fish set, late 19th century, serving platter, sauceboat, underplate and 12 plates, marked, minor hairline in platter, platter 24" l., plates 9-1/2" dia. **$375**

Courtesy of Neal Auction Co.

minimal wage. Domestic decoration of the blanks also meant that importers could select designs suited to the specific tastes of target audiences.

Because Limoges was a regional designation, rather than the identifier of a specific manufacturer, imported pieces were often marked with the name of the exporting firm, followed by the word "Limoges." Beginning in 1891, "France" was added. Some confusion has arisen from products marked "Limoges China Co." (aka "American Limoges"). This Ohio-based firm, in business from 1902-1955, has absolutely no connection to the porcelain produced in France.

The heyday of quality French Limoges lasted roughly into the 1930s. Production continues today, but after World War II, designs and painting techniques became much more standardized.

Vintage Limoges is highly sought-after by today's collectors. They're drawn to the delicacy of the porcelain as well as the colors and skill of decoration; viewing a well-conceived Limoges piece is like seeing a painting in a new form. Valuation is based on age, decorative execution and, as with any collectible, individual visual appeal.

For more information on Limoges, see *Antique Trader Pottery and Porcelain Ceramics Price Guide,* 7th edition.

Occupational shaving mug for insurance salesman, 19th century, inscribed "Charles W Varney" with burning building in background, stamped T & V Limoges France, 4" h....... **$3,600**

Courtesy of Pook & Pook, Inc.

Painted porcelain plaque of sheep and hounds, signed C. L. Juergens 1911, 9-1/2" x 13-3/4"... **$172**

Courtesy of Pook & Pook, Inc.

Pate-sur-pate porcelain plaque signed Limoges, 6-1/2" x 4-1/4".............................. **$424**

Courtesy of Cottone Auctions

Two Camille Tharaud pate-sur-pate plaques with maidens in diaphanous gowns, both impressed "Limoges France" with circular "CT" monogram and "Made in France" stamped in green on backs, tambourine dancer impressed "Grelerot" below rose sprig on front, both in beaded brass frames, excellent condition, 7" x 4-1/2"... **$275**

Courtesy of Mark Mussio, Humler & Nolan

Framed French enamel on copper plaque, L'eau Chaude, 201032, circa 1900, woman working hearthside, pouring hot water from teapot, marks: FAURÉ, Limoges, France, 5-1/2" x 4" x 2", frame 12-3/4" x 11-1/4" x 2"....... **$425**

Courtesy of Heritage Auctions

Pair of Rutherford B. Hayes Presidential pattern porcelain oyster plates, circa 1880, Haviland & Co., Limoges, France, designed by artist Theodore Russell Davis, fully marked, second edition, 8-1/2" dia. **$3,750**

Courtesy of Neal Auction Co.

CERAMICS

majolica

IN 1851, an English potter was hoping that his new interpretation of a centuries-old style of ceramics would be well received at the "Great Exhibition of the Industries of All Nations" set to open May 1 in London's Hyde Park.

Potter Herbert Minton had high hopes for his display. His father, Thomas Minton, founded a pottery works in the mid-1790s in Stoke-on-Trent, Staffordshire. Herbert Minton had designed a "new" line of pottery, and his chemist, Leon Arnoux, had developed a process that resulted in vibrant, colorful glazes that came to be called "majolica."

Trained as an engineer, Arnoux also studied the making of encaustic tiles, and had been appointed art director at Minton's works in 1848. His job was to introduce and promote new products. Victorian fascination with the natural world prompted Arnoux to reintroduce the work of Bernard Palissy, whose naturalistic, bright-colored "maiolica" wares had been created in the 16th century. But Arnoux used a thicker body to make pieces sturdier. This body was given a coating of opaque white glaze, which provided a surface for decoration.

Pieces were modeled in high relief, featuring butterflies and other insects, flowers and leaves, fruit, shells, animals, and fish. Queen Victoria's endorsement of the new pottery prompted its acceptance by the general public.

When Minton introduced his wares at Philadelphia's 1876 Centennial Exhibition, American potters also began to produce majolica.

For more information on majolica, see *Warman's Majolica Identification and Price Guide* by Mark F. Moran.

Choisy-le-Roi inkwell with inserts, France, circa 1880, modeled as swan seated with leaf in mouth, removable wing lifts to reveal quill holder and ink reservoir, whole on scalloped basin, underside with Charles L. Washburne Antiques label, underglaze pottery mark, 9" h. **$1,300**

Courtesy of Clars Auction Gallery, www.clars.com

CERAMICS

George Jones fox dish, England, circa 1875, oval dish with raised leaf motif, fox head peers over one side, tail coiled about underside, raised factory mark, 10" l. **$400**

Courtesy of Skinner, Inc.; www.skinnerinc.com

George Jones figural saltcellar, England, circa 1875, upper body of dog peers over edge of shallow oval bowl, 2-5/8" h. **$492**

Courtesy of Skinner, Inc.; www.skinnerinc.com

George Jones jardiniere, England, circa 1875, classical shape with female head handles and floral festoons in high relief, impressed mark, 7-1/8 h., 8-1/4" dia.. **$615**

Courtesy of Skinner, Inc.; www.skinnerinc.com

George Jones figure of Grecian maiden, England, circa 1880, standing figure modeled holding urn atop her head, mounted on raised circular plinth with floral and foliate banded border, pad mark, urn professionally restored, 18-1/4" h. **$984**

Courtesy of Skinner, Inc.; www.skinnerinc.com

◄ George Jones tree trunk planter, England, circa 1875, circular form with floral handles and blossoms and foliage in relief to naturalistically textured ground, pad and impressed mark, 7" h................ **$492**

Courtesy of Skinner, Inc.; www.skinnerinc.com

Two George Jones figural matchboxes with strikers, circa 1868: Oval box with relief molded leaves, vines, and buds in green on brown ground, opening to lavender interior with striker on bottom, with label from dealer Charles L. Washburne, 2-1/2" h. x 3-3/4" w. x 3" d., and box with rabbit in brown and white on brown and green oval base with relief molded ferns, rabbit figure lid lifts off to reveal lavender teardrop-form box with striker on side, with label for dealer Charles L. Washburne, 3" h. x 5-1/2" w. x 3" d. **$4,000**

Courtesy of Clars Auction Gallery, www.clars.com

Minton model of boy resting on tall basket, England, 1865, standing figure with fruiting grapevines by his feet, impressed mark, 9-1/2" h. **$246**

Courtesy of Skinner, Inc.; www.skinnerinc.com

Minton taverner jug, England, 1866, tapered form decorated with tavern figures, impressed mark, 10" h. **$800**

Courtesy of Skinner, Inc.; www.skinnerinc.com

Minton figural Hugues Protât design ewer, England, 1867, barrel-form flat-sided body with Bacchanalian children to shoulder and fruiting grapevines in relief, branch handle, impressed mark, 15" h. **$1,230**

Courtesy of Skinner, Inc.; www.skinnerinc.com

Minton pigeon serving bowl, England, 1873, scalloped wicker-work bowl set upon backs of three fantailed pigeons perched atop oak branches, impressed mark, 9-1/4" dia. **$923**

Courtesy of Skinner, Inc.; www.skinnerinc.com

Minton Flemish-style candlestick, England, circa 1865, decorated in relief with face masks, goat heads, flowers, foliage, and fruiting festoons, impressed mark, 15-1/2" h. **$861**

Courtesy of Skinner, Inc.; www.skinnerinc.com

CERAMICS

Minton shell-form sweetmeat dish, 19th century, naturalistically modeled with half shells above shell-encrusted base, underside with Charles L. Washburne Antiques label, 5" h. $1,000

Courtesy of Clars Auction Gallery, www.clars.com

Rörstrand pedestal, 19th century, modeled in three sections, tapering standard with square capital molded with figural masks between volute scroll supports, incurvate base with hairy paw feet, each piece marked "Made in Sweden Rörstrand" with impressed Rörstrand mark, 46" h. **$2,750**

Courtesy of Neal Auction Co.

◀ Sarreguemines vase, France, late 19th century, heavily decorated with foliage and reeds to dark blue ground, impressed mark, 16-1/2" h....................**$461**

Courtesy of Skinner, Inc.; www.skinnerinc.com

Royal Worcester figure of hunter, England, circa 1875, standing figure supporting dead rabbit and pheasant upon his back, impressed mark, 17-7/8" h. **$1,968**

Courtesy of Skinner, Inc.; www.skinnerinc.com

▶ Wedgwood shell-form spoon warmer, 19th century, naturalistically modeled as large shell in sky blue and Amaranth, verso with Charles L. Washburne Antiques label, 5" h. **$700**

Courtesy of Clars Auction Gallery, www.clars.com

Two Wedgwood caterer jugs, England, circa 1870, each with bands of verse alternating with bands of turquoise jeweling, impressed marks, 7-1/2" h.. **$277**

Courtesy of Skinner, Inc.; www.skinnerinc.com

Monumental vase in Asian style, 19th century, flared rim above cylinder neck with applied naturalistic wood-form handles above bulbous body covered in high relief peapods, vines, and flowers on cobalt ground, 15-3/4" h. x 9" w. . **$800**

Courtesy of Clars Auction Gallery, www.clars.com

Pair of aesthetic tall vases, early 20th century, each baluster form with cobalt ground decorated with clouds and chinoiserie-style dragon, 25" h. **$1,250**

Courtesy of Neal Auction Co.

Continental figural compote, 19th century, boat-form bowl mounted with griffin handle and Bacchanalian mask spout with fruiting grapevine border, supported atop satyr seated on rock among waves on stepped circular base, 15-5/8" h...... **$308**

Courtesy of Skinner, Inc.; www.skinnerinc.com

Continental by Jose A. Cunha, Portugal: Footed plate with applied crabs and shells on brown ground, 10-1/2" dia., and figural bowl with applied snake, frog, and worms on naturalistic ground, 4-1/2" w. **$1,600**

Courtesy of Clars Auction Gallery, www.clars.com

English compote, 19th century, with treelike base, buffalo and beaver, loss to buffalo horns, small nick to rim, 10" h., 10-1/2" dia. **$7,750**

Courtesy of Cottone Auctions

▲ English bread tray, late 19th century, concave oval form, rim with wheat husks and foliage, faux basketweave ground, centering rosette medallion, 11" h. x 13-1/2" w. **$400**

Courtesy of Clars Auction Gallery, www.clars.com

◄ French oyster service, late 19th/20th century, eight plates, one server, each molded with central sauce reservoir and radiating shell pockets with burgundy rim and green and cream ground, 13" dia. **$600**

Courtesy of Clars Auction Gallery, www.clars.com

CERAMICS

marblehead

MARBLEHEAD POTTERY WAS organized in 1904 by Dr. Herbert J. Hall as a therapeutic aid to patients in a sanitarium he ran in Marblehead, Massachusetts. It was later separated from the sanitarium and directed by Arthur E. Baggs, a fine artist and designer, who bought out the factory in 1916 and operated it until its closing in 1936. Most wares were hand-thrown and decorated and carry the company mark of a stylized sailing vessel flanked by the letters "M" and "P."

Tapered vase with fruiting ivy branch, 1910s, attributed to Arthur Baggs, stamped ship mark MP, 6" x 5". **$4,800**

Courtesy of Rago Arts, www.ragoarts.com

Green-glazed earthenware vase designed by Arthur Irwin Hennesey, decorated by Sarah Tutt, impressed ship mark and incised H.T cipher, oval MARBLEHEAD POTTERY paper label, 3-1/2" h. **$9,375**

Courtesy of Bonhams

Green-glazed earthenware corseted vase with geometric decoration of stems and squares, designed by Arthur Irwin Hennesey, decorated by Sarah Tutt, impressed ship mark, incised HT cipher, oval MARBLEHEAD POTTERY paper label inscribed D1-1, 8-3/4" h................. **$40,000**

Courtesy of Bonhams

Tall blue-glazed earthenware vase, early 20th century, impressed ship mark, no artist cipher, inscribed MRS ReeD in ink, 13-1/2" h.................**$22,500**

Courtesy of Bonhams

VISIT WWW.ANTIQUETRADER.COM

WWW.FACEBOOK.COM/ANTIQUETRADER

Blue- and gray-glazed earthenware vase with incised band of geese, designed by Maude Milner, decorated by Sarah Tutt, impressed ship mark and incised AMT cipher, 8-5/8" h., 7-1/4" dia. **$8,750**

Courtesy of Bonhams

Green-glazed earthenware pitcher with incised tree band, designed by Arthur Baggs, impressed ship mark and with AB cipher, 6-1/4" h. **$2,375**

Courtesy of Bonhams

Blue-glazed earthenware vase with crane decoration, designed by Maude Milner, decorated by Sarah Tutt, impressed ship mark and incised MT cipher, 5-1/2" h. **$2,750**

Courtesy of Bonhams

Tall vase with stylized apple trees, 1910s, Arthur Hennessey, Sarah Tutt, stamped ship mark MP, signed HT, uncrazed, 10-1/2" h., 5-1/2" dia. **$21,760**

Courtesy of Rago Arts, www.ragoarts.com

Mustard-glazed earthenware vase with stylized flowering tree decoration, designed by Arthur Irwin Hennesey, decorated by Sarah Tutt, impressed ship mark, almost illegible HT cipher in glaze, 3-1/2" h. **$2,750**

Courtesy of Bonhams

Green-glazed earthenware bowl with incised quatrefoil band, designed by Maude Milner, decorated by Sarah Tutt, impressed ship mark over incised MT cipher, 3-1/2" h. **$2,000**

Courtesy of Bonhams

Green-glazed earthenware vase with geometric decoration, designed by Herbert J. Hall, decorated by Sarah Tutt, impressed ship mark, inscised HJH over T cipher, MARBLEHEAD POTTERY paper label inscribed B 006, 6" h. **$13,750**

Courtesy of Bonhams

Gray- and blue-glazed earthenware vase with stylized bellflower decoration, impressed ship mark, MARBLEHEAD POTTERY oval paper label, 7-1/4" h. **$5,625**

Courtesy of Bonhams

CERAMICS

martin brothers

MARTINWARE, THE TERM used for this pottery, dates from 1873 and is the product of the Martin brothers – Robert, Wallace, Edwin, Walter, and Charles – and is often considered the first British studio pottery. From first to final stages, the hand-thrown pottery was completely the work of the team. The early wares may be simple and conventional, but the Martin brothers built up their reputation by producing ornately engraved, incised, or carved designs as well as rather bizarre figural wares. The amusing face jugs are considered some of their finest work. After 1910, the work of the pottery declined and can be considered finished by 1915, though some attempts were made to fire pottery as late as the 1920s.

Rare sculptural vessel with four faces, England, circa 1900, signed "Martin Bros. London," 7" x 6". **$10,880**

Courtesy of Rago Arts, www.ragoarts.com

Glazed stoneware double-sided barrister face jug, England, circa 1910, signed "R.W. Martin + Bros. Southall," 6-3/4" x 5-1/2". **$10,880**

Courtesy of Rago Arts, www.ragoarts.com

CERAMICS

Glazed stoneware bird tobacco jar, inscribed on rim of lid and base, R.W. Martin & Bros., London & South Hall, 1887, very good condition, professional restoration to interior of neck, small age lines, hairline in tail, 11" h. x 9" d. **$64,130**

Courtesy of Cottone Auctions

Glazed stoneware bird tobacco jar, England, 1905, head signed "R.W. Martin + Bros. London + Southall 18.4.1905," base signed "Martin + Bros. London + Southall 18.4.1905," light wear to wood base, repaired chip to eyebrow, on base 8-3/4" x 4"....................**$19,200**

Courtesy of Rago Arts, www.ragoarts.com

Glazed stoneware double-sided face jug, English, late 19th century, base signed "R.W. Martin Bros. Southall," strap handle and deeply molded design, 4-3/4". **$2,976**

Courtesy of Brunk Auctions

CERAMICS

mccoy pottery

THE FIRST MCCOY with clay under his fingernails was W. Nelson McCoy. With his uncle, W.F. McCoy, he founded a pottery works in Putnam, Ohio, in 1848, making stoneware crocks and jugs.

That same year, W. Nelson's son, James W., was born in Zanesville, Ohio. James established the J.W. McCoy Pottery Co. in Roseville, Ohio, in the fall of 1899. The J.W. McCoy plant was destroyed by fire in 1903 and was rebuilt two years later.

It was at this time that the first examples of Loy-Nel-Art wares were produced. The line's distinctive title came from the names of James McCoy's three sons, Lloyd, Nelson, and Arthur. Like other "standard" glazed pieces produced at this time by several Ohio potteries, Loy-Nel-Art has a glossy finish on a dark brown-black body, but Loy-Nel-Art featured a splash of green color on the front and a burnt-orange splash on the back.

George Brush became general manager of J.W. McCoy Pottery Co. in 1909. The company became Brush-McCoy Pottery Co. in 1911, and in 1925 the name was shortened to Brush Pottery Co. This firm remained in business until 1982.

Separately, in 1910, Nelson McCoy Sr. founded the Nelson McCoy Sanitary and Stoneware Co., also in Roseville. By the early 1930s, production had shifted from utilitarian wares to art pottery, and the company name was changed to Nelson McCoy Pottery.

Tall Brush-McCoy Jewel vase, unmarked, excellent original condition, 11-5/8" h. **$250**

Courtesy of Mark Mussio, Humler & Nolan

Designer Sydney Cope was hired in 1934, and was joined by his son, Leslie, in 1936. The Copes' influence on McCoy wares continued until Sydney's death in 1966. That same year, Leslie opened a gallery devoted to his family's design heritage and featuring his own original art.

Nelson McCoy Sr. died in 1945, and was succeeded as company president by his nephew, Nelson McCoy Melick.

A fire destroyed the plant in 1950, but company officials – including Nelson McCoy Jr., then 29 – decided to rebuild, and the new Nelson McCoy Pottery Co. was up and running in just six months.

Nelson Melick died in 1954. Nelson Jr. became company president, and oversaw the company's continued growth. In 1967, the operation was sold to entrepreneur David Chase. At this time, the words "Mt. Clemens Pottery" were added to the company marks. In 1974, Chase sold the company to Lancaster Colony Corp., and the company marks included a stylized "LCC" logo. Nelson Jr. and his wife, Billie, who had served as a products supervisor, left the company in 1981.

In 1985, the company was sold again, this time to Designer Accents. The McCoy pottery factory closed in 1990.

For more information on McCoy pottery, see *Warman's McCoy Pottery*, 2nd edition, by Mark F. Moran.

Brush-McCoy Jewel art pottery vase, circa 1920, grayish background with jewel-tone enameling, excellent original condition, #042 marked on bottom, 9" h. **$236**

Courtesy of A-1 Auction

Mt. Pelee creamer, circa 1902, hand-molded and pinched form in green and yellow glaze with impressed Mt. Pelee mark on underside, 4-3/4" h. **$120**

Courtesy of Garth's Auctions, Inc.

Signed chicken cookie jar, all original, excellent condition, 10" h. **$36**

Courtesy of Milestone Auctions, www.milestoneauctions.com

Three pieces of pottery, mid-20th century, pair of skull mugs in cream and tan glaze, impressed marks under bases, 4" h., with Brush onyx musical jug with songs "How Dry I Am" and "Always Another Drop," 9-3/4" h. **$62**

Courtesy of Garth's Auctions, Inc.

◀ Brush-McCoy art pottery vase shaped like Aladdin's lamp, marked "Olympia," 5-1/2" **$47**

Courtesy of Woody Auction, LLC

CERAMICS

meissen

KNOWN FOR ITS finely detailed figurines and exceptional tableware, Meissen is recognized as the first European maker of fine porcelain.

The company owes its beginnings to Johann Friedrich Bottger's 1708 discovery of the process necessary for the manufacture of porcelain. "Rediscovery" might be a better term, since the secret of producing hard paste porcelain had been known to the Chinese for centuries. However, Bottger, a goldsmith and alchemist, was the first to successfully replicate the formula in Europe. Soon after, The Royal Saxon Porcelain Works set up shop in Dresden. Because Bottger's formula was highly sought after by would-be competitors, in 1710 the firm moved its base of operations to Albrechtburg Castle in Meissen, Saxony. There, in fortress-like surroundings, prying eyes could be successfully deflected. And, because of that move, the company name eventually became one with its locale: Meissen.

The earliest Meissen pieces were red stoneware, reminiscent of Chinese work, and incised with Chinese characters. Porcelain became the Meissen focus in 1713; early releases included figurines and teasets, the decorations reminiscent of baroque metal. In 1719, after Bottger's death, artist J.J. Horoldt took over the firm's direction. His Chinese-influenced designs, which employed a lavish use of color and decoration, are categorized as chinoiserie.

By the 1730s, Meissen employed nearly 100 workers, among them renowned modelers J.G. Kirchner and J.J. Kandler. The firm became known for its porcelain sculptures; subjects included birds, animals, and familiar figures from commedia dell'arte. Meissen dinnerware also won acclaim; in earlier attempts, the company's white porcelain had only managed to achieve off-white. Now, at last, there were dazzling white porcelain surfaces that proved ideal for the exquisite, richly colored decoration that became a Meissen trademark.

Following Horoldt's retirement in the mid-1700s, Victor Acier became Meissen's master modeler. Under Acier, the design focus relied heavily on mythological themes. By the early 1800s, however, Meissen's popularity began to wane. With production costs mounting and quality inconsistent, changes were instituted, especially technical improvements in production that allowed Meissen to operate more efficiently and profitably. More importantly, the Meissen designs, which had remained relatively stagnant for nearly a century, were refurbished. The goal: to connect with current popular culture. Meissen's artists (and its porcelain) proved perfectly capable of adapting to the prevailing tastes of the times. The range was wide: the ornate fussiness of the Rococo period; the more subdued Neoclassicism of the late 1700s; the nature-tinged voluptuousness of early 20th century Art Nouveau; and today's Meissen, which reinterprets, and builds on, all of these design eras.

Despite diligent efforts, Meissen eventually found its work widely copied. A crossed-swords trademark, applied to Meissen pieces from 1731 onward, is a good indicator of authenticity. However, even the markings had their imitators. Because Meissen originals, particularly those from the 18th and 19th centuries, are both rare and costly, the most reliable guarantee that a piece is authentic is to purchase from a reputable source.

Meissen porcelain is an acquired taste. Its gilded glory, lavish use of color, and almost

Porcelain tray, 19th century, oblong, with two shell-form handles, border decorated with green fish scales and gilded cartouches filled with molded flowers alternating with vignettes of musical instruments, center with polychrome enamel decoration of flower spray, first quality crossed swords mark, handle to handle 20-1/2" l...**$1,353**

Courtesy of Skinner, Inc.; www.skinnerinc.com

Two molded and hand-painted porcelain cups and saucers, late 19th/early 20th century, with raised grapevines, monochromatic scenes of putti and flower sprays, gilded dentil rims, first quality crossed swords marks, saucer 5-1/2" dia. **$861**

Courtesy of Skinner, Inc.; www.skinnerinc.com

Porcelain figural master salt, late 19th/early 20th century, blue enamel-decorated and modeled as reclining male figure offering basin in Blue Onion pattern, first quality crossed swords mark, incised "2872," impressed "86," small loss to big toe, 7" l.................**$338**

Courtesy of Skinner, Inc.; www.skinnerinc.com

Porcelain figure of girl with sheep, 20th century, girl wearing patterned kerchief and holding bouquet of flowers, on square base with canted corners, underside with first quality crossed swords mark, incised "Z134," impressed "48," 6-1/4" h......................**$1,230**

Courtesy of Skinner, Inc.; www.skinnerinc.com

Porcelain figure of mandarin duck, designed by Max Esser, 20th century, bird standing atop domed base mounted with foliage, with polychrome enamel accents, first quality crossed swords mark, incised "A1045," impressed "23," 14-5/8" h. **$1,353**

Courtesy of Skinner, Inc.; www.skinnerinc.com

overwhelmingly intricate detailing require just the right setting for effective display. Meissen is not background décor. These are three-dimensional artworks that demand full attention. Meissen pieces also often tell a story (although the plots may be long forgotten): a cherub and a woman in 18th century dress read a book, surrounded by a bevy of shepherdesses; the goddess Diana perches on a clock above a winged head of Father Time; the painted inset on a cobalt teacup depicts an ancient Dresden cathedral approached by devout churchgoers. Unforgettable images all, and all part of the miracle that is Meissen.

◀ Porcelain figural group emblematic of commerce, late 19th century, each piece signed with crossed swords and numbered #386 and #451, figure of Mercury in center surrounded by other figures in various production activities including mining and agriculture, professional restoration to some figures, 16" h. x 14-3/4" w. x 11-1/2" d **$25,410**

Courtesy of Cottone Auctions

Hand-painted porcelain cache pot, late 19th/early 20th century, with applied satyr mask handles and panoramic figural landscape divided between eight panels separated by tooled gilt bands, first quality crossed swords mark and incised "E174," 4-1/8" h., 4-1/2" dia. **$677**

Courtesy of Skinner, Inc., www.skinnerinc.com

◀ Porcelain figural group of Venus and Cupid in chariot, late 19th century, marked, engraved "2260.94," 7" h. x 6-3/4" w. x 6-1/2" d. **$1,188**

Courtesy of Neal Auction Co.

Pair of porcelain orioles, 19th century, after models by J. J. Kandler, each executed in yellow and black on naturalistic tree branch base, underside with blue crossed swords mark, incised model number 280 and impressed 111. .... **$1,600**

Courtesy of Clars Auction Gallery, www.clars.com

Figural parrot perched on naturalistic tree trunk base with floral accents, 12-1/2" h. **$750**

Courtesy of Clars Auction Gallery, www.clars.com

Large porcelain mirror, late 19th century, arched crest with winged cherubs, applied flowers and acanthus, sides with columns adorned with flowers and bowknots, beveled mirror plate, 76-1/2" h. x 48-1/2" w. **$13,750**

Courtesy of Neal Auction Co.

Coffeepot and sugar bowl, mid-20th century, each decorated with polychrome-painted applied flowers on white ground with gilt highlights, sugar bowl with rosebud finial, each with underglaze blue crossed swords mark, coffeepot 5-1/2" h. x 5-1/4" w., 4" dia., sugar bowl 3-3/4" h., 3-7/8" dia. **$275**

Courtesy of John Moran Auctioneers, Inc.

Two porcelain figurines, late 19th/early 20th century, each modeled by Johann Joachim Kandler, first with four children with flowers and fruit, second with four children playing musical instruments, each with underglaze blue crossed swords mark and incised "B60," first impressed "147," second impressed "28," first 10-1/2" h. x 6" w. x 5-3/4" d., second 10-1/4" h. x 6" w. x 5-3/4" d. **$2,250**

Courtesy of John Moran Auctioneers, Inc.

Three pugs at play figure, mid-20th century, each wearing blue collar with gold painted bells, underglaze blue crossed swords mark, impressed "1470" and incised "78836," signed with gilder's number "45," with applied sticker reading "Made in German Democratic Republic," 3-1/2" h. x 6-1/4" w. x 4" d. **$650**

Courtesy of John Moran Auctioneers, Inc.

Two figural dishes, late 19th/early 20th century, each modeled by Peter Reinicke, each with underglaze blue crossed swords mark; girl holding bouquet of flowers, sitting atop rims of two baskets, incised "3024" and impressed "147," marked with red overglaze painter's mark "12," and boy holding bouquet of flowers, sitting atop rims of two baskets, incised "3024" and impressed "8," marked with overglaze painter's marks "12" and "62," girl 4-3/4" h. x 5-1/2" w. x 3-1/4" d., boy 4-3/4" h. x 5-3/4" w. x 5-1/4" d. **$700**

Courtesy of John Moran Auctioneers, Inc.

◄ Porcelain figurine, late 19th/early 20th century, three figures gathered around birdcage on table, seated man playing flute, woman holding small dog and umbrella, and gentleman offering woman flower, underglaze blue crossed swords mark, incised "2897" and impressed "23," marked with overglaze painter's mark "74," 5-3/4" h. x 5-3/4" w. x 6-3/4" d. **$1,200**

Courtesy of John Moran Auctioneers, Inc.

Two porcelain figures personifying seasons, late 19th century, each polychrome enamel-decorated with gilded accents, with standing female figure, Spring holds garland of applied flowers, Summer holds sickle with sheath of wheat, each with first quality crossed swords mark, Spring incised "C84," Summer "C88," height to 7-3/4".................................**$1,230**

Courtesy of Skinner, Inc.; www.skinnerinc.com

Porcelain figure group of shepherd and shepherdess, 20th century, polychrome enamel-decorated, figures resting beneath tree, with first quality crossed swords mark and incised "D19," 9-1/4" h. **$800**

Courtesy of Skinner, Inc.; www.skinnerinc.com

Porcelain chocolate pot, late 19th/early 20th century, with pink rose finial and molded rose petal and leaf-form lid with gilt rim, above conforming molded rose petal teardrop form body with twining rosebuds and vines rising on circular stepped gilt base, blue underglaze crossed swords mark, 9-3/4" h. **$850**

Courtesy of Clars Auction Gallery, www.clars.com

Porcelain figure of girl in green dress holding gold ball, marked "Meissen," 15" h. x 9" w. .. **$1,300**

Courtesy of Kaminski Auctions

Figure of seated pug wearing blue collar with gold painted bells, mid-20th century, underglaze blue crossed swords mark, impressed "1(?)78L" and incised "78579," 9" h. x 8" w. x 5-1/4" d. **$900**

Courtesy of John Moran Auctioneers, Inc.

INSIDE INTEL

Mellon Scaife Estate Consignments Boost Bidding

CLARS AUCTION GALLERY of Oakland, California, has generously provided dozens of lots from recent auctions filled with consignments from the Richard Mellon Scaife Estate, illustrating several of the popular decorative arts categories within this book. The immensity, diversity, and quality of the Mellon Scaife collections of majolica, porcelains, and antique furnishings is a combination seldom seen, let alone put up for bids. The appearance of the offerings at auction has resulted in a surge in both interest and results in some collecting genres.

Redge Martin, president of Clars, gives perspective on the immensity of the consignments. He said Mellon Scaife "had four huge houses around the country," which were in Ligonier, Pennsylvania; Pittsburgh, Pennsylvania; Pebble Beach, Florida; and Nantucket, Massachusetts.

"The property came here in one 53' truck, plus one 26' truck, so there are thousands of items," Martin said.

Deric Torres, vice president and director of Decorative Arts and Furniture for Clars, represented Clars in meetings with the trustees of the estate. After bidders' enthusiastic reactions to the initial offering of Mellon Scaife estate consignments in January 2015, Torres commented, "The formidable global market reaction to this collection exceeded all of our expectations. Bidding was incredibly strong, particularly from Europe and Britain. A majority of the pieces offered sold for over high estimate with several going for two and three times the high and more. The provenance combined with the quality of the offerings resulted in prices not seen, particularly on majolica, since before the 2008 downturn."

Many lots illustrate the high desirability of the estate's holdings for collectors. Three 19th century Royal Worcester urchin and dolphin compotes sold for an impressive $10,115 – nearly 10 times the high estimate – setting a new auction record for the form. Two Copeland shell-form majolica vases, circa 1885, sold for $4,400 against an estimate of $800, and a Copeland 19th century swan and bulrush vase sold for $2,400, also against a high estimate of $800. Also, two William Brownfield and Son conch shell vases, circa 1880, sold for $4,100 against an estimate of $1,500.

Prime examples of Staffordshire also had bidders disregarding estimates. "Scaife bought and collected the finest throughout his life, as did his mother before him, so we are seeing these pieces come to the market that buyers have been thirsting for, and they are responding in an astonishing and very robust manner," Torres explained.

The top lot of the collection offered, which went for almost 10 times high estimate, were these three 19th century Royal Worcester urchin and dolphin compotes that sold for an impressive $10,115, setting a new auction record for this form.

Courtesy of Clars Auction Gallery, www.clars.com

This very rare Wedgwood bough pot, the only example of the form to ever make an appearance on the market, resulted in driving this group lot to $8,300.

Courtesy of Clars Auction Gallery, www.clars.com

This 19th century swan and bulrush vase from Copeland sold for $2,400 against its high estimate of $800.

Courtesy of Clars Auction Gallery, www.clars.com

A highlight of the Mellon Scaife Staffordshire offerings was this early 18th century Mary of Baptism porcelain table base attributed to Obadiah Sherratt, which sold for $6,500.

Courtesy of Clars Auction Gallery, www.clars.com

The top seller in majolica were these two Copeland shell-form vases, circa 1885, for $4,400 against an estimate of $800.

Courtesy of Clars Auction Gallery, www.clars.com

In the February 2015 auction, Staffordshire figural groups brought astonishing prices, earning three to five times high estimate across the board. During the sale, an early 18th century Staffordshire Mary of Baptism porcelain table base attributed to Obadiah Sherratt sold for $6,500; a circa 1810 pearlware bocage group brought $5,600; and a circa 1815 pearlware figural group, of Walton type, achieved $5,300.

Also of note: A rare Wedgwood bough pot that was the only example of the form to make an appearance on the market resulted in furious bidding from collectors, driving the sale price to $8,300.

Decorative arts and antiques collections such as this, of unfathomable scope and quality with hidden rarities, are seldom offered at public auction. Keeping abreast of what's going on in the marketplace with the help of antiques trade newsletters, websites, and publications enables collectors to be able to take advantage of these rare opportunities as they arise.

CERAMICS
===

CERAMICS

mettlach

CERAMICS WITH THE name Mettlach were produced by Villeroy & Boch and other potteries in the Mettlach area of Germany. Villeroy & Boch's finest years of production are thought to be from about 1890-1910.

No. 2765 etched stein of knight on white horse, .5L size, turret inlay lid, impressed marks under base, marked for 1902, 9-1/2" h. overall. **$1,093**

Courtesy of Jeffrey S. Evans & Associates

No. 1724 etched stein of fireman, .5L size, signed "CW" for Warth, inlay lid with helmet, impressed marks under base, marked for 1889, 9" h. overall...................**$1,035**

Courtesy of Jeffrey S. Evans & Associates

No. 2255 etched stein of wedding scene, 1.0L size, inlay lid with heart, impressed marks under base, marked for 1899, 11" h. overall....................**$546**

Courtesy of Jeffrey S. Evans & Associates

No. 2382 etched stein of thirsty rider/knight, .5L size, peaked inlay lid, impressed and inscribed marks under base, marked for 1897, 9" h. overall. **$345**

Courtesy of Jeffrey S. Evans & Associates

No. 2007 etched stein of black cat, .5L size, signed F. Stuck, inlay lid, impressed and inscribed marks under base, marked for 1896, 7" h. overall. **$345**

Courtesy of Jeffrey S. Evans & Associates

No. 2180 print-under-glaze master stein with decoration No. 955 of tavern scene, 3.3L size, signed Schlitt, pewter lid, impressed and printed marks under base, marked for 1898, 19-1/2" h. overall............... **$288**

Courtesy of Jeffrey S. Evans & Associates

No. 1914 etched 4f stein of man holding flag and dumbbell, .5L size, inlay lid, impressed and inscribed marks under base, marked for 1900, 9" h. overall. **$288**

Courtesy of Jeffrey S. Evans & Associates

No. 2123 etched stein of drinking knight, .5L size, signed Schlitt, inlay lid, impressed and inscribed marks under base, marked for 1897, 8" h. overall....................... **$690**

Courtesy of Jeffrey S. Evans & Associates

No. 2192 etched stein of student joke, .5L size, inlay lid, impressed marks under base, marked for 1897, 9" h. overall. **$374**

Courtesy of Jeffrey S. Evans & Associates

CERAMICS

---

minton

THOMAS MINTON ESTABLISHED the Minton factory in England in 1793. The factory made earthenware, especially the blue-printed variety, and Thomas Minton is sometimes credited with the invention of the blue "Willow" pattern. For a time, majolica and tiles were also important parts of production, but bone china soon became the principal ware.

For more information on Minton, see *Antique Trader Pottery & Porcelain Ceramics*, 6th edition, or *Warman's Antiques & Collectibles*, 2015 edition.

Pair of porcelain shell figural compotes, Stoke-on-Trent, Staffordshire, England, circa 1880, marks: MINTON, 1205, 12" h. **$1,563**

Courtesy of Heritage Auctions

Double gourd vase with stencil-like design of thistle blossoms on each side with leaves and other field flowers with high glaze, brown transfer, "Minton, England" crown and world logo below, excellent condition, 10-1/2" h. **$150**

Courtesy of Mark Mussio, Humler & Nolan

◀ Pate-sur-pate porcelain vase in white slip with birds and flowers against teal blue ground with gilt rim and foot, marked, previously repaired chip to gilt rim, foot shows some wear, 7-1/2" h..........**$438**

Courtesy of Leslie Hindman Auctioneers

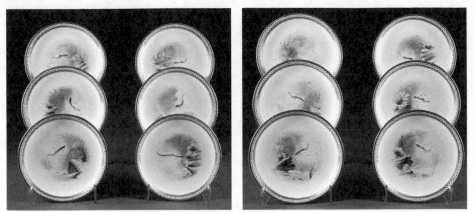

Twelve porcelain fish plates, marked, each well with different hand-painted aquatic scene signed by Albert H. Wright, gilt and patera rim, 9-1/8" dia. **$875**

Courtesy of Neal Auction Co.

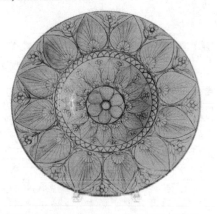

Art Nouveau charger or shallow bowl, stylized shell, leaf, and flower decoration in pale blue on pale yellow ground, impressed mark for Minton and underglaze blue decorator mark "WL? 1903," good condition, glaze flake at rim and shallow area of probable retouch, glaze crazing, 13-3/4" dia. **$186**

Courtesy of Brunk Auctions

Pate-sur-pate plate with gold enameling, 19th century, loss to gold on edges, 9-1/2" dia. **$1,331**

Courtesy of Cottone Auctions

Two framed Minton Hollins & Co. painted pottery tiles, each decorated with wild flowers and foliage on blue ground with arabesque border, 17" dia. overall. **$300**

Courtesy of Clars Auction Gallery, www.clars.com

CERAMICS

mochaware

MOCHA DECORATION IS found on basically utilitarian creamware or yellowware articles and is achieved by a simple chemical reaction. A color pigment of brown, blue, green, or black is given an acid nature by infusion of tobacco or hops. When this acid nature colorant is applied in blobs to an alkaline ground color, it reacts by spreading in feathery seaweed designs. This type of decoration is usually accompanied by horizontal bands of light color slip.

Produced in many Staffordshire potteries from the late 18th until the late 19th centuries, its name is derived from the similar markings found on mocha quartz. In addition to the Seaweed decoration, mocha wares are also seen with Earthworm and Cat's-Eye patterns or a marbleized effect.

Mocha-decorated pearlware double jug, England, circa 1830-1840, mouths decorated with doubled blue slip lines above dark brown slip field with tan and light blue Cat's-Eye decoration, triple wavy light brown slip banding on body above dark brown slip band bordered by doubled light blue slip bands with Cat's-Eye decoration, applied molded handle joins jugs at mouth along with marbled Cat's-Eye slip around area where bodies merge, imperfections, 10" h. x 14-1/2" w. x 7" d..... **$5,000**

Courtesy of Skinner, Inc.; www.skinnerinc.com

Two Mocha-decorated pearlware quart mugs, England, early 19th century.
Left: blue mouth and base band bordering triple light brown slip bands and light green field trailed with wavy brown lines and white slip dots, extruded handle with foliate ends, 5-7/8" h......**$1,300**
Right: mouth bordered by green rouletted band above orange slip band with white, blue, and sienna Cat's-Eye decoration above dark brown slip band with white, blue, and sienna cabling above orange slip band with white, blue, and sienna Cat's-Eye decoration, applied handle with foliate terminals, imperfections, 6" h. ... **$1,400**

Courtesy of Skinner, Inc.; www.skinnerinc.com

◄ Engine-turned mocha-decorated pearlware frog mug, England, late 18th century, with olive and blue bands flanking dark brown slip-filled engine-turned field, with alternating blue and brown bands, extruded handle with rust-painted outline with foliate terminals, interior bottom with applied frog figure, imperfections, 3-3/4" h.... **$1,500**

Courtesy of Skinner, Inc.; www.skinnerinc.com

Mocha-decorated pearlware pepper pot, England, early 19th century, blue-highlighted pierced sifter above gray slip body with Cat's-Eye decoration bordered by double deep brown bands, imperfections, sifter restored, 5" h...................... **$330**

Courtesy of Skinner, Inc.; www.skinnerinc.com

Double-handled mocha-decorated creamware covered bowl, England, circa 1800-1825, engine-turned body with applied handles with infilled rouletted dot and vine border at rim, two-color brown slip banding on body, handled lid with two-color brown slip banding and infilled rouletted dot and chain border, imperfections, lid with X-shape firing crack on lid and small chips on rim, bowl with hairline crack, 5-1/2" h., 7-3/4"dia. **$3,500**

Courtesy of Skinner, Inc.; www.skinnerinc.com

Wide-mouth mocha-decorated pearlware pitcher, England or America, 19th century, with three brown slip bands bordering blue slip field with cable decoration and two brown slip bands below, imperfections, hairline crack on lip, 7-3/4" h. **$461**

Courtesy of Skinner, Inc.; www.skinnerinc.com

Mocha-decorated creamware footed goblet, England, early 19th century, dark brown slip body with light brown banding on rim and foot with dipped fan decoration on sides, 4-3/8" h................ **$2,200**

Courtesy of Skinner, Inc.; www.skinnerinc.com

Marbleized mocha-decorated creamware teapot, England, late 18th century, cylindrical body with brown slip marbling and applied sprig-molded rosettes and swags, molded spout and applied extruded handle, imperfections, 4-3/4" h. **$1,400**

Courtesy of Skinner, Inc.; www.skinnerinc.com

CERAMICS

moorcroft

WILLIAM MOORCROFT WAS first employed as a potter by James Macintyre & Co., Ltd. of Burslem, Staffordshire, England, in 1897. He established the Moorcroft pottery in 1913. Walter Moorcroft, William's son, continued the business upon his father's death and made wares in the same style. The majority of the art pottery wares were hand thrown, resulting in a great variation among similarly styled pieces. Colors and marks are keys to determining age. The company initially used an impressed mark, "Moorcroft, Burslem." A signature mark, "W. Moorcroft," followed. Modern pieces are marked simply "Moorcroft," with export pieces also marked "Made in England."

Claremont vase, signed Moorcroft, 55, overall tight crazing, 5" h., 6-1/2" dia...................... **$4,235**

Courtesy of Cottone Auctions

Rare early Moorcroft-Macintyre landscape vase in blue and green with yellow, signed "W. Moorcroft Des." in green slip, registry number 397964, fine overall crazing, 12" h....... **$3,800**

Courtesy of Mark Mussio, Humler & Nolan

Two-handled Spanish vase, England, 1912, green signature W. Moorcroft 1912, uncrazed, 7-3/4" x 7"..................... **$5,440**

Courtesy of Rago Arts, www.ragoarts.com

Eventide ginger jar with sterling silver Shreve lid, England, 1918-1926, with letter from William Moorcroft's son, W. John S. Moorcroft, explaining date of vase and possible origins of lid, blue Moorcroft signature, stamped MOORCROFT MADE IN ENGLAND 769, lid stamped SHREVE & CO. STERLING 9810, 14-3/4" x 8-1/2" overall, jar 10" h., lid 12-1/2"...... **$6,400**

Courtesy of Rago Arts, www.ragoarts.com

Large two-handled ice bucket or bottle cooler, early 20th century, peach and grape decoration on blue/green ground, stamped and painted Moorcroft signatures, 7"; baluster-form vase with fruit decoration on blue ground, impressed and painted signatures, 6"; similar vase with poppy decoration on dark red ground, base with impressed and painted signatures with original paper label, 6"; small cup or vase with leaf and floral decoration on pale red ground, stamped Moorcroft signature, 3-1/4"; ice bucket with hairline crack in base. $1,860

Courtesy of Brunk Auctions

Cornflower teapot, signed, small nick to spout, repaired, 10" h. x 5-1/2" w. **$1,331**

Courtesy of Cottone Auctions

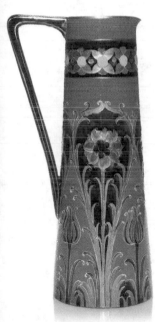

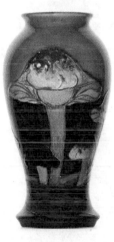

Claremont toadstool baluster vase, England, 1918-1929, stamped MOORCROFT MADE IN ENGLAND, painted initials, overall fine crazing, 7" x 3-1/2". **$3,200**

Courtesy of Rago Arts, www.ragoarts.com

Art Nouveau lidded loving cup, stylized leaf and flower decoration in green and pale blue with gilt highlights, cobalt handles, printed mark for Macintyre Burslem and script "WM" for William Moorcroft, underside of lid with "WM" signature, excellent condition with minor glaze crazing as made, minor areas of wear to gilding, 8-1/2" x 6" x 4-1/2". **$1,736**

Courtesy of Brunk Auctions

Tall Moorcroft-Macintyre Florian tankard in green, blue, and gold with stylized tulip designs, circa 1902 to 1913, Macintyre Burslem England ink stamp logo, "RdNo 404017" in red, "W.M. des." painted in green slip, excellent original condition with faint crazing and no wear to gold trim, 14" h........... **$1,500**

Courtesy of Mark Mussio, Humler & Nolan

Small pottery low bowl, interior with pansy and exterior with cobalt glaze, 1-1/2" h. x 4-1/4" dia. ... **$125**

Courtesy of Clars Auction Gallery, www.clars.com

CERAMICS

newcomb college

THIS POTTERY WAS established in the art department of Newcomb College in New Orleans in 1897. Each piece was hand-thrown and bore the potter's mark and decorator's monogram on the base. It was always studio business and never operated as a factory. Its pieces are, therefore, scarce, with the early wares eagerly sought. The pottery closed in 1940.

High glaze vase by Marie Levering Benson, 1908, with seven unfurled yellow irises, marks: Newcomb College logo, date code for 1908 (CN 77), impressed Q for buff clay, impressed monogram of potter Joseph Meyer, and incised and blue-tinted monogram of artist, excellent original condition with faint crazing, 12-3/8" h. .. **$7,750**

Courtesy of Mark Mussio, Humler & Nolan

Transitional period vase by Anna Francis Simpson, 1911, with painted and incised jonquils, marks: impressed Newcomb logo, date code for 1911 (E J 3), Simpson's initials in blue slip, incised mark of potter Joseph Meyer, 2" tight line from rim and faint crazing, 8" h. **$1,900**

Courtesy of Mark Mussio, Humler & Nolan

Carved scenic vase by Sadie Irvine, 1930, moss-laden oak trees beneath large full moon, impressed with Newcomb logo, date code for 1930, shape 4, incised initials of potter Kenneth Smith and incised mark of Irvine, excellent original condition, 5-1/2" h. **$2,600**

Courtesy of Mark Mussio, Humler & Nolan

Low vase by Henrietta Bailey, 1924, with carved and painted jonquils in band around shoulder in green, blue and yellow, marks: Newcomb logo, date code for 1924 (OE 71), shape number 65, impressed JM for potter Joseph Meyer, and incised monogram of artist, uncrazed, 4-1/2" h. x 7" w....................**$1,200**

Courtesy of Mark Mussio, Humler & Nolan

Four-handled vase by Sadie Irvine, 1926, bulbous squat form, matte glaze with blue and green underglaze, nicotina leaves, underside marked with Newcomb cipher, decorator's mark, Joseph Mayer potter's mark, shape no. 247, and reg. no. PL 50, with original Newcomb College paper label, 4" h., 5-1/2" dia. **$950**

Courtesy of Clars Auction Gallery, www.clars.com

Vase by Sadie Irvine, 1918, with relief-carved daffodils, matte glaze with blue, green and pink underglaze, base marked with Newcomb cipher, decorator's mark, Joseph Meyer's potter's mark, reg. no. JH 46, 8-3/4" h., 6" dia. **$5,938**

Courtesy of Neal Auction Co.

Mug by Harriet Coulter Joor, 1903, with relief-carved stylized alamanda blossoms and words "Come-Let-Us-Be-Happy-Together," high glaze with blue-green, green and blue underglaze, base marked with Newcomb cipher, decorator's mark, Joseph Meyer's potter's mark, reg. no. II52, 7-1/4" h....................**$8,125**

Courtesy of Neal Auction Co.

Vase by Henrietta Bailey, 1929, with stylized buds and foliage, blue, green and white underglaze, base marked with Newcomb cipher, decorator's mark, Jonathan Hunt's potter's mark, reg. no. RZ62, 5-1/2" h. **$2,500**

Courtesy of Neal Auction Co.

top lot

High glaze vase by Mary Givens Sheerer, 1904, with band of incised alamanda blossoms, dark blue, green and mustard yellow underglaze, base marked with Newcomb cipher, decorator's mark, Joseph Meyer's potter's mark, reg. no. VV35, and Q for buff clay body, 9-1/2" h., 6-3/4" dia. $21,250

COURTESY OF NEAL AUCTION CO.

Mug by Marie de Hoa LeBlanc, 1902, with carved artichokes, high glaze with blue-green and blue underglaze, base marked with Newcomb cipher, decorator's mark, reg. no. K7, Joseph Meyer's potter's mark, X indicating piece was reserved especially for decorator or college, and initials "GJ," 5-7/8" h. **$2,125**

Courtesy of Neal Auction Co.

Large high glaze tyg by Leona Fischer Nicholson, 1906, with blossoms, buds and banding in high relief, blue and blue-green underglaze, base marked with Newcomb cipher, decorator's mark, Joseph Meyer's potter's mark, reg. no. BJ70, and Q for buff clay body, 8-1/4" h., 8" dia............................ **$7,188**

Courtesy of Neal Auction Co.

Mug by Ada Wilt Lonnegan, circa 1902, with pattern of floral buds in low relief, high glaze with blue-green and blue underglaze, base marked with Newcomb cipher, decorator's mark, Joseph Meyer's potter's mark, reg. no. M19, and "GJ," 4-1/8" h., 3-3/4" dia. **$3,125**

Courtesy of Neal Auction Co.

Matte glaze tea tile by Anna Francis Simpson, pink phlox and green leaves over blue glaze, marks: incised initials of artist and impressed Newcomb College logo, letters Q and V and number 65, excellent condition, 5-5/8" dia. **$800**

Courtesy of Mark Mussio, Humler & Nolan

Two plates by Anna Frances Simpson, circa 1913, with border of chrysanthemums in low relief, semi-matte glaze with blue, blue-green, yellow and white underglaze, each base marked with Newcomb cipher, decorator's mark, Joseph Meyer's potter's mark, reg. no. FZ81, and "B" for buff clay body, 8-3/4" dia. **$5,000**

Courtesy of Neal Auction Co.

▲ Creamer by Sadie Irvine, 1907, low relief with grapes and foliage, high glaze with blue and green underglaze, base marked with Newcomb cipher, decorator's mark, Joseph Meyer's potter's mark, reg. no. CA39, 2-3/4" h., 4-1/2" dia. **$500**

Courtesy of Neal Auction Co.

Vase by Anna Frances Simpson, 1928, in Moon and Moss design, matte glaze with blue, green and pink underglaze, base marked with Newcomb cipher, decorator's mark, reg. no. QV76, and shape no. 32, 7" h. **$7,500**

Courtesy of Neal Auction Co.

Matte glaze vase by Anna Frances Simpson, 1929, with pink narcissus, blue, green, pink and yellow underglaze, base marked with Newcomb cipher, "Rd65," Joseph Hunt potter's mark, and shape no. 149, 7-1/2" h. **$6,875**

Courtesy of Neal Auction Co.

Bowl by Corinne Marie Chalaron, 1921, stylized design, matte glaze with blue and green underglaze, base marked with Newcomb cipher, decorator's mark, Joseph Meyer's potter's mark, reg. no. LQ94, and shape no. 10, 1-3/4" h., 3-3/4" dia. **$688**

Courtesy of Neal Auction Co.

CERAMICS

Lidded inkwell by Anna Frances Simpson, 1927, with narcissus in relief, matte glaze with blue, green, white and yellow underglaze, base marked with Newcomb cipher, decorator's mark, reg. no. Q096, and shape no. 225, 3-1/4" h. **$2,000**

Courtesy of Neal Auction Co.

High glaze creamer by Anna Frances Simpson, 1909, with gardenias in low relief, blue, green and yellow underglaze, base marked with Newcomb cipher, decorator's mark, Joseph Meyer's potter's mark, reg. no DA15, and "Q" for buff clay body, 3-1/4" h. **$2,250**

Courtesy of Neal Auction Co.

Vase by Marie de Hoa LeBlanc, 1909, with tulips in low relief, high glaze with blue and green underglaze, base marked with Newcomb cipher, decorator's mark, Joseph Meyer's potter's mark, reg. no. CX28, and Q for buff clay body, 10-5/8" h. ..**$16,250**

Courtesy of Neal Auction Co.

Vase by Henrietta Bailey, 1933, in pine cone motif, matte glaze with blue, green and pink underglaze, base marked with Newcomb cipher, decorator's mark, Kenneth Smith's potter's mark, and reg. no. UL47, 5" h., 6" dia. **$2,625**

Courtesy of Neal Auction Co.

High glaze plate by Marie de Hoa LeBlanc, 1909, with maple wing motif, blue, green and yellow underglaze, base marked with Newcomb cipher, decorator's mark, Joseph Meyer's potter's mark, reg. no. CU65, and Q for buff clay body, 8-1/4" dia.....**$1,750**

Courtesy of Neal Auction Co.

Bowl by Henrietta Davidson Bailey, 1927, with morning glories, matte glaze with blue, green, pink and yellow underglaze, base marked with Newcomb cipher, decorator's mark, Joseph Meyer's potter's mark, reg. no. QE82, and shape no. 65, 4-1/4" h., 6-1/2" dia........................**$1,375**

Courtesy of Neal Auction Co.

◄ Plaque by Anna Frances Simpson, 1918, with landscape design of moss-laden live oak before fence, matte glaze with blue, green and pink underglaze, cipher at lower left, reverse marked with Newcomb cipher, decorator's mark, reg. no. JI12, original paper label, 6" x 10", original molded wood frame with label from Farish Art Store, New Orleans, 10-1/2" x 14-1/2".............**$10,625**

Courtesy of Neal Auction Co.

CERAMICS

niloak

NILOAK POTTERY IS famous for its marbleized swirls of red, blue, gray, white, and other clay colors. Once produced in Benton, Arkansas, it has achieved center stage in national auctions. Rago Arts' auctions in recent years have seen the values paid for Niloak demonstrate a pottery that holds its value.

The pottery, founded by the Hyten family, derived its name from the backwards spelling of the clay type known as kaolin. In regular production from 1910 to 1934, Niloak was produced as vases, penholders, kitchenware, ewers, creamers, sand jars to douse cigarettes, umbrella jars, and even limited special-order production as tile. The family pottery produced housewares with the name "Hyten Brothers" and "Eagle Pottery" on it.

Charles "Bullet" Hyten was born in Benton in 1877. His father died while he was a child. Hyten learned the pottery trade from his stepfather, Frank Woosley. Woosley worked for the elder Hyten and cared for him until his death, while also keeping the family business going. Woosley married Bullet's mother, Harriet, in 1882.

In 1895, Woosley sold the family business to Bullet, who was 18. Soon after, tragedy struck. A fire consumed one of the kilns. Bullet almost lost the business.

In time, he and other potters in the area noticed the amazing colors of clay in the local

Pitcher, four tumblers, round platter, and unmarked trivet, pitcher 10" h., tumblers 3-3/4" h., platter 11" dia. **$1,331**

Courtesy of Briggs Auction, Inc., www.briggsauction.com

ground. He had a business connection with a potter in Hot Springs. Together they discovered that kiln heat burned out the unique colors of Saline County clays. They found a way to add chemicals and colors that duplicated the color of what was in the ground.

Hyten started to experiment seriously in 1909. In 1910 the Niloak process was perfected. Confident of success, Hyten sought financing for his company in 1911. Then fire destroyed the pottery a year later. Undaunted, Hyten built a brick factory alongside the railroad tracks, capitalizing on the rail line for ease of shipping and tourist traffic. At full strength, about 35 people worked there full-time, including four to five potters.

The Niloak pottery manufactured Eagle brand pottery and red clay flowerpots, thriving through World War I and the early 1920s recession years. But the company couldn't survive the Great Depression. Official Niloak production ceased in 1934. Then some Little Rock businessmen bought the business and Hyten worked for them.

The new pottery sold Hywood, which was a glazed cast ware, and produced Niloak in limited quantities. In time, the factory sold all pottery under the Niloak name because the brand was marketable.

Wartime limits on materials in the 1940s hurt the quality of production, and the factory closed in the 1950s.

— *John J. Archibald*

Candlestick with swirled decoration, early 20th century, 6-5/8" h., 3-5/8" dia. **$98**

Courtesy of Crescent City Auction Exchange

Vase with impressed mark and secondary paper label from an alternate retailer, 6-3/4" x 3-1/2". **$261**

Courtesy of Dirk Soulis Auctions

Waisted-form vase with impressed mark under base, 8" h. **$348**

Courtesy of Dirk Soulis Auctions

Early Mission Swirl trumpet vase, impressed "Niloak" on bottom, excellent original condition, 10-1/4". h. **$275**

Courtesy of Mark Mussio, Humler & Nolan

CERAMICS

nippon

"NIPPON" IS A TERM used to describe a wide range of porcelain wares produced in Japan from the late 19th century until about 1921. It was in 1891 that the United States implemented the McKinley Tariff Act, which required that all wares exported to the United States carry a marking indicating their country of origin. The Japanese chose to use "Nippon," their name for Japan. In 1921 the import laws were revised and the words "Made in" had to be added to the markings. Japan was also required to replace the "Nippon" with the English name "Japan" on all wares sent to the United States.

Many Japanese factories produced Nippon porcelain, much of it hand-painted with ornate floral or landscape decoration and heavy gold decoration, applied beading and slip-trailed designs referred to as moriage. Be aware that a number of Nippon markings have been reproduced and used on new porcelain wares.

Two-handled gourd vase, yellow tones with pink rose blossom decor and gold enamel leaf highlights, green leaf mark, 8-1/2" h. $35

Courtesy of Woody Auctions, LLC

Three-handled vase, green tones with large floral blossom décor, green leaf mark, 11-1/2" h. $94

Courtesy of Woody Auctions, LLC

Two-handled hand-painted vase, floral field of blossoms, artist signed Kojima, green wreath mark, small base chip, 15" h. $59

Courtesy of Woody Auctions, LLC

CERAMICS

Two-handled vase, blue and yellow with pink rose decor, gold highlights, blue leaf mark, 7-1/4" x 7-1/2".................**$106**

Courtesy of Woody Auctions, LLC

Monumental handled vase with continuous scene of tree-lined lake, large monument and birds flying across orange sky; neck, shoulder, and lower body with decorative relief designs and handles in gold, backstamped in green with M in wreath logo, nicks in raised gold design, excellent condition, 13-1/8" x 10" w. across shoulder........**$200**

Courtesy of Mark Mussio, Humler & Nolan

Large Coraline vase with irises front and back, three gold-over-cobalt blue fleur-de-lis ornaments at base, decorative trim inside and out on flaring rim, backstamped "U.S. Patent, NBR.91271, Feb 9, 1919, Japan" with character marks in pink, cracks and subsequent repairs at rim, some coraline missing, 8-1/4" flaring rim, 14" h.............................**$2,000**

Courtesy of Mark Mussio, Humler & Nolan

Large bolted and handled urn with conifer forest, lake and hills on horizon, raised gold trim on rim, shoulder and attached base, green M in wreath backstamp logo, excellent condition, 16-1/4" h. x 8-1/4" w. **$600**

Courtesy of Mark Mussio, Humler & Nolan

Two-handled vase, yellow background with scenic decor, blue floral highlights, green wreath mark, 6" h.................**$30**

Courtesy of Woody Auctions, LLC

Handled blow-out vase with raised poppies on square organic form, gold-beaded necklace at rim, blue-stamped "Nippon, Hand Painted" with maple leaf logo, some gold beads missing, 8-1/2" h...............................**$475**

Courtesy of Mark Mussio, Humler & Nolan

Handled vase with portrait of woman on one side and bouquet of roses on other side, gold applied to surround of designs and to handles, marked in green "Nippon, Hand Painted" with maple leaf logo, areas where gold was applied thin, minor uneven surface to portrait, 7-1/2" h. x 7" w. **$180**

Courtesy of Mark Mussio, Humler & Nolan

Monumental bolted and handled urn with Arabian oasis and ornamental designs on neck, shoulder, lower body, and attached base, green M in wreath backstamp, excellent original condition, 16-1/2" h. x 8-1/2" w. **$650**

Courtesy of Mark Mussio, Humler & Nolan

Small bolted and handled urn hand-painted with swans on pond, cabin on horizon enclosed by trees, decorative trim on shoulder and base, blue M in wreath backstamp, excellent condition, 11-1/2" h. **$275**

Courtesy of Mark Mussio, Humler & Nolan

Plaque with squirrel eating peanuts in molded relief and hand painted, marked on back with green "Nippon Hand Painted" wreath logo, excellent original condition, 10-1/2"....**$200**

Courtesy of Mark Mussio, Humler & Nolan

Plaque of bull moose in molded relief and hand painted, marked on back with green "Nippon Hand Painted" wreath logo, excellent original condition, 10-1/2"..............**$200**

Courtesy of Mark Mussio, Humler & Nolan

Plaque with elk bellowing to mate on other side of stream, in molded relief and hand painted, marked on back with green "Nippon Hand Painted" wreath logo, excellent original condition, 10-3/4"..............**$200**

Courtesy of Mark Mussio, Humler & Nolan

Blow-out boulder vase hand-painted with fall grape leaves with blue enameled fruit pods, green M in wreath backstamp logo beneath, excellent original condition, 9-3/4" h.............**$350**

Courtesy of Mark Mussio, Humler & Nolan

CERAMICS

george ohr

GEORGE OHR, the eccentric potter of Biloxi, Mississippi, worked from about 1883 to 1906. Some think he is one of the most expert throwers the craft will ever see. The majority of his works were hand-thrown, exceedingly thin-walled items, some of which have a crushed or folded appearance. He considered himself the foremost potter in world and declined to sell much of his production, instead accumulating a great horde to leave as a legacy to his children. In 1972 this collection was purchased for resale by an antiques dealer.

Twisted and double-handled ceramic loving cup, redware with brown glaze, base with stamped mark "GE Ohr Biloxi" (Mississippi, 1890-1910), 6" h. **$8,060**

Courtesy of Brunk Auctions

Small pitcher, dark green and brown sponged-on glaze, 1892-1894, stamped GEO. E. OHR BILOXI, 2-3/4" x 4-1/2" x 3". **$6,080**

Courtesy of Rago Arts, www.ragoarts.com

Bisque fired and folded clay novelty bank with coins inside, impressed G E Ohr Biloxi, Miss. on bottom, excellent original condition, 2-7/8" h. x 5" l... **$550**

Courtesy of Mark Mussio, Humler & Nolan

Large bisque pitcher with ribbon handle and in-body twist, 1897-1900, stamped G.E. OHR, Biloxi, Miss., overall very good condition, wear and minor flecks along rim, bottom of handle does not connect to body of vase, 8-3/4" x 5". **$5,120**

Courtesy of Rago Arts, www.ragoarts.com

Rare novelty woman's shoe, circa 1900, incised G. Ohr and E.W., repaired chip to top, two smaller chips at top edge, 3-1/2" x 2-3/4".............. **$3,840**

Courtesy of Rago Arts, www.ragoarts.com

Pinched pitcher with cutout handle in moss green glaze, circa 1895-1896, impressed GEO. E. OHR. / BILOXI, MISS., restoration to two chips at rim, 3" h. x 3-1/4" dia............ **$3,840**

Courtesy of Rago Arts, www.ragoarts.com

Teapot with ribbon handle, gunmetal glaze, 1895-1896, marked GEO. E. OHR BILOXI, MISS., touch-up to chip on tip of spout and touch-up to kiln kiss on body, lid associated, does not fit well, 4" x 7". **$3,840**

Courtesy of Rago Arts, www.ragoarts.com

Vase with crimped twisted body with yellow-brown and blue glaze, circa 1883-1898, impressed mark, 3-1/2" h., 5-1/8" dia. **$5,938**

Courtesy of Neal Auction Co.

CERAMICS

Vase with in-body twist, indigo glaze, 1897-1900, stamped G.E. OHR, Biloxi, Miss., excellent condition, minor wear to rim, 4-1/2" x 4". **$5,120**

Courtesy of Rago Arts, www.ragoarts.com

Vase with ruffled rim, ochre and brown speckled glaze, 1897-1900, stamped G.E. OHR, Biloxi, Miss., two small spots of restoration to ruffles, one chip to inner edge of one ruffle, 3-1/2" x 3-3/4". **$3,840**

Courtesy of Rago Arts, www.ragoarts.com

Redware vessel with mottled brown glaze, twisted and crimped top, base stamped GE Ohr Biloxi (Mississippi, 1890-1910), 2-3/4"................ **$2,232**

Courtesy of Brunk Auctions

Rare and important glazed earthenware vase with sculpted dragon, New Orleans, circa 1888, stamped NEW ORLEANS ART POTTERY COMPANY 249 BARONNE STREET, designed by artist Mary Reinfort, decorated by George Ohr, thrown by Joseph Meyer, 4" hairline from rim, several flakes and chips, loss to tip of top feather on wing, 10-1/2" x 6-3/4"........................**$25,600**

Courtesy of Rago Arts, www.ragoarts.com

Small crumpled vessel, pink volcanic glaze with speckled green interior, 1895-1896, stamped GEO. E. OHR BILOXI, MISS., fleabite to rim and light wear around foot ring, 2-1/4" x 4". **$5,440**

Courtesy of Rago Arts, www.ragoarts.com

CERAMICS

overbeck

THE OVERBECK STUDIO pottery was founded by four sisters, Hannah, Mary Frances, Elizabeth, and Harriet, in the Overbeck family home in Cambridge City, Indiana, in 1911. A fifth sister, Margaret, who worked as a decorator at Zanesville Art Pottery in 1910, was the catalyst for establishing the pottery, but died the same year. Launching at the tail end of the Arts & Crafts movement, and believing "borrowed art is bad art," the sister potters dedicated themselves to producing unique, quality pieces with original design elements, which often were inspired by the natural world. Pieces can also be found worked in the Art Nouveau and Art Deco styles, as well as unique figurines and grotesques. The studio used several marks through the years, including an incised "O" and incised "OBK," often accompanied by the artist's initials. The pottery ceased production in 1955.

Four-color bowl with exotic floral decoration by Elizabeth and Mary Frances Overbeck, mauve, teal, and cream-colored flowers against brown background, incised OBK logo and initials E and F for artists, excellent original condition, 3-1/4" h. x 4-5/8" dia. **$3,000**

Courtesy of Mark Mussio, Humler & Nolan

Goose figurine, polychrome glazed, marked, 5" w. x 3-1/2" h. **$762**

Courtesy of Treadway Toomey Auctions

Hand-sculpted turquoise and black dodo bird, marked, impressed logo on base, overall good condition, minor factory imperfections, 4-1/2" w. x 4" h. **$793**

Courtesy of Treadway Toomey Auctions

Rare hand-sculpted and hand-painted figurine, marked, 2-1/2" w. x 2" h. **$427**

Courtesy of Treadway Toomey Auctions

CERAMICS

owens

OWENS POTTERY WAS the product of J.B. Owens Pottery Co., which operated in Ohio from 1890 to 1929. In 1891 it was located in Zanesville and produced art pottery from 1896, introducing Utopian wares as its first art pottery. The company switched to tile after 1907. Efforts to rebuild after the factory burned in 1928 failed, and the company closed in 1929.

Uncommon mat Utopian umbrella stand with iris decoration, unmarked, chip on inside of rim, minor nicks at base, 20" h. . **$400**

Courtesy of Mark Mussio, Humler & Nolan

Mat two-tone green tankard with ice blockage spout and tall tulips and leaf design, impressed "Owens 1 A 13" beneath, excellent condition, 9" h. **$250**

Courtesy of Mark Mussio, Humler & Nolan

Gourd vase with cattail design in organic green glaze with slight texture, impressed "Owens" with shape number 050, excellent condition, glaze nick below base, 5-7/8" h. **$650**

Courtesy of Mark Mussio, Humler & Nolan

Two Cyrano items with ivory and blue applied design, unmarked square cylinder vase and covered rectangular container impressed with company logo and obscure number, both in good condition, vase 4-1/2" x 2-1/2", container 3-1/4" x 3-7/8"...**$160**

Courtesy of Mark Mussio, Humler & Nolan

Lotus vase with molded wisteria design in trio of mat glazes, impressed on bottom OWENS 220, excellent original condition, 8-1/4"................ **$300**

Courtesy of Mark Mussio, Humler & Nolan

CERAMICS

redware

RED EARTHENWARE POTTERY was made in the American colonies from the late 1600s. Bowls, crocks, and all types of utilitarian wares were turned out in great abundance to supplement pewter and hand-made treenware. The ready availability of the clay, the same used in making bricks and roof tiles, accounted for the vast production. The lead-glazed redware retained its reddish color, although a variety of colors could be obtained by adding various metals to the glaze. Interesting effects occurred accidentally through unsuspected impurities in the clay or uneven temperatures in the firing kiln, which sometimes resulted in streaks or mottled splotches. Redware pottery was seldom marked by the maker.

Pennsylvania pitcher, 19th century, with mottled green, orange, and brown glaze, rim and body with bands of potato stamp decoration and sgraffito flowers, 11" h. **$7,800**

Courtesy of Pook & Pook, Inc.

◀ Adams County, Pennsylvania bowl, inscribed "Solomon Miller Sept 14 1887," with mottled brown and orange glaze, 2-3/4" h., 5-1/4" dia. **$4,320**

Courtesy of Pook & Pook, Inc.

▲ Charger, dated 1802, probably German, with slip decoration of eagle with border and inscription, 13" dia................. **$780**

Courtesy of Pook & Pook, Inc.

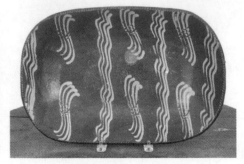

Pennsylvania loaf dish, 19th century, with yellow slip decoration, 12-1/4" h. x 18" w. **$1,320**

Courtesy of Pook & Pook, Inc.

New England pie plate, 19th century, with slip inscription "Mary," 10-1/8" dia. **$900**

Courtesy of Pook & Pook, Inc.

Pennsylvania pie plate, 19th century, with yellow slip decoration, 8-7/8" dia. **$450**

Courtesy of Pook & Pook, Inc.

Waynesboro, Pennsylvania crock, 19th century, impressed "D. M. Bakers Pottery, Waynesboro, PA," 6-3/4" h., 8-3/4" dia.............................. **$277**

Courtesy of Pook & Pook, Inc.

Two Pennsylvania pitchers, 19th century, 7-1/4" h. and 5-3/4" h. **$420**

Courtesy of Pook & Pook, Inc.

Three Pennsylvania bowls, 19th century, largest 3-3/4" h., 10" dia. **$123**

Courtesy of Pook & Pook, Inc.

Adams County, Pennsylvania bowl, inscribed Sol Miller 1872, with repeating manganese "S" decoration around body, 2-3/4" h., 5-5/8" dia. **$3,600**

Courtesy of Pook & Pook, Inc.

Adams County, Pennsylvania spittoon, inscribed on bottom "S.L. Miller near Hampton May 18-1864," with manganese pinwheel decoration, 3-1/2" h., 7-1/4" dia.......................... **$540**

Courtesy of Pook & Pook, Inc.

Rare Virginia three-handled vase, 19th century, impressed "J. Eberly & Bro Strasburg Va," 9" h. **$5,412**

Courtesy of Pook & Pook, Inc.

Pennsylvania shallow bowl, early 19th century, with brown and yellow slip bands, 9-3/8" dia. **$600**

Courtesy of Pook & Pook, Inc.

Small jug, 19th century, with manganese splash decoration, 5-1/2" h. **$600**

Courtesy of Pook & Pook, Inc.

Loaf dish, 19th century, inscribed in slip "St. Cecilia," 7-3/4" h. x 11-3/4" l. **$1,920**

Courtesy of Pook & Pook, Inc.

Lineboro, Maryland crock, 19th century, impressed "L. Kopp," 5-1/2" h. **$197**

Courtesy of Pook & Pook, Inc.

Pennsylvania shallow bowl, early 19th century, 6-3/4" dia. **$210**

Courtesy of Pook & Pook, Inc.

John Bell turk's cap mold, signed "John Bell / Waynesboro" (Pennsylvania), some wear, 6" h. x 8-1/2" w. **$575**

Courtesy of Cottone Auctions

CERAMICS

New England ovoid jug, early
19th century, 8-1/4" h........ **$300**

Courtesy of Pook & Pook, Inc.

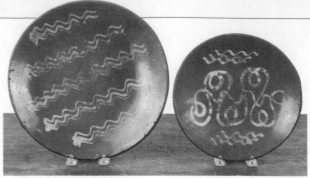

Two plates, 19th century, with yellow slip decoration, 9" dia. and 11-1/4" dia...**$381**

Courtesy of Pook & Pook, Inc.

Pennsylvania plate, 19th
century, with manganese
splotching, 9" dia.................**$62**

Courtesy of Pook & Pook, Inc.

Large Pennsylvania batter bowl,
19th century, 7" h., 13-1/2" dia...**$98**

Courtesy of Pook & Pook, Inc.

Pennsylvania bowl, 19th
century, attributed to Solomon
Miller, Hampton, Pennsylvania,
4" h., 10-1/4" dia. **$148**

Courtesy of Pook & Pook, Inc.

Pennsylvania ovoid jar, early
19th century, impressed
18-3/4 on underside, 7" h...**$123**

Courtesy of Pook & Pook, Inc.

Continental shallow bowl, 19th
century, with green and white
slip floral decoration, 2-1/2" h.,
11-1/2" dia..........................**$62**

Courtesy of Pook & Pook, Inc.

Oval loaf dish, 19th century, with
yellow and brown slip decoration,
11-3/4" x 14-1/4". **$664**

Courtesy of Pook & Pook, Inc.

Pennsylvania charger, 19th
century, with yellow slip decoration,
13-5/8" dia...........................**$1,680**

Courtesy of Pook & Pook, Inc.

Small Pennsylvania pie plate,
19th century, with yellow slip
decoration, 6-3/8" dia.........**$123**

Courtesy of Pook & Pook, Inc.

CERAMICS

red wing pottery

VARIOUS POTTERIES OPERATED in Red Wing, Minnesota, starting in 1868, the most successful being the Red Wing Stoneware Co., organized in 1877. Merged with other local potteries through the years, it became known as Red Wing Union Stoneware Co. in 1906 and was one of the largest producers of utilitarian stoneware items in the United States.

After a decline in the popularity of stoneware products, an art pottery line was introduced to compensate for the loss. This was reflected in a new name for the company, Red Wing Potteries, Inc., in 1936. Stoneware production ceased entirely in 1947, but vases, planters, cookie jars, and dinnerware of art pottery quality continued in production until 1967, when the pottery ceased operation altogether.

For more information on Red Wing pottery, see *Warman's Red Wing Pottery Identification and Price Guide* by Mark F. Moran.

Stoneware butter churn with lid, three-gallon mark with wing, unusual with wing under black ski oval, black number stamp, excellent condition, 15" h. **$330**

Courtesy of Rich Penn Auctions

Stoneware crock with salt glaze 20-gallon butterfly mark, back-stamped Red Wing Stoneware Co., excellent condition with chip on right handle and sliver missing on left handle, 22-1/2" h......... **$900**

Courtesy of Rich Penn Auctions

Three-gallon stoneware butter churn, circa 1900, 13-1/2" h. **$111**

Courtesy of Pook & Pook, Inc.

CERAMICS

Stoneware butter crock with lid advertising Semon's Fair Store / Athens, Wis., excellent condition, 6" h................... **$420**

Courtesy of Rich Penn Auctions

Stoneware koverwate, five-gallon size, excellent condition, 10" dia. **$300**

Courtesy of Rich Penn Auctions

Stoneware crock, salt glaze six-gallon ribcage with target mark, front stamped Red Wing Stoneware Company, small chip on each handle, minor chips on inside rim, 2" glued break on base at center, 14-1/2" h. ... **$780**

Courtesy of Rich Penn Auctions

Stoneware crock with 40-gallon birch leaf transitional mark, very good condition with 4-1/2" hairline at back and chip on inside rim, 29" h............. **$1,200**

Courtesy of Rich Penn Auctions

Two stoneware crocks: Reid, Murdoch & Co. advertising pickle crock with glass lid, excellent condition, 7-1/2" h. x 15" dia., and Red Wing 10-gallon wing crock with Red Wing Union oval, excellent condition, 16-1/2" h........... **$330**

Courtesy of Rich Penn Auctions

Stoneware poultry drinking fount and buttermilk feeder with plate, one-quart size, excellent-plus condition, 7" h................... **$480**

Courtesy of Rich Penn Auctions

Two stoneware Mason fruit jars, one- and two-quart size with black labels, pat. Jan 24, 1899 on bottoms, excellent condition, each with small base chip, 7" and 9" h... **$330**

Courtesy of Rich Penn Auctions

Blue and white pitcher in cherries and leaves design advertising L.M. Mann's General Store / De Soto, Iowa, excellent-plus condition with no chips or cracks, 9-1/2" h.. **$1,200**

Courtesy of Rich Penn Auctions

Stoneware water cooler with lid, unusual with bowtie oval over big wing, excellent condition, bar petal lid with minor hairline crack, 17" h. **$690**

Courtesy of Rich Penn Auctions

Brushed Ware umbrella stand or sand jar of deer in forest, bottom marked USA, excellent condition with minor chips on base, 15" h. x 12" dia. **$840**

Courtesy of Rich Penn Auctions

Stoneware water cooler with 50-gallon birch leaf with Red Wing ski oval and spigot hole, excellent condition, short hairlines at bottom, 33-1/2" h. **$2,040**

Courtesy of Rich Penn Auctions

Stoneware water cooler with advertising for St. Paul Book & Stationery Co. / St. Paul, Minn., bar handled lid, small wing and bail handles, no spigot, excellent condition with no chips or cracks, 16-1/2" h. **$420**

Courtesy of Rich Penn Auctions

Stoneware reamer with sponge band, unmarked, very good/ excellent condition with minor roughness on spout, 4" h. x 7" w. at spout. **$360**

Courtesy of Rich Penn Auctions

Stoneware water cooler with 60-gallon mark with wing, two factory holes at bottom and one on side, very good/excellent condition with old hairline crack, 43-1/2" h. **$3,960**

Courtesy of Rich Penn Auctions

CERAMICS

rookwood

MARIA LONGWORTH NICHOLS founded Rookwood Pottery in 1880. The name, she later reported, paid homage to the many crows (rooks) on her father's estate and was also designed to remind customers of Wedgwood. Production began on Thanksgiving Day 1880 when the first kiln was drawn.

Rookwood's earliest productions demonstrated a continued reliance on European precedents and the Japanese aesthetic. Although the firm offered a variety of wares (Dull Glaze, Cameo, and Limoges, for example), it lacked a clearly defined artistic identity. With the introduction of what became known as its "Standard Glaze" in 1884, Rookwood inaugurated a period in which the company won consistent recognition for its artistic merit and technical innovation.

Rookwood's first decade ended on a high note when the company was awarded two gold medals: one at the Exhibition of American Art Industry in Philadelphia and another later in the year at the Exposition Universelle in Paris. Significant, too, was Maria Longworth Nichols' decision to transfer her interest in the company to William W. Taylor, who had been the firm's manager since 1883. In May 1890, the board of a newly reorganized Rookwood Pottery Co. purchased "the real estate, personal property, goodwill, patents, trade-marks... now the sole property of William W. Taylor" for $40,000.

Under Taylor's leadership, Rookwood was transformed from a fledgling startup to successful business that expanded throughout the following decades to meet rising demand.

Throughout the 1890s, Rookwood continued to attract critical notice as it kept the tradition of innovation alive. Taylor rolled out three new glaze lines – Iris, Sea Green, and Aerial Blue – from late 1894 into early 1895.

At the Paris Exposition in 1900, Rookwood cemented its reputation by winning the Grand Prix, a feat largely due to the favorable reception of the new Iris glaze and its variants.

Over the next several years, Rookwood's record of achievement at domestic and international exhibitions remained unmatched.

Throughout the 1910s, Rookwood continued in a similar vein and began to more thoroughly embrace the simplified aesthetic promoted by many Arts & Crafts figures.

Vellum Glaze vase by Carrie Steinle, 1917, with blue bellflowers set inside ivory band at shoulder, deep blue ground, marks: Rookwood logo, date, shape 605, and artist's incised monogram, fine crazing, 5-1/2" h. **$350**

Courtesy of Mark Mussio, Humler & Nolan

Vase with bleeding heart decoration by E.T. Hurley, 1922, mauve and green on pumpkin-colored ground with brown-gray drip glaze on rim and shoulder, marks: company logo, date, shape number 112, and artist's initials in black slip with Rookwood II label from Cincinnati Art Galleries, uncrazed excellent original condition, 7" h. x 8" w. **$950**

Courtesy of Mark Mussio, Humler & Nolan

Vellum Glaze scenic vase by Alice Caven, 1917, lighter color palette with medium and light green fields and purple and blue mountains, single large tree in foreground with white clouds against blue and purple sky, marks: Rookwood logo, date, shape 901 D, impressed V for Vellum, and artist's incised initials, bottom also contains wheel ground X due to few short firing separations in body, fine overall crazing, 8" h. **$650**

Courtesy of Mark Mussio, Humler & Nolan

Wax Mat vase with pair of fish by Jens Jensen, 1944, marks: Rookwood logo, date, shape 6148 and Jensen's incised monogram, tiny grinding chip at base and open glaze bubbles, 5-1/2" h. **$800**

Courtesy of Mark Mussio, Humler & Nolan

Sea Green Glaze vase with single Easter lily by Mary Nourse, 1904, marks: Rookwood logo, date, shape 902 D, incised G for Sea Green glaze, and artist's incised initials, fine overall crazing, 6-3/4" h. **$2,500**

Courtesy of Mark Mussio, Humler & Nolan

Frog-shaped ash receiver in brown over green mat glazes, marks: Rookwood logo, 1931 date, shape 6097, and fan-shaped esoteric mark, uncrazed excellent condition, 2-7/8" h. **$300**

Courtesy of Mark Mussio, Humler & Nolan

Production of the Iris line, which had been instrumental in the firm's success at the Paris Exposition in 1900, ceased around 1912. Not only did the company abandon its older, fussier underglaze wares, but the newer lines the pottery introduced also trended toward simplicity.

Unfortunately, the collapse of the stock market in October 1929 and ensuing economic depression dealt Rookwood a blow from which it could not recover. The Great Depression took a toll on the company and eventually led to bankruptcy in April 1941.

Rookwood's history might have ended there were it not for the purchase of the firm by a group of investors led by automobile dealer Walter E. Schott and his wife, Margaret. Production started once again. In the years that followed, Rookwood changed hands a number of times before being moved to Starkville, Mississippi, in 1960. It finally closed its doors there in 1967.

ROOKWOOD MARKS

Rookwood employed a number of marks on the bottom of its vessels that denoted everything from the shape number, to the size, date, and color of the body, to the type of glaze to be used.

COMPANY MARKS

1880-1882

In this early period, a number of marks were used to identify the wares.

1. "ROOKWOOD" followed by the initials of the decorator, painted in gold. This is likely the earliest mark, and though the wares are not dated, it seems to have been discontinued by 1881-1882.
2. "ROOKWOOD / POTTERY. / [DATE] CIN. O." In Marks of American Potters (1904), Edwin AtLee Barber states, "The most common marks prior to 1882 were the name of the pottery and the date of manufacture, which were painted or incised on the base of each piece by the decorator."
3. "R. P. C. O. M. L. N." These initials stand for "Rookwood Pottery, Cincinnati, Ohio, Maria Longworth Nichols," and were either painted or incised on the base.
4. Kiln and crows stamp. Barber notes that in 1881 and 1882, the trademark designed by the artist Henry Farny was printed beneath the glaze.
5. Anchor stamp: Barber notes that this mark is "one of the rarest."
6. Oval stamp.
7. Ribbon or banner stamp: According to Barber, "In 1882 a special mark was used on a trade piece... the letters were impressed in a raised ribbon."
8. Ribbon or banner stamp II: A simpler variation of the above stamp, recorded by Herbert Peck.

1883-1886

1. Stamped name and date.
2. Impressed kiln: Appears only in 1883.

1886-1960

Virtually all of the pieces feature the conjoined RP monogram. Pieces fired in the anniversary kilns carry a special kiln-shaped mark with the number of the anniversary inside of it.

1955

A diamond-shaped mark that reads: "ROOKWOOD / 75th / ANNIVERSARY / POTTERY" was printed on wares.

1960-1967

Occasionally pieces are marked "ROOKWOOD POTTERY / STARKVILLE MISS"; from 1962 to 1967 a small "*" occasionally follows the monogram.

DATE MARKS

Unlike many of their contemporaries, Rookwood seems very early on to have adopted a method of marking its pottery that was accurate and easy to understand.

From 1882-1885, the company impressed the date, often with the company name, in block letters (see 1883-86, No. 1).

Although the date traditionally given for the conjoined RP mark is June 23, 1886, this marks the official introduction of the monogram rather than the first use.

Stanley Burt, in his record of the Rookwood at the Cincinnati Museum noted two pieces from 1883 (Nos. 2 and 3) that used the monogram. The monogram was likely designed by Alfred Brennan, since it first appears on his work.

From 1886 on, the date of the object was coded in the conjoined "RP" monogram.

1886: conjoined "RP" no additional flame marks.

1887-1900: conjoined "RP" with a flame added for each subsequent year. Thus, a monogram with seven flames would represent 1893.

1900-1967: conjoined "RP" with 14 flames and a Roman numeral below the mark to indicate the year after 1900. Thus, a monogram with 14 flames and the letters "XXXVI" below it signifies 1936.

CLAY-TYPE MARKS

From 1880 until around 1895, Rookwood used a number of different colored bodies for production and marked each color with a letter code. These letters were impressed and usually found grouped together with the shape number, sometimes following it, but more often below it.

The letter "S" is a particularly vexing designation since the same initial was used for two other unrelated designations. As a result, it is particularly important to take into account the relative position of the impressed letter.

R = Red
Y = Yellow
S = Sage
G = Ginger
W = White
O = Olive
P = From 1915 on, Rookwood used an impressed "P" (often found perpendicular to the orientation of the other marks) to denote the soft porcelain body.

SIZE AND SHAPE MARKS

Almost all Rookwood pieces have a shape code consisting of three or four numbers, followed by a size letter. "A" denotes the largest available size, "F" is the smallest. According to Herbert Peck, initial designs were given a "C" or "D" designation so that variations could be made. Not every shape model, however, features a variation in every size.

GLAZE MARKS

In addition to marking the size, shape and year of the piece, Rookwood's decorators also used a number of letters to designate the type of glaze to be used upon a piece. Generally speaking, these marks are either incised or impressed.

"S" = Standard Glaze to be used. (Incised.)

"L" = Decorators would often incise an "L" near their monogram to indicate that the light variation of the Standard Glaze was to be used. (Incised.)

"SG" = Sea Green Glaze to be used.

"Z" = from 1900-1904 designated any piece with a Mat Glaze. (Impressed)

"W" = Iris Glaze to be used.

"V" = Vellum Glaze to be used; variations include "GV" for Green Vellum and "YV" for Yellow Vellum.

OTHER MARKS

"S" = If found away from the shape number, this generally indicates a piece that was specially thrown at the pottery in the presence of visitors. (Impressed.)

"S" = If this precedes the shape number than it denotes a piece that was specifically thrown and decorated from a sketch with a corresponding number. Because of the size and quality of pieces this letter has been found on, this probably signifies a piece made specifically for an important exhibition.

"X" = Rookwood used a wheel ground "x" to indicate items that were not of first quality. There has been some suggestion that decorators and salespersons might have conspired to "x" certain pieces that they liked, since this designation would reduce the price. Since there are a number of items that appear to have been marked for no apparent reason, there may be some truth to this idea. Unfortunately, as this idea has gained credence, many pieces with obvious flaws have been listed as "marked x for no apparent reason," and collectors should be cautious.

Generally, the mark reduces the value and appeal of the piece. Peck describes a variation of the "x" that resembles an asterisk as indicating a piece that could be given away to employees.

"T" = An impressed T that precedes a shape number indicates a trial piece.

◗ ◆ ▲ = These shapes (crescents, diamonds, and triangles) are used to indicate a glaze trial.

"K1" and "K3" = circa 1922, used for matching teacups and saucers

"SC" = Cream and Sugar sets, circa 1946-1950

"2800" = Impressed on ship pattern tableware

SOME LINES OF NOTE

Aerial Blue: Commercially, this line was among the least successful. As a result, there are a limited number of pieces, and this scarcity has increased their values relative to other wares.

Black Iris: This line is among the most sought after by collectors, commanding significantly more than examples of similar size and design in virtually any other glaze. In fact, the current auction record for Rookwood – over $350,000 – was set in 2004 for a Black Iris vase decorated by Kitaro Shirayamadani in 1900.

Iris: Uncrazed examples are exceptionally rare, with large pieces featuring conventional designs commanding the highest prices. Smaller, naturalistically painted examples, though still desirable, are gradually becoming more affordable for the less advanced collector.

Production Ware: This commercial and mass-produced artware is significantly less expensive than pieces in most other lines.

Standard Glaze: These wares peaked in the 1970s-1980s, and the market has remained thin in recent years, but regardless of the state of the market, examples of superlative quality, including those with silver overlay, have found their places in the finest of collections.

Wax Mat: This is among the most affordable of the hand-decorated lines.

Vellum Glaze vase with floral decoration by Lorinda Epply, 1931, marks: Rookwood logo, date, shape 130, impressed fan-shaped esoteric mark and artist's monogram in brown slip, excellent original condition, 6-1/4" h. **$400**

Courtesy of Mark Mussio, Humler & Nolan

Carved mat bowl by William Hentschel, 1911, with trio of parrots and rose and green mat glazes, marks: Rookwood logo, date, shape 1393, impressed V for Vellum and artist's incised monogram, uncrazed excellent condition, 5-3/4" h., 11" dia. **$1,500**

Courtesy of Mark Mussio, Humler & Nolan

Iris Glaze vase with Japanese irises by Irene Bishop, 1903, marks: company logo, date, shape number 904 D, incised W for white (Iris) glaze, and incised initials of artist, fine overall crazing and two tight lines on opposite sides of rim, 8" h.......**$400**

Courtesy of Mark Mussio, Humler & Nolan

Black Opal vase by Harriet Wilcox, 1926, with repeating clematis decoration, interior lined in Nubian Black glaze, marks: company logo, date, shape number 2789, and artist's initials in black slip, uncrazed and clean, 10-7/8" h. **$2,500**

Courtesy of Mark Mussio, Humler & Nolan

Standard Glaze vase with oak leaves by Lena Hanscom, 1903, marks: Rookwood logo, date, shape 654 C, and artist's incised initials, faint crazing, 5-1/4" h. **$300**

Courtesy of Mark Mussio, Humler & Nolan

In 1920, Rookwood was celebrating its 40th anniversary with a display at the pottery. A newspaper account in the Nov. 22 *Cincinnati Times-Star* discussing the meritorious history of the pottery mentions the following: "It was a piece of Rookwood of the famous Tiger Eye type that won the Grand Prix at the Paris Exposition in 1900, and this wonderful vase, which may be seen in the display at the pottery, has been valued by some at $50,000." After barely surviving the Great Depression and bankruptcy, Rookwood revisited the Uranus vase during its 65th anniversary in 1945. Herbert Peck describes the scene in *The Book of Rookwood Pottery* on page 125: "In November, Rookwood marked it sixty-fifth anniversary quietly. Mayor Stewart of Cincinnati opened the ceremony at 2:00 p.m. on the Saturday following Thanksgiving, and tours of the plant were conducted both Saturday and Sunday." The famous Tiger Eye vase, which was shown at the 40th anniversary in 1920, was on display, but this time instead of being given an estimated value of $50,000, it was described as "a $10,000 vase." Never having been sold by Rookwood, the Uranus vase became the property (along with the pottery itself) of George Sperti and his St. Thomas Institute, and at some point was given by Sperti to a good friend, the father of the consignor. Sperti explained the significance of the vase to his friend, who passed it on to his son. The term "Uranus" seems to have been given to the vase in the 1960s when Rookwood produced a card featuring the great vessel, showing it with medals won by the company in its salad days. This vase is a major piece of Rookwood's history and that of the city of Cincinnati.

COURTESY OF MARK MUSSIO, HUMLER & NOLAN

Uranus Tiger Eye vase by Albert Valentien, circa 1899, a famous and, until recently, lost treasure, exhibited in 1900 Paris Exposition; incised design of cranes in flight with Tiger Eye effect, marks: Rookwood logo and shape number 139 A, date and artist signature obscured by glaze, several chips off base that occurred in production, glaze with flowed in chips, 18-1/2" h. **$31,000**

Pair of double owl bookends, William McDonald design, cast in 1921 and covered with dark blue over lighter blue mat glazes, marks: Rookwood logo, date, shape 2565, and artist's mold monogram, no crazing, short, tight firing line on bottom, tiny chip to bottom front corner of one, 6-7/8" h. **$400**

Courtesy of Mark Mussio, Humler & Nolan

Pair of rare black swan bookends, Sallie Toohey design, cast in 1928 and covered with trio of high glazes, marks: Rookwood logo, date, shape 6021, and artist's mold monogram, uncrazed excellent original condition, 4" h. **$1,500**

Courtesy of Mark Mussio, Humler & Nolan

Tall Arts & Crafts vase produced in 1911 with hand-tooled geometric design in early Ombroso glaze, marks: Rookwood logo, date, and shape 944 A, faint crazing and tiny open glaze bubbles, 17-1/2" h. **$1,000**

Courtesy of Mark Mussio, Humler & Nolan

Standard Glaze vase with winged demon, 1885, marks: impressed ROOKWOOD, 1885, shape 30 B, and R for red clay, fine overall crazing, overspray from repair to rim, 12" h.. **$2,000**

Courtesy of Mark Mussio, Humler & Nolan

Large Vellum glaze scenic vase by E.T. Hurley, 1913, with dark trees in foreground and peach-colored sky reflecting on lake, marks: Rookwood logo, date, shape 951 A, impressed V for Vellum, and artist's monogram, fine overall crazing and tight line descending from rim, 15-1/2" h. **$1,700**

Courtesy of Mark Mussio, Humler & Nolan

Mahogany (Standard) Glaze lidded potpourri jar by Kataro Shirayamadani, 1888, with butterfly handles and dragon, marks: Rookwood logo, shape 400, impressed R for red clay, and artist's incised initials, lid unmarked, fine overall crazing, 6" h. **$5,250**

Courtesy of Mark Mussio, Humler & Nolan

Standard Glaze four-handled presentation mug by Artus Van Briggle, 1896, with portrait of elderly gentleman on front and "Man doth not live by bread only," raised grape motif and "1896" carved on back, two large handles (one with tight line) and two slightly smaller handles, marks: Rookwood logo, shape S1249, and artist's incised initials, fine overall crazing, open glaze bubbles, 6-3/4" h. **$2,200**

Courtesy of Mark Mussio, Humler & Nolan

Mahogany vase with Goldstone and Tiger Eye effect by Matt Daly, 1893, with four small birds in flight, marks: company logo, date, shape number 684 C, R for red clay, and impressed monogram of artist, professional restoration to chip on underside of rim, faint crazing, 6-3/4" h. **$700**

Courtesy of Mark Mussio, Humler & Nolan

Porcelain bud vase with flowers by Arthur Conant, 1917, marks: Rookwood logo, date, shape 2307, sideways P for porcelain, artist's incised monogram and museum acquisition number on bottom, fine overall crazing, 6-3/4" h. **$1,100**

Courtesy of Mark Mussio, Humler & Nolan

Early Dull Finish covered urn by Fannie Auckland, 1881, incised flowering vines in blue against white ground, marks: "Rookwood Pottery Cin O 1881" incised on bottom with artist's initials, nicks to exterior of jar, interior of lid with several short, tight firing lines, high glaze used on interior of both pieces with fine overall crazing, no crazing to exterior of either piece, 7-7/8" h. **$800**

Courtesy of Mark Mussio, Humler & Nolan

CERAMICS

roseville pottery

ROSEVILLE IS ONE of the most widely recognizable of potteries across the United States. Having been sold in flower shops and drugstores around the country, its art and production wares became a staple in American homes through the time Roseville closed in the 1950s.

The Roseville Pottery Co., located in Roseville, Ohio, was incorporated on Jan. 4, 1892, with George F. Young as general manager. The company had been producing stoneware since 1890, when it purchased the J. B. Owens Pottery, also of Roseville.

The popularity of Roseville Pottery's original lines of stoneware continued to grow. The company acquired new plants in 1892 and 1898, and production started to shift to Zanesville, just a few miles away. By about 1910, all of the work was centered in Zanesville, but the company name was unchanged.

Young hired Ross C. Purdy as artistic designer in 1900, and Purdy created Rozane, a contraction of the words "Roseville" and "Zanesville." The first Roseville artwork pieces were marked either Rozane or RPCO, both impressed or ink-stamped on the bottom.

In 1902, a line was developed called Azurean. Some pieces were marked Azurean, but often RPCO. In 1904 at the St. Louis Exposition, Roseville's Rozane Mongol, a high-gloss oxblood red line, captured first prize, gaining recognition for the firm and its creator, John Herold.

Many Roseville lines were a response to the innovations of Weller Pottery, and in 1904 Frederick Rhead was hired away from Weller as artistic director. He created the Olympic and Della Robbia lines for Roseville. His brother Harry took over as artistic director in 1908, and in 1915 he introduced the popular Donatello line.

By 1908, all handcrafting ended except for Rozane Royal. Roseville was the first pottery in Ohio to install a tunnel kiln, which increased its production capacity.

Frank Ferrell, who was a top decorator at the Weller Pottery by 1904, was Roseville's artistic director from 1917 until 1954. This Zanesville native created many of the most popular lines, including Pine Cone, which had scores of individual pieces.

Many collectors believe Roseville's circa 1925 glazes were the best of any Zanesville pottery. George Krause, who in 1915 became Roseville's technical supervisor responsible for glaze, remained with Roseville until the 1950s.

Company sales declined after World War II, especially in the early 1950s when cheap Japanese imports began to replace American wares, and a simpler, more modern style made many of Roseville's elaborate floral designs seem old-fashioned.

In the late 1940s, Roseville began to issue lines with glossy glazes. Roseville tried to offset its flagging artware sales by launching a dinnerware line – Raymor – in 1953. The line was a commercial failure.

Roseville issued its last new designs in 1953. On Nov. 29, 1954, the facilities of Roseville were sold to the Mosaic Tile Co.

For more information on Roseville, see *Warman's Roseville Pottery, 2nd edition,* by Denise Rago.

BOTTOM MARKS

There is no consistency to Roseville bottom marks. Even within a single popular pattern like Pine Cone, the marks vary.

Several shape-numbering systems were implemented during the company's almost 70-year history, with some denoting a vessel style and some applied to separate lines. Though many pieces are unmarked, from 1900 until the late teens or early 1920s, Roseville used a variety of marks including "RPCo," "Roseville Pottery Company," and the word "Rozane," the last often with a line name, i.e., "Egypto."

The underglaze ink script "Rv" mark was used on lines introduced from the mid-to-late teens through the mid-1920s. Around 1926 or 1927, Roseville began to use a small, triangular black paper label on lines such as Futura and Imperial II. Silver or gold foil labels began to appear around 1930, continuing for several years on lines such as Blackberry and Tourmaline, and on some early Pine Cone.

From 1932 to 1937, an impressed script mark was added to the molds used on new lines, and around 1937 the raised script mark was added to the molds of new lines. The relief mark includes "U.S.A."

All of the following bottom mark images appear courtesy of Adamstown Antique Gallery, Adamstown, Pennsylvania.

Impressed mark on Azurean vase, 8" h.

Raised mark on Bushberry vase.

Ink stamp on Cherry Blossom pink vase, 10" h.

Wafer mark on Della Robbia vase, 10-1/2" h.

Gold foil label and grease pencil marks on Imperial II vase, 10" h.

Ink stamps on Wisteria bowl, 5" h.

Impressed marks on Rozane portrait vase, 13" h.

Impressed mark on Iris vase.

Artcraft pattern jardiniere in green, marked 629-8 on bottom in orange crayon, fine overall crazing, 7-3/4" h., 12" dia. ... **$500**

Courtesy of Mark Mussio, Humler & Nolan

Aztec pattern squatty pitcher, body encircled with angled Arts & Crafts design and white flower-like decorations applied via squeeze bag technique, unmarked, minor crazing, very good condition, 4-3/4" x 7-1/4" w. **$150**

Courtesy of Mark Mussio, Humler & Nolan

Apple Blossom pattern two-handled vase, 393-18", pink tones, minor base rim touch-up......................**$531**

Courtesy of Woody Auctions, LLC

▲ Two Juvenile pattern creamware pieces: Low bowl with wading ducks wearing boots and hats, 1-1/4" x 7-3/4", and mug with puppy front and back, 3" h.; both ink-stamped RV, usage scratches, glaze crazing............................**$70**

Courtesy of Mark Mussio, Humler & Nolan

Azurean pattern vase with bouquet of wild roses on front painted by Walter Myers, unmarked except for artist's signature on side of base, vase left factory with two tiny stilt nicks at base rim, excellent original condition, 9" h. **$700**

Courtesy of Mark Mussio, Humler & Nolan

◄ Juvenile pattern rolled rim plate with images of Santa Claus, marked on bottom with Roseville logo in black ink stamp, light wear and light scratches to surface, 1-3/8" x 7-3/4". **$475**

Courtesy of Mark Mussio, Humler & Nolan

Freesia pattern two-handled vase, 121-8", in brown tones. **$71**

Courtesy of Woody Auctions LLC

Rare Futura pattern "Chinese Pillow" vase, 430-9", unmarked, bruise at one foot, crisp mold, 9-1/8" h............................ **$1,100**

Courtesy of Mark Mussio, Humler & Nolan

Futura pattern "Christmas Tree" vase, 390-10, unmarked, faint overall crazing, professional restoration to chip at foot, 10-1/4" h............... **$170**

Courtesy of Mark Mussio, Humler & Nolan

Futura pattern triangle vase in blue, 388-9", unmarked, nick at top of plinth, 9-1/8" h..... **$300**

Courtesy of Mark Mussio, Humler & Nolan

Blackberry pattern twin-handled vase, 575-8", unmarked, good mold and color, 8-1/8" h.......**$400**

Courtesy of Mark Mussio, Humler & Nolan

Egypto pattern Arts & Crafts gourd vase with olive green over green glaze, arched branch handles flow into long curving stems with foliage and fruit and scrolling fronds, raised "Rozane Ware, Egypto" wafer, excellent original condition, minor glaze pull chip at base rim with glaze bursts, 5-1/8" h. x 7-1/2" w. **$600**

Courtesy of Mark Mussio, Humler & Nolan

Jardiniere with molded repeating design of scarabs in green mat glaze, shape number 510 on bottom, excellent original condition, 3-3/4" h. **$325**

Courtesy of Mark Mussio, Humler & Nolan

Rozane pattern ware vase, early 20th century, with hound portrait, signed and dated indistinctly, 19" h. **$738**

Courtesy of Pook & Pook, Inc.

Sunflower pattern wall pocket, 1265-7", unmarked, excellent original condition, faint crazing, 7-3/8" h. **$600**

Courtesy of Mark Mussio, Humler & Nolan

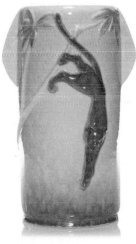

Early Velmoss pattern vase with six stalks of embossed leaves, unmarked, excellent original condition with superior mottled and striated glaze, faint crazing, 9-7/8" h. **$600**

Courtesy of Mark Mussio, Humler & Nolan

Wincraft pattern vase, 290-11", with panther leaping from tree branch, raised company marks and shape number on bottom, fine overall crazing, glaze flake at panther's ear, 10-1/2" h. **$250**

Courtesy of Mark Mussio, Humler & Nolan

Two Silhouette pattern items, 779-5" vase and 728-10" console bowl, both ivory with green. **$35**

Courtesy of Woody Auctions, LLC

CERAMICS
(sidebar)

CERAMICS

r.s. prussia

ORNATELY DECORATED CHINA marked "R.S. Prussia" and "R.S. Germany" continues to grow in popularity. According to the Third Series of Mary Frank Gaston's *Encyclopedia of R.S. Prussia* (Collector Books, Paducah, Kentucky), these marks were used by the Reinhold Schlegelmilch porcelain factories located in Suhl in the Germanic regions known as "Prussia" prior to World War I, and in Tillowitz, Silesia, which became part of Poland after World War II. Other marks sought by collectors include "R.S. Suhl," "R.S." steeple or church marks, and "R.S. Poland."

The Suhl factory was founded by Reinhold Schlegelmilch in 1869 and closed in 1917. The Tillowitz factory was established in 1895 by Erhard Schlegelmilch, Reinhold's son. This china customarily bears the phrase "R.S. Germany" and "R.S. Tillowitz." The Tillowitz factory closed in 1945, but it was reopened for a few years under Polish administration.

Prices are high and collectors should beware of the forgeries that sometimes find their way onto the market. Mold names and numbers are taken from Mary Frank Gaston's books on R.S. Prussia.

The "Prussia" and "R.S. Suhl" marks have been reproduced, so buy with care. Later copies of these marks are well done, but the quality of porcelain is inferior to the production in the 1890-1920 era.

Collectors are also interested in the porcelain products made by the Erdmann Schlegelmilch factory. This factory was founded by three brothers in Suhl in 1861. They named the factory in honor of their father, Erdmann Schlegelmilch. A variety of marks incorporating the "E.S." initials were used. The factory closed circa 1935. The Erdmann Schlegelmilch factory was an earlier and entirely separate business from the Reinhold Schlegelmilch factory. The two were not related to each other.

Stippled mold tankard in yellow and pink with floral décor, 13" h. **$106**

Courtesy of Woody Auctions, LLC

Charmers portrait plate, satin finish, winter scene, 8-1/2" dia....................................... **$885**

Courtesy of Woody Auctions, LLC

Chocolate pot and two matching cups and saucers, swan and gazebo décor, pot 9" h........ **$354**

Courtesy of Woody Auctions, LLC

Chocolate set: Pot, four cups and saucers, creamer and sugar, satin finish, cream and white with pink rose garland décor, gold stencil highlights, pot 10-3/4" h. **$266**

Courtesy of Woody Auctions, LLC

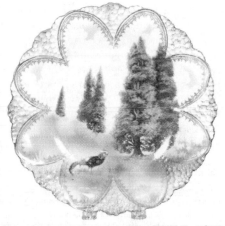

Plate, pheasant and evergreen décor, 8-1/2" dia....**$207**

Courtesy of Woody Auctions, LLC

Duck pictorial porcelain toothpick holder, two handles below scalloped rim, red star and demi-wreath mark to underside, late 19th/early 20th century, 2-3/8" h. overall. **$374**

Courtesy of Jeffrey S. Evans & Associates

Stippled mold plate, Lebrun portrait on green background, cobalt blue border with gold highlights, unmarked, 8" dia. **$885**

Courtesy of Woody Auctions, LLC

CERAMICS

satsuma

MEIJI SATSUMA EARTHENWARE reflects Japanese artistry, history and culture, from the featured themes and motifs to the art form's minute liquid gold embellishments and ivory to yellow fine-crackled glazes.

Although created expressly for export, Satsuma are richly hand-painted works with stylized Japanese themes that reflect how their creators believed Westerners perceived their country – or how they wanted it to be perceived.

The Satsuma art form was created during the Meiji Dynasty (1868-1912) in Kyushu, a historic ceramics center in southern Japan. By the late 19th century, Japan's artists began participating in the Great International Fairs. Their massive pairs of Satsuma vases, bowls and jardinières caused an immediate sensation through both America and Europe. To satisfy this craze, Satsuma techniques spread from Kyushu studios to those in Kyoto, Osaka, Nagoya, Tokyo, Yokohama, and elsewhere.

Many master painters, eager for business and fame, signed the bases of their creations with Japanese Kanji marks, often in cartouche. Some cleverly included their names or the names of their studios in their artwork, for example, written on scrolls. In this way, Sozan, Kinkozan, Kozan, and Ryozan became known for their characteristic techniques, style, subject matter, and harmony between form and design.

Noted for its dense ornamentation, Satsuma can be embellished with borders of varying types and patterns, including enamel, geometric, brocade, scroll, latticework, and florals. Many reflect the Japanese love of nature by including flocks of birds, sprays of wisteria, flowering trees, and winding streams. Others display picnics, market scenes, holidays, celebrations, processions, and the many festivals that enrich Japanese life. Themes can even include Samurai epics, Oriental mythological representations, or elements of demonology.

Dressed in kimonos, the human subjects include geishas, Noh actors, musicians, and wise men who are shown strolling, flying kites, conversing, playing flutes, offering gifts, reading scrolls, bestowing blessings, or observing the moon.

Although rendered with miniature brushstrokes – perhaps, at times, with single hairs from rats – the subjects' facial expressions reflect the full range of human emotions. Several personalities have actually been identified.

"Some today describe Satsuma as an undervalued art, neglected by both scholars and collectors," said collector Dr. Afshine Emrani, who displays his favorites at Some of My Favorite Things. "But they are valued very highly in price."

Vase, late 19th/early 20th century, of baluster form, with hand-painted enamel and gilt-highlighted chrysanthemums, banded neck and shoulder, signed with gilt four-character mark and blue mon, 24-1/4" h., 15-3/4" dia................ **$3,000**

Courtesy of John Moran Auctioneers, Inc.

Porcelain charger, Koshida character mark,
14-3/4" dia.. **$500**

Courtesy of Heritage Auctions

Porcelain charger, Koshida character mark,
15" dia... **$275**

Courtesy of Heritage Auctions

Pair of porcelain vases, 20th century, two-character
mark, 19-1/2" h. **$1,188**

Courtesy of Heritage Auctions

Pair of porcelain vases, early 20th century,
one-character mark, 9" h. **$1,125**

Courtesy of Heritage Auctions

Serious collectors seek pieces by Osakan Yabu Meizan, distinguished by their extremely fine work, or by Nakamura Baikei, which are very rare. Baikei's pieces always include lengthy inscriptions extolling the merits of his work and how much effort they took to paint.

"The time required to reproduce something that even remotely resembles a quality piece of Satsuma has kept reproductions out of the higher end of the market," dealer Matthew Baer of Ivory Tower Antiques said. The low end, however, is riddled with reproductions from China that bear little resemblance to Satsuma. They are often stamped "Royal Satsuma" or "Satsuma Made in China" in English.

Figural and sculpted Satsuma are purely decorative. Vari-shaped incense burners, vases, boxes, flowerpots, plates, and tea caddies were intended to be decorative as well. This is because earthenware stains with usage.

Satsuma: The Romance of Japan by Louis Lawrence shows fine examples of this unique art. It is only available through Satsuma Collector (www.satsumacollector.com).

— Melody Amsel-Ariel

CERAMICS

saturday evening girls (paul revere)

SATURDAY EVENING GIRLS (Paul Revere) pottery was established in Boston in 1906 by a group of philanthropists seeking to establish better conditions for underprivileged young girls of the area. Edith Brown served as supervisor of the small Saturday Evening Girls Club pottery operation, which was moved, in 1912, to a house close to the Old North Church where Paul Revere's signal lanterns had been placed. The wares were mostly hand-decorated in mineral colors, and both sgraffito and molded decorations were employed. Although it became popular, it was never a profitable operation and always depended on financial contributions to operate. After the death of Edith Brown in 1932, the pottery foundered and finally closed in 1942.

Bowl with 12 standing rabbits and initials MLR, produced in 1920 by unknown artist, marked in slip on bottom "S.E.G., DM, 6-20," small chip on outside of rim and bruise on inside of rim, 1-1/2" h., 6" dia................... **$300**

Courtesy of Mark Mussio, Humler & Nolan

Bowl with tan and white bands against yellow ground, white band with name "Honey" in black, work of Fannie Levine in 1919, marked in black slip on bottom "S.E.G., FL, 10-19," tight line descending from rim, 1-1/2" h., 6" dia. **$190**

Courtesy of Mark Mussio, Humler & Nolan

Large bowl in cuerda seca with geese, work of Fannie Levine in 1914, signed "3-14 S.E.G. FL," 5" x 11-1/2"............ **$9,600**

Courtesy of Rago Arts, www.ragoarts.com

Three-piece breakfast set: 3-3/8" h. mug; 2-1/4" h., 5-1/2" dia. bowl; and 7-5/8" dia. plate, each with child's name Joan Audrey Carlson and hand-decorated with racing rabbits borders, group stamped with company circular logo, stilt mark on mug. **$350**

Courtesy of Mark Mussio, Humler & Nolan

Two pitchers: Blue mat glaze with white tortoise and hare pattern at rim and wording "Slow But Sure," work of Rose Bacchini in 1911, marked on bottom in slip "154.1.11, S.E.G. R.B," glaze chip at spout, 4-1/4" h.; ivory mat glaze with yellow ring and three rabbits near rim, work of unknown artist in 1914, marked on bottom in black slip "S.E.G., 3-10-14, JG," two glaze chips at rim, 3-1/4" h. **$400**

Courtesy of Mark Mussio, Humler & Nolan

Lidded pitcher/coffeepot with band in blue and black with green leaves near rim, marked on bottom "S.E.G., JG, 3-7-14" in black slip, excellent original condition, chip on inside of spout, lid unmarked, slight gloss to glaze, 4-7/8" h.................**$275**

Courtesy of Mark Mussio, Humler & Nolan

Plate with ivory crackle glaze and Arts & Crafts-style trees around outer edge, work of Eva Geneco in 1912, marked in black slip on bottom "S.E.G., EG, 9-12" and smaller set of initials "RB" for Rose Bacchini, two chips on back of foot ring, 10" dia.............................. **$600**

Courtesy of Mark Mussio, Humler & Nolan

Plate with repeating rabbit pattern against yellow ring around outer edge, marked on bottom "S.E.G.," "3-16" and possibly artist's mark, all in black slip, fine crazing and tiny burst glaze bubbles, 7-1/2" dia. **$400**

Courtesy of Mark Mussio, Humler & Nolan

Tall vase in cuerda seca with band of trees, work of Sara Galner (1894-1982) in 1917, signed "S.E.G. 6-17 SG," short, shallow scratches, 10-1/2" x 5-1/2"............. **$6,080**

Courtesy of Rago Arts, www.ragoarts.com

Plate with four groups of three rabbits, work of Ida Goldstein in 1911, marked on bottom in black slip "292-9-11, S.E.G., IG," chips along outside edge of rim, 7-3/8" dia............... **$200**

Courtesy of Mark Mussio, Humler & Nolan

CERAMICS

sèvres

SÈVRES PORCELAIN, the grandest of ultimate luxury, artistic ceramics, was favored by European royalty, the aristocracy of the 19th century, and 20th century great collectors. Its story begins in 1708, when, following frenzied experimentation, German alchemist Johann Bottger discovered the formula for strong, delicate, translucent hard-paste porcelain. Unlike imported white "chinaware," Bottger's porcelain could also be painted and gilded. Soon potteries across Europe were producing decorative items a-swirl with fashionable gilt and flowers.

French potters lacked an ample source of kaolin, a requisite for hard-paste porcelain, however, so they developed a soft-paste formula from clay and powdered glass. Soft-paste, though more fragile, could be fired at a lower temperature than hard-paste. This allowed a wider variety of colors and glazes.

The Sèvres porcelain factory was originally founded at Chateau de Vincennes in 1738. Its soft-paste porcelain was prized for its characteristic whiteness and purity. By the time this workshop relocated to Sèvres in 1756, its craftsmen were creating small porcelain birds, figurals of children in white or delicate hues, and innovative pieces with characteristic rosy-hued backgrounds. They also produced detailed allegorical and thematic pieces like "Flute Lesson," "Jealousy," and "Justice and the Republic," which sparkle with transparent, colorless glazes.

The introduction of unglazed, natural-toned "biscuit" porcelain, a favorite of Madame de Pompadour, the mistress of Louis XV, followed. Many of these molded sculptures portray lifelike sentimental or Classical scenes. Biscuit porcelain is extremely fragile. Madame de Pompadour also adored Sèvres' porcelain flowers.

Glazed porcelain bud vase, Taxile Doat (1851-1939), 1902, signed DOAT 1902 SÈVRES G, 6-1/2" x 3-1/4"..................**$2,048**

Courtesy of Rago Arts, www.ragoarts.com

When Louis XV assumed full control of Sèvres porcelain in 1759, he insisted on flawless, extravagant creations, many of which he commissioned for his personal collection. The Sèvres mark, blue interlaced Ls, was born of his royal patronage, and helps determine dates of production. Other marks, either painted or incised, indicate specific Sèvres painters, gilders, sculptors, and potters by name. Louis XV's successor, Louis XVI, continued to support the royal Sèvres tradition.

Although kaolin deposits were discovered near Limoges in 1768, Sèvres began producing hard-paste porcelain commercially only from 1773. During this period, they continued to produce soft-paste items as well.

After suffering financial ruin during the French Revolution, Sèvres began producing simpler, less expensive items. During this period, its craftsmen also abandoned their old-fashioned soft-paste formula for hard-paste porcelain. Sèvres porcelain regained its former glory under Napoleon Bonaparte, who assumed power in 1804. He promoted elaborately ornamented pieces in the classical style. The range of Sèvres creations is extensive, varying in shape, historical styles, motifs, and ornamentation. Vases typically feature double round, oval, or elliptical finely painted scenes edged in white against pastel backgrounds. One

Footed bowl with hand-painted scenic decor with two cherubs, marked, artist signed "Boucher," cobalt blue border, gilt metal trim and feet, 4-1/4" x 12". .. **$531**

Courtesy of Woody Auctions, LLC

Ink stand, late 19th century, hand-painted amorous couple in landscape with pink and gilt borders flanked by two covered porcelain inkwells with berry finials, octagonal body with gilt stars in latticework design on blue ground, gilt and enameled scrolling feet, gilt loss to berry finials and stand, minor enamel losses, small flake to rear foot, chip to front foot, 3-1/2" x 14" x 6-1/2"................................. **$310**

Courtesy of Brunk Auctions

Twelve soft paste porcelain plates, 1763-1779, borders with molded basketweave design, thin cobalt blue bands, and gilt accents, centers with polychrome enameled flower sprays, each with painted factory marks, most in blue, with various date letters and decorators' marks, wear/loss to enamel and gilt, and surface abrasions/knife marks from usage wear, most with stacking wear, one with rim chip and foot rim chip, 9-5/8" dia. **$1,107**

Courtesy of Skinner, Inc., www.skinnerinc.com

Pair of reticulated porcelain baskets, circa 1800, marks: RF. dc, Sèvres, rubbing of gilt and minor wear, 5" h., 11-1/2" dia.............................. **$1,375**

Courtesy of Heritage Auctions

Two circular plaques, late 19th century, one of Louis XVI in profile, other of Marie Antoinette in profile, each with applied floral garlands within gilt bronze frame, each with incised interlaced "L" mark centered by letter "B," incised "A" with incised signature "Lecomte," each 7-1/2" dia. overall, excluding frame each 6-1/4" dia......... **$650**

Courtesy of John Moran Auctioneers, Inc.

CERAMICS

Porcelain box on stand in form of egg, lid with applied fruit and flower finial above scalloped piercings with cobalt and gilt accents, brass fittings at waist, lower half of egg with acanthus decoration, stepped parcel gilt standard, blue underglaze mark, inscription in French, "Modeled and decorated by hand," 8-1/2" h., 3-1/2" dia............ **$175**

Courtesy of Clars Auction Gallery, www.clars.com

Two soft paste porcelain teacups and saucers, France, 1757, painted en camaïeu rose with figures before rustic buildings within landscape vignettes and with birds, with gilt dentil rims, cups with twisted handles, each piece with blue interlaced "L" mark enclosing lower case date letter "e," with unidentified painter's mark of house, cup 2" h., saucer 4-3/4" dia...... **$3,198**

Courtesy of Skinner, Inc.; www.skinnerinc.com

side portrays figures, while the other features flower bouquets. Their lavish gilding, a royal touch reserved especially for Sèvres creations, is often embellished with engraved detail, like flowers or geometric motifs.

Simple plates and tea wares can be found for a few hundred dollars. Because large numbers were made to accompany dessert services, quite a few Sèvres biscuit porcelains have also survived. These fragile pieces command between $3,000 to as much as $70,000 apiece.

According to Errol Manners, author, lecturer, and proprietor of London's H & E Manners: Ceramics and Works of Art, the Sèvres market has strengthened considerably in recent years. "Pieces linked directly to the Court and very early experimental wares, which appeal to more serious and academic collectors, command the highest prices of all," he explains. "Major pieces can command a few hundred thousand dollars. A set of Sèvres vases can command over $1 million."

Manners recommends that would-be collectors visit museums and consult serious dealers and collectors before purchasing a Sèvres piece. "And read the books," he adds. "There are really no shortcuts. It takes serious study."

"While Sèvres-style pieces are not authentic Sèvres, they may be authentic antiques," counters Edan Sassoon, representing the Artes Antiques and Fine Art Gallery in Beverly Hills, Calif. "If they faithfully imitate Sèvres pieces in quality, style, and opulence, they may not only have decorative value, but may also be quite expensive. In today's market, a piece of Sèvres-style porcelain, depending on its color, condition, size, and quality, may command hundreds of thousands of dollars."

— *Melody Amsel-Arieli*

top lot!

Cobalt and gold enameled tureen from "Service Iconographique Grec," circa 1812, signed with double eagle heads, Sèvres mark and 1812 printed in red, gold script, 2juin BT, green numerals, 13.cv.12, minor fleck to rim of lid, 9-1/2" h. x 12" w. Descended in family of William Weightman. Tureen was used in his house in Mt. Airy, outside Philadelphia. After his death, that house, Raven Hill, was given to the Catholic church, which converted it into a girl's school. The china has been in family for over 100 years, thence by descent. The collection of Comtesse de Nadaillac (?) James B. Pooley, Philadelphia, 1888. The collection of William Weightman, "Ravenhill," Germantown, Philadelphia. By direct descent to present owner..................**$63,525**

COURTESY OF COTTONE AUCTIONS

Hand-painted porcelain and gilt bronze center bowl and pair of five-light candelabrum, late 19th/early 20th century: Oval center bowl, seated couple in garden landscape, signed "O. Gecl(?)," gilt metal and cobalt pedestal base on bronze platform, applied floral scrolling handles, 11-1/4" x 12-5/8" x 7"; and pair of cobalt hand-painted porcelain and gilt bronze candelabrum, 19th century, central flame finial over central post, acanthus leaf scrolling arms with candle nozzles with bobeches, cobalt porcelain pedestal bases, gilt bronze grape and vine circular bases on gilt bronze platform bases, one lacking bobeche, both damaged and repaired at porcelain base, one damaged and repaired at center of neck/top, one loose finial, 19-3/4"..**$1,860**

Courtesy of Brunk Auctions

Early pâte-sur-pâte portrait on porcelain, Taxile Doat (1851-1939), 1875, in original frame, signed and dated, short glazed-over firing lines, uncrazed, made before Doat began working at Sèvres, sight 10-1/2" x 8"........................**$1,280**

Courtesy of Rago Arts, www.ragoarts.com

CERAMICS

spatterware

SPATTERWARE TAKES ITS name from "spattered" decoration in various colors, used to trim pieces hand-painted with rustic center designs of flowers, birds, houses, etc. Popular in the early 19th century, most was imported from England.

Related wares, called "stick spatter," had freehand designs applied with pieces of cut sponge attached to sticks, hence the name. Examples date from the 19th and early 20th century and were produced in England, Europe, and America.

Some early spatter-decorated wares were marked by the manufacturers, but not many. Twentieth century reproductions are also sometimes marked, including those produced by Boleslaw Cybis.

Five blue plates with similar six-pointed stars within white stars, England, second quarter 19th century, light staining, 8-1/2" dia........................... **$960**

Courtesy of Garth's Auctions, Inc.

Three rainbow handleless cups and saucers in red and yellow with thistle pattern, England, second quarter 19th century, stains, one saucer with hairline crack, another with discoloration, one cup with roughness to glaze, one cup with large flake on foot. **$1,320**

Courtesy of Garth's Auctions, Inc.

Octagonal platter with blue rim and center with peafowl decoration, England, second quarter 19th century, glaze flakes on underside of rim, 14" x 18". **$1,200**

Courtesy of Garth's Auctions, Inc.

Blue teapot and handleless cup and saucer with rooster decorations, England, second quarter 19th century, cup and saucer in good condition, teapot with repairs to circular foot and lower portion of lid, teapot 6"h.. **$720**

Courtesy of Garth's Auctions, Inc.

CERAMICS

spongeware

SPONGEWARE: THE NAME SAYS IT ALL. A sponge dipped in colored pigment is daubed onto a piece of earthenware pottery of a contrasting color, creating an overall mottled, "sponged" pattern. A clear glaze is applied, and the piece fired. The final product, with its seemingly random, somewhat smudged coloration, conveys an overall impression of handmade folk art.

Most spongeware, however, was factory-made from the mid-1800s well into the 1930s. Any folk art appeal was secondary, the result of design simplicity intended to facilitate maximum production at minimum cost. Although mass-manufacturing produced most spongeware, it did in fact originate in the work of independent potters. Glasgow, Scotland, circa 1835, is recognized as the birthplace of spongeware. The goal: the production of utilitarian everyday pottery with appeal to the budget-conscious. Sponged surface decorations were a means of adding visual interest both easily and inexpensively.

Since early spongeware was quickly made, usually by amateur artisans, the base pottery was often insubstantial and the sponging perfunctory. However, due to its general usefulness, and especially because of its low cost, spongeware quickly found an audience. Production spread across Great Britain and Europe, finally reaching the United States. Eventually, quality improved, as even frugal buyers demanded more for their money.

The terms "spongeware" and "spatterware" are often used interchangeably. Spatterware took its name from the initial means of application: A pipe was used to blow colored pigment onto a piece of pottery, creating a spattered coloration. Since the process was tedious, sponging soon became the preferred means of color application, although the "spatterware" designation remained in use. Specific patterns were achieved by means of sponge printing (aka "stick spatter"): A small piece of sponge was cut in the pattern shape desired, attached to a stick, then dipped in color. The stick served as a more precise means of application, giving the decorator more control, creating designs with greater border definition. Applied colors varied, with blue on white proving most popular. Other colors included red, black, green, pink, yellow, brown, tan, and purple.

Stoneware jug, late 19th century, with unusual blue sponge decoration, 11" h. **$738**

Courtesy of Pook & Pook, Inc.

Because of the overlap in style, there really is no right or wrong way to classify a particular object as "spongeware" or "spatterware"; often the manufacturer's advertising designation is the one used. Spatterware, however, has become more closely identified with pottery in which the mottled color pattern (whether spattered or sponged) surrounds a central image, either stamped or painted free-hand. Spongeware usually has no central image; the entire visual consists of the applied "splotching." Any break in that pattern comes in the form of contrasting bands, either in a solid color matching the mottling, or in a portion of the base earthenware kept free of applied color. Some spongeware pieces also carry stampings indicating the name of an

CERAMICS

Blue spongeware platter, 19th century, 13-1/4" w.............**$111**

Courtesy of Pook & Pook, Inc.

Brown and green spongeware mixing bowl, early 20th century, 5-1/2" h., 12-1/2" dia. **$221**

Courtesy of Pook & Pook, Inc.

Blue and white spongeware tulip plate, 19th century, 8-3/4" dia............................**$74**

Courtesy of Pook & Pook, Inc.

◄ Nest of three spongeware bowls, 19th century, largest 4-1/4" h., 11-1/4" dia. **$221**

Courtesy of Pook & Pook, Inc.

Two large salt-glazed spongeware bowls decorated in blue and white with scalloped banding, first quarter 20th century, 6" and 6-1/8" h.......**$81**

Courtesy of Jeffrey S. Evans & Associates

▶ Salt-glazed spongeware umbrella stand with blue and white banding, first quarter 20th century, 20-1/2" h. overall. **$46**

Courtesy of Jeffrey S. Evans & Associates

Twelve blue and white spongeware plates, 19th/20th century, 10" dia. **$357**

Courtesy of Pook & Pook, Inc.

advertiser, or the use intent of a specific object ("Butter," "Coffee," "1 Qt.").

Much of what is classified as spatterware has a certain delicacy of purpose: tea sets, cups and saucers, sugar bowls, and the like. Spongeware is more down-to-earth, both in intended usage and sturdiness. Among the many examples of no-nonsense spongeware: crocks, washbowl and pitcher sets, jugs, jars, canisters, soap dishes, shaving mugs, spittoons, umbrella stands, washboards, and even chamber pots. These are pottery pieces that mean business; their shapes, stylings, and simple decoration are devoid of fussiness.

Spongeware was usually a secondary operation for the many companies that produced it and was marketed as bargain-priced service ware; it's seldom marked. Today, spongeware is an ideal collectible for those whose taste in 19th century pottery veers away from the overly detailed and ornate. Spongeware's major appeal is due in large part to the minimalism it represents.

CERAMICS

staffordshire

STAFFORDSHIRE FIGURES AND groups made of pottery were produced by the majority of the Staffordshire, England, potters of the 19th century and were used as mantle decorations or "chimney ornaments," as they were sometimes called. Pairs of dogs were favorites and were turned out by the carload, and 19th century pieces are still readily available.

The process of transfer-printing designs on earthenware developed in England in the late 18th century, and by the mid-19th century most common ceramic wares were decorated in this manner, most often with romantic European or Asian landscape scenes, animals, or flowers. The earliest transferwares were printed in dark blue, but a little later light blue, pink, purple, red, black, green, and brown were used. A majority of these wares were produced at various English potteries right up until the turn of the 20th century, but French and other European firms also made similar pieces and all are quite collectible.

Well-painted reproductions abound, and collectors are urged to exercise caution before purchasing.

The best reference on this area is Petra Williams' *Staffordshire Romantic Transfer Patterns – Cup Plates and Early Victorian China* (Fountain House East, 1978).

Figure of Ben Franklin, 19th century, mismarked Washington, overall crazing, 16" h. **$1,573**

Courtesy of Cottone Auctions

Blue transfer Millennium platter, 19th century, 19" w. **$640**

Courtesy of Pook & Pook, Inc.

CERAMICS

Historical blue Peace and Plenty platter, 19th century, impressed Clews, 13" x 17". **$360**

Courtesy of Pook & Pook, Inc.

Historical blue View of Washington plate, 19th century, 7-3/4" dia. **$210**

Courtesy of Pook & Pook, Inc.

Two porcelain hen on nest dishes, 19th century, one with chicks emerging from eggs, 6" h. **$300**

Courtesy of Pook & Pook, Inc.

Three porcelain hen on nest dishes, 19th century, tallest 7" h. **$480**

Courtesy of Pook & Pook, Inc.

Blue transfer platter with English landscape scene, 19th century, 17" w. **$160**

Courtesy of Pook & Pook, Inc.

Historical blue View of Treton Falls plate, 19th century, impressed Wood & Son, 7-1/2" dia. **$240**

Courtesy of Pook & Pook, Inc.

Figural group 1861,
unrecorded form of Sir Richard
riding camel, 7" h. **$325**

Courtesy of Clars Auction Gallery, www.clars.com

Five pearlware figural groups: Two lions, one with crown, two cows
with calves, and courting couple, each in front of bocage tree,
largest 9" h..**$3,500**

Courtesy of Clars Auction Gallery, www.clars.com

Pearlware figural spill vase,
circa 1820, with courting
couples playing musical
instruments in naturalistic
setting, stepped rockwork
flanking hollow tree, faux
marble base, 11-1/4" h.... **$1,200**

Courtesy of Clars Auction Gallery, www.clars.com

Two pearlware groups emblematic of Britain, circa 1820, crowned
model of recumbent unicorn in front of bocage tree and spill vase
modeled as crowned arms of United Kingdom flanked by lion and
unicorn supports, above motto banner inscribed "Dieu et mon droit"
with rose and thistle, larger 6" h **$5,500**

Courtesy of Clars Auction Gallery, www.clars.com

Figural group of shepherd
and sheep resting beside tree
in naturalistic setting, base
with foliage and polychrome
decorated roses, 11" h........ **$850**

Courtesy of Clars Auction Gallery, www.clars.com

Two figural groups, circa 1840, each depicting Arab groom and
stallion on naturalistic base, each with Oliver-Sutton Antiques,
Kensington UK label to underside, 9" h.....................................**$1,700**

Courtesy of Clars Auction Gallery, www.clars.com

CERAMICS

Three pearlware figural groups of lovebirds seated on branches, one
spill vase with lambs in front, 8-1/4" h....................................**$2,000**

Courtesy of Clars Auction Gallery, www.clars.com

Baptism of Mary porcelain
table base attributed to
Obadiah Sherratt pottery,
early 18th century, enamel
colors on pearlware glaze with
bocage sprays on footed base,
8" h. x 8" w. **$5,500**

Courtesy of Clars Auction Gallery, www.clars.com

Pearlware bocage group, circa
1810, possibly Wood and
Caldwell, children playing
with dog on naturalistic base,
9-1/2" h. x 9" w. **$4,750**

Courtesy of Clars Auction Gallery, www.clars.com

Pearlware figural group of Walton
type, circa 1815, itinerant
entertainers, one playing bagpipes
beside three toy dogs in costumes
perfoming tricks, in front of
bocage tree, on naturalistic base,
9-1/4" h..............................**$4,500**

Courtesy of Clars Auction Gallery, www.clars.com

Urn in Neo-classical style, circa
1875, glazed in teal with relief
molded gilt ram's head masks
and white fruit swags, ribbons,
and musical trophies, on
circular foot resting on square
base centering reliefs of putti,
12" h. x 7" dia. **$225**

Courtesy of Clars Auction Gallery, www.clars.com

Three figural groups: Pair of spill vases decorated with hunting dogs
and figure of hunter carrying rabbits with gun at front, standing
beside seated hunting dog, largest 16" h. **$3,750**

Courtesy of Clars Auction Gallery, www.clars.com

CERAMICS

Pair of figural groups of birds of prey, one grasping baby in its talons, other one a sheep, each on naturalistic base, 12" h. **$475**

Courtesy of Clars Auction Gallery, www.clars.com

Pearlware figure of brown bear, circa 1770, on green glazed base, molded with flowers, 2-3/4" h.............**$600**

Courtesy of Clars Auction Gallery, www.clars.com

Four pearlware figures of Four Seasons, late 18th or early 19th century, Spring, Summer, Autumn, and Winter personified as young women, each with polychrome decoration on square plinth, with labels for British dealer Earle D. Vandekar of Knightsbridge, 9" h. x 3-3/4" sq.................. **$2,250**

Courtesy of Clars Auction Gallery, www.clars.com

Three figural ewers: Two decorated with black and white spaniels and Minton majolica cat-form jug, late 19th century, largest 9-1/2" h. **$6,000**

Courtesy of Clars Auction Gallery, www.clars.com

Four figural groups, each with lion sejant seated beside lamb on naturalistic base, two smaller and two larger pairs, 10-1/2" h. **$8,000**

Courtesy of Clars Auction Gallery, www.clars.com

Pair of whippets after Thomas Parr, each modeled as opposing recumbent figures beside captured hare, 6-1/4" h. x 10-1/2" w............................. **$688**

Courtesy of Neal Auction Co.

Pair of lions, 19th century, each set with glass eyes, polychrome decorated bodies in hunting pose, 11" h. x 16" w. **$500**

Courtesy of Clars Auction Gallery, www.clars.com

CERAMICS

teco pottery

TECO POTTERY WAS the line of art pottery introduced by the American Terra Cotta and Ceramic Co. of Terra Cotta (Crystal Lake), Illinois, in 1902. Founded by William D. Gates in 1881, American Terra Cotta originally produced only bricks and drain tile. Because of superior facilities for experimentation, including a chemical laboratory, the company was able to develop an art pottery line favoring a matte green glaze in the earlier years but eventually achieving a wide range of colors including a metallic luster glaze and a crystalline glaze. Although some hand-thrown pottery was made, Gates favored a molded ware because it was less expensive to produce. By 1923, Teco Pottery was no longer being made, and in 1930 American Terra Cotta and Ceramic Co. was sold. For more information on Teco Pottery, see *Teco: Art Pottery of the Prairie School* by Sharon S. Darling (Erie Art Museum, 1990).

Vase with green over speckled brown mat glazes, some crystallization in green glaze at shoulder of piece, impressed TECO twice on bottom, excellent original condition, 5-3/4" h. ...**$425**

Courtesy of Mark Mussio, Humler & Nolan

Vase in light green mat glaze, impressed twice on bottom with Teco logo, excellent original condition, 4-1/2" h. ... **$275**

Courtesy of Mark Mussio, Humler & Nolan

Small buttressed vase, circa 1910, stamped TECO, 6-1/2" x 4"......**$1,408**

Courtesy of Rago Arts, www.ragoarts.com

Rare, tall vase with cattails, R.A. Hirschfeld, circa 1910, stamped TECO, 12" x 5"..............**$8,320**

Courtesy of Rago Arts, www.ragoarts.com

Large buttressed bowl, circa 1910, stamped TECO, 6" x 12"......**$3,584**

Courtesy of Rago Arts, www.ragoarts.com

◄ Oil lamp with Pomegranate shade, circa 1910, with original oil font, leaded slag glass, patinated metal, glazed ceramic, base stamped TECO, shade with metal tag stamped TIFFANY STUDIOS NEW YORK, 23-1/2" x 16-1/2" overall, vase 10" x 7-1/2", shade 6-1/2" x 16".........**$6,400**

Courtesy of Rago Arts, www.ragoarts.com

CERAMICS

teplitz (amphora) pottery

ANTIQUE DEALERS AND collectors often refer to Art Nouveau-era art pottery produced in the kaolin-rich Turn-Teplitz region of Bohemia (today Teplice region, Czech Republic) collectively as Teplitz. Over the years, however, this area boasted many different potteries. To add to the confusion, they opened, closed, changed owners, merged or shared common designers against a background of changing political borders.

Although all produced pottery, their techniques and products varied. Some ceramicists, like Josef Strnact and Julius Dressler, produced brightly glazed faience and majolica earthenware items. According to Elizabeth Dalton, Furniture and Decorative Arts Specialist at Michaan's Auctions, a strong earthenware body, rather than delicate, brittle porcelain, allowed more unusual manipulation of the ceramic surface of their vases, flowerpots and tobacco jars.

Alfred Stellmacher, who founded the Imperial and Royal Porcelain Factory in 1859, produced fanciful, sculptural creations noted for their fine design and quality. Many feature applied natural motifs, Mucha and Klimt-like portraits or simulated jewels.

According to Stuart Slavid, vice president and director of European Furniture, Decorative Arts and Fine Ceramics at Skinner Auctions, "The most collectible Teplitz pieces of all are those manufactured by the Riessner, Stellmacher and Kessel Amphora Porcelain Works (RStK), which was founded in 1892."

Archeology and history buffs may recognize amphoras as ceramic vessels used for storage and transport in the ancient world. Art collectors and dealers, however, know amphoras as RStK pieces that incorporate undulating, asymmetrical Art Nouveau interpretations of flora and fauna — both natural and fanciful — in their designs. Many RStK artists honed their skills at the Teplitz Imperial Technical School for Ceramics and Associated Applied Arts. Others drew on the fine ceramics manufacturing tradition of nearby Dresden.

Producing Amphora was time-consuming and prohibitively

Bust of draped woman wearing foliate crown over integral square base, after 1900, impressed "4263," titled "Daphne" to base, 28-3/4" h. x 18-1/2" w. x 7-1/2" d. **$3,500**

Courtesy of John Moran Auctioneers, Inc.

CERAMICS

expensive. Each piece began with an artist's drawing, which would typically include lifelike images of snakes, sea creatures, dragons, maidens, flora or fauna. Once approved, each drawing was assigned a style number, which would subsequently appear on the bottom of identically shaped pieces, along with the word "Amphora."

Porcelain vase enamel-decorated with portrait of maiden, Riessner, Stellmacher & Kessel, circa 1900, red RSTK stamp, impressed Amphora with crown 320 41, touch-ups to gilding, 10-1/4" x 4-1/2"............. **$3,840**

Courtesy of Rago Arts, www.ragoarts.com

Using these drawings as their guide, craftsmen carved and fired clay models, from which they created smooth plaster-of-Paris molds. These molds were then lined with thin layers of clay. Once the clay dried and the molds removed, the resulting Amphoras were fine-carved, hand-painted and glazed. Finally they were refired, sometimes as many as 10 times. Since each was decorated in a unique way, no two Amphoras were exactly alike. Since their manufacture was so complex, reproducing one is nearly impossible.

RStK's innovative pieces earned international acclaim almost immediately. After winning prizes at both the Chicago and St. Louis World's Fairs, exclusive establishments, including Tiffany & Co., marketed them in the United States.

Although many Amphoras retail for under $1,000, some are quite costly. Rare, larger pieces, probably commissioned or created expressly for exhibition, were far more prone to breakage in production and display, so they command far more.

In addition to lavish Amphoras, Riessner, Stellmacher and Kessel also produced highly detailed, intricately crafted female busts, both large and small. Beautiful virgins, nymphs and dancers, reflecting fashionable literary, religious, and mythological motifs and themes of the day, were popular choices. Larger busts, because they were so complex and so rarely made, were expensive from the start. Today these 100-year-old beauties, especially those who escaped the ravages of time, are extremely desirable.

In 1894, leading Viennese porcelain retailer Ernst Wahliss purchased the RStK Amphora. Paul Dachsel, a company designer and Stellmacher's son-in-law, soon left to open his own pottery. Dachsel was known for adorning fairly simple forms with unique, intricate, stylized Art Nouveau embellishments, as well as modern-looking applied handles and rims. These, along with his Secessionist works — those influenced by Austrian exploration of innovative artistic forms outside academic and historical traditions — are highly collectible today.

After Wahliss' death, the Amphora Porcelain Works — now known as the Alexandra Porcelain Works Ernst Wahliss — became known for Serapis-Wahliss, its fine white earthenware line that features intricate, colorful, stylized natural forms.

When Stellmacher established his own company in 1905, the firm continued operating as the Riessner and Kessel Amphora Works. After Kessel left five years later, Amphora Werke Riessner, as it became known, continued to produce Amphora pottery through the 1940s. In 1945, Amphora Werke Riessner was nationalized by the Czechoslovakian government.

— Melody Amsel-Arieli

Figural vessel with dished base molded with vines and applied with poppies and draped figure of nymph, standing with one arm outstretched, her head crowned with poppies forming bowl, whole glazed in matte yellow and iridescent blue with green and gilt accents,1892-1905, printed red "RStK" mark for Riessner, Stellmacher and Kessel, impressed mark "Amphora" within oval, impressed "798," incised "H / III," 27-3/4" h. x 17" w. x 14" d. **$2,000**

Courtesy of John Moran Auctioneers, Inc.

Painted and gilt porcelain vase, circa 1910, with molded female busts with green hair protruding from lip rim and throughout vase, applied gilt flower and spiderweb with gilt details to front, on circular mahogany base, vase has been glued to base, surface wear commensurate with age, 14-1/8" h. **$3,750**

Courtesy of Heritage Auctions

Vase with leaves and four handles, Riessner, Stellmacher & Kessel, circa 1900, stamped AMPHORA AUSTRIA CROWN 3947 42, small fleck inside foot ring and small irregularity to rim, 10-1/4" x 5-1/2"........**$2,048**

Courtesy of Rago Arts, www.ragoarts.com

Vase with pierced rosebush rim, decorated on side with large butterfly in raised gold paste and colored enamels on gold and green ground, Reissner, Stellmacher and Kessel, early 20th century, small chip on foot, firing anomalies, 7" h. **$1,054**

Courtesy of Brunk Auctions

Centerpiece with round platform foot with wide cylindrical stem supporting round bowl with pulled lip and pulled loops around body, in mottled blue and white glaze, with three girls dancing around stem, girls in muted green glaze with gilded highlights, signed on underside "Amphora Austria 1318" with incised crown mark, very good to excellent condition, 11" h. x 9" dia............................ **$1,007**

Courtesy of James D. Julia Auctioneers, Fairfield, Maine, www.jamesdjulia.com

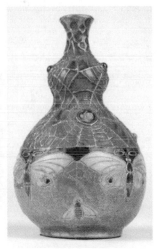

Vase of double-gourd form with short neck and flared lip, polychrome and gilt-decorated with moths beneath raised spiderwebs centered by "gres bijous" (porcelain "jewels") on iridescent blue-green ground, 1892-1918, impressed mark "Amphora" within oval, impressed "8777 / 25" and incised with heart-shaped mark, 7-3/4" h. x 4-1/2" dia.......................... **$600**

Courtesy of John Moran Auctioneers, Inc.

CERAMICS

Imperial vase molded with pelican heads and scrolls on neck and pairs of pelicans front and back of body among decorative motifs and textured ground, covered in gold and ruby luster, impressed mark "Imperial Amphora Turn" within medallion, Crown and "Amphora, Austria, 15002, 57" beneath, excellent original condition, 14-1/4" h. x 8-1/2" w. across base. **$600**

Courtesy of Mark Mussio, Humler & Nolan

Riessner, Stellmacher and Kessel "Allegory of Russia" vase with portrait of young woman, marked with red R.St. & K. ink stamp logo, excellent condition, some wear to gold trim, 6-1/8" h. **$1,200**

Courtesy of Mark Mussio, Humler & Nolan

Large porcelain vase enamel-decorated with maiden, Riessner, Stellmacher & Kessel, circa 1900, red RSTK stamp, small area of wear to gold inside rim, 10-3/4" x 8-1/4"............. **$3,584**

Courtesy of Rago Arts, www.ragoarts.com

Bust of young woman with iridescent glazes, after V. Pochini (Italian, 19th century), titled "Libellula" (genus of dragonfly) on rocky base, signed RStK for Reissner, Stellmacker, Kessel, old repair to end of ribbon, loss to end of cattail, 16" h. **$868**

Courtesy of Brunk Auctions

Vase decorated with raised designs and applied ceramic "jewels," gourd-form body rising to wide neck ending in crenellated mouth, 1898-1899, impressed marks "Amphora" and "Austria" within ovals, impressed "3668" and "55," gilt glaze fading to iridescent and matte purple nearer base, 13-1/2" h. x 7-3/4" w. x 6" d............... **$650**

Courtesy of John Moran Auctioneers, Inc.

Porcelain and enamel spiderweb vase, Riessner, Stellmacher & Kessler, circa 1905, gilt stylized handles and lip, neck with violet blossoms leading to painted and gilt spider to front and beetle with smaller bug stuck in web to verso, on molded and gilt foot, marks: RStK, TURN-TEPLITZ, BOHEMIA, MADE IN AUSTRIA, (impressed) 667, 49, AMPHORA, 6-1/8" h..... **$400**

Courtesy of Heritage Auctions

Porcelain and hardstone spiderweb jardinière, circa 1900, marks: (impressed crown), AMPHORA, AUSTRIA, 3655, 58, hairline crack to interior, 4" x 12-3/4" x 6-1/4".................... **$688**

Courtesy of Heritage Auctions

Figural, irregularly shaped, dished base ivory-glazed and molded with gilt-highlighted green-glazed irises entwining rim and figure of reclining maiden draped in polychrome-painted and gilt-patterned robe, hair ornamented with bird, raised left hand, circa 1910, impressed crown mark over impressed "Imperial Amphora / Turn" circular mark, impressed "Amphora" and "Austria" within ovals, "747" and "20," 18" h. x 20" w. x 12" d.................... **$1,100**

Courtesy of John Moran Auctioneers, Inc.

Pair of Reissner, Stellmacher & Kessler porcelain busts, circa 1900, marks to female: TURN-TEPLITZ BOHEMIA, R St. K., Made in Austria, 1005, surface scratches commensurate with age, each with small chips to protruding parts, 19-1/2" h............... **$500**

Courtesy of Heritage Auctions

Two items, first one constructed of twin bud vases, each of tapering ovoid form with flared, waved rims, connected at neck and body by four ceramic grapevine cordons impressed with Amphora crown mark and "Amphora" and "Austria" within ovals, impressed "3277" and "58"; second constructed of three matching ovoid bud vases with short necks rising to waved rims, arranged in triangular formation and connected at widest points by ceramic grapevine cordons; early 20th century, each glazed in mottled iridescent purple and blue with applied and gilt-highlighted grape leaves and green and purple grapes; first one 8" h. x 6-1/2" w. x 4-3/4" d., second one 4-1/2" h. x 6" dia.................... **$400**

Courtesy of John Moran Auctioneers, Inc.

Porcelain Art Nouveau-style figural bowl, Austria, late 19th century, gilt trimmed and enamel decorated model of nymph kneeling to front of lily plant-form bowl, printed mark, 19-1/2" l. x 11-1/2" h. **$800**

Courtesy of Skinner, Inc.; www.skinnerinc.com

CERAMICS

van briggle pottery

THE VAN BRIGGLE POTTERY was established by Artus Van Briggle, who formerly worked for Rookwood Pottery in Colorado Springs, Colorado at the turn of the 20th century. He died in 1904, but the pottery was carried on by his widow and others. From 1900 until 1920, the pieces were dated. It remains in production today, specializing in art pottery.

Pair of bear bookends in mulberry glaze, unmarked, one piece with two firing separations on plinth and glaze nicks, other piece with grinding chip at base, 4-1/4" h.........**$350**

Courtesy of Mark Mussio, Humler & Nolan

Ram on boulder bookend in purple mat glaze, possibly hand-modeled, incised with company logo within base, very good condition, thinness of glaze to high areas, 2" firing separation line inside bottom, 5" h. x 5-1/4" w. **$180**

Courtesy of Mark Mussio, Humler & Nolan

Bowl with molded clover design, 1907, reddish brown over green mat glazes, incised on bottom with company logo, Van Briggle, Colorado Springs, 1907, shape 499, finisher mark and finisher number, excellent original condition, 1-3/4" h., 5-1/2" dia. **$275**

Courtesy of Mark Mussio, Humler & Nolan

Heavy mug in light green mat finish, 1905, incised AA, Van Briggle, 1905 and 28 P, fine overall crazing, 5-1/4" h......**$120**

Courtesy of Mark Mussio, Humler & Nolan

Poppy plate in two-tone green mat glaze, 1912, incised AA, Van Briggle, Colo. Spgs. and 12, tight 2" line at rim, 8-1/2" dia..........................**$300**

Courtesy of Mark Mussio, Humler & Nolan

Early plate with five birds originating from swirl in dark maroon mat glaze, 1907-1912, marked with Van Briggle logo, Van Briggle Colo Spgs, and numbers 10 and 11, uncrazed with minor glaze skips on back edge, 6" ... **$300**

Courtesy of Mark Mussio, Humler & Nolan

Vintage tile carved with cardinal perched on leafy branch in natural mat glazes, unmarked, glaze bursts and minor roughness to edges, 6-1/4" sq. **$650**

Courtesy of Mark Mussio, Humler & Nolan

Bud vase with organic poppy design in green mat glaze, 1905, incised AA, Van Briggle, 1905, 326 with finisher's mark, 10-3/4" h. **$950**

Courtesy of Mark Mussio, Humler & Nolan

Early vase with embossed floral design in green mat glaze with crystallization, bottom marked with company logo, Van Briggle and 1904, excellent original condition, 5-5/8" h. **$600**

Courtesy of Mark Mussio, Humler & Nolan

Low vase with arrowroot decoration, green glaze over red clay body, only mark visible AA logo and faint "10," possibly 1907 to 1912 piece, excellent original condition, 4" h. x 6-1/2" w. **$850**

Courtesy of Mark Mussio, Humler & Nolan

Twin-handled vase with yucca leaf design in mulberry glaze, marked on bottom with company logo, Van Briggle and Colo. Sprgs., excellent original condition, 13" h. **$170**

Courtesy of Mark Mussio, Humler & Nolan

Vase in variegated shades of green mat glaze, dated 1905 or 1907, incised AA and Van Briggle along with date and obscure finisher's mark, excellent original condition with no crazing, 8-3/4" h. **$350**

Courtesy of Mark Mussio, Humler & Nolan

Vase in unusual form with stylized leaves in mulberry glaze, "dirty bottom" incised AA, Van Briggle and Colo. Spgs., excellent condition with some scattered crazing, 8-1/8" h. **$350**

Courtesy of Mark Mussio, Humler & Nolan

Vase with molded geometric design in white and purple mat glazes, 1906, marked on bottom with incised company logo, Van Briggle, date, 8 in circle, and impressed shape number 347, tight line inside vase does not break surface of exterior, 5-7/8" h. **$350**

Courtesy of Mark Mussio, Humler & Nolan

Large vase with leaves in curdled green glaze, 1914, incised AA 1914, 16" x 7". **$7,040**

Courtesy of Rago Arts, www.ragoarts.com

Early vase in light blue and green glaze, 1903, marked AA VAN BRIGGLE 1903, 8-1/2" x 7". ..**$2,432**

Courtesy of Rago Arts, www.ragoarts.com

Vase with poppy pods in ochre glaze, 1905, marked AA VAN BRIGGLE 340 1905 VX, 9" x 7-1/2". **$3,072**

Courtesy of Rago Arts, www.ragoarts.com

CERAMICS

wedgwood

IN 1754, JOSIAH WEDGWOOD and Thomas Whieldon of Fenton Vivian, Staffordshire, England, became partners in a pottery enterprise. Their products included marbled, agate, tortoiseshell, green glaze, and Egyptian black wares.

In 1759, Wedgwood opened his own pottery at the Ivy House works, Burslem. In 1764, he moved to the Brick House (Bell Works) at Burslem. The pottery concentrated on utilitarian pieces.

Between 1766 and 1769, Wedgwood built the famous works at Etruria. Among the most-renowned products of this plant were the Empress Catherina of Russia dinner service (1774) and the Portland Vase (1790s). The firm also made caneware, unglazed earthenwares (drabwares), piecrust wares, variegated and marbled wares, black basalt (developed in 1768), Queen's or creamware, and Jasperware (perfected in 1774).

Bone china was produced under the direction of Josiah Wedgwood II between 1812 and 1822, and was revived in 1878. Moonlight Lustre was made from 1805 to 1815. Fairyland Lustre began in 1920. All Lustre production ended in 1932.

A museum was established at the Etruria pottery in 1906. When Wedgwood moved to its modern plant at Barlaston, North Staffordshire, the museum was expanded.

Fairyland Lustre bowl with Picnic by River pattern on interior with fairies and imps by river with flowers and trees against Daylight Lustre background, exterior in Woodland Bridge pattern with trees, bridge, and fairies against Midnight Lustre background, signed on underside with gold Portland vase mark "Wedgwood, Made in England Z4968," very good to excellent condition, 8-1/8" dia. **$3,555**

Courtesy of James D. Julia Auctioneers, Fairfield, Maine, www.jamesdjulia.com

top lot

Christopher Dresser design terracotta fish vase, England, circa 1872, gilt trim and polychrome enamel decorated flat fish design to either side, impressed mark, 6-1/2" h. $23,370

Black basalt sphinxes, England, late 20th century, each atop raised rectangular base molded with hieroglyph border, impressed mark, 8-3/4" h. ... **$2,091**

Courtesy of Skinner, Inc.; www.skinnerinc.com

Black basalt Cupid and Psyche figures, England, circa 1900, each upon rock on circular base with molded band of palmettes, impressed mark, 8", 8-1/4" h. **$1,476**

Courtesy of Skinner, Inc.; www.skinnerinc.com

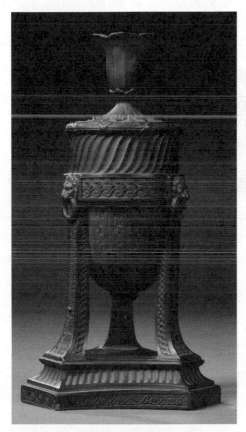

Three enameled black basalt tea wares, England, 19th century, impressed marks, each with polychrome and gilded flowers, covered teapot with ball finial, 8" l.; covered sugar bowl with Sybil finial, 5-1/4" h.; and cream jug, 4-1/8" h. **$554**

Courtesy of Skinner, Inc.; www.skinnerinc.com

Black basalt cassolette, England, early 19th century, cover with candle nozzle to one side and floral finial to reverse, bowl set on tripod base molded with foliage and set on triangular plinth, impressed mark, 11" h. with candle nozzle. **$800**

Courtesy of Skinner, Inc.; www.skinnerinc.com

Encaustic decorated black basalt sucrier and cover, England, 19th century, squat shape with loop handles, iron red and white decorated bands with florets between drapery swags, impressed mark, 4-1/2" dia. **$1,722**

Courtesy of Skinner, Inc.; www.skinnerinc.com

Fairyland Lustre lily tray with center medallion of "The King Watching Physicians Duel," medallion set against green iridescent glaze background with geometric gilded border, exterior finished in same glaze with matching geometric gilded band surrounding side, signed on underside with gold Portland vase mark "Wedgwood Made in England Z5494," very good to excellent condition, 6-1/8" dia. **$948**

Courtesy of James D. Julia Auctioneers, Fairfield, Maine, www.jamesdjulia.com

Fairyland Lustre commemorative bowl No. 1 in limited edition of 100, Woodland Bridge pattern against Daylight Lustre background on interior and against Midnight Lustre background on exterior, octagonal bowl marked on underside "Fairyland Lustre Woodland Bridge based upon original design by Daisy Makeig-Jones Wedgwood Designer 1914-1931 Number 1 in limited edition of 100 Wedgwood Bone China Made in England," with original fitted box, very good to excellent condition, 9" dia. at widest. **$3,088**

Courtesy of James D. Julia Auctioneers, Fairfield, Maine, www.jamesdjulia.com

◄ Fairyland Lustre covered vase in Candlemas pattern with three panels, each with lavender candle with woman's head against blue glaze background, each panel separated by green glaze vertical band with purple fairies, decorated cover with green flowers against blue background and black flame border with gilded trim, signed on underside in gold Portland vase mark "Wedgwood Made in England Z5461," very good to excellent condition, 9" h..... **$6,518**

Courtesy of James D. Julia Auctioneers, Fairfield, Maine, www.jamesdjulia.com

◄ Fairyland Lustre vase and cover, England, circa 1920, pattern Z5360 Ghostly Wood to flame sky, with coral enameling, printed factory mark, finial off and cleanly repaired, 11-1/4" h. **$15,600**

Courtesy of Skinner, Inc.; www.skinnerinc.com

Moonlight Lustre nautilus shell and stand, England, early 19th century, purple, pink, and orange glazes, impressed mark, shell in very good condition, stand with 4-1/2" two-part piece cut from one end and reglued, shell 10-1/4" l., dish 11-3/8" l. **$1,140**

Courtesy of Skinner, Inc.; www.skinnerinc.com

Dark blue Jasper dip pendant/ brooch, England, late 19th century, roundel decorated in white relief with putti holding stag head, impressed mark, set in silver frame, 2-7/8" dia...... **$677**

Courtesy of Skinner, Inc.; www.skinnerinc.com

Pair of dark blue Jasper dip candlesticks, England, early 19th century, columnar shape with applied white angular bands of foliage, impressed mark, 7-7/8" h. **$923**

Courtesy of Skinner, Inc.; www.skinnerinc.com

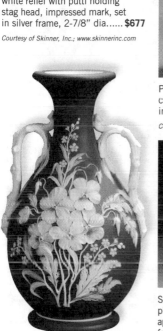

Free-form relief dark blue Jasper dip vase, England, mid-19th century, bottle shape with branch handles, floral and foliate decoration to either side, impressed mark, 10" h. ... **$4,305**

Courtesy of Skinner, Inc.; www.skinnerinc.com

▶ Solid light blue Jasper vase and cover, England, 19th century, applied white relief with lovebird finial and bands of arabesque flowers above shell border, impressed mark, 7" h. **$431**

Courtesy of Skinner, Inc.; www.skinnerinc.com

Solid light blue Jasper trophy plate, England, 19th century, applied white classical figures with fruiting festoons terminating at ram's heads and with trophy drops, impressed mark, 8" dia. **$523**

Courtesy of Skinner, Inc.; www.skinnerinc.com

Dark blue Jasper dip oenochoe ewer, England, early 19th century, foliate molded loop handle terminating at female mask head, body with applied white classical figures in relief, atop raised square plinth with florets and foliage, impressed mark, 14-1/4" h. **$2,337**

Courtesy of Skinner, Inc.; www.skinnerinc.com

CERAMICS

Pair of dark blue Jasper dip vases, England, 19th century, white free-form relief with white twig-form bail handles and flowers in high relief, impressed mark, 10-1/2" h., 10-7/8" h. **$5,228**

Courtesy of Skinner, Inc.; www.skinnerinc.com

▶ Solid black Jasper Portland vase, England, late 19th century, applied white classical figures, man wearing Phrygian cap below base, impressed mark, 9-3/4" h. **$800**

Courtesy of Skinner, Inc.; www.skinnerinc.com

Black Jasper dip vase and cover, England, 19th century, scrolled foliate handles, applied white classical medallions below floral festoons with band of zodiac motifs to shoulder, impressed mark, 12-1/2" h. **$1,722**

Courtesy of Skinner, Inc.; www.skinnerinc.com

Pair of three-color Jasper dip vases and covers, England, late 19th century, each cup-form with bell-shaped cover, wide center band lilac ground bordered in green and with applied white classical figures and foliage in relief, impressed marks, 8" h.............. **$3,075**

Courtesy of Skinner, Inc.; www.skinnerinc.com

Three-color Jasper torches vase and cover, England, 19th century, lovebird finial, solid white body with applied green torches and foliate borders, topped with blue flames and rope bands, impressed mark, 8-3/8" h. **$4,613**

Courtesy of Skinner, Inc.; www.skinnerinc.com

Rosso Antico incense burner and cover, England, early 19th century, applied black basalt foliate relief to pierced lid, bowl with foliate festoons and set atop tails of three dolphins mounted on triangular base, impressed mark, cover: finial replaced, small break and loss to open trellis, burner: slight chips to tip of one tail and to lips of one dolphin; 5-1/2" h.................. **$1,020**

Courtesy of Skinner, Inc.; www.skinnerinc.com

Three-piece Rosso Antico Egyptian tea set, England, 19th century, each with applied black hieroglyphs above meandering bands, impressed marks, crocodile finials to covered teapot, 3-7/8 h.; covered sugar bowl, 3-5/8 h.; and creamer, handle 2-3/4" h......**$2,091**

Courtesy of Skinner, Inc.; www.skinnerinc.com

Rosso Antico dolphin incense burner, England, early 19th century, bowl with black relief and supported atop three dolphin feet set on triangular base, with pierced cover and insert disc, impressed mark, 5-3/8" h. ...**$1,353**

Courtesy of Skinner, Inc.; www.skinnerinc.com

▲ Rosso Antico potpourri vase, England, late 18th century, slightly tapering sides with engine-turned dicing to black wash, meander and floret borders, with pierced lid, impressed mark, 5-7/8" h....**$1,107**

Courtesy of Skinner, Inc.; www.skinnerinc.com

◄ Rosso Antico Egyptian plate, England, early 19th century, applied white hieroglyph border in relief, impressed mark, 7" dia................................**$923**

Courtesy of Skinner, Inc.; www.skinnerinc.com

Three-color white smear glazed stoneware potpourri vase and cover, England, circa 1820, lilac bellflowers with alternating green acanthus leaves and fruiting grapevine border, impressed mark, 5" h. **$431**

Courtesy of Skinner, Inc.; www.skinnerinc.com

CERAMICS

CERAMICS

weller pottery

WELLER POTTERY WAS made from 1872 to 1945 at a pottery established originally by Samuel A. Weller at Fultonham, Ohio. It moved to Zanesville, Ohio in 1882.

Weller's famous pottery slugged it out with several other important Zanesville potteries for decades. Cross-town rivals such as Roseville, Owens, La Moro, and McCoy were all serious fish in a fairly small and well-stocked lake. While Weller occasionally landed some solid body punches with many of his better art lines, the prevailing thought was that his later production ware just wasn't up to snuff.

Samuel Weller was a notorious copier and, it is said, a bit of a scallywag. He paid designers such as William Long to bring their famous discoveries to Zanesville. He then attempted to steal their secrets, and, when successful, renamed them and made them his own.

After World War I, when the cost of materials became less expensive than the cost of labor, many companies, including the famous Rookwood Pottery, increased their output of less expensive production ware. Weller Pottery followed along in the trend of production ware by introducing scores of interesting and unique lines, the likes of which have never been created anywhere else, before or since.

In addition to a number of noteworthy production lines, Weller continued in the creation of hand-painted ware long after Roseville abandoned them. Some of the more interesting Hudson pieces, for example, are post-World War I pieces. Even later lines, such as Bonito, were hand painted and often signed by important artists such as Hester Pillsbury. The closer you look at Weller's output after 1920, the more obvious the fact that it was the only Zanesville company still producing both quality art ware and quality production ware.

For more information on Weller pottery, see *Warman's Weller Pottery Identification and Price Guide* by Denise Rago and David Rago.

FAR RIGHT Chase vase with molded scene of fox hunter on horseback with dogs, all covered in white glaze against deep blue ground, marked on bottom with Weller Pottery in script, impressed H and 3 in black slip, fine crazing in areas of white glaze. **$150**

Courtesy of Mark Mussio, Humler & Nolan

RIGHT Camelot bud vase in yellow and white glaze with coiled tendril design, impressed Weller beneath, dark crazing, otherwise excellent original condition, 4-1/4" h............. **$225**

Courtesy of Mark Mussio, Humler & Nolan

Coppertone-glazed simple form vase, incised "Weller Hand Made" with initial B on bottom, two small skips at rim, 5-7/8" h. **$120**

Courtesy of Mark Mussio, Humler & Nolan

Cretone vase with gazelles, leaves, and flowers in brown slip against yellow ground, by artist Hester Pillsbury, marked on bottom with script "Weller Pottery" with artist's initials in brown slip on side of piece, fine overall crazing and small glaze chips at base, 8-1/4" h. **$90**

Courtesy of Mark Mussio, Humler & Nolan

Dickensware vase with jonquils, impressed on bottom "Weller Dickens Ware" and "324," fine overall crazing, 10-3/4" h.... **$200**

Courtesy of Mark Mussio, Humler & Nolan

Dickensware vase with scene of maiden, castle, and three white knights on horseback, marked "Weller Dickens Ware" on bottom with label from White Pillars Museum, fine overall crazing, rough areas at rim, 14-1/2" h. **$1,500**

Courtesy of Mark Mussio, Humler & Nolan

Eocean vase with leafy woodbine sprig and berries by Levi J. Burgess, autumnal leaves against dappled blue over pink backdrop, initialed on side, incised "Eocean Weller" with numbers, excellent condition, 11" h. **$400**

Courtesy of Mark Mussio, Humler & Nolan

Eocean four-side "twist" vase decorated with pansy flower heads falling on two sides, artist signature obscured by glaze, excellent condition, 6-3/8" h. **$170**

Courtesy of Mark Mussio, Humler & Nolan

top lot

Rare Etruscan jardinière by decorator Fredrick Hurten Rhead, terra cotta vessel with ebony glazed backdrop with design of classical warriors within wreath of hearts encircling rim and base, signed beneath base in black slip "Etruscan" and "Rhead" with incised number 100/2, 6-7/8" h..............$1,800

COURTESY OF MARK MUSSIO, HUMLER & NOLAN

Eocean vase with solitary fish, incised on bottom "Weller" and "Eocean" and impressed "9055," fine overall crazing, 4-5/8" h. **$350**

Courtesy of Mark Mussio, Humler & Nolan

Etched Matt Sunflower jardiniere on pedestal, signed by Frank Ferrell, 10" jardiniere with inscribed signature of artist, tight line at rim of jardiniere and top of pedestal, combined 31" h. **$450**

Courtesy of Mark Mussio, Humler & Nolan

Hudson vase with wild rose decoration by artist Hester Pillsbury, signed on side by artist and incised "Weller Pottery" on bottom, small chip and bruise on base, 8-7/8" h.................**$160**

Courtesy of Mark Mussio, Humler & Nolan

Hudson vase with lilac decoration, possibly experimental piece, by Sarah Reid McLaughlin, flowers in pink, blue and white extend from bottom to top of vase, glaze with faint crazing, marked Weller in large block letters and incised "1-X" on bottom, indicating an experiment by McLaughlin or Weller or both, 13-1/2" h. **$325**

Courtesy of Mark Mussio, Humler & Nolan

LaSa scenic vase with trees in foreground and purple mountains against red and gold sky, signed Weller LaSa on side, excellent original condition, 5-3/4" h.............**$275**

Courtesy of Mark Mussio, Humler & Nolan

Lebanon or Burntwood vase of spring plowing by teams of oxen guided by Egyptian workers, finger scrolls decorate shoulder and lower body, chip on rim and some nicks, 9-7/8" h.............**$100**

Courtesy of Mark Mussio, Humler & Nolan

Louwelsa portrait mug by E. Sulcer with visage of Native American with long hair and buckskin attire, artist's name appears below handle, painted in brown slip, base impressed with circular "Louwelsa Weller" logo and shape 562, fine overall crazing, repair at rim, 5-3/4" h. **$250**

Courtesy of Mark Mussio, Humler & Nolan

Tall Louwelsa vase with yellowish and reddish nasturtiums and foliage arranged at top, unmarked, excellent condition, 13-1/4" h.............................**$200**

Courtesy of Mark Mussio, Humler & Nolan

CERAMICS

Blue Louwelsa vase with cherries, impressed on bottom "Weller Louwelsa X 519," fine overall crazing, 5-3/8" h...... **$300**

Courtesy of Mark Mussio, Humler & Nolan

Louwelsa ewer with pansies by artist Madge Hurst, impressed on bottom with circular Weller Louwelsa stamp and artist's signature near base, glaze chip on handle, crazing and burst glaze bubbles on back side of piece, 14-1/4" h. **$110**

Courtesy of Mark Mussio, Humler & Nolan

Marengo orange six-sided vase, overall crazing with spots of white within orange iridescent glaze, faint Weller mark on bottom, 8-1/4" h. **$160**

Courtesy of Mark Mussio, Humler & Nolan

◄ Matt Green vase with twisted fabric-like body, patina-like glaze, excellent original condition, 6" h................... **$400**

Courtesy of Mark Mussio, Humler & Nolan

◄ Matt Green urn with berry and leaf band, attached to four-leg stand, stand with minor glaze miss on side and flat glaze chip beneath, 7-3/4" h........**$375**

Courtesy of Mark Mussio, Humler & Nolan

▲ Matt ware vase with white daisies and green stems against mottled pink ground, impressed Weller mark on bottom, light overall crazing, 3-1/4" h......**$250**

Courtesy of Mark Mussio, Humler & Nolan

Matt ware two-handled vase with embossed holly decoration in dark green and red on light green ground, impressed Weller mark in small block letters, overall crazing, 4-3/4" h......**$275**

Courtesy of Mark Mussio, Humler & Nolan

▲ Matt ware handled vase with holly leaves and berries surrounding base, impressed "Weller" in medium block letters, mottled glaze of red and green over blue, excellent original condition, 4-5/8" h.....................**$250**

Courtesy of Mark Mussio, Humler & Nolan

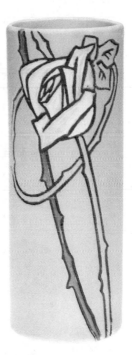

◄ Roma jardinière cast with repeating scene of pair of foxes and treed rooster and three hens, unmarked with fine overall crazing, 8-1/2" h., 10" dia................**$190**

Courtesy of Mark Mussio, Humler & Nolan

▲ Modeled etched matt vase with stems and single white rose against yellow ground, incised Weller on base, fine overall crazing, 8-1/2" h. **$300**

Courtesy of Mark Mussio, Humler & Nolan

CERAMICS

zsolnay

ZSOLNAY POTTERY WAS made in Pecs, Hungary, in a factory founded in 1862 by Vilmos Zsolnay. Utilitarian earthenware was originally produced with an increase in art pottery production from as early as 1870. The highest level of production employed more than 1,000 workers.

The Art Nouveau era produced the most collectible and valuable pieces in today's marketplace. Examples are displayed in major art museums worldwide. Zsolnay is always well marked and easy to identify. One specialty was the metallic eosin glaze.

With more than 10,000 different forms created over the years, and dozens of glaze variations for each form, there is always something new being discovered in Zsolnay. Today the original factory size has been significantly reduced with pieces being made in a new factory.

Plaque with nude maidens and satyr, Lajos Mack (attr.), eosin glaze, circa 1900, raised five churches seal, stamped 6873/36/0, restoration to several areas, 13" dia. **$2,176**

Courtesy of Rago Arts, www.ragoarts.com

Large bowl with two parrots, marbleized and red eosin glaze, circa 1930, gold five churches mark, stamped MADE IN HUNGARY, incised 8805E, overall excellent condition, 6-1/2" x 15". .. **$1,664**

Courtesy of Rago Arts, www.ragoarts.com

VISIT WWW.ANTIQUETRADER.COM

WWW.FACEBOOK.COM/ANTIQUETRADER

Pecs ceramic figural dish, post-1940, marks: ZSOLNAY HUNGARY, 1868, PÉCS, HAND PAINTED (gold mark), 3-1/8" x 11-5/8" x 11-1/4".............. **$500**

Courtesy of Heritage Auctions

Lustre ceramic fish bowl, circa 1906-1910, marks: ZSOLNAY, PECS (impressed five tower mark), 8221, 36, 3-1/2" h., 5-1/8" dia...................... **$2,500**

Courtesy of Heritage Auctions

Eosin-glazed figural in form of steeple with animal head fountains on each corner, marked with gold ink stamp "Zsolnay Pecs Made in Hungary," excellent original condition, 5-3/8" h............. **$150**

Courtesy of Mark Mussio, Humler & Nolan

Iridescent pitcher with two women, early 20th century, signed "Zsolnay Hungary," 6-1/2" h. **$333**

Courtesy of Cottone Auctions

"Wave" vase with figures of mermaid and merman reaching for catfish on ocean surface, another catfish on obverse, marked "Made in Hungary, Zsolnay Pecs" with five churches mark and unreadable pressed marks under glaze, excellent condition, 8-1/2" x 10" w. **$2,500**

Courtesy of Mark Mussio, Humler & Nolan

Gourd vase in red glaze with figure of nude maiden leaning over rim, glaze on maiden in mat-like finish, vase glossy, circular raised Zsolnay logo and impressed numbers beneath, very good condition, 8" h. ... **$800**

Courtesy of Mark Mussio, Humler & Nolan

Ceramic figure of man in hat and cloak seated beneath tree stump playing flute, circa 1930, marks: 9412 E, (five tower, shield mark), 8-1/4" h. **$250**

Courtesy of Heritage Auctions

Lustre ceramic figural water pitcher, circa 1902-1904, marks: ZSOLNAY, PECS (impressed five tower mark), 7117, 13-3/4" h. **$5,750**

Courtesy of Heritage Auctions

top lot

Rare cobra plate, eosin glaze, circa 1900, raised five churches seal, incised 8900, overall very good condition, small flecks inside foot ring and to high points, minor shallow scratches, 3" x 13"......................... **$33,280**

Iridescent decorated vase, early 20th century, footed bulbous form with stylized floral motifs and geometric neoclassical borders, five church steeples over ZSOLNAY PECS in circle, glaze on shoulder with slight wear, firing anomalies, 10-3/4" h. **$2,356**

Courtesy of Brunk Auctions

Two centerpieces, early 20th century, green iridescent-glazed example with four maidens, impressed seal and "No. S882"(?), small chip with retouch at maiden's toe, glaze roughness and possible retouch at another maiden's foot, other light surface wear and crazing, 7-1/4" x 10"; and figure of mother and child at fountain's edge with flowers on iridescent blue ground, underside with seal mark for Zsolnay, good condition, light surface wear and scratches, 7" x 15". **$4,712**

Courtesy of Brunk Auctions

Stoneware jardinière, circa 1900, probably by Sandor A. Pati, low-relief hunt scene of hounds chasing rabbit through trees, red glaze outside, green glaze inside, relief five church steeples mark on bottom, scratches in exterior glaze, interior crazed, 7-3/4" h. **$2,480**

Courtesy of Brunk Auctions

Pair of massive vases, marbleized eosin glaze, circa 1900, both with raised five churches seal, stamped 19, one vase in excellent condition, other with extensive professional restoration, 21" x 10". **$2,432**

Courtesy of Rago Arts, www.ragoarts.com

Rare plaque of chameleon on branch and lidded vessel with snake, eosin glaze, 1900/1911; plaque with original paper label, stamped ZSOLNAY PECS 6411 on reverse, incised CHAMALEON and illegible artist cipher to front; vessel with five churches mark and MADE IN HUNGARY, overall excellent condition, lid of vessel possibly associated, 4-1/2" dia. **$1,664**

Courtesy of Rago Arts, www.ragoarts.com

CHRISTMAS COLLECTIBLES

CHRISTMAS COLLECTIBLES REPRESENT the Christian holiday celebrating the birth of Jesus Christ. Collectibles include ornaments, kugels, feather trees, candy containers, household décor, art, games, cards, and a plethora of other items from every corner of the world.

Original Christmas card art signed by Art Riley, 1950s, gouache and tempera on 13" x 16" paper, fine condition. Riley joined Disney Studios as a background artist in 1938 and created a series of Christmas card paintings for California Artists Christmas cards....**$10,000**

Courtesy of Profiles in History

Four vintage blown glass Christmas tree ornaments, two comic strip characters from 1880s, two pipe-shaped ornaments, normal expected wear. **$650**

Courtesy of Woody Auction

German feather Christmas tree with round wooden base, some losses, 46" h...................... **$350**

Courtesy of Strawser Auctions

VISIT WWW.ANTIQUETRADER.COM

WWW.FACEBOOK.COM/ANTIQUETRADER

1930s Coca-Cola Christmas carriers, moderate wear and soiling on better carrier, heavier on lesser carrier, very good to excellent condition, larger carrier 7-1/2" l... **$100**

Courtesy of Morphy Auctions

Blue Roseville Futura Christmas Tree vase, original Roseville black paper label, excellent condition, 10-1/2" h. **$850**

Courtesy of Morphy Auctions

Original production cel from "How the Grinch Stole Christmas!" (MGM Studios, 1966), untrimmed animation cel, very fine condition, image 8-1/2" x 5", 10-1/2" x 12-1/2" on color copy background..............**$1,700**

Courtesy of Profiles in History

Pressed cardboard Santa roly poly Christmas tree ornament, Germany, Dresden trim body, composition face with rabbit fur beard, holding feather tree sprig, 7" l. **$175**

Courtesy of Bertoia Auctions

Popeye Christmas tree set with box, Mazda Lamps, plastic shades with decals, not tested, some wear to decals, tearing to box, box 6" x 16-1/4" l. **$375**

Courtesy of Bertoia Auctions

Pair of cobalt-colored grape-form kugels, 6" l **$1,094**

Courtesy of Pook & Pook, Inc.

KUGELS

A kugel – the German word for sphere or ball – is a traditional holiday and even year-round decoration originating in central Europe. First invented by craftsmen in Germany in the Biedermeier period, about 1830, these hollow glass ball ornaments didn't appear in the United States until the late 1800s, where they are often called "friendship balls."

The hole left in the glassblowing process is filled with an ornamental brass cap and fastened to the ball with twisted wire, allowing for ease of hanging. The earliest kugels were thick-walled and too heavy to hang on the branches of a tree; instead, they were often hung from the ceiling. Smaller, lighter ornaments were later created to adorn the tannenbaum, sometimes in the shapes of fruits.

The invention of the Bunsen burner in 1855 allowed glassblowers to craft much thinner-walled creations. Modern glass artisans continue to create one-of-a-kind kugels in a full spectrum of colors and broad range of shapes.

According to The Golden Glow of Christmas Past, a non-profit group dedicated to studying the historical and educational background of antique and vintage Christmas items prior to 1966, you should learn as much as you can about kugels before you begin investing in them.

Large ribbed kugel, silver color, excellent condition, 4" h. **$741**

Courtesy of Bertoia Auctions

Five grape-form kugels, Germany, late 19th century, largest 7". **$188**

Courtesy of Rago Arts, www.ragoarts.com

Three silver kugels in assorted sizes and shapes, good to very good condition, some minor areas of finish loss, 2" to 5" l. **$463**

Courtesy of Bertoia Auctions

Color and form are the keys to desirability and value. The Golden Glow maintains balls are the most common kugel form, but an amethyst-colored ball would be uncommon. Grapes are the next most common shape. They were blown in many different molded patterns with the rarest being red and amethyst grapes. Free blown shapes like eggs, pears, and teardrops are more desirable, especially in more uncommon colors like red and amethyst. Some eggs and balls were blown in a ribbed design that is highly sought after. Rare and hard-to-find shapes include artichokes, berry clusters, pinecones, and other fruit shapes that were mold blown.

The Golden Glow of Christmas Past is a wealth of information on many Christmas-related collectibles, including angels, belsnickles, books, candy containers, postcards and cards, clip-on ornaments, feather trees, candy and chocolate molds, nativity figures, Victorian ornaments and more.

Each year in July, the group holds a convention in a different host city in the United States, which is attended by approximately 600 dedicated Christmas enthusiasts from around the world. Convention activities include an auction, sales room, lectures, workshops, roundtable discussions, expert panels, displays of members' collections, and more.

"For collectors of antique Christmas, there is no better opportunity to add to their collections than at a Glow convention," says Golden Glow spokesman Bill Steely. "There is a wide variety of Christmas available to sell or purchase from many different time periods. No matter what your collecting interest, you will find something rare at a Glow convention."

— *Karen Knapstein*

CHRISTMAS

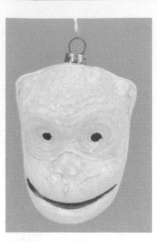

Blown glass chimpanzee ornament, excellent condition, 2-1/2" l............................ **$400**

Courtesy of Bertoia Auctions

Eight vintage Christmas tree ornament gift pockets with cardboard Santa cut-outs and miscellaneous designs, normal expected wear. **$225**

Courtesy of Woody Auction

Composition Father Christmas in red fur-trimmed robe, feather tree sprig in arm, stern facial expression, excellent condition, 12" h. **$1,700**

Courtesy of Bertoia Auctions

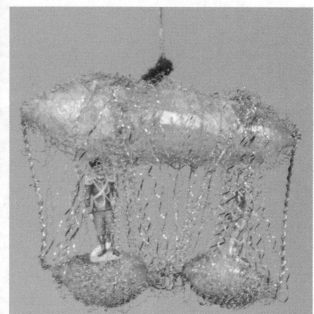

Zeppelin with two baskets ornament, wire wrap, blown glass airship with two suspended baskets with Prussian soldiers, very good to excellent condition, some loss of paint to airship, 5-1/2" l........... **$325**

Courtesy of Bertoia Auctions

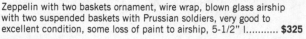

◄ Composition St. Nicholas, Germany, in wine-color robe with hood decorated with holly and berries, folded arms hold red berry-tipped feather tree, base of candy container sleeve reglued to legs, overall crazing, 19"..**$4,750**

Courtesy of Bertoia Auctions

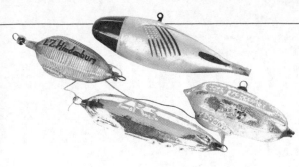

◀ Saint Nicholas in long red fur robe, composition face, full rabbit fur beard, articulated arms, composition hands, holding paper feather tree with candles, mounted on snow-covered wood platform base, Germany, excellent condition, 16-1/2" h. **$1,700**

Courtesy of Bertoia Auctions

▲ Four vintage blown glass Christmas tree ornaments: Hindenberg, Graf Zeppelin, Los Angeles Air Ship, and Stars & Stripes decorated air ship, normal expected wear.......... **$250**

Courtesy of Woody Auction

Composition Santa in red top and blue pants on lichen-trimmed wicker sleigh loaded with Christmas toys and feather tree, very good to excellent condition, Santa with one loose boot, 24" overall. **$750**

Courtesy of Bertoia Auctions

Early faux book Merry Christmas cigar box, signed Schmitt & Co., inside label with girl and "Holiday Greetings," near mint condition, light wear, 9-1/4" l.......**$100**

Courtesy of Morphy Auctions

Christmas peanut butter pail with bail handle, pre-1900, children sledding in Christmas scene, excellent-plus condition, 3-1/4" h. **$100**

Courtesy of Morphy Auctions

top lot

"The Day After Christmas" oil painting, George Hinke, first published by *Ideals Magazine* to accompany story "Jolly Old Santa Claus" in 1961, fine condition, 25-1/2" x 15-3/4" artists' board. George Hinke (1883-1953) was a German-born painter who came to the United States in 1923. After working in a printing shop, he eventually opened his own studio. From 1944 until his death in 1953, he was commissioned by *Ideals Magazine* to create works for publication depicting American small-town life, religious scenes, and Christmas themes in his classic nostalgic style.. $95,000

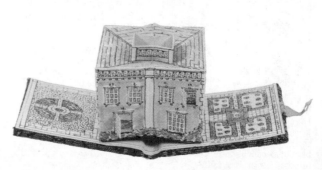

Christmas Dinner: An ABC Advent Calendar, miniature, illustrated by Maryline Poole Adams, brocade cover, gilt hinge, pictorial cover label, no. 8 of 100 copies, with signature of Adams on rear paste-down, light wear to covers, one side coming apart where glued together, near fine condition, 70mm x 76mm. $110

Courtesy of PBA Galleries

Cardboard Jack Frost Beverages Christmas sign, very good condition, edge bumping and some creases, 15" l. $50

Courtesy of Morphy Auctions

Thirteen Lalique annual Christmas plates in original boxes, France, 1970-1976, all marked, 8-1/2" dia. $250

Courtesy of Rago Arts, www.ragoarts.com

1942 Christmas Santa stand-up displays, moderate bumping and minor creasing, very good condition, 18" l. ... $150

Courtesy of Morphy Auctions

Early German Belsnickle in long robe trimmed in white, composition face with rabbit fur beard, basket of glass balls on one arm, multi-branch feather tree in other hand, very good to excellent condition, minor flaking near top of boots, 15" h. $3,250

Courtesy of Bertoia Auctions

Large German Santa Claus candy container with glass beard, Gottlieb Zinner & Söhne of Schalkau, Thuringia, papier-mâché and composition figure in mica-flecked dark purple robe with holly leaves and berries decorating hood, painted blue eyes, glass icicle beard, holding Christmas tree on his shoulder, separates at waist, 19-3/4" h. without tree. .... $13,000-$20,000

Courtesy of Auction Team Breker

Cast iron poinsettia Christmas tree stand, painted red, green, and white with applied mica, touch-up to paint, needs rewiring, good condition, 6-1/8" h. x 13" dia............... $25

Courtesy of Morphy Auctions

CIRCUS COLLECTIBLES

THE 200TH ANNIVERSARY of Phineas Taylor Barnum's birth in 2010 triggered a renewed interest in collecting circus memorabilia. Collectibles range from broadsides announcing the circus is coming to town, to banners with brightly embellished visages of freakish sideshow acts, to windup tin toys depicting the lions, tigers, elephants, and clowns that no circus or sideshow would be complete without.

Coca-Cola Circus Cutout sheet, 1932, 15" l. **$120**

Courtesy of Morphy Auctions

World's Greatest Circus child's pedal car with cage, restored, red with yellow pinstriping and tiger, clown, and lion stickers, 53" x 18". **$300**

Courtesy of Morphy Auctions

VISIT WWW.ANTIQUETRADER.COM

WWW.FACEBOOK.COM/ANTIQUETRADER

Hubley Royal Circus cage wagon, cast iron, blue cage-style body, marquee sides read "Royal Circus," yellow spoke wheels and hitch, drawn by two black horses trimmed in red and gold, 15-1/2" l..... **$309**

Courtesy of Bertoia Auctions

Etched circus goats and ringmaster goblet, colorless, deep bowl with circus gentleman with hat and mug of beer, flanked by two goats with one leg raised on barrel, 19th century, 6-7/8" h............... **$360**

Courtesy of Jeffrey S. Evans & Associates

Circus Boy tin toy, Japan, lithographed tin, young boy in colorful outfit holding circus placard and bell in hand that rings when clockwork is activated, with original box, 6-1/4" h. **$185**

Courtesy of Bertoia Auctions

Fisher-Price circus wagon, #156, circa 1942, long calliope wagon with ringmaster, keyboard and tall pipes, emits sounds while man plays instrument, 13" l..................**$93**

Courtesy of Bertoia Auctions

Buddy L Wild Animal Circus Truck, pressed steel, clear plastic top, plastic side gates housing lion and tiger, six Buddy L tires with "B" wheels, 25" l. **$210**

Courtesy of Morphy Auctions

top lot

Large metal Barnum and Bailey circus elephant sign, very good condition, some old repaint, metal damage near tusks, between Barnum and Bailey and legs, seven small holes, 96" x 72". $8,775

Lionel Mickey Mouse Circus Train, No. 1536, with wind-up Lionel Lines engine, Mickey Mouse stoker tender, and three circus cars: band car, circus car and dining car, excellent condition, 17" l............... **$1,800**

Hubley calliope circus wagon, circa 1920s, heavily embossed open body with interior bells and cast organ pipes on sides, painted blue with gold trim, black parade horses, ornate red and gold spoke wheels, 16" l. **$1,359**
Courtesy of Bertoia Auctions

Buddy L Wild Animal Circus truck with original box, No. 5477, circa 1969, pressed steel, red cab pulls long cage-sided body housing three plastic animals, ornately embossed, with decals, 26" l. **$463**
Courtesy of Bertoia Auctions

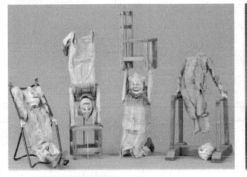

Auto Circus Performing Clowns in cloth outfits, hand-painted composition heads, each able to stand on wood chairs, ladder, 10" l. **$400**
Courtesy of Bertoia Auctions

Schoenhut Cracker Jack the Clever Clown circus clown performer with tub, ladder and chair accessories, cover of box reads "Cracker Jack...1001 New Tricks," figure 8" h. **$926**
Courtesy of Bertoia Auctions

Marx Musical Circus Horse lithographed tin horse-drawn circus drum that emits sounds, with colorful graphics overall, 10" l. **$309**
Courtesy of Bertoia Auctions

Schoenhut Humpty Dumpty Circus canvas top tent with banner streamers, large rectangular blue wooden base with red circus ring at center, paper label on front reads "Humpty Dumpty Circus," 24" d. x 35" w. x 36" h. **$1,359**
Courtesy of Bertoia Auctions

Marx Ring-A-Ling Circus lithographed tin wind-up toy with center ring with ring master, three performing animals and clown, 7" dia. **$740**

Courtesy of Bertoia Auctions

Tom Mix Circus and Wild West show poster, 47" x 15". **$270**

Courtesy of Morphy Auctions

◄ Circus World Museum poster advertising "Holter's Wrestling Tigers," nicks around bottom, very good condition, 28" x 42". **$60**

Courtesy of Morphy Auctions

Arcade Big Six circus wagon, 14-1/2 l. **$400**

Courtesy of Bertoia Auctions

Pressed steel Keystone truck, "World's Greatest Circus" side decal, opening back gate, red tractor and green trailer, restored, 20" l. **$210**

Courtesy of Morphy Auctions

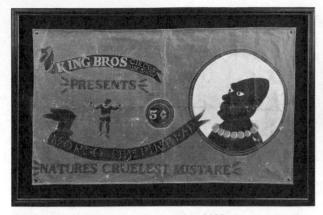

King Brothers Circus Sideshow banner, circa 1920s, heavy canvas, framed under plexiglass, 66" x 43" framed.............................**$2,160**

Courtesy of Morphy Auctions

Giant Salted Peanuts tin manufactured by Superior Peanut Co., Cleveland, Ohio, imagery of circus surrounding pail, 3-1/2" x 4"............. **$1,100**

Courtesy of Morphy Auctions

King Reid Shows circus poster, 1950s, 30" x 24". **$48**

Courtesy of Morphy Auctions

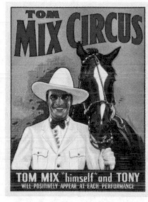

Tom Mix Circus poster, mid-1930s, portrait of Mix and his horse, Tony, at height of Mix's fame, 21" x 28"................. **$896**

Courtesy of Heritage Auctions

Britains Circus Diorama Set, No. 8665, original set in box. **$105**

Courtesy of Lloyd Ralston Gallery

Strongbox given to Buffalo Bill by queen of England, kept in Buffalo Bill's Traveling Circus wagon, 22" l. x 17" w. x 12" h. **$3,600**

Courtesy of Morphy Auctions

Corgi Chipperfields Circus Crane Truck, No. 1121, 1964-1969, with original box, 8" l. **$144**

Courtesy of Lloyd Ralston Gallery

CIRCUS

Dinky Pinder Circus Peugeot with caravan, No. FR882, with original box.. **$1,100**

Courtesy of Lloyd Ralston Gallery

"The Sideshow" one-sheet movie poster, Style B, Columbia, 1928, 27" x 41". **$1,315**

Courtesy of Heritage Auctions

James Montgomery Flagg (American, 1877-1960), Ringling Brothers Barnum and Bailey Circus program cover, oil on canvas, circa 1950, signed lower left, 33" x 25". **$8,365**

Courtesy of Heritage Auctions

"Charlie Chan at the Circus" window card, 20th Century Fox, 1936, 14" x 22"................ **$350**

Courtesy of Heritage Auctions

"Marx Bros. At the Circus" lobby card, MGM, 1939, 11" x 14"....................... **$3,250**

Courtesy of Heritage Auctions

Hazel Finck (American, 1894-1977), "Circus Backyard," 1941, oil on canvas, signed "H. Finck," 25-1/4" x 30-1/4"......................**$3,645**

Courtesy of Skinner, Inc.; www.skinnerinc.com

Polychrome-painted Masonite circus wagon panel, Connecticut, 20th century, 48" x 52-1/2".................... **$520**

Courtesy of Skinner, Inc.; www.skinnerinc.com

Ringling Bros. Circus Printing Set, original box, missing crayons................................ **$95**

Courtesy of Philip Weiss Auctions

Canada's Traditional Favorite Conklin Shows circus banner depicting traditional theme park, circa 1950, Fred Johnson, 94" x 117"......... **$550**

Courtesy of Leslie Hindman Auctioneers

Baranger Studios circus bandwagon, No. M-209 in book *Baranger – Window Displays in Motion*, 18" x 18" x 15"...........................**$8,060**

Courtesy of Noel Barrett Antiques & Auctions

CIVIL WAR COLLECTIBLES

THE CIVIL WAR began on April 12, 1861, at Fort Sumter, the Confederates surrendered at Appomattox Courthouse on April 9, 1865, and all official fighting ceased on May 26, 1865.

Between the beginning and end of the Civil War, the way wars were fought and the tools soldiers used changed irrevocably. When troops first formed battle lines to face each other near Bull Run Creek in Virginia on June 21, 1861, they were dressed in a widely disparate assemblage of uniforms. They carried state-issued, federally supplied, or brought-from-home weapons, some of which dated back to the Revolutionary War, and marched to the orders and rhythms of tactics that had served land forces for at least the previous 100 years.

Four short years later, the generals and soldiers had made major leaps in the art of warfare on the North American continent, having developed the repeating rifle, the movement of siege artillery by rail, the extensive employment of trenches and field fortifications, the use of ironclad ships for naval combat, the widespread use of portable telegraph units on the battlefield, the draft, the organized use of African-American troops in combat, and even the levying of an income tax to finance the war.

For some Civil War enthusiasts, collecting war relics is the best way to understand the heritage and role of the thousands who served. Collecting mementoes and artifacts from the Civil War is not a new hobby. Even before the war ended, people were gathering remembrances. As with any

Commercially produced 14th New Hampshire forage cap with original specially produced set of silver insignia and brass "simulated embroidered" hunting horn, worn by unknown member of Co. A, 14th N.H. Vol. Infantry, which served from Sept. 24, 1862 to July 8, 1865; body of cap in fine condition with no damage, bound edge tarred leather visor with typical crazing, original leather chinstrap attached by small eagle side buttons, leather sweatband intact with tight original stitching, lightly padded black polished cotton lining with minor wear, chinstrap 5/8", sweatband 1-1/4". ...**$20,000**

Courtesy of Heritage Auctions

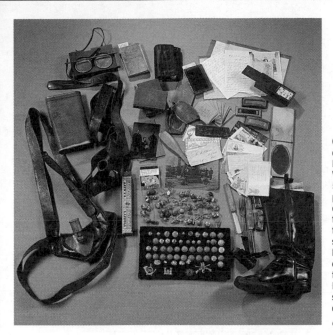

Group of Civil War objects, circa 1861-1865: Identified housewife carried by Private William D. Deadman, Co. E, 50th Massachusetts Regiment; patriotic match cases, playing cards, dominoes, two leather flag carriers, tin dispatch case, two mirrors, three officers shoulder straps, manuals, buttons, letters, boot, and equipment stencil identified to Col. Shatzwell of 1st Massachusetts Heavy Artillery; shoe horn and other related objects. **$3,198**

Courtesy of Skinner, Inc.; www.skinnerinc.com

period of warfare, the first collectors were the participants themselves. Soldiers sent home scraps of flags, collected minie-ball shattered logs, purchased privately marketed unit insignias, or obtained a musket or carbine for their own use after the war. Civilians wrote to prominent officers asking for autographs, exchanged photographs *(carte de visites)* with soldiers, or kept scrapbooks of items that represented the progress of the conflict.

After the war, the passion for owning a piece of it did not subside. Early collectors gathered representative weapons, collected battlefield-found relics, and created personal or public memorials to the veterans. Simultaneously, surplus sales emerged on a grand scale. This was the heyday of Civil War collecting. Dealers such as Francis Bannerman made hundreds of Civil War relics available to the general public.

Following World War II, a new wave of collecting emerged. Reveling in the victories in Japan and in Europe, Americans were charged with a renewed sense of patriotism and heritage. At the same time, newspapers started to track the passing of the last few veterans of the Civil War. As the nation paid tribute to the few survivors of the Rebellion, it also acknowledged that the 100-year anniversary of the war was fast upon them. In an effort to capture a sense of the heritage, Civil War buffs began collecting in earnest.

During the Civil War Centennial in the 1960s, thousands of outstanding relics emerged from closets, attics, and long-forgotten chests, while collectors eagerly bought and sold firearms, swords, and uniforms. It was during this time that metal detectors first played a large role in Civil War collecting, as hundreds donned headphones and swept battlefields and campsites, uncovering thousands of spent bullets, buttons, belt plates, and artillery projectiles.

By the 1970s, as this first wave of prominent and easily recognized collectibles disappeared into collections, Civil War buffs discovered carte de visites, tintypes, and ambrotypes. Accoutrements reached prices that far outstretched what surplus dealers could have only hoped for just a few years prior. The demand for soldiers' letters and diaries prompted people to open boxes and drawers to rediscover long-forgotten manuscript records of battles and campaigns.

By the end of the 20th century, collectors who had once provided good homes for the objects began to disperse their collections, and Civil War relics reemerged on the market. It is this era of

Civil War relic reemergence in which we currently live. The fabulous collections assembled in the late 1940s and early 1950s are reappearing.

It has become commonplace to have major sales of Civil War artifacts by a few major auction houses, in addition to the private trading, local auctions, and Internet sales of these items. These auction houses handle the majority of significant Civil War items coming to the marketplace.

The majority of these valuable items are in repositories of museums, universities, and colleges, but many items were also traded between private citizens. Items that are being released by museums and from private collections make up the base of items currently being traded and sold to collectors of Civil War material culture. In addition, many family collections acquired over the years have been recently coming to the marketplace as new generations have decided to liquidate some of them.

Civil War items are now acquired by collectors in the same fashion as any material cultural item. Individuals interested in antiques and collectibles find items at farm auction sales, yard sales, estate sales, specialized auctions, private collectors trading or selling items, and the Internet and online auction sales.

Provenance is important in Civil War collectibles – maybe even more important than with most other collectibles. Also, many Civil War items have well-documented provenance as they come from family collections or their authenticity has been previously documented by auction houses, museums, or other experts in the field. For more information on Civil War memorabilia, see *Warman's Civil War Collectibles Identification and Price Guide*, 3rd edition, by Russell L. Lewis.

Civil War-era doeskin gauntlets, small size, split cuffs, bound and lined in doeskin................... **$469**

Courtesy of Heritage Auctions

▲ Two pairs of Civil War-era boots, circa mid-to-late 19th century: Tall black leather boots with pegged soles, half-soles, and heels, leather pulls, and maker's mark "FISH BOOT/WARRENTED" on knee flap; low black boots with sewn soles and cloth pulls. **$615**

Courtesy of Skinner, Inc.; www.skinnerinc.com

◄ Rare Civil War sky-blue enlisted trousers made of kersey, no back pockets, belted back (buckle missing), front pockets and waistband watch pocket, cotton waist linings and pockets, all suspender buttons present, five tin-button fly, single-button closure at waist, brown polished cotton button fly facings. **$6,875**

Courtesy of Heritage Auctions

Civil War-era civilian frock coat in blue wool lined in cotton, 10-button front, five wooden buttons missing. **$656**

Courtesy of Heritage Auctions

▲ Civil War coat, cape, and kepi, kepi with 129 pin, together with World War I-era hat. **$390**

Courtesy of Pook & Pook, Inc.

▶ Civil War cased brass-frame sunglasses and brass pocket compass, brass frames with adjustable temples and green glass lenses, left lens with vertical crack, period tin case, rare; brass pocket compass with screw-off lid, appears to function correctly, very good condition, approximately 1-1/2" dia..... **$200**

Courtesy of Heritage Auctions

Civil War-era brass combination lock, circa 1862, four rotating barrels with engraved letters, 1-1/2" h. **$615**

Courtesy of Skinner, Inc.; www.skinnerinc.com

Black leather saddle valise with decorative metal corps badges to either end, possibly badge of XIX Corps, large size, 16-3/4"......................**$431**

Courtesy of Skinner, Inc.; www.skinnerinc.com

Rare Confederate cipher disc, brass mechanical wheel cipher consisting of two concentric discs that share common axle, each with 26 letters from Latin alphabet written out clockwise, inner disc stamped at center CSA / S.S. (Confederate States of America Secret Service), reverse stamped with maker's mark F. Labarre / Richmond, VA., outer disc approximately 57mm dia., inner disc approximately 41mm, housed in book-style presentation case produced specifically for disc by Lakeside Press, Chicago, spine labeled in gilt Decoding Device – C.S.A. Secret Service. **$18,000**

Courtesy of Cowan's Auctions

Three pairs of Civil War officer's shoulder straps: Major's straps with single bullion borders, metal rank devices, apparently converted from cavalry to infantry as evidenced by remnants of infantry blue felt on original yellow field lacking one major's leaf, lacking original tie strings, with significant insect damage, good condition, 1-1/2" x 4"; infantry captain's straps with false-embroidered brass single borders and rank devices on blue felt field, Smith's patent paper labels on verso, wool underlay mostly lacking, insect damage to blue field, good condition; and artillery second lieutenant's bullion single-borders on red field, very good condition. **$469**

Courtesy of Heritage Auctions

Five Civil War canteens, circa 1861-1865, three with jean cloth covers, two without covers. **$861**

Courtesy of Skinner, Inc.; www.skinnerinc.com

B. Kittredge & Co. copper Civil War cartridge box............. **$1,400**

Courtesy of Fontaine's Auction Gallery

Pair of First Division, 12th Corps badges: Larger badge with commercially produced star-shaped silhouette etched brass frame with red painted-paper center and mounting pin, 70 percent of red paint in center remains, approximately 1-3/4" x 1-3/4"; smaller badge commercially produced stamped brass with mounting pin, excellent condition, 1-1/4" x 1-1/4"................... **$594**

Courtesy of Heritage Auctions

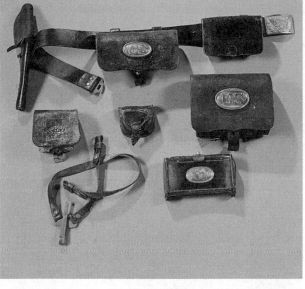

◄ Civil War-era accoutrements, circa mid-to late-19th century: Model 1855 cartridge box, belt with carbine cartridge box, pistol cartridge box, and holster, cavalry saber sling, two cap boxes, and McKeever cartridge box with lead-filled brass plate marked NJ...**$1,599**

Courtesy of Skinner, Inc.; www.skinnerinc.com

Civil War surgeon's leather trunk that may have belonged to surgeon JAM Craw of 157th N.Y. Volunteers, trunk lined with 1883 Boston newspaper, "M.A. Craw" written inside (M.A. Craw was JAM Craw's father), very good condition, 18" l. **$120**

Courtesy of Morphy Auctions

Two Civil War veteran's badges and 84th Pennsylvania Volunteer Infantry ladder badge: Co. C 84th Pennsylvania Volunteer Infantry badge with four nickel silver bars on light blue ribbon, missing final drop, very good condition; Sept. 1889 Chattanooga Army of Cumberland, 14th Corps souvenir badge, excellent condition, drop 1-1/4" dia.; 14th Corps Veterans reunion badge, Whitehead & Hoag back mark, excellent condition, drop 1-1/4" dia. with celluloid 14th Corps insignia mounted in center. **$375**

Courtesy of Heritage Auctions

Drum, sticks, and stick holder, circa mid-to-late-19th century, rope tension drum with wooden shell, brass tacks around vent, worn maker label from Philadelphia, wooden hoops, calfskin heads, wooden sticks, and brass stick holder, 12" h., 16-3/4" dia........................ **$400**

Courtesy of Skinner, Inc.; www.skinnerinc.com

◄ Combination fork, spoon, and knife set and two Civil War-era tin cups, Worman Elk & Co. maker-marked, 1861 patent dated, lead-handle knife and fork, tin spoon, excellent condition, each cup 4" h., 4-1/4" dia........................ **$813**

Courtesy of Heritage Auctions

Carved folk art pipe, America, circa 1861, cylindrical bowl with leaf garland border carved with crossed rifles, soldier brandishing sword and words "BULL RUN," held by cupped hand carved with presentation "JIM to SAM," continuing to stem and separate mouthpiece, old surface, imperfections, 11-1/2"............................ **$615**

Courtesy of Skinner, Inc.; www.skinnerinc.com

Carved pipe-bowl, circa 1861-1865, on front with "CHANCELLORSVILLE & FRDKSBURG/GETTYSBURG" over "USA," 3" l.............. **$3,198**

Courtesy of Skinner, Inc.; www.skinnerinc.com

Post-Civil War snare drum made by Lyon and Healy, wooden shell and rims, metal tension hooks and rope tensions, skin batters, paper maker's label visible through vent hole, tension ropes frayed, 10" h., 14-1/4" dia. **$250**

Courtesy of Heritage Auctions

Powder horn, no engraving, wooden stop, 6". **$40**

Courtesy of Affiliated Auctions

Small 11-star First National Confederate flag, circa 1861, hand-sewn red, white, and red-striped field, blue canton with white embroidered yarn stars and white cotton hoist, with testament from H.B. Wallis, 12-1/2" h. x 16-1/2" w. **$7,380**

Courtesy of Skinner, Inc.; www.skinnerinc.com

◀ Engraved pewter flask belonging to Maj. Bob Lansing, with floral and geometric designs, engraved within floral wreath "Maj. Bob Lansing," 6-1/4" h. x 3-1/2" w. **$625**

Courtesy of Heritage Auctions

Two Civil War flags, Confederate flag and Union flag with 13 stars, larger flag 67-1/2" l. **$13,200**

Courtesy of Morphy Auctions

Cased hand-tinted tintype of Union enlisted man holding early model Burnside carbine in shoulder sling on left and cavalry saber on right, smoking cigar, gutta-percha case lined with maroon velvet, 2-1/2" x 3-5/8"...**$2,188**

Courtesy of Sotheby's

Hand-colored albumen photograph of Union soldier with Starr revolver by P.H. Benedict, Syracuse, New York, soldier rests left arm on table and points at Starr revolver, indicating importance of revolver to him, photograph in original mount inscribed at bottom, "Photographed by P.H. Benedict, Syracuse, N.Y.," 8-1/2" x 6-1/2"........................**$938**

Courtesy of Sotheby's

Civil War soldier letter in fancy envelope, postmarked Feb. 10, 1862, from soldier stationed at camp to friend at home, cover with Baltimore & Ohio railroad postmark, 5-1/4" l..............**$120**

Courtesy of Morphy Auctions

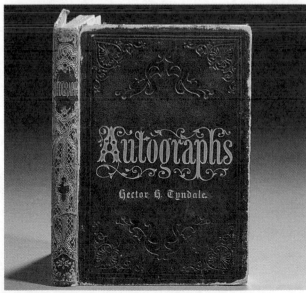

Ulysses S. Grant (1822-1885) autograph album containing his signature and those of associated political figures, octavo autograph book, formerly property of Civil War Gen. Hector Tyndale (1821-1880), with his name tooled in gilt on front cover, with signatures of Grant, Vice President Schuyler Colfax, Secretary of Treasury George S. Boutwell, Secretary of War William W. Belknap, Attorney General George H. Williams, Secretary of Navy George M. Robeson, Secretary of Interior Columbus Delano, and others, with signatures of 63 senators and 142 members of House of Representatives; bound in full sheepskin, blocked in blind on front and back boards, gilt-tooled spine and front board, a.e.g.; binding rubbed, title page discolored, 6-1/4" x 5"......**$1,353**

Courtesy of Skinner, Inc.; www.skinnerinc.com

top lot

Civil War-era book of signatures of members of U.S. Navy............ **$360**

Courtesy of Pook & Pook, Inc.

▲ Civil War Treasury Department document, 1872, payable to father of deceased soldier................. **$110**

Courtesy of Vero Beach Auction

CLOCKS

THE MEASUREMENT AND RECORDING of time has been a vital part of human civilization for thousands of years, and the clock, an instrument that measures and shows time, is one of the oldest human inventions.

Mechanical, weight-driven clocks were first developed and came into use in the Middle Ages. Since the 16th century, Western societies have become more concerned with keeping accurate time and developing timekeeping devices that were available to a wider public. By the mid-1600s, spring-driven clocks were keeping much more accurate time using minute and seconds hands. The clock became a common object in most households in the early 19th century.

Clocks are a prime example of form following function. In its earliest incarnations, the functionality of a timepiece was of paramount importance. Was it telling the time? More importantly, was it telling the correct time? Once those basic questions had been answered, designers could experiment with form. With the introduction of electronics in the 20th century, almost all traditional clockwork parts were eliminated, allowing clocks to become much more compact and stylistically adaptable.

In lavish Art Deco styles of the 1920s and 1930s, clocks featured the same attention to exterior detail as a painting or sculpture. Fashioned of materials ranging from exotic woods to marble, bronze, and even wedges of Bakelite, Art Deco clocks were so lovely that it was actually an unexpected bonus if they kept perfect time. The Parisian firm, Leon Hatot, for instance, offered a clear glass stunner with hands and numerals of silver.

For the budget-conscious, particularly during the 1930s Depression years, inexpensive novelty clocks found favor. Prominent among these were molded-wood clocks by Syroco (Syracuse Ornamental Co.). Offering the look of hand carving at a fraction of the cost, Syroco clocks featured an interior mechanism by Lux.

Also popular: affordable clocks ideally suited for a specific room in the home, such as the Seth Thomas line of kitchen-ready "Red Apple" clocks. Other companies specialized in attractively priced clocks with added whimsy. Haddon's "Ship Ahoy" clock lamp had a sailboat rocking on its painted waves, while MasterCrafters ceramic clocks replicated a pendulum effect with moving figures, such as children on swings or old folks in rocking chairs. Another best-seller, still in production today, is the "Kit-Cat Clock" with pendulum tail and hypnotic moving eyes.

And possessing an irresistible kitschy charm: "souvenir" clocks from locales as diverse as New York and Las Vegas. What better way to travel back in time than with a "Statue of Liberty Clock" (complete with glowing torch) or a sparkly Vegas version with casino dice marking the hours?

After the production restraints of World War II, postwar clock designers found inspiration in fresh shapes and materials. Among the most unusual: "clock lamps" by San Francisco's Moss Manufacturing. These Plexiglas eye-poppers exhibit a mastery of multi-purposing. They tell time. They light up. They hold flowers. Many even include a rotating platform: flick

top lot

Inlaid mahogany tall case clock, Simon Willard, Roxbury, Massachusetts, late 18th century, case with arched cresting above inlaid and brass-lined glazed door, painted iron dial flanked by reeded brass stop-fluted columns, arched string inlaid crossbanded waist door flanked by reeded and brass stop-fluted quarter-columns on quarter-fans and string-inlaid and crossbanded base, refinished, restored, label reads: "Clock manufactory Simon Willard at his clock dial in Roxbury printed by I. Thomas, Worcester" on interior of waist door, 94" h. with finial...**$13,530**

Grain-painted patent timepiece or "banjo" clock, 19th century, painted tin Roman numeral dial over grain-painted case and reverse-painted tablets of flowering urn and homestead, imperfections, 29" h........... **$369**

Courtesy of Skinner, Inc.; www.skinnerinc.com

Federal grain-painted tall case clock, Plymouth, Connecticut, circa 1825, with works by Silas Hoadley, original surface, 84-1/2" h. x 17-5/8" w. x 10" d.... **$1,107**

Courtesy of Skinner, Inc.; www.skinnerinc.com

Mahogany patent timepiece or "banjo" clock, circa 1820, painted Roman numeral dial above rope-turned frames enclosing reverse-painted tablets, brass side ornaments, eight-day, time-only movement with pendulum and lead weight, 34" h.................. **$1,107**

Courtesy of Skinner, Inc.; www.skinnerinc.com

Rare Chippendale figured mahogany tall case clock, James Jacks, New York, circa 1780, case of English origin, dial inscribed James Jacks N York, 95-1/2" h. x 23-3/4" w. x 11" d. **$6,875**

Courtesy of Sotheby's

Red-stained birch tall case clock, probably Exeter/Concord area, New Hampshire, circa 1790, case with scrolled cresting carved rosettes on hood, with freestanding columns flanking glazed arched door, painted iron dial with eight-day time and strike movement, on waist with rectangular thumb-molded door and bracket base, original surface, 85" h. **$2,460**

Courtesy of Skinner, Inc.; www.skinnerinc.com

New England tiger maple tall clock, circa 1810, scroll-top case above freestanding reeded columns, painted Arabic numeral dial with geometric and floral spandrels and arch decoration, serpentine waist door, cove molded base with scalloped apron, 30-hour time and hour strike, pull-up movement, 89" h. **$677**

Courtesy of Skinner, Inc.; www.skinnerinc.com

the switch, and a ceramic figurine (often by a prominent design name, such as deLee, Hedi Schoop, or Lefton) begins to twirl.

Equally modern yet less over-the-top were fused glass clocks by Higgins Glass Studio of Chicago. Although artisans such as Georges Briard also designed glass clocks, those by Michael and Frances Higgins are among the mid-century's most innovative. Clocks were a natural outgrowth for these pioneers of practical design, whose decorative housewares ran the gamut from cigarette boxes to candleholders.

According to Michael Higgins, "We try to make things which may be thought beautiful. But we are not ashamed if our pieces are useful. It makes them easier to sell."

A 1954 Higgins clock for GE, featuring ball-tipped rays radiating outward on the glass face, is as unexpectedly glorious as an alien sun. A later line of glass-on-glass clocks was created for Haddon during the Higgins' stay at Dearborn Glass Co. The hours are indicated by colorful glass chunks fused to a vibrantly patterned glass slab. While from the mid-century, a Higgins clock is not of the mid-century. Simplicity and clarity of line, coupled with a bold use of color, make Higgins clocks right at home in any age.

There's no time like the present to explore the limitless treasure trove of mid-20th century clocks. Which will be your favorite? Only time will tell.

Pennsylvania walnut tall clock, circa 1800, flat-top hood with freestanding columns flanking Roman numeral painted iron dial with floral spandrels and decorated arch, full-length tombstone door, step molded base, 30-hour, time and hour strike, pull-up movement, with unmarked false plate, regulated by two cast iron weights and pendulum, 90" h............... **$369**

Courtesy of Skinner, Inc.; www.skinnerinc.com

Ten clock dials: Silvered brass 6-3/4" dial marked C.A. Whelan 1877, engraved brass bracket clock dial with 5-1/4" silvered chapter ring and two subsidiary dials marked K.C. Co. Germany, five painted wooden dials, two square Roman numeral painted zinc dials, and 7-1/2" round zinc dial.. **$215**

Courtesy of Skinner, Inc.; www.skinnerinc.com

Two brass and glass carriage clocks, each of typical form with white enameled dial and Roman numerals and with unmarked works, one 5" h., other with original leather case, 2-3/4" h.......................... **$492**

Courtesy of Skinner, Inc.; www.skinnerinc.com

Howard Miller Museum wall clock, 20th century, designed by Nathan George Horwitt, with quartz movement and minimalist dial, 12-3/4" d.....**$98**

Courtesy of Skinner, Inc.; www.skinnerinc.com

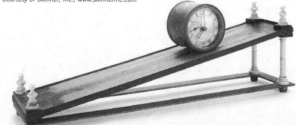

French gilt-bronze and ivory-mounted gravity clock, late 19th century, dial signed Renda/Paris, 8-1/4" h. x 25" l. **$5,625**

Courtesy of Sotheby's

Wedgwood Jasper mounted ormolu mantel clock, England, late 19th century, two light blue medallions with applied white relief of classical figures inset to clock case modeled as tall clock with enameled dial and child finial, 15-1/4" h. overall. **$1,845**

Courtesy of Skinner, Inc.; www.skinnerinc.com

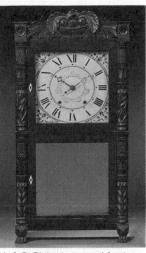

M. & E. Blakeslee carved-front mahogany clock, Plymouth, Connecticut, circa 1832, fruit basket splat over two doors flanked by carved half columns, painted wood Roman numeral dial, mirrored lower tablet, 30-hour, time and strike wooden movement powered by two cast iron weights, paw feet, 34" h. **$615**

Courtesy of Skinner, Inc.; www.skinnerinc.com

Engraved brass carriage clock, 19th century, case allover engraved with images of hunting dogs and game amid scrollwork, steel dial with Roman numerals engraved with scrolling foliage, works unmarked, 4-1/2" h. **$800**

Courtesy of Skinner, Inc.; www.skinnerinc.com

Miniature silver-mounted shell carriage clock, late 19th/early 20th century, steel dial with Arabic numerals, on four bun feet, works stamped "French Movement," case 3" h. **$800**

Courtesy of Skinner, Inc.; www.skinnerinc.com

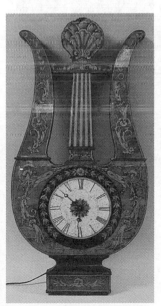

French reverse-painted wall clock, 20th century, lyre-form clock with shell finial, green-painted ground with gilt foliage surrounding Roman numeral dial, 34-3/4" h. x 17-1/4" w. **$369**

Courtesy of Skinner, Inc.; www.skinnerinc.com

Rodney Brace mahogany shelf clock, North Bridgewater, Massachusetts, circa 1825, scroll-top case, flat columns with contrasting wood inlays flanking both doors, painted wood Arabic numeral dial, reverse-painted glass of rural scene in lower door, 30-hour, time and strike wooden movement, two cast iron weights and pendulum, 41" h. **$554**

Courtesy of Skinner, Inc.; www.skinnerinc.com

CLOCKS

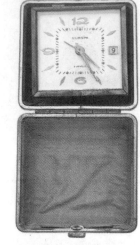

Phinney-Walker eight-day car clock, black metal dial, seconds bits, wind in back set, numerals, gold skeleton hands, sub-seconds, dash mount nickel case, 2-1/2" x 3-1/2" x 3/4"..................... **$113**

Courtesy of Heritage Auctions

Europa manual-wind alarm clock with original outer box, white metal dial, gold numerals and markers, date at 3, manual wind movement, seven jewels, metal case, 2" x 2", red case 3" x 3", folds out for clock to stand................................. **$20**

Courtesy of Heritage Auctions

Continental wood temple-form mantle clock, 19th century, marks: Dec 31, 1813, N. Hummdagard etched to front bottom edge of cabinet, 22-1/2" x 20-1/2" x 7"....... **$525**

Courtesy of Heritage Auctions

Louis XV-style boulle tortoiseshell and brass mantle clock with gilt bronze mounts, 19th century, 25" x 11-1/4" x 6".................................. **$1,375**

Courtesy of Heritage Auctions

Waltham eight-day military aircraft vintage clock, black metal dial, luminescent numerals, kite hands and center seconds sweep, manual wind movement, black metal case, 2-1/2" x 2-1/2" x 1-1/4"..... **$350**

Courtesy of Heritage Auctions

English oak and brass tall case clock attributed to Robert Davis, 18th century, marks to clock face: Robert Davis, 80" x 17-1/2" x 9-1/2"............. **$1,500**

Courtesy of Heritage Auctions

Empire-style marble, gilt, and patinated bronze mantle clock, circa 1900, marks to clock face: Charles Toucy, 16-1/2" x 22" x 7-1/8"................... **$2,500**

Courtesy of Heritage Auctions

French marble, gilt, and patinated bronze figural mantle clock, circa 1850, marks to suspension bracket: E. Pannard Stelleret; marks to pendulum: Thieble, 21-1/2" x 15-1/2" x 5".... **$3,250**

Courtesy of Heritage Auctions

French Louis XV-style japanned and gilt bronze mantle clock, circa 1915, marks: Bièsta A PARIS (to clock face), 5511 PLANCHON PARIS, Made in France (to movement), 24" h. **$1,250**

Courtesy of Heritage Auctions

Louis XVI-style spelter mantle clock, circa 1850, 27-1/4" x 19" x 9-1/2"....................... **$425**

Courtesy of Heritage Auctions

Brass and red marble Meridian Anèroid clock and barometer, France, late 19th century, barometer inscribed Baromètre Anèroide, base fronted by ruban engraved pendule mèridiènne, 21-3/4" h. **$4,375**

Courtesy of Sotheby's

Automobile vanity set with clock, 1920s, with two glass bottles, mirror, and pill box, 4-1/4" x 9" x 3".................. **$688**

Courtesy of Heritage Auctions

Louis XVI-style marble, gilt, and patinated bronze mounted mantle clock, circa 1880, marks to face: FRANCE, 15" h... **$2,750**

Courtesy of Heritage Auctions

Tiffany & Co. table clock, metal gold tone case, silver metal dial, raised applied gold numerals, day/date at 6, gold Dauphine hands, manual wind, 4-1/4" x 4" x 1-3/4"........... **$275**

Courtesy of Heritage Auctions

Late Louis XVI Ormolu mantle clock, late 18th century, 12-1/4" h. x 10-1/2" w. x 6" d...... **$5,000**

Courtesy of Sotheby's

Silver and enamel desk timepiece, No. 12533, circa 1930, nickel lever movement, silvered dial with guilloche sunburst from 12 o'clock, painted Roman numerals in plain reserve, outer minute track, star and pierced hands, silver case with green and black enamel bezel, hinged stand to back, dial signed Cartier, case stamped European Watch & Clock Co. and with Cartier reference numbers, 3-3/4" h........... **$8,750**

Courtesy of Sotheby's

R. Lalique frosted glass desk timepiece, circa 1930, electric movement, frosted glass dial with feathers in relief, painted black Arabic numerals in relief, large circular frosted glass case, rossignols in relief, case signed R. Lalique, 8" h. ... **$7,500**

Courtesy of Sotheby's

World time travel clock, Hermès, Paris, circular clock with date aperture and alarm, framed by various world cities according to time zone, mechanical movement, dial signed Hermès Paris, case back numbered 1005, with signed and fitted case. **$6,875**

Courtesy of Sotheby's

Raingo Frerès architectural gilt and silvered bronze mantle clock, 1830, Paris, case numbered 1886, 31-1/2" h. **$5,625**

Courtesy of Sotheby's

Raingo Frerès Louis XVI-style gilt and patinated bronze mounted white marble mantle clock, Paris, third quarter 19th century, surmounted by figure of musician inscribed A. COYZEVOX / 1709, clock dial signed RAINGO FRES / A PARIS, 29-1/2" h. x 17-3/4" w. x 13-1/4" d................ **$3,125**

Courtesy of Sotheby's

Austrian silver and enamel tower clock, Vienna, late 19th century, square base raised on paw feet, tower-form with openwork scrolling foliate borders, each side set with enameled plaque of classical figures, front set with enameled clock dial, columns at corners surmounted by knight figures, enameled domed top with finial of winged man riding bird, unmarked, 8-1/8" h......... **$8,125**

Courtesy of Sotheby's

COCA-COLA
& other soda pop collectibles

COLLECTIBLES PROVIDE a nostalgic look at our youth and a time when things were simpler and easier to understand. Through collecting, many adults try to recapture this time loaded with fond memories.

The American soft drink industry has always been part of this collectible nostalgia phenomenon. It fits all the criteria associated with the good times, fond memories, and fun. The world of soda pop collecting has been one of the mainstays of modern collectibles since the start of the genre.

Can soda pop advertising be considered true art? Without a doubt! The very best artists in America were an integral part of that honorary place in art history. Renowned artists like Rockwell, Sundbloom, Elvgren, and Wyeth helped take a quality product and advance it to the status of an American icon and all that exemplifies the very best about America.

This beautiful advertising directly reflects the history of our country: its styles and fashion, patriotism, family life, the best of times, and the worst of times. Nearly everything this country has gone through can be seen in these wonderful images.

Organized Coca-Cola collecting began in the early 1970s. The Coca-Cola Co., since its conception in 1886, has taken advertising to a whole new level. This advertising art, which used to be thought of as a simple area of collecting, has reached a whole new level of appreciation. So much so, that it has been studied and dissected by scholars as to why it has proved to be so successful for more than 120 years.

For more information on Coca-Cola collectibles, see *Petretti's Coca-Cola Collectibles Price Guide,* 12th edition, by Allan Petretti.

Coca-Cola festoon, "Girl on Hammock," 1913, framed, near mint condition.
$94,400

Courtesy of Richard Opfer Auctioneering

Coca-Cola Pam thermometer, 1959, 12" dia. ...**$1,416**

Courtesy of Richard Opfer Auctioneering

Startup's Chocolates outside box lid for Coca-Cola Chocolates, 1924. ....**$885**

Courtesy of Richard Opfer Auctioneering

Coca-Cola coasters, 1950s, 10 assorted color aluminum and one Hyde Park embossed metal 50th anniversary Coca-Cola Bottling Co. **$225**

Courtesy of Richard Opfer Auctioneering

Coca-Cola lollipop sign, 1930s, 64" x 30". **$2,480**

Courtesy of Richard Opfer Auctioneering

Coca-Cola 12-pack carrier, aluminum, heavy pitting, 16" l. **$53**

Courtesy of Richard Opfer Auctioneering

Early leaded Coca-Cola glass globe with original hardware, near mint condition, 13". **$165,200**

Courtesy of Richard Opfer Auctioneering

Coca-Cola cameo paper sign, circa 1896, "Cures Headache, Relieves Exhaustion," printed by J. Ottmann Litho. Co., New York, restored, 30" x 40".........**$120,750**

Courtesy of Richard Opfer Auctioneering

Coca-Cola Vendo vending machine, Model 81D-VT1D, serial no. 70627288, brass San Diego Coca-Cola label, 58" h. x 28" w. **$2,006**

Courtesy of Richard Opfer Auctioneering

Coca-Cola Victorian girl tray, 1897, thought to be first tin lithographed tray used by The Coca-Cola Co., 9-1/4"...**$112,100**

Courtesy of Richard Opfer Auctioneering

Coca-Cola roller skates, 1930s, premium given away by The Coca-Cola Bottler, extremely hard to find with key, "Coca-Cola In Bottles" engraved on each steel skate. **$885**

Courtesy of Richard Opfer Auctioneering

Holiday Coca-Cola Santa Claus die-cut easel back cardboard advertisement display sign, circa 1955, 10" x 19" h. **$96**

Courtesy of Morphy Las Vegas

Coca-Cola die-cut tin six-pack sign, 13" x 11". **$1,535**

Courtesy of Richard Opfer Auctioneering

INSIDE INTEL
with
ROBERT BARRON

Bottles Galore,
Commemorative Bottles
& Coca-Cola Memorabilia,
Bobme3rd@yahoo.com

WHAT'S HOT: The older the better: porcelain signs, pre-1923 bottles, trays from the 1920s through the 1930s.

TOP TIP: The key with any Coke item is to keep it out of the sun. Especially with commemorative bottles and those that are shrink-wrapped. If you're keeping bottles with original metal caps on them, I'd apply a thin coat of petroleum jelly to them just to make sure they don't start rusting.

Coca-Cola French Canadian double-sided flange porcelain sign, 18" x 19". **$240**

Courtesy of Morphy Las Vegas

Coca-Cola red leather golf bag marked "TR 9-99." **$150**

Courtesy of Morphy Las Vegas

Cavalier Coca-Cola chest cooler, old repaint, 35" x 69". **$118**

Courtesy of Richard Opfer Auctioneering

Coca-Cola calendar, 1900, one of two known to exist, framed, 16" x 20"....$211,200

Coca-Cola Fountain Service sign, porcelain, late 1930s, die-cut, 14" x 27"......$1,180

Courtesy of Richard Opfer Auctioneering

Frozen Coca-Cola doll, 1969, 14" h. $130

Courtesy of Richard Opfer Auctioneering

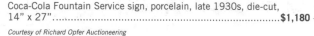

▲ Coca-Cola porcelain advertising sign, slightly curved, "DRINK Coca-Cola ICE COLD" with metal mounting brackets attached on back, 50" x 10". $1,020

Courtesy of Morphy Las Vegas

"Coca Cola" Hutchinson bottle, block letters, correct spelling, repaired fracture on back (top). $945

Courtesy of Richard Opfer Auctioneering

Coca-Cola menu board sign with "Drink Coca-Cola" button, 12" dia. metal button, total 17" x 35"......$720

Courtesy of Morphy Las Vegas

Drink Coca-Cola soda fountain syrup dispenser, No. C-6741, mounted on wood base with lid and pump, under Coca-Cola license by Dole Valve Co. $1,440

Courtesy of Morphy Las Vegas

◄ Drink Coca-Cola cooler couch on casters, embossed red metal frame with white leather upholstery, 69" l. x 27" d. x 32" h. **$1,560**

Courtesy of Morphy Las Vegas

Coca-Cola bus bench model sculpture by Michael Garman, 1977, American Moments Series with two of Garman's favorite characters from Magic Town series, 15" x 11" x 10"........**$300**

Courtesy of Morphy Las Vegas

Coca-Cola embossed metal bottle carrier, 1950s, sold with 13 embossed glass Coca-Cola bottles. **$180**

Courtesy of Morphy Las Vega

▲ Coca-Cola wood/metal toy delivery truck, Smith-Miller, circa 1940s, "SMITTY Toys, California," with wood blocks stamped "Coca Cola," repainted, 14" l. **$300**

Courtesy of Morphy Las Vegas

▲ The McGuire Sisters Coca-Cola cardboard advertisement, "King Size – Be Really Refreshed!," 36" x 20". **$210**

Courtesy of Morphy Las Vegas

Original Coca-Cola glass and plastic hanging advertisement sign, "Please Pay When Served," B-78, 18" x 13"..............**$600**

Courtesy of Morphy Las Vegas

Reproduction Pepsi-Cola pottery syrup dispenser, glazed and decorated with Arts & Crafts-style trees and rabbits, marked "Drink Pepsi Cola, 5 cents, Satisfying, Invigorating," 18" h., 8-1/2" dia. **$1,107**

Courtesy of New Orleans Auction Gallery

Pepsi-Cola cardboard advertisement sign in frame, "Pepsi's Best – Take No Less," good condition, 29" x 21"...**$396**

Courtesy of Morphy Auctions

▲ Pepsi-Cola porcelain advertising push bar, reverse marked "Thank you – Call Again," circa 1950, 31-1/2" l. **$300**

Courtesy of Jeffrey S. Evans & Associates

► Pepsi-Cola double dot metal barrel, 17" x 15"................**$201**

Courtesy of Kennedy Auction Service

Pepsi-Cola "Say Pepsi, Please" tin sign, 47" h. x 16-3/4" w. **$194**

Courtesy of Conestaga Auction Co.

Pepsi-Cola child's pedal car, Pepsi & Pete, PepsiCo. Inc., 1999, 34" x 15"................**$390**

Courtesy of Morphy Auctions

Moxie tin horse in toy car, very good condition, 8" l. **$1,440**
Courtesy of Morphy Auctions

Moxie Boy die-cut embossed
tin litho sign, circa 1910,
slight restoration, 6-3/4" h. . **$270**
Courtesy of Morphy Auctions

Moxie cardboard cutout sign,
artwork by Walt Otto, good/very
good condition, 34" x 26-3/4"...**$360**
Courtesy of Morphy Auctions

Moxie cardboard fan, 1924,
excellent condition, 8" l. **$360**
Courtesy of Morphy Auctions

Moxie tip tray and sign, 1910,
very good condition, 6" h. ... **$240**
Courtesy of Morphy Auctions

◀ "Say Hires" tin sign,
1907, excellent condition,
24" h. **$3,000**
Courtesy of Morphy Auctions

▲ Hires Root Beer tin sign,
paint touch up to edges,
30" l. x 12" h. **$105**
Courtesy of Meissner's Auction Service

"7Up Likes You" steel sign, 39" x 27".......................... **$118**

Courtesy of Duane Merrill & Co.

7Up wooden frame advertising cooler with tin interior and drainage hole, 20-1/2" h. x 72" l. x 21" w.. **$272**

Courtesy of Conestoga Auction Co.

◄ 7Up "DRINK UN ANYTIME" plastic light-up sign, with "7Up" neon sign on metal frame, 2' 9" x 2' 1"............ **$120**

Courtesy of Morphy Auctions

▲ Marx prototype 7Up truck, pressed steel, hand-painted model, marked "92646 Glendale" on bottom, 23-1/2" l. **$1,440**

Courtesy of Morphy Auctions

"Hires Rootbeer" advertising mug, salt glaze, 5-1/8" h., 3-1/4" dia.......................... **$105**

Courtesy of Turkey Creek Auctions

Hires Root Beer molded plastic lion sign, excellent condition with minor crack at top edge.. **$72**

Courtesy of Milestone Auctions, www.milestoneauctions.com

7Up topper, 1960s, 11-1/2" h. **$28**

Courtesy of Nevermore Antiques & Curiosities

COIN-OPS

DID YOU KNOW coin-operated dispensers date back to ancient times when they were used in houses of worship to deliver holy water? You'd be hard-pressed to find one of those offered at auction today, but many other types of coin-operated gadget-like gizmos certainly come up for sale, and there are always eager buyers lining up to add them to collections.

Coin-ops, as they're often referenced by both marketers and aficionados, come in all shapes and sizes and fall into three main categories: gambling, including slot machines and trade stimulators; vending machines with service devices like scales and shoe shiners as a subcategory; and arcade machines. From simple post-World War II gumball and peanut machines that can usually be found for under $100, to rare antique arcade machines that bring to mind the fortune teller amusement working magic in the popular movie "Big" starring Tom Hanks, these are all considered collectible.

Today one of those talking fortune-teller machines can easily bring five figures at auction. Other interesting models without talking features can be purchased more reasonably, in the $1,000-5,000 range, but none of them come cheap when they're in good working order.

Amusements such as these originated in penny arcades of the late 1800s. There were machines allowing patrons to demonstrate their skill at bowling, shooting or golf, among other pastimes, along with the familiar strength testers that sprang to life at a penny a pop. Some machines known as "shockers" were marketed as medical devices. In fact, one made

Art Deco-style Stoner Junior red mirror front six-way floor model vending machine, circa 1940s, accepts nickels and dimes, used for movie theater concession between 1930s and 1950s, with key, restored condition, 64" x 23" x 14". ..**$5,700**

Courtesy of Morphy Auctions

by Mills, a huge manufacturer of coin-ops, was actually named "Electricity is Life," and it would supposedly cure what ails you, according to Bill Petrochuk, an avid collector actively involved with the Coin Operated Collectors Association (http://coinopclub.org). Another lung tester, which operated by blowing into a mouthpiece attached to a hose causing water to rise in the device as a measurement tool, was eventually banned, ironically, due to the spread of tuberculosis.

There are also those aforementioned trade stimulators, some of which skirted gambling laws, according to Larry DeBaugh, a frequent consultant for Morphy Auctions (www.morphyauctions.com), who knows his stuff when it comes to devices powered by pocket change. These machines stimulated the trade of businesses like tobacco stores and bars by offering patrons a chance to win products, many times by spinning reels or playing a game. Later machines dispensed gum on the side for each coin spent. Customers received something for their money, and presto, law enforcement couldn't technically deem it gambling.

The earliest trade stimulators were cigar machines with no gambling involved, however. They were truly cigar dispensers, and for a nickel a customer would get a cigar. What made it different from buying from the guy down the block is that you might get two or three for the same nickel using the machine. Petrochuk adds that these were used to free up some of the tobacco shop clerk's time as well. When taxes were imposed on cigars, requiring that they be sold from original boxes, these machines were no longer serviceable. They're now considered rare collectibles and sell for $10,000 and up in most instances, when you can find them.

There were also slot machines designed for use outside casinos that would vend a pack of mints, or do a bit of fortune telling, in the same way as later trade stimulators. These machines were fought by authorities for decades, according to DeBaugh. Finally, in the 1950s and 1960s, vending-style gambling machines of this sort were outlawed, and their makers concentrated their marketing efforts on Las Vegas going forward.

Traditional slot machines are quite popular today as well, and collectors like DeBaugh, who've studied, bought and sold these types of items for 35-40 years, have seen a bit of everything including those in pretty rough shape.

"An average machine, one that's seen a lot of play from the '40s or late '30s and is basically worn out, will run about $1,000. But they won't be worth anything unless they are restored. After they're running, you might have a $3,000 machine."

Petrochuk notes that collectors of coin-ops in general look for "nice, clean, original machines," but a very small percentage fall into that category. He likes to use the term "preservation" when referring to giving old coin-ops new life, as in keeping things as original as possible. He sees restoration as more of a redo that might require totally new paint or extensive re-plating. "These old machines took a real beating. A few battle scars are acceptable," he adds.

Preserving coin-ops means using as many original parts as possible to replace those that are worn, and fabricating new ones out of appropriate materials when needed. DeBaugh supplies Rick Dale of the History Channel's hit television series "American Restoration" with many parts salvaged from old slot machines that can't be repaired. He also notes that it's tough to find older slots from the early 1900s in anything but poor condition. The wood usually needs work, and sometimes the nickel or copper finishes will need to be re-plated as well.

Other unusual coin-ops beyond the familiar "one-armed bandits" include devices that sold matchbooks, collar buttons, and sprays of perfume. Going even further into the unimaginable zone are machines that actually dispensed live lobsters via a game of sorts. Others even provided live bait for fishing excursions.

Nut and gum dispensers are the most common vending models, but unusual brands in this category most definitely appeal to advertising collectors in addition to coin-op enthusiasts. In fact, many coin-ops are direct extensions of advertising collectibles since vending machines made in the 1920s and '30s, unlike those that dispense multiple types of snacks today, usually focused on a single brand. Hershey's machines dispensed chocolate bars. Wrigley's dispensers rotated to deliver packs of gum. There were even coin-operated dispensers for Dixie Cups. Add an unusual shape or size to the equation and advanced collectors will pay big bucks to own them.

Even those old-fashioned red, white, and blue stamp dispensers used in post offices 30-40 years ago appeal to collectors of newer machines, and those can be found for less than $100. If you want a slot machine for use in a "man cave" or game room, DeBaugh suggests looking at a Mills machine from the 1940s or '50s. Both high top and half-top models can be found for around $1,000 in good working order. What's even better, they're dependable and reliable for home use for hours of coin-op fun.

— Pamela Y. Wiggins

Wurlitzer remote jukebox selector, chrome wall box with 104 selections with 26 green push buttons and one red coin return at top, very good condition, 12-1/2" x 11-1/2" x 7-1/2"................................ **$570**

Courtesy of Morphy Auctions

Wurlitzer Model 1015 bubbler jukebox fully restored with coin equipment, 33" x 25" x 60"................................ **$5,100**

Courtesy of Morphy Auctions

Caille Ben Hur counter wheel slot machine, circa 1908, European coin but will play on U.S. half dollar, with keys, good condition, 16" x 10" x 25".............. **$1,020**

Courtesy of Morphy Auctions

"Marvel's Pop-Up" baseball flip ball countertop skill game, circa 1947, no key.............. **$570**

Courtesy of Morphy Auctions

"Roll Out the Barrel" countertop reel trade stimulator vendor, excellent condition, 18" x 9" x 24"................ **$1,680**

Courtesy of Morphy Auctions

Cigarette trade stimulator flip ballgame countertop in wood cabinet, with key, very good condition, 29" x 6-1/2" x 19".. **$480**

Courtesy of Morphy Auctions

Daval Mfg. Co. "Races" three-wheel 5¢ trade stimulator, circa 1936, reels and lever working and in good condition, case with old repainted finish, gum dispenser mechanism missing, no key, 10" h. x 9-1/2" w. x 8-1/2" d. **$240**

Courtesy of Fontaine's Auction Gallery

◄ Silver King "Hunter" shooting gallery pistol skill game, aka "Shoot the Duck," lightweight metal countertop cabinet with lower gumball vendor, plastic top globe with rounded edges, with keys, very good condition, 24" x 18-1/4" x 9-1/2". **$600**

Courtesy of Morphy Auctions

Saloon Mutoscope viewer manufactured by International Mutoscope Reel Co. of New York with marquee for feature "Saloon," with keys, restored condition, 52" h. **$2,400**

Courtesy of Morphy Auctions

J.F. Frantz Mfg. Silver Dollar "Test Your Skill" pistol shooter arcade game in western saloon motif, marked "Limited Edition 1000 of 1000 Patent 1925," excellent condition, 58" x 28-1/2" x 14"... **$1,200**

Courtesy of Morphy Auctions

Bryans Four-Square Allwin arcade machine, circa 1950s, rare four-sided wood floor machine with original red and black crackled paint, square top on pedestal stand houses two Twelvewin clock skill games, Pat. 353451; one Fivewin flip ball game; and one Pilwin clown flip ball game (inside of Pilwin marked "Bryans Variable Payout Machines"); with cash door key, one-player machine made for early English pennies (will accept 50¢ pieces), good to very good condition, 68" x 33" x 29-1/2"..... **$1,140**

Courtesy of Morphy Auctions

Williams' "Nags" horse race turntable pinball floor arcade machine, circa 1960, with key. **$2,160**

Courtesy of Morphy Auctions

Marvel Mfg. "Pop-Up" countertop skill game in wood cabinet, circa 1946, one knob to flip ball and another to catch ball, with keys, very good condition, 19" x 8" x 12-1/2". **$570**

Courtesy of Morphy Auctions

Early countertop roulette wheel trade stimulator, wood and glass case with ball for wheel, circa 1894, missing cash door, excellent condition, 11" x 11" x 7". **$1,440**

Courtesy of Morphy Auctions

COINS & CURRENCY

IN 2016, the U.S. rare coin and currency market is solid gold.

Total sales of U.S. coins in 2014 reached about $5 billion, across auctions and private transactions such as shows, online sales, mail order and stores. Prices for U.S. coins at auction reached about $536 million, a 36 percent increase over 2013, as tabulated in a survey by the Professional Numismatists Guild (PNG), a nonprofit composed of many of the country's top rare coin and paper money dealers.

1787 Brasher doubloon, grade MS-63 (NGC), only pre-federal American gold coin. **$4,582,500**

Courtesy of Heritage Auctions

Respondents told PNG that demand was solid with a marked trend of high prices for high-quality, historic rare coins. Records were also set among sales of rare currency. That category also saw record prices during the last few years as an 1890 Grand Watermelon note sold for $3.29 million and an 1891 $1,000 Treasury Note sold for $2.58 million.

Among the factors contributing to the category's growth include a rising stock market, a declining precious metals market, and a general improvement in total economic recovery worldwide. This trend is only expected to increase as the economies of many nations stabilize and unemployment rates decline.

In 2014, the world's largest numismatic auctioneer Heritage Auctions' share of the $536 million in U.S. coin auction sales was 62%, or $334.5 million. The house sold nine of the year's 12 coins that sold for more than $1 million, including the 2014 record for the most valuable coin sold at auction – a 1787-dated gold Brasher Doubloon for nearly $4.6 million.

"We're seeing many high-profile collections coming to market now and the market is responding better than any of us could have estimated," said Todd Imhof, executive vice president at Heritage Auctions. "Significant growth is taking place in Hong Kong and in other affluent countries. We expect the world coin segment to grow exponentially in the next three to five years."

The United States has a rich history of coinage. Many of the early states created their own coins until April 1792, when Congress passed an act establishing the U.S. Mint. By 1796, in addition to half-cents and cents, the Mint was producing silver half-dimes, dimes, quarters, half-dollars, and dollars, and gold $2.50, $5, and $10 coins. By the mid-1800s, the Mint was producing about 17 million coins annually in 12 denominations.

The coinage act of 1873 brought sweeping changes to the U.S. monetary and coinage systems and to the Mint's governing structure. The act established the main mint at Philadelphia. President Theodore Roosevelt is credited with encouraging Congress to pass legislation for providing new coin designs. Designs on coins continue to change to reflect events.

The first U.S. paper money was issued during the Colonial era, but notes issued by states and the Continental Congress during this time, and around the time of the Revolutionary War, were not reliable due to the lack of a central bank. Demand notes of 1861 were the first paper money issued by the U.S. government as an emergency measure during the Civil War. The nickname "greenback" for paper money began with these notes, which have a distinctive green back.

The paper money used today in the United States is issued by the Federal Reserve bank, which is chartered under the Federal Reserve System created in 1913.

Coins may be pursed by series, type, and theme, but there really are no limits or rules on how coins can be collected.

ODDITIES HOLD VALUE

More than a billion U.S. quarters are in circulation right now, and more than 1.65 trillion U.S. pennies are in circulation with a date of 2009 alone. For a coin to skyrocket in value, it must be remarkable in some way to help it stand out from the billions of bills and coins in circulation at any given time.

Collectors are drawn to low mint rates and low or unusual serial numbers. Similar to any other collecting category, numismatists love to pursue, study, and collect the oddities of the coin world. One-of-a-kind coins such as die errors, unusual alloys, rare survivors, odd colorations, and experimental strikes are generally the most valuable of all coins.

But like all collectibles, condition often creates a wide gulf among values, and that rule is especially true in rare U.S. coins and currency.

CONDITION SETS THE MARKET

To those unfamiliar with coin collecting, the grading scale can seem complicated. It is actually a very effective means to describe a coin in just a handful of numerical grades. This format was adopted in the late 1980s, or around the time grading services began to encapsulate coins in plastic holders. This third-party grading system commoditized the coin market and made trade much easier. The grading scale used by Numismatic Guaranty Corp. (NGC) is printed below to help you understand the grades assigned to the coins featured in this guide.

NGC grades coins on a numerical scale from 1 to 70, with 70 being the highest grade assigned.

PREFIX	NUMERICAL GRADE	DESCRIPTION
MS	60-70	Mint State (Uncirculated)
AU	50, 53, 55, 58	About Uncirculated
XF	40, 45	Extremely Fine
VF	20, 25, 30, 35	Very Fine
F	12, 15	Fine
VG	8, 10	Very Good
G	4, 6	Good
AG	3	About Good
FA	2	Fair
PR	1	Poor

What is a 70? NGC defines a Mint State or Proof 70 coin as having no post-production imperfections at 5x magnification. Coins exhibiting 70 are extremely rare and extremely valuable to collectors.

For more information on U.S. coins and currency, see *Warman's U.S. Coins and Currency Field Guide*, 5th edition, by Arlyn G. Sieber.

1925-S Lincoln cent, red MS-64 (Professional Coin Grading Service), date and mint mark elusive in gem red condition. **$2,820**

Courtesy of Heritage Auctions

1943 Lincoln cent, MS-67 (NGC). **$89**

Courtesy of Heritage Auctions

1888 Liberty nickel, proof-67 (PCGS), one of just six 1888 proof nickels (4,582 minted) to earn the proof-67 grade from PCGS........................... **$3,642**

Courtesy of Heritage Auctions

1929 Buffalo nickel, MS-64 (PCGS). **$89**

Courtesy of Heritage Auctions

1879 Seated Liberty dime, deep-cameo proof-66 (PCGS), white on black contrast, one of 1,100 proofs struck in 1879. .... **$6,462**

Courtesy of Heritage Auctions

1949-S Roosevelt dime, MS-65 (PCGS). **$42**

Courtesy of Heritage Auctions

1934 Washington quarter, MS-67 (PCGS), "light motto" (soft definition in "In God We Trust").... **$2,585**

Courtesy of Heritage Auctions

1999-P New Jersey quarter, struck on experimental planchet, MS-66 (PCGS); gold-colored alloy experiments were conducted in 1999 using 50 State Quarters dies, and those experiments led to manganese-alloy Sacagawea dollar. **$2,820**

Courtesy of Heritage Auctions

U.S. CURRENCY

National Bank Note, $1,000 face proof, Fourth National Bank of New York, charter No. 290, Chittenden-Spinner signatures. **$96,050**

Courtesy of Philip Weiss Auctions

Federal Reserve note, 1934 $20, World War II emergency issue "mule," star note (L * block). **$3,835**

Courtesy of Archives International

Specimen note, 1879 $10,000, Bank of America (New York City), clearinghouse certificate...... **$1,888**

Courtesy of Archives International

Federal Reserve note, 1981 $1, gem uncirculated-65 (Paper Money Guaranty), Federal Reserve Bank of Philadelphia. **$69**

Courtesy of Archives International

Federal Reserve notes, 1914 $5, set of two, grade fine, Federal Reserve banks of Atlanta and St. Louis. **$105**

Courtesy of Archives International

Gold certificate, 1928 $10, 15PPQ (PCGS). **$258**

Courtesy of Archives International

Federal Reserve notes, 1995, $1, I, 10 examples, unusual serial numbers including 3333335 to 33335553..... **$84**

Courtesy of Archives International

Treasury note, 1890 $1,000, small seal, extremely fine 40 (PCGS), "watermelon note," nickname
derived from three large zeros that resemble watermelons on back. **$3,290,000**

Courtesy of Archives International

Federal Reserve Note, 1928A $20, very choice new 64 (PCGS). **$305**

Courtesy of Archives International

Federal Reserve note, 1934 $10,000, very choice new 64 (PCGS), formerly part of $1 million display
at Binion's Horseshoe Casino in Las Vegas; $5,000 and $10,000 Federal Reserve notes were used
primarily in bank-to-bank transactions. **$188,000**

Courtesy of Archives International

WORLD COINS & CURRENCY

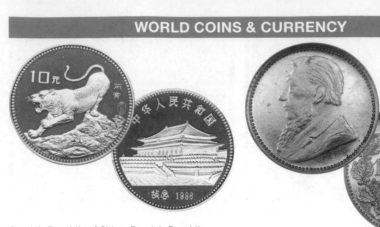

People's Republic of China, People's Republic, 1986 10 yuan, gem cameo proof. **$141**

Courtesy of Archives International

Republic of South Africa, gold pattern 1897 6 pence, cameo proof-63 (NGC)................... **$329,000**

Courtesy of Archives International

Korea, Yung Hi gold 20 won, year 3 (1909), perfect strike, full deep-mirror fields, few tiny contact marks, only two known, other permanently housed in Japanese museum. **$632,500**

Courtesy of Archives International

Australia, 1984 $20 note, Commonwealth of Australia Reserve Bank, serial No. 1. .... **$2,242**

Courtesy of Archives International

Venezuela, 1929 $10 "Discovery" note, Banco Commercial de Maracaibo. **$2,596**

Courtesy of Archives International

ANCIENT COINS

Italy, Venice, Ludovico Manin gold ducat, no date, 1789-1797, about uncirculated, strong original golden luster. **$258**

Courtesy of Archives International

Mexico, Carlos & Joanna 4 reales, no date (1544), late series, Mexico City mint, assayer Alonso Rincon, very fine... **$493**

Courtesy of Archives International

Rome, Priscus Attalus solidus, first reign (AD 409-410), draped and cuirassed bust of Attalus standing right in military attire, one of two known..**$188,000**

Courtesy of Archives International

Rome, Galla Placidia solidus, circa AD 426-430, mother of Valentinian III, 3.88 grams. **$10,350**

Courtesy of Archives International

Japan, Manen gold oban, no date (1860-1862), choice uncirculated, monetary ovoid gold plate, largest denomination of Tokugawa coinage............**$44,062**

Courtesy of Archives International

COMIC BOOKS

BACK IN 1993, Sotheby's auctioned a copy of *Fantastic Four #1* (1961) that was said to be the finest copy known to exist. It sold for $27,600, which at the time was considered an unheard-of price for a 1960s comic. Last year, Heritage Auctions sold that same copy for $203,000 ... and it's not even the finest known copy anymore.

It used to be that only comics from the 1930s or 1940s could be worth thousands of dollars. Now, truly high-grade copies of comics from the Silver Age (1956-1969 by most people's reckoning) can sell for four, five, or even six figures. Note I said truly high-grade. Long gone are the days when a near mint condition copy was only worth triple the price of a good condition copy. Now near mint is more like 10-20 times good, and sometimes it's as much as a factor of 1,000.

A trend of the last couple of years has been that the "key" issues have separated even further from the pack, value-wise. Note that not every key is a "#1" issue – if you have *Amazing Fantasy #15*, *Tales of Suspense #39*, and *Journey into Mystery #83*, you've got the first appearances of Spider-Man, Iron Man, and Thor. (Beware of reprints and replica editions, however.)

The most expensive comics of all remain the Golden Age (1938-1949) first appearances, like Superman's 1938 debut in *Action Comics #1*, several copies of which have sold for $1

Wonder Woman #1 (DC, 1987), CGC-graded 9.8 (near mint, mint), white pages, first Modern Age appearances of Themyscira, Gaea's Girdle, Hippolyte, Ares, and Olympian Gods. **$95**

Courtesy of Heritage Auctions

The Amazing Spider-Man #156 (Marvel, 1976), CGC-graded 9.8 (near mint, mint), white pages, story of marriage of Betty Brant and Ned Leeds, first appearance of Mirage, appearance by Doctor Octopus. **$1,912**

Courtesy of Heritage Auctions

Justice League of America #1 (DC, 1960), CGC-graded 7.5 (very fine), off-white pages, origin and first appearance of Despero, facing off against Aquaman, Batman, Flash, Green Lantern, Martian Manhunter, Superman, and Wonder Woman. **$4,541**

Courtesy of Heritage Auctions

million or more. However, not every single comic from the old days is going up in value. Take western-themed comics. Values are actually going down in this genre as the generation that grew up watching westerns is at the age where they're looking to sell, and there are more sellers than potential buyers.

Comics from the 1970s and later, while increasing in value, rarely reach anywhere near the same value as 1960s issues, primarily because in the 1970s, the general public began to look at comics as a potentially valuable collectible. People took better care of them, and in many cases hoarded multiple copies.

What about 1980s favorites like *The Dark Knight Returns* and *Watchmen?* Here the demand is high, but the supply is really high. These series were heavily hyped at the time and were done by well-known creators, so copies were socked away in great quantities. We've come across more than one dealer who has 20-30 mint copies of every single 1980s comic socked away in a warehouse, waiting for the day when they're worth selling.

I should mention one surprise hit of the last couple of years. When Image Comics published *The Walking Dead #1* in 2003, it had a low print run and made no particular splash in the comics world. Once AMC made it into a television series, however, it was a whole different story. High-grade copies of #1 have been fetching $1,000 and up lately.

If you've bought comics at an auction house or on eBay, you might have seen some in CGC holders. Certified Guaranty Co., or CGC, is a third-party grading service that grades a comic book on a scale from 0.5 to 10. These numbers correspond with traditional descriptive grades of good, very fine, near mint and mint, with the higher numbers indicating a better grade. Once graded, CGC encapsulates the comic book in plastic. The grade remains valid as long as the plastic holder is not broken open. CGC has been a boon to the hobby, allowing people to buy comics with more confidence and with the subjectivity of grading taken out of the equation. Unless extremely rare, it's usually only high-grade comics that are worth certifying.

One aspect of collecting that has absolutely exploded in the last 20 years has been original comic art, and not just art for the vintage stuff. In fact, the most expensive piece Heritage Auctions has ever sold was from 1990: Todd McFarlane's cover art for *Amazing Spider-Man #328*, which sold for more than $650,000. It's not unusual for a page that was bought for $20 in the 1980s to be worth $5,000 now.

If you want to get into collecting original comic art, McFarlane would not be the place to start unless you've got a really fat wallet. I suggest picking a current comic artist you like who isn't yet a major "name." Chances are his originals will be a lot more affordable. Another idea is to collect the original art for comic strips. You can find originals for as little as $20, as long as you're not expecting a Peanuts or a Prince Valiant. Heritage Auctions (HA.com) maintains a free online archive of every piece of art they've sold and it is an excellent research tool.

As expensive as both comic books and comic art can be at the high-end of the spectrum, in many ways this is a buyer's market. In the old days you might search for years to find a given issue of a comic; now you can often search eBay and see 10 different copies for sale. Also, comic conventions seem to be thriving in almost every major city – and while the people in crazy costumes get all the publicity, you can also find plenty of vintage comic dealers at these shows. From that point of view, it's a great time to be a comic collector.

— *Barry Sandoval*

Barry Sandoval is Director of Operations for Comics and Comic Art, Heritage Auctions. In addition to managing Heritage's Comics division, which sells some $20 million worth of comics and original comic art each year, Sandoval is a noted comic book evaluator and serves as an advisor to the *Overstreet Comic Book Price Guide*.

Archie Annual #1 (Archie, 1950), CGC-graded 7.5 (very fine), scarce version. **$5,078**

Courtesy of Heritage Auctions

All-Flash #1 (DC, 1941), CGC-graded 8.0 (very fine), off-white to white pages, first solo comic for Flash in Golden Age. ... **$5,019**

Courtesy of Heritage Auctions

Batman #25 Pennsylvania pedigree (DC, 1944), CGC-graded 9.0 (very fine, near mint), off-white to white pages, marked first pairing of two prime villains, with Joker and Penguin teaming up **$10,157**

Courtesy of Heritage Auctions

Blue Beetle #32 Mile High pedigree (Fox Features Syndicate, 1944), CGC-graded 9.4 (near mint)............... **$5,526**

Courtesy of Heritage Auctions

Detective Comics #31 (DC, 1939), CGC-graded 1.0 (fair), white pages, blue-label copy, split spine re-attached with tape. **$19,120**

Courtesy of Heritage Auctions

Doc Savage Comics #1 Denver pedigree (Street & Smith, 1940), CGC-graded 9.0 (very fine, near mint), off-white to white pages, with other pulp heroes including Norgil the Magician......................... **$9,560**

Courtesy of Heritage Auctions

◀ Looney Tunes and Merrie Melodies Comics #1 (Dell, 1941), CGC-graded 8.0, off-white to white pages, first comic book appearance of Bugs Bunny, Daffy Duck, Porky Pig, and Elmer Fudd............... **$9,261**

Courtesy of Heritage Auctions

Fantastic Four #1 (Marvel, 1961), CBCS-graded 8.5 (very fine), white pages, Marvel's first superhero team, first appearance of Mole Man...................**$65,728**

Courtesy of Heritage Auctions

Fantastic Four #9 (Marvel, 1962), CGC-graded 9.6 (near mint), white pages, Fantastic Four get thrown out of their headquarters for first time....................**$13,145**

Courtesy of Heritage Auctions

Frankenstein Comics #1 (Prize, 1945), CGC-graded 8.5 (very fine) cream to off-white pages, stick on top of CGC holder missing...........................**$3,346**

Courtesy of Heritage Auctions

Gene Autry Comics #1 Lost Valley pedigree (Fawcett Publications, 1942), CGC-graded 8.0 (very fine), off-white pages, one of the most in-demand Western comic books. **$1,912**

Courtesy of Heritage Auctions

The Human Torch #12 (Timely, 1943), CGC-graded 7.0 (near fine/very fine), with Alex Schomburg-designed Japanese War/bondage cover deemed "classic" by Overstreet. **$4,630**

Courtesy of Heritage Auctions

Jackpot Comics #4 (MLJ, 1941), CGC-graded 5.0 (very good, fine), cream to off-white pages, Archie's first cover appearance. **$10,755**

Courtesy of Heritage Auctions

COMIC BOOKS

The Amazing Spider-Man #3 (Marvel, 1963), CGC-graded 9.2 (near mint), off-white to white pages, origin and first appearance of villain Doctor Octopus, appearance by Human Torch, with first full version of Spider-Man's story and Spider-Man pin-up. $10,157

Courtesy of Heritage Auctions

Little Dot #1 file copy (Harvey, 1953), CGC-graded 9.2 (near mint), first appearance of Richie Rich and Little Lotta, most scarce "Harvey World" comic to find in high grade. $21,510

Courtesy of Heritage Auctions

Teenage Mutant Ninja Turtles #1 (Mirage Studios, 1984), CGC-graded 9.8 (near mint, mint), white pages, origin and first appearance of Teenage Mutant Ninja Turtles, their mentor Splinter, and archenemy Shredder. $14,937

Courtesy of Heritage Auctions

Mad #1 (EC, 1952), CGC-graded 9.4 (near mint), off-white to white pages, first issue of first satire comic. $11,950

Courtesy of Heritage Auctions

Marvel Spotlight #5 Ghost Rider (1972), GCG-graded 9.6 (near mint), white pages, first appearance of Ghost Rider and Roxanne Simpson. $4,302

Courtesy of Heritage Auctions

New York World's Fair Comics 1939 (DC, 1939), CGC-graded 6.5 (near fine), light tan to off-white pages, first appearance of Sandman and blond Superman on cover's masthead......... $7,170

Courtesy of Heritage Auctions

COMIC BOOKS

X-Factor #6 (Marvel, 1986), CGC-graded 9.8 (near mint, mint), white pages, first full appearance of Apocalypse, appearance of Alliance of Evil. **$298**

Courtesy of Heritage Auctions

Sensation Comics #1 (DC, 1942), CGC-graded 5.0 (very good, fine), light tan to off-white pages, second appearance of Wonder Woman prior to launch of her own series. **$16,132**

Courtesy of Heritage Auctions

Strange Tales #110 Signature Series (Marvel, 1963), CGC-graded 6.0 (fine), off-white pages, first appearance of Dr. Strange, Ancient One, Nightmare and Wong, first pairing of Paste-Pot Pete and Wizard, Stan Lee signature on cover. **$3,824**

Courtesy of Heritage Auctions

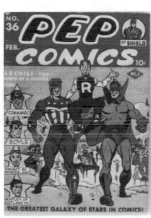

Tales of Suspense #39 (Marvel, 1963), CGC-graded 9.2 (near mint), off-white to white pages, first appearance and origin of Iron Man. **$59,750**

Courtesy of Heritage Auctions

Pep Comics #36 (MLJ, 1943), CGC-grade 5.5 (fine), light tan to off white pages, first Archie cover of series, appearances include Shield, Captain Commando, Sgt. Boyle, Bently of Scotland Yard, and Danny in Wonderland. **$5,377**

Courtesy of Heritage Auctions

X-Men #2 (Marvel, 1963), CGC-graded 9.4 (near mint), team of mutants faces Vanisher in his debut appearance... **$6,273**

Courtesy of Heritage Auctions

Zap Comix #1 Plymell Edition (Apex Novelties, 1967), CGC-graded 9.0 (very fine, near mint), cream to off-white pages, said to be start of "Underground Comix" movement; it's said that when comic was first printed, the wife of artist R. Crumb sold copies from an old baby buggy in the Haight-Ashbury district in San Francisco. **$2,629**

Courtesy of Heritage Auctions

Superman #2 (DC, 1939), CGC-graded 7.0 (fine, very good), cream to off-white pages, unusual cover design of diagonal lines, from collection of actor Nicholas Cage, light edge and spine wear. **$14,937**

Courtesy of Heritage Auctions

Miracleman #1 Gold Variant–Don/Maggie Thompson Collection pedigree (Eclipse, 1985), CGC-graded 9.8 (near mint, mint), from limited-edition run of 400 copies, "Alan Moore" and "368/400" written on first page in marker. **$1,792**

Courtesy of Heritage Auctions

Action Comics #1 (DC, 1938), CGC-graded 3.0 (good, very good), cream to off-white pages, unrestored copy of first appearance of Superman, cover detached. **$310,700**

Courtesy of Heritage Auctions

All Star Comics #8 (DC, 1942), CGC-graded 5.0 (very good, fine), off-white pages, origin and first appearance of Wonder Woman, also union of Starman and Dr. Mid-Nite with Justice Society of America..........**$28,688**

Courtesy of Heritage Auctions

The Amazing Spider-Man #100 (Marvel, 1971), CGC-graded 9.6 (near mint), white pages, milestone issue, with Green Goblin, Vulture Lizard, Doctor Octopus, and Kingpin as part of dream sequence. **$836**

Courtesy of Heritage Auctions

Batman #234 (DC, 1971),
CGC-graded 9.4, white pages,
first new story with Two-Face
since 1954, with Robin backup
story. **$597**

Courtesy of Heritage Auctions

The Thing! #1 (Charlton, 1952),
CGC-graded 7.5 (very fine), off-
white to white pages, shrunken
head on cover. **$657**

Courtesy of Heritage Auctions

Batman #232 (DC, 1971), CGC-
graded 8.5 (very fine), white
pages, first appearance of Ra's
Al Ghul, Talia cameo, origin of
Batman and Robin retold..... **$550**

Courtesy of Heritage Auctions

Funnies on Parade #nn (Eastern
Color, 1933), CGC-graded
8.0 (very fine), light tan to
off-white pages, considered
to be first comic book ever
published, promotional piece
for Proctor and Gamble, with
reprinted Sunday funnies strips,
unrestored condition. **$11,950**

Courtesy of Heritage Auctions

Green Lantern #16 Don/Maggie
Thompson Collection pedigree
(DC, 1962), CGC-graded 9.6
(near mint), white pages,
origin and first appearance of
Sapphire, along with backup
story about Abin Sur. **$7,767**

Courtesy of Heritage Auctions

Journey Into Mystery #83
(Marvel, 1962), CGC-graded 9.4
(near mint), white pages, first
appearance of Thor. **$179,250**

Courtesy of Heritage Auctions

COOKIE JARS

COOKIE JARS EVOLVED from the elegant British biscuit jars found on Victorian-era tables. These 19th century containers featured bail handles and were often made of sterling silver and cut crystal.

As the biscuit jar was adapted for use in America, it migrated from the dining table to the kitchen and, by the late 1920s, it was common to find a green-glass jar (or pink or clear), often with an applied label and a screw-top lid, on kitchen counters in the typical American home.

During the Great Depression – when stoneware was still popular but before the arrival of widespread electric refrigeration – cookie jars in round and barrel shapes arrived. These heavy-bodied jars could be hand-painted after firing. These decorations were easily worn away by eager hands reaching for Mom's baked goodies. The lids of many stoneware jars typically had small tapering finials or knobs that also contributed to cracks and chips.

The golden age of cookie jars began in the 1940s and lasted for less than three decades, but the examples that survive represent an exuberance and style that have captivated collectors.

It wasn't until the 1970s that many collectors decided – instead of hiding their money in cookie jars – to invest their money in cookie jars. It was also at this time that cookie jars ceased to be simply storage vessels for bakery and evolved into a contemporary art form.

The Brush Pottery Co. of Zanesville, Ohio, produced one of the first ceramic cookie jars in about 1929, and Red Wing's spongeware line from the late 1920s also included a ridged, barrel-shaped jar. Many established potteries began adding a selection of cookie jars in the 1930s.

The 1940s saw the arrival of two of the most famous cookie jars: Shawnee's Smiley and Winnie, two portly, bashful little pigs who stand with eyes closed and heads cocked, he in overalls and bandana, she in flowered hat and long coat. A host of Disney characters also made their way into American kitchens.

In the 1950s, the first television-influenced jars appeared, including images of Davy Crockett and Popeye. This decade also saw the end of several prominent American potteries, including Roseville, and the continued rise of imported ceramics.

A new collection of cartoon-inspired jars was popular in the 1960s, featuring characters drawn from the Flintstones, Yogi Bear, Woody Woodpecker, and Casper the Friendly Ghost. Jars reflecting the race for space included examples from McCoy and American Bisque. This decade also marked the peak production era for a host of West Coast manufacturers, led by twin brothers Don and Ross Winton.

For more information on cookie jars, see *Warman's Cookie Jars Identification and Price Guide* by Mark F. Moran.

Red Wing cookie jars, blue and brown Cattails pattern, both in excellent condition and stamped Red Wing on bottom, blue jar with small chip on inside rim, 8-1/2" h. **$150**

Courtesy of Rich Penn Auctions

Red Wing cookie jars: Green Dancing Dutch Peasants, small chip on base, otherwise excellent condition; brown Katrina – The Dutch Girl, hairline crack on apron and nick on one tip of cap; 11" and 10" h.....................................$40

Courtesy of Rich Penn Auctions

Red Wing cookie jars: Yellow Katrina – The Dutch Girl, excellent condition; brown Dancing Dutch Peasants, small chip on base, otherwise excellent condition; 11" and 10" h.................................$40

Courtesy of Rich Penn Auctions

◀ Six Little Red Riding Hood items: Cookie jar, teapot, large and small salt and pepper shakers, some minor wear, largest 13-1/2" h................$125

Courtesy of Morphy Auctions

▶ Hull Red Riding Hood cookie jar with red flowers. $90

Courtesy of Strawser Auctions

▲ Hull Little Red Riding Hood cookie jar with stars on apron, crazing to base. $75

Courtesy of Strawser Auctions

top lot

Rare large German majolica Wizard Owl cookie jar, circa 1890, owl dressed as wizard with large pink ruff and clutching a spell book, head forms lid surmounted by owl's oil funnel hat, "CURATED & CATALOGUED BY NICOLAUS BOSTON," 13" h. $1,850

Brayton Laguna figural Mammy cookie jar, turquoise dress, good condition, no chips, cracks or repairs, 12" h....... **$225**

Courtesy of Woody Auction

Brayton Laguna Mammy cookie jar, circa 1947, green dress, white apron with plaid trim, minor chip on tip of kerchief, 13"..................................... **$125**

Courtesy of A-1 Auction

Black Americana Chef/Cook figural cookie jar, hand-painted, 10" h. **$90**

Courtesy of Morphy Las Vegas

McCoy Mammy cookie jar, painted ceramic, good condition, uniform crazing, minor inner rim chip and hairlines, staining, 11" h..... **$100**

Courtesy of Richard Opfer Auctioneering, Inc.

Original early 1930s black Americana Mammy porcelain cookie jar and matching set of Aunt Jemima salt and pepper shakers, cookie jar with some paint loss, 1-1/4" x 7" x 6-1/4"............................. **$40**

Courtesy of North American Auction Co.

Majolica black boy cookie jar, 11-1/2" h. **$150**

Courtesy of Don Presley Auctions

Soldier cookie jar, painted ceramic, good to very good condition, 11-1/2" h.............**$50**

Courtesy of Richard Opfer Auctioneering, Inc.

Train cookie jar, approximately 11" h. **$10**

Courtesy of Pioneer Auction Gallery

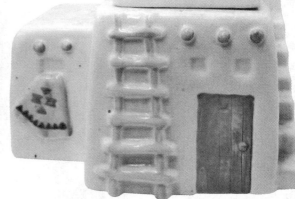

Vintage Elsie the Cow cookie jar, barrel-shaped, top shaped like Elsie's torso, 12" h. **$90**

Courtesy of Manor Auctions

▲ Treasure Craft Adobe House cookie jar with original box, approximately 11" h. **$12**

Courtesy of Pioneer Auction Gallery

◄ Twin Winton Pot O Cookies cookie jar, approximately 9" h. ....**$40-$80**

Courtesy of Pioneer Auction Gallery

Lefton Japan Chicken Basket cookie jar, approximately 11" h...**$12**

Courtesy of Pioneer Auction Gallery

Franciscan Apple cookie jar. ..**$60**

Courtesy of Strawser Auctions

INSIDE INTEL
with
LEONARD GIBSON

Retired social worker and owner of Mary V's Antiques & More

TOP TIP: Pay people a fair price and it will always come back to you. It's a tip that's as good today and tomorrow as it was yesterday. You can sleep at night. Once you get greedy you'll end up with three or four garages full of stuff. It's all about the numbers. It's all about volume.

BEST SHOW TIP: Always wear a brightly colored hat. People will see you rows away and they'll always remember you.

▲ Shawnee Pottery Corn cookie jar, 10-1/2" h......................**$30**

Courtesy of Martin Auction Co.

Roseville green Clematis pattern cookie jar, 3-8"..........**$90**

Courtesy of Strawser Auctions

Shawnee Pottery Smiley Pig cookie jar with green scarf and clover decorations...............**$120**

Courtesy of Strawser Auctions

◄ Shawnee Pottery Winnie Pig cookie jar with blue collar, good condition, 11" h.....**$70**

Courtesy of Woody Auction

American Bisque Flintstones cookie jar with Barney and Betty Rubble, circa 1960s, near mint-plus condition, 10" x 7" x 6". ....**$50-$100**

Courtesy of Morphy Auctions

McCoy Kitten cookie jar, green, made to look like ball of yarn, good condition, 9" h. x 8-1/4" dia.... **$35**

Courtesy of North American Auction Co.

▶ Yelloware End of Day cookie jar, American, clown holding his stout belly, firing damage, 11" h. **$100**

Courtesy of Cowan's Auctions

Fredericksburg Art Pottery Co. of Ohio Hungry Polar Bear cookie jar, circa 1925, marked on underside, good condition, 12-1/2" h. **$35**

Courtesy of Thomaston Place Auction Galleries

Coca-Cola jukebox cookie jar, good condition, 11-1/2" x 7"x 7". **$45**

Courtesy of Martin Auction Co.

◀ McCoy rocking horse cookie jar, mint condition, marked on bottom McCoy USA, hand-painted accents, 9-1/2" h. x 11" x 5". **$90**

Courtesy of North American Auction Co.

COUNTRY STORE

FEW CATEGORIES OF fine collectibles are as fun and colorful as country store memorabilia. The staple of quality antiques shows and shops nationwide, the phrase often refers to such an expansive field of items that it's often difficult to decide where "country store collectibles" begin and "advertising collectibles" end. However, that's one of the very reasons why the category remains so popular and one of the the the reasons why this market is growing in value and appeal.

Country store collectibles are associated with items in use in general or frontier retail establishments dating from the mid-1800s until well into the 1940s. The country store was a natural evolution of the pioneer trading post as the more affordable source of day-to-day living items, baking and cooking supplies, or goods for general household and home garden use. Country store furniture is rare, but larger pieces usually include retail countertops and dry goods bins.

The appeal of country store memorabilia has never really waned during the last 40 years, however, the emergence of online trading in the late 1990s redefined items dealers once described as rare. Much like how mid-20th century rock and roll and entertainment memorabilia is used to decorate Applebee's Bar and Grill restaurants, so have country store collectibles been used to line the walls of Cracker Barrel Restaurant and Old Country Store establishments to evoke big appetites for comfort food.

Among items in high demand are original and complete store displays in top condition. These displays were originally intended to hold the product sold to customers and were not generally available for private ownership. Those that survive are highly sought after by collectors for their graphic appeal and their rarity. Until recently, restoration of these items would negatively impact auction prices. However, recent auction results show strong prices for these items if they are rare and retain most of the original graphics.

A great deal of time, talent, and production value was invested in these store displays. Think of them as the Super Bowl commercials of their day. With limited counter space and a captive audience, marketers used every technique and theme available to catch customers' eyes. And here is where the appeal of country store collectibles crosses over so many different categories of collectibles. A store display of a fine paper poster advertising DeLaval Cream Separators may appeal to those who collect farming items, cows, and country maidens in addition to country store items. The same principal applies to store displays. Are they collected as country store items or as well-preserved examples of vintage advertising, or both? The definition takes shape when the items are added to a well-curated collection, like the one Bill and Kathie Gasperino amassed over the last 35 years.

The couple sold off the collection in April 2013 with Showtime Auction Services, as part of a massive collectibles event that realized more than 2.2 million. Together the couple happily traveled across the Pacific Northwest and beyond cultivating a collection of obscure and unusual items. It was a true team effort. "Kathie and I drove all over Montana, Idaho, and Oregon," Bill said. "Half the fun was finding the stuff. We loved crawling around attics and basements of old stores finding things."

The Gasperino collection was displayed next to the couple's Washington state home in a large building designed to look like a circa 1880s country store. "We had dry goods on one side, and on the other was a combination of things you'd find in a store of that period," Bill

General Electric lightbulb advertising store display, mid-20th century, metal and glass with interior bulb and socket for two different exterior bulbs, with original cord; frame in good condition, grime and wear to metal, glass in excellent condition, spots of paint loss on edges, 20-1/2" w. x 13" h. $960

Courtesy of Jeffrey S. Evans & Associates

Three jars, mid-20th century, Lance, Inc., Charlotte, North Carolina, maker of crackers, cookies and chips; embossed Lance logo cracker jar with glass lid, other two snack jars with metal lids; condition undamaged, one lid with light rust, 8" h. and 13" h., respectively. $204

Courtesy of Jeffrey S. Evans & Associates

Coca-Cola light-up motion advertising counter top sign, working condition, "Pause" version with metal case and "Thank You – Call Again" on metal base, circa 1955; good condition overall with wear to metal and letters on base, 19-1/2" w. x 4-3/4" d. x 9" h. $840

Courtesy of Jeffrey S. Evans & Associates

Oak bread/meat slicer, fourth quarter 19th century, rectangular form with cast iron handle and maker's plate, meat gauge, marked "ARCADIA MANUFACTURING CO. / NEWARK, NEW YORK / PATD. 1885-1891"; excellent condition with expected minor wear, 21-1/2" l. x 10" h. $156

Courtesy of Jeffrey S. Evans & Associates

said. As they encountered more items, the two began branching out to larger and larger items, such as country spool cabinets and eventually back bars, a bank teller booth, and even a 19th century soda fountain.

When it came time to downsize, the Gasperino collection hit the hobby like a comet. It remains one of the most important collections offered in recent years. Even the Gasperinos were surprised at the prices collectors were willing to pay for especially rare items in top condition.

"People called us and let us know how much they appreciated the collection and the quality," said Bill, a retired police officer. "We knew it was special to us, but it was interesting to hear from collectors who said they hadn't seen some of these items."

The Gasperino Collection is a good example of why the country store collectibles category continues to hold its own. The category was extremely popular between the late 1970s and the mid-1990s. It appears the hobby is reaching a point at which longtime collectors are ready to begin a new phase of their lives – one that requires fewer items and less space – and are offering these collections for the first time in decades.

So if the old adage, "The best time to buy an antique is when you see it" is true, the country store collectibles category stands grow as these large collections come to market and the crossover appeal catches the attention of a wide variety of collectors.

J. & P. Coats spool cabinet, late 19th century, six drawers with original inset tin panels and hardware, paneled sides and back; J. & P. Coats was founded in 1830 in Paisley, Scotland; fair condition, top loose and in three pieces, lower drawer cracked, wear throughout, 24-1/2" w. x 17-1/2" d. x 19-1/2" h..........**$192**

Courtesy of Jeffrey S. Evans & Associates

Embossed tin advertising figural wall match holder, Ceresota Flour, chromolithograph, early 20th century, marked for Northwestern Consolidated Milling Co., with Ceresota Flour advertising card in frame; condition excellent with some wear, match holder 5-1/4" h., card 3" w. x 4-1/2" h.......... **$204**

Courtesy of Jeffrey S. Evans & Associates

Two Pepsi-Cola tin menu boards, self-framed, 20th century; both with losses in color, scratches, wear, dents and areas of rusting, 19-1/2" w. x 30" h. **$120**

Courtesy of Jeffrey S. Evans & Associates

Zeno Gum diminutive oak advertising showcase with original carved pediment/marquee and possibly original finish, early 19th century, excellent condition with minor wear to surface, nails possibly added later to support glass shelves, 10-1/2" w. x 8" d. x 18" h.............................. **$600**

Courtesy of Jeffrey S. Evans & Associates

Eberhard Faber Stationer sign, original oak frame, late 19th/ early 20th century, lithograph, marked "Sole Agent for A.W. Faber's Lead Pencils and Agent for L.W. Fairchild & Co.'s Gold Pens and Pencil Cases," New York and Chicago, Ketterlinus lithographer; very good condition, some water staining, horizontal crease, minor toning and foxing, 25-1/2" w. x 31-1/2" h. **$204**

Courtesy of Jeffrey S. Evans & Associates

Ceramic syrup dispenser, early 20th century, Jersey Crème with red, green, and gilt decoration, marked with "The Perfect Drink" at center, "Strawberry" on handle and "L. Fischman & Sons / Philadelphia, Pa." at base, retains period pump; loss to mouth and chip to foot rim, small hairline crack to mouth, staining, crazing and wear to gilt, 14-1/2" h..................... **$840**

Courtesy of Jeffrey S. Evans & Associates

Two-wheel cast iron coffee mill, late 19th century, Enterprise Manufacturing Co., Philadelphia, countertop model with swivel top, iron drawer, and lettering on wheels and body, mounted on original wood base, original paint and decals with remnants of "No. 2" on drawer, excellent condition with minor wear, 12-1/2" h. x 8-3/4" d. **$840**

Courtesy of Jeffrey S. Evans & Associates

C. C. Conrad whiskey flask, Harrisonburg, Virginia, original label reads "Merry Christmas & A happy New Year, Compliments of...," original glass and cork stopper, with three pieces of Conrad paper ephemera including price list; bottle neck with two open bubbles, as made, one piece of ephemera stained, bottle 6-1/2" h. **$540**

Courtesy of Jeffrey S. Evans & Associates

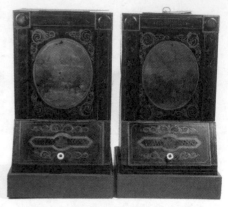

Decorated tin counter bins, fourth quarter 19th century, each topped with inset cover, hand-painted rustic scenes of outdoors and farming, lower hinged front door, custom-made unattached wood bases, 20" h. without bases. **$600**

Courtesy of Jeffrey S. Evans & Associates

Two advertising items from first half of 20th century: Wooden tub with lid stenciled "Tidewater Brand Hard Cured Cut Herring, Richmond, Va." and wooden hinged-top display box with lithographed label from Heinrich Haeberlein, gingerbread and chocolate company in Nuremberg, Germany; good to very good condition, tub 11-1/2" h., 16" dia. **$84**

Courtesy of Jeffrey S. Evans & Associates

Poplar countertop box with pigeonholes, applied molding to top and base, old dry surface, late 19th/early 20th century; good condition with expected wear, lacking base molding on one end, 2-1/2" cut out of base molding in front, several dividers removed to make larger compartments, 61-1/2" w. x 10-1/2" d. x 24" h. **$216**

Courtesy of Jeffrey S. Evans & Associates

Tin countertop displays, early 20th century: Rit Dyes three-drawer cabinet with cardboard insert, "New Improved RIT Guaranteed to Fast-Dye or Tint Washes as it Dyes" printed on side, and Art Deco Pepsodent multi-tier rack; very good condition or better with some staining and light rust, 8-1/4" h. and 26" h., respectively. **$96**

Courtesy of Jeffrey S. Evans & Associates

Green River Whiskey tin sign, early 20th century, lithographed image of African-American man with horse with "She Was Bred In Old Kentucky" at lower edge, likely in original frame with lettering for "McCullough the Distiller, Owensboro, KY" at bottom, 40-3/4" w. x 31" h. **$1,440**

Courtesy of Jeffrey S. Evans & Associates

Green River Whiskey tin circular sign in concave/plaque form, early 20th century, lithographed image of African-American man with horse at Green River Inn, "Copyright Owned By J.W. McCulloch/Chas. W. Shonk Co. Litho Chicago, No. C 1029" printed on bottom edge reverse; excellent condition with minor wear, 24" d.................... **$2,280**

Courtesy of Jeffrey S. Evans & Associates

Six glass seltzer bottles by La Salle, Stanley, Pocono, L.K. Lazarus, Tay-Sty, and Chester, 20th century, company names etched or embossed on body of bottles, metal soda siphons with each bottle, largest 12-1/2" h.. **$210**

Courtesy of Morphy Auctions

Seldom-seen six-pack cone tops cardboard carrier with unopened six-ounce cans of Dr Pepper soda, circa 1950s, packaged by Mead-Atlanta Paper Co., Atlanta, cans read "the friendly 'Pepper-Upper'" on bottom; excellent condition with light soiling, stains, and rusting, 6-1/2" l...**$2,160**

Courtesy of Morphy Auctions

Buss Clear Window Fuses display, tin, early 20th century, front of display has functional and blown fuses above image of woman, "A few cents spent now will save you delay and annoyance when the lights go out" printed on side of display; very good condition, paint flaking on image and other small areas, 14-1/4" w. x 15-1/2" h. **$120**

Courtesy of Morphy Auctions

Scarce Whistle soda bag rack, circa 1930s-1940s, metal; soda manufactured by Sylvester Jones of St. Louis, beginning in 1925, Whistle elves pictured on rack sign introduced to market in late 1930s; very good condition, medium wear and soiling with some shallow dents, 36-1/4" l...**$1,080**

Courtesy of Morphy Auctions

Wooden Paris Garters display, circa 1920s, A. Stein & Co., Chicago and New York, original label inside slots, with original boxes; company filed a patent for men's garters and became largest manufacturer of garters in the world during early 20th century; very good condition, 13-1/2" h. **$330**

Courtesy of Morphy Auctions

Four tin, paper, and glass coffee containers: Hoffman's Old Time Coffee (liquid in jar), pre-1900 Madura Coffee, three-pound Caswell Blend coffee with paper label, and Old Judge Coffee in glass jar with embossed logo; fair to excellent condition for group, largest 8-3/4" h. **$180**

Courtesy of Morphy Auctions

Porcelain sign for Star Tobacco with image of plug tobacco, circa 1920s, printed on star at center "Star Trade Mark Registered No. 4026"; very good condition, 12" h. x 24" w............................... **$480**

Courtesy of Morphy Auctions

Die-cut match holder, tin, advertising De Laval Separator Co., founded in Sweden in late 19th century before offices in U.S. and Canada opened; with components of separator system shown, "Save $15 per cow per year" printed near top bowl; very good condition with light wear and marks on color, rubbing of silver finish on bucket and bowl, 6-1/2" h... **$330**

Courtesy of Morphy Auctions

Wooden countertop advertising root beer keg, Hunters, Inc., Williamston, Michigan, mid-20th century, barrel form fitted with metal straps, wooden mock spout, "Hunter's Root Beer" embossed on reverse of barrel, "Mfd. By Multiplex Faucet Co., St. Louis U.S.A. Patented" on side of barrel; good condition, minor wear and fading to lettering, 14" h.. **$270**

Courtesy of Jeffrey S. Evans & Associates

Eskimo Pie container counter display, Thermos Co. for Eskimo Pie Corp., Louisville, Kentucky, circa 1920s, lithographed blue metal ice cream cooler, glass-lined, polished brass lid, plated base with three cast figural Eskimo feet supporting cooler, minor scratches, 16" h. ... **$1,650**

Courtesy of Philip Weiss Auctions

Sioux Bee Honey display, mid-20th century, painted wood, metal, and glass, six graduated shelves with lighted back; very good condition, some wear, lights not operational, 36" w. x 18" d. x 63" h. **$192**

Courtesy of Jeffrey S. Evans & Associates

Scull's Famous Blends Coffee tin lithographed store bin, late 19th century/early 20th century, William S. Scull & Co., Camden, New Jersey, "Java & Mocha" below illustration of woman with coffee grinder, "Grind It As / You Want It." printed on either side of woman; paint loss with scuffing and scratches, rusting, top of lid damaged along hinge, 19" w. x 15" d. x 18-1/2" h.... **$130**

Courtesy of Philip Weiss Auctions

Multi-tier paper/string rack, cast iron and wood, early 20th century, two string dispensers mounted on top of three graduated paper dispensers, each stamped "THE WRIGHT" and each with different number; excellent condition with original surfaces and lacking wooden rods, 25" w. x 46" h. **$660**

Courtesy of Jeffrey S. Evans & Associates

Round clear glass display jar, "Honey Creams / 3 for 1 Cent / Pieratt & Collins. Co.," one of three jars, other two (not shown) from The Nut House and Borden's, 20th century, excellent condition, 9" w. x 10" h. **$180**

Courtesy of Morphy Auctions

Cheer Up beverage sign with embossed lettering, mid-20th century, by Stout Sign Co., St. Louis, for Orange Smile Syrup Co., makers of Cheer Up soft drink and others; some wear, scuffs and scratches, minor dents, mounting holes at corners, 19" w. x 19" h. **$85**

Courtesy of Philip Weiss Auctions

Dixie Salted Peanuts tin and single-serving bag, circa 1900-1910, The Kelly Peanut Co., Boston, tin with fitted lid holds 10 pounds of peanuts; very good to near mint condition, no wear to bag, light to moderate marks and wear on tin, tin 9-3/4" h. **$275**

Courtesy of Morphy Auctions

DECOYS

THE ORIGIN OF THE DECOY in America lies in early American history, pre-dating the American pioneer by at least 1,000, perhaps 2,000 years. In 1924, at an archeological site in Nevada, the Lovelock Cave excavations yielded a group of 11 decoys preserved in protective containers. The careful manner of their storage preserved them for us to enjoy an estimated 1,000 to 2,000 years later.

When the first settlers came to North America, their survival was just as dependent upon hunting wild game for food as it was for the Indians. They began to fashion likenesses of their prey out of different materials, ultimately finding that wood was an ideal raw material. Thus the carving of wildfowl decoys was born out of necessity for food.

Historical records indicate wooden decoys were in general use as early as the 1770s, but it seems likely that they would have been widely used before then.

Until the middle of the 1800s, there was not sufficient commercial demand for decoys to enable carvers to make a living selling them, so most decoys were made for themselves and friends. Then the middle of the 19th century saw the birth of the market gunners. During the market-gunning period, many carvers began making a living with their decoys, and the first factory-made decoys came into existence. The huge numbers of decoys needed to supply the market hunters and the rising numbers of hunters for sport or sustenance made commercial decoy carving possible.

The market hunters and other hunters killed anything that flew. This indiscriminate destruction of wildfowl was the coup de grace for many bird species, rendering them extinct.

The United States Congress, with the passage of the Migratory Bird Treaty Act in 1918, outlawed the killing of waterfowl for sale. Following the passage of the 1918 act came the demise of the factory decoys of the day.

Today a few contemporary carvers carry on their tradition. They produce incredibly intricate, lifelike birds. What these contemporary carvings represent is that decoy carving is one of the few early American folk arts that has survived into our modern times and is still being pursued.

For more information on decoys, see *Warman's Duck Decoys* by Russell E. Lewis.

Carved and painted black duck decoy attributed to Joe Lincoln, early 20th century, glass tack eyes, old paint, minor wear to paint, minor chips to beak, 16-1/2" l. **$615**

Courtesy of Skinner, Inc.; www.skinnerinc.com

Black duck decoy by A. Elmer Crowell, East Harwich, Massachusetts, glass eyes, head turned slightly to right, oval brand, minor touch-up to head and crack to neck, paint loss. **$950**

Courtesy of Eldred's

Black duck decoy by A. Elmer Crowell, East Harwich, Massachusetts, glass eyes, oval brand, minor repaint to head, in-use wear................ **$1,100**

Courtesy of Eldred's

DECOYS

Miniature bufflehead drake decoy by Joe Lincoln, Accord, Massachusetts, early 20th century, original paint... **$1,500**

Courtesy of Eldred's

Oversize black duck decoy by A. Elmer Crowell, East Harwich, Massachusetts, circa 1920s, glass eyes, head turned slightly left, original paint, oval brand on bottom, minor wear. **$3,250**

Courtesy of Eldred's

Bluebill drake decoy by Fred Bradshaw and Canada goose decoy, American, 20th century; finely carved and painted wooden bluebill signed by Bradshaw, dated 1972, in good condition, 5-3/4" x 15" x 6-1/4"; unsigned carved and painted wooden goose, good condition, old break and repair to neck at body and under bill with partial repair, 18-1/2" x 22-1/4" x 8-1/2"................ **$558**

Courtesy of Brunk Auctions

Carved and painted Canada goose decoy attributed to Ben Schmidt, Centerline, Michigan, circa 1950s, hollow, light surface wear and abrasions, approximately 25" l. **$279**

Courtesy of Midwest Auction Galleries

Delaware Valley feeding Canada goose decoy with glass eyes, early 20th century, 5" x 26" x 7". **$288**

Courtesy of Rago Arts, www.ragoarts.com

Canvasback drake decoy by Roger Dolson, Sr. (1911-1979), Chatham, Mitchell's Bay, Ontario, original paint with yellow glass eyes and humpback, weighted bottom, paint faded on head and bill, minor nicks and dings throughout body, slightly hit by shot in rear, 15" l. overall. **$1,046**

Courtesy of Cowan's Auctions

Mason canvasback drake premier grade decoy, circa 1920-1930, carved and painted wood, solid body, applied head with glass eyes, lacking lead weight, good condition, crack under base, typical restorations, worn later paint, 7" h. x 16-3/4" l. **$450**

Courtesy of Jeffrey S. Evans & Associates

◄ Golden-eye drake decoy, New England, early 20th century, early paint, loss at top of tail, two gouges to back, paint crackling and surface losses, 7-7/8" x 12-1/4" x 6". **$744**

Courtesy of Brunk Auctions

top lot !

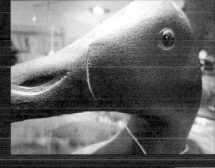

Canvasback drake decoy by Elmer Crowell, East Harwich, Massachusetts, early 20th century, glass eyes and original paint, stamped twice, overall good condition, 15". Provenance: From the collection of Allen Hendershott Eaton, Dean of American Crafts... $9,375

Mallard drake decoy by A. Elmer Crowell, East Harwich, Massachusetts, circa 1920s, glass eyes, old in-use repaint by Crowell, oval brand, animal damage to bill, head cracked in multiple places, significant tail chip. **$550**

Courtesy of Eldred's

Hooded merganser decoy, American, carved and painted wooden decoy, tack eyes, lead weight on base, ringlet below neck, paint loss and flaking to surface consistent with age and use, 6" x 18-1/2" x 5". **$558**

Courtesy of Brunk Auctions

Carved and painted pigeon decoy, circa 1900, lead beak, minor shot damage, minor abrasions to tail, three holes in bottom, 13" l. **$1,046**

Courtesy of Pook & Pook, Inc.

Mason-type merganser hen decoy, first quarter 20th century, carved and painted wood, solid body, applied head and tack eyes, lead weight to bottom, old worn working paint, cracks to bottom and likely restoration to head, 6-3/4" h. overall x 16" l. overall...................**$390**

Courtesy of Jeffrey S. Evans & Associates

Pintail drake decoy by Henry Ellis, hand-carved and painted with beaded eyes, signed "Henry Ellis, 146 Good St, Burnt Hills, Ny 12027. (c. 1989)," 19-1/2" l. **$121**

Courtesy of Fontaine's Auction Gallery

Two wooden barn owl decoys, carved and painted, owl on base and hanging owl initials B.B.D. (Back Bay Decoys), very good condition, 25" h. and 16" h. without chain. **$145**

Courtesy of Conestoga Auction Co.

▶ Black-bellied plover decoy, circa 1900, Cape Cod, Massachusetts, maker unknown, bone eyes, hit by shot, original paint with wear.....................**$650**

Courtesy of Eldred's

Plover decoy, 19th century, maker unknown, in feeding form, carved wing detail, hit by shot, paint worn off, stamp under tail........................ **$1,200**

Courtesy of Eldred's

Shorebird field decoys, northern Michigan, circa 1950s, carved and painted wooden bodies with metal heads and legs, overall surface wear and rusting to metal, 11-1/2" h. **$186**

Courtesy of Midwest Auction Galleries

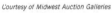

Black-bellied plover decoy, south shore of Massachusetts, red band painted around neck for owner identification, feathers done in folk art-style paint pattern, average in-use wear, bill missing. **$160**

Courtesy of Eldred's

Two carved and painted swan decoys, repaired necks, use wear, 18" h. x 28" x 31" l. **$1,150**

Courtesy of Conestoga Auction Co.

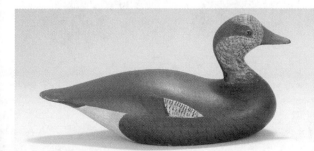

◀ Widgeon drake decoy by Joe Lincoln, Accord, Massachusetts, early 20th century, branded "C.N. Smith" on bottom, lightly hit by shot on left side of head, paint restored. **$1,300**

Courtesy of Eldred's

Canvas-covered swan decoy, early 20th century.............. **$431**

Courtesy of Pook & Pook, Inc.

Mason wood duck decoy, circa 1920-1930, carved and painted, solid body, applied head set with glass eyes, branded "WJM" under base, lacking lead weight, good condition with typical restorations, worn later paint, 6" h. x 13-1/2" l.. **$720**

Courtesy of Jeffrey S. Evans & Associates

American carved and painted preening decoy with painted eyes, 20th century, lead weight and ring to base, good condition overall with crack to back, shot holes, wear, 6" h. overall x 13" l. overall.......... **$390**

Courtesy of Jeffrey S. Evans & Associates

Carved and painted decoy by Reggie Birch, Chincoteague, Virginia, 20th/21st century, large example in swimming posture, signed "R. Birch" on bottom, antique polychrome-painted surface, very good condition, 24" l. overall. **$720**

Courtesy of Jeffrey S. Evans & Associates

Carved and painted duck decoy, mid-20th century, retailed by Abercrombie & Fitch, signed on base, 14-3/4" l. overall x 7-1/2" h. **$308**

Courtesy of Skinner, Inc.; www.skinnerinc.com

Two early wooden decoys with original paint, American, each 16". **$677**

Courtesy of Kaminski Auctions

Three fish decoys, very good condition, largest 8" l. **$150**

Courtesy of Morphy Auctions

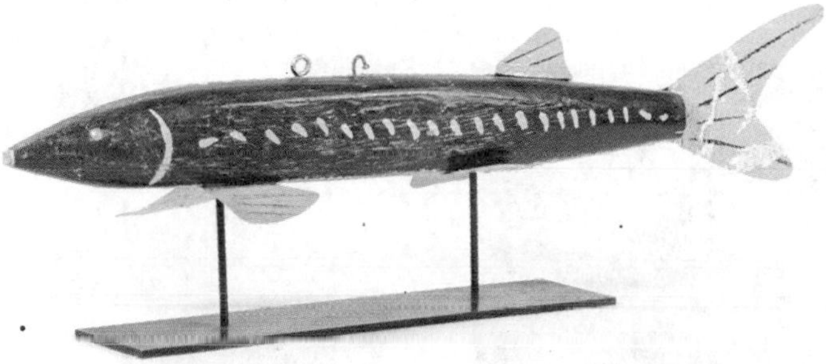

Large carved and painted fish decoy, American, 20th century, 4" x 29" x 9"...........**$188**

Courtesy of Material Culture

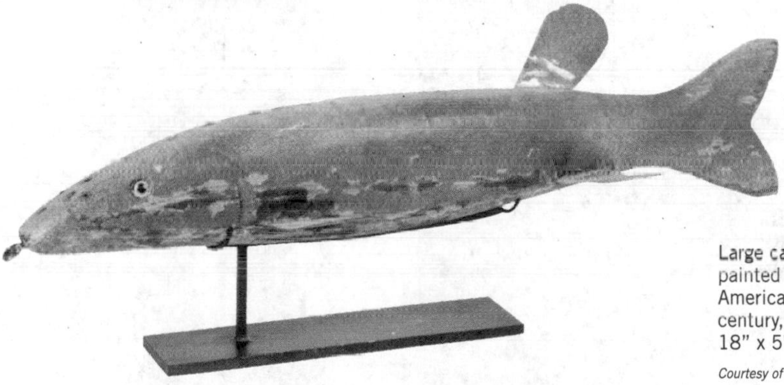

Large carved and painted fish decoy, American, 20th century, 4" x 18" x 5".............**$188**

Courtesy of Material Culture

Two fish decoys including one rainbow trout, excellent condition, larger 13-1/4" l. **$72**

Courtesy of Morphy Auctions

DISNEY

COLLECTIBLES THAT FEATURE Mickey Mouse, Donald Duck, and other famous characters of cartoon icon Walt Disney are everywhere. They can be found with little effort at flea markets, garage sales, local antiques and toys shows, and online as well as through auction houses and specialty catalogs.

Of Disney toys, comics, posters, and other items produced from 1930s through 1960s, prewar Disney material is by far the most desirable.

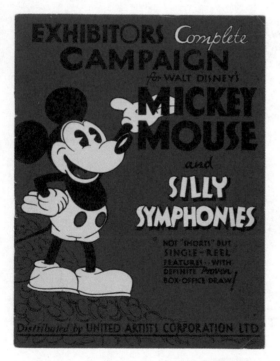

Mickey Mouse and Silly Symphonies English Exhibitors Complete Campaign book, 1932, 40 pages, published by Rawlings & Walsh, Ltd., and only sent to English theater owners/managers, 9" x 12". **$6,276**

Courtesy of Hake's Americana

Mickey Mouse largest size bisque, 1930s, movable arms, 8-3/4" h. **$5,819**

Courtesy of Hake's Americana

Mickey and Minnie Mouse large embossed French sand pail, mid-1930s, marked "EGDA" with "Par Aut. Walt Disney – Mickey Mouse S.A." text, 8-1/2" h. **$4,175**

Courtesy of Hake's Americana

Donald Duck, Goofy, Pluto and Mickey's nephew's sand pail, 1930s, Ohio Art, non-embossed variety, 5-5/8" h. **$1,600**

Courtesy of Hake's Americana

Mickey Mouse Savings Bank, Alex Harvey & Sons, Ltd., New Zealand, circa 1930s, 3-1/4" x 4-7/8" x 2". **$1,645**

Courtesy of Hake's Americana

Mickey Mouse original black-and-white nitrate production film cel, 1934, produced for animated short "Two-Gun Mickey" released Dec. 15, 1934, 9-3/4" x 12". **$13,800**

Courtesy of Hake's Americana

Nifty Mickey Mouse drummer tin toy, no. 173, distributed by Geo. Borgfeldt under its Nifty brand name, 6-1/2" h. **$2,657**

Courtesy of Hake's Americana

Cinderella prototype bank, Marx Toys, 2-1/2" x 4" x 4-1/8" h. $1,107

Courtesy of Hake's Americana

Mickey and Minnie Mouse child's chair, Kroehler Manufacturing Co., 1930s, 16-3/4" x 20" x 27-1/2"...$1,044

Courtesy of Hake's Americana

Mickey Mouse Steiff doll, 1930s, stuffed felt with oilcloth eyes and four mother-of-pearl pants buttons, smallest size, 4-1/2" h.....................$759

Courtesy of Hake's Americana

Walt Disney's Snow White boxed Timex wristwatch, rare, 1950s, Great Britain version, 7/8" x 1-1/4".................$1,392

Courtesy of Hake's Americana

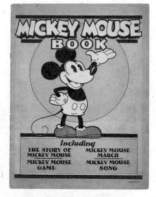

Mickey Mouse Book, first licensed Disney publication, by Bibo & Lang, copyright 1930, 16 pages, 9" x 12".............$968

Courtesy of Hake's Americana

Mickey Mouse boxed bank, Zell Products Co., 1930s, cream with gold luster side panels, bank 2-1/4" x 4-1/4" x 2"...$633

Courtesy of Hake's Americana

Large Pinocchio Belgium biscuit tin, "Par Aut. Walt Disney – Mickey Mouse S.A. – Etabl. J. Schuybroek S.A. Hoboken-Anvers," circa 1940, 7-3/4" x 12-3/4" x 2-1/2"...$512

Courtesy of Hake's Americana

"Dance of the Hours" ostrich storyboard original art from Walt Disney's 1940 animated musical "Fantasia," dated July 11, 1939, 7-3/4" x 10-1/4"..... **$1,173**

Courtesy of Hake's Americana

Mickey Mouse Uruguayan tea set, 1930s, three-person setting with three 3" dia. saucers, three 3/4" handled cups, 2" h. teapot, and 4-3/4" x 7-3/4" serving tray.. **$535**

Courtesy of Hake's Americana

Mickey and Minnie Mouse child's clothing/shoe rack made by Kroehler, 15" x 25-1/2" x 42-1/2"............................. **$557**

Courtesy of Hake's Americana

Matador animation cel from "Ferdinand the Bull," 1938, 4-1/2" x 5-1/8"................... **$460**

Courtesy of Hake's Americana

Mickey Mouse & Friends chalkboard made in England by LB, Ltd., 1930s, 20-1/2" x 45-1/2"............................... **$417**

Courtesy of Hake's Americana

Mickey Mouse wristwatch, Ingersoll, boxed version from fall/winter 1933, "5" beside Mickey's knee rather than above or below it, 1-1/4" dia. **$639**

Courtesy of Hake's Americana

Mickey Mouse and Felix the Cat wheel spinner toy, 1930s, missing generic wooden handle, 8-3/4" dia.......................... **$575**

Courtesy of Hake's Americana

top lot

Old King Cole Mickey and Minnie Mouse mechanical store displays, circa 1935, two-dimensional with original wood bracing/framework attached to reverse, motors and electric cords professionally replaced with modern devices and hardware, Mickey 30" x 40-3/4", Minnie 28-3/4" x 42"..... $29,222

COURTESY OF HAKE'S AMERICANA

Mickey Mouse Kolynos toothpaste premium BLB advertising sign, 7" x 11". $382

Courtesy of Hake's Americana

Pinocchio doll, Ideal, 1940s, painted composition head and torso, jointed wood limbs, 8" h. ..$62

Courtesy of Bertoia Auctions

Mickey Mouse full-figure Catalin plastic pencil sharpener, 1930s, 1-1/8" dia. $380

Courtesy of Hake's Americana

Mickey Mouse Palmolive soap premium, 1937 calendar, 3" x 5-7/8".........................$286

Courtesy of Hake's Americana

The Walt Disney Paint Book coloring book, no. 2080, Whitman, 1937, 11" x 13-3/4"................$510

Courtesy of Heritage Auctions

"Snow White and the Seven Dwarfs" Dec. 21, 1937 world premier movie program, Carthay Circle Theater in Los Angeles, 24 pages, 10" x 13"...........$381

Courtesy of Hake's Americana

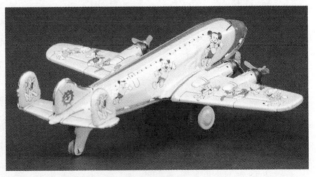

Four-prop jetliner lithographed tin toy, Linemar, Japan, with Disney character graphics, 7-1/2" wingspan. $432

Courtesy of Bertoia Auctions

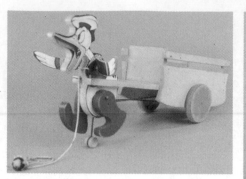

Trotting Donald Duck, Fisher-Price, 1937, No. 741, Walt Disney Enterprises, 19-1/2" l. **$990**

Courtesy of Bertoia Auctions

Pluto Mechanical Tricycle toy, Linemar, Japan, with original box, 3-3/4" h.............................. **$123**

Courtesy of Bertoia Auctions

Mickey Mouse Club MMM Movers, Inc. truck, Linemar, Japan, copyright Walt Disney Productions, friction-powered, 12-3/4" l...**$309**

Courtesy of Bertoia Auctions

Cheerios premium Y1 from "Donald Duck's Atom Bomb," signed by Carl Barks, Walt Disney Productions, 1947................**$300**
Courtesy of Heritage Auctions

Dumbo the Acrobat Elephant, Marx, Walt Disney Prod., 1941, lithographed tin wind-up toy that flips and leaps, 4" h. **$155**

Courtesy of Bertoia Auctions

"The Fox and the Hound" animation production cel original art, signed by Thomas and Johnston (Disney, 1980), 13" x 7". **$480**

Courtesy of Heritage Auctions

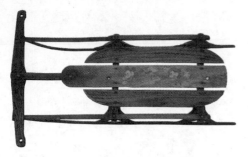

Child's sled with Mickey and Minnie decal,
1930s. **$378**

Courtesy of Philip Weiss Auctions

Official Walt Disney Mouseketeers costume play
outfit, size small, complete. **$47**

Courtesy of Philip Weiss Auctions

Three wooden carnival heads: Donald, Mickey
Mouse, and Horace Horsecollar. **$236**

Courtesy of Philip Weiss Auctions

Pinocchio marionette by Pelham Puppets,
England, copyright Walt Disney Productions,
painted and clothed, with strings and wooden
control bar, 2' h. **$480**

Courtesy of Morphy Auctions

Davy Crockett board game, 1955, Whitman. **$95**

Courtesy of Philip Weiss Auctions

DISNEY

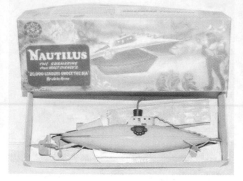

Nautilus submarine from Walt Disney's "20,000 Leagues Under the Sea," Sutcliff........................$170

Courtesy of Philip Weiss Auctions

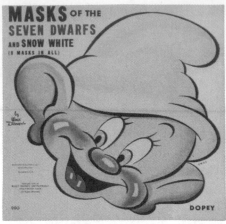

Masks of the Seven Dwarfs and Snow White set, complete. $96

Courtesy of Morphy Auctions

▲ Mary Poppins vinyl lunch box, circa 1973, Aladdin....................... $48

Courtesy of Morphy Auctions

◀ Matador doll from Walt Disney's "Ferdinand the Bull," Knickerbocker Toy Co., 23" h. $1,600

Courtesy of Philip Weiss Auctions

Hallowe'en With Mickey Mouse party set with table centerpiece, table covers, napkins, and other items.. $570

Courtesy of Morphy Auctions

Mickey Mouse Club Auto-Magic Picture gun with three Auto-Magic films, 1944....................$120

Courtesy of Morphy Auctions

DOLLS & DOLLHOUSES

DOLLS HAVE BEEN children's playthings for centuries. Dolls also have served other functions. From the 14th through 18th centuries, doll-making was centered in Europe, mainly in Germany and France. The French dolls produced in this era were representations of adults and dressed in the latest styles. They were not children's toys.

During the mid-19th century, child and baby dolls made of wax, cloth, bisque and porcelain were introduced. Facial features were hand-painted, wigs were made of mohair and human hair, and they were dressed in the current fashions for babies or children.

Doll-making in the United States began to flourish in the 1900s with companies such as Effanbee, Madame Alexander, and Ideal.

During the years of World War II, the development of new manmade products in the scientific community was centered on items allocated for military use. After the war, the emphasis changed.

Manmade products that had been put on hold because of the war or that had been used by the military were now made available for general use. Petroleum-based fibers such as nylon and later Dacron and Orlon were introduced to the clothing industry, and their ease of care and cleaning made life much easier for women who had worked so hard and sacrificed so much during the war years. Other petroleum-based products such as hard plastic were now more available, and vinyl soon followed.

These new manmade products did not go unnoticed by doll manufacturers. The development of new and innovative dolls had not been a priority for several years, but things were about to change. The new manmade products were exactly what the doll world had been waiting for. During the 1940s, hard plastic was being used in limited supply. Shortly after the war, a variation of plastic – called vinyl – was developed. Hard plastic, vinyl, or a combination of the two became the material of choice for doll manufacturers in the late 1940s and 1950s.

The major American doll companies now had what they needed to manufacturer a quality product, but how could they sell this product to a generation that had learned to do without?

The manufacturers looked at their major consumers: the women of America. These women were no longer restrained from buying as they had been. Many now had families with young children, nice homes, husbands with good jobs and good salaries, cars and, for the first time in many years, they were being exposed to glamour and fashion. Magazines and

Georgene Novelties Raggedy Ann with outlined nose, original dress with fading, facial and body watermarks, some hair missing, 18" h. **$30**

Courtesy of McMasters Harris Auction Co.

Carved and painted peg wooden doll, early 19th century, with original clothing, together with two miniature baskets and note, inscribed, "Sarah M. Tibbits her doll," 18" h. **$5,520**

Courtesy of Pook & Pook, Inc.

Multi-face doll, stamped C.B. for Carl Bergner, German bisque head with three faces – sleeping, crying and smiling, smiling face with glass eyes, crying face with tears and glass eyes, sleeping face with closed mouth; five-piece papier-mâché flapper-type body with molded shoes and socks with attached hood that hides unwanted faces, 14" h. **$840**

Courtesy of Morphy Auctions

Life-size Kestner baby doll, German bisque socket head incised "Q made in Germany 20 211 JDK" with sleeping eyes, light multi-stroked eyebrows, open mouth with two lower teeth, replaced wig, composition baby body, new cotton dress, three layered long antique baby slips, antique leather booties, 23" h. **$480**

Courtesy of Morphy Auctions

Flirty-eyed French walking doll, German bisque socket head "1039 Germany Simon & Halbig S & H" with flirty eyes, multi-stroked eyebrows, painted upper and lower lashes, open mouth with four upper teeth, pierced ears, curly mohair wig; French walking body turns head as legs move; extra navy blue silk two-piece dress with deterioration, hat and small leather purse and brooch on dress, 23" h. **$420**

Courtesy of Morphy Auctions

Flirty S & H doll, German bisque socket head incised "S.H. 1039 DEP 6 Germany" with red Wimpern stamp, molded eyebrows, flirty eyes, open mouth with upper teeth, pierced ears, replaced human hair wig; bisque shoulder plate, kid body with bisque lower arms; redressed in princess outfit, 18" h. **$240**

Courtesy of Morphy Auctions

newspapers were filled with advertisements for beauty products and stylish couture. No more painting seams on legs to represent stockings. No more coats and jackets made from blankets. No more dresses made and remade from old fabric. No more fingernails worn down because of work on military machinery, and no more hair hidden under bandanas. After five years of drabness, it was now time to shine – not only for ladies but also for dolls.

The doll manufacturers observed the popularity of the beauty products and the fashions flooding the pages of magazines and newspapers. The marketing people also realized that associating their dolls with a popular product would certainly increase sales. A popular product name would mean a popular product – at least that was the plan.

One of the earliest doll manufacturers to take advantage of this sales idea was the Ideal Toy Co. Ideal was known for its fine dolls and had been in business since the early 1900s, but the postwar period was a new market and the company was eager to compete.

Toni Home Permanents had become an overnight sensation for ladies and children. Now, home permanents could be done in the comfort of your home, and if the mother could give a permanent, why not the child? The Toni Co. allowed the Ideal Toy Co. to produce a doll that had hair that could be combed, washed and curled with a perm-type solution (not harmful). The perm rods and perm box looked just like the adult version. It even came with perm papers. While the perms were not always satisfactory, the sales proved very successful for Ideal and the idea spread.

A variation of the Toni doll was the Harriet Hubbard Ayer doll. This doll by Ideal used the Toni body but had a vinyl head and vinyl arms. The Harriet Hubbard Ayer Cosmetic Co. provided a cosmetic kit with each doll. "Child-safe" makeup including eyebrow pencil, eyeliner, rouge, lipstick, and fingernail polish came with the doll and could be applied to the vinyl face and to the unusual long fingernails. The popularity of these dolls was more limited than the Toni doll because the makeup was difficult to remove completely, and often the results were not pretty.

Revlon Cosmetics lent its name to another Ideal doll, the Revlon doll. Unlike the Toni doll, which represented a child, the Revlon doll had a lady's figure with a small waist and a bust, and she wore high heels. She could wear the high fashions seen in magazines, plus she could wear high heels and hose. Her fashions were influenced by designers such as Dior, but the names for the fashions were influenced by the names from the Revlon Cosmetic line. Names such as "Cherries a la Mode" given to one of the most popular Revlon doll outfits came directly from the introduction of the Revlon lipstick and nail polish color.

Like Ideal, the Arranbee Doll Co. needed a glamorous name association and formed an alliance with Coty Cosmetics. While Coty did not influence the doll directly, the name association paid off, and the little fashion ladies were quite popular in the late 1950s.

One of the largest doll manufacturers, Madame Alexander Doll Co., also saw the advantages of name recognition. Madame Alexander was a masterful businesswoman and drew up an agreement with the Yardley Cosmetic Co. A selection of the popular Cissy lady

Boxed Ideal Toni doll, all hard plastic with original blonde wig in original set, lashed sleeping eyes, rosy cheeks; tagged original dress with attached slip and matching panties, shoes and socks, wrist tag and Toni Playwave set; in original doll box, seam split on one upper leg, excellent condition, 14". $210

Courtesy of Morphy Auctions

Heinrich Handwerck 109 bisque socket head child doll, glass sleep eyes, open mouth, pierced ears, original mohair wig, jointed composition body with original finish; two fingers missing on right hand, one on left, damage to coat, 1" hairline crack between holes on back of head, 17-1/2" h...... **$275**

Courtesy of McMasters Harris Auction Co.

German bisque head boy, 14" h. **$190**

Courtesy of McMasters Harris Auction Co.

Jumeau "portrait" Bebe, closed mouth, 14" h. **$3,750**

Courtesy of McMasters Harris Auction Co

Large Armand Marseille bisque head doll, inscribed AM 17, with sleep eyes and open mouth, 38" h. **$615**

Courtesy of Pook & Pook, Inc.

French fashion lady, bisque swivel head on shoulder plate, perimeter stitched mohair wig over original cork pate, unmarked, 17" h. **$1,200**

Courtesy of McMasters Harris Auction Co.

Terri Lee doll on roller skates, tagged purple organdy dress with tulle, with extra pair of fur-trimmed slippers, 16" h. **$170**

Courtesy of McMasters Harris Auction Co.

dolls were to be used in the Yardley advertisements, which were seen in many popular ladies magazines. This proved to be a great sales boost to both Yardley Cosmetics and the Madame Alexander Cissy doll.

A child doll by Alexander was not to be left out. A "Little Lady" 8" Wendy Kin was produced that came with "Little Lady" cosmetics, including toilet water, bubble bath, and perfume.

Partnering the name of a doll firm with a name associated with beauty was a brilliant move. This, plus the utilization of manmade advances in manufacturing technology, established the U.S. doll industry as the best in the world.

— Sherry Minton

Side-glancing male china doll with painted brushstrokes, probably ABG, exposed ears, cloth body with replaced china hands and feet, 21" h.........................$60

Courtesy of McMasters Harris Auction Co.

Eugenie Poir all-original cloth doll, French, circa 1930s, mask pressed and painted facial features, blue side-glancing eyes with applied upper eyelashes, blue eye shadow, painted lower lashes, closed mouth with bow-shaped lips, light brown mohair wig, jointed arms and legs; original organdy dress with felt trim, felt jacket, hat, organdy undergarments, woven socks, and felt shoes, 19".............$100

Courtesy of Frasher's Doll Auction

French Tete Jumeau bisque head doll, inscribed Depose Tete Jumeau Bte S. G. D. G. 8, with jointed composition body, fixed eyes, closed mouth, 19" h....$3,120

Courtesy of Pook & Pook, Inc.

Kathe Kruse "Rose" X, made in Germany, painted hair and face, wrist and neck tag, in original clothes, 14" h. $1,250

Courtesy of McMasters Harris Auction Co.

Martha Chase-type stockinette doll with painted blue eyes, closed mouth, textured blond hair, stitched and jointed stockinette limbs, and cloth body, unmarked, with white cotton tunic, linen pants, and plaid shirt, 16" h................$185

Courtesy of Skinner Inc.; www.skinnerinc.com

Madame Alexander Jacqueline, vinyl, in tagged riding outfit, with additional newer clothes and travel trunks (not shown), 21" h. $300

Courtesy of McMasters Harris Auction Co.

333

Two Sasha dolls including #119 Cora in blue corduroy dress, and #309 Caleb in sweater and khakis, both in original boxes. **$170**

Courtesy of McMasters Harris Auction Co.

German bisque head character doll, 14" h. **$200**

Courtesy of McMasters Harris Auction Co.

German bisque head googly-eye doll, inscribed Demalcol 10/0 Germany, with a composition body, 7" h. **$461**

Courtesy of Pook & Pook, Inc.

LHK child doll, German bisque socket head incised "LHK made in Germany," dark multi-stroked eyebrows, large blue stationary eyes, painted upper and lower eyelashes, antique human hair wig; original early composition and wood jointed body, old repaint, head needs to be attached; dress and underwear appear original, replaced shoes and socks, good condition, 20". **$270**

Courtesy of Morphy Auctions

Composition Uncle Sam doll in original patriotic costume, 11-1/2" h. **$360**

Courtesy of Pook & Pook, Inc.

Huebach Kopplesdorf bisque head doll, inscribed 250.3, with sleep eyes and open mouth, 23" h. **$154**

Courtesy of Pook & Pook, Inc.

Leo Moss-type Amanda doll by RQ, with glass eyes, molded tears and red check dress, 21" h. **$850**

Courtesy of McMasters Harris Auction Co.

German bisque Parian lady with decorated blonde curls, bisque shoulder head with molded bodice, sculpted blonde hair in ringlet curls, floral decoration, pierced ears, painted features, blue eyes, red and black lid lines, closed mouth, old cloth body with leather arms, lace and silk two-piece gown, very good quality bisque and decoration, sturdy body, leather arms discolored, 17"..**$400**

Courtesy of Frasher's Doll Auctions

Bisque boy doll, 19th century, with fixed eyes, closed mouth, molded hair, kid leather body, and original miner's outfit, 19" h. **$240**

Courtesy of Pook & Pook, Inc.

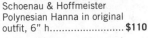

Shirley Temple doll in curly top dress, marks: "Shirley Temple 13," composition socket head on five-piece jointed body, original blonde wig in original set, sleep eyes, applied and painted lashes, open mouth, upper teeth; pink organdy dress, white teddy with slip, white leatherette shoes, Shirley pin, 13" h..........................**$225**

Courtesy of Frasher's Doll Auctions

Cubeb boudoir smoker doll, 25" h. **$650**

Courtesy of McMasters Harris Auction Co.

Schoenau & Hoffmeister Polynesian Hanna in original outfit, 6" h..........................**$110**

Courtesy of McMasters Harris Auction Co.

White and green-painted wood two-story dollhouse with white-painted brick-pattern exterior, white-painted wood portico and double front doors, green-trimmed windows, slate-pattern roof, and two red brick-pattern chimneys, together with painted and turned wood stand. $240

Courtesy of Skinner Inc.; www.skinnerinc.com

Wooden dollhouse, 14" l. $60

Courtesy of Morphy Auctions

Schoenhut wooden dollhouse bedroom set, circa 1930, wooden furnishings with painted green finish, applied decals, 10" h. x 9-1/2" w. wardrobe closet with double doors, poster bed with mattress, dresser with two drawers and mirror, dressing table with single drawer and mirror, and side chair. $200

Courtesy of Frasher's Doll Auction

Painted and electrified dollhouse, 20th century, two-story structure with shingled roof, front stoop, and five rooms, 28" h. x 21-3/4" w. x 15-1/2" d. $246

Courtesy of Skinner Inc.; www.skinnerinc.com

Gottschalck blue-roofed wooden two-story dollhouse, circa 1900, lithographed paper exterior to simulate architectural details such as brick, stonework, railings, and window detail, attic gable dormer with applied decoration, recessed right side with front porch, second floor balcony, seven curtained glass windows, front door with latch, hinged front opens to reveal originally papered interior, wooden base and steps, 18" h. x 12" w. x 9-1/2" d. $750

Courtesy of Frasher's Doll Auction

Dollhouse barn and shed, circa 1950, 21" l. **$120**

Courtesy of Morphy Auctions

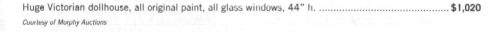

Huge Victorian dollhouse, all original paint, all glass windows, 44" h. **$1,020**

Courtesy of Morphy Auctions

Dollhouse, circa 1920, with all but one original glass window, one missing balcony post, 27-1/2" h. **$600**

Courtesy of Morphy Auctions

Large two-story dollhouse, 42" l. **$480**

Courtesy of Morphy Auctions

DOORSTOPS

DOORSTOPS HAVE BEEN AROUND as long as there have been doors. They were originally improvised from garden stones, wedges of wood, pieces of furniture, or any other objects heavy enough to prop doors open to ensure air circulation. Early decorative ones, which date from the late 1700s, were generally round and made of sand-cast brass or metal with flat, hollow backs.

By the early 19th century, scores of French and English households boasted fashionable three-dimensional iron doorstops in the shape of animals, flowers, and figurines. Some, called door porters, incorporated convenient long handles that were used to lift and place them easily.

Homes with French double doors often featured matching pairs, like eagles or horse hooves, Punch and Judy, or lions opposing unicorns. Today these sets range from $400-$900 each, depending on condition and themes.

Doorstops migrated to American shores after the Civil War, where due to Yankee frugality, they became smaller and lighter than European models.

During the height of their popularity – the 1920s through the mid-1940s – American homemakers could purchase doorstops, or coordinated sets that included doorknockers and bookends, for pennies in gift stores and through mail-order catalogs. Fashionable Art Deco, circus, and nursery rhyme themes, along with figures like organ grinders, dapper gentlemen, Southern belles and flappers, reflected the times.

Cheery flower and flower basket doorstops featuring bouquets of tulips, zinnias, pansies, black-eyed Susans or sunflowers, for example, celebrated the arrival of spring. Although some currently start at around $100 apiece, those that have survived with original paint in prime condition may fetch many times that amount.

Hubley's dog breed doorstops, which portray lifelike, highly detailed Doberman pinschers, German shepherds, cocker spaniels, French bulldogs, beagles and various types of terriers, and more, were also extremely popular. So were arched, curled, springing, or sleeping cats.

John and Nancy Smith, avid collectors and leading doorstop and figural cast iron authorities, as well as authors of *The Doorstop Book: An*

Boston terrier bulldog doorstop, Old Danish silver, circa 1920, marked Bradley & Hubbard, W. Meriden, CT, catalog #7924, original paint with some fading and oxidation, 9" h. x 11" w. **$585**

Courtesy of Copake Auction, Inc.

Dapper Dan cast iron doorstop, circa 1920, marked "H.L. Judd, New Britain, CT," original paint with some fading, scratches and scuff marks, 9" h. **$936**

Courtesy of Copake Auction, Inc.

Bathing girls doorstop, Hubley Manufacturing Co., Lancaster, Pennsylvania, circa 1920, marked "Fish" on front and "250" on backside, original paint, 11-1/2" h.............. **$2,223**

Courtesy of Copake Auction, Inc.

Bathing beauties doorstop, Hubley Manufacturing Co., Lancaster, Pennsylvania, circa 1920, popular Art Deco design of two young women in bathing gear sharing two-toned parasol, designed by Anne Harriet Fish, marked "© FISH 250" on base, minor paint chipping on parasol and figures, 11" h. x 5-1/4" w. **$2,100**

Courtesy of Bertoia Auctions

◀ Owl on stump pedestal electroplated doorstop, circa 1920, Hubley Manufacturing Co., Lancaster, Pennsylvania, catalog #254, original surface with some oxidation, 10" h..**$351**

Courtesy of Copake Auction, Inc.

▶ Owl on pedestal cast iron doorstop, circa 1920, Bradley & Hubbard, W. Meriden, Connecticut, marked "7797" and "B & H" on backside, original paint, detailed illustration of beak, feathers and talons, 16" h. **$3,480**

Courtesy of Copake Auction, Inc.

Four cast iron doorstops: Painted tulip basket, blue-painted cat with darker bow and black base attributed to Hubley Manufacturing Co., Lancaster, Pennsylvania, white cat with blue eyes attributed to Hubley, and painted kitten in playful pose with red bow, all circa early 20th century, most with minimal paint wear. **$861**

Courtesy Case Antiques, Inc. Auctions & Appraisals

Encyclopedia of Doorstop Collecting, find that beginners generally concentrate on certain themes like flowers, animals, people, or wildlife. Some seek doorstops produced by a particular foundry, including Albany, National, Eastern Specialty, Judd, Wilton, Litto, Virginia Metalcrafters, Waverly, or Spencer.

As their collections grow, however, many explore other themes as well. Nautical enthusiasts may collect clipper ship, sailor, lighthouse, and anchor doorstops. Sports fans may seek skiers, golfers, caddies, or football players. Animal lovers may populate menageries with Hubley honey bears and horses or Bradley & Hubbard parrots. Some prefer pets portrayed in character, like rabbits in evening dress, Peter Rabbits chomping on carrots, and strutting ducks in tophats. These fancies currently sell from $300-$2,000.

Other collectors search for bright, sassy, desirable and pricey Anne Fish Art Deco pieces like bathing beauties, Charleston dancers, and parrots, or Taylor Cook's brightly colored elephants on barrels, koalas, or fawns.

"In addition to their beauty," observed Lewis Keister, proprietor of East Meets West Antiques based in Los Angeles, "the historical value of many of these doorstops can be significant. One highly desirable doorstop, the yellow-slickered Old Salt fisherman, for example, is very appealing to both antique collectors and folk art collectors." So are nostalgic, mellow-hued stagecoach, Conestoga wagon, Aunt Jemima, Victorian lady, fruit basket, horns of plenty, and cozy, rose-covered cottage doorstops. Even when doorstops outnumber doors, home decorators, charmed by their appeal, often display them as colorful accent pieces, bookends, or works of art lined up in custom-built shelving, antique cupboards, or along staircases.

Doorstops that feature outstanding sculptural quality, form and character are the most desirable of all. If they also bear identifying stamps, signatures, copyrights, studio names, or production numbers (that often appear on their backs), their values rise even further.

In addition to desirability, rarity – possibly due to high production costs, short foundry existence, or even bad design – raises the value of vintage doorstops. Condition, however, determines their ultimate worth. Collectors should certainly buy doorstops that they like within a price range that they find comfortable. But they should be in the very best condition that they can afford. According to experts, only these will retain or increase in value over time. And some may increase considerably.

Today, for example, a rare, unusual, desirable doorstop that is also in mint condition – perhaps a vintage Uncle Sam, Halloween girl, or Whistling Jim, may command as much as $10,000.

Cottage in Woods cast iron doorstop, Albany, and Castle in Woods cast iron doorstop, repainted, good condition, larger 8-5/8" h. **$240**

Courtesy of Morphy Auctions, Inc.

Because doorstops are cast objects, however, they lend themselves to reproduction. In addition to reuse of old molds, new designs are continually in production. "Older doorstops usually have smoother, more refined castings than reproductions, which are rougher or pebbly," the Smiths said. "Seams, if any, are usually tighter. Originals feature slotted screws or rivets, while reproductions, if cast in two or more pieces, are usually assembled with Philips-head screws. Moreover, artists generally painstakingly smoothed mold marks of vintage castings with hand files. Reproductions, however, are finished in minutes with power tools and tumblers. These leave coarser grinding marks."

Collectors should also look carefully at the wear patterns on possible buys. Most old doorstops were used for their original purpose – holding doors open. So potential buyers are advised to look for wear in the logical places: on their tops, where they were handled, and around their bases, where they were scuffed along the floor. Reproductions rarely resemble the real thing.

By studying as many collections as possible, by actually handling as many doorstops as possible, beginners can learn to differentiate between vintage pieces and reproductions.

Doorstops are readily found at antique shows, shops, and auctions. It is recommended, however, to purchase them from reputable dealers who not only specialize in cast iron items, but also guarantee their authenticity.

— Melody Amsel-Arieli

Highland Lighthouse cast iron doorstop, marked "Highland Light, Cape Code" on front of base, circa 1920, unknown foundry, hand painted, original, some fading of color on top of roofs and along base, chipping on lighthouse, 9" h. x 9" w. **$1,053**

Courtesy of Copake Auction, Inc.

Bronze Spanish galleon doorstop, multi-mast model with base crafted to mimic ocean waves, cast mark "ARG" on bottom with hand-inscribed 1928, patina appearing where waves and bottom of ship meet and on topmost flag on bow, 12-1/2" h. x 14" w. **$146**

Courtesy of Copake Auction, Inc.

Pair of footmen cast iron doorstops, circa 1930, smaller and scarcer of two sizes produced, Hubley Manufacturing Co., Lancaster, Pennsylvania, designed by illustrator and cartoonist Anne Harriet Fish, marked "FISH" on left front corner of base and "272" on backside, original paint, marks and wear on faces of footmen, 9" h. **$870**

Courtesy of Copake Auction, Inc.

Caddie cast iron doorstop, Hubley Manufacturing Co., Lancaster, Pennsylvania, circa 1920, seldom-seen example with detailed patterns on caddie's pants, jacket and golf bag, some chipping to original paint on caddie's jacket and cap, good condition overall, 8-1/4" h. **$1,897**

Courtesy of RSL Auction Co.

Hand-painted cast iron sculptural golfer doorstop, foundry unknown, circa 1925, good condition, 8" h. x 7" w. x 2-1/2" d., 4-1/2 lbs. **$218**

Courtesy of Louis J. Dianni, LLC

Putting Golfer cast iron doorstop, Hubley #34, red jacket and tan knee breeches on green-shaped base, original painted surface, Hubley Manufacturing Co., Lancaster, Pennsylvania, first quarter 20th century, 8-1/2" h. x 7" w..... **$371**

Courtesy of Jeffrey S. Evans & Associates

Parrot on stoop cast iron doorstop, marked "Made by Blodgett Studio, Lake George, Wisconsin" on bottom of base, hand-painted color with usual wear with time, overall excellent condition, 12 1/4" l. **$420**

Courtesy of Morphy Auctions, Inc.

Charleston Dancers cast iron doorstop, circa 1920, seldom-seen example of one of six Art Deco-style doorstops created by U.K. illustrator Anne Harriet Fish for Hubley Manufacturing Co., Lancaster, Pennsylvania, marked "FISH," original paint, some paint chipping on dancers' arms and legs, 8-3/4" h................... **$660**

Courtesy of Stanton Auctions

Standing English bulldog doorstop, Hubley Manufacturing Co., Lancaster, Pennsylvania, catalog #460, with turned head and animated expression, original paint, some chipping along spine and face, excellent condition overall, 5-1/2" l. **$900**

Courtesy of Morphy Auctions, Inc.

▶ Black Americana cast iron doorstops: Hand-painted figure with red dress and blue polka dot scarf, no markings, 9" h., and another figure with black dress and red polka dot scarf, stamped Copyright Hubley, 12" h.; overall good condition, paint chips throughout both doorstops........................... **$300**

Courtesy of Morphy Auctions, Inc.

Art Deco girl cast iron doorstop, first quarter 20th century, outstretched arms grasping flowing gown, impressed "1251" reverse side, original painted surface, 9-1/4" h. x 7-1/4" w. **$463**

Courtesy of Jeffrey S. Evans & Associates

Three Little Kittens cast iron doorstop, detailed facial features and illustration of open book, Bradley & Hubbard, paint chipping along top of pages and noses of cats. **$1,888**

Courtesy of Bertoia Auctions

Foundry worker cast iron doorstop, double-sided with detailed cap, gloves, goggles and apron, holding full pot, "Hill Clutch" marked along side of pot, overall excellent condition, paint chipping on areas of face, top of cap, and along base with wear along fingers of glove, 6" h. **$2,040**

Courtesy of Morphy Auctions

◀ Scarce full-figure casting of black man in top hat holding box of matches while sitting on bale of cotton, figure in pot metal and cotton bale in cast iron, Judd Co., "1248," detailed pattern to figure's pants and shirt, some paint chipping on figure's elbows, knees and hands, overall excellent-plus condition, 9" h. **$3,300**

Courtesy of Morphy Auctions

Rare tiger iron doorstop with glass eyes created for "The Jungle Boy," meant to sit beside another doorstop of Jungle Boy hugging tiger, 19th century, intricate details on face and body of tiger, including two canine teeth... **$455**

Courtesy of Pangea Auctions

Marblehead pottery doorstops, deep blue matte glaze with bas relief decoration of galleon and Viking ship, latter retains original paper label, overall very good condition, 5-1/4" and 5-1/2" h., respectively.......... **$402**

Courtesy of Thomaston Place Auction Galleries

Cast iron doorstops: Spirit of St. Louis airplane in nickel over cast iron perched on detailed base and Graf Zeppelin at mooring tower, both in good condition, some oxidation on base, color fading along body of Graf Zeppelin, 8-3/4" h....... **$390**

Courtesy of Morphy Auctions

Graf Zeppelin cast iron doorstop, scarce example marked "Graf Zeppelin" on lower front of airship, first quarter 20th century, 8-3/4" h. x 13" w. **$371**

Courtesy of Jeffrey S. Evans & Associates

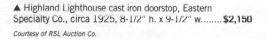

Cat cold-painted cast iron doorstop, hand-painted gray and white with two yellow eyes of varying shapes, paint chipping on chest and face, 7" h. x 13" w. **$118**

Courtesy of Hartzells Auction Gallery

▲ Highland Lighthouse cast iron doorstop, Eastern Specialty Co., circa 1925, 8-1/2" h. x 9-1/2" w........**$2,150**

Courtesy of RSL Auction Co.

Red Riding Hood and Wolf cast iron doorstop, Nuydea Co., U.K. producer of doorstops, sprinklers, and bookends, scarce model, early 20th century, 7-1/2" h. x 9-1/2" w...**$1,771**

Courtesy of RSL Auction Co.

Relief-decorated cast iron dog doorstop facing left with heavy base representing grass, early 20th century, Bradley & Hubbard, original paint, good condition with no breaks or repairs, 9-3/4" h. x 12" w. x 3" d.........................**$484**

Courtesy of Fontaine's Auction Gallery

top lot

Football player cast iron doorstop in full uniform holding football in rushing stance, jersey marked "STATE," 20th century, scarce, excellent condition overall, some paint chipping on face and helmet, 11" h...$11,400

Full-figure dog doorstop, one of largest produced by Hubley Manufacturing Co., Lancaster, Pennsylvania, catalog #454, realistic size and original hand painting, scarce, overall very good condition, paint chipping throughout, specifically to dog's nose, normal wear on bottom of paws, 9-3/4" h. **$1,800**

FIGURINES
=========

hummel figurines & collectibles

THE GOEBEL COMPANY of Oeslau, Germany, first produced M.I. Hummel porcelain figurines in 1934, having obtained the rights to adapt the beautiful pastel sketches of children by Sister Maria Innocentia (Berta) Hummel. Every design by the Goebel artisans was approved by the nun until her death in 1946. Goebel produced these charming collectibles until Sept. 30, 2008. Manufaktur Rödental GmbH resumed production in 2009.

For more information on M.I. Hummel collectibles, see *The Official M.I. Hummel Price Guide,* 2nd edition, by Heidi Ann von Recklinghausen.

HUMMEL TRADEMARKS

Since 1935, there have been several changes in the trademarks on M.I. Hummel items. In later years of production, each new trademark design merely replaced the old one, but in the earlier years, frequently the new design trademark would be placed on a figurine that already bore the older style trademark.

THE CROWN MARK (TMK-1): 1934-1950

The Crown Mark (TMK-1 or CM), sometimes referred to as the "Crown-WG," was used by Goebel on all of its products in 1935, when M.I. Hummel figurines were first made commercially available. The letters WG below the crown in the mark are the initials of William Goebel, one of the founders of the company. The crown signifies his loyalty to the imperial family of Germany at the time of the mark's design, around 1900. The mark is sometimes found in an incised circle.

Another Crown-type mark is sometimes confusing to collectors; some refer to it as the "Narrow Crown" and others the "Wide Ducal Crown." This mark was introduced by Goebel in 1937 and used on many of its products.

Often, the Crown Mark will appear twice on the same piece, more often one mark incised and the other stamped. This is, as we know, the "Double Crown."

When World War II ended and the United States Occupation Forces allowed Goebel to begin exporting, the pieces were marked as having been made in the occupied zone.

These marks were applied to the bases of the figurines, along with the other markings, from 1946 through 1948. They were sometimes applied under the glaze and often over the glaze. Between 1948 and 1949, the U.S. Zone mark requirement was dropped, and the word "Germany" took its place. With the partitioning of Germany into East and West, "W. Germany," "West Germany," or "Western Germany" began to appear most of the time instead.

Incised Crown Mark

Stamped Crown Mark

Wide Ducal Crown Mark

THE FULL BEE MARK (TMK-2): 1940-1959

In 1950, Goebel made a major change in its trademark. The company incorporated a bee in a V. It is thought that the bumblebee part of the mark was derived from a childhood nickname of Sister Maria Innocentia Hummel, meaning bumblebee. The bee flies within a V, which is the first letter of the German word for distributing company, Verkaufsgesellschaft.

There are actually 12 variations of the Bee marks to be found on Goebel-produced M.I. Hummel items.

The Full Bee mark, also referred to as TMK-2 or abbreviated FB, is the first of the Bee marks to appear. The mark evolved over nearly 20 years until the company began to modernize it. It is sometimes found in an incised circle.

The very large bee flying in the V remained until around 1956, when the bee was reduced in size and lowered into the V. It can be found incised, stamped in black, or stamped in blue, in that order, through its evolution.

Incised Full Bee   Stamped Full Bee

High Bee   Small Bee. Note that the   Baby Bee   Vee Bee
            bee's wingtips are level with
            the top of the V.

THE STYLIZED BEE (TMK-3): 1958-1972

A major change in the way the bee is rendered in the trademark made its appearance in 1960. The Stylized Bee (TMK-3), sometimes abbreviated as Sty-Bee, as the major component of the trademark appeared in three basic forms through 1972. The first two are both classified as the Stylized Bee (TMK-3), but the third is considered a fourth step in the evolution, the Three Line Mark (TMK-4).

The Large Stylized Bee: This trademark was used primarily from 1960 through 1963. The color of the mark will be black or blue. It is sometimes found inside an incised circle. When you find the Large Stylized Bee mark, you will normally find a stamped "West" or "Western Germany" in black elsewhere on the base, but not always.

The Small Stylized Bee: This mark is also considered to be TMK-3. It was used concurrently with the Large Stylized Bee from about 1960 and continued in this use until about 1972. The mark is usually rendered in blue, and it too is often accompanied by a stamped black "West" or "Western Germany." Collectors and dealers sometimes refer to the mark as the One Line Mark.

Large Stylized Bee

W. Germany
Small Stylized Bee

THE THREE LINE MARK (TMK-4): 1964-1972

This trademark is sometimes abbreviated 3-line or 3LM in print. The trademark used the same stylized V and bee as the others, but also included three lines of wording beside it. This major change appeared in blue.

Three Line Mark

THE LAST BEE MARK (TMK-5): 1972-1979

Developed and occasionally used as early as 1970, this major change was known by some collectors as the Last Bee Mark because the next change in the trademark no longer incorporated any form of the V and the bee. However, with the reinstatement of a bee in TMK-8 with the turn of the century, TMK-5 is not technically the "Last Bee" any longer. The mark was used until about mid-1979. There are three minor variations in the mark shown in the illustration. Generally, the mark was placed under the glaze from 1972 through 1976 and is found placed over the glaze from 1976 through 1979.

Last Bee Mark

THE MISSING BEE MARK (TMK 6): 1979-1991

The transition to this trademark began in 1979 and was complete by mid-1980. Goebel removed the V and bee from the mark altogether, calling it the Missing Bee. In conjunction with this change, the company instituted the practice of adding to the traditional artist's mark the date the artist finished painting the piece.

Missing Bee Mark

THE HUMMEL MARK (TMK-7): 1991-1999

In 1991, Goebel changed the trademark once again. This time, the change was not only symbolic of the reunification of the two Germanys by removal of the "West" from the mark, but very significant in another way. Until then, Goebel used the same trademark on virtually all of its products. The mark illustrated here was for exclusive use on Goebel products made from the paintings and drawings of M.I. Hummel.

Hummel Mark

THE MILLENNIUM BEE (TMK-8): 2000-2008

Goebel decided to celebrate the beginning of a new century with a revival in a bee-adorned trademark. Seeking once again to honor the memory of Sister Maria Innocentia Hummel, a bumblebee, this time flying solo without the V, was reinstated into the mark in 2000 and ended in 2008. Goebel stopped production of the M.I. Hummel figurines on Sept. 30, 2008.

Millennium Bee Mark

THE MANUFAKTUR RÖDENTAL MARK (TKM-9): 2009-PRESENT

Manufaktur Rödental purchased the rights to produce M.I. Hummel figurines from Goebel in 2009. This trademark signified a new era for Hummel figurines while maintaining the same quality and workmanship from the master sculptors and master painters at the Rödental factory. This trademark has a full bee using yellow and black for the bumblebee, which circles around the words "Original M.I. Hummel Germany" with the copyright sign next to M.I. Hummel. Manufaktur Rödental is underneath the circle with a copyright sign.

Manufaktur Rödental Mark

FIGURINES

For purposes of simplification, the various trademarks have been abbreviated in the list below. Generally speaking, earlier trademarks are worth more than later trademarks.

TRADEMARK	ABBREVIATIONS	DATES
Crown	TMK-1	1934-1950
Full Bee	TMK-2	1940-1959
Stylized Bee	TMK-3	1958-1972
Three Line Mark	TMK-4	1964-1972
Last Bee	TMK-5	1972-1979
Missing Bee	TMK-6	1979-1991
Hummel Mark	TMK-7	1991-1999
Millennium Bee/Goebel Bee	TMK-8	2000-2008
Manufaktur Rödental Mark	TMK-9	2009-present

Hum 1: Puppy Love, trademarks 1-6 .... **$200-$2,900**

Hum 2: Little Fiddler, trademarks 1-8 .. **$175-$2,000**

Hum 3: Book Worm, trademarks 1-8..... **$200-$2,500**

Hum 4: Little Fiddler, trademarks 1-8 .. **$200-$1,500**
The left piece features the doll face with pale hands and face, different head position, and lack of neckerchief.

Hum 5: Strolling Along,
trademarks 1-6...........**$150-$425**

Hum 6: Sensitive Hunter,
trademarks 1-8........**$125-$1,500**

Hum 7: Merry Wanderer,
trademarks 1-8................................$200-$25,000

Hum 9: Begging His Share,
trademarks 1-9...................................$150-$1,000

Hum 8: Book Worm,
trademarks 1-8...........**$200-$475**
*This image shows the
comparison between the normal
skin coloration (left) and the
pale coloration.*

RIGHT: Hum 10: Flower Madonna,
trademarks 1-7...........**$200-$800**

FAR RIGHT: Hum 11: Merry Wanderer,
trademarks 1-8+1.......**$100-$625**

Hum 12: Chimney Sweep,
trademarks 1-8.............**$99-$550**

Hum 14/A, 14/B: Book Worm bookends, trademarks 1-8+1......**$350-$800**

Hum 13: Meditation,
trademarks 1-9..........**$99-$2,750**

Hum 15: Hear Ye, Hear Ye,
trademarks 1-8...........**$125-$650**

Hum 16: Little Hiker,
trademarks 1-8...........**$140-$500**

Hum 18: Christ Child, trademarks 1-7................................**$125-$250**

◄ Hum 17: Congratulations, trademarks 1-7 ....**$175-$2,000**

Hum 20: Prayer Before Battle, trademarks 1-8...........**$200-$450**

Hum 21: Heavenly Angel, trademarks 1-8.............**$100-$800**

Hum 22: Angel With Bird holy water font, trademarks 1-8 ....**$50-$300**

Hum 24: Lullaby candleholder, trademarks 1-7...........**$150-$900**

Hum 26: Child Jesus holy water font, trademarks 1-7 .....**$40-$450**

Hum 23: Adoration, trademarks 1-8 ....**$250-$900**

Hum 25: Angelic Sleep candleholder, trademarks 1-6......................................**$150-$450**

Hum 27: Joyous News, trademarks 1-7....**$225-$750**

FIGURINES

lladró

LLADRÓ FIGURINES – distinctive, elegant creations often glazed in the trademark colors of blue and white – hail from a Spanish company founded by three brothers 60 years ago.

Juan, José, and Vicente Lladró began producing ceramic sculptures in their parents' home near Valencia, Spain in the mid-1950s. In 1955 they established their own retail shop where they sold some of their earliest wares. In 1958 they moved to a factory in the town of Tavernes Blanques.

The 1960s were a decade of such strong growth and development, the Lladró company enlarged its facilities seven times before finally breaking ground for a new factory in 1967. This factory/office building complex, known as the City of Porcelain, was inaugurated in October 1969.

The 1970s were marked by Lladró's consolidation in the American market. In 1974, the first blue emblem – a bellflower and an ancient chemical symbol – appeared on the sculptures. Lladró's success continued into the 1980s, and in 1985, the Lladró Collectors Society was launched. It lasted for more than 15 years. During the 1990s the Lladró brothers received several awards for their creations, which were exhibited in several cities throughout the world, and the company continued expanding. In 2001, the Lladró Collectors Society gave way to Lladró Privilege, a customer loyalty program.

Today Lladró – still headquartered at the City of Porcelain – employs 2,000 people and markets its creations in more than 100 countries across the globe.

A "G" after the identification number refers to a glazed finish; "M" refers to a matte finish. "G/M" means both glazed and matte finishes.

"Clown," 4618, glossy finish, originally issued in 1970, 13-3/4" l.
$100

Courtesy of Elite Decorative Arts

"Angela," 5211, originally issued in 1984, retired in 2003, 8-1/2" h. **$75**

Courtesy of Elite Decorative Arts

"Angel," 4537, originally issued in 1970, retired in 2005, 4-3/4" x 4-3/4". **$30**

Courtesy of Manor Auctions

"Best Friend," 7620, Lladró Collectors Society piece, originally issued in 1993, retired in 1995, glossy finish, 6-1/4" x 5". **$75**

Courtesy of Elite Decorative Arts

"Boy on Carousel Horse," 1470, originally issued in 1985, retired in 2001, 15" h. **$125**

Courtesy of Elite Decorative Arts

"Cinderella," 4828, originally issued in 1972, retired in 1998, 10" h. **$60**

Courtesy of Phoebus Auction Gallery

▲ "Duck," 1057, originally issued in 1970, retired in 1986, approximately 7" l. x 6" h. **$50**

Courtesy of Elite Decorative Arts

◀ "Dressmaker," 4700, in original box marked "700," originally issued in 1970, retired, 14" h. **$125**

Courtesy of Kaminski Auctions

▲ "Hebrew Student," 4684, seated male student reading book, originally issued in 1970, retired in 1985, 11-1/2" h. .. **$110**

Courtesy of Clars Auction Gallery, www.clars.com

◀ "For Me?," 5454, originally issued in 1988, retired in 1998, 6-1/2" h, x 9-1/2" l, x 5-3/4" w. **$150**

Courtesy of Elite Decorative Arts

◀ "Japanese Girl Decorating," 4840, originally issued in 1973, retired in 1998, approximately 8" h. **$75**

Courtesy of Elite Decorative Arts

"Japanese With Fan," 4991, glossy finish, originally issued in 1978, retired in 1998, 11-3/4" h. **$75**

Courtesy of Elite Decorative Arts

357

"Japanese With Parasol,"
4988, originally issued in
1978, retired in 1996,
11-1/2" h. **$80**

Courtesy of Omega Auction Corp.

"Little Sister," 1534, two
sisters with sleeping pet cat,
originally issued in 1988,
retired in 1992, 7" h. **$100**

Courtesy of Elite Decorative Arts

"Love's Tender Tokens," 6521,
girl with flower cart, originally
issued in 1998, approximately
9" h. **$400**

Courtesy of Elite Decorative Arts

◀ "Marketing Day," 4502, matte
finish, originally issued in 1970,
retired in 1985, 14" h. **$90**

Courtesy of Stephenson's Auction

"Madonna
Head," 4649,
Virgin Mary
in bust form,
originally issued
in 1970, retired
in 2002.....**$70**

*Courtesy of ATM Antiques
& Auctions, LLC*

▲ "Melchior King," 4673,
originally issued in 1970, retired,
approximately 6-3/4" h. **$25**

Courtesy of Pioneer Auction Gallery

"Sea-Breeze," 4922, young woman leaning into wind while holding book at her back, on green and white stepped plinth, maker's marks in blue to underside, impressed "12" and with various incised marks, originally issued in 1974, retired, 14-3/4" high. **$50**

Courtesy of Jeffrey S. Evans & Associates

"Sitting Pretty Ballerina," 5499, originally issued in 1988, retired in 1998, good condition with no damage, 6" h. **$60**

Courtesy of Vero Beach Auction

"The Snowman," 5713, holding broom, standing next to two children and dog, originally issued in 1990, 8-1/4" h.........**$90**

Courtesy of Vero Beach Auction

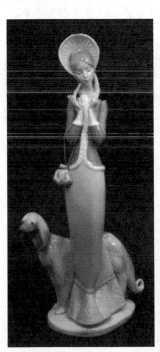

"Surprised Cat," 5114, originally issued in 1982, 5" l. **$50**

Courtesy of Elite Decorative Arts

▲ "Teaching to Pray," 4779, older sister teaching younger brother to pray, originally issued in 1971, retired. **$70**

Courtesy of ATM Antiques & Auctions, LLC

"Stepping Out," 1537, originally issued in 1988, retired, 13" h.....................**$125**

Courtesy of Elite Decorative Arts

◄ "Teresa," 5411, glossy finish, originally issued in 1987, retired in 1990, 6" h......................**$200**

Courtesy of Elite Decorative Arts

FIGURINES

"Teruko," 1451, originally issued in 1983, retired in 2013, 10-3/4" h. **$125**

Courtesy of Elite Decorative Arts

"Wedding," 4808, originally issued in 1972, retired in 2005, mint condition, 7-1/2" h. **$55**

Courtesy of Omega Auction Corp.

"Winged Companions," 6242, originally issued in 1996 and retired in 2000, 7-1/2" x 7" x 5-1/2". **$120**

Courtesy of Manor Auctions

"Woman with Cow & Calf," 4953, glossy finish, originally issued in 1977, retired in 1981, rare, 11-3/4" h. **$400**

Courtesy of Elite Decorative Arts

"You're So Cute," 6826, originally issued in 2002, 8" h. **$75**

Courtesy of Elite Decorative Arts

"Winter," 5220, originally issued in 1984, retired in 2002, 8-1/4" h. **$50**

Courtesy of Elite Decorative Arts

◄ "Yuki," 1448, originally issued in 1983, retired in 1998, 7-3/4" h. **$150**

Courtesy of Elite Decorative Arts

FIGURINES
=========

doulton and royal doulton

DOULTON & COMPANY, Ltd., was founded in Lambeth, London, in about 1858. It operated there until 1956 and often incorporated the words "Doulton" and "Lambeth" in its marks. Pinder, Bourne & Co. Burslem was purchased by the Doultons in 1878 and in 1882 became Doulton & Co., Ltd. It added porcelain to its earthenware production in 1884. The "Royal Doulton" mark has been used since 1902 by this factory, which is still in operation.

John Doulton, the founder, was born in 1793. He became an apprentice at the age of 12 to a potter in south London. Five years later he was employed in another small pottery near Lambeth. His two sons, John and Henry, subsequently joined their father in 1830 in a partnership he had formed with the name of Doulton & Watts. Watts retired in 1864 and the partnership was dissolved. Henry formed a new company that traded as Doulton and Co.

In the early 1870s the proprietor of Pinder, Bourne & Co., located in Burslem, Staffordshire, offered Henry a partnership. Pinder, Bourne & Co. was purchased by Henry in 1878 and became part of Doulton & Co. in 1882.

With the passage of time, the demand for the Lambeth industrial and decorative stoneware declined whereas demand for the Burslem manufactured and decorated bone china wares increased.

Doulton & Co. was incorporated as a limited liability company in 1899. In 1901 the company was allowed to use the word "Royal" on its trademarks by Royal Charter. The well-known "lion on crown" logo came into use in 1902. In 2000 the logo was changed on the company's advertising literature to one showing a more stylized lion's head in profile.

Today Royal Doulton is one of the world's leading manufacturers and distributors of premium grade ceramic tabletop wares and collectibles. The Doulton Group comprises Minton, Royal Albert, Caithness Glass, Holland Studio Craft, and Royal Doulton. Royal Crown Derby was part of the group from 1971 until 2000, when it became an independent company. These companies market collectibles using their own brand names.

"Adrienne," HN 2152, designed by Peggy Davies, issued 1964-1976, 7-1/4" h.....**$40**

Courtesy of DuMouchelles

"All Aboard," HN 2940, designed by Robert Tabbenor, issued 1982-1986, 9" h.....**$110**

Courtesy of Vero Beach Auction

"Autumn Breezes," HN 1934, vintage figurine designed by Leslie Harradine from 1940-1997, excellent condition, 7-1/2" h. **$15**

Courtesy of Homestead Auctions

"Balloon Clown," HN 2894, excellent condition, 9-1/4" h. **$50**

Courtesy of Premiere Auction Co.

"Balloon Man," HN 1954, designed by Leslie Harradine from 1940-2009, 7-1/2" h. **$50**

Courtesy of Elite Decorative Arts

"Bess," HN 2003, designed by Leslie Harradine, issued 1947-1950, small glaze flaw on front, scratches on back, no chips, cracks, crazing, or restorations, 7-1/4" h. **$50**

Courtesy of Premiere Auction Gallery

"Biddy Penny Farthing," HN 1843, designed by Leslie Harradine from 1938-2009, 9" h. **$250**

Courtesy of Leonard's Auction Service

"Captain MacHeath," HN 464, designed by Leslie Harradine, from Beggar's Opera, 7" h. ...**$125**

Courtesy of Premiere Auction Co.

"Catrina," HN 2327, first designed in 1964, 7-1/2" h...**$75**

Courtesy of Elite Decorative Arts

"Cissie," HN 1809, vintage, designed by Leslie Harradine, issued 1937-1993, 5" h. **$40**

Courtesy of Pioneer Auction Gallery

"Clarissa," HN 2345, vintage, designed by Peggy Davies, issued 1968-1981, original price tag on bottom, approximately 7-3/4" h. **$30**

Courtesy of Pioneer Auction Gallery

"The Cobbler," HN 1706, designed by Charles J. Noke, issued 1935-1969, 8-1/2" h.....**$50**

Courtesy of Elite Decorative Arts

FIGURINES

"Falstaff," HN 2054, designed by Charles J. Noke, issued 1950-1992, 7" h.................**$60**

Courtesy of Vero Beach Auction

"Flora," HN 2349, designed by Mary Nicoll, issued 1966-1973, Character Series, 7-3/4" h.......**$30**

Courtesy of Premiere Auction Co.

"Forty Winks," HN 1974, designed by H. Fenton from 1945-1973, 6-3/4" h...........**$50**

Courtesy of Leonard's Auction Service

"Frodo Middle Earth," HN 2912, designed by D. Lyttleton, Tolkien Series, excellent condition, 4-1/2" h..............**$26**

Courtesy of Premiere Auction Co.

"George Washington at Prayer," Winter at Valley Forge, artist Laszlo Ispanky, #74 of 750, excellent condition, 13" h. plus custom wooden base...........**$700**

Courtesy of Richard D. Hatch & Associates

"A Gentlewoman," HN 1632, designed by Leslie Harradine, issued 1934-1949, Pretty Ladies Series, excellent condition, no chips, cracks, crazing or restorations, 7-1/4" h..............**$150**

Courtesy of Premiere Auction Co.

"Jester," HH 2016, designed
by Charles J. Noke, issued
1949-1997, 9-1/4" h. **$75**

Courtesy of Elite Decorative Arts

"Joker," HN 2252, designed
by Mary Nicoll, issued 1990-
1992, Clowns Series, excellent
condition, 8-1/4" h................**$84**

Courtesy of Premiere Auction Gallery

"Lady Charmain," HN 1949,
designed by Leslie Harradine
from 1940-1967, 5-1/2" h. ..**$35**

Courtesy of ATM Antiques & Auctions, LLC

"The Laird," HN 2361,
designed by Mary Nicoll, issued
in 1969, 8" h. **$90**

Courtesy of Vero Beach Auction

"Lidia," HN 1908, designed by
Leslie Harradine, issued 1939-
1995, 5" h...............................**$50**

Courtesy of Turkey Creek Auctions, Inc.

"Lily," HN 1798, vintage,
markings on base include "Lily
H N 1798, Copr 1937, Doulton
& Co., Ltd.," mint condition,
5-1/4" h. ....**$60-$100**

Courtesy of John Coker, Ltd.

FIGURINES

"Long John Silver," HN 2204, excellent condition, 9" h. **$130**

Courtesy of Premiere Auction Co.

"Michele," HN 1809, vintage, designed by Leslie Harradine from 1937-1993, 5" h. **$30**

Courtesy of Pioneer Auction Gallery

"Lorna," HN 2311, designed by M. Davies, 8-1/4" h. **$70**

Courtesy of ATM Antiques & Auctions, LLC

"Orange Lady," HN 1953, designed by Leslie Harradine, issued 1940-1975, 8-1/2" h..... **$25**

Courtesy of Elite Decorative Arts

"The Potter," HN 1493, designed by Charles J. Noke, issued 1932-1992, 7" x 7-1/2". **$100**

Courtesy of Echoes Antiques & Auction Gallery

"The China Repairer," HN 2943, designed by Robert Tabbenor, issued 1983, Character Studies Series, 6-3/4" h. **$110**

Courtesy of Vero Beach Auction

"Silks and Ribbons," HN 2017, 1948, designed by Leslie Harradine, marked on bottom, 6-1/2" x 5-1/2" x 4"......**$30**

Courtesy of Arus Auctions

▲ "Schoolmarm," HN 2223, designed by M. Davies, issued 1958-1991, 6-3/4" h. **$25**

Courtesy of Elite Decorative Arts

◀ "Rustic Swain," HN 1745, designed by Leslie Harradine, issued 1935-1949, professional restoration to boy's hat and right foot, 5-1/4" h. **$110**

Courtesy of Premiere Auction Co.

"Goody Two Shoes," "Bedtime," "Melanie" (8" h.), "Top o' the Hill," "Delight" (7-1/4" h.), and "Marie." **$140**

Courtesy of Michaan's Auctions

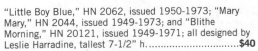

"Little Boy Blue," HN 2062, issued 1950-1973; "Mary Mary," HN 2044, issued 1949-1973; and "Blithe Morning," HN 20121, issued 1949-1971; all designed by Leslie Harradine, tallest 7-1/2" h.................................**$40**

Courtesy of Leslie Hindman Auctioneers

"Tinsmith," HN 2146, designed by Mary Nicoll, issued 1962-1967, excellent condition, 6-1/4" h..............**$58**

Courtesy of Premiere Auction Gallery

"Valerie," HN 2107, vintage, designed by M. Davies, issued 1953-1995, approximately 5" h. **$30**

Courtesy of Pioneer Auction Gallery

"Veneta," HN 2722, 1973, designed by William K. Harper, markings on base include "Veneta, H. N. 2722, Doulton & Co., Ltd., 1973," mint condition, 8-1/4" h. .... **$60-$100**

Courtesy of John Coker, Ltd.

"Victorian Lady," HN 0728, designed by Leslie Harradine, issued between 1925 and 1952, 7-3/4" h. **$100**

Courtesy of Premiere Auction Co.

"Wendy," HN 2109, designed by Leslie Harradine, issued 1953-1995, 5" h. **$30**

Courtesy of Pioneer Auction Gallery

"Wizard," HN 2877, designed by Alan Maslankowski, issued 1979-present, excellent condition, 9-3/4" h. **$50**

Courtesy of Premiere Auction Gallery

FINE ART

THE GREAT RECESSION is finally over.

At least that's the consensus among art market watchers after recording the largest market ever in recent years. Roughly $53.9 billion changed hands in 2014 in transactions involving fine and decorative art. The figure marks the first time such sales neared the pre-recession record of $51 billion in 2007.

Who are the players driving these sales? What are they after and when will it stop? The answers in a nutshell show rich Americans pouring new profits into modern and post-war and contemporary art with absolutely no end in sight, according to the annual *TEFAF Art Market Report* by Art Economics.

According to Holly Sherratt, a consignment director of modern and contemporary art at Heritage Auctions, Dallas, "Despite longstanding rumors of an art bubble, the contemporary art market continues to be strong, mostly driven by top-performing artists in the market and the trendsetting galleries that promote them."

The global hub for all art sales is the United States (39 percent of all transactions) and specifically New York, where post-war and contemporary art lead sales at auction houses and galleries. China, however, remains the largest emerging market although sales are still haunted by non-paying bidders and a high percentage of unsold lots. In some cases the rate of unsold lots in China surpasses half of all lots offered.

Online sales are also a leading driver of fine art sales, which may surprise some. But collectors and dealers are comfortable making purchases with only a website between them. This segment is expected to grow a whopping 25 percent per year and is estimated to reach $10 billion in five years.

Although multi-million dollar auction records tend to capture the most headlines, the market is seeing more art in general sold and at faster rates, and the market is currently growing by six percent a year, according to Arts Economics' annual report.

These customers are much more selective about what they buy. So as condition sets the market for collectibles, the best examples of an artist's work influences prices. An artist's key works continue to bring the best prices as collectors remain mindful of both aesthetics and resale.

"Collectors are looking for established names such as Andy Warhol, Roy Lichtenstein, Jasper Johns, Robert Rauschenberg, and Frank Stella," Sherratt said. "American artists like Jeff Koons, Jean Michel Basquiat, Christopher Wool, and Richard Prince top the charts. U.K. artists Peter Droig and Damien Hirst are also at the top of the list along with German artist Martin Kippenberg, and Chinese artists Zeng Fanzhi, Luo Zhongli, Chen Yifei, and Zhang Xioagang."

"Peyton Falls, Va.," John Gadsby Chapman (Dec. 3, 1808-Nov. 28, 1889), 1862, oil on board, 12" h. x 8" w.................... **$7,470**

Courtesy of Louis J. Dianni, LLC

GLOBAL ART MARKET BY THE NUMBERS

2.8 MILLION
People employed by the art and antiques business

180 Number of art and antiques shows worldwide

$3.5 BILLION
Annual online sales of fine art

300,000
Number of companies around the world that buy and sell art and antiques

$10.5 BILLION
Amount sold at art and antiques shows worldwide

Source: 2014 TEFAF Art Market Report by Art Economics, Clare McAndrew, released March 11, 2015.

In the middle market, post-war art is still very strong and less speculative than contemporary art, Sherratt said. The Art Economics report shows sales that take place in this middle market are mainly valued between $1,000 and $50,000.

"Prints account for many of these sales and provide an easier entry point and safer investment for many collectors," Sherratt said. "But even in this market, there is strong demand for star contemporary artists like Jeff Koons and Takashi Murakami, often in the form of editions."

With so few contemporary artists dominating the market, a lot of great art remains at reasonable prices, said Sherratt, who also points out robust demand on the West Coast. The region offers a substantial market and a source of very good art that has not yet fully maximized its enthusiast base.

"In the United States, Los Angeles is experiencing an art renaissance with international galleries like Hauser, Wirth & Schimmel opening satellite offices, superstar dealers like Larry Gagosian operating galleries, and The Broad museum opening in 2015," she said. "The California art community is incredibly strong, but with the exception of a few artists like Ed Ruscha, Chris Burden, and John Baldessari, most California artists have not sold for their potential."

"California art offers great investment opportunities for investors and dealers alike," she said. "With so much wealth, celebrity, and fashion concentrated in one area, I wouldn't be surprised to see prices for West Coast art increase in the coming years."

"Femme endormie," Pierre-Auguste Renoir (French, 1841-1919), circa 1890-1894, oil on canvas laid to board, initialed R. lower right, 6-7/8" x 5-3/4". **$272,500**

Courtesy of Leslie Hindman Auctioneers

"The Pet Lamb," Eastman Johnson (American, 1824-1906), 1873, oil on board, signed E. Johnson and dated lower left, 13" x 18".....**$284,500**

Courtesy of Leslie Hindman Auctioneers

"The Viviparous Quadrupeds of North America," Audubon, John James, and John Bachman, New York: J.J. Audubon, 1845-1848, 3 vols. **$290,500**

Courtesy of Leslie Hindman Auctioneers

"Reclining Nude with Books and Pencils on Lawn," Fernando Botero (Columbian, b. 1932), 1982, oil on canvas, signed Botero and dated, 44" x 60"........ **$494,500**

Courtesy of Leslie Hindman Auctioneers

"Babylone d'Allemange," Henri de Toulouse-Lautrec (French, 1864-1901), 1894, lithography, signed..........**$10,200**

Courtesy of Los Angeles Auction House

"Paysage aver un Bosquet," Jean Metzinger (French, 1883-1956), 1905, oil on canvas, signed Jean Metzinger, lower right, 17" x 25-1/4". **$150,000**

Courtesy of A.B. Levy's

INSIDE INTEL
with
HOLLY SHERRATT

Consignment Director, Modern & Contemporary Art, Heritage Auctions

WHAT'S HOT: The contemporary art market continues to be strong, mostly driven by top-performing artists in the market and the trendsetting galleries that promote them.

TOP TIP: The California art community is incredibly strong, but with the exception of a few artists like Ed Ruscha, Chris Burden, and John Baldessari, most California artists have not sold to their potential. California art offers great investment opportunities for investors and dealers alike.

"Le Bouquet Rouge Et Jaune," Marc Chagall, Paris, France, 1974, lithograph on arches paper, signed in pencil lower right, numbered 42/50 sheet, 25-3/8" h. x 18-13/16" w. .. **$7,200**

Courtesy of Los Angeles Auction House

"Venus et L'Amour, d'Apres Cranach," Pablo Picasso (Spanish, 1881-1973), 1949, aquatint on woven paper, signed Picasso lower right, numbered 23/50 lower left, (Bloch 1835, Baer 836), image 21-1/2" x 15-3/4", plate 30-7/8" x 16-7/8". **$650**

Courtesy of A.B. Levy's

"Untitled (Spin Painting)," Damien Hirst (British, b. 1965), 2011, acrylic and metallic paint on paper, inscribed and signed, 20-1/2" x 20-1/2". **$28,000**

Courtesy of A.B. Levy's

"William L. Austin," Georg Papperitz (German, 1846-1918), 74" x 46-1/2". Provenance: From the estate of John E. DuPont. **$4,305**

Courtesy of Gordon S. Converse & Co.

"Tyrolean Couple with Chalet and Mountainous Landscape," Emil Rau (German, 1858-1937), oil on canvas, signed E. Rau, lower right, 38" x 30"................. **$4,305**

Courtesy of A.B. Levy's

"Stillleben (Still Life)," Reinhold Ludwig Krassnig (Austrian, 1898-1947), oil on canvas, monogrammed lower right, 39-1/2" x 31-1/2". . **$4,840**

Courtesy of Ahlers & Ogletree Auction Gallery

"The Night Before Christmas," Charles Burchfield (American, 1893-1967), card, signed "Bertha & Charles Burchfield," 6-1/4" h. x 10-1/2" w. **$786**

Courtesy of Cottone Auctions

"Sacred Lotus of the Nile," Hovsep Pushman (Armenian/American, 1877-1966), oil on wood panel, signed lower right, 28" x 20"......................**$60,500**

Courtesy of Ahlers & Ogletree Auction Gallery

"Mother & Daughters in Springtime," William John Hennessy (Irish/Canadian, 1839-1917), oil on canvas, signed lower left W. J. Hennessey, 30" x 54".....**$12,100**

Courtesy of Cottone Auctions

"Classical Landscape with Figures Strolling on a Path," George Lambert (British, circa 1700-1765), oil on canvas, apparently unsigned, 34" x 47"... **$20,600**

Courtesy of Ahlers & Ogletree Auction Gallery

"Funeral Procession," Clementine Hunter (1887-1988), circa 1970, oil on board, signed center right, framed, 11-3/4" h. x 15-3/4" w. **$6,500**

Courtesy of Crescent City Auction Gallery

"Concert in the Classroom," Charles Bertrand D'entraygues (French, b. 1851), oil on canvas, 15" x 22".. **$8,750**

Courtesy of Heritage Auctions

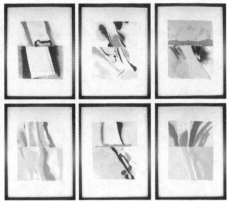

"Flashback: Six Plates," John Chamberlain (American, b. 1927), silkscreens in color, each signed in pencil "Chamberlain" and numbered VIII, IX, (2) XXXIV, (2) XXXIII, respectively, with London Arts, Inc., 28" x 19-1/2". **$6,500**

Courtesy of A.B. Levy's

"Working Hayers," Jules Jacques Veyrassat (1828-1893), oil on canvas, signed lower left J. Veyrassat, 35" x 49"..................................**$22,800**

Courtesy of Nadeau's Auction Gallery

"Rainy Day, New York," Paul Cornoyer, American (1864-1923), oil on canvas, signed lower left, 18" x 24"..$78,000

Courtesy of Shannon's Fine Art Auctioneers

"Woman with Bales of Cotton on the Docks," William Aiken Walker (1838-1921, South Carolina), oil on academy board, unsigned, period gilt and gesso frame, perhaps original, 7-3/4" h. x 3-3/4" w. **$3,444**

Courtesy of Crescent City Auction Gallery

"Loops Filled In," Alexander Calder (American, 1898-1976), gouache on paper, signed lower right and dated (1972), 23" x 31"........ **$78,200**

Courtesy of Cottone Auctions

"Great White Heron," John James Audubon (1785-1851), No. 57, Plate CCLXXXI, from *Birds of America*, hand-colored engraving by Robert Havell, elephant folio watermarked "J. Whatman 1836," unframed, 25-1/4" h. x 39-5/8" w. ... **$19,680**

Courtesy of Crescent City Auction Gallery

"Japonette," Charles Dana Gibson (American, 1867-1944), circa 1912, ink on paper, 20-5/8" x 12-1/4". **$6,250**

Courtesy of Heritage Auctions

"Butcher Boy," Max Band (Lithuanian, 1900-1974), oil on canvas, 24-1/2" x 39". **$8,470**

Courtesy of Elite Decorative Arts

"Spring in Florence," Francesco Vinea (Italian, 1845-1902), oil on canvas, 18-1/2" x 14-3/8". **$7,500**

Courtesy of Heritage Auctions

"Stri-Arc," Victor Vasarely, French (1906-1997), oil on canvas, signed lower right, signed, titled and dated 1974 on reverse, n. 2825, 31-3/4" x 31-3/4"..........................$72,000

Courtesy of Shannon's Fine Art Auctioneers

"Girl with Doll," John George Brown, American (1831-1913), oil on canvas, signed lower left, 22-1/2" x 14-1/2".........$78,000

Courtesy of Shannon's Fine Art Auctioneers

"Souper Dress," Andy Warhol (American, 1928-1987), circa 1968, color screenprint on cellulose and cotton, 37-1/2" x 21-1/2". $10,625

Courtesy of Heritage Auctions

"Provincetown Studios," Blanche Lazzell, American (1878-1956), woodcut, signed lower right and dated 1933, titled lower left, signed, titled and dated Aug 17, 1933 on reverse, No. 358/4, 7-7/8" h. x 4-7/8" w. $44,400

Courtesy of Shannon's Fine Art Auctioneers

"Wall Street," Laurence Campbell, American (b. 1939), oil on canvas, signed lower left, signed and titled on reverse, 30" x 24".....................$45,600

Courtesy of Shannon's Fine Art Auctioneers

"Feed Folks," David Hammons (American, b. 1943), 1974, mixed media, 39-3/4" x 29-1/2"....................$1,205,000

Courtesy of Heritage Auctions

"Alpine Glow, Kitzbuehel Village," Alois Arnegger (Austrian, 1879-1963), oil on canvas, 27-1/2" x 39-3/8". $4,375

Courtesy of Heritage Auctions

◄ "Untitled, pl. 3 (from portfolio Joan Miró Lithographs I), 1972," Joan Miró (Spanish, 1893-1983), lithograph in colors, ed. XXI/LXXX, 17-3/4" x 14-1/2".......................... $1,875

Courtesy of Heritage Auctions

SCULPTURES

Russian Deisis, set of three icons, 19th century, on curved wooden panels with silvered and brass oklads, depicting Virgin Mary, Christ, and John the Baptist, 23" h. x 17-1/2" w. **$5,000**

Courtesy of Crescent City Auction Gallery

Russian bronze grouping, Vassili Yacovlevitch Grachev (1831-1905, Russian Federation), signed by artist in Cyrillic character for Vassili Grachev, foundry mark for Fab. C. F. Woerffel Foundry of St. Petersburg, 9" h. x 20" w. x 11" d. **$12,750**

Courtesy of Fontaine's Auction Gallery

Icon, Imperial Russian silver with silver oklad, depicting Mary and Christ, oil on multi-layered panel, circa 1844. .... **$13,200**

Courtesy of Los Angeles Auction House

Sculpture of nude bronze, Jean-Baptiste Clésinger (French, 1814-1883), 1857, 29" h. **$5,082**

Courtesy of Elite Decorative Arts

Russian icon, gilt silver over wood panel, crown set with colored stones, 17" x 13-1/4"........ **$15,600**

Courtesy of Nadeau's Auction Gallery

Sculptural pair, C. (Cesare) Lapini, 19th century, Italian carrara marble, signed (Italian, 1848-after 1891), one putto in seashell, titled "Amour de la Mer," 25" h. x 15" w. x 20" d., and one putto in nest interspersed with flowers, titled "Amour de la Terre," 26-1/5" h. x 16-1/5" w. x 19" d...**$30,250**

Courtesy of Great Gatsby's Antiques & Auctions

"Horse with Dog Pulling on Reins" in style of Paul Edouard Delabrierre (French, 1829-1912), patinated bronze sculpture, indistinguishably signed, 9-1/4" h. x 16-1/9" w. x 7-1/4" d........................ **$3,630**

Courtesy of Ahlers & Ogletree Auction Gallery

"Gloria Victis," Marius-Jean-Antonin Mercie (French, 1845-1916), late 19th century, 1874, cast in bronze by Barbedienne shortly after, signed "A. MERCIE" on base, titled and impressed "F. BARBEDIENNE, Fondeur. Paris" on circular plinth, 6' h........ **$90,000**

Courtesy of A.B. Levy's

FIREARMS

GUN COLLECTING HAS been going on since the first chunks of lead were fired out of old muskets, but it wasn't until the Industrial Revolution that things got interesting. Early manufacturers and inventors changed the way firearms were produced and conceived and, as a result, hundreds of makes and models of handguns, shotguns, and rifles have been produced. Some of these guns have changed the world through their use in wars, exploration, and hunting.

Collectible guns receiving the most attention are ones used by famous and infamous people alike. In the last decade, the guns of Theodore Roosevelt, Ernest Hemingway, and baseball great Ted Williams have sold for staggering amounts of money. For example, Roosevelt's specially made double-barreled shotgun set a world record when it sold for $862,500 at a James D. Julia auction, while a Hemingway-owned Westley Richards side-by-side safari rifle sold for $340,000. Two pistols found on the bodies of famed Depression-era outlaws Bonnie Parker and Clyde Barrow after they were killed in 1934 sold for $504,000.

In these rare cases provenance is everything, according to Wes Dillon, head of James D. Julia Rare Firearm & Military Division. "The results (from the Roosevelt sale) were a direct reflection of the significance and importance of the man and his gun," Dillon said.

Keep in mind, however, that these are exceptional, historical finds in the gun-collecting world and command extraordinary prices befitting the historical figure associated with the weapon. Some of these high prices are certainly driven by vanity – the desire to own a one-of-a-kind gun – while others are seen as investments. Either way, the right gun with the right history can realize staggering results at auction.

UNDERSTANDING VALUE

Like any collectible item, it is important to understand that the value of a used firearm greatly depends on its condition. There are six grades of gun conditions, and how a gun is graded is key to its value:

New in Box: The gun is in its original box with the papers that came with it. But this grade also means that the gun has never been fired, and there is no sign whatsoever that the gun has been handled or used. This is the highest grade for a used gun.

Excellent: The gun may have been used but so gently and lightly that 98 percent of its finish remains as if it were brand new. All of its parts are still original and have not been swapped out with foreign ones. That includes no repairs or alternations.

Very Good: The gun is in good working order and 100 percent original but may have had some minor repair work or alterations. Finish should be around 92 percent.

Good: The gun must have 80 percent of its original finish remaining. Alterations, repairs, or additions are acceptable as long as they are not major ones. Must be safe to fire and in decent working condition.

Fair: The gun is safe and in working order but only about 30 percent of its original finish remains. May have had a major overhaul in a refinishing process or some other kind of alteration.

Pair of 1857 Colt Walker Type 3 Dragoons with consecutive serial numbers, ordered and purchased between 1856-1857 by Lambert B. Wolfe, captain with 142nd Ohio Infantry Regiment during Civil War; excellent condition, pistols solid, cylinders smooth, all metal cleaned, retains Colt markings. **$54,000**

Courtesy of Morphy Auctions

Poor: Gun is piece of junk and unsafe to fire – rusty, cracked wood. Unless the gun has some incredible historical significance, it is not worth your time or money to mess around with other than hanging it above a fireplace as a conversation piece.

It is important not to deceive yourself about a gun's value. Professional gun appraisers will notice small details that were missed in your amateur inspection. If you think you have an old gun of value, or you are contemplating buying one, please do your homework. The landscape is pockmarked with unscrupulous people more than happy to separate you from your hard-earned money for something of dubious value. As always, knowledge is power. An excellent reference for antique American arms is *Flayderman's Guide to Antique American Firearms and Their Values.* Norm Flayderman is arguably the world's best-known antique arms dealer and authority. Gun collectors and historians have long considered his book an indispensable tool. Other excellent resources are the *Standard Catalog of Firearms* and *The Blue Book of Gun Values.* Both offer an impressive depth and breadth of knowledge to the gun-collecting hobby.

Even with the help of a dependable reference such as *Flayderman's,* you may be well served getting the advice of a professional gun appraiser, especially if you think there is something unique or special about the gun you have or are considering buying. Armed with that knowledge, you can make an intelligent buying or selling decision.

COLLECTIBLE GUNS AS AN INVESTMENT

On Internet message boards, there is considerable debate about collectible guns as an investment. There are arguments for and against the idea that acquiring guns could enhance your financial portfolio. It's true that certain collectible firearms have realized substantial return on investment. As with any investment, however, there is risk.

Here are some points to consider before you decide to include collectible firearms in your investment portfolio:

Don't venture into gun collecting as an investment unless you know what you're doing.

To get to the point of knowing could take years of study of both guns and the marketplace.

If you decide to invest in firearms, it's often wise to choose a specialty, preferably with a type of gun that you are personally interested in. There are numerous manufacturer-specific gun collector associations and they are a great place to start your research.

Investing in anything entails risk.

— *James Card,*
Editor, *Gun Digest Magazine*

Handguns

PISTOLS

Two Colt Snake Eyes pistols (one shown), SN EYES412 and 412EYES, .357 caliber, 2-1/2" barrel, rare unfired condition, one stainless, one blued; near mint condition, original boxes..**$13,200**

Courtesy of Morphy Auctions

Colt Model 1918 pistol, SN 39897, .38 caliber, 5-3/4" barrel, standard model military automatic pistol, 99% of original factory blue, all casing on spur hammer, lanyard ring; mint bore. **$5,100**

Courtesy of Morphy Auctions

Remington-UMC prototype 1911 semi-automatic pistol, NSN, .45 ACP, 5" barrel, seldom-seen pre-production or prototype World War I-era Model 1911 contract pistol, marked on slide with "Made by B.M. Kuperstock June-17th-1918. Bridgeport, Conn.," fitted with all-blued barrel; very fine condition with 95% of faded period matte blue finish showing. **$5,750**

Courtesy of Rock Island Auction Co.

Pair of English percussion pistols with custom case and accessories (one pistol shown), SN NSN, .67 caliber, 5" octagon barrel, each barrel with golden band and plaque marked "LONDON" at breech, each with bead front and notch rear sights, scroll engraving throughout; fine condition, each barrel with mixture of brown finish and patina. **$2,300**

Courtesy of Rock Island Auction Co.

Colt pocket hammerless semi-automatic pistol, SN 463471, 1925, .32 ACP, 3-3/4" barrel, with mother-of-pearl grips, fixed sights, mirror-polished nickel finish; excellent condition with more than 98% of original polished nickel finish present, grips non-factory period replacements. **$2,587**

Courtesy of Rock Island Auction Co.

Ludwig Loewe Borchardt semi-automatic pistol, SN 817, 1893, 7-1/2" barrel, early development in semi-automatic firearms, toggle breech locking system, fixed blade front and adjustable rear sights, checkered wood grips, wood magazine base, and blue finish.......................**$10,925**

Courtesy of Rock Island Auction Co.

Mauser Luger semi-automatic pistol, SN 7784y, 9mm, 4" barrel, date "1942" on chamber and police "eagle/swastika L" proof present on right side of extension, full-blue components, checkered walnut grips; fine condition, partially refinished, showing 80% of blue finish with areas of brown patina............................. **$1,955**

Courtesy of Rock Island Auction Co.

Webley & Scott semi-automatic pistol with holster, SN 66375, 1911, .38 caliber, one of only 486 believed to be made in this configuration; partridge blade front and windage adjustable notch rear sights, Webley "winged bullet" log on left side of slide; fine condition with more than 40% of original blush finish showing. **$2,070**

Courtesy of Rock Island Auction Co.

Colt Lightning Shop Keeper or Sheriff's Model revolver, SN 57871, 1866, .38 caliber, 3-1/2" barrel, never fired, with case and factory letter, six-shot, double-action, blue and case-colored, rubber grip, no rubs, finish wear, or powder residue, perfect factory stamps. **$8,400**

Courtesy of Morphy Auctions

REVOLVERS

Deluxe factory-engraved Colt Army revolver, .SN 169814, circa 1860, .44 caliber, 8" barrel, barrel marked "Saml Colt New York City America," deluxe blue finish with case, color frame, hammer, and lever, hand-engraved cylinder scene, backstrap engraved inscription reads "Cavalry Brigade to General Seldon E. Marvin 1867." **$43,475**

Courtesy of Cowan's Auctions

Colt single-action Army revolver, SN 24029, 1876, .45 Long Colt, 7-1/2" round barrel, with official statement that revolver was carried by Gratton (Grat) Dalton in double bank robbery in Coffeyville, Kansas, by members of Dalton gang in 1892; walnut grip and blue/case hardened finish; fair condition, cleaned and touched up. **$20,700**

Courtesy of Rock Island Auction Co.

Colt single-action Army revolver, SN 235942, 1902, .45 Colt, 5-1/2" barrel, with factory letter confirming shipment to K.L. Hart, backstrap inscribed "Wm. S. Hart from K. L. Hart 12-25-02," grips with oval pearl inserts and heart on each lower grip panel. **$5,175**

Courtesy of Rock Island Auction Co.

Tranter double-trigger percussion revolver, SN 9191T, .44 caliber carbine, common scrollwork and border engraving on barrel, loading arm, grip cap and frame, with maker's marking "THO.S. BLISSET SOUTH CASTLE ST LIVERPOOL" on top strap; with wooden case with lubricating wax, bullets, tin of percussion caps, oiler, wrench, cleaning rod and powder flask. **$3,450**

Courtesy of Rock Island Auction Co.

Colt double-action revolver, SN 57929, .45 Long Colt, 7-1/2" round barrel, 1912, knurled hammer, cylinder catch, and smooth trigger finished in niter blue, with polished side on hammer, fitted with lanyard swivel and pair of "COLT" imprint grips; excellent condition with 98% plus of original high polish blue finish................................ **$4,025**

Courtesy of Rock Island Auction Co.

Custom Colt double-action revolver, SN 250450, 1919, .45 Long Colt, 5-1/2" barrel, custom-engraved with three-quarter coverage fine floral scrollwork, fitted with smooth maple grips and silver Colt medallions; very fine condition as custom engraved and rebarreled. **$1,955**

Courtesy of Rock Island Auction Co.

Wells Fargo-marked Smith & Wesson revolver, SN 1494, .45 caliber, 5" solid rib barrel; 3,035 of this revolver were manufactured in 1875 with 7" barrels, walnut grips and blue finish, and a number were purchased and had barrels shortened for use by Wells Fargo agents; retains 25% of original blue finish mixed with gray or brown patina on balance. **$6,325**

Courtesy of Rock Island Auction Co.

Webley-Fosbery automatic revolver, SN 1750, .455 caliber, 6" solid rib barrel, six-shot cylinder, section of revolver shifts backwards, cocks hammer, mechanism allows for faster firing while maintaining low trigger pull of single-action revolver, with leather holster made by Martin's of Birmingham in 1918; excellent condition, retains more than 85% of original blue finish with gray/ brown patina on grip straps..........................**$17,250**

Courtesy of Rock Island Auction Co.

LONG GUNS

Colt full-stock military percussion revolving rifle, SN 8248, 1856-1864, .56 caliber, 37-1/2" part octagon barrel, root-type side hammer, brass trigger guard, five-shot fluted cylinder, ratchet-type loading lever and three-leaf rear sight, stock and full forearm varnished black walnut with brass forend tip and sling swivel on rear barrel band; fair condition, extensively repaired, markings clear and action fine.... **$5,750**

Courtesy of Rock Island Auction Co.

Henry lever-action rifle, SN 4083, 1864, New Haven Arms Co., .44 caliber, 24" octagon barrel, early rounded profile brass buttplate, loading lever latch and sling swivel on left side of stock, top of barrel marked "HENRY'S PAT.OCT.16.1860/MANUFACT'D BY NEWHAVEN ARMS CO. NEWHAVEN. CT." **$25,875**

Courtesy of Rock Island Auction Co.

Civil War production Henry lever-action rifle, SN 7252, circa 1864, New Haven Arms Co., .44 Henry, 24" octagon barrel, with distinctive brass receiver and buttplate and 15-shot magazine, straight grain walnut stock fitted with factory sling swivel on left side; history shows many Federal soldiers in Western regiments during Civil War were armed with privately purchased Henry rifles; very good condition..... **$34,500**

Courtesy of Rock Island Auction Co.

Springfield Marksman rifle, .45-.70 caliber, 28" round barrel, large "VP" eagle "P.," engraved 1881 on receiver, engraved tang, breechblock, receiver, lock, buttplate, and front band; silver plaque in butt pistol grip reads, "Third Prize Marksman Rifle awarded by War Department to First Sergeant E.P. Wells Co H 2nd Infantry Division Of Pacific 1881 Two scores Five consecutive shots at 200, 400, 600 yards total score 124." **$76,375**

Courtesy of Cowan's Auctions

Smith & Wesson 320 revolving rifle, circa 1871, blue gone to patina and finish on shoulder stock turned to patina; good condition, barrel and action show cleaned rust, old repair to crack on left grip, bore very good condition. **$7,200**

Courtesy of Morphy Auctions

Johnson semi-automatic rifle, SN 6252, 1941, .30-06 caliber, 22" barrel, 10-round magazine, post front sight with protecting ears, aperture rear sight, two-piece walnut stock, recoil operated semi-automatic, perforated steel ventilated bandguard, checkered steel buttplate with trap door; mint condition stock, bore, and action...**$7,800**

Courtesy of Morphy Auctions

Jennings breechloading rifle, SN 691, circa 1850-1851, Robbins and Lawrence, Windsor, Vermont, .54 percussion, 26" round barrel, believed to be one of fewer than 1,000 of all variations made; "Rocket Ball" cartridge loaded through right side of frame, converted to muzzle-loading; fair condition, mottled gray and brown patina on surfaces...**$6,900**

Courtesy of Rock Island Auction Co.

Swiss K-31 straight pull bolt-action sniper rifle, SN 450371, 26" barrel, introduced in 1944, variation of Schmidt-Rubin rifle, with periscope head that lies against stock for storage and transport, Swiss Cross on top of receiver, smooth pistol grip stock with forearm grasping grooves; very fine condition, as arsenal refurbished with 90% of blue finish showing. **$3,162**

Courtesy of Rock Island Auction Co.

Sharps rifle, SN 54391, .52 caliber, 30" barrel, marked "New Model 1859," issued to Hiram Berdan's 1st and 2nd Regiments of U.S. Sharpshooters, three barrel bands, military sights, walnut stock, factory markings on barrel and frame, with metal patchbox on right side and sling swivels, double-set triggers, with Springfield Research letter. **$10,800**

Courtesy of Morphy Auctions

Springfield U.S. Officer's Trapdoor rifle, SN NSN, .45-70 govt. caliber, 26" full round barrel, manufactured on special order for commissioned officers only from 1875 to 1885; folding globe front sight, wooden ramrod with nickel finial, engraved German nickel nose cap, VP-proofed barrel, coarsely checkered walnut stock, and engraved U.S.-stamped buttplate. **$13,200**

Courtesy of Morphy Auctions

Ulrich engraved Winchester lever action rifle, SN 128866, 1876, .44 caliber, 24" octagon barrel, with Winchester factory letter confirming rifle, silver-plating, and factory engraving; blade front sight, ladder rear sight, extensive floral scroll on receiver, panel scene of elk on left side plate. **$25,875**

Courtesy of Rock Island Auction Co.

Winchester Model .50 Express rifle, SN 140407, circa 1906, lever action, 26" octagon barrel, blue/brown patina barrel with more blue on tube than barrel, folding leaf rear sight. **$11,400**

Courtesy of Morphy Auctions

Winchester Model 1896 Takedown rifle, SN 106817, .45-.90 caliber, 26" octagon barrel, 70% of original blue on barrel, thinning on edges, sides of tube retaining 70-80% of original bluing, strong case colors on hammer and lever; very good condition, strong clean bore...**$7,800**

Courtesy of Morphy Auctions

Winchester rifle, SN 418448B, 1892, .44-40 caliber, barrel, tube, nose cap and frame retain 90% or more of original factory blue finish, hammer and lever retain most of original case colors, original stocks, bore and action, with factory letter; near mint condition. **$8,400**

Courtesy of Morphy Auctions

Winchester lever-action rifle, SN 2262, 1878, .45 caliber, first model with checkered thumbprint dust cover guide rail secured to receiver with two screws; combination front sight, rear sight filler block; good condition as factory rebarreled, retains traces of original blue finish with mix to mottled brown patina, legible markings on barrel. **$5,462**

Courtesy of Rock Island Auction Co.

Nickel-plated Winchester lever-action saddle ring carbine, SN 77290, 1871, .44 caliber, factory-engraved model, receiver, tangs and bottom of cartridge carrier with floral scroll designs, dovetailed blade front sight mounted on front barrel band and fixed iron rear sight, saddle ring and staple on left side of receiver; fine condition, retains 70% original untouched nickel finish with scattered flaking and edge wear. **$23,000**

Courtesy of Rock Island Auction Co.

FOLK ART/ AMERICANA

FOR A NATION that takes deep pride in calling itself a nation of immigrants, American folk art and Americana acts like the ribbon tying our collective heritage together. Rich with evidence of German woodworking, Scottish ship-carving, or perhaps African tribal motifs, each work is one-of-a-kind and stands on its own, backed by good ol' American individuality. The fact that most works were completed by self-taught artists who had little to no formal training enhances the appeal to the collectors of American folk art and Americana. In one sense, the vernacular charm symbolizes the country's reputation for ambition, ingenuity, and imagination. There's little wonder why American folk art and Americana is more popular than ever.

The last few years saw several large folk art and Americana collections come to market with spectacular results. It also saw preservationists and scholars take major steps to ensure folk art remains an important art form in our national heritage.

Sotheby's presentation of the Ralph Esmerian collection of American folk art in early 2014 generated the highest proceeds ever for an American folk art collection. The 228-lot selection from the former chairman emeritus of the American Folk Art Museum was as noteworthy as its owner was notorious. Esmerian is serving a six-year federal sentence for fraud associated with the sale of jewelry and collectibles worth millions. The collection was ordered to be sold to provide restitution to victims and generated more than $10.5 million.

The collection held true American treasures. The top lot was a carved figure of Santa Claus by master carver Samuel Robb, the last figure he ever carved, in fact. Famous for his cigar store American Indian figures, Robb completed the 38" Santa in 1923 as a Christmas present to his daughter, Elizabeth. The figure more than doubled its pre-auction estimate to hammer for $875,000.

"Abraham Lincoln," oil on canvas, possibly done from life as it does not match any known photographs or prints; prior to cleaning, relining and varnishing, inscription and date ("E.P. 1863") were visible on back of canvas, touch-up on tip of nose and some in-painting above necktie, 25" x 30", framed to 32" x 37", Donald Dow-designed frame produced by Newcomb Macklin of Chicago. **$11,250**

Courtesy of Heritage Auctions

"Sugar Cane Cutting," May Kugler (American, 1915-2005), 1983, acrylic on board, signed by artist in lower right corner, with additional signature and annotation on verso, moisture stains to paper lining verso, slight bow to board, 12" x 16"........**$163**

Courtesy of Heritage Auctions

Native American scissor-cut, hand-colored scherenschnitte, dated 1844, issued in wake of New York City election in 1844, eagle clutches two American flags and dispatches snake, "The American Republican Victory April 8th 1844. Beware of Foreign Influence"; name of owner, Robert W. Lawrence, appears below with various carpentry tools; light stains and minor aging, 18" x 14" framed...................................... **$2,750**

Courtesy of Heritage Auctions

"Cotton Picking Time," Helene Delcambre, circa 1925, oil on board, signed by artist, very good condition, framed to 24-1/2" x 20-1/4"........... **$138**

Courtesy of Heritage Auctions

"New Girl in Town," Velox Benjamin Ward (American, 1901-1994), 1962, oil on board, signed and dated lower left: Velox Ward / 12/62, 19" x 38-1/4"... **$9,375**

Courtesy of Heritage Auctions

"Lively Gathering in Town Square," Ethel Spears (American, 1903-1974), oil on canvas, signed lower right: Ethel Spears, 29-7/8" x 40-1/4". **$3,250**

Courtesy of Heritage Auctions

Oil on panel of ship near shore, framed, unsigned, good condition, 9" x 12"................................ **$275** .

Courtesy of Rago Fine Arts, www.ragoarts.com

American carved whirligig of man in coat with tails on high-wheeler on custom wooden stand, weathered original painted surface, circa 1930, loss of paddles and other areas of wear and loss, 19-3/4" h. overall x 20-1/8" w. overall. **$1,600**

Courtesy of Jeffrey S. Evans & Associates

Wooden lantern slide with paper label, "Assassination of Lincoln – Figure of Booth – Movable," made by T. M. McAllister of New York, wooden stop prevents slide from going out of position, likely used in 1865-1875 period, 7" x 4", with standard 4" x 3" slide of same scene, circa 1900. Central portion shows Lincoln and guests viewing "Our American Cousin" from Presidential Box at Ford's Theatre; John Wilkes Booth, with derringer drawn, appears out of sight. By pulling glass slide to right, Booth makes dramatic entrance, pulling up directly behind Lincoln. **$1,500**

Courtesy of Heritage Auctions

Mid-Atlantic hooked floral scatter rug, circa 1930, brown field with large basket of multicolor tulips, scallop and floral border, attached sleeve for hanging, good overall condition, expected wear and edges with some raveling, 35-1/2" x 41-1/2". **$250**

Courtesy of Jeffrey S. Evans & Associates

The sale meant that two Samuel Robb-carved figures achieved world records within just months of each other. The Maryland-based auction firm of Guyette, Schmidt and Deeter sold a rare Robb cigar store American Indian princess, circa 1880, in late 2013 for a record $747,000.

Another sign of this category's growing interest with collectors and the general public is the popularity of the only museum dedicated to the scholarly study and exhibition of the country's self-taught artisans. In 2013, the American Folk Art Museum had record attendance with over 100,000 visitors. The museum's more than 5,000 items were collected almost entirely through gifts. Collectors cheered in December 2013 when the museum digitized and gave away free 118 issues of *Folk Art* magazine (formerly *The Clarion*), originally published between winter 1971 and fall 2008. The trove may be accessed online (as of 2015) at issuu.com/american_folk_art_museum.

"Found Upon Field of Battle at Gettysburg" Civil War brass eagle finial mounted on folk art plaque, 16" x 10" ledger board cover, eagle lacks legs, mounted to board via wire, surrounded by painted rays emanating from above, crossed U.S. flags and oak leaf wreath; painted on ribbon banner beneath scene: "Presented to New York G.A.R. In memory of Duryee's Zouaves 165th Regt. Of Inf. By Mrs. L. R. Sullivan May 7, 1895 New York / Eagle standard finial found upon field of battle at Gettysburg Pa. By Dr. R. Sullivan June 14, 1882," lower right corner stamped G.A.R. medal and number 63.......................**$2,250**

Courtesy of Heritage Auctions

Folk art hickory chair, 20" h. ....**$50-$100**

Courtesy of Clars Auction Gallery, www.clars.com

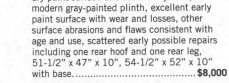

Miniatures by E. Fairchild, both dated 1830: Portrait of young woman in black dress, watercolor and ink on card, inscribed "Jane L. King's miniature July 1830," also inscribed "E. Fairchild presented to Wm. B. Blakesley," 2-5/8" x 4-1/8"; man in blue coat, arms folded, inscribed "Wm. B. Blakesley's miniature AD 1830," verso inscribed "Hand painted by E. Fairchild" (in different hand) and "Miss Elizabeth Cross," 2-1/4" x 3-1/2", both with some toning and stains, in matching cartouche-form bird's-eye maple frames with poplar and pine secondary. **$700**

Courtesy of Brunk Auctions

Carousel horse, American, late 19th century, possibly Charles Looff, with early dry paint surface and set with "jewels," on modern gray-painted plinth, excellent early paint surface with wear and losses, other surface abrasions and flaws consistent with age and use, scattered early possible repairs including one rear hoof and one rear leg, 51-1/2" x 47" x 10", 54-1/2" x 52" x 10" with base..**$8,000**

Courtesy of Brunk Auctions

top lot

This whaling journal records 3-1/2 years at sea seeking whales, with an array of watercolors of whales, ships and boats engaged in this maritime exercise of the 19th century. The Geo. Howland set out from New Bedford on May 20, 1842, and did not return until November 1845. Most of the time she was cruising up and down the west coast of South America, occasionally stopping at various ports for supplies, recruiting replacements for crew, and social diversions. Mostly it was searching for whales, sighting whales, lowering boats, striking whales, and bringing them alongside for rendering. In the 19th century whale oil had a variety of uses, from lubricants and soap to lamp fuel and more. Many of the whales described as struck and caught in the journal were sperm whales, prized because they produced oil that was considered to be superior to that of other whales, and which sold for more money.

The watercolors in the journal include three full-page paintings of two whales being attacked by two whaleboats with a ship in the background; two whales surrounded by four whaleboats with two large ships in the background; and a large ship, likely the Geo. Howland herself, with the mountainous shore at right. In addition, there are 13 smaller views, about a quarter page each, of ships and whales, and some with whaleboats. One of these depicts a capsized whaleboat with a coffin floating in the sea, and accompanying text relates how one Samuel Watson was drowned when the boat was overturned. Thirty-eight watercolors depict whale tails (some with more than one), indicating whales sighted but not struck; 22 depict one or more whole whales, indicating whales caught; eight depict whales with ships or boats; and 15 depict ships with fellow whalers or merchantmen that they encountered.

Whaling journal with watercolor illustrations, Aaron C. Cushman, "Manuscript journal and log book of ship Geo. Howland out of New Bedford, commanded by Aaron C. Cushman, with watercolor illustrations," 1842-1845, approximately 178 leaves plus blanks at end; with daily or nearly daily entries recording weather, sailing conditions, route, longitude and latitude, plus whaling activities such as sighting whales, lowering boats, striking whales, pulling them alongside ship, cutting them up and boiling them down to whale oil. Also such activities as stowing barrels of oil, mending sails, painting the boat, and when ashore or at harbor gathering or purchasing supplies, water, timber, etc. Running headings throughout describe general course. Journal enhanced by approximately 100 watercolor drawings ranging from simple depictions of whale tails to indicate sighting to three full-page watercolors of ship and whaling activities. Original quarter vellum and boards, with remains of watercolor of ship mounted on front cover, 15" x 10"............... $25,000

Three Noah's Arks with animals, carved and painted, early 20th century, tallest 3-1/2" h. $175

Courtesy of Rago Fine Arts and Auction Center

Handmade Depression-era tramp art clock housing, chip-carved wooden clock cabinet with cross motif, unsigned, circa 1930s, original hinged door in rear, made from cigar box panels assembled in up to 11 layers, overall very good condition, solid and tight, metal strip at top appears to have additional glued pieces lacking, rear door bowed, chipping and scratching, 14-1/4" x 12", opening in front 5" x 5"................................$94

Courtesy of Heritage Auctions

Figure of reclining lion in manner of Bernard Langlais (1923-1977), constructed from roughly hewn sections of pine logs, knots, and limbs, with jute twine mane and tail, seashell eyes, sitting on custom-made pine table with casters, good condition, 43" h., 69" x 20" overall with table, not including 46" removable tail..........$2,000-$3,000

Courtesy of Thomaston Place Auction Galleries

American inlaid walnut desk box, second half 19th century, double-sided example, possibly partner's desk, with stylized inlaid decorations of tree, birds, quarter fans, perched eagle with arc above, pine secondary wood, mellow color and some sun-bleaching, areas of bottom boards and base molding possibly restored, otherwise very good condition, 6" h. x 24" l. x 16-1/4" d. $160

Courtesy of Jeffrey S. Evans & Associates

10 Things You Didn't Know
About the Women's Suffrage Movement

1 The month of August was a pivotal month for the women's suffrage movement in America. On Aug. 18, 1920, the 19th amendment, giving women the right to vote, was ratified by a two-thirds majority of states, and it took affect Aug. 26, 1920. The amendment reads: "The right of citizens of the United States to vote shall not be denied or abridged by the United States or by any State on account of sex."

2 A seldom-seen woman's suffrage button, showing the personi-fication of the movement – a woman blowing a clarion trumpet – inscribed with "National Woman Suffrage Congressional Union," and listing Irwin Hodson Co. of Portland, Oregon on the back paper, sold for $687.50 during Heritage Auctions' July 2014 Americana & Political Signature Auction.

Women's suffrage button, inscribed with "National Woman Suffrage Congressional Union," fetched nearly $688 at auction in July 2014.

Courtesy of Heritage Auctions

3 In light of the ratification of the amendment, a number of individuals and groups brought the validity of the ratification to the courts, which was eventually met with the Supreme Court's unanimous dismissal in 1922 of the arguments for invalidation of the amendment. While the majority of the states ratified the amendment in 1920, there were 10 states that delayed formal ratification of the amendment. Some held out for a couple of years, some for much longer; with the last state ratifying the 19th amendment in 1984.

4 A women's suffrage movement cup and saucer set in mint condition, produced by Hutschenreuther of Bavaria, Germany, featuring gold trim and three panels which read "Votes for Women," sold for $562.50 in November 2013 by Heritage Auctions.

5 More than 70 years before the 19th amendment went into affect, the first women's rights con-vention was held in Seneca Falls, New York. The event was held in 1848 and was organized by reformers Elizabeth Cady Stanton and Lucretia Mott, among others.

6 In the late 19th century/early 20th century, various organizations were formed and became the driving forces in the women's suffrage movement, among them the National American Woman Suffrage Association and the National Woman's party. The NAWSA was said to be a moderate lobbying group, focusing efforts on education, lobbying congress, and campaigning. The National Woman's Party, formed by Alice Paul, was seen as more radical and militant in its approach, which included picketing at the White House and Congress, which often led to arrests.

7 In 2011, a bound two-volume set of first issues of *The Revolution*, the weekly newspaper that reported on the women's rights movement and discussed more controversial concerns including divorce and birth control, sold for $3,585 during an auction offered by Heritage Auctions. The magazine was published from 1868 until 1872, and was established by suffragists Susan B. Anthony, Elizabeth Cady Staton, and Parker Pillsbury.

8 As historical accounts state, the women's suffragist movement was largely peaceful, but there were some acts deemed radical at the time, including the act by Susan B. Anthony and a small group of women of registering and then voting in the 1872 election in Rochester, New York. Antho-ny was arrested on the charge of "knowingly, wrongfully and unlawfully vot[ing] for a representative to the Congress of the United States," convicted, and fined $100 by the State of New York, a fine that she fought during her trial, saying: "May it please your honor, I shall never pay a dollar of your unjust penalty." According to historical accounts, Anthony never did pay the fine.

9 A 9" x 29" women's suffrage pennant featuring a figure representing jus-tice, emblazoned with the slogan "Equal Rights" and "Votes for Women," with some moderate soiling, commanded $2,569.25 during a December 2012 auction at Heritage Auctions.

▼ Women's suffrage pennant commanded $2,569 during a December 2012 auction at Heritage Auctions.

Courtesy of Heritage Auctions

10 American women could run for office long before they could vote. In fact, Jeannette Rankin, R-Montana, the first congresswoman elected to the House of Representatives, served for a single term in 1917 – three years before the ratification of the 19th amendment.

– Compiled by Antoinette Rahn

Sources: *Constitutioncenter.org*, New York Times Op-Ed, *August 2010*; History.com, http://www.ipu.org/wmn-e/suffrage.htm

VOTES FOR WOM

◀ Molded copper running horse weathervane with brass or bronze weighted head and mounted on custom wooden stand, 19th/20th century, good condition, 16-3/4" h. overall x 32" l. overall................... **$1,100**

Courtesy of Jeffrey S. Evans & Associates

Painting of George Washington on horseback, oil on board, signed C. H. Mitchell, 12" x 11"............ **$250**

Courtesy of Pook & Pook, Inc.

◀ Carved and painted bird on water pump, American, with movable pump handle, on square base, chips to wood and paint loss, bird can be removed from water pump, 10" h. x 11-1/4" w............................ **$125**

Courtesy of Cowan's Auctions

Cross-cut saw blade cut and assembled in form of shark, 20th century, welded fin and tail, applied eye and fin elements, mounted on weathered wood fragment, areas of rust and corrosion, 13-1/2" x 44-1/2" x 7-1/2"... **$400**

Courtesy of Brunk Auctions

Painted turned and bent wood armchair in red, white, and blue, early 20th century, sporadic paint wear, overall good condition.................... **$450**

Courtesy of Pook & Pook, Inc.

Mirrored gun rack, 19th century, elaborately painted with flowers, fish and other motifs, center top with two drawers, central section with bird-form brackets for four long guns, scattered pest damage with some associated losses at lower molding, break and glue repair at one bracket, scattered paint losses and retouch, wear and other surface distress, 53-1/2" x 72" x 8"............. **$300**

Courtesy of Brunk Auctions

Carved wood eagle head, 11-3/4" h. x 23-1/2" w. x 10" d. **$750**

Courtesy of Kaminski Auctions

Molded-copper steer weathervane, circa 1950, three-dimensional form with bronze/brass horns and original mounting rod with directionals, mounted on homemade stand (not stable), very good condition overall with minor wear, 28-1/2" w. overall x 62-3/8" h. overall including stand. **$3,250**

Courtesy of Jeffrey S. Evans & Associates

Rare Virginia molded sheet iron rooster weathervane, second half 19th century, swelled breast, scrolled cut-out tail feathers and primitive strutting pose, mounted on large orb above likely original arrow directional with cut-out embellishment to end, mounted on custom iron black-painted stand, early paint-decorated surface in red, yellow, blue, and white, areas of wear, dents, and small losses to body, wear to paint-decorated surface, otherwise very good condition, 36-1/2" h. overall x 34-3/4" l. overall. **$5,000**

Courtesy of Jeffrey S. Evans & Associates

Miniature walnut two-drawer chest, probably made by child, Augusta County, Shenandoah Valley of Virginia, circa 1880, rectangular top with chip-carved edges over two drawers set with original turned wooden knobs, raised on turned feet doweled into bottom board, numerous inscriptions, sketches, signatures, and dates throughout, including "William / Jane / 1880 / Price 25 cents," early, possibly original dry surface with warm color, crack to bottom board and front feet secured with new nails, otherwise excellent condition, 4-3/4" h. x 5" w. x 3-1/2" d. **$140**

Courtesy of Jeffrey S. Evans & Associates

Theorem/panel, Loudoun County, Virginia, circa 1849, appliquéd fabric on cotton with inked embellishments, composition in manner of album quilt block with patterned two-handled vase overflowing with floral elements, bottom left corner with inked design of eagle/dove holding banner marked "Amanda H. Donohoe" above inscription for what appears to be "Philomont, Va," bottom right corner with inked "December 25th 1849" date in banner, in maple and walnut cornerblock frame, fine condition overall, 9-3/4" sq. sight, 13" sq. overall. **$2,800**

Courtesy of Jeffrey S. Evans & Associates

Decorated bentwood box, fourth quarter 19th/early 20th century, circular form with upright handle, one side painted with red cabin by lake, other with windmill, bottom attached with small wooden pins, original dry painted surfaces, very good condition, horizontal crack at bottom of both handles, 5-1/2" h. overall, 3-3/4" h. rim, 5-1/2" dia. **$90**

Courtesy of Jeffrey S. Evans & Associates

Carved and painted wood whirligig of man wearing tin hat fashioned from can lid, fitted with paddle arms on modern wooden stand, 20th century, carved by John Jacobson, Sparta, Wisconsin, very good condition with wear and weathering to paint, 12" h... **$600**

Courtesy of Jeffrey S. Evans & Associates

Rare 1819 Anna Magdalena Scherertz (Wythe County, Virginia, b. 1819) fraktur birth and baptismal certificate, circa 1819, watercolor and ink on paper by Southern folk artist; facing turkeys flank inscribed heart above central reserve inscribed "Anna Magdalena Scherertz / Anno 1819 / 12th of February" over another heart flanked by Maltese crosses resting on scrolled arms, whole flanked by large stylized tulips rising from small urns, unframed and loosely secured in unsealed modern matte under glass, 12-1/2" x 7-3/4" sheet. **$24,000**

The so-called "Wild Turkey Artist" worked in Wythe County, Virginia during the fourth quarter of the 18th century and first quarter of the 19th century, executing fraktur birth and baptismal certificates for German clientele who had settled in the area. Likely a schoolmaster whose identity remains unclear at present, he used both fraktur lettering and script and almost always employed facing turkey-like figures as important design elements in the overall composition. Approximately 30 examples by the artist are known, and most remain in the families for whom they were originally made.

Courtesy of Jeffrey S. Evans & Associates

Carved wood-handled frame, circa 1920-1930, end of handle depicting relief-carved bust, possibly of African American, frame with half-inch deep center possibly to hold mirror, original varnished and black-painted surfaces, very good condition with some expected wear, 14" l., frame 6" d. **$850**

Courtesy of Jeffrey S. Evans & Associates

Carved wooden plaque with facing roosters forming crest above central fielded reserve of potted plant within oval floral surround, dated "1883" at bottom, old worn surface with mellow color, losses of one rooster's head and wear to edges, 23" h. x 14-3/4" w. ...**$350**

Courtesy of Jeffrey S. Evans & Associates

FOLK ART/AMERICANA

Prior-Hamblin School portrait of child, oil on artist's board, New England, mid-19th century, young child with strawberry blond hair and blue eyes, wearing ochre dress with white lace edging and holding cherry-laden branch, unsigned, modern paint-decorated frame, 12" x 8-3/4" sight, 15-3/4" x 12-1/2" overall.........**$4,000**

Courtesy of Jeffrey S. Evans & Associates

▶ Virginia pictorial hooked scatter rug, fourth quarter 19th century, rectangular-form medial with red field and potted plant between butterflies pattern, tan and faded red fleur-de-lis pattern on wide brown field border, stitched to fabric-covered contemporary wooden mount for hanging, good overall condition, moderate wear, some losses to pile and faded areas, 2' 2" x 3' 3-1/2".....................**$225**

Courtesy of Jeffrey S. Evans & Associates

American or English oak apothecary trade sign carved in the round, mid-19th century, with iron hook for hanging, old refinished surface, large split to one side and areas of wear to base, 15" h. overall, 9" dia. **$375**

Courtesy of Jeffrey S. Evans & Associates

American carved and paint-decorated work box of pine, poplar, and chestnut, mid-19th century, applied carved and painted elements including tulips, foliate sprays, and large central cherry tree to lid, original paint-decorated and varnished surface, good condition with minor wear and areas of replaced sawtooth edge molding, 6-3/4" h. x 13-1/8" w. x 9-1/4" d. **$450**

Courtesy of Jeffrey S. Evans & Associates

10 Things You Didn't Know About Weathervanes

1 It's said the largest existing weathervane sits along the shore of Michigan's White Lake. Produced by Whitehall Products, the structure measures 48 feet tall and boasts a 26-foot-long arrow that indicates the direction of the wind.

2 A rare molded copper Liberty weathervane, attributed to Cushing and White, Waltham, Massachusetts, circa 1865, with a swell-bodied stylized figure of Liberty holding a painted 13-star American flag, measuring 29 inches by 18 inches, sold for $22,500 during an Important Americana Auction Jan. 24, 2014 at Sotheby's.

Molded copper Liberty weathervane, circa 1865.............. **$22,500**

Courtesy of Sotheby's

3 One of the most well-known of the earliest weathervanes is in the shape of the Greek god Triton, and it sat atop a marble clock tower structure built in 48 B.C. While the vane has been long since lost, the tower (named the Tower of the Winds) still stands in Athens, Greece. However, evidence from relatively recent discoveries mentions use of wind vanes in ancient Mesopotamian civilizations dating back to 1600 B.C.

4 A large white-painted sheet iron and wood three-masted ship weathervane, American, early 20th century, with sheet iron sails and pennants, wire rigging, turned wood masts, and carved wood bowsprit and hull, measuring 81 inches high by 69 inches long, positioned on a custom stand, fetched $3,321 during an American Furniture & Decorative Arts Auction presented by Skinner Auctions on Aug. 4, 2014.

5 Shapes and designs of weathervanes are an eclectic bunch. Patriotic images and designs were popular themes for vanes in the 19th century, while racing horses, birds, and roosters came into fashion in the mid-19th and early 20th centuries. Some of the more unique and whimsical designs of weathervanes have included cherubs, ships, sea creatures, and wild animals.

6 President George Washington, who is said to have been a bit of an amateur weatherman, requested a weathervane be manufactured for use at Mount Vernon. As a nod to the end of the Revolutionary War, the weathervane was built in the shape of a dove of peace.

7 There is no shortage of sources to learn more about this timeless topic. According to Denninger Weather Vanes & Finials' bibliography page, there have been no less than 105 books written on the topic of weathervanes. Among the most referenced works are *A Gallery of American Weathervanes and Whirligigs* by Robert Bishop and Patricia Coblentz and *Yankee Weathervanes* by Myrna Kaye and Corinne Pascoe.

8 While wrought iron became the most popular materials from which weathervanes were manufactured, over the years examples made of wood, copper, tin and brass, among other materials, have been discovered.

9 The functionality of weathervanes may center on their use as weather forecasting tools, but in the Middle Ages and even 19th century American culture they were also status symbols and even served as some company's advertising interests.

10 One of the most talked-about collections of weathervanes resides at the Shelburne Museum in Shelburne, Vermont. The majority of the 125-plus weathervanes are from the 19th and 20th centuries, and it was the museum's founder, Electra Havemeyer Webb, who began collecting the vanes in the late 1940s.

Weathervane, early 20th century, sheet metal in form of liquor distillery, old surface, unusual, 17" h. x 36" w.......**$1,400**

Courtesy of Cottone Auctions

– Compiled by Antoinette Rahn

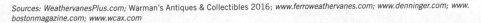

Sources: WeathervanesPlus.com; Warman's Antiques & Collectibles 2016; *www.ferroweathervanes.com; www.denninger.com; www.bostonmagazine.com; www.wcax.com*

FURNITURE
===============

antique furniture

FURNITURE COLLECTING HAS been a major part of the world of collecting for more than 100 years. It is interesting to note how this marketplace has evolved.

In past decades, 18th century and early 19th century furniture was the mainstay of the American furniture market, but in recent years there has been a growing demand for furniture manufactured since the 1920s. Factory-made furniture from the 1920s and 1930s, often featuring Colonial Revival style, has seen a growing appreciation among collectors. It is well made and features solid wood and fine veneers rather than the cheap compressed wood materials often used since the 1960s. Also much in demand in recent years is furniture in the Modernistic and Mid-Century taste, ranging from Art Deco through quality designer furniture of the 1950s through the1970s (see "Modern Furniture" later in this section).

These latest trends have offered even the less well-heeled buyer the opportunity to purchase fine furniture at often reasonable prices. Buying antique and collectible furniture is no longer the domain of millionaires and museums.

Today more furniture is showing up on Internet sites, and sometimes good buys can be made. However, it is important to deal with honest, well-informed sellers and have a good knowledge of what you want to purchase.

As in the past, it makes sense to purchase the best pieces you can find, whatever the style or era of production. Condition is still very important if you want your example to continue to appreciate in value in the coming years. For 18th century and early 19th century pieces, the original finish and hardware are especially important as it is with good furniture of the early 20th century Arts & Crafts era. These features are not quite as important for most manufactured furniture of the Victorian era and furniture from the 1920s and later. However, be aware that a good finish and original hardware will mean a stronger market when the pieces are resold. Of course, whatever style of furniture you buy, you are better off with examples that have not had major repair or replacements. On really early furniture, repairs and replacements will definitely have an impact on the sale value, but they will also be a factor on newer designs from the 20th century.

As with all types of antiques and collectibles, there is often a regional preference for certain furniture types. Although the American market is much more homogenous than it was in past decades, there still tends to be a preference for 18th century and early 19th century furniture along the Eastern Seaboard, whereas Victorian designs tend to have a larger market in the Midwest and South. In the West, country furniture and "western" designs definitely have the edge except in major cities along the West Coast.

Whatever your favorite furniture style, there are still fine examples to be found. Just study the history of your favorites and the important points of their construction before you invest heavily. A wise shopper will be a happy shopper and have a collection certain to continue to appreciate as time marches along.

For more information on furniture, see *Antique Trader Furniture Price Guide* by Kyle Husfloen.

FURNITURE STYLES

american

PILGRIM CENTURY 1620–1700

MAJOR WOOD(S): Oak

GENERAL CHARACTERISTICS:

- **Case pieces:** Rectilinear low-relief carved panels; blocky and bulbous turnings; splint-spindle trim

- **Seating pieces:** Shallow carved panels; spindle turnings

WILLIAM AND MARY 1685–1720

MAJOR WOOD(S): Maple and walnut

GENERAL CHARACTERISTICS:

- **Case pieces:** Paint decorated chests on ball feet; chests on frames; chests with two-part construction; trumpet-turned legs; slant-front desks

- **Seating pieces:** Molded, carved crest rails; banister backs; cane, rush (leather) seats; baluster, ball and block turnings; ball and Spanish feet

QUEEN ANNE 1720–1750

MAJOR WOOD(S): Walnut

GENERAL CHARACTERISTICS:

- **Case pieces:**
  Mathematical proportions
  of elements; use of the
  cyma or S-curve broken-
  arch pediments; arched
  panels, shell carving, star
  inlay; blocked fronts;
  cabriole legs and pad feet

- **Seating pieces:** Molded
  yoke-shaped crest
  rails; solid vase-shaped
  splats; rush or upholstered seats; cabriole legs; baluster, ring, ball and block-turned
  stretchers; pad and slipper feet

CHIPPENDALE 1750–1785

MAJOR WOOD(S): Mahogany and walnut

GENERAL CHARACTERISTICS:

- **Case pieces:** Relief-carved broken-arch pediments; foliate, scroll, shell, fretwork
  carving; straight, bow or serpentine fronts; carved cabriole legs; claw and ball,
  bracket or ogee feet

- **Seating pieces:** Carved, shaped crest rails with out-turned ears; pierced,
  shaped splats; ladder (ribbon) backs; upholstered seats; scrolled arms;
  carved cabriole legs or straight (Marlboro) legs; claw and ball feet

FEDERAL (HEPPLEWHITE) 1785–1800

MAJOR WOOD(S): Mahogany and light inlays

GENERAL CHARACTERISTICS:

- **Case pieces:** More delicate rectilinear forms; inlay with eagle and classical motifs; bow, serpentine or tambour fronts; reeded quarter columns at sides; flared bracket feet

- **Seating pieces:** Shield backs; upholstered seats; tapered square legs

FEDERAL (SHERATON) 1800–1820

MAJOR WOOD(S): Mahogany, mahogany veneer, and maple

GENERAL CHARACTERISTICS:

- **Case pieces:** Architectural pediments; acanthus carving; outset (cookie or ovolu) corners and reeded columns; paneled sides; tapered, turned, reeded or spiral-turned legs; bow or tambour fronts; mirrors on dressing tables

- **Seating pieces:** Rectangular or square backs; slender carved banisters; tapered, turned or reeded legs

FURNITURE

CLASSICAL (AMERICAN EMPIRE) 1815–1850

MAJOR WOOD(S): Mahogany, mahogany veneer, and rosewood

GENERAL CHARACTERISTICS:

- **Case pieces:** Increasingly heavy proportions; pillar and scroll construction; lyre, eagle, Greco-Roman and Egyptian motifs; marble tops; projecting top drawer; large ball feet, tapered fluted feet or hairy paw feet; brass, ormolu decoration

- **Seating pieces:** High-relief carving; curved backs; out-scrolled arms; ring turnings; sabre legs, curule (scrolled-S) legs; brass-capped feet, casters

VICTORIAN – EARLY VICTORIAN 1840–1850

MAJOR WOOD(S): Mahogany veneer, black walnut, and rosewood

GENERAL CHARACTERISTICS:

- **Case pieces:** Pieces tend to carry over the Classical style with the beginnings of the Rococo substyle, especially in seating pieces.

F

VICTORIAN – GOTHIC REVIVAL 1840–1890

MAJOR WOOD(S): Black walnut, mahogany, and rosewood

GENERAL CHARACTERISTICS:

- **Case pieces:** Architectural motifs; triangular arched pediments; arched panels; marble tops; paneled or molded drawer fronts; cluster columns; bracket feet, block feet or plinth bases

- **Seating pieces:** Tall backs; pierced arabesque backs with trefoils or quatrefoils; spool turning; drop pendants

VICTORIAN – ROCOCO (LOUIS XV) 1845–1870

MAJOR WOOD(S): Black walnut, mahogany, and rosewood

GENERAL CHARACTERISTICS:

- **Case pieces:** Arched carved pediments; high-relief carving, S- and C-scrolls, floral, fruit motifs, busts and cartouches; mirror panels; carved slender cabriole legs; scroll feet; bedroom suites (bed, dresser, commode)

- **Seating pieces:** High-relief carved crest rails; balloon-shaped backs; urn-shaped splats; upholstery (tufting); demi-cabriole legs; laminated, pierced and carved construction (Belter and Meeks); parlor suites (sets of chairs, love seats, sofas)

FURNITURE

VICTORIAN – RENAISSANCE REVIVAL 1860–1885

MAJOR WOOD(S): Black walnut, burl veneer, painted and grained pine

GENERAL CHARACTERISTICS:

- **Case pieces:** Rectilinear arched pediments; arched panels; burl veneer; applied moldings; bracket feet, block feet, plinth bases; medium and high-relief carving, floral and fruit, cartouches, masks and animal heads; cyma-curve brackets; Wooton patent desks

- **Seating pieces:** Oval or rectangular backs with floral or figural cresting; upholstery outlined with brass tacks; padded armrests; tapered turned front legs, flared square rear legs

VICTORIAN – LOUIS XVI 1865–1875

MAJOR WOOD(S): Black walnut and ebonized maple

GENERAL CHARACTERISTICS:

- **Case pieces:** Gilt decoration, marquetry, inlay; egg and dart carving; tapered turned legs, fluted

- **Seating pieces:** Molded, slightly arched crest rails; keystone-shaped backs; circular seats; fluted tapered legs

VICTORIAN – EASTLAKE 1870–1895

MAJOR WOOD(S): Black walnut, burl veneer, cherry, and oak

GENERAL CHARACTERISTICS:

- **Case pieces:** Flat cornices; stile and rail construction; burl veneer panels; low-relief geometric and floral machine carving; incised horizontal lines

- **Seating pieces:** Rectilinear; spindles; tapered, turned legs, trumpet-shaped legs

VICTORIAN JACOBEAN AND TURKISH REVIVAL 1870–1890

MAJOR WOOD(S): Black walnut and maple

GENERAL CHARACTERISTICS:

- **Case pieces:** A revival of some heavy 17th century forms, most commonly in dining room pieces

- **Seating pieces:** Turkish Revival style features: oversized, low forms; overstuffed upholstery; padded arms; short baluster, vase-turned legs; ottomans, circular sofas

- **Jacobean Revival style features:** heavy bold carving; spool and spiral turnings

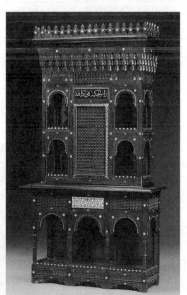

VICTORIAN – AESTHETIC MOVEMENT 1880–1900

MAJOR WOOD(S): Painted hardwoods, black walnut, ebonized finishes

GENERAL CHARACTERISTICS:

- **Case pieces:** Rectilinear forms; bamboo turnings, spaced ball turnings; incised stylized geometric and floral designs, sometimes highlighted with gilt

- **Seating pieces:** Bamboo turning; rectangular backs; patented folding chairs

ART NOUVEAU 1895–1918

MAJOR WOOD(S): Ebonized hardwoods, fruitwoods

GENERAL CHARACTERISTICS:

- **Case pieces:** Curvilinear shapes; floral marquetry; whiplash curves

- **Seating pieces:** Elongated forms; relief-carved floral decoration; spindle backs, pierced floral backs; cabriole legs

TURN-OF-THE-CENTURY (EARLY 20TH CENTURY) 1895–1910

MAJOR WOOD(S): Golden (quarter-sawn) oak, mahogany, hardwood stained to resemble mahogany

GENERAL CHARACTERISTICS:

- **Case pieces:** Rectilinear and bulky forms; applied scroll carving or machine-pressed designs; some Colonial and Classical Revival detailing

- **Seating pieces:** Heavy framing or high spindle-trimmed backs; applied carved or machine-pressed back designs; heavy scrolled or slender turned legs; Colonial Revival or Classical Revival detailing such as claw and ball feet

MISSION (ARTS & CRAFTS MOVEMENT) 1900–1915

MAJOR WOOD(S): Oak

GENERAL CHARACTERISTICS:

- **Case pieces:** Rectilinear through-tenon construction; copper decoration, hand-hammered hardware; square legs

- **Seating pieces:** Rectangular splats; medial and side stretchers; exposed pegs; corbel supports

COLONIAL REVIVAL 1890–1930

MAJOR WOOD(S): Oak, walnut and walnut veneer, mahogany veneer

GENERAL CHARACTERISTICS:

- **Case pieces:** Forms generally following designs of the 17th, 18th, and early 19th centuries; details for the styles such as William and Mary, Federal, Queen Anne, Chippendale, or early Classical were used but often in a simplified or stylized form; mass-production in the early 20th century flooded the market with pieces that often mixed and matched design details and used a great deal of thin veneering to dress up designs; dining room and bedroom suites were especially popular.

- **Seating pieces:** Designs again generally followed early period designs with some mixing of design elements.

ART DECO 1925–1940

MAJOR WOOD(S): Bleached woods, exotic woods, steel, and chrome

GENERAL CHARACTERISTICS:

- **Case pieces:** Heavy geometric forms
- **Seating pieces:** Streamlined, attenuated geometric forms; overstuffed upholstery

MODERNIST OR MID-CENTURY 1945-1970

MAJOR WOOD(S): Plywood, hardwood, or metal frames

GENERAL CHARACTERISTICS: Modernistic designers such as the Eames, Vladimir Kagan, George Nelson, and Isamu Noguchi led the way in post-war design. Carrying on the tradition of Modernist designers of the 1920s and 1930s, they focused on designs for the machine age that could be mass-produced for the popular market. By the late 1950s many of their pieces were used in commercial office spaces and schools as well as in private homes.

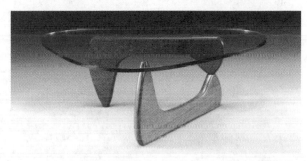

- **Case pieces:** Streamlined or curvilinear abstract designs with simple detailing; plain round or flattened legs and arms; mixed materials including wood, plywood, metal, glass, and molded plastics

- **Seating pieces:** Streamlined or abstract curvilinear designs generally using newer materials such as plywood or simple hardwood framing; fabric and synthetics such as vinyl used for upholstery with finer fabrics and real leather featured on more expensive pieces; seating made of molded plastic shells on metal frames and legs used on many mass-produced designs

DANISH MODERN 1950 1970

MAJOR WOOD(S): Teak

GENERAL CHARACTERISTICS:

- **Case and seating pieces:** This variation of Modernistic post-war design originated in Scandinavia, hence the name; designs were simple and restrained with case pieces often having simple boxy forms with short rounded tapering legs; seating pieces have a simple teak framework with lines coordinating with case pieces; vinyl or natural fabric were most often used for upholstery; in the United States dining room suites were the most popular use for this style although some bedroom suites and general seating pieces were available.

FURNITURE

BEDROOM ITEMS

Uncommon Modern Gothic maple and woven wire daybed, circa 1876, George Hunzinger, stamped with patent date, turned crest rail terminating in applied bosses, adjustable back, curved arms with cone finials, rectangular seat, and original fabric-wrapped metal wire wedding, spindle stretchers, tapered legs, 35" h. x 72" w. x 24" d. **$8,125**
Courtesy of Neal Auction Co.

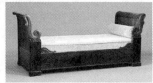

Classical mahogany daybed, circa early 19th century, scrolled headboard and footboard, fronted by swan's necks, shaped rail, block feet, 34-1/2" h. x 69-1/2" w. x 29-1/2" d. **$875**

Courtesy of Neal Auction Co.

Rococo carved rosewood bedroom suite, circa 1860, Cincinnati, bedstead, mirror-back dresser, washstand, and commode, carved and reticulated crest on headboard, dresser crest shield and foliage, washstand and commode with marble tops, washstand 47-1/8" h. x 35-1/2" w. x 20-1/2" d., commode 35-3/4" h. x 25-3/4" w. x 18-1/4" d., dresser 109" h. x 47-1/4" w. x 24-3/4" d., bed 109" h. x 75" l. x 56-1/2" w...**$33,750**

Courtesy of Neal Auction Co.

William IV mahogany bowfront bed step, circa 19th century, three leather inset treads, one with lift lid, another with pull-out chamber pot compartment, on turned legs, 27" h. x 30-1/2" w. x 20-3/8" d. **$812**

Courtesy of Neal Auction Co.

CHESTS/DRESSERS

Queen Anne cherry highboy, mid-18th century, two-part highboy with nine drawers on top section and four on bottom, deep center drawers with concave shell carvings with leaf decoration, carved cabriole legs with acanthus carved knees, good condition, refinished and restored in 1916, 37" x 20" x 71"... **$1,718**

Courtesy of James D. Julia Auctioneers, Fairfield, Maine, www.jamesdjulia.com

Queen Anne carved and figured mahogany bonnet top high chest of drawers highboy, circa mid-18th century, three corkscrew-form finials in middle with three short pull-out drawers below and four graduated pull-out drawers with brass metal pulls, four cabriole legs terminating on pad and disk feet, 86-1/4" x 39" x 22"......................**$39,325**

Courtesy of Ahlers & Ogletree Auction Gallery

Late Federal carved and inlaid cherry wood tall chest of drawers, circa early 19th century, cove molded cornice, crossbanded frieze, three-over-five graduated drawers flanked by arched chevron inlaid stiles, turned feet, 64-1/2" h. x 44-1/4" w. x 20-1/2" d.... **$2,375**

Courtesy of Neal Auction Co.

Regency Kingwood and marble-top commode, circa 18th century, bowl and shaped rectangular top above conforming bombe case fitted with two upper drawers flanking small drawer over two long drawers, splayed feet ending in sabots, excellent condition, small veneer chip on lower right side, minor imperfections and veneer chips, 34-1/2" x 57-1/2" x 26-1/2".........**$24,600**

Courtesy of New Orleans Auction Galleries, Inc.

Continental carved walnut chest, circa 18th century, likely Italian, lid opens to void interior, case carved with figures, acanthus scrolls and foliate moldings, anthropomorphic feet, casters, 24" h. x 46" w. x 22-1/2" d.. **$875**

Courtesy of Neal Auction Co.

CUPBOARDS • CABINETS • ARMOIRES

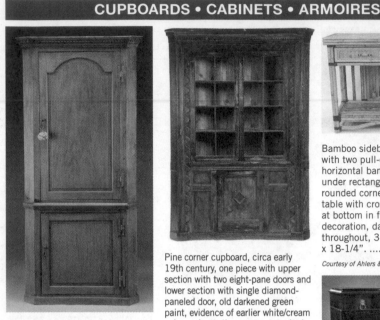

Bamboo sideboard or server with two pull-out drawers with horizontal bamboo handles under rectangular top with rounded corners, console table with cross stretcher self at bottom in front of arched decoration, darker accents throughout, 34-3/4" x 47-3/4" x 18-1/4". **$302**

Courtesy of Ahlers & Ogletree Auction Gallery

Pine corner cupboard, circa early 19th century, one piece with upper section with two eight-pane doors and lower section with single diamond-paneled door, old darkened green paint, evidence of earlier white/cream color underneath, one pane cracked, repairs to cornice, interior finished, green paint old and oxidized, 87" x 60" x 27". **$10,200**

Courtesy of Garth's Auctioneers & Appraisers

Federal walnut corner cupboard, early 19th century, Pennsylvania, two doors with raised panels, top door of tombstone form, stepped crown molding with Greek key detail, original brass "H" hinges, very good condition, 82" x 36"... **$355**

Courtesy of James D. Julia Auctioneers, Fairfield, Maine, www.jamesdjulia.com

Pair of English carved mahogany pedestal cabinets, 19th century, plinth tops, blind fretwork carved doors, cellarette drawers, rest with sliding trays, ball and claw feet, 45-1/2" h. x 27-1/2" w. x 23" d. **$2,187**

Courtesy of Neal Auction Co.

Classical carved mahogany armoire, circa early 19th century, probably Baltimore, flared cornice, inset arch frieze, paneled doors flanked by Ionic columnar pilasters, shelf interior, each end with paneled doors, molded base, massive paw feet, 87" h. x 73-7/8" w. x 28" d. **$2,125**

Courtesy of Neal Auction Co.

Four-piece stacking cabinet, circa late 18th century, New England, hinged paneled doors and open shelves, forged iron drop handles on sides with shaped backing plates, two pieces marked on top in black paint script "Rev. J.B. Condit, Long Meadow, Mass. Care of Col. S. Warriner, Springfield, Mass," pastor served during Civil War, 90" h. assembled, 46" x 16 1/2".....**$3,835**

Courtesy of Thomaston Place Auction Galleries

French Provincial walnut buffet, 18th century, rectangular top with molded edge and angled corners above conforming case, fitted with long drawer above pair of covered doors and recessed panels, scrolling molded edges, good condition with original hardware, chestnut secondary wood, shrinkage on top, minor repairs, 39" x 54" x 25". **$1,185**

Courtesy of James D. Julia Auctioneers, Fairfield, Maine, www.jamesdjulia.com

DESKS

Edwardian mahogany and paint-decorated lady's writing desk, circa 1900, galleried superstructure with bracketed shelves flanked by glazed doors, base with frieze drawer, square tapered legs, and stretcher shelf, 49-1/4" h. x 27" w. x 17-1/2" d......... **$1,250**

Courtesy of Neal Auction Co.

Russian Neoclassical-style gilt bronze-mounted inlaid mahogany bureau cylindre, galleried top with eagle head mounts, cylinder lid enclosing fitted interior, pull-out tooled leather writing surface, kneehole flanked by pedestals of drawers, 47" h. x 54-3/4" w. x 28" d.......................... **$6,250**

Courtesy of Neal Auction Co.

Two-part campaign chest with desk, 19th century, hinged compartment folds out to sloping baize-lined writing surface below row of three drawers above two aligned short drawers, good condition, 37-1/2" x 35-1/2" x 18".. **$1,777**

Courtesy of James D. Julia Auctioneers, Fairfield, Maine, www.jamesdjulia.com

SEATING

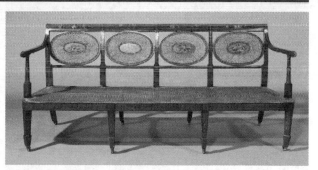

American aesthetic carved giltwood slipper chair, circa late 19th century, open latticework back with centering floral panels, beaded front seat rail, turned block legs with rosettes, stretchers........................... **$812**

Courtesy of Neal Auction Co.

George III polychromed satinwood and caned settee, circa late 18th century, back of four oval panels with putti and flowers, scrolled arms, caned seat, square tapered legs, spade feet, casters, 34-1/2" h. x 75" w. x 27-1/4" d..**$2,500**

Courtesy of Neal Auction Co.

Louis XVI oak bench/coffer, 18th century, rectangular seat with raised ends, hinged compartments flanking hinged panel top, supported on stiles, four-panel front with original brass key escutcheons, 37" w. x 74-1/4" h. x 21" d........ **$1,500**

Courtesy of Neal Auction Co.

Pair of Chinese hardwood folding horseshoe-back armchairs, likely Qing Dynasty (1644-1912), possibly lichimu, with rounded rails and outswept hand rests and curved extensions attached to front legs, backsplat carved with two dragons, seats in diamond pattern made of woven hemp, 41-1/2" h. x 27-7/8" w. x 21-1/2" d.................. **$625**

Courtesy of Neal Auction Co.

Windsor writing chair, circa early 19th century, New England, shaped crest, medial rail over turned spindles, shaped writing arm and scrolled arms, plank seat, turned splayed legs, stretchers and old rubbed paint decoration. **$531**

Courtesy of Neal Auction Co.

Eight Irish country Queen Anne-style dining chairs, late 20th century, six straight and two arm chairs, bench-made examples set to emulate 18th century country Irish, with half-spindled back and pad feet with balls, very good condition, 40" h. **$1,185**

Courtesy of James D. Julia Auctioneers, Fairfield, Maine, www.jamesdjulia.com

Six Shaker ladderback side chairs, late 19th/early 20th century, New Hampshire, simple form with straight back posts and turned finials, fitted with three broad arch-top slats and one slat held in place with small wooden peg, very good condition, 43"..................... **$592**

Courtesy of James D. Julia Auctioneers, Fairfield, Maine, www.jamesdjulia.com

Pair of square back armchairs with marble inserts, 19th century, China, scrolling backs and arms centering basketry seats, square frontal legs with foot rests, 36-1/2" x 20" x 24-1/2". **$2,470**

Courtesy of James D. Julia Auctioneers, Fairfield, Maine, www.jamesdjulia.com

TABLES

FURNITURE

Louis XVI-style inlaid Kingwood side table, early 20th century, probably Paris, shaped bronze molded top with radial and banded inlay, frieze drawer, cabriole legs ending in sabots and connected by stretcher shelf, 28-3/8" h. x 17-1/2" w. x 12-1/2" d.................... **$1,125**

Courtesy of Neal Auction Co.

Federal inlaid mahogany card table, circa 1810-1815, manufactured in Salem, Massachusetts, hinged mahogany top with half serpentine side, ovolo corners, and elliptic front above conforming frieze, very good condition, original surfaces professionally cleaned and polished, 29-1/2" x 36-1/2" x 18-1/2"......................... **$1,358**

Courtesy of James D. Julia Auctioneers, Fairfield, Maine, www.jamesdjulia.com

Federal mahogany sewing stand, early 19th century, bird's-eye maple drawer fronts, thin overhanging top above two dovetailed drawers faced in bird's-eye maple with mahogany banding, fitted with silk-lined sewing drawer, very good condition, old refinish, silk cloth bag and frame replacement, 14" x 19-1/2" x 28-1/2"............................ **$948**

Courtesy of James D. Julia Auctioneers, Fairfield, Maine, www.jamesdjulia.com

Regency yew center table, late 18th/early 19th century, circular top with conforming green leather inset with impressed gilt floral border within bird's-eye crossbanded edge, apron fitted with four drawers alternating with rectangular panels, all with bird's-eye figural surface, condition structurally good, early replaced hardware and original leather top, 29-1/2" x 33-1/2"........................... **$1,066**

Courtesy of James D. Julia Auctioneers, Fairfield, Maine, www.jamesdjulia.com

Queen Anne-style mahogany tray-top tea table, mid-19th century, rectangular top with molded edges above conforming frieze, tapering cabriole legs terminating in spoon pad feet, very good condition, minimal and minor roughness and shrinkage crack within inner edge of top molding, 27" x 29-1/2" x 18-3/4"......................... **$711**

Courtesy of James D. Julia Auctioneers, Fairfield, Maine, www.jamesdjulia.com

Hepplewhite Pembroke drop-leaf table in cherry and tiger maple, circa early 19th century, figured single plank top, two drop leaves joined by rule joints, cherry base and tall tapering square legs, very good condition, one replacement hinge and two chips along rule joints, 36" x 18-1/2" x 29". **$2,370**

Courtesy of James D. Julia Auctioneers, Fairfield, Maine, www.jamesdjulia.com

Lacquered short table inset with cloisonné, 20th century, four short hoof legs, top with three large chargers with floral motif, some wear and damage, 50" x 18" x 16".................. **$592**

Courtesy of James D. Julia Auctioneers, Fairfield, Maine, www.jamesdjulia.com

Chinese altar table, late 19th/ early 20th century, tall narrow form with scrolling open work on front and paneled ends, mitered corners and inset paneled top, light celadon green painted surface, very good condition, inset patch on top, 74" x 16" x 32-1/2". ... **$948**

Courtesy of James D. Julia Auctioneers, Fairfield, Maine, www.jamesdjulia.com

Painted sawbuck table, circa early 19th century, pine, original ochre and brown grained paint, single board pegged square cleats beneath, affixed square X-base legs, very good condition, minor abrasions, 26-1/2" x 60" x 29"............ **$741**

Courtesy of James D. Julia Auctioneers, Fairfield, Maine, www.jamesdjulia.com

Empire table with white square marble top, circa early 19th century, Charles Honore Lannuier, canted corners above bronze ormolu metal mounts on mahogany apron in form of rosettes and scrolled accents, four winged harpy figures raised on horn-shaped ebonized shafts, signed "H. Lannuier NEW YORK" under marble top, one gilt wing repair, minor cracking to veneer, regilded, 33" x 32-1/2"................**$36,300**

Courtesy of Ahlers & Ogletree Auction Gallery

James III oval gate-leg dining table, circa late 17th century, oak with oval top, two drop leaves, six-leg base with two legs that swing outward to support leaves, apron with cupid bow scallop, fair to good condition, minor glue repairs, losses and slight worm damage to bottom of feet, 51" x 59" x 28"............ **$948**

Courtesy of James D. Julia Auctioneers, Fairfield, Maine, www.jamesdjulia.com

George II mahogany wood tilt-top table, circa mid-18th century, floral carved border raised on beaded and gadrooned shaft on tripod base with acanthus leaf motif and scrolled legs, 29-1/5" x 39-3/4". **$36,300**

Courtesy of Ahlers & Ogletree Auction Gallery

top lot

American Gothic rosewood and marble-top center table, circa 1840-1850, probably executed by cabinet shop of Alexander Roux, New York, and after design by Alexander Jackson Davis, original hexagonal white marble top with double "bull's-nose" edge over conforming frame with ripple molding along upper edge, turned drop finials with ball tips supported by cluster columns, base with extended trefoil feet and applied beaded moldings, underside of marble with faint penciled inscription "W Clarke," 31" h. x 37" w. x 37" d........**$93,480**

Courtesy of New Orleans Auction Galleries, Inc.

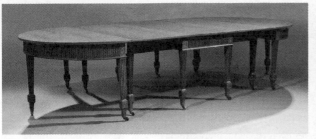

Georgian carved mahogany four-part banquet table in Adam style, circa late 18th century, ends with two drop-leaf center sections, fluted frieze, fluted tapered square legs, brass cuffs, casters, 29-1/2" h. x 60" w., extended length 202"..........**$537**

Courtesy of Neal Auction Co.

George III-style carved mahogany serving table in style of Robert Adam, early 20th century, serpentine top, conforming highly carved frieze, tapered square bellflower carved legs, spade feet, 35-7/8" h. x 60" w. x 25" d. **$1,750**

Courtesy of Neal Auction Co.

George III inlaid mahogany dressing table, circa late 18th century, shield-shaped mirror above inlaid cupboards, shaped tray top, drawers to each side, center slide, two drawers centered by patera, shaped apron, tapered and cuffed legs, 58" h. x 26-1/2" w. x 19" d....................**$1,375**

Courtesy of Neal Auction Co.

Dining table from Arizona Biltmore Hotel, Phoenix, 1927, iron and enameled steel, designed by Warren McArthur, good condition, craquelure throughout table top, 27-3/4" x 30-7/8" x 35-1/4"..........**$11,250**

Courtesy of Heritage Auctions

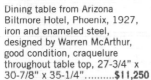

MISCELLANEOUS

Rococo carved rosewood console étagère, circa 1850-1860, John Henry Belter, paper "broadside" label, serpentine tiered superstructure with three shelves, mirrored back, base with shaped and molded white marble top, cabriole legs carved with floral clusters joined by stretchers and casters, 71-3/4" h. x 41" w. x 21" d. **$17,500**

Courtesy of Neal Auction Co.

Georgian mahogany bookcase, circa late 18th century and later elements, dentil molded broken pediment, glazed doors, adjustable shelves, drawer in base, ogee bracket feet, interior lined with velvet, 90" h. x 61" w. x 22-1/2" d. **$1,875**

Courtesy of Neal Auction Co.

Regency inlaid mahogany sofa table, circa early 19th century, cross-banded drop-leaf top, two frieze drawers, trestle supports connected by stretcher, sabre legs, brass caps, casters, 28-3/4" h. x 59-1/2" w. x 25-7/8" d. **$1,500**

Courtesy of Neal Auction Co.

FURNITURE
==========

modern furniture

MODERN DESIGN IS EVERYWHERE, evergreen and increasingly popular. Modernism has never gone out of style. Its reach into the present day is as deep as its roots in the past. Just as it can be seen and felt ubiquitously in the mass media of today – on film, television, in magazines and department stores – it can be traced to the mid-1800s post-Empire non-conformity of the Biedermeier Movement, the turn of the 20th century anti-Victorianism of the Vienna Secessionists, the radical reductionism of Frank Lloyd Wright and the revolutionary post-Depression thinking of Walter Gropius and the Bauhaus school in Germany.

"The Modernists really changed the way the world looked," said John Sollo, a partner in Sollo Rago Auction of Lambertville, New Jersey. Sollo's partner in business, and one of the most recognizable names in the field, David Rago, takes Sollo's idea a little further by saying that Modernism is actually more about the names behind the design than the design itself, at least as far as buying goes.

No discussion of Modern can be complete, however, without examining its genesis and enduring influence. Modernism is everywhere in today's pop culture. Austere Scandinavian furniture dominates the television commercials that hawk hotels and mutual funds. Post-war American design ranges across sitcom set dressings to movie sets patterned after Frank Lloyd Wright houses and Hollywood Modernist classics set high in the hills.

You have to look at the dorm rooms of college students and the apartments of young people whose living spaces are packed with the undeniably Modern mass-produced products of IKEA, Target, Design Within Reach and the like.

There can be no denying that the post-World War II manufacturing techniques and subsequent boom led to the widespread acceptance of plastic and bent plywood chairs along with low-sitting coffee tables, couches and recliners.

"The modern aesthetic grew out of a perfect storm of post-war optimism, innovative materials and an incredible crop of designers," said Lisanne Dickson, director of 1950s/Modern Design at Treadway-Toomey.

"I think that the people who designed the furniture were maybe ahead of society's ability to accept and understand what they were doing," Sollo said. "It's taken people another 30 to 40 years to catch up to it."

There are hundreds of great Modern designers, many who worked across categories – furniture, architecture, fine art, etc. – and many contributed to the work of other big names without ever seeking that glory for themselves.

For more information on Modernism, see *Warman's Modernism Furniture & Accessories Identification and Price Guide* by Noah Fleisher.

RAR rocker, circa 1950, designed by Charles Eames and Ray Kaiser Eames for Herman Miller, fiberglass shell, zinc wire, walnut, retains original label, molded HERMAN MILLER, good condition, 27" x 25" x 27"................ **$687**

Courtesy of Heritage Auctions

— Noah Fleisher

Isamu Noguchi "Rudder" dinette table, circa 1944, birch and zinc-plated steel for Herman Miller, free-form top over three parabolic legs, structurally sound, marks, scratches and nicks commensurate with age and use, 16" l. **$20,400**
Three "Rudder" stools, circa 1944, birch and zinc-plated steel......... **One for $33,000; two for $30,625 ea.**

Courtesy of John Moran Auctioneers

Pair of swan chairs, circa mid-20th century, Arne Jacobsen for Fritz Hansen, continuous blue vinyl upholstered back and seat, raised on adjustable four-prong aluminum base, good condition, minor scuffing on base, 31-1/2" x 28-3/4" x 19-1/2". **$3,120**

Courtesy of Garth's Auctioneers & Appraisers

Pair of Elizabeth lounge chairs, mid-20th century, by I.B. Kofod-Larsen for Christensen & Larsen, continuous shaped back and seat flanked by shaped arms transitioning to circular tapering legs joined by stretchers, good condition, original upholstery, original bill of sale/lading included, 28" x 31" x 29".......................................**$17,400**

Courtesy of Garth's Auctioneers & Appraisers. Delaware, Ohio www.garths.com

Coffee table, circa 1950, model AT-10, designed by Andreas Tuck, teak, oak, and caning, large dent to one of long sides, light surface wear commensurate with age, 20" x 63-1/4" x 20"..................... **$1,500**

Courtesy of Heritage Auctions

Italian mid-century design card table with chairs, Mascagni Furniture Co., Bologna, chromed metal trim on red square top, overskirt and tapered cylindrical legs with maroon upholstered cover, capped feet, table 29-3/4" h. x 29-3/4" w., chairs 38" h. x 17-1/2" w. x 18-1/2" d. **$332**

Courtesy of Austin Auction Gallery

Coffee table, circa 1951, Model No. 5042, Johnson Furniture Co., Paul Frankl design, pioneer of American modernist design movement, 14-1/4" x 60"..**$15,360**

Courtesy of Los Angeles Modern Auctions

FURNITURE

Five-piece suite of furniture, circa 1960, designed by Marcel Breuer, two chairs, two end tables (shown), and coffee table, chairs 29" x 31" x 27", coffee table 13-1/2" x 53-1/2" x 18-3/4", end tables 18" x 21-1/2" x 19"......**$1,920**

Courtesy of Los Angeles Modern Auctions

Diamond chair, circa 1952, Knoll Corp., designed by Harry Bertoia, welded steel with chrome finish, upholstered seat cushion, good condition with minor rusting and oxidation at joints, 30-1/2" x 33" x 27"........**$1,187**

Courtesy of Heritage Auctions

Modern chair and ottoman, tilting swivel chair with rolled back and arms of brown fabric, back and sides in vinyl, on quadripartite angled metal supports, chair tagged "design and crafted for Levitz Furniture," 41" h. x 35" w. x 35" d., matching footstool 14-1/2" h. x 26" w. x 21" d. **$423**

Courtesy of Austin Auction Gallery

Five-piece bedroom suite, circa 1951, designed by Paul Frankl for Johnson Furniture Co., two nightstands, dresser, highboy, and headboard, nightstands 24-1/4" x 24" x 17", headboard 34" x 80" x 3-1/2", dresser 36" x 73" x 22-1/2", highboy 45" x 40" x 20-1/2". **$4,160**

Courtesy of Los Angeles Modern Auctions

Pair of Mid-Century Modern black leather chairs, circa 1960s, Germany, arched back with arms flanking shaped integral seat, three long chrome steel legs with castors, several tears along seams of both chairs, 36-1/2" h. x 27-3/4" w. x 27" d...........................**$2,722**

Courtesy of Austin Auction Gallery

Danish mid-century modern rosewood executive desk, 1960s, design by Arne Vodder for Sibast Furniture, Virum, "floating" rectangular top with slightly upturned edges at two ends, two drawers at one side, other side supported by return cabinet with sliding doors, end door and drawer, turned legs, desk top 29-1/4" h. x 80" l. x 35-1/4"d., return 25-1/4" h. x 66" l. x 16-3/4" d. **$7,260**

Courtesy of Austin Auction Gallery

Pair of lounge chairs, circa 1960, designed by John Masheroni, tubular aluminum frame, linen sling seating, scratch to front right leg of one chair, new upholstery, surface wear commensurate with age, 29" x 32" x 35"............. **$2,125**

Courtesy of Heritage Auctions

Large modern hammered copper table lamp with shade, dual socket, circa 1960s, Dunbar Furniture Co., 29-1/2" h. **$1,694**

Courtesy of Austin Auction Gallery

Table and four chairs, circa 1970, designed by Robert Josten, cast aluminum, steel, maple, multiple scratches to table top, scuffing to legs, some scratching on seats, minor rubbing and color shift to finish on crossbars, 29-1/4" x 27-1/2" x 27-3/4". **$2,750**

Courtesy of Heritage Auctions

Danish modern brass flared cone pendant single-light lamp, design by Claus Bonderup and Thorsten Thorup for Fog and Morup, Denmark, circa 1960, 13" h. x 27" dia................. **$484**

Courtesy of Austin Auction Gallery

Set of eight Eco-Eden chairs, circa 1982, ash plywood, designed by Peter Danko, surface wear indicative of use, 32-3/4" x 21-1/8" x 21". Provenance: Museum of Modern Art Collection, New York. **$1,375**

Courtesy of Heritage Auctions

GLASS

GLASS

art glass

ART GLASS IS ARTISTIC novelty glassware created for decorative purposes. Types of art glass include leaded glass, molded glass, blown glass, and sandblasted glass. Tiffany, Lalique, and Steuben are some of the best-known types of art glass. Daum Nancy, Baccarat, Gallé, Moser, Mt. Washington, Fenton, and Quezal are a few others.

Alexandrite bowl with purple and blue shading to amber body and pressed honeycomb pattern, ruffled and pinched rim, unsigned, very good to excellent condition, 5" dia. **$593**

Courtesy of James D. Julia Auctioneers, Fairfield, Maine, www.jamesdjulia.com

Desire Christian vase with red cameo, berries, stems and leaves with two cameo butterflies hovering above, cameo decoration with gilded highlights against translucent green background, signed on underside "D. Christian Meisenthal," very good to excellent condition with minor acid burns on side of foot, 7" h.....**$1,185**

Courtesy of James D. Julia Auctioneers, Fairfield, Maine, www.jamesdjulia.com

Monumental Charder Art Deco cameo vase on foot with chestnut foliage and fruit nuts in repeating design around shoulder, glossy design in autumnal colors against acid backdrop of frost with orange and cream, cameo marked "Charder" below group arrangement, excellent original condition, 6-1/2" x 12" w........**$3,000**

Courtesy of Mark Mussio, Humler & Nolan

VISIT WWW.ANTIQUETRADER.COM

WWW.FACEBOOK.COM/ANTIQUETRADER

English cameo vase attributed to Webb, wheel-carved floral decoration in white against frosted deep red background, neck decorated with panels of stylized leaves and flowers, unsigned, very good to excellent condition, 7-1/8" h. **$1,185**

Courtesy of James D. Julia Auctioneers, Fairfield, Maine, www.jamesdjulia.com

Burgun & Schverer vase with cameo thistle decoration, each thistle with green enamel stems and leaves and pink and blue enameled flowers, brown background with etched thistle flowers, signed on underside with etched and gilded thistle signature "Verrerie D'Art De Lorraine B.S. & Co.," very good to excellent condition, 7" h. **$2,963**

Courtesy of James D. Julia Auctioneers, Fairfield, Maine, www.jamesdjulia.com

Dale Chihuly conical vase in blue glass with gold foil inclusions and applied swirling band leading to applied stylized flame in red glass with gold foil inclusions, applied red foot and lip, signed on side with etched signature "Chihuly" and marked on underside "PP 99," very good to excellent condition, 16-1/4" h. **$2,963**

Courtesy of James D. Julia Auctioneers, Fairfield, Maine, www.jamesdjulia.com

Trumpet vase, H. C. Fry Glass Co., first quarter 20th century, Foval with jade connector and foot, polished pontil mark, 9-1/4" h., 5" dia. overall..... **$374**

Courtesy of Jeffrey S. Evans & Associates

LeVerre Francais footed bowl in Primerolles pattern with mottled brown and orange cameo floral decoration against mottled yellow background, signed "LeVerrre Francais" and marked on underside "France," very good to excellent condition, 9" h. **$1,126**

Courtesy of James D. Julia Auctioneers, Fairfield, Maine, www.jamesdjulia.com

LeVerre Francais vase in Papillons pattern with mottled orange and blue cameo butterflies against mottled light blue and cream background, signed "LeVerre Francais France," very good to excellent condition, 13-3/4" h........ **$2,489**

Courtesy of James D. Julia Auctioneers, Fairfield, Maine, www.jamesdjulia.com

Monumental LeVerre Francais vase in Mirettes pattern with royal blue foot and blue cameo stems extending to mottled brown and orange stylized flowers against yellow background, signed "LeVerre Francais," very good to excellent condition, 18-1/2" h. **$2,370**

Courtesy of James D. Julia Auctioneers, Fairfield, Maine, www.jamesdjulia.com

English cameo vase with white cameo foxglove flowers with stems and leaves on front and ferns and butterfly on reverse on blue ground, single white cameo band at top and double band at foot, unsigned but attributed to Webb, very good to excellent condition, 7" h. **$1,659**

Courtesy of James D. Julia Auctioneers, Fairfield, Maine, www.jamesdjulia.com

Lamartine cabinet vase with cameo decoration of large tree with pond in background and forest on distant shore, signed "Lamartine," very good to excellent condition, 3-1/2" h................................ **$1,659**

Courtesy of James D. Julia Auctioneers, Fairfield, Maine, www.jamesdjulia.com

Large Legras Art Deco vase with round bulbous body and flaring ruffled rim with large turquoise and white stylized flowers and cobalt blue and brown stylized leaves, signed on side in black "Leg," marked on bottom in acid-etched block letters "MADE IN FRANCE," very good to excellent condition, tiny black inclusion on lip of vase (from making), 10-1/2" h. **$415**

Courtesy of James D. Julia Auctioneers, Fairfield, Maine, www.jamesdjulia.com

Cranberry and vaseline overshot bud vase, 9" h. **$266**

Courtesy of Woody Auctions, LLC

Monumental D'Argental four-color cameo vase with scene of trees before lake and mountain range on horizon on front and back, oval windows connected by cameo cuttings of branches within triangular forms, D'Argental signature in cameo within each scene, excellent condition, 12" h. x 8" w. at shoulder...................... **$1,700**

Courtesy of Mark Mussio, Humler & Nolan

Gold iridescent goblet with applied puntes on bowl and stem, attributed to Steuben, strong color, 6". **$944**

Courtesy of Woody Auctions, LLC

Continental flashed glass wheel-carved vase, 19th century, tapered form in green and purple with intertwined floral and geometric patterns, retains Mallett Gallery New York and London labels to underside, 12" h. **$4,000**

Courtesy of Clars Auction Gallery, www.clars.com

Baluster-form acid-etched vase, circa 1900, with iridescent blue-green long-stemmed irises on iridescent pale gold ground, incised signature to underside "Cristallerie de Pantin / STVC" (for Stumpf, Touvier and Viollet Cie), 13-1/4" h. x 5-1/2" dia. **$2,000**

Courtesy of John Moran Auctioneers, Inc.

Flared-rim vase in Primrose pattern, circa 1925, with attenuated cylindrical body on spreading circular foot and stylized flowers and foliage in orange shading to brown on mottled yellow and orange ground, etched signature to top of foot "Le Verre Francais," 24-1/2" h. x 7-1/2" dia.... **$3,500**

Courtesy of John Moran Auctioneers, Inc.

GLASS

Early Charles Lotton Mandarin red gourd vase, signed by Lotton with production year 1981, excellent original condition, 5-3/8" h. x 6" w..................**$500**

Courtesy of Mark Mussio, Humler & Nolan

President Abraham Lincoln acid-cut overlay glass pane, fourth quarter 19th/early 20th century, ruby to colorless glass, rectangular form with image of Lincoln standing and holding rolled-up paper in one hand, within arched border flanked by columns surmounted by winged griffins, lettered "LINCOLN" in reserve at bottom, 29" x 18-1/2"........**$1,495**

Courtesy of Jeffrey S. Evans & Associates

Early Lundberg Studios miniature blue Aurene vase with night scene of red-eyed dragonflies hovering before "King Tut" watery backdrop, engraved "Lundberg Studios, 1976," possibly designed and created by one of Lundberg founders, excellent condition, 3-1/4" h. **$225**

Courtesy of Mark Mussio, Humler & Nolan

John Fields Monet Series pillow vase with gardens of pink flowers beneath blue sky, white mottled interior, engraved "Fields & Fields, 2001," excellent condition, 9-1/2" h. **$110**

Courtesy of Mark Mussio, Humler & Nolan

▲ California Glass Studio free-form vase with resemblance of white swan in center surrounded by magenta and teal blue glass, signed "CGS" with 1995 creative year, excellent condition, 9-3/4" h. x 17" w. **$190**

Courtesy of Mark Mussio, Humler & Nolan

▶ Dale Chihuly Portland Press glass vase, late 20th century, lime green lip above free-form crimson body with mottled taupe and black, signed to underside, 8" h. x 12" w. ...**$4,500**

Courtesy of Clars Auction Gallery, www.clars.com

top lot!

Burgun & Schverer vase with cameo decoration of Roman soldier holding spear, soldier and female figure standing by cameo pillar set against gilded textured background with blue and white enameled highlights to clothing, sides and back of vase with cameo medallions with eagles in center and diagonal band of cameo animals, blue and white enameled band at foot and neck, signed on underside with engraved and gilded thistle signature "Verrerie de'art de Lorraine BS & Co Depose," very good to excellent condition, 9" h. $11,850

GLASS

baccarat

BACCARAT GLASS HAS been made by Cristalleries de Baccarat, France, since 1765. The firm has produced various glassware of excellent quality as well as paperweights. Baccarat's Rose Tiente is often referred to as Baccarat's Amberina.

Antique paperweight with scattered millefiori with gridel animal canes (horse, goat, dog, monkey, elephant, partridge), shamrock, and flower cane on upset white muslin, signed in cane "B1847," very good to excellent condition, 3" dia. **$2,015**

Courtesy of James D. Julia Auctioneers, Fairfield, Maine, www.jamesdjulia.com

Vase in opalescent glass, foot pressed in shape of rocky ground and applied glass snake coiled around cylindrical neck impressed with bamboo shoots with large insect near lip, enameled insect and snake, gilded bamboo shoots, signed on underside in raised block letters "Baccarat," very good condition, 8-3/4" h..... **$2,963**

Courtesy of James D. Julia Auctioneers, Fairfield, Maine, www.jamesdjulia.com

Two five-light candelabra, Baccarat, 20th century, marks: BACCARAT, FRANCE, 22-3/4" h........ **$2,500**

Courtesy of Heritage Auctions

VISIT WWW.ANTIQUETRADER.COM

WWW.FACEBOOK.COM/ANTIQUETRADER

Pair of Mille Nuits two-light candelabra, 20th century, each with tapering central post supporting two clear arms with candle nozzles and cut-crystal teardrops, circular base stamped "Baccarat" and signed in script at base rim, both in good condition, 18-7/8"............................ **$868**

Courtesy of Brunk Auctions

Pair of crystal candleholders, barley twist form, baluster standards and circular bases, etched mark, 9" h., 4-3/4" dia. **$225**

Courtesy of Clars Auction Gallery, www.clars.com

Christian Dior glass perfume bottle with stopper, circa 1950, red cut-to-clear with faceted panels to stopper and body, gilt painted label faintly reads Diorama, Christian Dior, marks: BACCARAT, FRANCE, PARIS (acid-etched mark), 7-1/4" h. including stopper........ **$375**

Courtesy of Heritage Auctions

Antique interlocking garland paperweight with two garlands, one in blue and white and one in salmon and blue, surrounding central cane with row of green millefiori on white upset muslin with six and one faceting, very good to excellent condition, 3-1/4" dia. **$1,359**

Courtesy of James D. Julia Auctioneers, Fairfield, Maine, www.jamesdjulia.com

GLASS

bride's baskets

THESE BERRY OR fruit bowls were popular late Victorian wedding gifts, hence the name. They were produced in a variety of quality art glass wares and sometimes were fitted in ornate silver plate holders.

Windows pattern air-trap mother-of-pearl satin bowl, ruby to colorless, applied blue rim and polished pontil mark, late 19th/early 20th century, 4-1/2" h. overall, 8-1/2" dia. overall. **$184**

Courtesy of Jeffrey S. Evans & Associates

Poinsettia pattern basket, cranberry opalescent, crimped and ruffled rim, fitted in unsigned quadruple-plate frame with floral decoration, Northwood Glass Co., circa 1903, 11-1/2" h., bowl 10-1/2" dia. overall. **$288**

Courtesy of Jeffrey S. Evans & Associates

Victorian cased glass bride's basket, shaded blue with polychrome enamel decoration, applied vaseline and opal crimped rim, fitted in Wilcox Silver Plate Co. quadruple-plate stand, numbered "7666," fourth quarter 19th century, 11" h. overall, bowl 10-1/4" dia. overall. **$184**

Courtesy of Jeffrey S. Evans & Associates

Victorian cased glass bride's basket, shaded blue with polychrome enamel decoration, applied vaseline and opal crimped rim, fitted in Toronto Silver Plate Co. quadruple-plate stand, numbered "232," fourth quarter 19th century, 11" h. overall, bowl 10-1/4" dia. overall. **$196**

Courtesy of Jeffrey S. Evans & Associates

Blue satin ruffled bowl with Coralene-style rose décor, on French gilt metal stand (marriage), 3-1/2" x 12". **$83**

Courtesy of Woody Auctions, LLC

Victorian cased glass bride's bowl, shaded amethyst interior, ribbed bowl with fancy scalloped and ruffled rim, fitted in unmarked quadruple-plate stand, fourth quarter 19th century, 11-1/4" h. overall, bowl 12" dia. overall..........**$219**

Courtesy of Jeffrey S. Evans & Associates

Two Lattice pattern bowls, cranberry opalescent and colorless, square forms, crimped and ruffled rims, late 19th/early 20th century, 3-3/8" and 3-3/4" h. overall, 7-3/4" dia. overall.........................$104

Courtesy of Jeffrey S. Evans & Associates

Three Swirling Maze pattern bowls, green, cranberry, and colorless opalescent, each with crimped and ruffled rims, Jefferson Glass Co., circa 1905, 3 1/4" to 3 3/4" h. overall, 8-3/4" to 9-3/4" dia. overall.............$184

Courtesy of Jeffrey S. Evans & Associates

Victorian cased glass bride's basket, shaded amethyst with polychrome enamel decoration, applied vaseline and opal crimped rim, fitted in loose-fitting Waldorf Silver Co. quadruple-plate stand, numbered "521," fourth quarter 19th century, 13-1/2" h. overall, bowl 11-1/2" dia. overall. $259

Courtesy of Jeffrey S. Evans & Associates

Victorian cased glass bride's basket, cranberry opalescent with polychrome enamel decoration, lattice motif with fancy scalloped and ruffled rim, fitted in E.G. Webster and Son quadruple-plate stand numbered "180," fourth quarter 19th century, 15" h. overall, bowl 12-1/2" dia. overall. $259

Courtesy of Jeffrey S. Evans & Associates

Victorian cased glass bride's basket, transparent yellow green to opal with enamel scroll and floral decorations, lobbed bowl with ruffled rim, fitted in quadruple-plate and brass stand marked for Meriden Silver Plate Co. and numbered "7064," fourth quarter 19th century, 10" h. overall, bowl 10-1/2" dia. overall. $184

Courtesy of Jeffrey S. Evans & Associates

Victorian cased glass bride's basket, shaded blue interior with polychrome enamel and gilt decoration, crimped rim, fitted in James W. Tufts of Boston quadruple-plate stand and numbered "172," fourth quarter 19th century, 9-3/4" h. overall, bowl 9-1/2" dia. overall. $138

Courtesy of Jeffrey S. Evans & Associates

GLASS

carnival glass

CARNIVAL GLASS IS what is fondly called mass-produced iridescent glassware. The term "carnival glass" has evolved through the years as glass collectors have responded to the idea that much of this beautiful glassware was made as give-away glass at local carnivals and fairs. However, more of it was made and sold through the same channels as pattern glass and Depression glass. Some patterns were indeed giveaways, and others were used as advertising premiums, souvenirs, etc. Whatever the origin, the term "carnival glass" today encompasses glassware that is usually pattern molded and treated with metallic salts, creating that unique coloration that is so desirable to collectors.

Early names for iridescent glassware, which early 20th century consumers believed to have all come from foreign manufacturers, include Pompeiian Iridescent, Venetian Art, and Mexican Aurora. Another popular early name was "Nancy Glass," as some patterns were believed to have come from the Daum, Nancy, glassmaking area in France. This was at a time when the artistic cameo glass was enjoying great success. While the iridescent glassware being made by such European glassmakers as Loetz influenced the American market place, it was Louis Tiffany's Favrile glass that really caught the eye of glass consumers of the early 1900s. It seems an easy leap to transform Tiffany's shimmering glassware to something that could be mass produced, allowing what we call carnival glass today to become "poor man's Tiffany."

Carnival glass is iridized glassware that is created by pressing hot molten glass into molds, just as pattern glass had evolved. Some forms are hand finished, while others are completely formed by molds. To achieve the marvelous iridescent colors that carnival glass collectors seek, a process was developed where a liquid solution of metallic salts was put onto the still hot glass form after it was unmolded. As the liquid evaporated, a fine metallic surface was left which refracts light into wonderful colors. The name given to the iridescent spray by early glassmakers was "dope."

Many of the forms created by carnival glass manufacturers were accessories to the china American housewives so loved. By the early 1900s, consumers could find carnival glassware at such popular stores as F. W. Woolworth and McCrory's. To capitalize on the popular fancy for these colored wares, some other industries bought large quantities of carnival glass and turned them into "packers." This term reflects the practice where baking powder, mustard, or other household products were packed into a special piece of glass that could take on another life after the original product was used. Lee Manufacturing Co. used iridized carnival glass as premiums for its baking powder and other products, causing some early carnival glass to be known by the generic term "Baking Powder Glass."

Classic carnival glass production began in the early 1900s and continued about twenty years, but no one really documented or researched production until the first collecting wave struck in 1960

It is important to remember that carnival glasswares were sold in department stores as well as mass merchants rather than through the general store often associated with a young America. Glassware by this time was mass-produced and sold in large quantities by such enterprising companies as Butler Brothers. When the economics of the country soured in the 1920s, those interested in purchasing iridized glassware were not spared. Many of the leftover inventories of glasshouses that hoped to sell this mass-produced glassware found their way to wholesalers who in

Acorn Burrs pattern 12-piece punch set in green iridescent, ruffled and scalloped rim bowl, pedestal base, and 10 cups, each with maker's mark in base, Northwood Glass Co., pattern introduced circa 1911, 11" h. overall, bowl 6-1/4" h., 11-1/4" dia., pedestal 5-1/2" h., cups 2-1/2" h................ **$345**

Courtesy of Jeffrey S. Evans & Associates

turn sold the wares to those who offered the glittering glass as prizes at carnivals, fairs, circuses, etc. Possibly because this was the last venue people associated the iridized glassware with, it became known as "carnival glass."

For more information on carnival glass, see *Warman's Carnival Glass Identification and Price Guide,* 2nd edition, by Ellen T. Schroy.

CARNIVAL GLASS COMPANIES

Much of vintage American carnival glassware was created in the Ohio valley, in the glasshouse-rich areas of Pennsylvania, Ohio, and West Virginia. The abundance of natural materials, good transportation, and skilled craftsmen that created the early American pattern glass manufacturing companies allowed many of them to add carnival glass to their production lines. Brief company histories of the major carnival glass manufacturers follow:

CAMBRIDGE GLASS CO. (CAMBRIDGE)

Cambridge Glass was a rather minor player in the carnival glass marketplace. Founded in 1901 as a new factory in Cambridge, Ohio, it focused on producing fine crystal tablewares. What carnival glass it did produce was imitation cut-glass patterns.

Colors used by Cambridge include marigold, as well as few others. Forms found in carnival glass by Cambridge include tablewares and vases, some with its trademark "Near-Cut."

DIAMOND GLASS CO. (DIAMOND)

This company was started as the Dugan brothers (see Dugan Glass Co.) departed the carnival glass-making scene in 1913. However, Alfred Dugan returned and became general manager until his death in 1928. After a disastrous fire in June of 1931, the factory closed.

DUGAN GLASS CO. (DUGAN)

The history of the Dugan Glass Co. is closely related to Harry Northwood (see Northwood Glass Co.), whose cousin, Thomas Dugan, became plant manager at the Northwood Glass Co. in Indiana, Pennsylvania, in 1895. By 1904, Dugan and his partner W. G. Minnemayer bought the former Northwood factory from the now defunct National Glass conglomerate and opened as the Dugan Glass Co. Dugan's brother, Alfred, joined the company and stayed until it became the Diamond

Glass Co. in 1913. At this time, Thomas Dugan moved to the Cambridge Glass Co., later Duncan and Miller and finally Hocking, Lancaster. Alfred left Diamond Glass, too, but later returned.

Understanding how the Northwood and Dugan families were connected helps collectors understand the linkage of these three companies. Their productions were similar; molds were swapped, retooled, etc.

Colors attributed to Dugan and Diamond include amethyst, marigold, peach opalescent, and white. The company developed deep amethyst shades, some almost black.

Forms made by both Dugan and Diamond mirrored what other glass companies were producing. The significant contribution by Dugan and later Diamond were feet – either ball or spatula shapes. They are also known for deeply crimped edges.

FENTON ART GLASS CO. (FENTON)

Frank Leslie Fenton and his brothers, John W. Fenton and Charles H. Fenton, founded this truly American glassmaker in 1905 in Martins Ferry, Ohio. Early production was of blanks, which the brothers soon learned to decorate themselves. They moved to a larger factory in Williamstown, West Virginia.

By 1907, Fenton was experimenting with iridescent glass, developing patterns and the metallic salt formulas that it became so famous for. Production of carnival glass continued at Fenton until the early 1930s. In 1970, Fenton began to reissue carnival glass, creating new colors and forms as well as using traditional patterns.

Colors developed by Fenton are numerous. The company developed red and Celeste blue in the 1920s; a translucent pale blue, known as Persian blue, is also one of its more distinctive colors, as is a light yellow-green color known as vaseline. Fenton also produced delicate opalescent colors including amethyst opalescent and red opalescent. Because the Fenton brothers learned how to decorate their own blanks, they also promoted the addition of enamel decoration to some of their carnival glass patterns.

Forms made by Fenton are also numerous. What distinguishes Fenton from other glassmakers is its attention to detail and hand finishing processes. Edges are found scalloped, fluted, tightly crimped, frilled, or pinched into a candy ribbon edge, also referred to as 3-in-1 edge.

IMPERIAL GLASS CO. (IMPERIAL)

Edward Muhleman and a syndicate founded the Imperial Glass Co. at Bellaire, Ohio, in 1901, with production beginning in 1904. It started with pressed glass tableware patterns as well as lighting fixtures. The company's marketing strategy included selling to important retailers of its day, such as F. W. Woolworth and McCrory and Kresge, to get glassware into the hands of American housewives. Imperial also became a major exporter of glassware, including its brilliant carnival patterns. During the Depression, it filed for bankruptcy in 1931, but was able to continue on. By 1962, it was again producing carnival glass patterns. By April 1985, the factory was closed and the molds sold.

Colors made by Imperial include typical carnival colors such as marigold. It added interesting shades of green, known as helios, a pale ginger ale shade known as clambroth, and a brownish smoke shade.

Forms created by Imperial tend to be functional, such as berry sets and table sets. Patterns vary from wonderful imitation cut glass patterns to detailed florals and naturalistic designs.

MILLERSBURG GLASS CO. (MILLERSBURG)

John W. Fenton started the Millersburg Glass Co. in September 1908. Perhaps it was the factory's more obscure location or the lack of business experience by John Fenton, but the company failed by 1911.

The factory was bought by Samuel Fair and John Fenton, and renamed the Radium Glass Co., but it lasted only a year.

Colors produced by Millersburg are amethyst, green, and marigold. Shades such as blue and vaseline were added on rare occasions. The company is well known for its bright radium finishes.

Forms produced at Millersburg are mostly bowls and vases. Pattern designers at Millersburg often took one theme and developed several patterns from it. Millersburg often used one pattern for the interior and a different pattern for the exterior.

NORTHWOOD GLASS CO. (NORTHWOOD)

Englishman Harry Northwood founded the Northwood Glass Co. He developed his glass formulas for carnival glass, naming it "Golden Iris" in 1908. Northwood was one of the pioneers of the glass manufacturers who marked his wares. Marks range from a full script signature to a simple underscored capital N in a circle. However, not all Northwood glassware is marked.

Colors that Northwood created were many. Collectors prefer its pastels, such as ice blue, ice green, and white. It is also known for several stunning blue shades. The one color that Northwood did not develop was red.

Forms of Northwood patterns range from typical table sets, bowls, and water sets to whimsical novelties, such as a pattern known as Corn, which realistically depicts an ear of corn.

UNITED STATES GLASS CO. (U.S. GLASS)

In 1891, a consortium of 15 American glass manufacturers joined together as the United States Glass Co. This company was successful in continuing pattern glass production, as well as developing new glass lines. By 1911, it had begun limited production of carnival glass lines, often using existing pattern glass tableware molds. By the time a tornado destroyed the last of its glass factories in Glassport in 1963, it was no longer producing glassware.

Colors associated with US Glass are marigold, white, and a rich honey amber.

Forms tend to be table sets and functional forms.

WESTMORELAND GLASS CO. (WESTMORELAND)

Started as the Westmoreland Specialty Co., Grapeville, Pennsylvania, in 1889, this company originally made novelties and glass packing containers, such as candy containers. Researchers have identified its patterns being advertised by Butler Brothers as early as 1908. Carnival glass production continued into the 1920s. In the 1970s, Westmoreland, too, begin to reissue carnival glass patterns and novelties. However, this ceased in February of 1996 when the factory burned.

Colors originally used by Westmoreland were typical carnival colors, such as blue and marigold.

Forms include tablewares and functional forms, containers, etc.

— Ellen T. Schroy

Big Basketweave pattern vase in ice blue iridescent, slightly flared and scalloped rim, Dugan Glass Co., circa 1914, 9-3/4" h. overall, 4" dia. overall rim...... **$184**

Courtesy of Jeffrey S. Evans & Associates

Acorn Burrs pattern bowl in green, Northwood Glass Co., 9-1/4"......**$207**

Courtesy of Woody Auctions, LLC

Big Fish pattern bowl in amethyst iridescent, three-in-one crimped rim, wide-paneled exterior, Millersburg Glass Co., circa 1909-1911, 2-1/2" h. overall, 8-1/2" dia... **$316**

Courtesy of Jeffrey S. Evans & Associates

Corn pattern figural vase in green iridescent, maker's mark in base, Northwood Glass Co., circa 1912, 6-1/2" h., 3-1/8" dia. foot.............................. **$173**

Courtesy of Jeffrey S. Evans & Associates

Embroidered Mums pattern bowl, ice blue iridescent, ruffled and scalloped rim, unpatterned exterior, Northwood Glass Co., first quarter 20th century, 2-5/8" h. overall, 9" dia. overall......... **$219**

Courtesy of Jeffrey S. Evans & Associates

◀ Candlestick holder in pattern #657, Flute, Northwood Glass Co., 8-1/4" h. **$47**

Courtesy of Woody Auctions, LLC

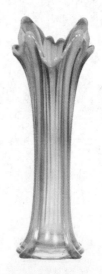

◀ Fleur De Lis pattern bowl in marigold iridescent, ice cream shape, scallop and saw-tooth rim, Country Kitchen exterior, Millersburg Glass Co., circa 1909-1911, 2-7/8" h. overall, 9-1/2" dia.......................... **$173**

Courtesy of Jeffrey S. Evans & Associates

Four Pillars pattern vase by Northwood Glass Co., aqua opalescent, 10-1/2" h......... **$266**

Courtesy of Woody Auctions, LLC

Good Luck pattern footed plate in marigold iridescent, circular even-scalloped rim, unstippled pattern, basketweave exterior, maker's mark in base, Northwood Glass Co., first quarter 20th century, 1-5/8" h., 9" dia.................................**$115**

Courtesy of Jeffrey S. Evans & Associates

Grape Arbor pattern pitcher in marigold, Northwood Glass Co., 11-3/4"................................**$59**

Courtesy of Woody Auctions, LLC

Hearts and Flowers pattern bowl, aqua iridescent, ruffled and scalloped rim, ribbed exterior, Northwood Glass Co., pattern introduced circa 1912, 2-1/2" h. overall, 9" dia. overall. **$230**

Courtesy of Jeffrey S. Evans & Associates

◀ Imperial Grape pattern decanter and six wine glasses in marigold. **$71**

Courtesy of Woody Auctions, LLC

▲ Lined Lattice pattern squat-form vase, black amethyst iridescent, flared and scalloped rim, Dugan Glass Co., first quarter 20th century, 5-1/8" h. overall, 6" dia. overall rim.....**$115**

Courtesy of Jeffrey S. Evans & Associates

◀ Two three-footed Orange Tree pattern bowls in marigold, Fenton Art Glass Co., 5" x 10". **$71**

Courtesy of Woody Auctions, LLC

GLASS

Peacocks on the Fence pattern ruffled bowl in electric blue with ribbed exterior, Northwood Glass Co., minor edge nick not on point, 8-1/2" h. **$106**

Courtesy of Woody Auctions, LLC

Peacock at the Fountain pattern six-piece water set in amethyst, Northwood Glass Co., 8-1/2". **$413**

Courtesy of Woody Auctions, LLC

Peacocks on the Fence pattern bowl, blue/electric blue iridescent, ruffled and lightly scalloped rim, ribbed exterior, maker's mark in base, Northwood Glass Co., pattern introduced 1912, 2" h. overall, 8-3/4" dia........................... **$259**

Courtesy of Jeffrey S. Evans & Associates

Persian Garden pattern two-piece fruit bowl in marigold iridescent, circular form with ruffled and scalloped rim, Big Basket pedestal base with scallop foot, Dugan Glass Co., first quarter 20th century, 8" h. overall, 10" dia. overall. **$115**

Courtesy of Jeffrey S. Evans & Associates

Rose Show pattern bowl in aqua opalescent and iridescent, ruffled plain rim, Northwood Glass Co., circa 1910, 2-3/4" h., 9" dia. overall. **$489**

Courtesy of Jeffrey S. Evans & Associates

Seacoast pattern pin tray in green iridescent, figural fish below lighthouse and within leaf-form wreath, Millersburg Glass Co., circa 1909-1911, 7/8" h., 3-7/8" x 5-1/2"................... **$431**

Courtesy of Jeffrey S. Evans & Associates

Singing Birds pattern blue mug, Northwood Glass Co., 3-1/2". **$47**

Courtesy of Woody Auctions, LLC

Two-row open weave basket shape, true red coloring, 5-1/2" h. **$106**

Courtesy of Woody Auctions, LLC

Tree Trunk pattern vase by Northwood Glass Co., amethyst, 12-1/2" h. **$354**

Courtesy of Woody Auctions, LLC

Trout and Fly pattern bowl in green iridescent, three-in-one crimped rim, wide-paneled exterior, Millersburg Glass Co., circa 1909-1911, 2-1/2" h. overall, 9" dia. **$345**

Courtesy of Jeffrey S. Evans & Associates

Trout and Fly pattern bowl in marigold iridescent, crimped rim, unpatterned exterior, Millersburg Glass Co., circa 1909-1911, 2-1/2" h. overall, 9" dia. **$198**

Courtesy of Jeffrey S. Evans & Associates

Wide Panel pattern epergne in green iridescent, circular scalloped rim base supporting four trumpets/lilies, faint maker's mark in base, Northwood Glass Co., circa 1909, 16-1/4" h. overall, 11-1/2" w. **$288**

Courtesy of Jeffrey S. Evans & Associates

Two-part amethyst punch bowl and six cups in Wreath of Roses pattern, Persian Medallion pattern interior, Fenton Art Glass Co., 10" x 12". **$413**

Courtesy of Woody Auctions, LLC

GLASS

consolidated glass

THE CONSOLIDATED LAMP & GLASS CO. of Coraopolis, Pennsylvania, was founded in 1894. For a number of years it was noted for its lighting wares but also produced popular lines of pressed and blown tableware. Highly collectible glass patterns of this early era include the Cone, Cosmos, Florette, and Guttate lines.

Lamps and shades continued to be good sellers, but in 1926 a new "art" line of molded decorative wares was introduced. This "Martelè" line was developed as a direct imitation of the fine glassware being produced by Renè Lalique of France, and many Consolidated patterns resembled their French counterparts. Other popular lines produced during the 1920s and 1930s were Dancing Nymph, the delightfully Art Deco Ruba Rombic introduced in 1928, and the Catalonian line, which debuted in 1927 and imitated 17th-century Spanish glass.

Although the factory closed in 1933, it was reopened under new management in 1936 and prospered through the 1940s. It finally closed in 1967. Collectors should note that many later Consolidated patterns closely resemble wares of other competing firms, especially the Phoenix Glass Co. Careful study is needed to determine the maker of pieces from the 1920-1940 era.

A book that will be of help to collectors is *Phoenix & Consolidated Art Glass, 1926-1980,* by Jack D. Wilson (Antique Publications, 1989).

Florette/Quilt pattern condiment set, cased pink, two shakers and mustard of varying shades of pink, in matching holder, late 19th/early 20th century, 7-1/4" h. overall, 5-1/2" dia. overall. .**$81**

Courtesy of Jeffrey S. Evans & Associates

Criss-Cross pattern large berry bowls, cranberry opalescent, each with factory polished rim, circa 1888, 2" h., 4-1/4" dia. **$161**

Courtesy of Jeffrey S. Evans & Associates

Criss-Cross pattern salt and pepper shakers, cranberry opalescent, near matching period lids, circa 1894, 3-1/4" h. overall. **$184**

Courtesy of Jeffrey S. Evans & Associates

Ruba Rombic pattern jade-green glass perfume bottle, circa 1928, satin finish, 4-3/4" h. x 3-3/4" w. x 1-3/4" d. **$2,375**

Photo courtesy of Neal Auction Co.

Criss-Cross pattern toothpick holder, colorless opalescent, factory polished rim, circa 1894, 2-1/4" h. **$150**

Courtesy of Jeffrey S. Evans & Associates

Two Criss-Cross pattern toothpick holders, cranberry opalescent, circa 1894, 2" and 2-3/8" h. **$127**

Courtesy of Jeffrey S. Evans & Associates

Bulging Loop pattern toothpick holders, opal-cased blue, opal-cased pink, and two shades of Pigeon Blood/ruby, each with factory polished rim, circa 1894, 2-3/8" h. **$196**

Courtesy of Jeffrey S. Evans & Associates

Criss-Cross pattern creamer, cranberry opalescent, factory polished circular rim, applied colorless handle, circa 1888, 4" h. overall. **$138**

Courtesy of Jeffrey S. Evans & Associates

GLASS

cranberry glass

GOLD WAS ADDED to glass batches to give cranberry glass its color on reheating. It has been made by numerous glasshouses for years and is currently being reproduced. Both blown and molded articles were produced. A less expensive type of cranberry glass was made with the substitution of copper for gold.

Big Windows pattern creamer, cranberry opalescent, circular rim, applied colorless handle with pressed-fan design to upper terminal, Buckeye Glass Co., fourth quarter 19th century, 5-3/8" h................ **$374**

Courtesy of Jeffrey S. Evans & Associates

Big Windows pattern syrup pitcher, cranberry opalescent, applied colorless handle, period lid, Buckeye Glass Co., fourth quarter 19th century, 6-3/4" h. overall. ... **$374**

Courtesy of Jeffrey S. Evans & Associates

Bullseye pattern water pitcher, cranberry opalescent, applied base and handle, polished pontil mark, fourth quarter 19th century, 6-3/4" h........ **$489**

Courtesy of Jeffrey S. Evans & Associates

Christmas Snowflake pattern ribbed water pitcher, cranberry opalescent, applied colorless handle, Northwood Glass Co./ Dugan Glass Co., circa 1895, 8-7/8" h. overall................. **$863**

Courtesy of Jeffrey S. Evans & Associates

Chrysanthemum Swirl pattern syrup pitcher, cranberry opalescent, satin finish, applied colorless satin finished handle, period lid with patent date, Northwood Glass Co./Buckeye Glass Co., circa 1893, 7" h.....**$219**

Courtesy of Jeffrey S. Evans & Associates

Coinspot pattern three-tier tankard water pitcher, cranberry opalescent, applied colorless handle, Northwood Glass Co., late 19th/early 20th century, 11-1/4" h. overall, 6-1/2" dia. overall. **$863**

Courtesy of Jeffrey S. Evans & Associates

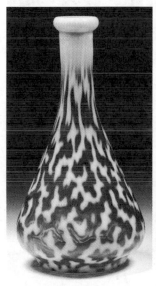

Coral Reef pattern bitters/ barber's bottle, ruby/cranberry opalescent, conical tapered form, polished pontil mark, Hobbs, Brockunier & Co./ Beaumont Glass Co., circa 1890s, 7" h., 3-3/4" dia. overall. **$259**

Courtesy of Jeffrey S. Evans & Associates

Coinspot pattern bulbous syrup pitcher, cranberry opalescent, applied colorless handle, period lid, late 19th/early 20th century, 5-3/4" h. **$150**

Courtesy of Jeffrey S. Evans & Associates

Criss-Cross pattern toothpick holder, cranberry opalescent, factory polished rim, Consolidated Lamp & Glass Co., circa 1894, 2-1/4" h. .. **$184**

Courtesy of Jeffrey S. Evans & Associates

Diamond Wave pattern water pitcher, colorless to cranberry opalescent, tankard-form with applied colorless angled handle, polished pontil mark, Harrach Glassworks, Czechoslovakia, early 20th century, 9-1/4" h. **$805**

Courtesy of Jeffrey S. Evans & Associates

Coral Reef pattern bitters/ barber's bottle, ruby/cranberry opalescent, square form, polished pontil mark, Hobbs, Brockunier & Co./Beaumont Glass Co., circa 1890s, bottle 8-1/4" h., 2-1/2" sq. **$259**

Courtesy of Jeffrey S. Evans & Associates

Drapery pattern blown tankard water pitcher, cranberry opalescent, applied colorless handle, possibly Buckeye Glass Co., late 19th/early 20th century, 13" h. overall. **$690**

Courtesy of Jeffrey S. Evans & Associates

Herringbone pattern tumbler, cranberry opalescent, factory polished rim, fourth quarter 19th century, 3-3/4" h........ **$259**

Courtesy of Jeffrey S. Evans & Associates

Fern pattern bitters/barber's bottle, cranberry opalescent, six-lobe melon rib form, probably Beaumont Glass Co., circa 1894, 7" h. **$374**

Courtesy of Jeffrey S. Evans & Associates

Fern pattern bitters/barber's bottle, cranberry opalescent, square form, West Virginia Glass Co. or Beaumont Glass Co., circa 1894, 8-3/8" h., 2-3/4" sq. **$460**

Courtesy of Jeffrey S. Evans & Associates

Hobbs No. 326/Windows Swirl pattern toothpick holder, ruby/cranberry opalescent, oval form, factory polished rim, Hobbs, Brockunier & Co., circa 1888, 2-5/8" h. **$184**

Courtesy of Jeffrey S. Evans & Associates

Hobbs No. 326/Windows Swirl pattern covered sugar bowl and creamer, ruby/cranberry opalescent, oval forms, creamer with applied colorless handle and cover with applied faceted finial, Hobbs, Brockunier & Co., circa 1888, creamer 3-1/2" h., covered sugar bowl 5-1/2" h. overall. **$259**

Courtesy of Jeffrey S. Evans & Associates

▶ Hobbs No. 326/Windows Swirl pattern sugar shaker, ruby/cranberry opalescent with satin finish, period lid, Hobbs, Brockunier & Co., circa 1888, 5-1/8" h. **$259**

Courtesy of Jeffrey S. Evans & Associates

Inverted Thumbprint pattern tapered syrup pitcher, cranberry, applied colorless handle, period lid with patent information under lid, fourth quarter 19th century, 7-1/2" h. overall................... **$81**

Courtesy of Jeffrey S. Evans & Associates

Lattice pattern water carafe, cranberry opalescent, bulge form, factory polished rim, late 19th/early 20th century, 7-7/8" h., 5-3/4" dia. overall. **$374**

Courtesy of Jeffrey S. Evans & Associates

Polka Dot/Fancy Fans pattern mold sugar shaker, cranberry opalescent, period lid, possibly Northwood Glass Co., circa 1893, 4-1/4" h. **$633**

Courtesy of Jeffrey S. Evans & Associates

Stars and Stripes pattern bitters/barber's bottle, cranberry opalescent, three rows of stars, lower end of stripes flow to left above stars, period spout, polished pontil mark, Beaumont Glass Co., circa 1899, 7" h. **$345**

Courtesy of Jeffrey S. Evans & Associates

Stripe/Wide Nickel pattern mold sugar shaker, cranberry opalescent, period lid, Nickel Plate Glass Co., fourth quarter 19th century, 4" h. overall... **$403**

Courtesy of Jeffrey S. Evans & Associates

Swirl pattern tankard water pitcher, cranberry opalescent, applied colorless reeded handle, late 19th/early 20th century, 9-1/8" h. **$1,150**

Courtesy of Jeffrey S. Evans & Associates

▶ Wide Stripe pattern bitters/barber's bottle, cranberry opalescent, six-lobe melon rib form, later spout, late 19th/early 20th century, 7-1/4" h. **$374**

Courtesy of Jeffrey S. Evans & Associates

Swirl pattern bitters/barber's bottle, ruby/cranberry opalescent, square form, probably Hobbs, Brockunier & Co. or Beaumont Glass Co., late 19th/early 20th century, 8-1/8" h., 2-1/2" sq. **$431**

Courtesy of Jeffrey S. Evans & Associates

GLASS

custard glass

"CUSTARD GLASS," AS collectors call it today, came on the American scene in the 1890s, more than a decade after similar colors were made in Europe and England. The Sowerby firm of Gateshead-on-Tyne, England had marketed its patented "Queen's Ivory Ware" successfully in the late 1870s and early 1880s.

There were many glass tableware factories operating in Pennsylvania and Ohio in the 1890s and early 1900s, and the competition among them was keen. Each company sought to capture the public's favor with distinctive colors and, often, hand-painted decoration. That is when "custard glass" appeared on the American scene.

The opaque yellow color of this glass varies from a rich, vivid yellow to a lustrous light yellow. Regardless of intensity, the hue was originally called "ivory" by several glass manufacturers who also used superlative sounding terms such as "Ivorina Verde" and "Carnelian." Most custard glass contains uranium, so it will "glow" under a black light.

The most important producer of custard glass was certainly Harry Northwood, who first made it at his plants in Indiana, Pennsylvania, in the late 1890s and, later, in his Wheeling, West Virginia, factory. Northwood marked some of his most famous patterns, but much early

Argonaut Shell pattern butter dish, Northwood Glass Co., marked, 5-1/2". **$83**

Courtesy of Woody Auctions, LLC

custard is unmarked. Other key manufacturers include the Heisey Glass Co., Newark, Ohio; the Jefferson Glass Co., Steubenville, Ohio; the Tarentum Glass Co., Tarentum, Pennsylvania; and the Fenton Art Glass Co., Williamstown, West Virginia.

Custard glass fanciers are particular about condition and generally insist on pristine quality decorations free from fading or wear. Souvenir custard pieces with events, places, and dates on them usually bring the best prices in the areas commemorated on them rather than from the specialist collector. Also, collectors who specialize in pieces such as cruets, syrups, or salt and pepper shakers will often pay higher prices for these pieces than would a custard collector.

Key reference sources include William Heacock's *Custard Glass from A to Z*, published in 1976 but not out of print, and the book *Harry Northwood: The Early Years*, available from Glass Press. Heisey's custard glass is discussed in Shirley Dunbar's *Heisey Glass: The Early Years* (Krause Publications, 2000), and Coudersport's production is well-documented in Tulla Majot's book, *Coudersport's Glass 1900-1904* (Glass Press, 1999). The Custard Glass Society holds a yearly convention and maintains a website: www.homestead.com/custardsociety.

— James Measell

Argonaut Shell/Nautilus (OMN) pattern creamer and spooner, green and gilt decoration, Northwood Glass Co./Dugan Glass Co, circa 1900, each signed "Northwood," 4-3/4" and 4-7/8" h. overall. **$46**

Courtesy of Jeffrey S. Evans & Associates

Argonaut Shell/Nautilus (OMN) pattern salt and pepper shakers, gilt decoration, period lids, Northwood Glass Co./Dugan Glass Co., circa 1900, 3" h. overall. **$345**

Courtesy of Jeffrey S. Evans & Associates

Argonaut Shell/Nautilus pattern toothpick holder, green and gilt decoration, Northwood Glass Co./Dugan Glass Co., circa 1900, 2-7/8" h. **$184**

Courtesy of Jeffrey S. Evans & Associates

Chrysanthemum Sprig/Pagoda (OMN) pattern five-piece water set, signed water pitcher and four tumblers, green and pink staining and gilt decoration, factory polished bases, Northwood Glass Co, circa 1899, 3-3/4" to 8-3/8" h. overall. **$104**

Courtesy of Jeffrey S. Evans & Associates

Chrysanthemum Sprig/Pagoda (OMN) pattern four-piece table set, butter dish, covered sugar, creamer, and spooner, green and pink staining and gilt decoration, Northwood Glass Co, circa 1899, each piece except sugar signed "Northwood," with jelly compote, five pieces total, 4-1/4" to 6-1/2" h. overall. **$138**

Courtesy of Jeffrey S. Evans & Associates

Chrysanthemum Sprig/Pagoda (OMN) pattern master berry bowl, toothpick holder, and salt and pepper shakers, green and pink staining and gilt decoration, Northwood Glass Co., circa 1899, master berry and toothpick signed "Northwood," 2-5/8" to 4-3/4" h. overall, master berry 10-1/2" dia. overall. **$115**

Courtesy of Jeffrey S. Evans & Associates

GLASS

Five Fan pattern ice cream dishes, gilt decoration, Dugan Glass Co, circa 1906, 5" dia. overall. **$35**

Courtesy of Jeffrey S. Evans & Associates

Intaglio pattern covered butter, creamer, and spooner, green and blue staining and gilt decoration, Northwood Glass Co./Dugan Glass Co., late 19th/early 20th century, 4-3/4" to 6-1/2" h. overall. **$58**

Courtesy of Jeffrey S. Evans & Associates

Inverted Fan and Feather pattern five-piece berry set, master berry bowl and four individual berry dishes, pink stain and gilt decoration, Northwood Glass Co./Dugan Glass Co., circa 1904, 4-3/8" to 6-1/2" h. overall...**$92**

Courtesy of Jeffrey S. Evans & Associates

Inverted Fan and Feather pattern toothpick holder, pink and gilt decoration, Northwood Glass Co./Dugan Glass Co., circa 1904, 2-1/2" h. **$161**

Courtesy of Jeffrey S. Evans & Associates

Inverted Fan and Feather pattern three-piece water set, water pitcher and two tumblers, pink stain and gilt decoration, Northwood Glass Co./Dugan Glass Co., circa 1904, 4" to 7-3/4" h. overall. **$127**

Courtesy of Jeffrey S. Evans & Associates

Maple Leaf pattern salt and pepper shakers, green stain and gilt decoration, period lids, Northwood Glass Co., early 20th century, 3-3/8" h. **$489**

Courtesy of Jeffrey S. Evans & Associates

Maple Leaf pattern toothpick holder, green and gilt decoration, Northwood Glass Co., early 20th century, 2-3/8" h. overall...........................**$259**

Courtesy of Jeffrey S. Evans & Associates

GLASS

cut glass

CUT GLASS IS made by grinding decorations into glass by means of abrasive-carrying metal or stone wheels. An ancient craft, it was revived in 1600 by Bohemians and spread through Europe to Great Britain and America.

American cut glass came of age at the Centennial Exposition in 1876 and the World Columbian Exposition in 1893. America's most significant output of high-quality glass occurred from 1880 to 1917, a period now known as the Brilliant Period. Glass from this period is the most eagerly sought glass by collectors.

No. 41/A. G. Brilliant cut glass trumpet vase, T. B. Clark and Co., colorless, scalloped and sawtooth rim, large hobstar over concave flutes and notched prisms, circular foot with rayed pattern, script maker's signature to underside of base, circa 1901, 16" h. overall, 6-1/4" dia. rim, 5-1/2" dia. base. **$230**

Courtesy of Jeffrey S. Evans & Associates

American Brilliant cut glass vase, colorless, baluster form, flared-in scallop rim over three large hobstars divided by sprays of notched prisms, pinched base with horizontal bars over 10-panel flared base with triple horizontal bands, fourth quarter 19th/first quarter 20th century, 14-5/8" h., 6" dia. base, 5-1/4" dia. rim.................. **$633**

Courtesy of Jeffrey S. Evans & Associates

Glass cruet, ruby cut to vaseline, late 19th/early 20th century, baluster-form with stopper, unsigned, 13-1/2" h. **$800**

Courtesy of Skinner, Inc.; www.skinnerinc.com

Monarch Brilliant cut glass flower center vase, J. Hoare & Co., colorless, compressed form, 10 large flared scallops around rim over horizontal stepping, six large hobstars with fans, cross-hatching, and hobstars in diamond field, underside of base with maker's mark, fourth quarter 19th/early 20th century, 7" h. overall, 9-7/8" dia. overall. **$288**

Courtesy of Jeffrey S. Evans & Associates

Marquis 13-piece water set, T. G. Hawkes & Co., colorless, water pitcher with applied handle and 12 tumblers (one shown), notched prisms between hobstar bands, handle with facet-like cuttings, pitcher with maker's mark and name below lower handle terminal and tumblers to underside of base, early 20th century, excellent condition overall, pitcher 7-5/8" h. overall, tumblers 3-5/8" to 3-3/4" h. **$1,495**

Courtesy of Jeffrey S. Evans & Associates

American Brilliant cut glass ewer, late 19th/early 20th century, flared mouth, narrow neck, and bulbous lower body cut with hobstars, 9-3/4" h. **$308**

Courtesy of Skinner, Inc., www.skinnerinc.com

Decanter with green cut to clear pattern of stork in flight amid cut glass flowers and vines that open on backside to reveal cut glass bumblebee, faceted neck and applied clear glass handle, faceted stopper and cut starburst on underside, unsigned, very good to excellent condition, 9" h. **$1,776**

Courtesy of James D. Julia Auctioneers, Fairfield, Maine, www.jamesdjulia.com

Glass cruet, ruby to clear, late 19th/early 20th century, flared base and stopper, unsigned, 12-1/4" h. **$400**

Courtesy of Skinner, Inc.; www.skinnerinc.com

Pair of Hawkes cut glass engraved candlesticks, circa 1900, signed, Floral and Honeycomb, 14" h., 5-1/2" dia...................... **$2,178**

Courtesy of Cottone Auctions

Pair of glass decanters, green to clear, late 19th/early 20th century, mint green cased glass bodies and stoppers, unsigned, 13" h. **$1,353**

Courtesy of Skinner, Inc.; www.skinnerinc.com

Bowl, Hobstar, Vesica with deep lattice-cut hobs, and Nailhead Diamond motif, 3-3/4" x 9"........................ **$295**

Courtesy of Woody Auctions, LLC

Bohemian goblet, amber cut to clear, thick scalloped base, engraved scene of man standing near pedestal, nine optic window on reverse, monogrammed "E.R.," 6-1/4". **$413**

Courtesy of Woody Auctions, LLC

Pedestal vase, Claire pattern by Bergen, fine blank with vertical hobstar panels, pattern cut base, ruffled rim, very rare, 12-1/2"......................... **$1,770**

Courtesy of Woody Auctions, LLC

Cologne bottle, cranberry cut to clear Star and Block pattern attributed to Boston & Sandwich Glass Co., 7-3/4"............... **$472**

Courtesy of Woody Auctions, LLC

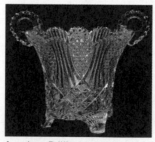

American Brilliant cut glass three-footed ice tub with two triple-notched handles, flared shape, Diamond, Prism, Cane and Fan motif, clear blank, 7-3/4" x 9"......................... **$531**

Courtesy of Woody Auctions, LLC

American Brilliant cut glass table lamp with mushroom shade, Pinwheel, Hobstar, Strawberry Diamond and Fan motif, 19" x 10". **$708**

Courtesy of Woody Auctions, LLC

Round tray, Hobstar, Vesica, Nailhead Diamond and Strawberry Diamond motif, 11-3/4" dia. **$502**

Courtesy of Woody Auctions, LLC

Rare low bowl, Arabesque pattern by J. Hoare, 2-1/4" x 11"................................. **$1,652**

Courtesy of Woody Auctions, LLC

Flared bowl, Rose Cut Diamond pattern by Meriden, museum quality, 3" x 9-3/4". **$4,130**

Courtesy of Woody Auctions, LLC

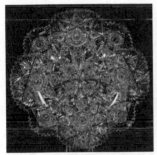

Round tray, Hobstar with clear buttons, Strawberry Diamond, circular Hobstars and Fan motif, Libbey blank mark, attributed to W. C. Anderson, 13-1/2".... **$4,130**

Courtesy of Woody Auctions, LLC

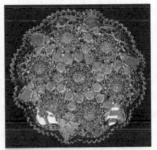

American Brilliant cut glass round tray, interlocking circular rings with Hobstar, Vesica, Strawberry Diamond and Fan highlights, clear blank, 12". **$1,121**

Courtesy of Woody Auctions, LLC

Round tray, Seneca pattern by Empire, 10" dia. **$1,121**

Courtesy of Woody Auctions, LLC

Deep one-piece punch bowl, Hobstar, Cane, Geometric Bar, Strawberry Diamond, Fern and Star motif, pattern attributed to J. Hoare, 7-1/2" x 12"........ **$826**

Courtesy of Woody Auctions, LLC

Round tray, Alhambra pattern by Meriden, no repair, 13-3/4" dia... **$4,425**

Courtesy of Woody Auctions, LLC

American Brilliant cut glass bowl, Florence pattern, designed by W.C. Anderson for Libbey, flashed hobstar center, Hobstar, Kite, Star and Fan motif, extra thick blank, 4" x 8-1/2"................................ **$354**

Courtesy of Woody Auctions, LLC

GLASS

czechoslovakian glass

THE COUNTRY OF Czechoslovakia, including the glassmaking region of Bohemia, was not founded as an independent republic until after the close of World War I in 1918. The new country soon developed a large export industry, including a wide range of colored and hand-painted glasswares such as vases, tableware, and perfume bottles. Fine quality cut crystal or Bohemian-type etched wares were also produced for the American market. Some Bohemian glass carries faint acid-etched markings on the base.

With the breakup of Czechoslovakia into two republics, the wares produced between World War I and II should gain added collector appeal.

Bohemian gilded and enameled cranberry glass decanter, late 19th century, bottle-form with four lobes with ornate strapwork and scrolling foliage, neck and stopper with conforming design, unmarked, 13-1/2" h. **$1,169**

Courtesy of Jeffrey S. Evans & Associates

Bohemian gilded and enameled lavender glass pitcher, late 19th century, pear-form, with polychrome leaves and insects, applied salamander handle and three feet, etched factory number, 9-3/4" h. **$1,968**

Courtesy of Jeffrey S. Evans & Associates

Bohemian gilded and enameled cranberry glass decanter, late 19th century, flask-form, body and stopper with polychrome oak leaves and acorns, unmarked, 12-1/2" h. **$1,046**

Courtesy of Jeffrey S. Evans & Associates

Two Bohemian Moser-type gilded and enameled green glass goblets, late 19th century, each with applied prunts, one lacking factory mark, 6-3/8" h., other marked "BE," 9-1/4" h................... **$492**

Courtesy of Jeffrey S. Evans & Associates

Bohemian gilded and enameled emerald glass vase, late 19th century, urn-form with central medallion polychrome hand-painted with portrait of woman, unmarked, 11-1/4" h.......... **$246**

Courtesy of Jeffrey S. Evans & Associates

Bohemian gilded and enameled gray glass urns and covers, late 19th/early 20th century, each with central polychrome medallion, one of woman assisting beggar, other of woman helping elderly man, unmarked, 9" h.................. **$246**

Courtesy of Skinner, Inc.; www.skinnerinc.com

Pair of Bohemian cranberry candle lustres with white overlay, gold stencil highlights, 11-3/4" h. **$1,298**

Courtesy of Woody Auctions, LLC

Czechoslovakian rippled gourd vase with red-orange "flaming" leaves alternating with tall stalks against opaline pink backdrop, acid-marked "Czechoslovakia" beneath, excellent original condition, 9-1/4" h. x 9-1/4" w. **$80**

Courtesy of Mark Mussio, Humler & Nolan

Bohemian pilsner glass, eight-sided with acid-cut vine decor with applied jewels, 8" h....... **$83**

Courtesy of Woody Auctions, LLC

Bohemian multicolor decanter, amber, blue and pink tones, engraved floral highlights, decanter cut down, 10-1/2" h. **$106**

Courtesy of Woody Auctions, LLC

LOETZ

Loetz vase with gold iridescent body with green highlights, encircled by band of silver overlay of stylized poppies with second poppy band descending from lip, unsigned, very good condition, small open bubbles in side of base (from making), 4" h. **$1,778**

Courtesy of James D. Julia Auctioneers, Fairfield, Maine, www.jamesdjulia.com

Loetz Cytus vase with blue iridescent body with platinum iridescent oil spots against iridescent amber glass body, silver overlay of Art Nouveau design flower on each side with silver rim and foot, silver stamped with "Alvin Silver Co." hallmark, "999/1000 fine" and "103," very good to excellent condition, 5" h. **$2,470**

Courtesy of James D. Julia Auctioneers, Fairfield, Maine, www.jamesdjulia.com

Loetz vase with pinched sides near foot with rounded shoulder and slightly flaring rim, decorated with swirling green bands giving way to swirling silvery blue bands against cobalt blue ground, unsigned, very good to excellent condition, 7" h. **$2,133**

Courtesy of James D. Julia Auctioneers, Fairfield, Maine, www.jamesdjulia.com

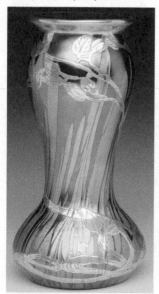

Loetz vase in Medici pattern with blue iridescent oil spots against olive green iridescent background, sterling silver overlay of vines and leaves, center cartouche near foot unengraved, unsigned, very good to excellent condition, 6" h... **$1,896**

Courtesy of James D. Julia Auctioneers, Fairfield, Maine, www.jamesdjulia.com

Loetz Lava vase with bulbous body, pinched sides, square neck with tendrils extending from each corner onto body, green iridescence with purple, blue, and red highlights, unsigned, one tendril missing at tip, hairline crack at lip, 6-3/4" h. **$652**

Courtesy of James D. Julia Auctioneers, Fairfield, Maine, www.jamesdjulia.com

Early Loetz vase in Octopus pattern with cream-colored controlled bubble octopus lines against shaded brown ground, gilded free-form design around octopus pattern and ruffled lip decorated on interior with gilded stylized vines, marked in polished pontil "Patent 9159," very good to excellent condition, 6" h. **$1,067**

Courtesy of James D. Julia Auctioneers, Fairfield, Maine, www.jamesdjulia.com

Loetz oil spot desk lamp with dome-shaped shade with blue iridescent wavy lines around bottom, platinum iridescent oil spot decoration with green, purple, and blue highlights, shade supported by bronze adjustable desk clamp with two-arm socket cluster, shade held in place by matching bronze floral openwork heat cap with acorn finial, base unsigned, very good to excellent condition, base rewired with appropriate cloth cord, 18-3/4" h. **$6,221**

Courtesy of James D. Julia Auctioneers, Fairfield, Maine, www.jamesdjulia.com

Loetz Titania vase with silvery blue dragged loop design against yellow background, three pinched sides and tricorn lip, floral sterling silver overlay with openwork band around foot with rose stems extending to spray of roses around lip, unsigned, very good to excellent condition, 10" h. **$7,110**

Courtesy of James D. Julia Auctioneers, Fairfield, Maine, www.jamesdjulia.com

Loetz silver overlay vase in Phanomen genre 1/158 with gold iridescent body with swirls of green and blue iridescence and purple and pink highlights, overlaid with silver stems and leaves of Art Nouveau design, unsigned, very good to excellent condition, 6-1/2" h. **$5,333**

Courtesy of James D. Julia Auctioneers, Fairfield, Maine, www.jamesdjulia.com

Large Loetz vase in shape of swan in white glass with applied dark amber bill and eyes, wings and tail decorated with gold iridescent Papillon design, applied green iridescent textured foot with purple and blue highlights, unsigned, very good to excellent condition, 12" h. **$2,370**

Courtesy of James D. Julia Auctioneers, Fairfield, Maine, www.jamesdjulia.com

Loetz tri-color Phanomen genre PG299 vase with bulbous body, pinched neck and rolled ruffled rim in translucent cranberry, green, and blue with gold iridescent oil spots, signed in polished pontil "Loetz Austria," very good to excellent condition, 5-1/2" h. **$7,999**

Courtesy of James D. Julia Auctioneers, Fairfield, Maine, www.jamesdjulia.com

Loetz cigar-shaped Titania vase with green and silvery blue wave decoration against cobalt blue background, tricorn lip, unsigned, very good to excellent condition, 11" h. **$2,370**

Courtesy of James D. Julia Auctioneers, Fairfield, Maine, www.jamesdjulia.com

MO3ER

Moser square cranberry glass bowl with flowers and scrolls surrounding bottom and sides, double row of fishscale design with enameled beads in center, exterior of bowl with matching fishscale border, unsigned, very good to excellent condition, 9-1/4" sq............................ **$356**

Courtesy of James D. Julia Auctioneers, Fairfield, Maine, www.jamesdjulia.com

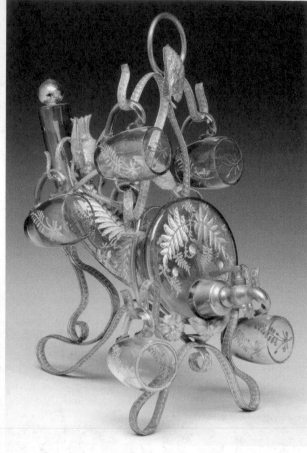

Moser cordial set with blue glass cornucopia-shaped decanter and six matching miniature mugs with enameled fern design in brass frame with leaf design, unsigned, very good condition, 9" h. x 7" l. overall..........**$741**

Courtesy of James D. Julia Auctioneers, Fairfield, Maine, www.jamesdjulia.com

Moser clear glass vase with faceted sides and gold and orange enameled stylized leaves descending from lip and ascending from foot, gilded lip and foot edge, very good to excellent condition, 12-3/4" h. **$185**

Courtesy of James D. Julia Auctioneers, Fairfield, Maine, www.jamesdjulia.com

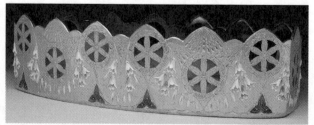

Large Moser center bowl with gilded background and cutout wheels with cranberry staining behind, wheels surrounded by sculptural applied and enameled bellflowers in swags around openings, gilded background with gold enamel geometric designs, very good to excellent condition, 16" l. x 7-3/8" w. x 4-3/8" h. **$474**

Courtesy of James D. Julia Auctioneers, Fairfield, Maine, www.jamesdjulia.com

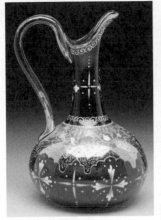

Moser letter rack with cranberry body and gold enameled floral decoration with applied free-form leaf and vine decoration forming three feet, very good condition, 9-1/4" l **$494**

Courtesy of James D. Julia Auctioneers, Fairfield, Maine, www.jamesdjulia.com

Moser ewer with gilded collar surrounding shoulder with enameled stylized flowers, leaves and vines, neck and bulbous body with blue and white stylized crosses surrounded by beaded design, applied and gilded clear glass handle, very good condition with wear to gilding on handle and discoloration and scratching to gilded collar, 10" h **$371**

Courtesy of James D. Julia Auctioneers, Fairfield, Maine, www.jamesdjulia.com

Moser green glass vase with vertically ribbed body and flaring ruffled lip, each side with solid gilded panel with blue, white and red flowers and yellow enameled beading, unsigned, very good condition, 4" h **$178**

Courtesy of James D. Julia Auctioneers, Fairfield, Maine, www.jamesdjulia.com

Moser green glass vase with vertically ribbed body and heavy gold enameled flowers and scrolls, three applied green glass handles with heavy gold enameled scrolls, gilded lip and foot, very good to excellent condition, 11-1/4" h **$593**

Courtesy of James D. Julia Auctioneers, Fairfield, Maine, www.jamesdjulia.com

Two Moser wines: Shaded green glass bowl with gold and platinum grape leaves and vines and applied glass grape clusters with gilding, concentric circle stem with gilded banding, very good to excellent condition; and shaded cranberry glass bowl with gold enameled flowers, stems, and leaves with three clusters of pink and white enameled flowers, very good to excellent condition, 8" h **$309**

Courtesy of James D. Julia Auctioneers, Fairfield, Maine, www.jamesdjulia.com

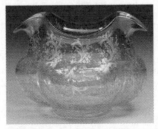

Moser melon-ribbed vase with green shading to clear glass body, gold enameled foliage and gilded ruffled rim, very good to excellent condition, 5-1/2" h. **$178**

Courtesy of James D. Julia Auctioneers, Fairfield, Maine, www.jamesdjulia.com

Moser vase with applied and enameled multi-level floral bouquets against gilded background with scrolled enamel borders against green glass ground, very good to excellent condition, 5-1/2" h. x 8-1/2" w. **$432**

Courtesy of James D. Julia Auctioneers, Fairfield, Maine, www.jamesdjulia.com

GLASS

daum nancy

DAUM NANCY FINE glass, much of it cameo, was made by Auguste and Antonin Daum, who founded the factory in 1875 in Nancy, France. Most of their cameo and enameled glass was made from the 1890s into the early 20th century.

Cameo glass is made by carving into multiple layers of colored glass to create a design in relief. It is at least as old as the Romans.

Winter scene vase with cameo trees on front and back, trees enameled in brown with patches of white snow, internally decorated background of mottled yellow shading to orange, irregular lip, signed on underside with faint etched signature "Daum Nancy" with Cross of Lorraine, very good to excellent condition, 9-5/8" h........ **$7,703**

Courtesy of James D. Julia Auctioneers, Fairfield, Maine, www.jamesdjulia.com

Vase with black cameo stems and leaves and red-over-white padded and wheel-carved poppies, mottled cream-colored martele background, cameo decorated foot of stylized leaves, signed on side of foot with engraved signature with "Daum Nancy" with Cross of Lorraine, very good to excellent condition, 7-1/8" h.......... **$8,295**

Courtesy of James D. Julia Auctioneers, Fairfield, Maine, www.jamesdjulia.com

Small square vase with cameo decoration of stems, leaves, and flowers on each side, stems and leaves enameled in green, flowers enameled in violet, mottled brown, yellow, and cream background, signed on side in cameo "Daum Nancy" with Cross of Lorraine, very good to excellent condition, 3-3/4" h. **$1,778**

Courtesy of James D. Julia Auctioneers, Fairfield, Maine, www.jamesdjulia.com

Vase with mottled yellow, green, and brown cameo trees and grass against mottled lavender background, signed on underside with engraved signature "Daum Nancy" with Cross of Lorraine, very good to excellent condition, 12" h. **$6,518**

Courtesy of James D. Julia Auctioneers, Fairfield, Maine, www.jamesdjulia.com

Vase with brown mottled internal decoration at foot, opalescent body with gold oil inclusions, four padded medallions, two with blue cameo floral decoration and two with blue cameo Celtic symbols, signed on side with engraved signature "Daum Nancy" with Cross of Lorraine, very good to excellent condition, 7" h. **$1,541**

Courtesy of James D. Julia Auctioneers, Fairfield, Maine, www.jamesdjulia.com

Scent bottle with cameo waterlilies and lily pads surrounding cylindrical body, waterlilies and buds enameled in purple, lily pads shaded in gray with gilded highlights, acid-textured light blue background, original stopper with cameo lily pads with gilded highlights against gilded background, signed on underside with gilded signature "Daum Nancy" with Cross of Lorraine, very good to excellent condition, 2-3/4" h. **$3,259**

Courtesy of James D. Julia Auctioneers, Fairfield, Maine, www.jamesdjulia.com

Vase with dark maroon wheel-carved flowers, stems and leaves against frosted white body, areas of martele throughout background, signed on underside with large engraved signature "Daum Nancy" with Cross of Lorraine, very good to excellent condition, 7-1/2" h. **$3,555**

Courtesy of James D. Julia Auctioneers, Fairfield, Maine, www.jamesdjulia.com

◀ Square vase with cameo Dutch winter scenes on each side: snow-covered windmills, cabin in woods, snow-covered trees with church in background, and snow-covered homes; enameled in white, black, and yellow against mottled white and orange background, signed on underside "Daum Nancy S" with Cross of Lorraine, very good to excellent condition, 4-1/2" h. **$2,607**

Courtesy of James D. Julia Auctioneers, Fairfield, Maine, www.jamesdjulia.com

GLASS

Vase in form of wine barrel with center band of cameo flowers, stems, and leaves, leaves enameled in gray with gilded detail, stems and flowers enameled in red with gilded detail, cameo barrel staves enameled in translucent light blue with dark blue enameled outline, barrel cork with gilded cameo Star of David, acid-textured light amber glass body, signed in polished pontil with engraved and gilded signature "Daum Nancy" with Cross of Lorraine, very good to excellent condition, 8" h............... **$4,148**

Courtesy of James D. Julia Auctioneers, Fairfield, Maine, www.jamesdjulia.com

Square vase decorated on each side with cameo violets, stems, and leaves enameled in green with gilded highlights, violets enameled in purple, acid-textured mottled purple shading to white background, signed on side in cameo "Daum Nancy" with Cross of Lorraine, very good to excellent condition, 4-3/4" h.......... **$3,851**

Courtesy of James D. Julia Auctioneers, Fairfield, Maine, www.jamesdjulia.com

Monumental vase with square foot supporting square tapered vase, internal decoration of mottled brown, orange, green, and yellow with areas of color striation, signed on side with engraved signature "Daum Nancy" with Cross of Lorraine, paper label on underside "N.C. Museum of Art ACC. NO. 12," very good to excellent condition, 24-1/4" h........ **$1,422**

Courtesy of James D. Julia Auctioneers, Fairfield, Maine, www.jamesdjulia.com

Large charger with yellow, green, and brown cameo seaweed swirling in bottom of bowl against blue translucent background, signed on side of charger with engraved signature "Daum Nancy" with Cross of Lorraine, very good to excellent condition, 14" dia. **$2,074**

Courtesy of James D. Julia Auctioneers, Fairfield, Maine, www.jamesdjulia.com

Bowl with cameo lily pond decoration with green lily pads surrounding bottom, mottled blue shading to cream shading to purple background, purple and orange padded and wheel-carved lilies, random areas of martele, signed on underside with engraved signature "Daum Nancy" with Cross of Lorraine, very good to excellent condition, 3-3/4" h. x 11-1/2" l. x 8" w. **$6,221**

Courtesy of James D. Julia Auctioneers, Fairfield, Maine, www.jamesdjulia.com

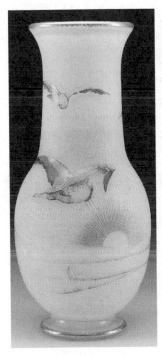

Vase with vitrified glass cameo autumn leaves and thorn stems in brown and green extending from foot to lip on all sides, frosted mottled white background with patches of yellow and orange, signed on side in cameo "Daum Nancy" with Cross of Lorraine, very good to excellent condition, 11-3/4" h...........................**$1,482**

Courtesy of James D. Julia Auctioneers, Fairfield, Maine, www.jamesdjulia.com

Monumental vase with cameo and enameled seagulls above ocean with cameo and enameled sea turtle, sun setting beyond ocean, cameo cut rays highlighted with gilding, frosted opalescent background, signed on underside in gold "Daum Nancy" with Cross of Lorraine, very good to excellent condition, 16" h............**$10,073**

Courtesy of James D. Julia Auctioneers, Fairfield, Maine, www.jamesdjulia.com

Bottle with green cameo vines and leaves encircling cylindrical body against green acid-textured background, leaves and stems highlighted with gilded detail and cameo decoration highlighted with white enameled berries, sterling silver collar and hinged lid with matching leaf, vine, and berry decoration, lid opens to reveal matching cameo glass gilded stopper, silver hallmarked on side, bottle signed on underside with gilded signature "Daum Nancy" with Cross of Lorraine, very good to excellent condition, 4" h. **$652**

Courtesy of James D. Julia Auctioneers, Fairfield, Maine, www.jamesdjulia.com

Peach-colored bowl with applied and enameled stylized flowers against acid-textured background, enamel stylized dragon, signed on underside with etched signature "Daum Nancy" with Cross of Lorraine, very good to excellent condition, 5" h., 7" dia.... **$3,911**

Courtesy of James D. Julia Auctioneers, Fairfield, Maine, www.jamesdjulia.com

top lot

Cabinet vase with cameo floral design encircling bulbous body, stems and leaves enameled in green, flowers enameled in red, mottled background of orange shading to white, signed on side in cameo "Daum Nancy" with Cross of Lorraine, very good to excellent condition, 3-1/4" h. **$1,541**

Courtesy of James D. Julia Auctioneers, Fairfield, Maine, www.jamesdjulia.com

Cabinet vase in amber-colored glass with gilded cameo flowers covering front of vase, neck and side inscribed with cameo words "A Tout Seigneur" and "Tout Honneur," acid-textured background, silver stamped "G. Falconberg" with two hallmarks, very good to excellent condition, 3-5/8" h. **$770**

Courtesy of James D. Julia Auctioneers, Fairfield, Maine, www.jamesdjulia.com

Rare prairie vase with cameo and enameled flowers against green background of internal decoration, gray enameled forest and pond with village in background, mottled pink sky, signed on underside with gilded signature "Daum Nancy" with Cross of Lorraine, very good to excellent condition, 8" h. $18,368

COURTESY OF JAMES D. JULIA AUCTIONEERS, FAIRFIELD, MAINE, WWW.JAMESDJULIA.COM

Ewer with cameo vines, leaves, and berries, vines and leaves enameled in gray and black, berries enameled in red, three polished horizontal bands and enameled center cartouche against acid-textured opalescent background, bands inscribed "Souvenir de l'Exposition 1900 / Le plus grand foudre du monde," signed on underside with engraved and gilded signature "Daum Nancy" with Cross of Lorraine, very good to excellent condition, 12" h.............. **$5,333**

Courtesy of James D. Julia Auctioneers, Fairfield, Maine, www.jamesdjulia.com

Nautical vase with black cameo sailboats surrounding body and outline of distant shore against mottled blue, orange, yellow, and green background, signed on side in cameo "Daum Nancy" with Cross of Lorraine, very good to excellent condition, 11-1/2" h........ **$2,666**

Courtesy of James D. Julia Auctioneers, Fairfield, Maine, www.jamesdjulia.com

Bud vase with vitrified glass cameo leaves and stems, pink padded and wheel-carved roses against frosted cream background, signed on underside with engraved signature "Daum Nancy" with Cross of Lorraine, very good to excellent condition, 7-3/4" h................ **$5,036**

Courtesy of James D. Julia Auctioneers, Fairfield, Maine, www.jamesdjulia.com

◄ Vase with black cameo stems and leaves and padded red-over-white wheel-carved poppies against mottled background of orange shading to white, background covered with martele carving, dark brown shading to black foot with stylized leaf cameo decoration, signed on side of foot with engraved signature "Daum Nancy" with Cross of Lorraine, very good to excellent condition, 7-1/4" h... **$5,036**

Courtesy of James D. Julia Auctioneers, Fairfield, Maine, www.jamesdjulia.com

Vase with cameo floral decoration surrounding body, stems and leaves enameled in green, flowers enameled in red and pink, mottled orange, brown, and yellow background, signed on side in cameo "Daum Nancy" with Cross of Lorraine, "France," very good to excellent condition, 6-1/4" h.......... **$2,844**

Courtesy of James D. Julia Auctioneers, Fairfield, Maine, www.jamesdjulia.com

GLASS

depression glass

DEPRESSION GLASS IS the name of colorful glassware collectors generally associated with mass-produced glassware found in pink, yellow, crystal, or green in the years surrounding the Great Depression in America.

The homemakers of the Depression-era were able to enjoy the wonderful colors offered in this new inexpensive glass dinnerware because they received pieces of their favorite patterns packed in boxes of soap, or as premiums given at "dish night" at the local movie theater. Merchandisers, such as Sears & Roebuck and F. W. Woolworth, enticed young brides with the colorful wares that they could afford even when economic times were harsh.

Because of advancements in glassware technology, Depression-era patterns were mass-produced and could be purchased for a fraction of what cut glass or lead crystal cost. As one manufacturer found a pattern that was pleasing to the buying public, other companies soon followed with their adaptation of a similar design. Patterns included several design motifs, such as florals, geometrics, and even patterns that looked back to Early American patterns like Sandwich glass.

As America emerged from the Great Depression and life became more leisure-oriented again, new glassware patterns were created to reflect the new tastes of this generation. More elegant shapes and forms were designed, leading to what is sometimes called "Elegant Glass." Today's collectors often include these more elegant patterns when they talk about Depression-era glassware.

Depression-era glassware is one of the best-researched collecting areas available to the American marketplace. This is due in large part to the careful research of several people, including Hazel Marie Weatherman, Gene Florence, Barbara Mauzy, Carl F. Luckey, and Kent Washburn. Their books are held in high regard by researchers and collectors today.

Regarding values for Depression glass, rarity does not always equate to a high dollar amount. Some more readily found items command lofty prices because of high demand or other factors, not because they are necessarily rare. As collectors' tastes range from the simple patterns to the more elaborate patterns, so does the ability of their budget to invest in inexpensive patterns to multi-hundreds of dollars per form patterns.

For more information on Depression glass, see *Warman's Depression Glass Identification and Price Guide, 6th Edition*, or *Warman's Depression Glass Field Guide, 5th Edition*, both by Ellen T. Schroy.

Tea Room green pitcher, 10" h. **$60**
Courtesy of Saca Valley Auctions

VISIT WWW.ANTIQUETRADER.COM

WWW.FACEBOOK.COM/ANTIQUETRADER

PATTERN SILHOUETTE Identification Guide

Depression-era glassware can be confusing. Many times a manufacturer came up with a neat new design, and as soon as it was successful, other companies started to make patterns that were similar. To help you figure out what pattern you might be trying to research, here's a quick identification guide. The patterns are broken down into several different classifications by design elements.

ART DECO

Ovide

BASKETS

Lorain

BEADED EDGES

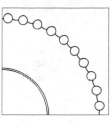

Beaded Edge

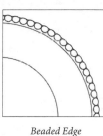

Candlewick

BIRDS

Delilah

Georgian

Parrot

Peacock & Wild Rose

BLOCKS

Beaded Block

Colonial Block

BOWS

Bowknot

COINS

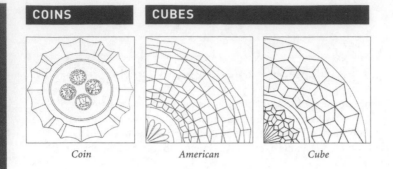

Coin

CUBES

American

Cube

DIAMONDS

Cape Cod

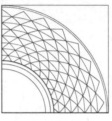

Diamond Quilted

English Hobnail

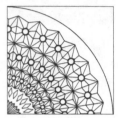

Holiday

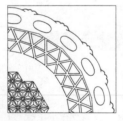

Laced Edge

Miss America

Peanut Butter

Waterford

Windsor

ELLIPSES (FANS)

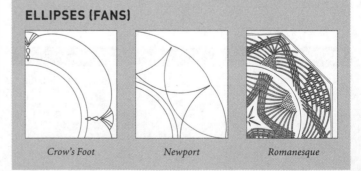

Crow's Foot

Newport

Romanesque

FIGURES

Cameo

Cupid

FLORALS

Alice

Cherry Blossom

Cloverleaf

Daisy

Dogwood

Doric

Doric & Pansy

Floragold

Floral

Floral and Diamond Band

Flower Garden with Butterflies

Indiana Custard

Iris

Jubilee

GLASS

Mayfair (Federal)

Mayfair (Open Rose)

Normandie

Orange Blossom

Pineapple & Floral

Primrose

Rosemary

Rose Cameo

Royal Lace

Seville

Sharon

Sunflower

Thistle

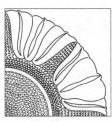

Tulip

Vitrock

Wild Rose

FRUITS

Avocado

Cherryberry

Della Robbia

Fruits

Paneled Grape

Strawberry

GEOMETRIC & LINE DESIGNS

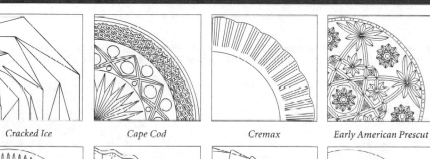

Cracked Ice

Cape Cod

Cremax

Early American Prescut

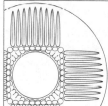

Park Avenue

Pioneer

Sierra

Star

Starlight

Tea Room

GLASS

HONEYCOMB

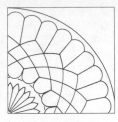

Aunt Polly *Hex Optic*

HORSESHOE

Horseshoe

LEAVES

Laurel Leaf *Sunburst*

LACY DESIGNS

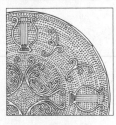

Harp *Heritage* *S-Pattern* *Sandwich (Duncan Miller)*

Sandwich (Hocking) *Sandwich (Indiana)*

LOOPS

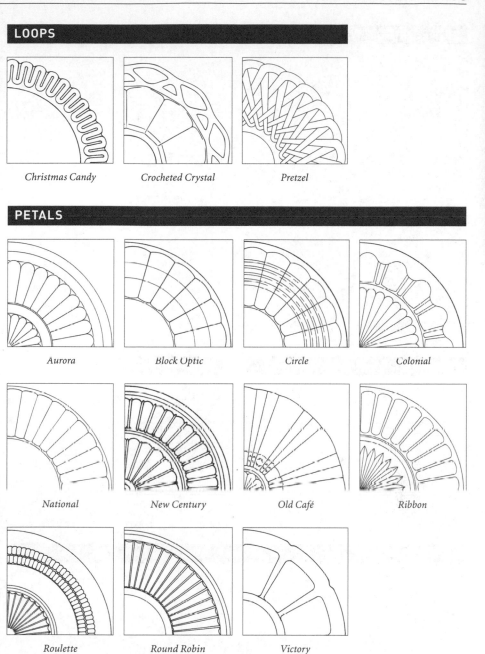

Christmas Candy   Crocheted Crystal   Pretzel

PETALS

Aurora   Block Optic   Circle   Colonial

National   New Century   Old Café   Ribbon

Roulette   Round Robin   Victory

PETALS/RIDGES WITH DIAMOND ACCENTS

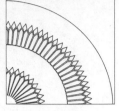

Anniversary

Coronation

Fortune

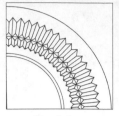

Lincoln Inn

Petalware

Queen Mary

PLAIN

PYRAMIDS

Charm

Mt. Pleasant

Pyramid

RAISED BAND

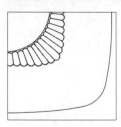

Charm

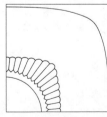

Forest Green

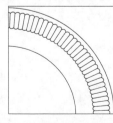

Jane Ray

Royal Ruby

GLASS

RAISED CIRCLES

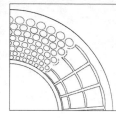

American Pioneer

Bubble

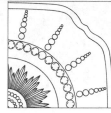

Columbia

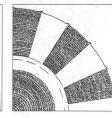

Dewdrop

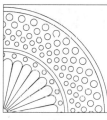

Hobnail

Moonstone

Oyster & Pearl

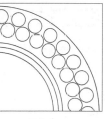

Raindrops

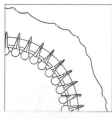

Radiance

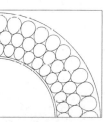

Ships

Teardrop

Thumbprint

RIBS

Homespun

RINGS (CIRCLES)

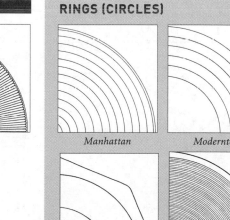

Manhattan

Moderntone

Moondrops

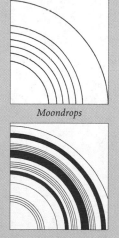

Moroccan Amethyst

Old English

Ring

SCENES

Chinex Classic

Lake Como

SCROLLING DESIGNS

Adam

American Sweetheart

Florentine No. 1

Florentine No. 2

Madrid

Patrick

Philbe

Primo

Princess

Rock Crystal

Roxana

Vernon

SWIRLS

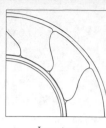

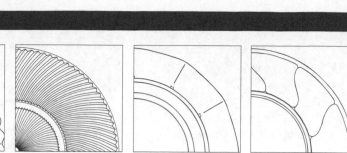

Colony

Diana

Fairfax

Jamestown

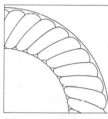

Spiral

Swirl

Swirl (Fire King)

Twisted Optic

TEXTURED

U.S. Swirl

By Cracky

Twiggy

Princess green salad
plate, 8" dia. **$15**

Courtesy of Vintique Vault

GLASS

Cherry Blossom pink creamer. **$30**
Cherry Blossom pink covered sugar. **$50**

Courtesy of The Saucon Valley Auction

Cherry Blossom pink cup. **$28**

Courtesy of The Saucon Valley Auction

Coin amber nappy with handle. ...**$14.50**

Courtesy of The Auction House Sacramento

Coin amber covered urn.........**$95**

Courtesy of The Auction House Sacramento

Coin Dot amber center bowl,
9" dia...................................**$28**

Courtesy of The Auction House Sacramento

Cube pink creamer, 3-9/16" h. **$6**
Cube pink sugar, 3" h. **$8**

Courtesy of Heritage Auction Gallery LLC

Colonial pattern green straw
holder with flared base,
circa 1915-1930, excellent
condition, 10 1/2" h. **$125**

Courtesy of Rich Penn Auctions

▲ English Hobnail pink plate,
5-1/2" **$10**

Courtesy of Top Hat Auctions, Appraisals & Sales

Della Robbia covered compote
with red trim and scalloped
edge, 7" h. **$35**

Courtesy of Specialists of the South

Floral (Poinsettia) pink salt and
pepper shakers. **$60**

Courtesy of Mooreland Auction Services

Floral (Poinsettia) pink covered
casserole. **$40**

Courtesy of Auctions Neapolitan

479

Florentine No. 2 green footed pitcher, 6-1/4" h. **$20**

Courtesy of Strawser Auctions

Six Georgian green tumblers, 5-1/4" h. .... **$135 ea.**

Courtesy of Jeffrey S. Evans & Associates

Iris crystal tumbler, 6-1/2" h. **$20**

Courtesy of Wickliff & Associates Auctioneers

Vintage 1930s Lancaster topaz etched two-handled serving bowl, 6-1/2" handle to handle. .....**$15-$22**

Courtesy of J&C Antiquities and Collectibles

Jubilee yellow sugar. **$15**
Jubilee yellow creamer. **$24**

Courtesy of Lancaster Glass Co.

Madrid amber ice lip pitcher, 80 oz. **$60**

Courtesy of Sunflower Auction

Miss America pink small plate, 5". ......**$65-$175**

Courtesy of Top Hat Auctions, Appraisals & Sales

Adam pink water pitcher....................**$75**
Cameo green water pitcher.................**$90**

Courtesy of Strawser Auctions

Set of Queen Mary pink wine and water goblets, 8" and 9".... **$80**

Courtesy of Vero Beach Auction

Royal Lace pink bowl,
10" dia...................... **$48**

Courtesy of Accurate Auctions

Royal Lace cobalt blue
butter dish. **$800**

Courtesy of Valley Auctions

Royal Lace cobalt blue ice
lip pitcher, 8" h............ **$320**
Six Royal Lace cobalt blue
tumblers. ....**$150 ea.**

Courtesy of Strawser Auctions

Royal Lace cobalt blue salt and pepper shakers.............................. **$265**

Courtesy of Valley Auctions

Royal Lace cobalt blue grill plate, 9-7/8" dia. **$40**

Courtesy of Valley Auctions

Sandwich, Hocking, desert gold candleholders...............**$70-$100**

Courtesy of Hollywood Auction Galleries

Sandwich, Hocking, forest green covered butter dish/cheese dish, 6-3/4" h. x 7-1/2" dia. **$10**

Courtesy of K&M Auction Liquidation Sales, Ltd.

Sharon amber covered cheese dish.......... **$225**

Courtesy of Rich Penn Auctions

Sharon pink dinner plate, excellent condition, 9" dia. **$4**

▶ Star amber sugar...............**$15**

Sunflower pink footed tumbler..........................**$32**

◀ Tea Room pink seven-piece water set.
Pitcher **$135**
Tumblers....................**$40 ea.**

Courtesy of Strawser Auctions

▲ Tea Room green handled bowl. **$65**

Courtesy of ATM Antiques & Auctions LLC

Thistle pink cup. **$24**
Thistle pink saucer............**$12**

GLASS

Tulip ice tubs, blue and amethyst..**$95 ea.**
Green. **$45**

Twisted Optic pink vase
with handles, 8" h...... **$50**

Courtesy of California Auctioneers

Vernon yellow
tumbler...... **$45**

Wild Rose With Leaves &
Berries iridescent bowl, 2-7/8"
h x 7-1/4" dia. **$15**

Courtesy of Showpiece Antique & Design Center

GLASS

durand

FINE DECORATIVE GLASS similar to that made by Tiffany and other outstanding glasshouses of its day was made by Vineland Flint Glass Works Co. in Vineland, New Jersey, first headed by Victor Durand Sr. and subsequently by his son, Victor Durand Jr., in the 1920s.

Iridescent gold vase, bulbous baluster form with high out-flaring foot and neck, 1924-1932, inscribed on bottom "DURAND 1991-9," pucker in iridescent finish, 9-1/4". **$310**

Courtesy of Brunk Auctions

King Tut vase, orange lustre with green King Tut decoration, applied lustre foot, shape 2028, polished pontil mark, signed "Durand," circa 1924-1931, 8-3/8" h. **$748**

Courtesy of Jeffrey S. Evans & Associates

Two King Tut vases, orange lustre with green King Tut decoration, applied lustre feet, shape 20120, each with polished pontil mark and signed under foot "Durand 20120-12," circa 1924-1931, 12-1/8" h. **$2,185**

Courtesy of Jeffrey S. Evans & Associates

King Tut pattern vase, early 20th century, signed Victor Durand, 7" h., 6" dia. **$908**

Courtesy of Cottone Auctions

Urn-form coil vase, dark green lustre with applied gold coil decoration, polished pontil mark, signed "Durand 1710-6," circa 1924-1931, 6-1/8" h., 6-1/4" dia. **$1,265**

Courtesy of Jeffrey S. Evans & Associates

VISIT WWW.ANTIQUETRADER.COM

WWW.FACEBOOK.COM/ANTIQUETRADER

GLASS

Coil vase, orange lustre with applied blue coil decoration, applied lustre foot and polished pontil mark, unsigned but matches Durand shape 2028 consistent with known examples, circa 1924-1931, 8-1/4" h. **$1,380**

Courtesy of Jeffrey S. Evans & Associates

Urn with cover in blue King Tut design against iridescent marigold backdrop, cover with ridged amber button finial and magenta halo, factory paper sticker beneath reads "No. 1964" (handwritten), "Price" (blank), and "Dec. OK" (handwritten), cloth tape adhered to bottom with writing in old ink of shape number and size 1964-8" with code lettering and price of "$30 pr.," excellent original condition, 10" h. x 8-1/2" w. across shoulder................ **$1,800**

Courtesy of Mark Mussio, Humler & Nolan

King Tut vase with blue and bronze iridescent lines with platinum highlights, interior of flaring mouth in gold iridescence, signed in polished pontil "Durand," very good to excellent condition, 9-1/2" h. **$1,955**

Courtesy of James D. Julia Auctioneers, Fairfield, Maine, www.jamesdjulia.com

Vase with platinum iridescent heart and vine decoration, light blue highlights against dark blue shading to black at foot, iridescent background, rolled and flared lip and interior with gold iridescence, unsigned, very good to excellent condition, 6-3/4" h. **$2,252**

Courtesy of James D. Julia Auctioneers, Fairfield, Maine, www.jamesdjulia.com

Pulled feather vase, early 20th century, unsigned, 8-1/2" h. **$333**

Courtesy of Cottone Auctions

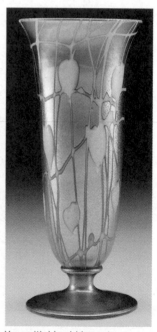

Vase with blue iridescent body and white heart and vine decoration, applied gold iridescent foot, unsigned, very good condition with some scratches to iridescence on foot, 10" h. **$711**

Courtesy of James D. Julia Auctioneers, Fairfield, Maine, www.jamesdjulia.com

Vase in silver blue lustre with opal heart and vine decoration, polished pontil mark, shape 1730, signed "Durand," circa 1924-1931, 6-5/8" h. overall.................. **$633**

Courtesy of Jeffrey S. Evans & Associates

Monumental stick vase in blue luster with magenta about shoulder and extending onto neck, signed in silver "Durand" with shape and height "1974-15" within polished pontil, excellent condition, 15-1/2" h. x 9" w. **$750**

Courtesy of Mark Mussio, Humler & Nolan

Twin vases in blue with round ribbed bodies above ribbed bases, purple and gold highlights on neck areas, unmarked, excellent original condition, 9-1/4" h. x 7" w. **$750**

Courtesy of Mark Mussio, Humler & Nolan

Moorish crackle vase, pink and white, 1920s, unmarked, 8-1/2" h., 6" dia. **$1,152**

Courtesy of Rago Arts, www.ragoarts.com

Crackle vase with lava decoration, blue and white with crystal and blue lava decoration, shape 1716, base with polished pontil mark, unsigned, circa 1924-1931, 9-3/4" h. overall.............. **$1,495**

Courtesy of Jeffrey S. Evans & Associates

Red lustre vase, circa 1930, enameled DURAND, 1812-8, 8-3/8" h. **$875**

Courtesy of Heritage Auctions

Moorish crackle vase, blue and white, 1920s, unmarked, 8-1/2" h., 4-1/2" dia. **$1,152**

Courtesy of Rago Arts, www.ragoarts.com

Moorish crackle table torchere, cranberry and white crackle with lustre, shape 1706, original base patina, cord and socket, circa 1924-1931, 20" h. overall, shade 8-1/2" h. overall. **$920**

Courtesy of Jeffrey S. Evans & Associates

Pulled feather vase, early 20th century, unsigned, applied thread decoration, 8-1/2" h. **$968**

Courtesy of Cottone Auctions

Decorated vase, early 20th century, signed Durand 31019-8, 10-1/2" h., 6" dia. **$1,331**

Courtesy of Cottone Auctions

Blue squat-bodied vase with aurora rings about shoulder, marked in silver "V. Durand" with shape and size, 1986-6-D, excellent condition, 5-5/8" h. x 7" w. **$550**

Courtesy of Mark Mussio, Humler & Nolan

Orange lustre vase, circa 1930, enameled DURAND, 1986-6, 5-7/8" h. **$625**

Courtesy of Heritage Auctions

Torchiere shade with three rows of blue and yellow iridescent leaves against cream-colored background, applied random gold iridescent threading and light gold iridescent interior, flake to fitter rim, minor thread loss, 9-1/4" h., 4-1/4" dia. fitter...................... **$237**

Courtesy of James D. Julia Auctioneers, Fairfield, Maine, www.jamesdjulia.com

Large bulbous vase with long flaring neck in platinum iridescence shading to gold on neck and lip, signed on underside in silver "Durand 1716-12," very good to excellent condition with minor scratches to side, 12-1/4" h. **$593**

Courtesy of James D. Julia Auctioneers, Fairfield, Maine, www.jamesdjulia.com

GLASS

fenton art glass

THE FENTON ART GLASS CO. was founded in 1905 by Frank L. Fenton and his brother John W. in Martins Ferry, Ohio. They initially sold hand-painted glass made by other manufacturers, but it wasn't long before they decided to produce their own glass. The new Fenton factory in Williamstown, West Virginia, opened on Jan. 2, 1907. From that point on, the company expanded by developing unusual colors and continued to decorate glassware in innovative ways.

Two more brothers, James and Robert, joined the firm. But despite the company's initial success, John W. left to establish the Millersburg Glass Co. of Millersburg, Ohio, in 1909. The first months of the new operation were devoted to the production of crystal glass only. Later iridized glass was called "Radium Glass." After only two years, Millersburg filed for bankruptcy.

Fenton's iridescent glass had a metallic luster over a colored, pressed pattern and was sold in dime stores. It was only after the sales of this glass decreased and it was sold in bulk as carnival prizes that it came to be known as carnival glass.

Fenton became the top producer of carnival glass with more than 150 patterns. The quality of the glass, and its popularity with the public, enabled the new company to be profitable through the late 1920s. As interest in carnival glass subsided, Fenton moved on to stretch glass and opalescent patterns. A line of colorful blown glass (called "off-hand" by Fenton) was also produced in the mid-1920s.

Spiral pattern decanter in cranberry opalescent, applied colorless crimped handle, original hobnail stopper, circa 1950, 12-1/2" h. overall. **$104**

Courtesy of Jeffrey S. Evans & Associates

During the Great Depression, Fenton survived by producing functional colored glass tableware and other household items, including water sets, table sets, bowls, mugs, plates, perfume bottles, and vases. Restrictions on European imports during World War II ushered in the arrival of Fenton's opaque colored glass, and the lines of "Crest" pieces soon followed. In the 1950s, production continued to diversify with a focus on milk glass, particularly in Hobnail patterns. In the third quarter of Fenton's history, the company returned to themes that had proved popular to preceding generations and began adding special lines, such as the Bicentennial series.

Innovations included the line of Colonial colors that debuted in 1963, including amber, blue, green, orange and ruby. Based on a special order for an Ohio museum, Fenton in 1969 revisited its early success with "Original Formula Carnival Glass." Fenton also started marking its glass in the molds for the first time.

The star of the 1970s was the yellow and blushing pink creation known as Burmese, which remains popular today. This was followed closely by a menagerie of animals, birds, and children. In 1975, Robert Barber was hired by Fenton to begin an artist-in-residence program, producing a limited line of art glass vases in a return to the off-hand, blown-glass creations of the mid-1920s. Shopping at home via television was a recent phenomenon in the late 1980s when the "Birthstone Bears" became the first Fenton product to appear on QVC. In August 2007, Fenton discontinued all but a few of its more popular lines, and the company ceased production altogether in 2011.

For more information on Fenton Art Glass, see *Warman's Fenton Glass Identification and Price Guide,* 2nd edition, by Mark F. Moran.

GLASS

Epergne in opaque white with Aqua Crest rims, ruffled-rim bowl fitted with four vases, Fenton Art Glass for L.G. Wright, mid-20th century, 17-1/4" h. overall, 12" dia. overall. **$173**

Courtesy of Jeffrey S. Evans & Associates

Drapery pattern five-piece water set in blue opalescent, globular-form pitcher with flared star-crimped rim and applied blue handle and four pressed tumblers with factory ground table rings, circa 1910, pitcher 9-1/4" h. overall, tumblers 3-3/4" h............................... **$196**

Courtesy of Jeffrey S. Evans & Associates

Drapery pattern water pitcher in green opalescent, globular form with flared star-crimped rim and applied green handle, circa 1910, 9" h. **$104**

Courtesy of Jeffrey S. Evans & Associates

Six Drapery pattern tumblers in green opalescent, each with factory polished base, circa 1910, 3-3/4" h... **$58**

Courtesy of Jeffrey S. Evans & Associates

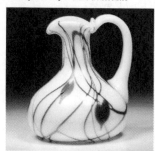

Hanging Hearts pattern cruet in custard iridescent, no stopper, factory polished base and rough pontil mark, mid-20th century, 4-3/4" h. overall................... **$92**

Courtesy of Jeffrey S. Evans & Associates

Hobnail seven-piece water set in cranberry opalescent, water pitcher with circular-form crimped rim, applied colorless crimped handle, six barrel-form tumblers, third quarter 20th century, 4-7/8" and 7-5/8" h. overall. **$173**

Courtesy of Jeffrey S. Evans & Associates

Opalescent Aqua Crest ewer with applied blue handle and floral decoration signed by Linda Fleming, second half 20th century, and Peachblow vase with polychrome foliate decoration, signed by Martha Reynolds and inscribed "Sample / (incorrect crimp)" under base, 9" and 10" h. **$127**

Courtesy of Jeffrey S. Evans & Associates

Six Waterlily and Cattails pattern tumblers in amethyst opalescent, circa 1908, 3-3/4" h. **$196**

Courtesy of Jeffrey S. Evans & Associates

Waterlily and Cattails pattern seven-piece water set in blue opalescent, water pitcher and six tumblers, circa 1908, 3-3/4" to 9" h. overall... **$219**

Courtesy of Jeffrey S. Evans & Associates

Six stretch glass iced tea tumblers in topaz/vaseline (uranium) iridescent, each with factory polished rim and applied cobalt blue handle, introduced in 1921, 5-1/8" h. **$230**

Courtesy of Jeffrey S. Evans & Associates

Waterlily and Cattails pattern seven-piece water set in ice blue opalescent, water pitcher and six tumblers, circa 1908, 3-3/4" to 8-3/4" h. overall. **$150**

Courtesy of Jeffrey S. Evans & Associates

Honeycomb and Clover pattern three-piece water set in green opalescent, water pitcher and two tumblers, circa 1909, 3-3/4" to 8-1/8" h. overall. **$150**

Courtesy of Jeffrey S. Evans & Associates

GLASS

FENTON CARNIVAL GLASS

Butterfly and Fern pattern carnival glass assembled five-piece water set in blue iridescent, water pitcher with hexagonal crimped rim and applied cobalt blue handle, four tumblers with polished table rings, first quarter 20th century, pitcher 9-1/2" h., tumblers 4" h. **$207**

Courtesy of Jeffrey S. Evans & Associates

Orange Tree pattern carnival glass hatpin holder in cobalt blue iridescent, folded-in rim, three scroll feet, circa 1911, 6-3/4" h. **$104**

Courtesy of Jeffrey S. Evans & Associates

Butterfly and Berry pattern carnival glass seven-piece water set in blue iridescent, water pitcher with circular sawtooth rim, six tumblers, circa 1911-1926, pitcher 9-1/8" h. overall, tumblers 4" to 4-1/8" h. **$184**

Courtesy of Jeffrey S. Evans & Associates

No. 349 Florentine pattern carnival glass candlesticks in red iridescent, soft stretch glass pattern, hexagonal form, circa 1922, 10-1/2" h., 4-3/4" dia. overall base. **$546**

Courtesy of Jeffrey S. Evans & Associates

Two carnival glass bowls: Stag and Holly pattern with ruffled rim and Two Flowers pattern in marigold iridescent, each with three ball feet, scalloped rims and paneled exteriors, first quarter 20th century, 4-1/4" h., 11" dia. and 4-3/4" h., 9-1/4" dia. **$92**

Courtesy of Jeffrey S. Evans & Associates

Panther pattern carnival glass eight-piece berry set in marigold iridescent, ruffled and scalloped rims, master berry bowl and seven individual bowls with slight variances in forms, each with three ball feet and Butterfly and Berry pattern exterior, circa 1914, undamaged, master 4" h., 9" dia. overall, individuals 2-1/4" to 2-1/2" h. overall, 5-1/2" to 6-1/2" dia. overall. **$138**

Courtesy of Jeffrey S. Evans & Associates

Orange Tree pattern carnival glass eight-piece punch set in marigold iridescent, flared-rim punch bowl, pedestal base of lighter shade and soft iridescence, and six cups, circa 1911, bowl 8-3/4" h. overall, 11-3/4" dia. overall, cups 2-3/8" h. **$104**

Courtesy of Jeffrey S. Evans & Associates

Thistle pattern carnival glass banana boat/bowl in blue iridescent, ovoid form with scalloped rim, four feet, Waterlily and Cattails pattern exterior, first quarter 20th century, 4-1/4" h. overall, 7-3/4" x 11". **$184**

Orange Tree pattern carnival glass orange bowl in blue iridescent, interior of base with band of daisies, slightly flared and scalloped rim, three ball feet, circa 1911, 5-1/2" h. overall, 10" dia. overall. **$92**

Courtesy of Jeffrey S. Evans & Associates

Dragon and Lotus pattern carnival glass ice cream bowl in red iridescent with amberina-like foot, scalloped rim, unpatterned exterior, circa 1915, 2-5/8" h. overall, 8-5/8" dia. **$633**

Courtesy of Jeffrey S. Evans & Associates

Grape and Cable pattern carnival glass orange bowl in emerald green iridescent, Persian Medallion pattern interior, ruffled and scalloped rim, three ball feet, circa 1911, 5-1/2" h. overall, 9-3/4" dia. overall. **$104**

Courtesy of Jeffrey S. Evans & Associates

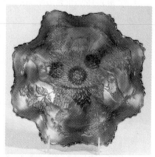

Stag and Holly pattern carnival glass bowl in blue iridescent, ruffled and scalloped rim, three ball feet, first quarter 20th century, 4-1/4" h. overall, 10-1/2" dia. overall. **$92**

Courtesy of Jeffrey S. Evans & Associates

Panther pattern carnival glass master berry bowl in green iridescent, ruffled and scalloped rims, three ball feet, and Butterfly and Berry pattern exterior, circa 1914, 4-1/4" h. overall, 9-1/4" dia. overall.. **$115**

Courtesy of Jeffrey S. Evans & Associates

GLASS

fostoria

THE FOSTORIA GLASS Co., founded in 1887, produced numerous types of fine glassware over the years. Its factory in Moundsville, West Virginia, closed in 1986.

Three No. 789/Wedding Bells toothpick holders, circa 1900, colorless, one with maiden's blush staining, 2-1/4" h. **$35**

Courtesy of Jeffrey S. Evans & Associates

Two No. 183/Victoria toothpick holders, circa 1888, colorless, one with satin finish, each with factory polished base, 2-3/8" h. **$104**

Courtesy of Jeffrey S. Evans & Associates

GLASS

gallé

GALLÉ GLASS WAS made in Nancy, France, by Emile Gallé, founder of the Nancy School and leader in the Art Nouveau movement in France. Much of his glass, both enameled and cameo, is decorated with naturalistic motifs. The finest pieces were made in the last two decades of the 19th century and the opening years of the 20th.

Pieces marked with a star preceding the name were made between 1904, the year of Gallé's death, and 1914.

Mold blown vase with pink fuchsia flowers and brown leaves descending from lip against shaded yellow, cream, and brown background, signed on side in cameo "Gallé," very good to excellent condition, 11-3/4" h. $11,850

Courtesy of James D. Julia Auctioneers, Fairfield, Maine, www.jamesdjulia.com

Mold blown vase with shaded red and white apple blossoms with reddish-brown limbs against frosted cream-colored background, signed on side in cameo "Gallé," very good to excellent condition, 13-3/4 h. $10,902

Courtesy of James D. Julia Auctioneers, Fairfield, Maine, www.jamesdjulia.com

Mold blown vase in pattern of brown leaves and green berries descending from neck against brown shading to yellow shading to frost background, signed on side in cameo "Gallé," very good to excellent condition, 11-1/2" h. $10,665

Courtesy of James D. Julia Auctioneers, Fairfield, Maine, www.jamesdjulia.com

Mold blown vase with allover floral decoration in purple, lavender, and light blue against light pink background, signed on side in cameo "Gallé," very good to excellent condition, 6-3/4" h. **$6,814**

Courtesy of James D. Julia Auctioneers, Fairfield, Maine, www.jamesdjulia.com

Scenic vase with purple cameo pine trees and rocks, blue pond and blue mountains in background, shaded yellow background, base has been ground, signed on side in cameo "Gallé," very good to excellent condition, 9-7/8" h. **$4,444**

Courtesy of James D. Julia Auctioneers, Fairfield, Maine, www.jamesdjulia.com

Vase with dark green cameo trees on front with green and yellow pond with green trees on distant shore against shaded yellow and cream background, signed on side in cameo "Gallé," very good condition, flake to outside edge of lip, 14-1/2" h. **$1,185**

Courtesy of James D. Julia Auctioneers, Fairfield, Maine, www.jamesdjulia.com

Double gourd-shape vase with brown and green cameo aquatic vegetation against green shading to brown background, small areas of controlled bubbles, signed on side in cameo "Gallé," very good to excellent condition, light grind marks to top of lip, most likely from factory, 8" h. **$1,185**

Courtesy of James D. Julia Auctioneers, Fairfield, Maine, www.jamesdjulia.com

Banjo vase with brown cameo lily pond scene with large dragonfly above lily pads, dragonfly's tail extends up neck, shaded cream and yellow background, signed on side in cameo "Gallé," very good to excellent condition, 6-1/2" h. **$2,548**

Courtesy of James D. Julia Auctioneers, Fairfield, Maine, www.jamesdjulia.com

497

Vase with red cameo glass leaves, stems, and flower clusters against frosted cream-colored background, signed "Gallé," very good to excellent condition, 8" h............... **$1,185**

Courtesy of James D. Julia Auctioneers, Fairfield, Maine, www.jamesdjulia.com

Vase with flared rim above tapering elongated body wheel-cut overall with vines, flowers, and berries, circa turn of 20th century, cameo signed "Gallé," 13-1/2" h. x 4-3/4" dia.... **$1,400**

Courtesy of John Moran Auctioneers, Inc.

Early bottle with enameled chrysanthemums on front and back with stylized stems and leaves in pink, gray, and blue, signed "E. Gallé Nancy," very good to excellent condition, shallow flake on bottom of stopper and minor staining to interior, 6" h. **$2,963**

Courtesy of James D. Julia Auctioneers, Fairfield, Maine, www.jamesdjulia.com

Vase with cameo decoration of grapevines, leaves, and clusters in brown and light yellow against background shading from pink to cream to salmon, signed "* GALLE," very good to excellent condition, 9-1/2" h. **$1,067**

Courtesy of James D. Julia Auctioneers, Fairfield, Maine, www.jamesdjulia.com

Large vase with green fern cameo design against shaded cream, yellow, and green background, signed "* Gallé," very good to excellent condition, 28" h.............. **$3,140**

Courtesy of James D. Julia Auctioneers, Fairfield, Maine, www.jamesdjulia.com

Overlay glass landscape vase, circa 1900, signed in cameo "Gallé," 16-1/2" h. **$3,250**

Courtesy of Heritage Auctions

Vase with dark amethyst cameo lily pond and other aquatic plants against frosted light yellow background, signed "Gallé," very good to excellent condition, 11" h. **$1,422**

Courtesy of James D. Julia Auctioneers, Fairfield, Maine, www.jamesdjulia.com

Vase of compressed ovoid form in deep brown over mottled blue-green and purple ground, circa 1900, wheel-cut with design commemorating Battle of Lorraine with Prussian eagle, cross of Lorraine, thistles, and date 1914, signed in cameo "Gallé," 10-1/4" h. x 5" w. x 4" dia............................ **$9,500**

Courtesy of John Moran Auctioneers, Inc.

Vase with amethyst cameo scenic decoration, cameo trees in foreground partially obscure small pond with forest on far shore against background of yellow shading to cream shading to yellow, signed on side with engraved signature "Gallé," very good to excellent condition, side of foot professionally polished, 10" h. **$2,963**

Courtesy of James D. Julia Auctioneers, Fairfield, Maine, www.jamesdjulia.com

Yellow etched glass and enamel two-handled vase with orchids, circa 1900, engraved Cristallerie, Emile Gallé, modéle et (effaced mark), 9-3/4" h. **$6,000**

Courtesy of Heritage Auctions

Overlay glass landscape vase, circa 1900, signed in cameo "Gallé," small flake missing to signature, light surface wear commensurate with age, 13" h. **$5,000**

Courtesy of Heritage Auctions

Overlay glass landscape vase,
circa 1900, signed in cameo
"Gallé," 5-1/4" h............. **$2,000**

Courtesy of Heritage Auctions

Cameo vase on foot with lilac
hydrangea cluster and falling
flower heads in green foliage
set over slightly textured white
backdrop, raised ring collar on
neck, cameo signature low on
side among leaves, excellent
condition, 6".....................**$475**

Courtesy of Mark Mussio, Humler & Nolan

Cameo vase in two-tone
blue with clusters of berries
attached to leafy branches,
reduced in height, surface
scratches to widest area and
polished rim with roughness
inside, 13-5/8" h. x 7" w.
across base. **$325**

Courtesy of Mark Mussio, Humler & Nolan

top lot

Rare dill table lamp of
acid-etched and wheel-
polished glass, blown glass,
and patinated metal, three
sockets, circa 1900, shade
signed Gallé, 30" x 15".
.............................**$83,200**

COURTESY OF RAGO ARTS,
WWW.RAGOARTS.COM

Monumental overlay glass
wisteria stick vase, circa 1900,
signed in cameo "Gallé," good
condition, fleabite to antenna
of one butterfly, 29-1/4" h.**$2,750**

Courtesy of Heritage Auctions

GLASS

heisey glass

NUMEROUS TYPES OF fine glass were made by A.H. Heisey & Co., Newark, Ohio, from 1895. The company's trademark, an H enclosed within a diamond, has become known to most glass collectors. The company's name and molds were acquired by Imperial Glass Co., Bellaire, Ohio, in 1958, and some pieces have been reissued.

No. 1205/Fancy Loop toothpick holders, green and colorless, colorless example with gilt decoration, circa 1896, 2-1/4" h. **$104**

Courtesy of Jeffrey S. Evans & Associates

No. 1235/Bead Panel and Sunburst toothpick holders, colorless, one example with maiden's blush staining, circa 1897, 2-1/2" h. **$150**

Courtesy of Jeffrey S. Evans & Associates

Two toothpick holders, colorless and green with gilt decoration, signed Prince of Wales and Winged Scroll example, circa 1902 and 1899, 2" and 2-3/8" h. **$92**

Courtesy of Jeffrey S. Evans & Associates

No. 337/Touraine ruby-stained toothpick holder, colorless, engraved "Gettysburg 1863," circa 1902, 2-1/4" h. **$259**

Courtesy of Jeffrey S. Evans & Associates

No. 1255/Pineapple & Fan ruby-stained toothpick holder, colorless, circa 1898, 2" h. ..**$345**

Courtesy of Jeffrey S. Evans & Associates

No. 356/Queen Anne toothpick holder, colorless, signed, circa 1907, 2-1/4" h. **$150**

Courtesy of Jeffrey S. Evans & Associates

GLASS

imperial

FROM 1902 UNTIL 1984, Imperial Glass Co. of Bellaire, Ohio, produced hand-made glass. Early pressed glass production often imitated cut glass and may bear the raised "NUCUT" mark in the interior center. In the second decade of the 1900s, Imperial was one of the dominant manufacturers of iridescent or carnival glass. When glass collecting gained popularity in the 1970s, Imperial again produced carnival glass and a line of multicolored slag glass. Imperial purchased molds from closing glasshouses and continued many lines popularized by others, including Central, Heisey, and Cambridge. These reissues may cause confusion but they were often marked.

No. 473 Grape pattern carnival glass seven-piece cordial set, decanter with correct stopper and six cordials with stippling to pattern in amethyst iridescent, pattern introduced 1914-1915, decanter 11-7/8" h. overall, cordials 4" h. **$138**

Courtesy of Jeffrey S. Evans & Associates

Corn pattern carnival glass figural bottle in smoke iridescent, factory polished rim, original cork stopper in interior of body, first half 20th century, 4-3/4" h., 2" dia. **$230**

Courtesy of Jeffrey S. Evans & Associates

Leaf and Vine pattern vase, early 20th century, unsigned, 7-1/2" h. **$545**

Courtesy of Cottone Auctions

Scroll Embossed pattern carnival glass plate in amethyst/purple iridescent, octagonal form with sawtooth edge rim, unpatterned exterior, star-patterned foot, first quarter 20th century, 1-1/2" h., 9-1/4" dia. overall............................ **$92**

Courtesy of Jeffrey S. Evans & Associates

Freehand vase in heavy iridescent marigold with applied red iridescent rim and stem, shape as catalog number FH 214, polished pontil mark, circa 1925, 13-1/2" h. **$690**

Courtesy of Jeffrey S. Evans & Associates

Leaf and Vine pattern vase, 6" h. **$424**

Courtesy of Cottone Auctions

Cobblestone pattern carnival glass bowl, amethyst iridescent, ruffled plain rim, Imperial Arcs exterior, first half 20th century, 2-3/4" h. overall, 9" dia........ **$81**

Courtesy of Jeffrey S. Evans & Associates

Broken Arches pattern carnival glass eight-piece punch set, punch bowl, pedestal base, and six cups in amethyst/purple iridescent, factory polished table rings, first half 20th century, punch bowl 10" h. overall, 12-1/4" dia., cups 2-1/8" h. **$115**

Courtesy of Jeffrey S. Evans & Associates

Fashion pattern carnival glass eight-piece punch set, punch bowl with ruffled and scalloped rim, pedestal base with scalloped foot, and six cups in marigold iridescent, first half 20th century, punch bowl 10" h. overall, 12-1/4" dia. overall, cups 2-1/4" to 2-1/8" h... **$69**

Courtesy of Jeffrey S. Evans & Associates

GLASS

lalique

RENÉ JULES LALIQUE was born on April 6, 1860, in the village of Ay, in the Champagne region of France. In 1862, his family moved to the suburbs of Paris.

In 1872, Lalique began attending College Turgot where he began studying drawing with Justin-Marie Lequien. After the death of his father in 1876, Lalique began working as an apprentice to Louis Aucoc, who was a prominent jeweler and goldsmith in Paris.

Lalique moved to London in 1878 to continue his studies. He spent two years attending Sydenham College, developing his graphic design skills. He returned to Paris in 1880 and worked as an illustrator of jewelry, creating designs for Cartier, among others. In 1884, Lalique's drawings were displayed at the National Exhibition of Industrial Arts, organized at the Louvre.

At the end of 1885, Lalique took over Jules Destapes' jewelry workshop. Lalique's design began to incorporate translucent enamels, semiprecious stones, ivory, and hard stones. In 1889, at the Universal Exhibition in Paris, the jewelry firms of Vever and Boucheron included collaborative works by Lalique in their displays.

In the early 1890s, Lalique began to incorporate glass into his jewelry, and in 1893 he took part in a competition organized by the Union Centrale des Arts Decoratifs to design a drinking vessel. He won second prize.

Lalique opened his first Paris retail shop in 1905, near the perfume business of François Coty. Coty commissioned Lalique to design his perfume labels in 1907, and he also created his first perfume bottles for Coty.

In the first decade of the 20th century, Lalique continued to experiment with glass manufacturing techniques, and mounted his first show devoted entirely to glass in 1911.

During World War I, Lalique's first factory was forced to close, but the construction of a new factory was soon begun in Wingen-sur-Moder, in the Alsace region. It was completed in 1921, and still produces Lalique crystal today.

In 1925, Lalique designed the first "car mascot" (hood ornament) for Citroën, the French automobile company. For the next six years, Lalique would design 29 models for companies such as Bentley, Bugatti, Delage, Hispano-Suiza, Rolls Royce, and Voisin.

Lalique's second boutique opened in 1931, and this location continues to serve as the main Lalique showroom today.

René Lalique died on May 5, 1945, at the age of 85. His son, Marc, took over the business at that time, and when Marc died in 1977, his daughter, Marie-Claude Lalique Dedouvre, assumed control of the company. She sold her interest in the firm and retired in 1994.

For more information on Lalique, see *Warman's Lalique Identification and Price Guide* by Mark F. Moran.

(Editor's Note: In some of the descriptions of Lalique pieces that follow, you will find notations like "M p. 478, No. 1100" or "Marcilhac 952, pg. 428." This refers to the page and serial numbers found in *René Lalique, maître-verrier, 1860-1945: Analyse de L'oeuvre et Catalogue Raisonné* by Félix Marcilhac, published in 1989 and revised in 1994. Printed entirely in French, this book of more than 1,000 pages is the definitive guide to Lalique's work, and listings from auction catalogs typically cite the Marcilhac guide as a reference.)

Gros Scarabees amber glass vase, model introduced 1923, Marcilhac 892, script signature "R. Lalique," 11-1/2" h..**$30,750**

Courtesy of A.B. Levy's Auctions

Oran clear and frosted glass vase with green patina, model introduced 1927, Marcilhac 999, wheel-carved "R. LALIQUE FRANCE," 10-1/2" h. **$13,530**

Courtesy of A.B. Levy's Auctions

Perruches cased yellow glass vase, model introduced 1919, Marcilhac 876, script signature "R. Lalique," good condition, very good rim, scratches on bottom consistent with age, rare model, 10" h. **$19,680**

Courtesy of A.B. Levy's Auctions

Trophee frosted clear crystal sculpture, engraved "Lalique France," molded as abstract stylized flame, 12-1/2" h., 8" dia............................. **$2,500**

Courtesy of Neal Auction Co.

Tortues amber glass vase, model introduced 1926, Marcilhac 966, 10-1/2" h. **$47,970**

Courtesy of A.B. Levy's Auctions

Grillons clear and frosted glass vase with black patina, model introduced 1931, Marcilhac 1063, wheel-carved "R. LALIQUE FRANCE," 8.8" h. **$15,990**

Courtesy of A.B. Levy's Auctions

Biches frosted turquoise vase with deer foraging in foliage, engraved "Lalique ® France" below disc base, excellent condition, 6-5/8" h. x 5-1/2" w. across shoulder...............**$650**

Courtesy of Mark Mussio, Humler & Nolan

Vase with three horizontal rows of raised opalescent diamond-shaped cabochons surrounded by allover impressed floral designs with green patination within floral design, signed on underside with acid-etched blocked letters "R. Lalique France," very good to excellent condition, 4-7/8" h.......... **$1,422**

Courtesy of James D. Julia Auctioneers, Fairfield, Maine, www.jamesdjulia.com

Renes pattern vase with central band of opalescent glass antelope with curling horns standing amid foliage, clear glass with opalescent foot, signed on underside "R. Lalique France," very good to excellent condition, 4-7/8" h. **$2,370**

Courtesy of James D. Julia Auctioneers, Fairfield, Maine, www.jamesdjulia.com

top lot

Nadica frosted glass vase with two handles, model introduced 1930, Marcilhac 1054, wheel-carved "R. Lalique," 10.6" h. Provenance: Formerly from the Royal Collection of King Tribhuvan Bir Bikram Shah of Nepal (1906-1955), ordered by the king directly from Lalique. $150,000

COURTESY OF A.B. LEVY'S AUCTIONS

Frosted cherub vase with horizontal bands of wavy lines with raised dots in each wave, center with indented clear windows, each separated by frosted panels of nude cherubs in various poses, signed on underside with etched script signature "Lalique France," very good to excellent condition with minor scratches to underside of vase, 7-5/8" h. **$948**

Courtesy of James D. Julia Auctioneers, Fairfield, Maine, www.jamesdjulia.com

Suzanne luminaire of nude woman with arms outstretched and shawl hanging down atop original bronze luminaire base with incised peacock design, figure signed with raised block letters "R. Lalique," base unsigned, chip to bottom edge on back corner of glass, grind mark to top of raised hand, fleabites to corners, drill hole on underside of glass approximately 1/2" d., 11-1/4" h. **$10,665**

Courtesy of James D. Julia Auctioneers, Fairfield, Maine, www.jamesdjulia.com

Sirenes Avec Bouchon stoppered vase in frosted glass with sides impressed with figures of nude sirens, figural stopper of kneeling nude siren, stopper and impressed sides with sepia patination, signed on underside with etched signature "R. Lalique France No. 883," very good to excellent condition, 14" h. to top of stopper................$17,775

Courtesy of James D. Julia Auctioneers, Fairfield, Maine, www.jamesdjulia.com

GLASS

Clear and frosted glass Versailles urn-form vase with frosted band and molded decoration of grapevines over conforming foot, square base, etched mark to side "Lalique, France," 13-3/4" h......... **$2,000**

Courtesy of Clars Auction Gallery, www.clars.com

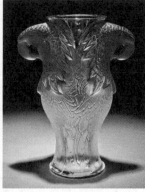

Macao frosted amber and clear crystal vase, designed 1999, engraved "Lalique France 13/99," base surmounted with colored cockatoo forms, with certificate of authenticity and original box, 13" h., 10" dia............... **$5,938**

Courtesy of Neal Auction Co.

Gui vase of entwined vines, leaves, and berries in white opalescent glass, signed on underside with etched script signature "R. Lalique France," very good condition, small flake and bruise on side of foot, 6-1/2" h. **$711**

Courtesy of James D. Julia Auctioneers, Fairfield, Maine, www.jamesdjulia.com

Oranges clear and frosted glass vase with black enamel, model introduced 1926, Marcilhac 964, molded signature "R. Lalique" and inscribed "R. Lalique France," 11.4" h............**$38,130**

Courtesy of A.B. Levy's Auctions

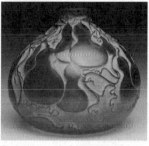

Courges vase in blue glass with impressed pattern of pears, neck possibly ground down, signed on underside with impressed block letters "Lalique" and engraved "France," very good to excellent condition, 7-3/8" h.........**$15,405**

Courtesy of James D. Julia Auctioneers, Fairfield, Maine, www.jamesdjulia.com

Ispahan red crystal vase embossed with roses, engraved "Lalique France," marked on base "MO72," with original box, 9 3/8" h., 7 3/4" dia. **$2,969**

Courtesy of Neal Auction Co.

Languedoc green glass vase, model introduced 1929, Marcilhac 1021, engraved "R. Lalique France," 8-3/4" h. **$27,060**

Courtesy of A.B. Levy's Auctions

Large Martigues frosted and molded glass serving plate with swimming fish in circular formation on frosted ground, 14-1/4" dia..................... **$1,600**

Courtesy of Clars Auction Gallery, www.clars.com

Clear and amber Lizard glass bowl with globular form in clear glass and molded reptile in amber, signed underside "Lalique, France," 9-1/2" h............ **$1,200**

Courtesy of Clars Auction Gallery, www.clars.com

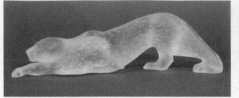

Frosted glass sculpture of Zella panther crouched and gazing outward, signed "Lalique, France" to underside, 4-1/2" h. x 13-1/2" w. **$850**

Courtesy of Clars Auction Gallery, www.clars.com

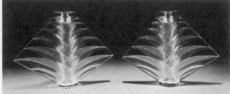

Ravelana frosted clear glass candlesticks engraved "Lalique France," diamond-form embossed with stylized palm leaves, surmounted with removable silver candle cups, 8" h. x 10-3/4" w. **$1,563**

Courtesy of Neal Auction Co.

Pair of Tanega frosted green and clear crystal vases, engraved "Lalique France," tapered form surmounted by molded leaves, 14-1/2" h., 9" dia......................**$6,250**

Courtesy of Neal Auction Co.

Limited edition Dragon ruby and clear glass vase, engraved "Lalique France," marked "Rubris" and numbered "05/99," bulbous form surmounted by molded dragons, 11-1/2" h. **$9,375**

Courtesy of Neal Auction Co.

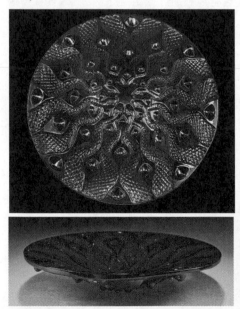

Serpentine red crystal bowl, engraved "Lalique France," embossed with snakes and radiating geometric pattern, with box, 2-3/8" h., 15-3/4" dia. **$3,125**

Courtesy of Neal Auction Co.

Antinea frosted green and clear crystal vase, engraved "Lalique France," tapered form body surmounted by nude female figures, 8" h., 9" dia................ **$1,563**

Courtesy of Neal Auction Co.v

GLASS

libbey glass

IN 1878, William L. Libbey obtained a lease on the New England Glass Co. of Cambridge, Massachusetts, changing the name to the New England Glass Works, W. L. Libbey and Son, Proprietors. After his death in 1883, his son, Edward D. Libbey, continued to operate the company at Cambridge until 1888, when the factory was closed. Edward Libbey moved to Toledo, Ohio, and set up the company subsequently known as Libbey Glass Co. During the 1880s, the firm's master technician, Joseph Locke, developed the now much desired colored art glass lines of Agata, Amberina, Peach Blow, and Pomona. Renowned for its cut glass of the Brilliant Period, the company continues in operation today as Libbey Glassware, a division of Owens-Illinois, Inc.

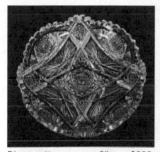

Diane pattern nappy, 6". **$236**
Courtesy of Woody Auctions, LLC

Ellsmere pattern flower center, signed Libbey, unusual corset neck, 8" x 10". **$6,490**

Courtesy of Woody Auctions, LLC

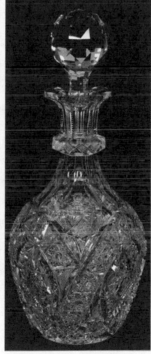

Rare Grand Prize pattern decanter, pattern cut ring neck, full hobstar base, signed Libbey, 13".................... **$9,145**

Courtesy of Woody Auctions, LLC

Maize pattern water bottle, custard with brown and green stained leaves, W. L. Libbey and Son, fourth quarter 19th century, 8" h..................... **$316**

Courtesy of Jeffrey S. Evans & Associates

Maize toothpick holder, custard, factory polished rim, W. L. Libbey and Son, circa 1889, 2-1/4" h. **$150**

Courtesy of Jeffrey S. Evans & Associates

GLASS

Maize toothpick holder, custard with blue staining and gilt decoration, factory polished rim, W. L. Libbey and Son, circa 1889, 2-1/4" h. ... **$403**

Courtesy of Jeffrey S. Evans & Associates

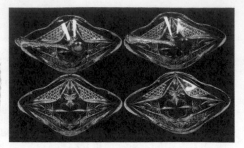

Four salt dips with engraved floral and nailhead diamond motif, signed Libbey, each with roughness, including two sterling salt spoons, 4". **$89**

Courtesy of Woody Auctions, LLC

Cobalt and clear cocktail set, early 20th century, cocktail shaker with silver-plated lid, stenciled Libbey mark, 12-3/4" h., and nine matching footed glasses (three shown), signed Libbey, 3" h., good condition, some tarnish, minor edge dents, possible solder repair, two glasses with chips at bases. **$744**

Courtesy of Brunk Auctions

Nash Spot-Optic threaded vase, colorless with blue threading, applied foot with polished pontil, signed "Libbey," Libbey Glass Co., second quarter 20th century, 8-5/8" h., 6" dia. overall............ **$173**

Courtesy of Jeffrey S. Evans & Associates

Silhouette goblets, set of four, colorless and opalescent, each with figural cat stem and acid-stamped Libbey in circle mark, Libbey Glass Co., second quarter 20th century, 7" h.................... **$288**

Courtesy of Jeffrey S. Evans & Associates

Brilliant period cut glass pitcher, late 19th/early 20th century, signed Libbey, good condition, top of handle with etched mark, chip at edge of handle, scattered minor flaws and typical scratches at bottom, 7-3/4" h........................ **$124**

Courtesy of Brunk Auctions

GLASS

mary gregory

GLASS ENAMELED IN white with silhouette-type figures, primarily of children, is now termed "Mary Gregory" and was attributed to the Boston and Sandwich Glass Co. However, recent research has proven conclusively that this was not decorated by Mary Gregory, nor was it made at the Sandwich plant. Miss Gregory was employed by Boston and Sandwich Glass Co. as a decorator; however, records show her assignment was the painting of naturalistic landscape scenes on larger items such as lamps and shades, but never the charming children for which her name has become synonymous. Further, in the inspection of fragments from the factory site, no paintings of children were found.

It is now known that all wares collectors call "Mary Gregory" originated in Bohemia beginning in the late 19th century and were extensively exported to England and the United States well into the 20th century.

For further information, see *The Glass Industry in Sandwich,* Volume #4 by Raymond E. Barlow and Joan E. Kaiser, and the book *Mary Gregory Glassware, 1880-1900* by R. & D. Truitt.

▶ Victorian Panel-Optic pattern water pitcher, amber, tapered tankard form with so-called Mary Gregory white enamel decoration of boy with walking stick, rough pontil mark, late 19th/early 20th century, 10" h. **$92**

Courtesy of Jeffrey S. Evans & Associates

Pair of vases with internally decorated bodies with blue modeling within clear glass, each with Mary Gregory winter scene, one with boy and girl ice skating on pond with clock tower in background, other with three boys having snowball fight on frozen pond, back of each with snow-covered ground, barren trees, and birds in flight; applied gilded glass handles and matching stoppers with gilded acorn finials, unsigned, very good condition, 13-1/4" h. to top of finial. **$741**

Courtesy of James D. Julia Auctioneers, Fairfield, Maine, www.jamesdjulia.com

Two Victorian Panel-Optic pattern items, blue dresser box with hinged cover and green pitcher with applied colorless reeded handle, each with so-called Mary Gregory white enamel decoration of young person within landscape with birds, late 19th/early 20th century, 3" and 7" h.......**$173**

Courtesy of Jeffrey S. Evans & Associates

GLASS

mt. washington

A WIDE DIVERSITY of glass was made by the Mt. Washington Glass Co. of New Bedford, Massachusetts, between 1869 and 1900. It was succeeded in 1900 by the Pairpoint Manufacturing Co. Throughout its history, the Mt. Washington Glass Co. made different types of glass including pressed, blown, art, lava, Napoli, cameo, cut, Albertine, Peachblow, Burmese, Crown Milano, Royal Flemish, and Verona.

◄ Two Burmese vases, late 19th century, two-handled short-neck vase with polychrome enameled Persian lily decoration, 10-1/8" h., and bottle shape with raised gold and enamel swirls, 9-3/4" h. **$2,58**

Courtesy of Skinner, Inc.; www.skinnerinc.com

▲ Four Burmese items, late 19th century, each with enameled flowers and foliage: Cylindrical vase with hexagonal scalloped rim, 9" h.; water pitcher, 8-7/8" h.; bottle-shaped bud vase, 8" h.; and biscuit jar with silver-plated rim, handle, and cover, 5-3/4" h. **$2,214**

Courtesy of Skinner, Inc.; www.skinnerinc.com

◄ Three Burmese vases, late 19th century, each with enameled flowers, bottle shape with trefoil spout, 9-7/8" h.; tall shouldered form, 9-1/8" h.; and squat form with cover, 3-7/8" h. **$2,337**

Courtesy of Skinner, Inc.; www.skinnerinc.com

Two Queen's pattern Burmese vases, late 19th century, each with raised gold vines and beaded enamel flowers; bottle-shape, 11-3/4" h., squat shape with quatrefoil rim atop four feet, 5-7/8" h. **$3,321**

Courtesy of Skinner, Inc.; www.skinnerinc.com

Burmese Queen's Lace ewer, late 19th century, gilded and enameled swirled bands with stylized flowers, 10" h. **$2,706**

Courtesy of Skinner, Inc.; www.skinnerinc.com

Colonial Ware vases, late 19th century, each with foliate molded handles and polychrome enameled figures within raised gold foliate framework, 17-7/8" h. **$2,460**

Courtesy of Skinner, Inc.; www.skinnerinc.com

Colonial Ware vase, late 19th century, Garden of Allah motif to three-handled bulbous form, one side with procession of camels and riders with pyramids in distance, reverse with camel and Arab to one side, painted mark, 12" h.................. **$3,198**

Courtesy of Skinner, Inc.; www.skinnerinc.com

Crown Milano aquatic vase, late 19th century, wide-mouth globular-shape, polychrome enameled and raised gold decoration of fish flanked by large shell and jeweled coral, 10-1/2" h. **$2,214**

Courtesy of Skinner, Inc.; www.skinnerinc.com

Two Crown Milano items, late 19th century, each with black enameling to gilded flowers and foliage, water pitcher, 8-1/8" h., and vase with quatrefoil spout, 12-7/8" h.......................... **$1,353**

Courtesy of Skinner, Inc.; www.skinnerinc.com

Three vases, late 19th century, each floral decorated in enamels and gold, pair of bottle-shaped Crown Milano vases, 9-3/4" h., and globular shape with scrolled leaf handles, 4-1/2" h. **$1,169**

Courtesy of Skinner, Inc.; www.skinnerinc.com

Two Crown Milano water pitchers, late 19th century, raised gold mum and foliate designs, 8-3/8" h. **$1,046**

Courtesy of Skinner, Inc.; www.skinnerinc.com

Two Crown Milano pitchers, late 19th century, each with colored ropetwist handle and decorated in gold with oak leaves and acorns, 9-3/4" h. and 10-1/2" h. **$1,722**

Courtesy of Skinner, Inc.; www.skinnerinc.com

GLASS

Three floral-decorated items, late 19th century, Crown Milano pitcher with ropetwist handle, 12-1/2" h., and two biscuit jars with silver-plated rims, handles, and covers, one with polychrome enameled flowers, other with gilded flowers, rim 5-3/4" h............................$615

Courtesy of Skinner, Inc.; www.skinnerinc.com

Lava glass toothpick holder with multicolored glass shards imbedded in pink lava glass body with gilded tracery, unsigned, very good to excellent condition, 2-5/8" h.............$11,850

Courtesy of James D. Julia Auctioneers, Fairfield, Maine, www.jamesdjulia.com

Peachblow ewer, late 19th century, beaded enamel flowers and gold vines, 10" h...... $1,968

Courtesy of Skinner, Inc.; www.skinnerinc.com

Pink flamingo vase, late 19th century, two-handled globular shape with wide mouth, enameled and gilded with ferns surrounding flamingos in flight to one side, wading in water to reverse, 9-1/4" h... $1,722

Courtesy of Skinner, Inc.; www.skinnerinc.com

Pink flamingo vase, late 19th century, two-handled globular shape with wide mouth, enameled and gilded with ferns bordering flamingos in flight to one side, wading in water to reverse, 9-3/4" h...$1,722

Courtesy of Skinner, Inc.; www.skinnerinc.com

Vase, late 19th century, teardrop shape with enameled and raised gold flowers and foliage to enameled ground with flowers and foliage, 8" h. $246

Courtesy of Skinner, Inc.; www.skinnerinc.com

Pink flamingo vase, late 19th century, two-handled bottle shape enameled and gilded with ferns surrounding flamingos in flight to one side and wading in water to reverse, 13" h........... $2,091

Courtesy of Skinner, Inc.; www.skinnerinc.com

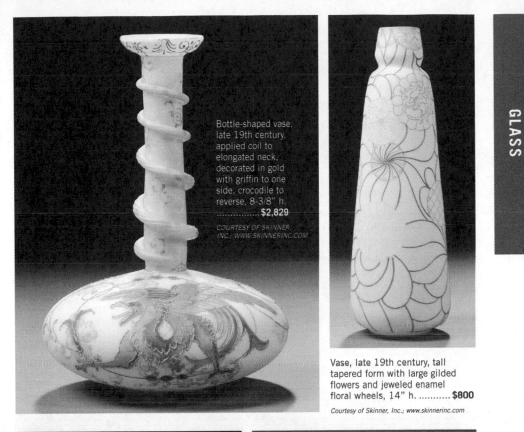

Bottle-shaped vase, late 19th century, applied coil to elongated neck, decorated in gold with griffin to one side, crocodile to reverse, 8-3/8" h. $2,829

COURTESY OF SKINNER, INC.; WWW.SKINNERINC.COM

Vase, late 19th century, tall tapered form with large gilded flowers and jeweled enamel floral wheels, 14" h. **$800**

Courtesy of Skinner, Inc.; www.skinnerinc.com

Vase, late 19th century, flat sided with turned spout, gilded and enamel decorated with scrolled foliage surrounding central figures of cherubs slaying mythological creatures, 10" h. **$5,228**

Courtesy of Skinner, Inc.; www.skinnerinc.com

Egg sugar shaker, opal with pale blue shaded ground, plush/satin finish, with polychrome spider mum and berry decoration, and period lid, fourth quarter 19th century, undamaged, 4" h. overall. .. **$196**

Courtesy of Jeffrey S. Evans & Associates

Chick head salt and pepper shakers, fourth quarter 19th century, opal with pale rose ground, glossy finish, each with polychrome floral decoration, one with original paper label, one lid with worn gilt decoration, undamaged, 2-1/8" h. overall. **$690**

Courtesy of Jeffrey S. Evans & Associates

Pillar-ribbed/ribbed three-piece condiment set, fourth quarter 19th century, opal shaded blue, plush/satin finish, salt and pepper shaker and mustard pot, each with polychrome leaf and berry decoration and period two-part hinged lids, fitted in quadruple-plate stand marked for Wilcox Silverplate Co. and numbered 3831, undamaged, condiments 3-1/8" to 3-7/8" h. overall, stand 6-5/8" h. overall. **$460**

Courtesy of Jeffrey S. Evans & Associates

Palmer Cox Brownie salt and pepper shakers, fourth quarter 19th century, opal, shaded blue, glossy finish, each with transfer decoration on front and reverse, matching period lids, glass undamaged, one with ill-fitting lid, 2-1/2" h. overall. **$489**

Courtesy of Jeffrey S. Evans & Associates

◀ Burmese pillar-ribbed/ribbed three-piece condiment set, circa 1885-1895, plush/satin finish, salt and pepper shakers with matching period two-part lids and oil bottle with painted inappropriate stopper, fitted in quadruple-plate stand marked for Pairpoint Manufacturing Co. and numbered 724-1/2, excellent condition overall, stopper with losses to paint, remainder undamaged, stand undamaged, condiments 3-7/8" to 5-3/4" h. overall, stand 7" h. **$230**

Courtesy of Jeffrey S. Evans & Associates

Pillar-ribbed/ribbed three-piece condiment set, fourth quarter 19th century, opal with yellow/cream ground, glossy finish, salt and pepper shakers and mustard pot, each with monochrome decoration, and period two-part hinged lids, mustard jar with marked silver spoon, fitted in quadruple-plate stand marked for E. G. Webster & Son and numbered 17, undamaged, 4-1/4" and 3-3/8" h. overall, stand 3-3/8" h. overall. **$150**

Courtesy of Jeffrey S. Evans & Associates

GLASS

murano

IN THE 1950S, the American home came alive with vibrant-colored decorative items, abstract art, and "futuristic"-designed furniture. The colorless geometry of the 1930s was out.

Over the last decade, mid-century design has once again gained favor with interior decorators, magazines, shows, and stores dedicated solely to this period. The bold colors and free-form shapes of mid-century modern Italian glass are emblematic of 1950s design. This distinctive glass has become a sought-after collectible.

Prices realized at auction for 1950s glass have seen a resurgence. However, there are still many items readily available and not always at a premium.

Italian glass can be found in many American homes. In fact, it is likely that some of the familiar glass items you grew up with were produced in Italy – the candy dish on the coffee table with the bright colors, the ashtray with the gold flecks inside. Modern glass objects from Italy were among the most widely distributed examples of 1950s design.

As with any decorative art form, there are varying levels of achievement in the design and execution of glass from this period. While you should always buy what you love, as there is never a guarantee return on investment, buying the best representation of an item is wise. In considering modern Italian glass, several points make one piece stand above another.

Italy has a centuries-old tradition of glassmaking, an industry whose center is the group of islands known as Murano in the lagoon of Venice. The most recognized and desirable Italian glass comes from three companies: Seguso, Venini, and Barovier & Toso.

Italy offers a vast array of talented glass artists. Top end collectors seem to favor Carlo Scarpa from Venini, Napoleone Martinuzzi (who worked at Venini from 1925-1932), and Dino Martens of Aureliano Toso. You can expect to pay several thousand dollars for a fine piece by one of these artists.

For slimmer collecting budgets, good quality examples by other artists are available and more affordable. Alfredo Barbini and Fulvio Biaconi (for Venini) are two of them. While some of their work does command top dollar, many of their pieces are priced for the novice collector.

A few mid-century designs can still be found that could prove to be sleepers in the near future. Look for Inciso vases by Venini, Aborigeni pieces by Barovier & Toso, and Soffiati examples by Giacomo Cappellin. Each of these designs is totally different from the other, yet all are reasonably priced in today's market.

Collectors should be aware that the most popular glass form is the vase, with glass

Reazioni policroma glass vase, Giulio Radi (1895-1952), A.V.E.M., circa 1948, unmarked, 7" x 4-1/4"......................**$1,408**

Courtesy of Rago Arts, www.ragoarts.com

Intarsio vase, Ercole Barovier (1889-1974), Barovier & Toso, 1960s, fused glass tessere with controlled air bubbles, unmarked, 7-1/4" x 7-1/2" x 4-1/2". **$1,664**

Courtesy of Rago Arts, www.ragoarts.com

Frammentati glass vase, Dino Martens (Italian, 1894-1970) for Aureliano Toso, original paper label, 10" h. **$5,100**

Courtesy of Cottone Auctions

sculpture following next in line. Popular sculptural forms include male or female nude figurals and pasta glass animals by Fulvio Biaconi.

Reproductions of the most famous forms of Italian glass are rampant. Some are marketed as such, while others are made to fool unsuspecting buyers. Also, and perhaps more confusing, many Italian glass designs are being produced to this day. The most common example of this is the Handkerchief vase. Originally produced by Piero Chiesa in 1937 for Fontana Arte, it was called the Paper Bag vase due to its crumpled shape. In the 1950s, Bianconi designed his own version for Venini. Since that time, generic manufacturers throughout Murano have produced countless unsigned imitations for the tourist trade. Almost all Venini handkerchief vases were signed, except for a few very valuable examples by Dino Martens.

Whether from the original manufacturer or another firm, Murano glass now being reproduced includes Sommerso designs, Barbini glass aquariums, and bowls along with Oriente designs. Venini lamps have also been reproduced. No doubt there will be more reproductions to come.

Enameled glass vase, Anzolo Fuga (1914-1988), S.A.L.I.R., circa 1930, remnant of original decal label, 9" x 7-3/4". **$1,216**

Courtesy of Rago Arts, www.ragoarts.com

Orlente glass vase no. 3121, Nabucco, Dino Martens (1894-1970), A.V.E.M., 1952-1961, unmarked, 9" x 9" x 4-1/2". **$7,680**

Courtesy of Rago Arts, www.ragoarts.com

Two Latticinio striped perfume bottles, colorless with blue and rainbow striping, each with colorless stopper with applied white, blue, and red flowers and mica flakes, rough pontil marks, 20th century, 5-1/8" h. overall. **$69**

Courtesy of Jeffrey S. Evans & Associates

Blown glass clessidre and five canne tumblers, Gio Ponti (1891-1979), Paolo Venini (1895-1959), Venini, 1946-1965, tumblers unmarked, clessidre with three-line acid-etched signature and Brevetta button, clessidre 6" x 2-1/4", tumblers 3-3/4" x 3-1/4". **$1,088**

Courtesy of Rago Arts, www.ragoarts.com

Six cordials from Commedia Dell'Arte series, Fulvio Bianconi (1915-1996), Venini, 1946-1965, Lattimo glass with applied elements, paper label, VENINI MURANO VENEZIA MADE IN ITALY, three-line etched signature, 5-1/2" x 3". **$1,408**

Courtesy of Rago Arts, www.ragoarts.com

◄ Polvere vase, Yoichi Ohira (b. 1946), 1998, blown glass, murrine and powder inserts, executed by Maestro Livio Serena, etched "Yoichi Ohira – Mo. L. Serena-1/1 unico 16.04.1998" with artist cipher, 8" x 5-3/4". **$20,480**

Courtesy of Rago Arts, www.ragoarts.com

Regional costumes figurine, Fulvio Bianconi (1915-1996), Venini, circa 1950, Zanfirico glass and murrine, unmarked, 13-1/2" x 4"................... **$1,024**

Courtesy of Rago Arts, www.ragoarts.com

Trailed-spiral glass bottle with stopper, Paolo Venini (1895-1959), Venini, designed 1952, paper label, VENINI MURANO VENEZIA MADE IN ITALY, 8-1/4" x 3"........................ **$768**

Courtesy of Rago Arts, www.ragoarts.com

Large spiral glass vase, Ercole Barovier (1889-1974), Barovier & Toso, 1950s, unmarked, 15-1/2" x 9"................... **$2,432**

Courtesy of Rago Arts, www.ragoarts.com

Cenedese pillow vase, turquoise blue with swirl pattern, surface acid-finished with "tugs" to each side of rim, acid-stamped "Cenedese," paper sticker on bottom reads "Cenedese Glass Murano, Made in Italy, 61/88/2/1," excellent condition, 10-1/2" h. x 10" w. x 7-1/2" d.............................**$70**

Courtesy of Mark Mussio, Humler & Nolan

Vase with school of angel fish, Alfredo Barbini, engraved "Barbini Murano" with clear Barbini Murano sticker, fish with millefiori tails fused into crystal glass, excellent condition, 15-1/4" h. x 7" w.............. **$300**

Courtesy of Mark Mussio, Humler & Nolan

Barovier & Toso pulled loop vase, no. 23888, original paper label, 13" h. **$1,210**

Courtesy of Cottone Auctions

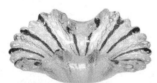

Folded bowl, red, green, and yellow lattice ribbon design with gold mica highlights, 7-3/4"................................**$59**

Courtesy of Woody Auctions, LLC

GLASS

GLASS

northwood glass co.

NORTHWOOD GLASS CO. was founded by Harry Northwood, son of prominent English glassmaker John Northwood, who was famous for his expertise in cameo glass.

Harry migrated to America in 1881 and, after working at various glass manufacturers, formed the Northwood Glass Co. in 1896 in Indiana, Pennsylvania. In 1902 he created H. Northwood and Co. in Wheeling, West Virginia. After Northwood died in 1919, H. Northwood and Co. began to falter and eventually closed in 1925.

Northwood produced a wide variety of opalescent, decorated, and special effect glasses and colors like iridescent blue and green, which were not widely seen at the time.

Blown Twist nine-panel mold sugar shaker, green opalescent, period lid, fourth quarter 19th century, undamaged, lid with some light corrosion, 4-5/8" h. overall. **$127**

Courtesy of Jeffrey S. Evans & Associates

Blown Twist wide-waist sugar shaker, colorless opalescent, period lid, fourth quarter 19th century, excellent condition, shoulder with light scratch, 4-7/8" h. overall................... **$58**

Courtesy of Jeffrey S. Evans & Associates

Blown Twist wide-waist sugar shaker, blue opalescent, period lid, fourth quarter 19th century, base edge with short crack, lid with light corrosion, 4-5/8" h. overall. **$58**

Courtesy of Jeffrey S. Evans & Associates

Chrysanthemum Swirl sugar shaker, cranberry opalescent, period lid, Northwood Glass Co./Buckeye Glass Co., circa 1890, undamaged, one base rib with manufacturing roughness, as made, 4-3/4" h. overall. **$184**

Courtesy of Jeffrey S. Evans & Associates

Chrysanthemum Swirl speckled sugar shaker, blue with opal frit, period lid, circa 1890, undamaged, lid with minor wear to finish, 4-5/8" h. overall. ...**$173**

Courtesy of Jeffrey S. Evans & Associates

◄ Chrysanthemum Swirl speckled syrup pitcher, cranberry with opal frit, satin finish, frosted colorless applied handle, period lid, Northwood Glass Co./Buckeye Glass Co., fourth quarter 19th century, very good condition overall, crack to upper handle terminal, 6-3/4" h. overall. **$81**

Courtesy of Jeffrey S. Evans & Associates

▲ Coinspot nine-panel mold sugar shakers, cranberry, colorless, and blue opalescent, each with period lid, circa 1894, blue and colorless examples undamaged, cranberry example with damage to base, lids undamaged, colorless opalescent example with normal flakes/roughness to rim, 4-5/8" h. overall. **$104**

Courtesy of Jeffrey S. Evans & Associates

Daisy and Fern/Parian Swirl miniature lamp shade, colorless opalescent, ball form, late 19th century, shallow chips to outer edge of one rim, 2-1/2" h., 2" fitter. **$173**

Courtesy of Jeffrey S. Evans & Associates

Daisy and Fern/Northwood Swirl mold sugar shaker, cranberry opalescent, period lid, circa 1894, undamaged, 4-3/8" h. overall. **$138**

Courtesy of Jeffrey S. Evans & Associates

Diamond Spearhead syrup pitcher, canary/vaseline (uranium) opalescent, period lid, Northwood Glass Co./ National Glass Co, circa 1902, crack to handle at upper terminal, minor flake and normal light wear/roughness to pattern high points, lid loose, 5-5/8" h. **$92**

Courtesy of Jeffrey S. Evans & Associates

Northwood No. 333/Leaf Mold pitcher and tumbler, canary/vaseline (uranium) with cranberry and opal spatter, water pitcher with applied matching handle and tumbler, pattern introduced in 1891, undamaged, pitcher 8" h., tumbler 4" h. **$748**

Courtesy of Jeffrey S. Evans & Associates

Northwood No. 263/Leaf Umbrella sugar shaker, cased cranberry and opal spatter, period lid, pattern introduced 1889, glass undamaged, lid with light denting, 4-5/8" h. overall. **$196**

Courtesy of Jeffrey S. Evans & Associates

Opaline Brocade/Spanish Lace wide-waist sugar shaker, cranberry opalescent, period lid, fourth quarter 19th century, undamaged, lid with minor imperfections, 4-1/2" h. overall. **$259**

Courtesy of Jeffrey S. Evans & Associates

Opaline Brocade/Spanish Lace wide-waist sugar shaker, vaseline (uranium) opalescent, period lid, fourth quarter 19th century, excellent condition, edge of base with flake, rim with normal flakes/roughness, as made, lid with minor wear to finish, 4-1/2" h. overall. **$150**

Courtesy of Jeffrey S. Evans & Associates

Opaline Brocade/Spanish Lace tumbler, bittersweet opalescent, tapered form, circa 1899, very good condition overall, two minor flakes to exterior of rim and small chip, 4-1/4" h. **$196**

Courtesy of Jeffrey S. Evans & Associates

Opaline Brocade/Spanish Lace tumbler, cranberry opalescent, straight-sided form, factory polished rim, circa 1899, excellent condition overall, minor flake to exterior of rim and mold roughness to rim, 3-5/8" h. **$69**

Courtesy of Jeffrey S. Evans & Associates

Opaline Brocade/Spanish Lace vase, cranberry opalescent, light melon-form body with vine flowing to left and slightly flared rim, circa 1899, very good condition overall, rim with small bruise, minor flake, and mold roughness, 4-1/4" h. **$207**

Courtesy of Jeffrey S. Evans & Associates

Poinsettia sugar shaker, blue opalescent, period lid, fourth quarter 19th century, excellent condition overall, normal flakes/roughness to rim, probably as made, hidden by lid, lid with light denting, 5" h. overall... **$288**

Courtesy of Jeffrey S. Evans & Associates

Poinsettia sugar shaker, colorless opalescent, period lid, fourth quarter 19th century, very good condition overall, normal flakes/roughness to rim and open bubble to body, as made, light interior residue and minor flake under base, lid with light splitting, 5" h. overall.... **$92**

Courtesy of Jeffrey S. Evans & Associates

Poinsettia tumbler, green opalescent, factory polished rim, circa 1903, undamaged, 4" h. **$127**

Courtesy of Jeffrey S. Evans & Associates

Poinsettia water pitcher, green opalescent, ringed bulbous-base tankard form on low foot with plain rim and applied handle, circa 1902, undamaged, 12-3/4" h. overall...**$316**

Courtesy of Jeffrey S. Evans & Associates

Poinsettia water pitcher, blue opalescent, tankard form on low foot with plain rim and applied reeded handle with pressed fan design to upper terminal, circa 1902, undamaged, 13-1/4" h. overall........**$207**

Courtesy of Jeffrey S. Evans & Associates

◄ Poinsettia water pitcher, colorless opalescent, ringed bulbous-base tankard form on low foot with plain rim and applied handle, circa 1902, undamaged, 13" h. **$127**

Courtesy of Jeffrey S. Evans & Associates

Quilted Phlox sugar shaker, cased light green, period lid, fourth quarter 19th century, excellent condition overall with moderate chip to rim, hidden by lid, lid with some splitting, 4-1/4" h. overall. **$69**

Courtesy of Jeffrey S. Evans & Associates

GLASS

opalescent glass

OPALESCENT GLASS IS one of the most popular areas of glass collecting. The opalescent effect was attained by adding bone ash chemicals to areas of an item while still hot and refiring the object at tremendous heat. Both pressed and mold-blown patterns are available to collectors. *Opalescent Glass from A to Z* by the late William Heacock is the definitive reference book for collectors. See more opalescent glass in the "Cranberry Glass" section.

Coinspot bitters/barber's bottle, blue opalescent, polished pontil mark, late 19th/early 20th century, 7" h.............. **$431**

Courtesy of Jeffrey S. Evans & Associates

Coral Reef bitters/barber's bottle, sapphire/blue opalescent, square form, later pour spout, polished pontil mark, Hobbs, Brockunier & Co./Beaumont Glass Co., circa 1890s, bottle 8-3/8" h., 2-1/2" sq........................... **$207**

Courtesy of Jeffrey S. Evans & Associates

Coral Reef bitters/barber's bottle, sapphire/blue opalescent, conical tapered form, polished pontil mark, Hobbs, Brockunier & Co./ Beaumont Glass Co., circa 1890s, 6-3/4" h., 3-3/4" dia. overall. **$219**

Courtesy of Jeffrey S. Evans & Associates

Coral Reef bitters/barber's bottle, crystal/colorless opalescent, tall tapered form, polished pontil mark, Hobbs, Brockunier & Co./Beaumont Glass Co., circa 1890s, 9-1/4" h., 2-5/8" dia. **$259**

Courtesy of Jeffrey S. Evans & Associates

Drapery bitters/barber's bottle, blue opalescent, pinched waist form, late 19th/early 20th century, 7" h. **$1,093**

Courtesy of Jeffrey S. Evans & Associates

Fern bitters/barber's bottle, blue opalescent, square form, West Virginia Glass Co. or Beaumont Glass Co., circa 1894, 8-1/4" h. overall, 2-1/2" sq. **$316**

Courtesy of Jeffrey S. Evans & Associates

Fern bitters/barber's bottle, blue opalescent, six-lobe melon rib form, polished pontil mark, West Virginia Glass Co. or Beaumont Glass Co., circa 1894, 7" h. **$374**

Courtesy of Jeffrey S. Evans & Associates

Polka Dot bitters/barber's bottle, blue opalescent, six-lobe melon rib form, later spout, probably West Virginia Glass Co. or Northwood Glass Co., circa 1894, 7" h. **$374**

Courtesy of Jeffrey S. Evans & Associates

Chrysanthemum Swirl covered butter dish, blue opalescent, circular form, cover with applied blue ball-form finial, Northwood Glass Co./Buckeye Glass Co., circa 1890, 5-1/4" h. overall, base 6" dia. overall. **$196**

Courtesy of Jeffrey S. Evans & Associates

Ribbed Opal Lattice covered butter dish, blue opalescent, blue finial, factory polished rims, maker unverified, possibly Northwood Glass Co., circa 1888, 4-3/8" h. overall, 5-1/2" dia......... **$250**

Courtesy of Jeffrey S. Evans & Associates

Crocus flower arranger, turquoise opalescent, factory polished rim, fitted with metal cover with floral decoration, possibly Northwood Glass Co. or Dugan, late 19th/early 20th century, 4" h. overall............ **$345**

Courtesy of Jeffrey S. Evans & Associates

Big Windows sugar shaker, blue opalescent, period lid, Buckeye Glass Co., fourth quarter 19th century, 4-7/8" h..,............ **$138**

Courtesy of Jeffrey S. Evans & Associates

Bubble Lattice/Buckeye's sugar shaker, blue opalescent, period lid, Buckeye Glass Co., circa 1889, 5-1/8" h. **$259**

Courtesy of Jeffrey S. Evans & Associates

Daffodil sugar shaker, colorless opalescent, period lid, H. Northwood and Co., circa 1903, 5" h. **$161**

Courtesy of Jeffrey S. Evans & Associates

Daisy and Fern/Apple Blossom mold sugar shaker, blue opalescent, period lid, Northwood Glass Co., circa 1895, 4-3/8" h. **$184**

Courtesy of Jeffrey S. Evans & Associates

Ribbed sugar shaker, pink opalescent with polychrome and gilt decoration, period lid, late 19th/early 20th century, 5-1/2" h. **230**

Courtesy of Jeffrey S. Evans & Associates

Stripe sugar shaker, blue opalescent, period lid, possibly Buckeye Glass Co., fourth quarter 19th century, 5" h. overall. **$288**

Courtesy of Jeffrey S. Evans & Associates

Stripe/Wide Nickel mold sugar shaker, blue opalescent, period lid, Nickel Plate Glass Co., fourth quarter 19th century, 4" h. overall. **$316**

Courtesy of Jeffrey S. Evans & Associates

Opaline Brocade/Spanish Lace ball-shape mold syrup pitcher, blue opalescent, applied blue reeded handle, period lid, late 19th/early 20th century, 5-7/8" h. **$196**

Courtesy of Jeffrey S. Evans & Associates

Daffodil tumbler, blue opalescent, factory polished rim, Northwood Glass Co., circa 1903, 4" h. **$288**

Courtesy of Jeffrey S. Evans & Associates

Criss-Cross toothpick holder, colorless opalescent, factory polished rim, Consolidated Lamp & Glass Co., circa 1894, 2-1/4" h.......... **$104**

Courtesy of Jeffrey S. Evans & Associates

Drapery/No. 528 Venetian tumbler, blue opalescent, factory polished rim, Buckeye Glass Co., circa 1888, 3-7/8" h. **$288**

Courtesy of Jeffrey S. Evans & Associates

Daisy and Fern tumblers, blue and colorless opalescent, factory polished rims, Northwood Glass Co., colorless example possibly L. G. Wright, circa 1895, 3-3/4" h. **$46**

Courtesy of Jeffrey S. Evans & Associates

▶ Scottish Moor tumbler, bittersweet opalescent with remnants of gilt decoration outlining pattern, factory polished rim, circa 1890, 3-3/4" h....**$633**

Courtesy of Jeffrey S. Evans & Associates

Arabian Nights water pitcher, colorless opalescent, crimped-triangular rim, applied colorless handle with pressed-fan design at upper terminal, possibly Beaumont Glass Co./Northwood Glass Co., circa 1895, 9" h. overall. **$546**

Courtesy of Jeffrey S. Evans & Associates

Big Windows/Honeycomb water pitcher, blue opalescent, star-crimped rim, applied blue handle with pressed-fan design to upper terminal, late 19th/early 20th century, 8-1/2" h. overall. **$633**

Courtesy of Jeffrey S. Evans & Associates

Christmas Snowflake ribbed water pitcher, colorless opalescent, applied colorless handle with pressed-leaf design to upper terminal, Northwood Glass Co./Dugan Glass Co., circa 1895, 8-7/8" h. overall. **$546**

Courtesy of Jeffrey S. Evans & Associates

Coinspot water pitcher, blue opalescent, tooled ruffled rim, applied blue handle, possibly Jefferson Glass Co. or Northwood Glass Co., late 19th/early 20th century, 10-3/4" h. overall. ...**$690**

Courtesy of Jeffrey S. Evans & Associates

Daffodil water pitcher, blue opalescent, ball form with circular crimped rim, applied blue handle, Northwood Glass Co., circa 1903, 9-1/2" h. overall...**$920**

Courtesy of Jeffrey S. Evans & Associates

Daffodil tankard water pitcher, green opalescent, applied green handle, Northwood Glass Co., circa 1903, 12" h. overall.................................. **$1,035**

Courtesy of Jeffrey S. Evans & Associates

top lot

Opaline Brocade/Spanish Lace water pitcher, vaseline (uranium) opalescent, shouldered-form with three-section crimped and ruffled rim, applied vaseline (uranium) reeded handle, National Glass Co., circa 1899, 9-3/4" h. overall. $1,265

GLASS

pairpoint

ORIGINALLY ORGANIZED IN New Bedford, Massachusetts, in 1880 as the Pairpoint Manufacturing Co. on land adjacent to the famed Mt. Washington Glass Co., Pairpoint first manufactured silver and plated wares. In 1894, the two famous factories merged as the Pairpoint Corp. and enjoyed great success for more than 40 years. The company was sold in 1939 to a group of local businessmen and eventually bought out by one of the group, who turned the management over to Robert M. Gundersen. Subsequently, it operated as the Gundersen Glass Works until 1952 when, after Gundersen's death, the name was changed to Gundersen-Pairpoint. The factory closed in 1956. Subsequently, Robert Bryden took charge of this glassworks, at first producing glass for Pairpoint abroad and eventually, in 1970, beginning glass production in Sagamore, Massachusetts. Today the Pairpoint Crystal Glass Co. is owned by Robert and June Bancroft. They continue to manufacture fine quality blown and pressed glass.

Controlled-bubble bowl, deep amethyst, shape B-369, applied foot and controlled-bubble stem, polished pontil mark, first half 20th century, 6-1/4" h., 12" dia. **$138**

Courtesy of Jeffrey S. Evans & Associates

Colias cut and engraved three-piece console set, colorless with frosted finish to pattern, footed circular-form center bowl with flared rim and two baluster-form candlesticks, spider webs, butterflies, flowers, and foliage pattern, first half 20th century, undamaged, one candlestick with some interior residue, candlestick 10-5/8" h., center bowl 5-1/2" h., 12" dia. rim................ **$259**

Courtesy of Jeffrey S. Evans & Associates

Two No. 632 engraved grape pattern decanters, 1915-1937, one Auroria, the other green, each unmarked, 8-1/2" h. **$338**

Courtesy of Skinner, Inc.; www.skinnerinc.com

Engraved centerpiece bowl, Auroria, shape A-106 with engraved fruits, nuts, and berries pattern, polished pontil mark, 15-1/8" dia. **$69**

Courtesy of Jeffrey S. Evans & Associates

Candlesticks with cut and etched floral sprays surrounding bulbous hollow blown stem, candle cup with faceted side and diamond cut rolled lip, cut starburst on underside of foot, unsigned, very good to excellent condition, 7" h. **$356**

Courtesy of James D. Julia Auctioneers, Fairfield, Maine, www.jamesdjulia.com

No. 1624 candlesticks engraved in Waterford pattern, 1915-1920, each with removable colorless bobeche, trimmed and threaded in Chrysopos, unmarked, 10" h.................**$615**

Courtesy of Skinner, Inc.; www.skinnerinc.com

Amethyst engraved Waterford pattern grape juice bowl, 1915-1920, unmarked, 8-5/8" h. **$277**

Courtesy of Skinner, Inc.; www.skinnerinc.com

Amber engraved grape pattern covered glass vase, late 19th/ early 20th century, trumpet-form with circular foot, etched grapevines throughout, unmarked, 14" h. to cover. **$154**

Courtesy of Skinner, Inc.; www.skinnerinc.com

Amethyst engraved grape pattern covered glass vase, late 19th/ early 20th century, trumpet-form with circular foot, etched grapevines throughout, unmarked, 14-1/2" h. to cover............. **$154**

Courtesy of Skinner, Inc., www.skinnerinc.com

Four toothpick holders in Burmese and Peachblow, one barrel-form and three hat-form examples, one with dragonfly and floral polychrome decoration, each with rough pontil mark, circa 1890s, 2" to 2-1/4" h. **$161**

Courtesy of Jeffrey S. Evans & Associates

Three toothpick holders, opal with painted decoration, two with buffalo and one with pointer, metal rim mounting, circa 1895, 2-1/4" h.............................**$288**

Courtesy of Jeffrey S. Evans & Associates

GLASS

pattern glass

THOUGH IT HAS never been ascertained whether glass was first pressed in the United States or abroad, the development of the glass-pressing machine revolutionized the glass industry in the United States, and this country receives the credit for improving the method to make this process feasible. The first wares pressed were probably small flat plates of the type now referred to as "lacy," the intricacy of the design concealing flaws.

In 1827, both the New England Glass Co., Cambridge, Massachusetts, and Bakewell & Co., Pittsburgh, took out patents for pressing glass furniture knobs; soon other pieces followed. This early pressed glass contained red lead, which made it clear and resonant when tapped (flint). Made primarily in clear, it is rarer in blue, amethyst, olive green, and yellow.

By the 1840s, early simple patterns such as Ashburton, Argus, and Excelsior appeared. Ribbed Bellflower seems to have been one of the earliest patterns to have had complete sets. By the 1860s, a wide range of patterns was available.

In 1864, William Leighton of Hobbs, Brockunier & Co., Wheeling, West Virginia, developed a formula for "soda lime" glass that did not require the expensive red lead for clarity. Although "soda lime" glass did not have the brilliance of the earlier flint glass, the formula came into widespread use because glass could be produced cheaply.

Ashburton large wine/claret, teal green, low-knop stem, polished pontil mark, Boston & Sandwich Glass Co., New England Glass Co., and probably others, third quarter 19th century, undamaged, 4-1/2" h., 2-1/4" dia. rim, 2-3/8" dia. foot. **$1,035**
Courtesy of Jeffrey S. Evans & Associates

Pressed Basket match/toothpick holder, translucent yellow-green, slightly tapered form with rope-edge rim and concave base with factory polished table ring, Boston & Sandwich Glass Co. and probably others, 1850-1870, minor inner-rim flake, 2" h., 2" dia. rim. **$115**

Courtesy of Jeffrey S. Evans & Associates

OL-15 Beaded Strawberry Diamond oval pressed open salt, purple-blue, high and low point rim, rare, Boston & Sandwich Glass Co., 1830-1850, loss of one low point and another tipped, 1-3/4" h. x 2-1/4" x 3-1/2". ...**$518**

Courtesy of Jeffrey S. Evans & Associates

▶ Bird and Strawberry seven-piece water set, colorless, pitcher and six tumblers, early 20th century, undamaged, 8-3/8" and 4-3/8" h. overall. **$374**

Courtesy of Jeffrey S. Evans & Associates

Pressed Circle and Ellipse vase, fiery opalescent to opaque white, small size, short conical bowl with gauffered six-petal rim, raised on hexagonal knop stem and flared base, single-piece construction, factory polished lower mold lines and under base to level, New England, 1850-1870, 7-1/8" h., 3-1/2" dia. overall rim, 3-3/4" dia. overall foot........**$345**

Courtesy of Jeffrey S. Evans & Associates

CN-1B Crown pressed open salt, fiery opalescent, on four scroll feet, rare, Boston & Sandwich Glass Co., 1830-1845, rim with minor flake to top edge and flake to inner rim, light mold roughness to upper corners and feet, 2-1/8" h. x 1-7/8" x 3-1/8"..................**$316**

Courtesy of Jeffrey S. Evans & Associates

Hobbs No. 101 Daisy and Button six-bottle caster set, vaseline (uranium), three vinegar/oil bottles with original stoppers, two shakers, and one mustard, each with cut-and-shut scar under base, fitted in quadruple-plate rotating stand marked for Mermod Jaccard & Co. and numbered 2173, fourth quarter 19th century, undamaged, 18" h. overall, bottles 5-1/2" to 8" h. overall. **$489**

Courtesy of Jeffrey S. Evans & Associates

EE-3B Eagle and Shield pressed open salt, light opalescent, on four feet, rare, Boston & Sandwich Glass Co., 1830-1845, shallow chip to interior of one foot and flake to interior of another, 2-1/8" h. x 2" x 3-1/4". **$316**

Courtesy of Jeffrey S. Evans & Associates

Pressed Diamond variant pickle caster, vaseline (uranium), polished table ring, fitted in unmarked quadruple-plate stand, fourth quarter 19th century, flake to base of jar, 11-3/4" h. overall.............. **$127**

Courtesy of Jeffrey S. Evans & Associates

Forget-Me-Not sugar shaker, opaque light to medium pink, period lid, Challinor, Taylor & Co., pattern introduced 1885, undamaged, 4" h. overall. **$81**

Courtesy of Jeffrey S. Evans & Associates

Forget-Me-Not syrup pitcher, opaque chartreuse, applied handle, period lid, Challinor, Taylor. & Co., pattern introduced 1885, 5-1/4" h. overall, undamaged............. **$184**

Courtesy of Jeffrey S. Evans & Associates

GA-4 variant Gothic Arch and Heart pressed open salt, opalescent medium blue, even scallop rim, on four bucket feet, base like GA-4a, rare, possibly Boston & Sandwich Glass Co., 1835-1845, large interior rim chip, shallow chip to outer rim, shallow chip under base, 1-3/4" h. x 2" x 2-3/4"...............**$184**

Courtesy of Jeffrey S. Evans & Associates

Greentown No. 450/Holly amber tumbler, Golden Agate, plain rim, Indiana Tumbler & Goblet Co., circa 1903, base edge with two flakes and area of moderate mold roughness, 3-7/8" h. **$184**

Courtesy of Jeffrey S. Evans & Associates

Greentown No. 450/Holly amber salt and pepper shakers, Golden Agate, with matching period lids, Indiana Tumbler & Goblet Co., circa 1903, very good condition overall, 3-1/8" h. overall.................................... **$748**

Courtesy of Jeffrey S. Evans & Associates

Gutatte covered sugar bowl, creamer, and water pitcher, opal-cased pink, glossy finish, Consolidated Glass Co., fourth quarter 19th century, sugar cover with significant damage, remainder undamaged, 4-3/4" to 9-1/4" h. overall. **$138**

Courtesy of Jeffrey S. Evans & Associates

Inverted Fan and Feather/Dugan No. 607 tumbler and punch cup, pink slag, Dugan Glass Co., circa 1901, cup undamaged, tumbler with chip off base edge, 2-1/4" and 3-7/8" h. **$127**

Courtesy of Jeffrey S. Evans & Associates

Inverted Fern and Feather salt and pepper shakers, opaque pink slag, non-matching period lids, Northwood Glass Co., fourth quarter 19th century, undamaged, 3" h. overall. **$403**

Courtesy of Jeffrey S. Evans & Associates

Horn of Plenty spoon holder/spill, alabaster/clambroth, polished pontil mark, Boston & Sandwich Glass Co. and others, 1850-1870, undamaged, no interior wear, 4-1/2" h., 3-1/2" dia. **$230**

Courtesy of Jeffrey S. Evans & Associates

Indiana No. 77 King's Crown table articles, colorless with cranberry stain, three compotes (one covered), cake stand, creamer, and sugar bowl, mid-20th century, compote cover with chip, remainder undamaged, 3" to 7-1/2" h. overall. .. **$69**

Courtesy of Jeffrey S. Evans & Associates

Klondike/Amberette amber-stained goblet, colorless with satin panels, Dalzell, Gilmore & Leighton Co., circa 1898, undamaged, 6-1/4" h. overall... **$575**

Courtesy of Jeffrey S. Evans & Associates

Pressed Lacy glass cup plates, American, early 19th century, one blue centered with bust of Henry Clay facing left (Lee-Rose 565-B), one cobalt blue centered with ship Cadmus (Lee-Rose 610A), one amber with radiating star motifs (Lee-Rose 323), and one amethyst with daisy with bull's-eye center (Lee-Rose 522), rim chips, 3-1/4" to 3-5/8" dia. **$431**

Courtesy of Skinner, Inc.; www.skinnerinc.com

Pressed Lacy Pointed Oval toy tumbler, electric blue, plain circular base with faint pontil mark, Boston & Sandwich Glass Co., 1830-1850, flake under base, probably as made, 1-3/4" h., 1-5/8" dia. rim. **$138**

Courtesy of Jeffrey S. Evans & Associates

Pressed Lacy Pointed Oval toy tumblers, green and amethyst, each with plain circular base and faint pontil mark, Boston & Sandwich Glass Co., 1830-1850, green with base chip, other with polished base, 1-3/4" h., 1-5/8" dia. rim. **$184**

Courtesy of Jeffrey S. Evans & Associates

No. 263 Leaf umbrella toothpick holder, cranberry with opal spatter, Northwood Glass Co., pattern introduced 1889, excellent condition overall, 2-1/2" h. **$173**

Courtesy of Jeffrey S. Evans & Associates

No. 333 Leaf mold tumbler, ruby, satin finish, Northwood Glass Co., pattern introduced in 1891, undamaged, 3-7/8" h. **$489**

Courtesy of Jeffrey S. Evans & Associates

No. 333 Leaf mold cruet, canary/vaseline (uranium) with cranberry and opal spatter, with appropriate stopper, Northwood Glass Co., pattern introduced in 1891, undamaged with wear to pattern high points, 6-1/2" h. **$431**

Courtesy of Jeffrey S. Evans & Associates

▶ No. 333 Leaf mold salt shaker, ruby, with period lid, Northwood Glass Co., pattern introduced in 1891, undamaged with minor wear to pattern high points, 2-1/2" h. overall. **$403**

Courtesy of Jeffrey S. Evans & Associates

top lot !

Pressed Loop/Leaf stand lamps, amethyst, each dome-top six-loop font with short disc-like extension, raised on compressed knop and hexagonal ringed standard and base with slight step, wafer construction, pewter fine-line collars and double-tube whale oil burners, reserve, New England, possibly Patrick Slane's American Glass Co., South Boston or Boston & Sandwich Glass Co., 1840-1860, some flakes, 9-1/2" h. to top of collars, 4-1/2" dia. base. $4,600

No. 333 Leaf mold sugar shaker, cased canary/vaseline (uranium) with cranberry and opal spatter, satin finish, period lid, Northwood Glass Co., pattern introduced in 1891, undamaged, 3-1/2" h. overall....................**$259**

Courtesy of Jeffrey S. Evans & Associates

No. 333 Leaf mold sugar shaker, canary/vaseline (uranium) with cranberry and opal spatter, with period lid, Northwood Glass Co., pattern introduced in 1891, undamaged, 3-5/8" h. overall. ...**$316**

Courtesy of Jeffrey S. Evans & Associates

No. 333 Leaf mold salt shaker, ruby, satin finish, with appropriate lid, Northwood Glass Co., pattern introduced in 1891, undamaged with minor wear to pattern high points, 2-5/8" h. overall. **$127**

Courtesy of Jeffrey S. Evans & Associates

No. 333 Leaf mold salt and pepper shakers, canary/vaseline (uranium) with cranberry and opal spatter, with period lids, Northwood Glass Co., pattern introduced in 1891, undamaged, minor wear/roughness to pattern high points, 2-5/8" h. overall. **$150**

Courtesy of Jeffrey S. Evans & Associates

No. 339 Leaf and Flower syrup pitcher, colorless with amber stain, colorless applied handle, period lid, Hobbs, Brockunier & Co., fourth quarter 19th century, excellent condition overall, 6-3/4" h. overall. **$196**

Courtesy of Jeffrey S. Evans & Associates

Pressed Loop vases in purple-blue, one with traces of gilt decoration, large size version, each with deep conical bowl with gauffered six-petal rim, raised on hexagonal double-knop stem and double-step base, no factory polishing to mold lines or under bases, single-piece construction, New England, 1850-1870, 10-1/2" h., minute flake to each base, 4-1/4" rim dia. overall, 4-5/8" base dia. overall. **$1,265**

Courtesy of Jeffrey S. Evans & Associates

Pressed Loop/Leaf compote/dish on foot, yellow (uranium), deep nine-loop bowl with conforming rim and unpatterned base, raised on hexagonal baluster-form standard stepped to circular panel-top foot, wafer construction, Boston & Sandwich Glass Co. and possibly others, 1845-1860, partially polished shallow chip to top edge of one rim scallop, normal light wear to bowl interior, 7-1/2" h., 10-3/8" dia. rim, 5-1/4" dia. foot. **$1,265**

Courtesy of Jeffrey S. Evans & Associates

MV-1 Mount Vernon pressed open salt, gray-blue, scallop and point rim, rare, Boston & Sandwich Glass Co., Mount Vernon or Saratoga Glass Co., 1835-1850, flaking/mold roughness, 1-3/4" h. x 2-1/8" x 2-7/8"..........**$546**

Courtesy of Jeffrey S. Evans & Associates

NE-1 variant New England marked pressed open salt, fiery opalescent, embossed under base, scallop and point rim, two sides and one end rim lacking decorative elements, other end with lower edge of elements, probably rare, New England Glass Co., 1835-1850, chip to under edge of one upper corner, minor mold roughness, 1-3/4" h. x 2-1/8" x 3". **$161**

Courtesy of Jeffrey S. Evans & Associates

Pigs in Corn right bent husk goblet, colorless, fourth quarter 19th century, flake to rim and flake to stem, 6" h............. **$259**

Courtesy of Jeffrey S. Evans & Associates

Scroll 13-piece water set, opaque blue, tankard-form pitcher and 12 tumblers, fourth quarter 20th century, excellent condition overall, 3-3/4" to 12-5/8" h. overall. **$115**

Courtesy of Jeffrey S. Evans & Associates

SL-1 Shell pressed open salt, red amethyst, shaped rim, rare, possibly Boston & Sandwich Glass Co., 1835-1850, excellent condition, 1-5/8" h. x 2" x 3"............................... **$489**

Courtesy of Jeffrey S. Evans & Associates

◀ SL-16 Shell and Star pressed open salt, unlisted cobalt blue, diamond point base, on four scroll feet, probably rare, possibly Boston & Sandwich Glass Co., 1830-1850, minute flake to one corner and light flaking/mold roughness to feet interior, 1-5/8" h. x 2" x 3-1/8".... **$1,035**

Courtesy of Jeffrey S. Evans & Associates

SD-7 Strawberry Diamond pressed open salt, medium yellow amber, scallop and point rim, rare, Boston & Sandwich Glass Co., 1827-1840, excellent condition, 2" h. x 2-1/8" x 2-7/8"................. **$489**

Courtesy of Jeffrey S. Evans & Associates

Squirrel goblet, colorless, standard version with flare and step at base of stem, fourth quarter 19th century, undamaged, 5-7/8" h. **$460**

Courtesy of Jeffrey S. Evans & Associates

Squirrel water pitcher, colorless, with plain rim and two squirrels on each side, Dalzell, Gilmore & Leighton Co., fourth quarter 19th century, undamaged, 9-1/4" h. overall. **$288**

Courtesy of Jeffrey S. Evans & Associates

▲ Victoria pattern compote, Pittsburgh, third quarter, 19th century, clear flint pressed glass, chipped edges of lid and chips to scalloped edge of compote, 15-1/2" h., 10" lid dia............ **$31**

Courtesy of Cowan's Auctions, Inc.

◀ SD-7 Strawberry Diamond pressed open salt, cobalt blue, scallop and point rim, scarce, Boston & Sandwich Glass Co., 1827-1840, very good condition, 2" h. x 2-1/8" x 2-7/8"............................... **$184**

Courtesy of Jeffrey S. Evans & Associates

GLASS

peach blow

SEVERAL TYPES OF glass lumped together by collectors as Peach Blow were produced by half a dozen glasshouses. Hobbs, Brockunier & Co., Wheeling, West Virginia, made Peach Blow as a plated ware that shaded from red at the top to yellow at the bottom and is referred to as Wheeling Peach Blow. Mt. Washington Glass Works produced a homogeneous Peach Blow shading from rose at the top to pale blue in the lower portion. The New England Glass Works' Peach Blow, called Wild Rose, shaded from rose at the top to white. Gundersen-Pairpoint Co. also reproduced some of the Mt. Washington Peach Blow in the early 1950s, and some glass of a somewhat similar type was made by Steuben Glass Works, Thomas Webb & Sons, and Stevens & Williams of England. New England Peach Blow is one-layered glass and the English is two-layered.

Another single-layered shaded art glass was produced early in the 20th century by New Martinsville Glass Mfg. Co. Originally called "Muranese," collectors today refer to it as New Martinsville Peach Blow.

◄ Tri-corner rim toothpick holder, plush finish, large polished pontil mark, possibly Mt. Washington Glass Co., circa 1886, 2-3/8" h. overall.......**$219**

Courtesy of Jeffrey S. Evans & Associates

Two New England Peach Blow toothpick holders, glossy finish, one with remnants of Agata decoration, each with square rim and polished pontil mark, New England Glass Co., circa 1888, 2-1/4" h. **$219**

Courtesy of Jeffrey S. Evans & Associates

New England Peach Blow lily vase, glossy finish, tri-corner rim, on applied foot with rough pontil mark, New England Glass Co., circa 1886, 6-1/4" h. **$150**

Courtesy of Jeffrey S. Evans & Associates

Wheeling Peach Blow double-gourd vase shading from deep fuchsia at top to amber at bottom with even color separation, unsigned, Hobbs, Brockunier & Co., very good to excellent condition, 7" h.......**$356**

Courtesy of James D. Julia Auctioneers, Fairfield, Maine, www.jamesdjulia.com

GLASS

phoenix glass

THE PHOENIX GLASS Co., Beaver, Pennsylvania, was established in 1880. Known primarily for commercial glassware, the firm also produced a molded, sculptured, cameo-type line from the 1930s until the 1950s.

Coinspot footed toothpick holder, blue opalescent, factory polished rim, circa 1883-1888, 2-3/4" h. $207
Courtesy of Jeffrey S. Evans & Associates

Large Diamond-Optic ewer, bittersweet opalescent, applied foot and colorless handle with polished lower terminal, circa 1883-1888, 13-3/4" h. overall. $546

Courtesy of Jeffrey S. Evans & Associates

Diamond-Optic punch cup, bittersweet opalescent with floral polychrome decoration, factory polished rim, applied colorless handle, circa 1883-1888, 2-7/8" h...$184
Courtesy of Jeffrey S. Evans & Associates

Diamond-Optic water pitcher, ruby die-away to opal sensitive crystal with opalescent diamond pattern, shoulder mold, applied colorless handle, polished pontil mark, circa 1883-1888, 8-1/4" h. **$460**

Courtesy of Jeffrey S. Evans & Associates

Diamond-Optic water pitcher, ruby die-away to opal sensitive crystal, shoulder mold with circular-form plain rim, colorless applied handle, polished pontil mark, circa 1883-1900, excellent condition with high-point wear, 8-1/8" h. overall. **$460**

Courtesy of Jeffrey S. Evans & Associates

Diamond-Optic water pitcher, ruby die-away to opal sensitive crystal, shoulder mold with circular-form plain rim, colorless applied handle, polished pontil mark, circa 1883-1900, body of upper terminal with V-shaped crack and light wear to body, 8-3/4" h. overall.....................**$127**

Courtesy of Jeffrey S. Evans & Associates

Water bottle and tumble-up, bottle in Diamond-Optic pattern and tumble-up in Spot-Optic pattern, cranberry die-away to colorless with opalescent pattern, each with factory polished rims, probably Phoenix Glass Co., circa 1883-1888, 7" h. **$345**

Courtesy of Jeffrey S. Evans & Associates

▶ Diamond-Optic Craquelle water pitcher, blue opalescent, ball-form with circular plain rim, applied translucent blue reeded handle, polished pontil mark, circa 1883-1888, 7-7/8" h. **$374**

Courtesy of Jeffrey S. Evans & Associates

Diamond-Optic Craquelle water pitcher, cranberry opalescent, ball-form with circular plain rim, applied colorless reeded handle, polished pontil mark, circa 1883-1888, 7-1/4" h...........**$374**

Courtesy of Jeffrey S. Evans & Associates

Wide stripe Diamond Quilted Optic bitters/barber bottle, cased cranberry with opal vertical stripes, applied colorless lip, polished pontil mark, probably Phoenix Glass Co., fourth quarter 19th century, 7-1/4" h., 3-1/2" dia. overall. **$288**

Courtesy of Jeffrey S. Evans & Associates

Drape footed creamer, cranberry opalescent with five applied colorless polished feet and reeded handle, polished pontil mark, circa 1883-1888, 4-3/4" h. overall.................**$403**

Courtesy of Jeffrey S. Evans & Associates

Drape cruet, Amberina with amber applied handle and facet-cut stopper, polished pontil mark, fourth quarter 19th century, cruet with annealing crack to upper handle terminal, stopper with chip to extension, 6-1/8" h. overall. **$127**

Courtesy of Jeffrey S. Evans & Associates

Drape pitcher, opal-cased Rubina, ball shape plain rim and applied colorless reeded handle, polished pontil mark, fourth quarter 19th century, undamaged, 5-1/4" h. **$115**

Courtesy of Jeffrey S. Evans & Associates

Drape-Optic punch cup, cranberry opalescent, factory polished rim, applied colorless reeded handle, probably Phoenix Glass Co., circa 1883-1888, 3" h. **$115**

Courtesy of Jeffrey S. Evans & Associates

Drape tumbler, cranberry opalescent, factory polished rim, circa 1883-1888, 3-5/8" h. **$207**

Courtesy of Jeffrey S. Evans & Associates

Drape vase, reverse Amberina, crimped and ruffled top, drawn foot with polished pontil mark, fourth quarter 19th century, undamaged, 7-3/4" h. overall, 3-1/2" dia. base. **$104**

Courtesy of Jeffrey S. Evans & Associates

◀ Drape water pitcher, cranberry opalescent, bulbous form, square rim, applied colorless reeded handle and polished pontil mark, circa 1883-1888, 8-1/4" h. overall. **$489**

Courtesy of Jeffrey S. Evans & Associates

Honeycomb Optic pitcher, amber opalescent, circular rim, applied amber reeded handle, polished pontil mark, circa 1883-1888, 7-1/4" h................................**$431**

Courtesy of Jeffrey S. Evans & Associates

Honeycomb Optic water pitcher, ruby cased over opal glass, triangular-form crimped rim, applied amber reeded handle, polished pontil mark, circa 1883-1888, 8-1/4" h. overall. **$575**

Courtesy of Jeffrey S. Evans & Associates

▲ Lattice punch cup, cranberry opalescent, factory polished rim, applied colorless reeded handle, probably Phoenix Glass Co., circa 1883-1888, 2-3/4" h. **$138**

Courtesy of Jeffrey S. Evans & Associates

◀ Panel-Optic pitcher, Rubina Verde, circular-form rim, applied verde/green reeded handle, circa 1883-1888, 4-1/2" h. **$460**

Courtesy of Jeffrey S. Evans & Associates

Panel-Optic water pitcher, cased opalescent with dark to light bronze shading, triangular-form crimped rim, applied colorless reeded handle, polished pontil mark, circa 1883-1888, pitcher 8-1/2" h. overall. **$259**

Courtesy of Jeffrey S. Evans & Associates

Peacock Eye air-trap mother-of-pearl satin glass milk pitcher, coral, ball-form with circular neck and plain rim, applied colorless satin reeded handle, polished pontil mark, probably Phoenix Glass Co., fourth quarter 19th century, undamaged, no bruises or markings, 6-1/2" h. ...**$518**

Courtesy of Jeffrey S. Evans & Associates

Polka Dot/Spot-Optic cruet, Amberina, applied amber handle, original amber facet-cut stopper, polished pontil mark, Phoenix Glass Co. and others, fourth quarter 19th century, undamaged, light basal residue, 5-1/2" h. overall. **$81**

Courtesy of Jeffrey S. Evans & Associates

Spot-Optic Craquelle waisted tall tumbler, blue opalescent, factory polished rim, circa 1883-1888, 4-3/4" h. **$161**

Courtesy of Jeffrey S. Evans & Associates

Spot-Optic Craquelle pitcher, cranberry opalescent, ball-form with circular plain rim, applied colorless handle, polished pontil mark, circa 1883-1888, 6-1/4" h. **$230**

Courtesy of Jeffrey S. Evans & Associates

Stripe-Optic pitcher, colorless opalescent with polychrome floral and bird decoration, ball-form with circular rim, applied colorless reeded handle, polished pontil mark, circa 1883-1888, 5-3/4" h. **$138**

Courtesy of Jeffrey S. Evans & Associates

Swirl pitcher, cranberry opalescent, ball-form, circular rim, applied amber handle, polished pontil mark, probably Phoenix Glass Co., circa 1883-1888, 5-1/2" h. overall. **$207**

Courtesy of Jeffrey S. Evans & Associates

Swirl pitcher, blue opalescent, ball-form with circular plain rim, applied amber handle, polished pontil mark, circa 1883-1888, 5" h. **$92**

Courtesy of Jeffrey S. Evans & Associates

GLASS

quezal

IN 1901, Martin Bach and Thomas Johnson, who had worked for Louis Tiffany, opened a competing glassworks in Brooklyn, New York, called the Quezal Art Glass and Decorating Co. Named for the quetzal, a bird with brilliantly colored features, Quezal produced wares closely resembling those of Tiffany until the plant closed in 1925. In general, Quezal pieces are more defined than Tiffany glass, and the decorations are brighter and more visible.

Shade in green and gold iridescent pulled design against light green and opal background, ruffled rim, interior with gold iridescence, very good to excellent condition, 4-1/2" h.......... **$5,629**

Courtesy of James D. Julia Auctioneers, Fairfield, Maine, www.jamesdjulia.com

Shade in green and gold iridescent fishnet design with vertical gold iridescent zipper design over fishnet, blue highlights on lip and purple at fitter, interior with gold iridescence, signed on fitter "Quezal," very good to excellent condition, 4" h............... **$2,844**

Courtesy of James D. Julia Auctioneers, Fairfield, Maine, www.jamesdjulia.com

Jack-in-the-pulpit vase with green pulled feather design extending from foot to back of vase with gold iridescent outline around top of each pulled feather, iridescent outline surrounded by green and white swirling King Tut design, face of jack-in-the-pulpit finished in gold iridescence with pink highlights, ruffled and stretched rim, signed in polished pontil "Quezal R70," very good to excellent condition, 11" h.............. **$5,925**

Courtesy of James D. Julia Auctioneers, Fairfield, Maine, www.jamesdjulia.com

Rare double-handled coil vase in gold iridescent with blue coil decoration, applied handles and foot, polished pontil mark, signed "Quezal," first quarter 20th century, 12" h. overall. **$2,760**

Courtesy of Jeffrey S. Evans & Associates

Darner, early 20th century, 7" l. ..**$787**

Courtesy of Cottone Auctions

Two shades: One shade with tall vertically ribbed body in gold iridescent King Tut design with purple highlights against shaded green background, interior of flaring mouth in gold iridescence, signed in fitter "Quezal," very good to excellent condition, 6-3/8" h.; other shade with light vertical ribbing in gold iridescent King Tut design with purple highlights at rim against shaded green background, interior of shade in gold iridescence, signed on fitter "Quezal," very good to excellent condition, 5-1/4" h.................................**$4,148**

Courtesy of James D. Julia Auctioneers, Fairfield, Maine, www.jamesdjulia.com

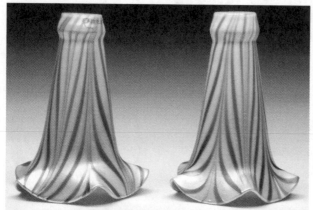

Pair of lily shades in green pulled design against gold iridescent background with gold iridescent interiors, each signed on fitter "Quezal," each in very good to excellent condition, 4-3/4" h. **$2,370**

Courtesy of James D. Julia Auctioneers, Fairfield, Maine, www.jamesdjulia.com

Three shades in allover light green pulled feather design with gold iridescent ribbons against lightly iridescent white background, each signed on fitter "Quezal," each in very good to excellent condition, 5-1/4" h............**$2,074**

Courtesy of James D. Julia Auctioneers, Fairfield, Maine, www.jamesdjulia.com

Lamp base with spherical body in gold iridescent wave design and gold iridescent vertical zipper design against cream-colored background, base finished with stamped brass foot and brass riser with two-socket cluster, unsigned, glass in very good to excellent condition, metal hardware with some discoloration to finish and some corrosion and deterioration to edge of foot, rewired with appropriate cloth cord, 19" h. **$830**

Courtesy of James D. Julia Auctioneers, Fairfield, Maine, www.jamesdjulia.com

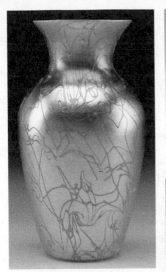

Vase in gold iridescent finish with pink highlights at neck, irregular swirling white threads, marked on underside with remnants of original paper label "Quezal Art Glass," very good to excellent condition, 9-1/2" h. **$474**

Courtesy of James D. Julia Auctioneers, Fairfield, Maine, www.jamesdjulia.com

Centerpiece bowl, early 20th century, signed "Quezal," 3-3/4" h., 14-1/2" dia.. **$666**

Courtesy of Cottone Auctions

Bowl with applied flaring foot with vertical ribbing and vertical ribbing on bulbous bowl with flaring lip, bowl and foot with shaded green iridescent body with purple and blue highlights to ribbing at foot and lip, interior in gold iridescence with pink, green, and blue highlights, signed on underside "Quezal," very good to excellent condition, 5-1/2" h., 9-3/4" dia... **$1,422**

Courtesy of James D. Julia Auctioneers, Fairfield, Maine, www.jamesdjulia.com

Vase in iridescent blue with gold, silver signed "Quezal" beneath, excellent condition, minor short surface scratches, 8". **$225**

Courtesy of Mark Mussio, Humler & Nolan

Vase with lily pads in dark green to gold iridescent, early 20th century, signed "Quezal, NY," 6-1/2" h., 5" dia...... **$3,993**

Courtesy of Cottone Auctions

Shade in green and gold iridescent fishnet design with gold iridescent zipper design over fishnet with green, purple, and blue highlights, interior in gold iridescence, signed on fitter "Quezal," very good to excellent condition, 5-1/4" h.......... **$2,015**

Courtesy of James D. Julia Auctioneers, Fairfield, Maine, www.jamesdjulia.com

GLASS

sandwich glass

NUMEROUS TYPES OF glass were produced at the Boston & Sandwich Glass Co. in Sandwich, Massachusetts, on Cape Cod, from 1826 to 1888. Founded by Deming Jarves, the company produced a wide variety of wares in differing levels of quality. The factory used free-blown, blown three-mold, and pressed glass manufacturing techniques. Both clear and colored glasses were used.

Jarves served as general manager from 1826-1858, and after he left, emphasis was placed on mass production. The development of a lime glass (non-flint) led to lower costs for pressed glass. Some free-blown and blown-and-molded pieces were made. By the 1880s the company was operating at a loss, and the factory closed on Jan. 1, 1888.

Pressed Dolphin double-step candlesticks, set of four, electric/copper blue, each six-petal socket with lower extension, raised on medium dolphin-form standard and square base, wafer construction, probably Boston & Sandwich Glass Co., circa 1845-1870, excellent condition, 9-7/8" h., 3-5/8" sq. base..........................**$4,600**

Courtesy of Jeffrey S. Evans & Associates

VISIT WWW.ANTIQUETRADER.COM

WWW.FACEBOOK.COM/ANTIQUETRADER

Pressed Petal and Hexagonal candlesticks, peacock blue, each six-petal socket with hexagonal extension, raised on hexagonal knop and flared base, wafer construction, Boston & Sandwich Glass Co. and Patrick F. Slane's American Glass Co., South Boston, 1840-1860, 7-1/4" h., 4-1/4" dia. overall base......................**$690**

Courtesy of Jeffrey S. Evans & Associates

Pressed Petal and Loop candlesticks, translucent blue over gray alabaster/clambroth, each six-petal socket with hexagonal extension, raised on hexagonal knop and seven-loop circular base with rough pontil mark, wafer construction, Boston & Sandwich Glass Co. and others, circa 1840-1860, 6-3/4" h., 4-1/4" dia. base.................**$978**

Courtesy of Jeffrey S. Evans & Associates

Pressed Petal and Loop candlesticks, yellow (uranium), each six-petal socket with hexagonal extension, raised on hexagonal knop and seven-loop circular base with rough pontil mark, wafer construction, Boston & Sandwich Glass Co. and others, circa 1840-1860, 6-7/8" h., 4-1/4" dia. base. **$127**

Courtesy of Jeffrey S. Evans & Associates

Pressed Loop/Leaf open compote/dish on foot, yellow (uranium), 12-loop bowl with 12 large beads in base, raised on high standard with six elongated loops, wafer construction, Boston & Sandwich Glass Co. and others, circa 1850-1870, 7" h., 9-1/4" dia. rim, 5" dia. foot...........**$920**

Courtesy of Jeffrey S. Evans & Associates

Pressed toy flat irons, violet blue, opalescent, and colorless, each factory polished at rear edge, colored examples also polished under base, Boston & Sandwich Glass Co. and others, 1850-1870, colorless example undamaged, others with crack to handle and normal base/rear edge flaking/chipping, 7/8" to 1" h. x 1-3/8" x 1". $259

Courtesy of Jeffrey S. Evans & Associates

Blown-molded paneled cruet or toilet bottle, cobalt blue, 12 panels from plain lip to plain base, single neck ring, Boston & Sandwich Glass Co. and others, circa 1835-1850, 6" h., 2-1/4" dia. base. $58

Courtesy of Jeffrey S. Evans & Associates

Pressed Lacy Heart and Scale creamer, fiery opalescent, circular body with medial ring, plain rim, molded handle, raised on plain circular foot, smooth underneath, circa 1840-1850, 4-1/2" h. overall, 3" dia. rim, 2-3/4" dia. foot....................$345

Courtesy of Jeffrey S. Evans & Associates

Pressed Lacy Gothic Arch sugar bowl and cover, fiery opalescent octagonal bowl with two different arch designs and plain rim, raised on eight-scallop foot, similar lighter opalescent cover with four arch designs and hexagonal finial on large platform, Boston & Sandwich Glass Co. and probably others, circa 1840-1850, bowl undamaged, cover with flaking/mold roughness to underside of rim and flake to finial, 5" h. overall, 3-1/2" h. rim, 5-1/8" dia. overall rim, 2-7/8" dia. foot.. $345

Courtesy of Jeffrey S. Evans & Associates

Frosted Dolphin standard epergne, colorless, in four sections with screw fittings, upper bowl with folded rim, trumpet vase with twisted-rib stem, circa 1870-1887, 22" h. overall, 11" dia. overall........................$403

Courtesy of Jeffrey S. Evans & Associates

▲ Open-work fruit basket on standard, fiery opalescent, bowl with 32-point rim above 16 vertical staves, 34-point star under slumped conical base, raised on hexagonal knop and flared base, wafer construction, rough snap ring under foot, circa 1840-1855, chip to lower edge of one bowl stave, snap-ring spall under foot, as made, 8" h., 8-1/4" dia. rim, 5-1/4" dia. overall foot. $8,050

Courtesy of Jeffrey S. Evans & Associates

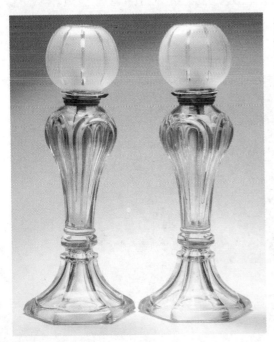

▲ Pressed Ring and Oval whale oil stand lamp, violet blue, inverted pyriform font with short ringed lower extension, raised on hexagonal knop and seven-loop circular base with rough pontil mark, wafer construction, original pewter collar fitted with pewter and sheet-iron double-tube burner, circa 1845-1860, proof condition, 7-1/2" h. to top of collar, 4-3/8" dia. base. $2,415

Courtesy of Jeffrey S. Evans & Associates

◄ Pressed Loop/Leaf whale oil stand lamps, yellow (uranium), each square, bulb-form font with four loops, raised on hexagonal base with compressed knop and flared foot, wafer construction, pewter fine-line collars, each fitted with pewter and tin double-tube whale oil burner, unusual slip-over circular shade holder with tripod fitter supports, roughed and cut ball-form shade, Boston & Sandwich Glass Co. and others, circa 1840-1860, excellent condition, 13-1/8" h. to top of shade, 10-3/8" h. to top of collar, 5-1/4" dia. overall base, shades 3" h., 2" dia. fitter............................$2,645

Courtesy of Jeffrey S. Evans & Associates

top lot

It is thought this frosted Madonna night-clock lamp is one of only two known complete specimens of this rare lighting and time-keeping device. Dr. Lewis Balch (1847-1909) was a well-respected New York State surgeon and teacher. After graduating from the College of Physicians and Surgeons at Columbia College in New York in 1870, he worked at Brooklyn City Hospital and was appointed Attending Surgeon to Northern Dispensary. In 1873, Lewis moved to Albany, New York, where he practiced at St. Peter's Hospital and was appointed Professor of Anatomy at City Hospital. He also served as city physician and the city's health officer. In 1886 the state appointed Balch secretary of the New York Board of Health, where he served two terms. During this time he witnessed the world's first execution by electrocution in 1890.

Frosted Madonna night-clock lamp, colorless, frosted figural Madonna stem raised on ribbed and scalloped foot, original brass connector supporting clockwork mechanism with small ball pendulum and tapered clock hand, original opaque white shade painted with black Roman numerals I through XII over horizontal band divided into quarters, top with brass trim ring; with original brass key; lacking kerosene font and burner; side of mechanism case engraved "To Dr. Lewis Balch / In pia facta vident," circa 1875, excellent working condition, 14-1/2" h. to top of shade, 4-3/4" dia. base. **$9,775**

COURTESY OF JEFFREY S. EVANS & ASSOCIATES

BT-4D Lafayet steamboat pressed open salt, deep cobalt blue with slight opalescent bloom in base, marked "B. &. S. / GLASS. / Co" on stern and "SANDWICH" on interior base, circa 1830-1845, bowsprit reattached, 1-5/8" h. x 2" x 3-5/8".. **$316**

Courtesy of Jeffrey S. Evans & Associates

◀ Pillar-molded and pressed Tulip vase, amethyst, deep bowl with eight ribs and lightly gauffered rim, raised on pressed hexagonal base with upper knop and flared foot, wafer construction, circa 1850-1860, proof condition, 10-1/2" h., 5-1/2" dia. rim, 5-3/8" dia. overall foot. ...**$4,025**

Courtesy of Jeffrey S. Evans & Associates

▲ Pressed Tulip vase, emerald green, deep octagonal bowl with flared rim, panels stop above lower peg extension, raised on flared, octagonal base, wafer construction, 1845-1865, undamaged, 10" h., 5-1/2" dia. overall rim, 4-5/8" dia. overall foot. **$2,300**

Courtesy of Jeffrey S. Evans & Associates

▶ Pressed Twisted Loop vase, cobalt blue, deep conical bowl with six loops twisted to right and plain rim, raised on compressed knop, octagonal baluster-form standard and square base, wafer construction, 1840-1860, near proof condition, 10-5/8" h., 4-1/2" dia. rim, 3-1/8" sq. base........ **$4,025**

Courtesy of Jeffrey S. Evans & Associates

◀ Pressed Tulip vase, forest/emerald green, deep octagonal bowl with flared rim and panels that continue to lower peg, raised on flared octagonal base, wafer construction, circa 1845-1865, undamaged, snap-ring flaking/roughness to interior of foot, as made, 10-1/8" h., 5-1/4" dia. rim, 4-3/4" dia. overall base. **$2,415**

Courtesy of Jeffrey S. Evans & Associates

GLASS

steuben

FREDERICK CARDER, AN Englishman, and Thomas G. Hawkes of Corning, New York, established the Steuben Glass Works in 1903 in Steuben County, New York. In 1918, the Corning Glass Co. purchased the Steuben company. Carder remained with the firm and designed many of the pieces bearing the Steuben mark. Probably the most widely recognized wares are Aurene, Verre De Soie, and Rosaline, but many other types were produced. The firm operated until 2011.

Five brown Aurene shades with white glass skirts and gold iridescent heart and vine pattern with vines extending to top portion of shade, gold iridescent thread where skirt meets brown Aurene, matching thread on bottom lip, white lightly iridescent interior, unsigned, all very good to excellent condition, two shades with minor roughness to fitter rim, 5-3/8" h.......... **$7,110**

Courtesy of James D. Julia Auctioneers, Fairfield, Maine, www.jamesdjulia.com

▼ Aurene three-handled urn-form vase, first quarter 20th century, blue iridescent glass, shape 6627, polished pontil mark, signed "Steuben Aurene 6627," 6-1/8" h., 7-1/4" dia...................... **$1,495**

Courtesy of Jeffrey S. Evans & Associates

Large Aurene deep-etched urn-form vase, first quarter 20th century, gold iridescent, shape 2689, large grapevine etched band around middle of body, second etched vine band around shoulder, polished pontil mark, signed "Steuben Aurene 2689," 10-1/2" h. overall, 9-1/4" dia. overall. **$2,070**

Courtesy of Jeffrey S. Evans & Associates

Aurene jack-in-the-pulpit vase, first quarter 20th century, blue iridescent glass, shape 2699, polished pontil mark, signed "Aurene 2699," 6-3/8" h. overall. **$1,093**

Courtesy of Jeffrey S. Evans & Associates

Art glass floriform three-light candleholder, circa 1932, mirror black and ivory glass, shape 7317, applied base, reeded stems and candleholders, polished pontil mark, 10-1/2" h. overall...... **$920**

Courtesy of Jeffrey S. Evans & Associates

Aurene vase with green pulled feather design extending from foot, each green feather with gold iridescent outline, remainder of vase covered with gold iridescent pulled feathers against white background, signed on underside "Aurene 521," very good to excellent condition with minor scratches to iridescence, 9" h. **$5,925**

Courtesy of James D. Julia Auctioneers, Fairfield, Maine, www.jamesdjulia.com

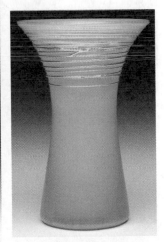

Rare iridescent green jade vase with light iridescent finish and platinum iridescent threading around top third of vase, very good to excellent condition, 6" h. **$593**

Courtesy of James D. Julia Auctioneers, Fairfield, Maine, www.jamesdjulia.com

Gold calcite vase, first quarter 20th century, iridescent glass, shape 2718, polished pontil mark, unsigned, 6-1/8" h. overall, 6-3/4" dia. overall......**$633**

Courtesy of Jeffrey S. Evans & Associates

GLASS

Scent bottle with square body in Oriental poppy pink with vertical ribbons of opalescence, original flower stopper, unsigned, very good to excellent condition, 5" h.................. **$1,778**

Courtesy of James D. Julia Auctioneers, Fairfield, Maine, www.jamesdjulia.com

Aurene urn-form vase, first quarter 20th century, blue iridescent glass, shape 2683, polished pontil mark, signed "Aurene 2683," 4-1/4" h.....**$460**

Courtesy of Jeffrey S. Evans & Associates

Art Deco vase with Rosaline acid cut-back stylized flowers against acid-textured alabaster background, alabaster inverted saucer foot, unsigned, very good to excellent condition, 6" h....**$770**

Courtesy of James D. Julia Auctioneers, Fairfield, Maine, www.jamesdjulia.com

Blue Aurene vase with inverted saucer foot and flaring body with swirled ribbing, green and purple highlights, signed on underside "Steuben Aurene 6034," very good to excellent condition, four fleabites to bottom edge of foot, 9-3/4" h.............................. **$593**

Courtesy of James D. Julia Auctioneers, Fairfield, Maine, www.jamesdjulia.com

Glass and metal sculpture titled "Thistle Rock" with carved crystal base in shape of jagged rock with metal gilded thistle extending from top, signed on underside "Steuben," very good to excellent condition, 7-1/2" h. **$4,740**

Courtesy of James D. Julia Auctioneers, Fairfield, Maine, www.jamesdjulia.com

Blue Aurene vase in form of three tree trunks extending from round base, blue iridescence with purple highlights, signed on underside "Aurene 2744," very good to excellent condition, 6" h.....**$948**

Courtesy of James D. Julia Auctioneers, Fairfield, Maine, www.jamesdjulia.com

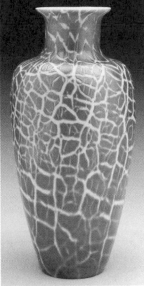

◄ Shade with gold iridescent heart and vine pattern against brown Aurene background, gold iridescent pattern with blue highlights at top, white slightly iridescent interior, flake at edge of mounting hole on interior and line into brown Aurene finish at mounting hole, 4-1/2" h.......**$1,718**

Courtesy of James D. Julia Auctioneers, Fairfield, Maine, www.jamesdjulia.com

Cobalt blue candlesticks with inverted saucer feet, cylindrical stems and wide, flat rims, one candlestick signed in polished pontil with etched signature in script "Steuben," very good to excellent condition, 4" h..........................**$237**

Courtesy of James D. Julia Auctioneers, Fairfield, Maine, www.jamesdjulia.com

Lamp shaft with green and white crackle decoration, rounded shoulder and slightly flaring lip, unsigned, very good to excellent condition, light roughness to top edge, 11" h......................**$1,185**

Courtesy of James D. Julia Auctioneers, Fairfield, Maine, www.jamesdjulia.com

Two red Aurene shades: Tulip shade with gold iridescent heart and vine decoration, blue highlights at lip, marked on fitter with remnants of silver fleur-de-lis mark "Steuben," very good to excellent condition, 4-1/4" h.; and shade with gold iridescent heart and vine pattern, blue and pink highlights, unsigned, very good to excellent condition, 4-1/2" h..........................**$7,110**

Courtesy of James D. Julia Auctioneers, Fairfield, Maine, www.jamesdjulia.com

Large gold Aurene vase with rounded shoulders and slightly flaring neck, gold iridescence with red highlights at neck, platinum iridescence at lip and pink highlights on interior, signed on underside "Steuben Aurene 2683," very good to excellent condition with minor scratches to iridescence, 10-1/2" h. **$830**

Courtesy of James D. Julia Auctioneers, Fairfield, Maine, www.jamesdjulia.com

Art glass melon-form cologne bottle, circa 1920-1930, yellow jade glass, shape 1455, original lobed stopper numbered to match bottle, polished pontil mark with original triangular paper label, 5-3/4" h. overall, bottle 3-1/2" h. $1,150

Courtesy of Jeffrey S. Evans & Associates

Aurene melon ribbed cosmetic jar, first quarter 20th century, blue iridescent glass, shape 2701, reeded feet and polished pontil mark, signed "Aurene 2701," 5" h. overall, 4-1/4" dia. overall. $1,725

Courtesy of Jeffrey S. Evans & Associates

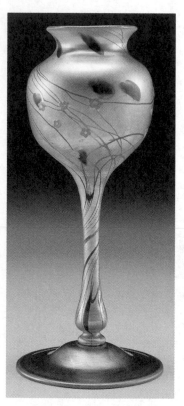

Flower form gold Aurene vase with green iridescent heart and vine decoration with vines encircling stem, white millefiori, inverted saucer foot, gold iridescence with platinum and pink highlights, signed on underside "Aurene 578" with silver ink-stamped mark "Aurene," very good to excellent condition, 7-3/4" h. **$5,925**

Courtesy of James D. Julia Auctioneers, Fairfield, Maine, www.jamesdjulia.com

Compote with lightly ribbed amethyst inverted saucer foot, clear twisted stem, and lightly ribbed amethyst bowl, signed on underside in etched block letters "Steuben," very good to excellent condition, 6-3/4" h., 7" dia. $371

Courtesy of James D. Julia Auctioneers, Fairfield, Maine, www.jamesdjulia.com

GLASS

sugar shakers

ONE OF THE most interesting aspects of collecting Victorian art glass shakers and condiment sets is that you can collect just about all types of Victorian art glass and display it in a small area.

These types of items include salt, pepper, and sugar shakers as well as mustard jars, small cruet bottles, and toothpick holders.

Some manufacturers that made these items are Mt. Washington, New England Glass, Consolidated Glass, Hobbs Brockunier, Challinor Taylor, Northwood, and others. They made the shakers from cased glass, decorated opalware, and many other forms of enameled glass. Shakers can be found in Amberina, Burmese, Peachblow, Findlay onyx, opalescent, chocolate glass, and many other colors and combinations.

Victorian-era shakers can have either a two-piece or one-piece cap. Two-piece caps contain a collar that is cemented to the shaker using plaster. This collar contains the threads onto which the top screws. The glass itself does not contain any threads.

A one-piece cap doesn't have a plaster collar, as the shaker's glass top has molded threads and the top screws on like modern-day tops. You will notice a thick rough top edge on most shakers that have a one-

Acorn sugar shaker, black amethyst with white enamel and gilt decoration, period lid, Beaumont Glass Co. and possibly others, 1890-1900, glass undamaged with normal roughness to rim, hidden by lid, 5" h. overall.......................**$138**

Courtesy of Jeffrey S. Evans & Associates

Acorn sugar shaker, green with polychrome decoration, period lid, Beaumont Glass Co. and possibly others, 1890-1900, excellent condition overall, normal flakes/roughness to rim, probably as made, hidden by lid, 5" h. overall. **$207**

Courtesy of Jeffrey S. Evans & Associates

Acorn sugar shaker, opaque light to dark pink with white enamel and gilt decoration, period lid, Beaumont Glass Co. and possibly others, 1890-1900, undamaged, base with minor manufacturing flaw and rim with two flakes/roughness, each as made, 4-1/2" h. overall. **$92**

Courtesy of Jeffrey S. Evans & Associates

Ribbed sugar shaker, blue opalescent, inappropriate period two-part lid, Beatty & Sons, circa 1889, undamaged, lid with dent, 5-3/8" h. overall. **$115**

Courtesy of Jeffrey S. Evans & Associates

Egg-based sugar shaker, yellow to white with polychrome decoration, period two-part lid, fourth quarter 19th century, undamaged, 4-1/4" h. overall. **$69**

Courtesy of Jeffrey S. Evans & Associates

Findlay onyx sugar shaker, ivory onyx with platinum flowers, period lid, Dalzell, Gilmore & Leighton Co., Findlay, Ohio, circa 1889, undamaged, 5-1/4" h. overall.....**$196**

Courtesy of Jeffrey S. Evans & Associates

piece cap. This rough, chipped edge is a telltale sign the shaker is an old one, but there are exceptions.

There are some reproductions out there; most of them will have a ground or smooth top edge and may be made of heavier glass. Not all old shakers have rough, chipped edges on the top; experience will give you the skills to differentiate old from new.

Every shaker and mustard had a cap of some sort. They were made of many types of materials – typically brass, nickel, pewter, and silver – and are either plain or embossed with designs and flowers. Specialty tops were reserved for certain shakers made by Mt. Washington and Monroe's Wavecrest line, to name two. For example, Mt. Washington made shakers in the forms of tomatoes, eggs, and figs with specific caps that served as part of the form's design.

When buying a Victorian-era shaker, don't be discouraged if it doesn't have a cap. Unless it's a shaker with a specific cap that is part of the identity of the shaker, you can always find a replacement. Most shaker collectors have a box of old caps for just this reason.

Mustard jars are a natural to go along with a shaker collection. They come in all the same patterns and glass types. Mustards are harder to find in most cases, as there was only one mustard made for every two shakers. Other "go-withs" are toothpick holders, small oil bottles, and larger cruets. And, if you are lucky, you may run across a silver-plate holder of the period that will hold the pieces. These holders can be very ornate and enhance the shakers.

Some of my favorite pieces are odd or non-production colors and slag glass shakers as well as old carnival glass shakers, none of which are found very often. Enameled shakers can be miniature works of art representing flowers, designs, Mary Gregory-type figures, and even flying insects like butterflies. Figural shakers, such as owls, chickens, and people, can be most interesting but hard to come by.

Shakers come in all price ranges. Some sell for less than $50. At the other end of the spectrum are unique pieces worth several thousand dollars. In my opinion, most of the better pieces fall between $75 and $300 each.

The Antique Glass Salt & Sugar Shaker Club unites many collectors from across the United States and Canada. The club produces a quarterly newsletter and has an ongoing shaker identification project as well as an annual convention. Visit www.antiquesaltshakers.com for more club information.

— *Scott Beale*

GLASS

tiffany glass

TIFFANY & CO. was founded by Charles Lewis Tiffany (1812-1902) and Teddy Young in New York City in 1837 as a "stationery and fancy goods emporium." The store operated as Tiffany, Young and Ellis in lower Manhattan, initially selling a wide variety of stationery items. The name was shortened to Tiffany & Co. in 1853, and the firm's emphasis on jewelry was established.

The first Tiffany catalog, known as the "Blue Book," was published in 1845. It is still being published today.

In 1862 Tiffany & Co. supplied the Union Army with swords, flags and surgical implements.

Charles' son, Louis Comfort Tiffany (1848-1933), was an American artist and designer who worked in the decorative arts and is best known for his work in stained glass. Louis established Tiffany Glass Co. in 1885, and in 1902 it became known as the Tiffany Studios. America's outstanding glass designer of the Art Nouveau period produced glass from the last quarter of the 19th century until the early 1930s. Tiffany revived early techniques and devised many new ones, becoming the most famous glassmaker in America.

(For Tiffany lamps, please see "Lighting" section.)

Gold Favrile vase with green Heart and Vine pattern against gold iridescence with green and pink highlights, signed on underside "L.C. Tiffany – Favrile 1029L," very good to excellent condition, 8-5/8" h. **$1,422**

Courtesy of James D. Julia Auctioneers, Fairfield, Maine, www.jamesdjulia.com

▼ Favrile cabinet vase, circa 1916, gold iridescent glass with green Heart and Vine pattern, polished pontil mark and base, signed "647 K L.C. Tiffany-Favrile," 2-3/4" h., 3-1/2" dia. **$1,265**

Courtesy of Jeffrey S. Evans & Associates; www.jeffreysevans.com

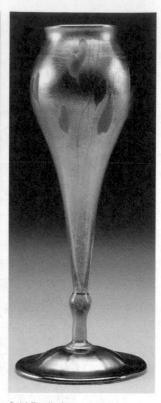

Favrile candle lamp, early 20th century, golden iridescent ribbed and swirled base with polished pontil mark, signed "L. C. T. Favrile," opaque white with green pulled leaves candlestick insert, fitted with gold lightly paneled and ruffled shade signed "L. C. T. Favrile," 13" h. overall, shade 7-1/8" dia. overall.................... **$1,495**

Courtesy of Jeffrey S. Evans & Associates; www.jeffreysevans.com

Gold Favrile flower form vase with green hearts and vines against gold iridescent background with purple and blue highlights, ribbed inverted saucer foot, signed on underside "L.C. Tiffany-Favrile 6408 G," very good to excellent condition, 9" h............... **$2,666**

Courtesy of James D. Julia Auctioneers, Fairfield, Maine, www.jamesdjulia.com

Vase with bronze Tiffany Studios holder with artichoke stem and stylized floral design cup, base signed "Tiffany Studios N.Y. 1043," gold Favrile glass vase flares at top to hexagonal lip, signed on underside "L.C.T. Favrile," very good to excellent condition, 15-7/8" h. **$1,606**

Courtesy of James D. Julia Auctioneers, Fairfield, Maine, www.jamesdjulia.com

Favrile vase, circa 1905, green body with gold iridescent pulled design, polished base and pontil mark, signed "L.C. Tiffany Y3435 Favrile," 4-1/8" h., 5" dia...................... **$2,875**

Courtesy of Jeffrey S. Evans & Associates; www.jeffreysevans.com

Early Favrile vase with translucent gold iridescent body with platinum iridescent hooked feather design surrounding center, shoulder decorated with band of platinum iridescence with green and purple highlights, center band of cream-colored swirling threads, button pontil, signed on underside "L.C.T. A1201," very good to excellent condition, blemish to iridescence on shoulder (from making), 9" h.................. **$7,110**

Courtesy of James D. Julia Auctioneers, Fairfield, Maine, www.jamesdjulia.com

Pastel candlestick with applied inverted saucer foot with white opalescent ribbons supporting clear glass ribbed stem leading to turquoise blue candle cup and bobeche, each with white opalescent ribbons, signed on underside "L.C.T.," very good to excellent condition, 11-3/4" h. **$1,067**

Courtesy of James D. Julia Auctioneers, Fairfield, Maine, www.jamesdjulia.com

Flower form vase with white inverted saucer foot with green pulled feather design that extends to stem and expands onto body of vase against white opalescent background, interior in gold iridescence, signed on underside "L.C.T. W3072," very good to excellent condition with spotting to interior (from making), 13-1/2" h.......... **$4,000**

Courtesy of James D. Julia Auctioneers, Fairfield, Maine, www.jamesdjulia.com

◄ Gold Favrile shade with gold iridescent hooked feather design against yellow shading to transparent gold iridescent background, shade signed in fitter "L.C.T.," very good to excellent condition, 5-3/8" h. **$1,235**

Courtesy of James D. Julia Auctioneers, Fairfield, Maine, www.jamesdjulia.com

Gold Favrile cabinet vase with row of five green wavy bands with orange coloration at point of each wave, above which a band of swirling lines surrounding shoulder gives way to band of four wavy lines around top of shoulder, all against gold iridescent background, signed on underside "L.C.T. A2876," very good to excellent condition, 2-3/4" h. **$3,705**

Courtesy of James D. Julia Auctioneers, Fairfield, Maine, www.jamesdjulia.com

top lot

Gold Favrile vase with vertically ribbed body with flared shoulder and lip, gold iridescent finish with pink highlights with platinum highlights at lip, foot and shoulder, signed on underside "L.C. Tiffany-Favrile X67 1078 8363," very good to excellent condition, 5-1/2" h.............. **$593**

Courtesy of James D. Julia Auctioneers, Fairfield, Maine, www.jamesdjulia.com

Gold Favrile vase with green and yellow hooked feather design from lip against gold iridescent background, signed on underside "L.C. Tiffany-Inc. Favrile 8351N," very good condition, scratches to iridescence on side of vase, 5" h. **$2,074**

Courtesy of James D. Julia Auctioneers, Fairfield, Maine, www.jamesdjulia.com

Favrile cameo vase in amber glass with shaded maroon and yellow five-petal flowers with green cameo leaves, signed on underside "L.C. Tiffany Favrile 8802B," very good to excellent condition, 11-1/2" h.............. $13,035

COURTESY OF JAMES D. JULIA AUCTIONEERS, FAIRFIELD, MAINE, WWW.JAMESDJULIA.COM

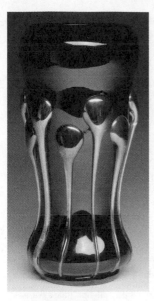

Favrile vase with shiny black body and applied gold iridescent tendrils in transparent glass, signed on underside "L.C. Tiffany-Inc. Favrile 5153N," very good to excellent condition with staining to interior of vase, 9-3/8" h. **$3,555**

Courtesy of James D. Julia Auctioneers, Fairfield, Maine, www.jamesdjulia.com

◄ Paperweight with gold iridescent turtleback tile with pink and green highlights in bronze frame with applied oval bronze feet in gold patina, signed on underside "Tiffany Studios New York 935," very good to excellent condition with minor wear and discoloration to patina, 5-3/4" x 4-5/8".... **$2,963**

Courtesy of James D. Julia Auctioneers, Fairfield, Maine, www.jamesdjulia.com

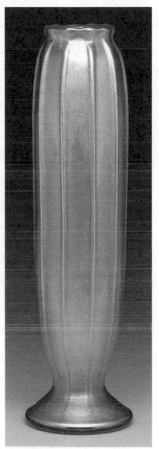

Vase with inverted saucer foot and light vertical ribbing on body with rolled lip at top, gold iridescence with platinum highlights near top, signed on underside "L.C.T. Y9593," very good to excellent condition, 6" h. **$494**

Courtesy of James D. Julia Auctioneers, Fairfield, Maine, www.jamesdjulia.com

◄ Red agate vase with faceted sides and neck and intaglio carved leaves separating faceted sections, signed on underside "L.C. Tiffany-Favrile C390," original Tiffany paper label, very good to excellent condition, 5-1/2" h.........**$10,498**

Courtesy of James D. Julia Auctioneers, Fairfield, Maine, www.jamesdjulia.com

Gold Favrile vase with vertically ribbed body with gold iridescent finish and blue highlights at edge of foot and pink highlights at ribbing, signed on underside "L.C. Tiffany-Inc. Favrile 1093-2237N," very good to excellent condition with staining to interior, 13-1/4" h. **$830**

Courtesy of James D. Julia Auctioneers, Fairfield, Maine, www.jamesdjulia.com

Trumpet vase with gold iridescent pulled feather design with each feather outlined in green iridescence against platinum iridescent background, Tiffany Studios bronze stand with artichoke stem and gold patina, vase marked "L.C.T.," stand marked "Tiffany Studios, New York 1043," very good condition with spotting to patina on stand and wear to iridescence on lip, 11-3/4" h. **$1,363**

Courtesy of James D. Julia Auctioneers, Fairfield, Maine, www.jamesdjulia.com

Green pastel trumpet vase with inverted saucer foot with white opalescent ribbons leading to opalescent stem, vase with vertical white opalescent ribbons and green pastel interior with stretched rim, signed on underside "L.C. Tiffany-Favrile, 1885" with original Tiffany label, very good to excellent condition, 10-1/2" h. **$2,015**

Courtesy of James D. Julia Auctioneers, Fairfield, Maine, www.jamesdjulia.com

Large gold Favrile bullet shade with green Heart and Vine decoration from fitter to bottom, shoulder with band of white millefiori inlays with gold iridescent flower petals surrounding millefiori against gold iridescent background with purple highlights, signed on fitter "L.C.T.," very good to excellent condition with minor roughness to bottom tip of shade (from making), 13-1/2" h. x 8" dia........**$11,258**

Courtesy of James D. Julia Auctioneers, Fairfield, Maine, www.jamesdjulia.com

Gold Favrile scent bottle with green leaf and vine decoration surrounding body and neck with green vines on stopper against gold iridescent background with pink and green highlights, signed on underside "L.C. Tiffany-Inc. Favrile 1053 4674 N," stopper numbered 4674 N, very good to excellent condition, flea bite to bottom edge of stopper, 4" h. **$4,148**

Courtesy of James D. Julia Auctioneers, Fairfield, Maine, www.jamesdjulia.com

Favrile flower form cabinet vase, circa 1913, blue iridescent glass, applied foot with polished base and pontil mark, signed "2964 H/L.C. Tiffany-Favrile," 4-1/2" h. overall, 6" dia. overall...... **$1,093**

Courtesy of Jeffrey S. Evans & Associates

Favrile ribbed floriform vase, circa 1918, blue iridescent glass with 12-rib body with flaring rim, domed 10-rib applied foot, polished base and pontil mark, signed "1526-3380 M L.C. Tiffany-Favrile Inc.," 12-3/8" h. overall... **$1,495**

Courtesy of Jeffrey S. Evans & Associates

Flower form vase with blue iridescent inverted saucer foot and double gourd body with flaring ruffled rim, stem in cobalt blue glass, interior in gold iridescence with red highlights, signed on underside with spurious "L.C. Tiffany-Favrile 4275F," spurious Tiffany Favrile paper label, very good to excellent condition, 11-1/4" h. **$618**

Courtesy of James D. Julia Auctioneers, Fairfield, Maine, www.jamesdjulia.com

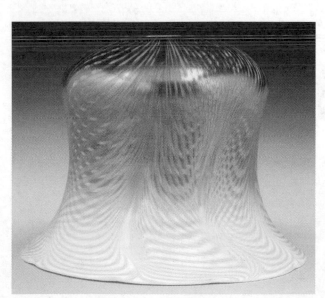

Bell-shaped shade with green pulled feather design overlaid with gold iridescent pulled feather design against white background, shade with 3/8" dia. hole in top for mounting, very good to excellent condition, minor roughness around mounting hole, 5-1/4" h., 6-3/4" dia..................**$1,112**

Courtesy of James D. Julia Auctioneers, Fairfield, Maine, www.jamesdjulia.com

GLASS

wave crest

NOW MUCH SOUGHT after, Wave Crest was produced by the C.F. Monroe Co., Meriden, Connecticut, in the late 19th and early 20th centuries. It was made from opaque white glass blown into molds, then hand-decorated in enamels, and metal trim was often added. Boudoir accessories such as jewel boxes, hair receivers, etc., predominated.

Scroll mold jardiniere, blue and yellow tones, pink floral décor, banner mark, 8" x 8". **$413**

Courtesy of Woody Auctions, LLC

Rare scroll mold wall plaque, blue and white with daisy decor, in elaborate gilt metal frame, overall frame 16" x 11-1/2".................................... **$4,838**

Courtesy of Woody Auctions, LLC

Scroll mold inkwell, yellow and white with pink rose décor, unmarked, 3" x 4". **$472**

Courtesy of Woody Auctions, LLC

Square dresser box, egg crate mold, embossed scroll design, floral décor, banner mark, 5" x 6-1/2". **$295**

Courtesy of Woody Auctions, LLC

Two-handled vase, pink and white tones with blue floral decor, gilt metal handles, banner mark, 8". $177

Courtesy of Woody Auctions, LLC

Toothpick holder on pedestal, opal with pink shading and gilt decoration, beaded rim and gilt-metal pedestal, circa 1900, 2-3/4" h. $92

Courtesy of Jeffrey S. Evans & Associates

Toothpick holder, opal with polychrome decoration, beaded rim, gilt-metal stand, circa 1898, signed, 2-1/2" h. $69

Courtesy of Jeffrey S. Evans & Associates

Two footed cylinder vases/ hatpin holders, one white with pink blossoms and banner mark, the other white with pink and yellow rose décor, unmarked, each 6" h. $207

Courtesy of Woody Auctions, LLC

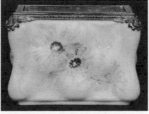

Egg crate mold letter holder, cream tones with floral decor, gilt metal rim, banner mark, 4" x 1/2". $106

Courtesy of Woody Auctions, LLC

Short-cylinder toothpick holder, opal with polychrome decoration, beaded rim, gilt-metal stand, circa 1898, unsigned, 2-1/4" h. $115

Courtesy of Jeffrey S. Evans & Associates

Scroll mold round hinged ring box, white with cottage scene décor, stamp mark, 3-1/2" x 3". $413

Courtesy of Woody Auctions, LLC

Jardiniere, white with pink blossoms and branch décor, unmarked, 7-3/4" x 9". $207

Courtesy of Woody Auctions, LLC

Five dresser boxes, opal with polychrome floral decoration, four circular and one square, late 19th/early 20th century, two signed, 3-1/4" to 5-1/4" dia. **$184**

Courtesy of Jeffrey S. Evans & Associates

Large cylinder vase hand-decorated with butterfly supporting maiden, blue flowers on obverse, bordered by raised scrolls in gold, with gilt metal scroll handles, rim and base, excellent condition, 14" h. x 8-1/4" w. across handles..... **$750**

Courtesy of Mark Mussio, Humler & Nolan

Two jewel stands, opal with polychrome floral decoration, each with gilt-metal mounts, late 19th/early 20th century, not signed, 3" and 3-1/2" h. **$127**

Courtesy of Jeffrey S. Evans & Associates

Fern dish with insert, opal with polychrome floral decoration, egg crate form, insert with original bail handles, late 19th/early 20th century, not signed, 3-1/2" h., 7" sq. **$104**

Courtesy of Jeffrey S. Evans & Associates

Two Erie Twist table articles, opal with mushroom/toadstool transfer decoration, spoon holder and sugar bowl lacking original rim mount, late 19th/early 20th century, not signed, 4" and 4-1/2" h. overall... **$104**

Courtesy of Jeffrey S. Evans & Associates

Puff mold round hinged dresser box, blue tones with pink floral décor, original lining, banner mark, 3-1/2" x 7"............... **$325**

Courtesy of Woody Auctions, LLC

GLASS

webb

THOMAS WEBB & Sons of Stourbridge was one of England's most prolific glasshouses. Many types of glass, including cameo, have been produced by this firm through the years. The company also produced various types of novelty and art glass during the late Victorian period.

Two cameo glass vases, one with butterflies, England, circa 1890, unmarked, attributed to Thomas Webb & Sons, 10", 9" h. **$1,000**

Courtesy of Rago Arts, www.ragoarts.com

Cameo glass vase, bulbous with wide white-banded mouth and foot, body decorated with white trailing vine of morning glories and butterfly to reverse, Stourbridge, England, late 19th/early 20th century, underside marked in demilune banner "THOMAS WEBB & SONS," nick ground to top rim, 8-5/8" h. **$960**

Courtesy of Skinner, Inc.; www.skinnerinc.com

Cameo glass bowl with sterling silver rim and foot, body decorated with white cameo vine with flowers to one side and butterfly to other, Stourbridge, circa 1900, rim marked London, 1900-01, "T.W&S" maker's mark, with presentation inscription, marked to underside "THOMAS WEBB & SONS/CAMEO" in banner, inscription reads "Happy 25th Sir George III from your good friends J.W. and family July 3, 1892," glass in very good condition, 9-3/4" dia. **$1,320**

Courtesy of Skinner, Inc.; www.skinnerinc.com

top lot

Cameo vase with white flowers, stems, and leaves against blue background, back of vase decorated with single white cameo butterfly, signed on underside "Thomas Webb & Sons," very good to excellent condition, 8-1/4" h. $2,074

Cameo glass bowl, squat with wide, triple-banded mouth, white cameo floral spray to red ground, Stourbridge, England, late 19th/early 20th century, marked ":THOS WEBB & SONS CAMEO:" to underside, nicks to inner and outer edge of rim, 3" h. **$960**

Courtesy of Skinner, Inc.; www.skinnerinc.com

Cameo glass ice bucket with two black and white cameo glass penguins against acid-cut snowy background, signed on underside "Made Exclusively for Rembrandt Guild Webb Made in England" and artist signed "Anna Fogelberg," very good to excellent condition, 8-7/8" dia., 5-1/4" h....................... **$593**

Courtesy of James D. Julia Auctioneers, Fairfield, Maine, www.jamesdjulia.com

Cameo cabinet vase attributed to Thomas Webb & Sons, wheel-carved vine and leaves descending from neck and encircling body of vase, white cameo decoration set against light blue background, very good to excellent condition, 3-1/2" h. **$474**

Courtesy of James D. Julia Auctioneers, Fairfield, Maine, www.jamesdjulia.com

Cameo glass vase with fruiting branches on red background, England, circa 1910, unmarked, attributed to Thomas Webb & Sons, 13-3/4" x 7-1/2". **$1,375**

Courtesy of Rago Arts, www.ragoarts.com

Cased rainbow glass vases, opal interiors, each square pinched-side form with swirled ribs, short neck with enamel decoration, factory polished rim, and slightly concave polished base inscribed "I / 32," probably Thomas Webb & Sons, late 19th/early 20th century, undamaged, 11" h. **$1,035**

Courtesy of James D. Julia Auctioneers, Fairfield, Maine, www.jamesdjulia.com

English cameo vase, yellow amber to colorless, slightly tapered form with acid cut-back and engraved Art Nouveau lily decoration on textured ground, cameo "Webb" script signature at base, polished pontil mark, Thomas Webb & Sons, first half 20th century, undamaged, 8" h., 5-3/4" dia. **$403**

Courtesy of James D. Julia Auctioneers, Fairfield, Maine, www.jamesdjulia.com

English cameo lay-down scent bottle attributed to Thomas Webb & Sons, wheel-carved cameo design of palms against yellow background with white cameo butterfly on one shoulder, finished with silver-plated hinged top and collar, glass in very good condition, catch on lid no longer working, 3-3/8" l. **$948**

Courtesy of James D. Julia Auctioneers, Fairfield, Maine, www.jamesdjulia.com

Cameo glass vase, inverted baluster with banded neck and foot, body decorated with wild rose motif on one side and two butterflies to other on Prussian blue ground, Stourbridge, late 19th/early 20th century, marked to underside "WEBB" in square cartouche, top rim slightly ground to exterior edge, 7-3/4" h. **$1,800**

Courtesy of Skinner, Inc.; www.skinnerinc.com

GLASS

whimsies

EVERY ONCE IN A WHILE you come across a piece of art glass that you just know must be one of a kind. Perhaps it's because of the design or the eclectic colors of the glass, but you just get this feeling that there's no other piece like it. If this is the impression you get, you may have just found a glasshouse whimsy.

From witch balls to top hats, gavels to cigarette holders, whimsies are representations of glass artisans' skills and imaginations in solid form.

Glasshouse whimsies – whether they are entirely free-form or created from production glass pieces – are items made by glassworkers to show off their skills. Whimsies, often given the misnomers "end-of-day" or "lunch-hour" pieces, are known as "friggers" in England. They are non-production pieces; other than the use of factory glass, the whimsies have no connection to the glass factory.

Dale Murschell is a life-long collector who has written many articles and books on aspects of glass collecting, including the 1989 publication "Glasshouse Whimsies: An Enhanced Reference," co-written with Joyce Blake. Murschell said these one-of-a-kind glass items had to be made on the glassblowers' own time; they didn't have the leisure to amuse themselves with their creations during working hours. Pay scales were equated to the volume of the product or numbers of piecework.

At some glass houses, workers took a "turn," meaning they worked a specified length of time, possibly four hours. During that "turn," the shop had to produce a "move," which

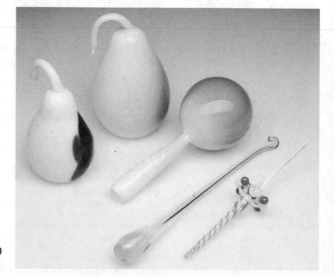

Assorted free-blown glass whimsies, including Peachblow pear with long stem and sock darner/darning ball, each with glossy finish and rough pontil mark, and opal pear with ruby inclusions, New England Glass Co., Libbey Glass Co., and others, fourth quarter 19th century and 20th century, undamaged, each pear stem with normal loss to end from blow pipe removal, as made, 4" h. and 4-3/4" h., 5-3/4" to 8" l. **$219**

Courtesy of Jeffrey S. Evans & Associates

Free-blown mottled darning ball, opal-cased, colorless with blue, rose, and teal green, handle with rough, open-pontil end, Boston & Sandwich Glass Co. and others, 1840-1880, undamaged, 6" l. **$230**

Courtesy of Jeffrey S. Evans & Associates

equaled a certain number of items. The number of items per "move" was determined through negotiations between the union and the company. Artisans working together enabled a shop to produce a "move" in a "turn," leaving no time for personal creations other than during a lunch break or at the end of the day.

Glass working was difficult because of the heat, the smoky, dusty air, and the pressure to complete a "move" to make the maximum wage. "The opportunity to make a useful item for home or just an attractive item for pleasure was one of the few benefits that had the owner's consent," Murschell said. Even though the glass workers had unions, they were unable to get many benefits because the glasshouse owners would stop production and close before giving in to union demands; this happened at Sandwich Glass Works of Sandwich, Massachusetts, in 1888.

Murschell noted one problem glassworkers faced when they made a whimsy was preventing someone else from taking it. The item had to cool overnight in the lehr, an oven that let the glass anneal slowly so as to prevent breakage; whoever was first to get to work the next morning had the opportunity to grab the whimsy if he was so inclined.

According to Ellen Schroy, author of *Warman's Depression Glass Identification and Price Guide,* "Glasshouse whimsies are wonderful creations: Whimsical because they often were made using the imagination of the glassblower, with materials and colors readily at hand, or so we believe."

Whimsies fuel glass enthusiasts' imaginations. "Perhaps if we had a time machine, we could travel back in time and watch how long elegant glass canes with stripes and swirls were blown so that they could be used in parades," Schroy continued. "Or watch as witch balls were gathered and again swirled. We could watch as the glassblowers crimped and prodded the molten gather into what they wished it to be."

In addition to witch balls, other desirable forms include chains, sock darners, bells, banks, powder horns, pipes, rolling pins, and many more items.

"Additional novelties surface each year, including witch wands, gavels, screwdrivers, pistols, and swords," Murschell said. "The pieces are unmarked, making creator identification difficult, if not impossible." The best lead to the maker would be a documentation of provenance; unfortunately, such a record is unlikely. The whimsies' color is also a clue to where the pieces may have been made.

Free-blown marbrie-loop-decorated pipe whimsy, opal cased with blue loopings, stem with tooled mouth and five-knop stem, bowl with plain rim, Boston and Sandwich Glass Co. and others, fourth quarter 19th century, undamaged, manufacturing roughness to bowl rim, 16" l...................**$259**

Courtesy of Jeffrey S. Evans & Associates

Some whimsies are made of clear or aqua glass. Others may be of a single color like amber or cobalt blue, while others may have many colors. "Some glasshouse whimsies also incorporate bits of color called spatter; think of it as raindrops of color on a pretty blue or olive green ground," said Schroy.

According to Murschell, the whimsies of aqua color were probably made at a window glass or bottle factory. "Bottle glass was usually aqua due to the natural iron in the sand that discolored the glass," he explained. "Window glass may have been chemically treated to produce a somewhat clearer glass."

Green, amber, cobalt blue, or ruby red glass were seldom available to bottle and window glass workers. The more colorful whimsy items may have originated in larger glassworks that had several colors available.

The 19th century was the heyday for glasshouse whimsies, and it extended into the 20th century until machines finally took over production at all of the glass factories; when the machines took over, the glass was no longer accessible to the glassblowers, ending the practice.

"All glasshouse whimsies are one-of-a-kind and therefore should be judged on their own individual quality and beauty and not necessarily on their age," Murschell said. "This is especially important with glass because it is difficult to judge its age."

According to American glass specialist Jeffrey S. Evans, board member of the Museum of American Glass in West Virginia and principle of Jeffrey S. Evans & Associates, "Pieces made from known objects can be dated by the time period of the object. Blown off-hand pieces are much more difficult to assign a date. One has to be familiar with the techniques employed to make the piece and the type of glass being used. Whimsies have been made as long as there have been glassmakers."

However, there are some types of whimsies still being made today. "In today's market pretty much any seemingly whimsical object it referred to as a whimsy," Evans said.

Reproduction efforts are usually thick and clumsy. Modern art glass houses (like Murano) attempting to recreate the look of the 19th and early 20th century whimsies are usually marked. "One should have a good general knowledge of glass in order to avoid modern production pieces," Evans advised. "While these are not a big problem at the moment, this is the type of thing that can begin coming out of China at any time."

When asked how to tell a whimsy from a production piece, Evans replied, "True whimsies are objects that are produced by manipulating previously established utilitarian forms into a totally different article. Whimsies can still serve a useful purpose, or they can be strictly

Free-blown glass darning balls:
opal-cased yellow example
with opal marbrie loops and
cobalt blue example, each
with rough, open-pontil end
handle, and aqua example with
opal and blue-green swirls,
powder-coated interior, and
closed-end handle; second half
19th century, undamaged, blue
example with light wear, aqua
example with losses to interior
coating, 5-1/4" to 9" l. **$374**

Courtesy of Jeffrey S. Evans & Associates

Decorated free-blown parade
staff, opal with applied green
and gray swirled ribs, open tip,
late 19th/early 20th century,
undamaged, 58" l. **$316**

Courtesy of Jeffrey S. Evans & Associates

decorative in nature.

"Many times pieces, such as powder-horn form bottles, were actual production pieces that
were sold as novelty containers. When these were made from colorful decorated glass and
raised on a standard or foot, they were often sold as mantle decorations. So technically these
objects are not whimsies – although they are certainly whimsical."

Many whimsies are bought and sold at antique bottle shows, with some appearing at glass
shows and auctions. Evans, whose Mount Crawford, Virginia, firm sells approximately 50 to
100 whimsies per year through its glass and lighting sales, says bottles and/or fruit jars made
into hats or other forms see the most interest at auction. The most extraordinary piece he has
sold is a pressed Greentown Holly Amber pattern shelf support or hat stand made by joining
two compote bases top-to-top. The 9"-high piece brought a remarkable $8,250 (including 10
percent buyer's premium) in a 2007 glass auction.

"A general collector should collect whimsies for fun and not investment," Evans advised.
And just like any other collectible venture, the buyer needs to be educated on the subject. He
says most whimsies are fairly inexpensive and trade for less than $200. But there are some
extreme examples. "Whimsies that were produced from American historical flasks would
probably fetch in excess of $100,000 if one ever came on the market," he said.

— *Karen Knapstein* Print Editor, *Antique Trader* magazine

HUNTING & FISHING COLLECTIBLES

FOR DIE-HARD HUNTERS, there's nothing better than spending time surrounded by vintage examples of the brands and tools they use in the field and on the water. The market for vintage hunting and fishing collectibles has seen prices creep ever northward out of the hundreds and into the thousands in recent years. The diverse category touches on thousands of different items and price points, with even nominally priced items finding new homes every day.

DECOYS

Collectors may be drawn to derelicts or those carved by the most well-respected carvers in North America. "There has been established, over the past 40 years or so, a 'pecking order' of the most collectible carvers of old decoys," said Stan VanEtten, publisher of *Hunting & Fishing Collectibles Magazine.* "But by no means is there within our hobby/business an agreed-upon list of these renowned artisans; and, in fact, there is no universal agreement as to what is old." A rare back-preening elder hen carved in the early 1900s by Augustus "Gus" Aaron Wilson sold for $36,000 at a Slotin folk art auction in late 2014, against an $8,000 estimate. It's estimated that Wilson, a prolific carver from South Portland, Maine, carved the decoy while he was employed as a lighthouse keeper.

Black-bellied plover decoy, circa 1912, A. E. Crowell, original paint, head turned back approximately 110 degrees over right shoulder and terminating in carved bill, split tail with raised wingtips and seldom-seen carved split lower tail feathers....................**$40,250**

Courtesy of Decoys Unlimited

EPHEMERA

Hunting and fishing ephemera is among the scarcest of all collectibles in this category. It doesn't always have to be paper, as the word is so often associated. Ephemera, including wooden boxes, labels, hunting tags and licenses, and even specialty magazines, all find a price among hunting and fishing collectors.

At Lang's Auction, the world's largest fishing tackle auction house, a rare catalog crossed the block in 2014. Plainly titled *Jim Heddon's Fishing Tackle,* the catalog held 46 pages of the Heddon company's inventory for 1913, including James Heddon's last invention, the Dummy Double. It even showed a crisp image of the #1400 Single Hook Minnow, widely considered the most desirable of all Heddon baits. When the hammer fell, the catalog sold for $1,200.

ADVERTISING

Hunting- and fishing-themed advertising items are among the most sought-after today. The market bull's-eye still revolves around the biggest names in advertising displays:

Bufflehead drake decoy, A. E. (Elmer) Crowell, deeply carved and crossed wingtips with fluted tail feather carving, tiny split crest carved into rear of head, rare and important. **$207,000**

Courtesy of Decoys Unlimited

Winchester, Peters, Remington, and Western Powder. Even pieces in compromised condition are bringing good prices on eBay: A center panel for a circa 1915 Winchester die-cut window advertising "Hunter and Guide" display recently sold for $3,150, and an 1896 Winchester calendar, showing water markings, fading, and glued to a board, brought $900.

Demand is so great for early Winchester paper that aluminum signs are being mass-produced by the thousands in the United States – not overseas. These fakes and fantasy pieces are designed after 19th century cartridge boards. Rectangular signs measure 12-1/5" x 16" and 16" x 8-1/2", and circular signs are often 11" or 12" in diameter. The popularity of the these signs is overwhelming, mostly because prices are less than $10 shipped and lots of collectors really want a piece of Winchester lore and history.

Documented examples of spring-operated mechanical traps to capture animals and humans first appeared in the 1500s, but collectors think they were used far earlier. They are often called "gin traps," as derived from the word "engine." Their effectiveness is directly related to the strength of the spring and the teeth in the jaws.

LURES

Perhaps unsurprisingly, a nice collection of vintage lures spanning a full century can be assembled for less than $500. Most lures sell at auction for between $1 and $100. Lures valued greater than $1,000 are generally early examples, uncataloged examples, in excellent condition, rare finds with original boxes, or prototypes.

An early folk art minnow dating from the late 1880s to the early 1900s brought $1,180 at a sale held by Crossroads Angling Auctions. The lure was likely made by employees active in the shops of Pflueger (Trory), Friend, Pardee/Manco or Kent; or the shops of Shaeffer/Holzwarth/Woods. The lure displays distinctive hat-shaped, oval props with integral thrusters that are generally associated with an Ohio-based carriage-manufacturing company. It proved irresistible for collectors of folk art lures – a very active and passionate subset of the lure-collecting hobby.

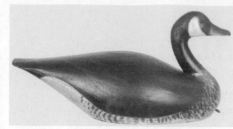

Goose decoy, A.E. Crowell, deep rasping to breast and to rear of two-piece head and neck, original Crowell paint with outstanding painted feather detail...**$31,050**

Courtesy of Decoys Unlimited

Rare boxed birdcage fly reel, Billinghurst, 1859, Rochester, New York, credited as first patented American fly reel and only fourth reel patented in United States, brass with folding handle with walnut grasp, circular green box, 3-1/4" dia..**$36,000**

Courtesy of Lang's Auction

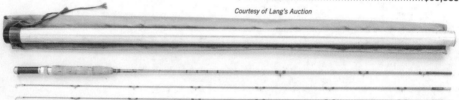

Rare 7' Dickerson Model 7012 fly rod, circa 1962, made by master rod maker Lyle Dickerson of Michigan, 2/2 rod, chrome guides, light brown wraps, tipped black, four signature wraps on butt section, swelled butt, and walnut reel seat with aluminum screw down-locking hardware, cork handle, light ridging on some rings, nearly 7' l. **$6,050**

Courtesy of Lang's Auction

Gear, circa 1900, rope with wood floats, collapsible oak net, Hardy Brothers bamboo rod, Hardy Brothers combination fishing gaff and scale, marks to reel: Hardy Bros Ltd, England, "The Perfect," 3-7/8", circa 1891; net 48" l. ...**$300**

Courtesy of Heritage Auctions

Display, Peters Cartridge Co., die-cut, Rustless Shells, 13-1/4" w. x 9" h. ....**$600-$900**

Courtesy of Hal Bogguss

Lure, Hosmer Mechanical Froggie, by J. D. Hosmer of Dearborn, Michigan, mid-1930s, green frog spot model with off-white belly and red accents, appears to be "unfished," original box, 5" l. **$15,000**

Courtesy of Lang's Auction

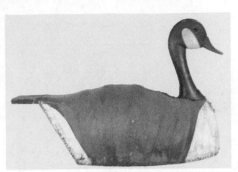

Decoy, circa 1902, Captain Clarence Bailey, folk art carving of canvas-over-frame goose, 36-1/2" from tip of tail to breast and 23-3/4" from bottom board to top of head................................... **$7,475**

Courtesy of Decoys Unlimited

Greater yellowlegs decoy, Joseph Lincoln of Hingham, Massachusetts, elaborate plumage, paint applied with variety of patterns achieved with matchstick and trimmed paint brush. **$8,625**

Courtesy of Decoys Unlimited

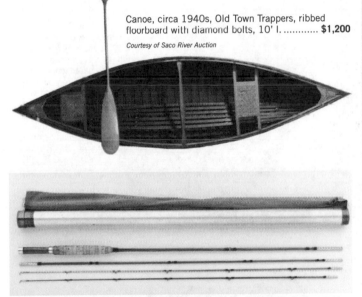

Canoe, circa 1940s, Old Town Trappers, ribbed floorboard with diamond bolts, 10' l. **$1,200**

Courtesy of Saco River Auction

Spear, early 20th century, hand-forged, unknown maker but likely upstate New York, spring-loaded with iron rivets securing two sections, 15" l. **$550**

Courtesy of Lang's Auction

Leonard rod, circa 1930s, 3/2 model, black wraps tipped in red, English twist snake guides, guides wrapped with black, red, and olive tipping, reel seat butternut, extra thin "Tournament" stamped cap and ring hardware......... **$1,200**

Courtesy of Lang's Auction

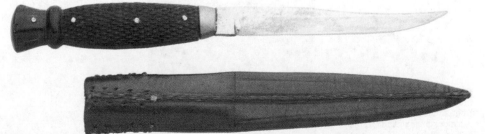

Hunting knife, unmarked, brass ferrule, leather scabbard with integral belt loop, 5" l. $40

Courtesy of Heritage Auctions

Lure, Bug-a-Moth, by Creek Chub, marked 501, 20th century, original "open top" box, rare...$3,100

Courtesy of Lang's Auction

Philbrook & Payne reel, circa 1877, marked Bangor, ME, early example with tapered ivory grasp, conical rear journal, marbleized side plates, raised pillar frame, only one known with rare company stamp, 2-3/8" dia., 13/16" w. ...$7,260

Courtesy of Lang's Auction

Fish trap, Philippine Islands, 20th century, 67" h., 18" dia...............................$88

Courtesy of Heritage Auctions

Banner, Daisy Air Rifle Co., "Happy Daisy Boy," 1913, Graphics Arts Co., top and bottom bands, 14" w. x 20-7/8" h. ....$6,000-$7,000

Courtesy of Hal Bogguss

Raised pillar multiplying reel, bronze frame and aluminum front and rear end plate inserts, 6 o'clock handle, knurled rear sliding click switch and knurled and removable end caps... $1,200

Courtesy of Lang's Auction

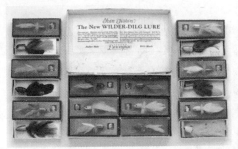

Store display, Heddon, Wilder-Dilg picture box set, circa 1930s, with one each of all 12 picture boxes produced, rare, individual boxes 1-1/2" h. x 7/8" d. x 3-7/8" w., display 5" h. x 1-7/8" d. x 8" w...**$7,500**

Courtesy of Lang's Auction

Licenses, set of 36 Pennsylvania metal hunting back tag, 14 non-residents, seven special deer licenses, seven specific county licenses, and eight residents.. **$1,180**

Courtesy of Blanchard's Auction Service

Rare reel by Edward R. Hewitt (1866-1957), handmade by noted Catskill fly fisherman, one of only eight known, marked with low number "7" on aluminum foot and hand-etched on tail plate "Made by Edward R. Hewitt," aluminum and nickel silver, 3-1/2" dia., reel (pillar to pillar) with 3/4"-wide spool sports and oversized roller pillar positioned for left-hand wind angler and large spool screw, eight-position drag arm fitted to rear plate.............**$10,000**

Courtesy of Lang's Auction

Nine Wisconsin bowhunters' pins, 1942-1949, hand-stamped "43" and extra "44" pin, very good condition... **$3,993**

Courtesy of Lang's Auction

Rare Mitchell Model 410 global spinning reel, 1971, 29 country names around rotor, of two styles made to commemorate special event, one of five known, commemorative item to celebrate 20 million reels sold. **$6,957**

Courtesy of Lang's Auction

Royal Malleable Crystal Body Fly lure, circa 1883, Enterprise Mfg. Co., "Luminous Crystal Minnow," original feather dressing, hackle, wire-wrapped peacock herl tail, and stationary single hook, glass body "filled with a luminous substance" that still produces strong glow, hand-cut glass beads fore and aft, with original 1883 patent paper filed by Ernest F. Pflueger, rare, 1-3/8" l. **$3,393**

Courtesy of Lang's Auction

Game launcher made by Cook, Mark III bird release (used to train dogs for hunting), 7" h. x 15" w. **$12**

Courtesy of Affiliated Auctions

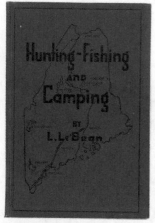

L.L. Bean, *Hunting-Fishing and Camping*, Freeport, Maine: L.L. Bean, 1944, fifth edition, octavo, original cloth binding. **$65**

Courtesy of Heritage Auctions

Hunting permit, 1936, $1 Canada Geese, top plate number single, o.g., never hinged...............................**$426**

Courtesy of Heritage Auctions

Western Shells rare die-cut cardboard advertising manifest, hunter with pheasants at approximately half of life-size, advertised shotgun shell and two types of shells, "New Chief" and "Record," sold by Western Shells brand, rare, 26-1/5" h. x 38" w. **$760**

Courtesy of Manifest Auctions

Zane Grey, *Fly Fishing*, Utica: Horrocks-Ibbotson Co., 1936, first edition, small octavo, publisher's original pictorial wrappers bound with two staples, Horrocks-Ibbotson fishing equipment catalog with seven-page Grey essay.........**$468**

Courtesy of Heritage Auctions

"Mallard or Anas Platyrhynchos," Athos Rudolfo Menaboni (Italian/American, 1895-1990), gouache, signed and titled, No. 32L, 38-1/5" h. x 27-1/5" w. **$12,100**

Courtesy of Ahlers & Ogletree

1889 N8 Allen & Ginter "Fish from American Waters" near set (49/50) cards, circa 1889. ....**$3,107**

Courtesy of Heritage Auctions

Tintype, hunter and dog, 19th century, quarter plate tintype in half embossed leather frame. ...**$150**

Courtesy of Heritage Auctions

ILLUSTRATION ART

EXPOSURE PLAYS AN important role in collector demand and values for illustration art, which has proven itself over the last decade as one of the most popular and dynamic art genres in the country.

Take for instance "Hello Everybody!," a calendar illustration originally produced for Brown & Bigelow in the late 1920s. Artist Rolf Armstrong created the carefree pastel on board of a young lady with a bright smile at the onset of the Roaring '20s and the Great Depression. Popular reaction was enthusiastic. The artwork appeared as a calendar illustration, on playing cards, puzzles, a die-cut advertising sign for Orange Kist soda pop, and as the cover for the March 1929 edition of *College Humor* magazine. According to Janet Dobson's *Pin Up Dreams: The Glamour Art of Rolf Armstrong*, early works such as "Hello Everybody!" defined the vision of feminine beauty for the next 40 years and earned Armstrong the title of "Father of the Pin-Up Artists." The exposure and reputation of the artist generated strong demand when the original work finally came up for auction and its sale price was pushed to $30,000.

"Hello Everybody!" represents the type of subject matter that is attracting mainstream attention.

"It's really what we think of as classic images in all genres that speak directly and powerfully to a specific time period – whether it's a 1940s *Saturday Evening Post* cover, 1950s science-fiction paperback cover, or 1960s Gil Elvgren calendar pin-up," said Todd Hignite, director of illustration art at Heritage Auctions, the world's largest auctioneer of illustration art and related works.

Attributed to Frederick Sands Brunner, Royal Crown Cola advertisement, circa 1942, oil on board, part of advertising campaign with Hollywood starlets, restretched over original stretcher with restoration, 20-1/2" x 12-1/2"..........**$1,500**

Courtesy of Swann Auction Galleries

Interestingly, as the market for illustration art matures, auctioneers are reclassifying works as American fine art and offering works by artists with household names along with other artists such as Grandma Moses, Leroy Neiman, or by the Wyeths. Norman Rockwell's works now routinely bring in excess of $2 million at auction, but his early illustration art, steeped in sentimentality and strong national pride, may be found for less than $100,000.

"Well-known artists such as Rockwell did indeed work in advertising – many illustrators did – and it's certainly less expensive than a magazine cover by the same artist," Hignite said.

Although industry watchers are excited to see many illustration artists make the leap from illustration art to American fine art, there are dozens, perhaps thousands, of artists whose identity is still lost but whose art lives on. Currently these works are anonymously attributed

Walter Baumhofer, "Dr. Walters glanced back. Howell was whispering to Louise as though the savagery around them were a thousand miles away," oil on canvas, illustration published as part of story "Test Swamp" by Wyatt Blassingame in *American Magazine*, February 1955, 27" x 38"...$1,063

Courtesy of Swann Auction Galleries

James Neil Boyle, "Bikini," acrylic and colored pencil illustration for advertisement, circa early 1960s, signed in image, lower right, old matte attached to perimeter, 24" x 18-1/2"............................. **$650**

Courtesy of Swann Auction Galleries

simply as "American artist," but that doesn't mean research has stopped looking into the identity of these artists. Scholars have been given a boost in recent years thanks to collectors who remain fascinated by various styles.

"The scholarship and research in the field is very active and, between exhibitions, publications, and more dealers handling the work, is increasing all the time, but there's still a lot of work to be done in terms of identifying art," Hignite said. "Oftentimes artists didn't sign their paintings, and if their style isn't immediately identifiable, there's a good deal of digging to do. Much of the best research actually comes from devoted fans and collectors, who doggedly put together extensive checklists and track down publication histories, check stubs from publishers, biographies, etc., to try and enhance our understanding of the history."

This confluence of awareness, appreciation, and a growing nostalgia for mid-century works has more than doubled values for pieces offered just a few short years ago. Gil Elvgren's original pin-up art from the collection of author Charles Martignette was sold at auction beginning in 2009 for amounts ranging from $40,000 to $60,000. However, purchase offers are now hovering between $120,000 to as much as $155,000 for the works.

Hignite credits the increase to a matter of supply and demand. "I think simply the opportunity to see a steady supply of great art by Elvgren has increased the demand," he said. "If you see one of his paintings in person, there's no question of his painting talent, and collector confidence increases as we see such a steady growth and consistent sales results."

Dan Andreasen, "Felicity Reading," oil on gessoed illustration board, original illustration for poster to promote reading and "Felicity" series of *American Girl* books, circa 1980s, monogrammed in image, lower right corner, signed by Andreasen in pencil below image on mount, 25" x 17" on 28" x 20" board mount. **$1,000**

Courtesy of Swann Auction Galleries

Benton Henderson Clark, "Buggywhipped," oil on canvas, signed and dated 1942 in lower right corner, 33-1/2" x 24-1/2". **$2,500**

Courtesy of Swann Auction Galleries

George Barbier, perfume box design, gouache, ink and watercolor heightened in gold, on paper, circa 1920, likely done for Paul Poiret's perfume company, archivally matted and framed, 5-7/8" x 5-7/8". **$1,500**

Courtesy of Swann Auction Galleries

Lucille Corcos, "Everybody's Downtown," tempera on board, circa 1950, small town Main Street at night, signed lower left, mounted to page in album containing 10 printed copies of Corcos' covers and fold-out illustrations, 14-1/2" x 11-1/8". **$8,125**

Courtesy of Swann Auction Galleries

Joseph Keppler, "U.S. Senate," watercolor, ink and pencil over lithographed background on paper, enraged citizens throwing a half dozen senators out of two windows, signed lower left, matted and framed, 18-3/4" x 12-1/4"; Keppler was one of the most popular political cartoonists of the 19th century. **$750**

Courtesy of Swann Auction Galleries

Aubrey Beardsley, "A Young Tough," pen and ink on paper, published in *The Bon-Mots of Samuel Foote and Theodore Hook*, March 1894, 4-1/2" x 2-3/8"............**$13,750**

Courtesy of Swann Auction Galleries

Walt Disney Studios, "The Aristocats," group of 11 hand-painted animation cels (one shown), circa 1970, with "Big Chief from Peter Pan" color production layout drawing on paper, circa 1953; "The Aristocats" 7-3/4" x 9-3/4", "Big Chief" 11-1/2" x 15"............**$3,380**

Courtesy of Swann Auction Galleries

Edward McKnight Kauffer, "Ranger," gouache on board, advertisement for Charles Eneu Johnson Printing Inks, signed and dated lower right, artist's ink stamp verso "Designed by E Mck Kauffer, 26 Aug 1925" and his original copyright label signed in ink, tipped to archival matte, 12-1/4" x 9-1/2"... **$1,875**

Courtesy of Swann Auction Galleries

Edith Head, costume design for Olivia de Havilland in role of Catherine Sloper in "The Heiress," watercolor, ink and pencil on paper, circa 1949, signed in pencil, lower right, 10" x 7-1/2"; Head won an Academy Award for Best Costume Design for the movie................... **$4,000**

Courtesy of Swann Auction Galleries

Peter Arno, "We've Lost Our Tour," pen, ink and gouache on paper, cartoon for *The New Yorker*, July 4, 1953, with *The New Yorker* stamps and printing marks on verso, signed lower right margin, framed with captioned matter, 18" x 13"...........**$4,500**

Courtesy of Swann Auction Galleries

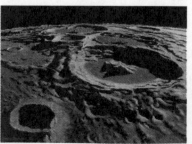

Chesley Bonestell (American, 1888-1986), "50 Miles Above the Moon (Conquest of Space)," mixed media on board, signed lower left, framed and matted under glass, no visible condition issues, 21-3/4" x 25-3/4".......**$17,500**

Courtesy of Heritage Auctions

Stanley Meltzoff (American, 1917-2006), "Hetty Green, The Witch of Wall Street," oil on board, story illustration for *Argosy* magazine, February 1959, initialed lower left, 16-1/4" x 11-3/4, 28-3/4" x 22" framed; Green was America's first female financial titan, responsible for helping bail out New York City in 1907 and twice more..............**$10,000**

Courtesy of Heritage Auctions

Bart Forbes (American, b. 1939), "Joe Dimaggio," oil on canvas, circa 1999, signed lower right, unlined canvas, canvas slightly loose on stretcher, 21" x 16", 24-3/4" x 18-3/4" framed............. **$2,750**

Courtesy of Heritage Auctions

Jack Thurston (American, 20th century), "Star Trek: The Final Frontier, STARLOG #1," accompanied by framed magazine cover, August 1976, gouache on board, 20-1/2" x 16-1/2"..............**$11,875**

Courtesy of Heritage Auctions

Garth Williams, "The Rabbits' Wedding," ink wash, pencil, and charcoal on board, published as double-page illustration, circa 1958, 11-3/4" x 18-3/4"; book made news when segregationist Senator E.O. Eddins demanded it be removed from all libraries in his home state of Alabama because he found the marriage of a white rabbit and a black rabbit to be racially offensive. **$10,625**

Courtesy of Swann Auction Galleries

Nick Hufford (American, 20th century), billboard advertisement for Esso Motor Oil, oil on canvas board with paper appliqué, circa 1952, signed lower left, light surface grime, flecks of paint loss in text, 17" x 37-3/4", 22-1/4" x 42-1/4" framed. **$1,750**

Courtesy of Heritage Auctions

Florence Scovell Shinn, "Mrs. Wiggs of the Cabbage Patch," pen and ink with color wash on paper, original illustration for first illustrated edition of Alice Caldwell's Hegan's *Mrs. Wiggs of the Cabbage Patch*, circa 1903, signed at bottom, with first edition of book, matted and laid over cardboard, 9-3/4" x 7-3/4".......................... **$2,000**

Courtesy of Swann Auction Galleries

Frederick Sands Brunner, Par-T-Pack Cola advertisement of woman with U.S. servicemen, oil on canvas, circa 1934, signed in image, lower left, restretched on original stretcher in contemporary frame, 41" x 33"; Rita Hayworth may have been the model for the advertisement. **$6,250**

Courtesy of Swann Auction Galleries

Arthur Rackham, "Frost," watercolor, ink and gouache on paper, circa 1922, signed in full, lower right image, with archivally removed matte with Rackham's caption, in ink: "Frost. Hawthrone's Wonder Book / Arthur Rackham," 9-3/4" x 8"..**$11,250**

Courtesy of Swann Auction Galleries

Howard Chandler Christy, "The farmer crossed the plowed strip to Saxon, and joined her on the rail," ink, watercolor and gouache on board, illustration for first appearance of Jack London's novel *The Valley of the Moon, Cosmopolitan Magazine*, September 1913, signed in full, lower left, contemporary wooden frame, 39" x 29-1/2".. **$3,500**

Courtesy of Swann Auction Galleries

Alice and Martin Provensen, "Maple Hill Farm Animals," watercolor and ink on thin parchment paper, original illustration from book *Our Animal Friends at Maple Hill Farm*, circa 1974, signed in lower image, 13" x 19". **$1,188**

Courtesy of Swann Auction Galleries

John Conrad Berkey (American, 1932-2008), "New York City: The 22nd Century," gouache on board, faint dots of possible surface residue in sky and distant city skyline, 22" x 13", 24-1/2" x 17-1/4" framed............... **$2,375**

Courtesy of Heritage Auctions

Bob Mackie (American, b. 1940), design sketch of The Supremes, felt tip pen and marked on paper, circa 1968, signed, titled and dated along bottom edge, 18" x 13-1/2", 23-1/2" x 19" framed...... **$3,750**

Courtesy of Heritage Auctions

Robert C. Kaufmann (American, 1900-1999), "Art Deco Ski Bunny," oil on canvas, published as magazine cover image, circa 1933-1938, signed lower right, professional varnish, framed, 38" x 19"...................... **$9,375**

Courtesy of Heritage Auctions

Willy Pogany (Hungarian/American, 1882-1955), chapter head illustration in *Down the Rabbit-Hole, Alice's Adventures in Wonderland*, appliqué, pen, ink, and white highlight on paper, circa 1929, signed lower left, light overall paper discoloration, light soiling along sheet corners, scattered minor surface smudges, faint possible water stains in left and right margins, 13" x 11"....................... **$2,000**

Courtesy of Heritage Auctions

Frank Kelly Freas (American, 1922-2005), "Double Star," pen and ink with white highlights on paper, interior illustration in *Astounding Science Fiction* magazine, initialed lower right, pinpoints of foxing in upper right quadrant, 5-3/4" x 6-2/3" matted and framed.........**$5,625**

Courtesy of Heritage Auctions

Gil Elvgren (American, 1914-1980), "Doggone Good (Puppy Love)," oil on canvas, Brown & Bigelow calendar illustration, circa 1959, signed lower right, unlined and stretcher creases visible, 30" x 24", 37" x 31" framed. $59,375

Courtesy of Heritage Auctions

Allen Anderson (American, 1908-1995), "The Shootout," oil on canvas, published as cover of *Western Aces*, April 1943, signed lower right, faint stretcher crease with light craquelure on top edge, light accretions to right of horse's nose, 30" x 21". $11,250

Courtesy of Heritage Auctions

Harry Anderson (American, 1906-1996), "The Oldest House, St. Augustine, Florida, 1934 Chrysler Airflow," Great Moments in Early American Motoring calendar illustration, gouache on board, signed lower right, 21" x 26", 28-3/4" x 33-3/4" framed. **$4,375**

Courtesy of Heritage Auctions

Gilbert Adrian, "Fantasy Wedding," graphite and pastel on blue wove paper, created for the "Well-Groomed Africa" series of works, circa 1950, signed in red pastel, lower right corner, matted and framed, 17-1/2" x 23-1/2". **$4,000**

Courtesy of Swann Auction Galleries

Tomi Ungerer, "One Fine Morning," mixed media illustration on paper, on page mock-up for first English edition of *Warwick's Three (3) Bottles* by Ungerer and Andre Hodier, circa 1966, signed in pencil, lower margin, printer marks along outer margins, 5-1/2" x 7-1/4". **$2,080**

Courtesy of Swann Auction Galleries

JEWELRY

JEWELRY HAS HELD a special place for humankind since prehistoric times, both as an emblem of personal status and as a decorative adornment worn for its sheer beauty. This tradition continues today. We should keep in mind, however, that it was only with the growth of the Industrial Revolution that jewelry first became cheap enough so that even the person of modest means could win a piece or two.

Only since around the mid-19th century did certain forms of jewelry, especially pins and brooches, begin to appear on the general market as a mass-produced commodity and the Victorians took to it immediately. Major production centers for the finest pieces of jewelry remained in Europe, especially Italy and England, but less expensive pieces were also exported to the booming American market and soon some American manufacturers also joined in the trade. Especially during the Civil War era, when silver and gold supplies grew tremendously in the U.S., did jewelry in silver or with silver, brass or gold-filled (i.e. gold-plated or goldplate) mounts begin to flood the market here. By the turn of the 20th century all the major mail-order companies and small town jewelry shops could offer a huge variety of inexpensive jewelry pieces aimed at not only the feminine buyer but also her male counterpart.

Inexpensive jewelry of the late 19th and early 20th century is still widely available and often at modest prices. Even more in demand today is costume jewelry, well-designed jewelry produced of inexpensive materials and meant to carefully accent a woman's ensemble. Today costume jewelry of the 20th century has become one of the most active areas in the field of collecting and some of the finest pieces, signed by noted designers and manufacturers, can reach price levels nearly equal to much earlier and scarcer examples.

Jewelry prices, as in every other major collecting field, are influenced by a number of factors including local demand, quality, condition and rarity. As market prices have risen in recent years it has become even more important for the collector to shop and buy with care. Learn as much as you can about your favorite area of jewelry and keep abreast of market trends and stay alert to warnings about alterations, repairs or reproductions that can be found on the market.

For more information on jewelry, see *Warman's Jewelry Identification and Price Guide, 5th edition.*

Jewelry Styles

Jewelry has been a part of every culture throughout time, reflecting the times as well as social and aesthetic movements. Jewelry is usually divided into periods and styles. Each period may have several styles, with some of the same styles and types of jewelry being made in both precious and non-precious materials. Elements of one period may also overlap into others.

Georgian, 1760-1837. Fine jewelry from this period is quite desirable, but few good-quality pieces have found their way to auction in recent years. Sadly, much jewelry from this period has been lost.

Victorian, 1837-1901. Queen Victoria of England ascended to the throne in 1837 and remained queen until her death in 1901. The Victorian period is a long and prolific one, abundant with many styles of jewelry. It warrants being divided into three sub-periods: Early or Romantic period dating from 1837-1860; Mid or Grand period dating from 1860-1880; and Late or Aesthetic period dating from 1880-1901.

Sentiment and romance were significant factors in Victorian jewelry. Often, jewelry and clothing represented love and affection, with symbolic motifs such as hearts, crosses, hands, flowers, anchors, doves, crowns, knots, stars, thistles, wheat, garlands, horseshoes and moons. The materials of the time were also abundant and varied. They included silver, gold, diamonds, onyx, glass, cameo, paste, carnelian, agate, coral, amber, garnet, emeralds, opals, pearls, peridot, rubies, sapphires, marcasites, cut steel, enameling, tortoiseshell, topaz, turquoise, bog oak, ivory, jet, hair, gutta percha and vulcanite.

Sentiments of love were often expressed in miniatures. Sometimes they were representative of deceased loved ones, but often the miniatures were of the living. Occasionally, the miniatures depicted landscapes, cherubs or religious themes.

Hair jewelry was a popular expression of love and sentiment. The hair of a loved one was placed in a special compartment in a brooch or a locket, or used to form a picture under a glass compartment. Later in the mid-19th century, pieces of jewelry were made completely of woven hair. Individual strands of hair would be woven together to create necklaces, watch chains, brooches, earrings and rings.

In 1861, Queen Victoria's husband, Prince Albert, died. The queen went into mourning for the rest of her life, and

Georgian multi-stone and gold brooch with cabochon, oval, and pear-shaped cabochon-cut opals weighing 0.60 carat, cushion-cut rubies weighing 0.25 carat, cushion-cut emeralds weighing 0.15 carat each, set in 14k gold, 2-1/2" x 1"...........................**$325**

Courtesy of Heritage Auctions

Antique tortoiseshell suite, brooch and earpendants each with floral motifs and suspending drops, gilt-metal findings, 2-7/8" l., 3". ...**$984**

Courtesy of Skinner, Inc.; www.skinnerinc.com

◀ Antique gold and hairwork sentimental suite, pair of bracelets and brooch (not shown), each braided strap of hair with shaped gold and hairwork clasp with enamel border of entwined snakes and flowers, each inscribed and in original fitted box, 6-1/2" l., 1-1/4".......................**$2,000-$3,000**

Courtesy of Skinner, Inc.; www.skinnerinc.com

Victorian diamond and silver-topped gold necklace with rose-cut diamonds weighing 10.00 carats, set in silver-topped 14k pink gold, 16-1/2" l........ **$5,313**

Courtesy of Heritage Auctions

Edwardian diamond heart pendant/brooch, scrolling foliate heart set with old mine-cut diamonds, approximately 2.48 carats, platinum-topped 18k gold mount, and suspended from platinum and diamond chain set with 21 old European- and old mine-cut diamonds bead-set in octagonal bezels, approximately 5.09 carats, 1-3/16" l., 29-1/4"..... **$15,990**

Courtesy of Skinner, Inc.; www.skinnerinc.com

Victoria required that the royal court wear black. This atmosphere spread to the populace and created a demand for mourning jewelry, which is typically black. When it first came into fashion, it was made from jet, fossilized wood. By 1850, there were dozens of English workshops making jet brooches, lockets, bracelets and necklaces. As the supply of jet dwindled, other materials were used such as vulcanite, gutta percha, bog oak and French jet.

By the 1880s, somber mourning jewelry was losing popularity. Fashions had changed and the clothing was simpler and had an air of delicacy. The Industrial Revolution, which had begun in the early part of the century, was now in full swing and machine-manufactured jewelry was affordable to the working class.

Edwardian, 1890-1920. The Edwardian period takes its name from England's King Edward VII. Though he ascended to the throne in 1901, he and his wife, Alexandra of Denmark, exerted influence over the period before and after his ascension.

The 1890s were known as La Belle Epoque. This was a time known for ostentation and extravagance. As the years passed, jewelry became simpler and smaller. Instead of wearing one large brooch, women were often found wearing several small lapel pins.

In the early 1900s, platinum, diamonds and pearls were prevalent in the jewelry of the wealthy, while paste was being used by the masses to imitate the real thing. The styles were reminiscent of the neo-classical and rococo motifs. The jewelry was lacy and ornate, feminine and delicate.

Arts & Crafts, 1890-1920. The Arts & Crafts movement was focused on artisans and craftsmanship. There was a simplification of form where the material was secondary to the design. Guilds of artisans banded together. Some jewelry was mass-produced, but the most highly prized examples of this period are handmade and signed by their makers. The pieces were simple and at times abstract. They could be hammered, patinated and acid etched. Common materials were brass, bronze, copper, silver, blister pearls, freshwater pearls, turquoise, agate, opals, moonstones, coral, horn, ivory, base metals, amber, cabochon-cut garnets and amethysts.

Art Nouveau, 1895-1910. In 1895, Samuel Bing opened a shop called "Maison de l'Art Nouveau" at 22 Rue de Provence in Paris. Art Nouveau designs in the jewelry were characterized by a sensuality that took on the forms of the female figure, butterflies, dragonflies, peacocks, snakes, wasps, swans, bats, orchids, irises and other exotic flowers. The lines used whiplash curves to create a feeling of lushness and opulence.

Arts & Crafts 14k gold, moonstone, sapphire, and split pearl bracelet with bezel-set moonstones and foliate panels set with circular-cut sapphires and split pearls, 7-3/8" l.. **$4,920**

Courtesy of Skinner, Inc.; www.skinnerinc.com

▼ Art Nouveau 14k gold and amethyst bracelet, Krementz & Co., hinged bangle with floral and foliate motifs, set with five circular-cut amethysts, 11.1 dwt, maker's mark, 7" interior circumference. **$2,214**

Courtesy of Skinner, Inc.; www.skinnerinc.com

1920s-1930s. Costume jewelry began its steady ascent to popularity in the 1920s. Since it was relatively inexpensive to produce, it was mass-produced. The sizes and designs of the jewelry varied. Often, it was worn a few times, disposed of and then replaced with a new piece. It was thought of as expendable, a cheap throwaway to dress up an outfit. Costume jewelry became so popular that it was sold in both upscale and "five and dime" stores.

During the 1920s, fashions were often accompanied by jewelry that drew on the Art Deco movement, which got its beginning in Paris at the "Exposition Internationale des Arts Décoratifs et Industriels Modernes" held in 1925. The idea behind this movement was that form follows function. The style was characterized by simple, straight, clean lines, stylized motifs and geometric shapes. Favored materials included chrome, rhodium, pot metal, glass, rhinestones, Bakelite and celluloid.

One designer who played an important role was Coco Chanel. Though previously reserved for evening wear, the jewelry was worn by Chanel during the day, making it fashionable for millions of other women to do so, too.

With the 1930s came the Depression and the advent of World War II. Perhaps in response to the gloom, designers began using enameling and brightly colored rhinestones to create whimsical birds, flowers, circus animals, bows, dogs and just about every other figural form imaginable.

Retro Modern, 1939-1950. Other jewelry designs of the 1940s were big and bold. Retro Modern had a more substantial feel to it and designers began using larger stones to enhance the dramatic pieces. The jewelry was stylized and exaggerated. Common motifs included flowing scrolls, bows, ribbons, birds, animals, snakes, flowers and knots.

Sterling silver now became the metal of choice, often dipped in a gold wash known as vermeil.

Designers often incorporated patriotic themes of American flags, the V-sign, Uncle Sam's hat, airplanes, anchors and eagles.

Post-War Modern, 1945-1965. This was a movement that emphasized the artistic approach to jewelry making. It is also referred to as Mid-Century Modern. This approach was occurring at a time when the Beat Generation was prevalent. These avant-garde designers created jewelry that was handcrafted to illustrate the artist's own concepts and ideas. The materials often used were sterling, gold, copper, brass, enamel, cabochons, wood, quartz and amber.

1950s-1960s. The 1950s saw the rise of jewelry that was made purely of rhinestones: necklaces, bracelets, earrings and pins. The focus of the early 1960s was on clean lines: Pillbox hats and A-line dresses with short jackets were a mainstay for the conservative woman. The large, bold rhinestone pieces were no longer the must-have accessory. They were now replaced with smaller, more delicate gold-tone metal and faux pearls with only a hint of rhinestones.

At the other end of the spectrum were psychedelic-colored clothing, Nehru jackets, thigh-high miniskirts and go-go boots. These clothes were accessorized with beads, large metal pendants and occasionally big, bold rhinestones. By the late 1960s, there was a movement back to Mother Nature and the "hippie" look was born. Ethnic clothing, tie-dye, long skirts, fringe and jeans were the prevalent style, and the rhinestone had, for the most part, been left behind.

BRACELETS

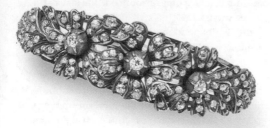

Antique diamond bracelet, hinged bangle set with silver and old mine-cut diamond flowers, 18k gold mount, 26.8 dwt, 6-1/2" interior circumference...... **$3,690**

Courtesy of Skinner, Inc.; www.skinnerinc.com

Vintage crystal rock, diamond, and gold bracelet, 14k white gold, with one small diamond, very good condition, rock crystal 17mm x 19mm, 6-1/2". **$203**

Courtesy of Heritage Auctions

Art Deco colored diamond, diamond, and platinum bracelet with square-cut brown diamond measuring 6.00mm x 5.60mm x 3.80mm and weighing 0.95 carat, square-cut diamonds weighing 1.60 carats, square-cut pink diamond weighing 0.35 carat, outlined by European and single-cut diamonds weighing 8.25 carats, cut-cornered rectangle-shaped diamonds weighing 0.65 carat, set in platinum, Austrian hallmark, 7-1/4" x-1/2". **$21,250**

Courtesy of Heritage Auctions

Art Deco aquamarine, diamond, and gold "Reflections" bracelet, Trabert & Hoeffer-Mauboussin, hinged bangle with emerald-cut aquamarine measuring 24.94mm x 16.84mm x 13.40mm and weighing 38.25 carats, shield- and kite-shaped diamonds weighing 1.00 carat, full-cut diamonds weighing 4.40 carats, and emerald-cut diamonds weighing 1.80 carats, set in 18k gold with applied "Reflections" plaque, 6" x-3/4"......................**$18,750**

Courtesy of Heritage Auctions

Antique gold and garnet carbuncle bracelet, circa 1835, with bezel-set oval cabochon garnets within textured mounts with scrolling foliate frames, 6-5/8" l.......... **$2,583**

Courtesy of Skinner, Inc.; www.skinnerinc.com

Antique multi-stone and gold charm bracelet, 18k gold, with eight charms: silver gilt heart set with rose- and European-cut garnets; silver gilt crescent charm set with rose-cut garnets; 18k gold claw set with oval turquoise cabochon measuring 5.91mm x 4.91mm; 14k gold charm set with cultured pearl measuring 4.21mm x 4.03mm and European-cut diamonds weighing 0.05 carat; 14k gold charm set with seed pearls and round rubies weighing 0.10 carat; 18k gold enamel bird set with European- and native-cut diamonds; 14k charm set with European-cut diamond weighing 0.03 carat; and 14k gold face-engraved charm; 7" l.. **$625**

Courtesy Heritage Auctions

BROOCHES/PINS

◀ Seed pearl, glass, and gold brooch with round, oval, and pear-shaped glass stones, 2.00mm seed pearls set in 9k white and pink gold, 1-5/8" x 1-1/8"......**$43**

Courtesy of Heritage Auctions

▶ Gold pendant-brooch with photograph of man on front and photograph of woman on reverse, set in 10k gold, with bail, pinstem, and catch on reverse, 2-1/8" x 1-5/8".................**$250**

Courtesy of Heritage Auctions

Edwardian diamond swallow brooch, Bailey, Banks & Biddle, set throughout with old European-cut diamonds, cabochon ruby eye, platinum-topped 18k gold mount, No. 39053, signed, 2" l.........**$4,613**

Courtesy of Skinner, Inc.; www.skinnerinc.com

Antique sapphire, diamond, and platinum-topped gold brooch with oval sapphire measuring 7.70mm x 6.40mm x 3.80mm and weighing 1.50 carats, round-cut sapphire weighing 0.35 carat, European- and rose-cut diamonds weighing 2.50 carats, set in platinum-topped 14k gold, 1-3/8" x 1-3/8"...............**$4,688**

Courtesy of Heritage Auctions

Victorian garnet, peridot, and gold brooch with emerald-cut rhodolite garnet, 12.50mm x 9.00mm and weighing 6.00 carats, with round-cut peridot weighing 1.00 carat, set in 18k gold, with pinstem, "C" catch, and safety chain, 1-1/2" x 1-1/4"...............................**$325**

Courtesy of Heritage Auctions

▶ Egyptian Revival gold, hardstone, and enamel brooch set with hardstone scarab with bezel-set old European-cut diamonds, flanked by serpents and polychrome enamel wings, 3-5/8" l. **$2,706**

Courtesy of Skinner, Inc.; www.skinnerinc.com

Edwardian platinum, pearl, and diamond plaque brooch, Cartier, New York, center gray button pearl measuring 13.72mm x 13.25mm x 10.04mm, and old European-, old mine-, and single-cut diamonds, millegrain accents, signed, 1-3/4" l. **$110,700**

Courtesy of Skinner, Inc.; www.skinnerinc.com

Art Deco diamond, platinum, and white gold brooch with marquise-cut diamond measuring 8.80mm x 5.25mm x 3.00mm and weighing 0.80 carat, marquise-cut diamonds weighing 0.70 carat, single-cut diamonds weighing 0.95 carat, and baguette-cut diamonds, set in platinum with 14k white gold pinstem and catch, 1-3/4" x 7/8"...............**$2,000**

Courtesy of Heritage Auctions

Vintage pearl, peridot, and gold flower pin, 14k yellow gold, petal set with pearls and tipped with three small peridots on each end, with bale to wear as pendant, very good condition, 28mm. **$180**

Courtesy of Heritage Auctions

Vintage gold shell cameo, 10k yellow gold, with bale, very good condition, 47mm x 38mm. **$138**

Courtesy of Heritage Auctions

Baroque pearl and diamond brooch of stork with pearl and rose-cut diamond body, silver-topped 14k gold mount, 1-3/4" l.............**$2,706**

Courtesy of Skinner, Inc.; www.skinnerinc.com

Antique multi-stone and gold stickpin with pear-shaped pink topaz measuring 14.50mm x 6.50mm, oval chrysoberyl measuring 5.50mm x 4.50mm, and turquoise cabochons, set in 18k gold, 10k gold pin, 3-3/4" x 1/2"................ **$438**

Courtesy of Heritage Auctions

CLIPS & CUFFLINKS

Art Deco platinum gem-set clip brooch of geometric form, Oscar Heyman, set with carved moonstones, channel-set French-cut sapphires and step-cut aquamarines, buff-top coral accent, and sapphire beads, with full- and single-cut diamonds, engraved gallery, chips to moonstones, 1-1/2" l............. **$13,530**

Courtesy of Skinner, Inc.; www.skinnerinc.com

Platinum and diamond dress clips set with old European-, old single-, and baguette-cut diamonds, approximately 2.50 carats, with white gold finding for brooch conversion, in original fitted box, each 7/8" l. **$2,337**

Courtesy of Skinner, Inc.; www.skinnerinc.com

Antique 18k gold cufflinks, Tiffany & Co., each double link designed as cushion with engraved accents, signed......**$1,230**

Courtesy of Skinner, Inc.; www.skinnerinc.com

Antique 18k gold cufflinks, Tiffany & Co., with engraved Prince of Wales' feathers, signed..... **$1,107**

Courtesy of Skinner, Inc.; www.skinnerinc.com

EARRINGS

◀ Antique diamond, ruby, and gold earrings with rose- and native-cut diamonds and round rubies, set in 10k gold, 2-1/8" x-3/4"... **$6,250**

Courtesy of Heritage Auctions

Edwardian platinum and diamond earpendants, Cartier, New York, each set with faceted pear-shape diamond drop, 10.50 carats, suspended from old mine- and old European-cut diamond scroll tops, millegrain accents, signed, 1-1/4" l................**$159,000**

Courtesy of Skinner, Inc.; www.skinnerinc.com

top lot

Antique pearl and diamond earpendants, France, white button pearls measuring approximately 15.30mm x 15.05mm and 15.10mm x 14.70mm, old mine-cut diamond accents, silver and 18k gold mounts, guarantee stamps. $315,000

Art Deco diamond, sapphire, and platinum earrings with European-cut diamonds, one measuring 9.16-9.21mm x 4.80mm and weighing 2.66 carats, other measuring 9.09-9.20mm x 4.73mm and weighing 2.45 carats, with triangle- and rectangle-shaped sapphires and European-cut diamonds, set in platinum, posts with le pousette backs, 1-1/2" x 3/8".......**$15,000**

Courtesy of Heritage Auctions

Art Deco natural pearl, diamond, platinum, and white gold earrings with natural pearls measuring 8.50mm and 8.64mm, European-, single-, and rose-cut diamonds weighing 1.00 carat, set in platinum, 18k white gold screw backs, with Austrian and French hallmarks, 1-15/16" x-3/8"...**$9,063**

Courtesy of Heritage Auctions

Antique sapphire, diamond, and silver-topped gold earrings with cushion-cut sapphires measuring 7.35mm x 6.20mm x 3.90mm and weighing 2.25 carats, European- and rose-cut diamonds weighing 1.25 carats, set in silver-topped 18k gold, 1-7/8" x 1/2"........... **$1,250**

Courtesy of Heritage Auctions

LOCKETS/NECKLACES/PENDANTS

Antique ruby and diamond necklace, India, designed as fringe of alternating star-set cushion-cut rubies and old European-cut diamonds, suspended from bead-set old European-cut and old mine-cut diamonds, completed by fancy links, approximately 5.80 carats, silver-topped gold mount, 14-1/8" l.......................................**$5,843**

Courtesy of Skinner, Inc., www.skinnerinc.com

Victorian diamond, emerald, and silver-topped gold necklace with cushion-, mine-, European-, Swiss-, single-, and rose-cut diamonds weighing 19.00 carats, set in silver topped gold with antique cushion-shaped emerald measuring 13.00mm x 11.00mm x 4.45mm and weighing 4.20 carats, mine-cut diamond measuring 5.80mm x 5.85mm x 4.25mm and weighing 1.00 carat, pear-shaped emerald measuring 13.00mm x 9.00mm x 4.30mm and weighing 2.30 carats, set in 18k gold, 18" l. **$15,625**

Courtesy of Heritage Auctions

Egyptian Revival 18k gold and plique-a-jour enamel gem-set necklace, Marcus & Co., designed as hammered gold scarab with plique-a-jour enamel wings, lapis and carnelian accents, and suspended from swags of lapis, coral, jade, and green hardstone beads, and hammered gold scarabs with enamel hieroglyphics on reverse, signed, 19-1/2" l. **$18,450**

Courtesy of Skinner, Inc.; www.skinnerinc.com

Victorian Archeological Revival cave pearl and gold necklace, Carlo Giuliano, with high karat gold loop-in-loop chained ribbon suspending "cave pearls" topped to resemble amphorae, with original signed Carlo Giuliano fitted leather box, 15-1/2" l. **$75,000**

Courtesy of Heritage Auctions

Antique 14k gold and citrine necklace, fancy links suspending seven faceted citrine drops, 14-5/8" l. ....$1,000-$1,500

Courtesy of Skinner, Inc.; www.skinnerinc.com

Antique 14k gold, coral, and diamond locket, star motif with rose-cut diamond center with coral cabochons and blue enamel border, opening to two frames, 2" l. **$1,968**

Courtesy of Skinner, Inc.; www.skinnerinc.com

Antique gold and turquoise snake necklace, head set with turquoise cabochons and rose-cut diamond eyes, suspending heart-shaped drop from its teeth, engraved accents, and completed by flexible scale links, 15-3/4" l. **$2,829**

*Courtesy of Skinner, Inc.;
www.skinnerinc.com*

Arts & Crafts 14k gold and hardstone necklace, centering one pear-shaped and four oval cabochon hardstones each within floral and foliate bezel, with navette link chain, 14-1/4" l.....................$1,107

Courtesy of Skinner, Inc.; www.skinnerinc.com

Antique gold and amethyst necklace designed as fringe of rectangular cushion-cut amethysts and suspending removable drop set with pear- and circular-cut amethysts, 14-3/4" l., 1-3/4". **$5,228**

Courtesy of Skinner, Inc.; www.skinnerinc.com

Art Nouveau 14k gold, opal, and freshwater pearl necklace, Durand & Co., set with oval cabochon opals with lotus flower motifs and swags of trace link chain with freshwater pearls, maker's mark, 15-3/4" l.........................**$2,583**

Courtesy of Skinner, Inc.; www.skinnerinc.com

Antique emerald and diamond pendant, centering emerald-cut emerald measuring 15.55 x 11.20mm x 3.92mm, and weighing 3.50 carats, framed by old mine-cut diamonds, suspended from bar set with emerald- and pear-shape emeralds and old mine-cut diamonds, silver-topped gold mount, and suspended from trace link chain.....**$107,625**

Courtesy of Skinner, Inc.; www.skinnerinc.com

Etruscan Revival 18k gold, enamel, and diamond pendant, France, central matte enamel panel of Bacchante within rose-cut diamond frame, reverse with fine ropework panel, central floret, and applied bead and ropework accents, conforming bail, and opening to compartment, guarantee stamp, 2-1/4" l. total..................**$4,920**

Courtesy of Skinner, Inc.; www.skinnerinc.com

▶ Renaissance Revival gold, amethyst, and enamel pendant, Carlo Giuliano, prong-set with large cushion-cut amethyst within enamel grillework frame, button pearl accents, and suspended from chain with conforming plaques, signed on reverse with signature plaque C.G., 3" l., chain 14-1/2" l..................**$17,220**

Courtesy of Skinner, Inc.; www.skinnerinc.com

Renaissance Revival Pendant Renaissance Revival silver gem-set pendant, shaped enamel plaque with carved rock crystal and suspending green beryl drops, caps set with circular-cut rubies, pearl and emerald bead chain, 5-3/4" l..............**$3,000-$5,000**

Courtesy of Skinner, Inc.; www.skinnerinc.com

Art Nouveau 18k gold, plique-a-jour enamel, and diamond pendant/brooch, Henri Vever Paris, designed as butterfly with plique-a-jour enamel wings and bezel-set old mine-cut diamonds, framed by foliate motifs set with old mine- and rose-cut diamonds, diamond-set bail, with removable findings for pendant or brooch conversion, with original screwdriver, French import stamps, signed VEVER PARIS, in original fitted box for Vever, 14 rue de la Paix, 2-1/4" l. **$28,290**

Courtesy of Skinner, Inc.; www.skinnerinc.com

Art Nouveau 18k gold, enamel, and diamond pendant/brooch designed as pair of griffins flanking flower blossom, rose-cut diamond accents, with old European-cut diamond accents, suspended from platinum chain, 1-3/4" l. **$2,091**

Courtesy of Skinner, Inc.; www.skinnerinc.com

Antique gold, emerald, and diamond starburst pendant/brooch, prong-set with circular-cut emerald measuring 9.25mm x 9.20mm x 4.73mm, and further set with old mine-cut diamonds, approximately 3.00 carats, 1-1/2" l. **$29,520**

Courtesy of Skinner, Inc.; www.skinnerinc.com

Edwardian amethyst and diamond cross pendant, fancy square-cut amethysts within foliate border set with rose-cut diamonds, platinum-topped 18k gold mount with millegrain accents, suspended from purple cord with rose-cut diamond flower slide, 2-1/8" l.........**$2,337**

Courtesy of Skinner, Inc.; www.skinnerinc.com

Rare Art Nouveau 18k gold and enamel pendant/brooch, Gabriel Falguieres, "Fecundite," female personification of fecundity with long hair among branches with pearl and diamond accents, 3-1/2" l. ....**$30,000-$40,000**

Courtesy of Skinner, Inc.; www.skinnerinc.com

Art Nouveau plique-a-jour enamel and enamel pendant, Switzerland, designed as woman wearing necklace and earpendants set with single-cut diamonds against plique-a-jour enamel ground within shaped frame with floral and foliate motifs and full-cut diamonds, silver and 18k gold mount, hallmarks, 1-3/4" l. **$1,353**

Courtesy of Skinner, Inc.; www.skinnerinc.com

RINGS

Vintage gold and jade ring, 14k yellow gold, with small pearls and two-tone gold on flowers, very good condition, size 7-1/2, 25mm x 20mm. **$478**

Courtesy of Heritage Auctions

Vintage diamond and gold ring, 14k yellow gold, 1.0 carat, very good condition, size 8-1/4. .... **$388**

Courtesy of Heritage Auctions

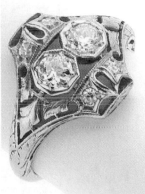

Art Deco diamond and white gold ring with European-cut diamonds measuring 3.50mm and weighing 0.30 carat and single-cut diamonds weighing 0.05 carat, set in 18k white gold, size 5-3/4. .... **$501**

Courtesy of Heritage Auctions

Art Deco diamond, ruby, and platinum ring with marquise-cut diamond measuring 12.00mm x 6.65mm x 4.40mm and weighing 2.25 carats, square rubies weighing 0.70 carat, single-cut diamonds, set in 18k gold and platinum, size 5. ....**$32,500**

Courtesy of Heritage Auctions

Antique sapphire, diamond, and platinum ring with oval sapphire measuring 16.28mm x 11.73mm x 7.20mm and weighing 11.00 carats and European- and single-cut diamonds weighing 1.20 carats, set in platinum, size 5-1/2.............................**$12,500**

Courtesy of Heritage Auctions

Art Deco diamond and platinum ring with European-cut diamonds weighing 0.55 carat, set in platinum, size 5.
.... **$775**

Courtesy of Heritage Auctions

Art Deco diamond and platinum ring with European- and single-cut diamonds weighing 0.50 carat, set in platinum, size 6-1/2................................. **$938**

Courtesy of Heritage Auctions

Art Deco diamond and platinum ring with European-cut diamonds weighing 1.50 carats, set in platinum, size 8-1/4................................. **$813**

Courtesy of Heritage Auctions

MISCELLANEOUS

▶ Victorian coral and gold suite, brooch with round and oval coral cabochons, surrounded by carved coral scrolls and tassels, earrings with oval coral cabochons, surmounted by coral cabochons, surrounded by carved coral scrolls and tassel drops, set in 10k gold, brooch 2-7/8" x 2-3/4" (including tassel drops), earrings 2-3/4" x 3/4"....................**$4,063**

Courtesy of Heritage Auctions

◀ Edwardian 18k gold and pearl convertible suite, France, designed as chain of navette-form garland links set with pearls, separating into pair of bracelets, maker's marks and guarantee stamps, chain 16-1/2" l., bracelets each 7-1/4" l.
..................................**$3,000-$4,000**

Courtesy of Skinner, Inc.; www.skinnerinc.com

Antique gold and enamel suite, comprising brooch and earpendants, each designed as dome with black tracery enamel within beaded border and suspending baton and bead drops, in box for Bigelow Brothers & Kennard, Boston, 2-5/8" l., 2-1/2". **$2,091**

Courtesy of Skinner, Inc.; www.skinnerinc.com

◄ Art Deco Swiss lady's diamond, sapphire, and platinum wristwatch, case: 26.00mm x 13.00mm, platinum, engraved J.M.S.; dial: off-white enamel, black Arabic numerals, black spade hands; movement: Swiss, 15 jewels, adjusted, manual wind; bracelet: 6-1/4" l., platinum, diamond, and sapphire; stones: marquise- and single-cut diamonds weighing 1.40 carats, square and baguette-cut sapphires weighing 1.75 carats; signed Brenad Watch Co. on movement, in working order. **$2,500**

Courtesy of Heritage Auctions

▲ Art Deco sapphire and gold cigarette case, French, 18k gold with sapphire cabochon thumb push and prism-shaped sapphires at each corner, engraved "D.D.D. - J.A.D. October 23, 1931," unknown maker's mark, 01454, FRANCE, BREVETE, French hallmarks, retailed by Cartier, 3-7/8" x 2-7/8" x 5/16"................ **$10,000**

Courtesy of Heritage Auctions

◄ Antique silver and hairwork watch key, one side depicting inkwork cow in bucolic ink and hairwork landscape with houses, other with hairwork spray of flowers, silver floral and foliate motifs, Dutch hallmarks, 3" l. ....**$700-$900**

Courtesy of Skinner, Inc.; www.skinnerinc.com

◄ Edwardian platinum, ruby, diamond, and pearl sautoir, circular pendant centering circular-cut ruby weighing 1.50 carats, with palmette motifs set with old mine- and rose-cut diamonds and calibre-cut rubies, millegrain accents, suspended from woven pearl strap with conforming bosses, 1-3/4" dia., 22-1/2" l. **$8,610**

Courtesy of Skinner, Inc.; www.skinnerinc.com

▲ Late Georgian diamond ornament, circa 1840, designed as feather and set throughout with 140 old mine-cut diamonds, approximately 12 carats, silver-topped gold mount, reverse with pinstem, 3-3/4" l. **$17,220**

Courtesy of Skinner, Inc.; www.skinnerinc.com

▼ Late Georgian gold muff chain, dated 1828, longchain of circular links, 45.7 dwt, 52" l. **$3,690**

Courtesy of Skinner, Inc.; www.skinnerinc.com

KITCHENWARE

EVERYONE KNOWS THAT the kitchen is the hub of the home. So when the wildly successful "Downton Abbey" series streamed across television screens earlier this year, the show's Edwardian kitchen became a visual primer on class and comfort in our increasingly uncertain times.

That vision not only riveted viewers to each "Downton Abbey" installment, but the show's anti-snobbery theme created a new market niche for antique kitchen collectibles.

When stoic butler Mr. Carson chides housekeeper Mrs. Hughes about a new-fangled electric toaster, antique dealers nationwide said vintage toasters flew off the shelves.

"We simply could not believe how much interest 'Downton Abbey' has sparked in antique kitchen utensils," said Rege Woodley, a retired antique dealer in Washington, Pennsylvania. "I sold one of my antique rolling pins to my neighbor for $100 because it looked like the one used by Mrs. Patmore, the cook in 'Downton Abbey.'"

Pat Greene, owner of Nothing New Antiques, said she is excited about all the "Downton Abbey" fuss and hopes her antique kitchenwares fetch some lasting prices, too. "My rolling pins usually go for $5 to $10, but I'm seeing a big rush on my cookie cutters," said Greene of Pittsburgh.

Mary Kirk of New Alexandria, Pennsylvania, said she collects antique cookbooks and was especially interested in trying to prepare some of the food served in the "Downton Abbey" show. "I am extremely interested in trying to prepare the eggs poached with spinach – a dish that poor young kitchen maid Daisy had to prepare during one show scene," said Kirk,

Three-piece ceramic canister set in graduated sizes, Torquay pattern, each canister with wooden top and brass feet, coordinating decorated trivet, marked "MacKenzie-Childs, Ltd., 1983, Aurora, New York." **$600**

Courtesy of Northgate Gallery

a retired librarian. Because of the show's lengthy shooting schedule, producers have reported that most of the food served during production consists of light salads.

Jimmy Roark of Nashville, Tennessee, said he has not seen as large a rush for his kitchen collectibles as a result of the show. "What I see is a more gradual demand for these items," said Roark, who operates a small antique collectible shop in his garage. "I sell a lot of my cookie cutters, antique wooden bowls, and vintage mixer beaters during the holidays."

Still, the "Downton Abbey" magic continues to seed interest in a broad swath of antique kitchen utensils and artifacts from Bennington mixing bowls to turn-of-the-century tiger wood rolling pins.

Stephen White of White & White Antiques & Interiors of Skaneateles, New York, said interest in antique kitchenware remains steady. At the ninth annual Antique Show

English copper and metal plate warmer, W.A.S. Benson, circa 1900, fitted with scalloped, D-shaped copper panel supporting two metal trivets raised on out-set legs, 22" h. x 12" d. x 11" w... **$200**

Courtesy of Stair Auctioneers & Appraisers

at Oakmont Country Club March 9-10, 2013, near Pittsburgh, kitchenwares were front and center with collectors. The show, a benefit for the Kerr Memorial Museum, sports a broad mix of antiques for all ages.

White was quick to feature his rare whale ivory crested Nantucket rolling pin valued at $425. "I have unusual kitchen antiques from hand food choppers to copper pots," said White.

Other dealers at the Oakmont show featured kitchen antiques from old historical companies instrumental in the economic growth of western Pennsylvania.

"When you think of Pittsburgh, you can't escape the long history that the H.J. Heinz Co. has here," said Toni Bahnak of Candlewood Antiques in Ardara, Pennsylvania. "We have rare old vinegar bottles and ketchup bottles that denote an era when the Heinz Co. made its own glass," said Bahnak.

And industry experts say ketchup and pickle collectibles will continue to soar in value because the H.J. Heinz Co. announced a $23.3 billion deal to be purchased by Warren Buffett's Berkshire Hathaway and 3G Capital, co-founded by Jorge Lemann, one of Brazil's richest men.

Even before the blockbuster deal was announced, some Heinz memorabilia collectors reported that their antique bottles and jars were fetching higher prices than normal.

"I had one of my antique vinegar bottles sell for about $225 and I think I could have gotten more for it," said Ruth Oslet, an antique collector from Waynesburg, Pennsylvania. She sold it to a marketing executive who collects business memorabilia.

Tom Purdue, a longtime collector of food company antiques, said history and nostalgia play an important role in what people remember and want to save for their modern kitchens. "I can remember the distinct smell of my grandmother's old pickle jars and Heinz horseradish in her musty old kitchen where she used a hand pump to wash dishes," said Purdue, an 89-year-old former blacksmith from Wheeling, West Virginia.

Art Deco green ceramic enameled coffee set from Mexico, 20th century, octagonal coffee pot (shown), lidded sugar and creamer and four cups with four saucers that depict figures of men, women, burros and dog in tropical landscape, minor flakes, glazing cracks and firing flaws. $177

Courtesy of Brunk Auctions

The ever-expanding business reaches back to 1869 when Henry John Heinz and neighbor L. Clarence Noble began selling grated horseradish, bottled in clear glass to showcase its purity. It wasn't until 1876 that the company introduced its flagship product, marketing the country's first commercial ketchup.

Not all history, though, is tied to corporate America. Family memories still stoke the embers of home cooking although many young people today find fast food the fuel of the future.

"I still have my family's old cornbread recipe and I use it all the time," said Elizabeth Schwan, gallery director for Aspire Auctions in Pittsburgh.

Schwan, who scans the country for antiques, admits she has a soft spot for old kitchen utensils. "Flower-sifters, antique copper mixing bowls, and rolling pins were all part of my heritage because my family grew up on a Kentucky farm," Schwan said. "I can still smell the homemade bread and jams."

And like most farm families, the kitchen served as a meeting place and refuge from a long day's work. "Between verbal debates about what to plant on the south flats, we would help our parents churn butter and chop wood for the old country stove," said Myrtle Bench, 91, of Washington, Pennsylvania.

But as a young America turned from the agricultural frontier in the late 1890s and began to embrace a manufacturing economy, automation replaced handcrafts, and the kitchen became a new testing ground for a variety of modern gizmos like the automatic dishwasher.

The automatic dishwasher was a toy for the rich when an electric model was introduced on 1913 by Willard and Forrest Walker, two Syracuse, New York brothers who ran a hardware store when they were not tinkering with kitchen machines. The new dishwasher sold for $120 (the equivalent of $1,429 in today's dollars), a hefty premium over the $20 the Walkers charged for their popular hand-cranked model and also more expensive than a gasoline-powered washer the brothers put on the market in 1911.

"You can still find some of the old hand-crank washers, but I like to spend my time finding kitchen utensils that reflect how people prepared their food," said Dirk Hayes, a freelance cook from Uniontown, Pennsylvania. "I love watching 'Downton Abbey' because the kitchen scenes really give you a flavor of how the food was prepared. I never had that kind of staff, but it's fun to dream," said Hayes, who collects rolling pins and antique carving knives.

— Chriss Swaney

Modern Kitchen Collectibles

The diverse area of kitchenware/household objects offers a world of collecting opportunities. Your interests may lead you to antique rarities more than 100 years old or to items of more recent manufacture. Any and all territory should be considered fair game. As with other collectibles, your primary motivation should be your individual likes and preferences.

There is a great deal of interest in kitchenware and related items from 35 to 60 years old; these objects rekindle old memories and represent a different, less-complicated era for

many. They represent a broad spectrum of kitchen items and cooking activities. These include just about every task you would want to try to master in your kitchen of yesteryear. There are gadgets of all types and all sorts of accessories, sets, holders, and miscellaneous gizmos. Most of the items are non-electrical and small in scale.

For more information on kitchen collectibles, see *Spiffy Kitchen Collectibles* or *Warman's Kitschy Kitchen Collectibles Field Guide,* both by Brian S. Alexander.

Hamilton Beach teal enamel and chrome mixer, circa 1930s-1940s, very good overall condition, six mixer cups in 18/8 heavy-duty stainless steel, one original, plus larger-size mixer, 18.25" h. **$59**

Courtesy of Midwest Auction Galleries

Five graduated copper kitchen
pots...................................$106

Courtesy of A.H. Wilkens Antiques & Appraisals

Trio of 19th century copper jelly molds. $292

Courtesy of A.H. Wilkens Antiques & Appraisals

Dutch and English colanders, 18th to 19th century,
blue and white Delft colander with pierced basin over
solid bowl with one cut handle on side, long crack,
professional restoration at base ring, earthenware
example pale yellow with manganese decoration and
pierced with stylized quatrefoil decoration, chip on
underside of one handle, 13-1/2".........................$300

Courtesy of Brunk Auctions

Antique copper basin and
covered hot water pot......$265

*Courtesy of A.H. Wilkens
Antiques & Appraisals*

Two antique copper kitchen pots. ...$137

Courtesy of A.H. Wilkens Antiques & Appraisals

◄ Brass pie crimper and
rosewood-handled chopper
with thin, 6-1/2" wrought iron
blade, American or English,
19th century. $90

Courtesy of Garth's Auctioneers & Appraisers

\Vintage cherry stoner with table screw mount, marked "Enterprise Mfg. Co., Phila. USA, 29848 Cherry Stoner Pat. May 15, 1917," black painted finish with age-appropriate wear, 14" l. x 9 w. x 5" d.. **$18**

Courtesy of Dargate Auction Galleries

Colonial silver toasting fork, handle with intricate spiral carving, 22" l. **$477**

Courtesy of A.H. Wilkens Antiques & Appraisals

Sunkist electric juicer, circa 1920s-1930s, very good working condition, general medium plating loss and wear, 16" h............ **$210**

Courtesy of Morphy Auctions

Two aluminum champagne buckets for Cordon Rouge Brut and Bessarat de Bellefon, 8" h. **$159**

Courtesy of A.H. Wilkens Antiques & Appraisals

1950s-era Kelvinator refrigerator in working order, Australian, faulty wiring, 58" h. x 31-1/2" w. **$62**

Courtesy of Theodore Bruce Auctions

Four vintage-style glassware pieces: cobalt-colored juicer (not shown), jadeite biscuit jar with lid (not shown), and jadeite graduated measuring cups, largest piece 7" h. x 6" dia..................**$75**

Courtesy of Clars Auction Gallery, www.clars.com

Crandall and Godley hand-crank mixer, New York, circa late 19th century to early 20th century, iron and tin, side-mounted crank operates internal beaters, 12" h........**$90**

Courtesy of Garth's Auctioneers & Appraisers

Wendell sterling pie server,
9" l., 2.11 troy oz........................**$35**

Courtesy of William J. Jenack Auctioneers

Art Deco-style cocktail shaker and traveling bar in zeppelin form, J.A. Henkels Twin Works, Germany, circa 1928, silver-plated brass, signed with impressed manufacturer's mark to individual elements; four nesting spoons, three nesting cups, removable flask, juicer and funnel with stopper, 12" h. x 3-1/4" dia. x 4-1/4" w. **$21,250**

Courtesy of Wright Auctions

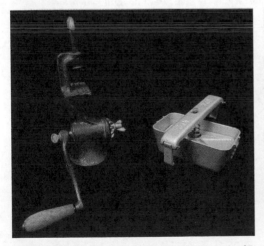

Vintage meat grinder and vintage tureen press........... **$5**

Courtesy of Theodore Bruce Auctions

Sterling silver coffee pot, 11" h., 27.5 troy oz....**$425**

Courtesy of Sandwich Auction House

LIGHTING

COLORED GLASS LOOKS beautiful when it's illuminated, and therein lies the problem. In the case of leaded glass, or stained glass lamps, even poorly designed, cheaply made examples look attractive when the lights go on, making it critically important to be able to look beyond the pretty colors when determining any lamp's aesthetic, structural and intrinsic value.

Despite less than acceptable condition, some lamps will retain a good portion of their value due to their pedigree. A rare Tiffany or Duffner & Kimberley lamp, for instance, will still hold great value despite conditions that would otherwise render an unknown maker's lamp depreciated.

I've identified 10 items you should consider when looking at or buying a leaded glass lamp. These are not the end-all and be-all of qualitative evaluations, but should form a reliable framework to better recognize quality in leaded glass lamps.

OVERALL BEAUTY

This may seem obvious, but a lamp can display beauty in any number of ways; it can be colorful (the most disarming of qualities); it can be pretty (again, sometimes disarming); it can be fascinating (due to the glass pattern or design); or it can be downright stunning when all of the visual characteristics of its shape, design, color, pattern, and aesthetics gel into one harmonious delight.

DESIGN EXCELLENCE

Conscientious lamp designers instinctively address certain design conventions when outlining artwork to be translated onto a three-dimensional lamp mold. One primary consideration is how the design assumes the shape of the lamp. Are large flat pieces of glass expected to span a tight curvature of the form, or are the pieces sized to assume the shape gracefully, giving the impression that the glass is bent? Poor designers overlook this condition, resulting in lamps whose surfaces seem rough, jagged and harsh to the touch.

Lamp designs are based on components such as border, background, primary image,

ILLUS. 1

secondary image, support elements (stems and flower buds, for instance), and geometrics. Any number of these can be combined to create a design. The more intelligent the use of these elements, the more elegant the result, be it a pure geometric or an intensely naturalistic design (Illus. 1).

Another design factor to consider is flow. Does the design sit comfortably on the shape of the lamp? Are lead lines jagged or out of character with the rest of the design? Are there areas of awkward dead space between design elements? If the design repeats itself, which many do, are the repeats balanced and seamless? A simple spinning of the shade on its base will tell. In more elaborate designs, do the elements such as borders and geometric areas enhance the viewing experience or do they compete with the primary imagery, whatever that may be? A basic sense of these relationships is helpful when evaluating the many aesthetic properties of lamp design.

ILLUS. 2

CHOICE OF GLASS

Strong, contrasting colors can be attractive. For the longest time, production lamp manufacturers were aware that combining a neutral background glass such as bone, beige or amber, some pretty opal colors for flower or image glass, and a strong leaf green was a slam dunk of successful color selection. I can't begin to tell you how many leaded glass lamps have been crafted over the last century using this simple recipe of coloration. Compare a lamp of this caliber (Illus. 2) with one where the selection of color, tone and texture is sensitive and painterly (Illus. 3).

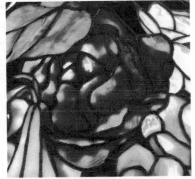

ILLUS. 3

TYPES OF GLASS

Two major types of glass dominate the leaded glass lamp landscape: mass-produced, machine-made glass and hand-rolled or art glass. Both are opalescent rather than translucent. Machine-made glass appears very uniform and consistent in color. It portrays very little variance of depth, tone or movement; it tends to look flat. Although some examples have good light to dark areas, machine-made glass provides a very two-dimensional visual experience. Hand-rolled art glass, in which case no two pieces of glass can ever be the same due to their handcrafted nature, when carefully selected portrays all of the values and visual excitement of a well-executed painting. Depth, shadow, intense light to dark transitions and strong movement of color within the individual pieces of glass prove a very satisfying, dimensional visual experience. At its best, you can easily forget that you are looking at glass.

STRUCTURAL INTEGRITY

You must judge a lamp not only when it is lit and at its most disarming, but also when it is unlit and off its base, when all of its scars, warts and flaws are visible and tangible. A well-crafted lamp should feel sturdy and substantial when in hand — not flimsy. If light pressure to the widest expanse of the shade results in flexing, it is reasonable to believe that the shade has not been properly reinforced during construction. Proper reinforcement here would consist of a rod or thick wire of brass or copper set and soldered onto the bottom edge. This also applies to the upper opening or aperture of the shade. If the lamp is built to sit on a ring or base support, and has a opening at the top to accommodate such, this area of the lamp should be properly reinforced with a strong band of metal preferably made of copper or brass and be intact. The aperture of the lamp should also be free from any damage that may render the opening a threat to the safety of the lamp (Illus. 4).

If the lamp has a finial or heat cap fastened to its aperture, that fitting should be properly fastened to a metal reinforcement at the opening and not simply to the copper-foiled glass border. The latter usually results in the cap or finial pulling away from the shade in reaction to heat from lightbulbs building up at the top of the shade. If this occurs, it is possible that the lead/tin solder used in securing the fitting could gradually soften and fail. The full weight of the shade pulling down on this joint compounds the problem. This type of repair or restoration can prove expensive, especially if the damage includes the upper row of glass. Ideally, support should come from underneath the aperture. It is important to remember that the most vulnerable parts of any leaded glass lamp are its aperture and bottom edge.

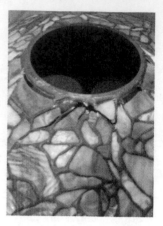

ILLUS. 4

QUALITY CRAFTSMANSHIP

Many skills come together in the construction and crafting of a leaded glass lamp: glass cutting, glass shaping, copper foiling, assembly, soldering and finishing, among others. Knowing how to examine the execution of each of these component skills is necessary to evaluate not only the quality of a leaded glass lamp but also its physical condition and the possibility for any restoration or repair.

First and foremost: Are the individual pieces of glass cut and shaped accurately? If examining a geometric lamp, or section of a lamp that includes geometrics, do the resulting leaded lines line up, or are the crossing lines mismatched or carelessly assembled? Are curved lines smooth? Are border pieces either at the top or bottom, or both, set straight? A skillful glass cutter or glazier is careful to create pieces that accurately reflect the pattern or template used without creating pieces that have irregular edges or are bigger or smaller than the template. Additionally, a skillful assembler will position each glass piece carefully – in its proper position according to the established design.

ILLUS. 5

Each piece of glass in a leaded glass lamp has its edges wrapped with a thin copper foil to facilitate assembly. This foil should be applied so the resulting lead lines are consistent in size. Lead lines that vary from thin to wide or are unusually wide throughout are telltale signs of shoddy workmanship, or areas of poor repair technique (Illus. 5).

A lead/tin-based solder is used to join each piece of glass to its neighbor and to fill the gaps between each piece of glass with a smooth, slightly mounded bead of solder. Rough, blotchy, lumpy or inconsistent solder lines are, again, a sign of shoddy workmanship, or if isolated, signs of less-than-professional repair or restoration (Illus. 6). The character of the lead lines should be consistent throughout the shade. It should be noted that many

ILLUS. 6

lamp makers favor the outside, or "show" side, of the shade, and the quality of the lead lines may vary from the inside to the outside of the shade, reflecting this preference.

PATINA AND FINISH

Patina is the color produced on the metal surfaces of the lamp, i.e., the lead lines, top and bottom edges and any added components to the lamp such as filigree or finials. Patina finishes will vary from light to dark brown, to a combination of brown and green (this finish being, historically, the most desirable) to black. On a well-preserved lamp, or one that has been professionally repaired or restored, the patina color will be consistent throughout. The color should be uniform, and there should be no areas where the patina color is either missing or wrong.

ILLUS. 7

BASE AND SHADE PROPORTIONS

The marriage of shade and base should be pleasing to the eye. Most importantly, does the shade sit properly on its base? Does it seem to tilt to the left or right? This could be a sign of damage or the shade's aperture joint being compromised. Such defects are subject to expensive repair. Beyond that, is the marriage a good one? Simply put, the diameter of the shade in relation to the height and width of the base should not look extreme or unsteady in any way (Illus. 7).

COMPARISON TO OTHER EXAMPLES

Many leaded glass lamp designs were made in multiples utilizing the same design, templates and mold to make similar models that differed in color and mood. Comparisons to the same models by the same maker are useful in determining whether the item in question lives up to or surpasses those it compares to. A little research through auction catalogs and books is indispensable when making these comparisons.

PROVENANCE

Finally, where did the shade come from? Can its history be traced? Is it a contemporary shade or a reproduction? Has it been repaired or restored? Was the work done by a well-known craftsperson or a hobbyist? The availability of this information would certainly be valuable.

Developing a working knowledge of leaded glass lamps and how they are designed and constructed is an ongoing process. These few guidelines are a good place to start to ensure that your choice and/or purchase of a leaded glass lamp—whether privately, through a gallery, or at auction—will be an informed and intelligent one.

— *Joseph Porcelli,* Porcelli Studio

Illustrations 1 and 3 courtesy of James D. Julia Auctioneers, Fairfield, Maine, www.jamesdjulia.com
Illustrations 2, 4, 5, 6, 7 courtesy of Porcelli Studio

EARLY NON-ELECTRIC LIGHTING

Hobbs No. 341/ Snowflake stand lamp, ruby/cranberry opalescent font, colorless base, metal screw connector, No. 1 Taplin-Brown collar, fitted with period No. 1 "Eldorado" slip burner and chimney with serrated-scallop top, Hobbs, Brockunier & Co., fourth quarter 19th century, 8-1/2" h. to top of collar, 4-1/2" dia. base.......... **$228**

Courtesy of Jeffrey S. Evans & Associates

Free-blown Lutz-type striped stand lamp, colorless, compressed pyriform font with rose and opal stripes, raised on hollow baluster-form stem and domed foot with opal stripes, wafer construction, brass No. 1 collar, hand-written label under base attributing lamp to Nicholas Lutz at Sandwich, signed by J. I. Dawes, circa 1860-1880, undamaged, 10" h., 5-3/8" dia. base................. **$1,080**

Courtesy of Jeffrey S. Evans & Associates

Sunken Hollyhock/ Button Tufted carnival glass parlor lamp, marigold iridescent, matching patterned ball-form shade with brass trim ring, tapered-globular form glass font holder, fitted with metal liner, rim flares out in scroll ornamentation, cast-iron base with scroll ornamentation, brass drop-in font, fitted with electrified Success slip burner and colorless slip chimney, Pittsburgh Lamp, Brass & Glass Co., first quarter 20th century, 24-1/4" h. to top of shade, lamp 13-1/2" h. to top of collar, 8" sq. base, shade 10-1/2" h., 4-1/8" dia. fitter................. **$540**

Courtesy of Jeffrey S. Evans & Associates

Marbrie Loop kerosene stand lamp, colorless pyriform font with eight groups of ruby and opal loops, stamped brass stem and single-step marble base, No. 1 fine-line collar, fitted with period set-up comprising hinged E. Miller No. 1 lip burner with hinged cap refill feature adjacent to wick tube, thumbwheel marked "E MILLER MERIDEN CONN," cast brass Julius Ives tripod shade holder marked "PATD. JULY 18-65" on one petal, colorless cone-form frosted and engraved shade with double-banded disk over berry and foliage pattern decoration, colorless lip chimney, Boston & Sandwich Glass Co., third quarter 19th century, undamaged, 15-1/4" h. to top of shade, 9-1/4" h. to top of collar, 4" sq. base, shade 4-7/8" h., 7-3/4" dia. fitter. **$2,760**

Courtesy of Jeffrey S. Evans & Associates

Monumental cut overlay kerosene banquet stand lamp, green cut to colorless compressed pyriform font with punties and oval panels, shaded green punty stem, raised on triple-step marble base with cast brass ornamentation, brass connector, No. 3 fine-line collar, fitted with period set-up comprising E. F. Jones No. 3 lip burner, thumbwheel marked "E. F. JONES PATENT JANUARY. 11. 1859," with Merrill's air director, marked "R. S. MERRILL'S PATENT. JUNE 14. 1859," 6-1/8" dia. shade ring with coining to edge, cut and frosted waisted bell-form shade with foliate and berry pattern, and colorless lip chimney, Boston & Sandwich Glass Co., third quarter 19th century, excellent condition, 39" h. to top of shade, 28" h. to top of collar, 8" sq. base, shade 9-5/8" h., 6-1/8" dia. fitter. **$19,200**

Courtesy of Jeffrey S. Evans & Associates

Coolidge Drape kerosene stand lamp, opaque green, No. 2 Taplin-Brown collar, matching patterned translucent light green chimney-shade, fitted with period Manhattan Brass Co. "Arctic" slip burner, fourth quarter 19th century, flake to one stem drape, edge of font shoulder with broken bubble, as made, 19" h. to top of chimney shade, 9-3/4" h. to top of collar, 7-1/4" dia. base...................**$840**

Courtesy of Jeffrey S. Evans & Associates

Cut overlay Moorish Windows kerosene stand lamp, white to emerald green pyriform font, brass stem and double-step marble base with stamped-brass ornamentation, No. 1 fine-line collar, fitted with period set-up comprising E. F. Jones No. 1 lip burner, thumbwheel marked "JONES PAT. JAN. 11. 1856," brass 3-1/2" standard shade ring with coining to edge, and green frosted and engraved Oregon shade with Vintage pattern decoration, probably Boston & Sandwich Glass Co., third quarter 19th century, 17" h. to top of shade, 10-5/8" h. to top of collar, 4-1/8" sq. base, shade 6" h. overall, 3-3/8" dia. fitter.......**$1,440**

Courtesy of Jeffrey S. Evans & Associates

Onion/Eaton kerosene stand lamp, opaque white, blown-molded vertical-ribbed font and matching pressed base, brass Atterbury screw connector with patent date, No. 2 fine-line collar, fitted with period set-up comprising Holmes, Booth & Haydens No. 2 lip burner with George Nielson's corrugated deflector, thumbwheel marked "HOLMES BOOTH & HAYDENS PAT JAN 24 1860 / E. F. JONES PAT. JAN 11TH 1859," 4" standard shade ring with coining to edge, matching patterned opaque white ball-form shade with brass trim ring, colorless lip chimney, Atterbury & Co., circa 1865-1880, undamaged, 21" h. to top of shade, 13-1/4" h. to top of collar, 6-3/4" dia. base, shade 7-1/8" h., 4" dia. fitter.........**$1,560**

Courtesy of Jeffrey S. Evans & Associates

◀ Rare English cameo miniature oil lamp, cased white, pink, and citron with satin finish, floral and butterfly decoration, squatty base raised on three applied feet and polished pontil mark, matching globular crimped-top shade, period "Silber Light" burner, Thomas Webb & Son, late 19th/ early 20th century, excellent condition, 7-1/2" h. to top of shade, shade 3-1/4" h., fitter 1-15/16" dia., base 3-1/2" h. to top of collar, 4-3/4" dia. **$16,800**

Courtesy of Jeffrey S. Evans & Associates

Pair of Pressed Loop/Leaf whale oil stand lamps, yellow (uranium), bulb-form font with four loops, raised on hexagonal base with compressed knop and flared foot, wafer construction, pewter fine-line collars, each fitted with pewter and tin double-tube whale oil burner, unusual slip-over circular shade holder with tripod fitter supports, and roughed and cut ball-form shade, Boston & Sandwich Glass Co. and others, circa 1840-1860, excellent condition, 13-1/8" h. to top of shade, 10-3/8" h. to top of collar, 5-1/4" dia. overall base, shades 3" h., 2" dia. fitter. **$2,760**

Courtesy of Jeffrey S. Evans & Associates

ELECTRIC LIGHTING

Tiffany Studios gilt bronze floor lamp with bronze shade, 20th century, dome-top bronze damascene unsigned shade with slag glass border band and numbered "85-1-42" on bottom rim, gilt bronze base with graduated scrolling knobs, four-petal support on stepped circular base, stamped "Tiffany Studios New York," "577," shade possibly replacement, tarnish to gilding, 56" h. **$5,208**

Courtesy of Brunk Auctions

Tiffany Studios patinated bronze floor lamp, early 20th century, heart-shaped adjustable harp with octagonal gold damascene glass shade signed "Louis Comfort Tiffany, Tiffany Studios Favrile," central support with pod-form separators, platform base with scrolling feet, signed "Tiffany Studios New York," "455" on one foot, good condition, 53-1/2" h. **$7,440**

Courtesy of Brunk Auctions

Reverse Tiffany acorn floor lamp, shade signed "Tiffany's Studio New York," base signed "29444 Tiffany's Studio New York," excellent condition, shade 22" dia. **$31,200**

Courtesy of Morphy Auctions

Art Nouveau gilt bronze and brass floor lamp with mica shade, probably French, circa 1900, stylized leaf-form feet, paneled mica shade with polychrome decoration, good condition overall, losses to gilding at central upper part of column, mica shade generally good condition with minor flaws at center top, 68-1/2". **$1,364**

Courtesy of Brunk Auctions

Arts & Crafts slag glass lamp, four-panel green glass shade with black-painted metal surround, stepped pedestal base, removable painted tole fluid lamp with glass chimney, good condition, one metal support slightly bent, scattered surface wear, minor paint losses to metal mounts, corner of one glass panel at side broken at corner edge, 24"................**$310**

Courtesy of Brunk Auctions

Roycroft hammered copper lamp, made in 1913 for Grove Park Inn, model 901, stamped "R" in orb-and-cross mark, original patina, replaced vintage isinglass shade, rewired, 6-1/2" w. across base, 16-1/2" h. to top of shade. **$1,054**

Courtesy of Brunk Auctions

▲ Leaded glass hanging lamp, American, early 20th century, brass fixture with two lights, large green-to-amber leaded glass shade with scalloped lower edge, surface wear and finish losses to brass cap, shade generally good condition with scattered minor cracks, 17" x 23-1/2". **$1,488**

Courtesy of Brunk Auctions

▶ Art glass lamp and shade, possibly Durand, circa 1900, baluster-form base with wide foot, squared shade and large knob finial, white glass with pale green leaves and dark green vines covered overall in iridescent threading, gold aurene lining, brass frame, unsigned, broken threads, brass frame corroded, 16-1/4" h. **$1,178**

Courtesy of Brunk Auctions

Roycroft Arts & Crafts hammered copper and mica table lamp, East Aurora, New York, early 20th century, hammered copper and mica shade with strapwork decoration over column support and circular base, underside with Roycroft orb-and-cross mark, excellent condition, fine original patination, 14-1/2". **$3,224**

Courtesy of Brunk Auctions

Tiffany Studios leaded glass peony lamp on bronze base, ribbed bronze three-light base signed "Tiffany Studios New York 370," shade signed "Tiffany Studios New York," shade in excellent condition overall, five minor cracks, chimney cap likely associated, with scattered minor dents, shade 18-1/4" dia. **$86,800**

Courtesy of Brunk Auctions

Handel painted glass and patinated metal table lamp, base signed "Handel," patinated three-socket stand with Art Nouveau decoration in relief, original patination, circular chipped-ice shade with tall green reeds against yellow ground and signed verso "Handel 5351"(?), excellent condition, shade with slight roughness at lower edge, base with some patination variation, shade 18" dia. **$5,456**

Courtesy of Brunk Auctions

Tiffany Studios arrowroot leaded glass and bronze table lamp, shade signed "Tiffany Studios," patinated bronze base with original patination and unsigned, attributed to Tiffany, adjustable shade support, original Tiffany chimney cap, base in excellent condition with some spotting and variation to original patination, shade with scattered cracks to panels, shade 20-1/4" dia. **$18,600**

Courtesy of Brunk Auctions

Handel leaded glass lamp on Handel embossed tree lamp base, three sockets, excellent condition, 24" h., shade 18" dia. **$3,000**

Courtesy of Morphy Auctions

Brilliant-period cut glass mushroom-form table lamp, American, late 19th century, brass rim hung with prism drops, excellent condition, one chip at top of shade, brass mounts with corrosion and surface wear, shade 12-3/4" dia., 24-1/2" h. overall. **$620**

Courtesy of Brunk Auctions

Italian millefiore boudoir lamp, mushroom shade in multicolor murrini, surmounting single light socket, rising on conforming base, 14" h. **$671**

Courtesy of Clars Auction Gallery, www.clars.com

Daum etched and enameled glass Rain lamp, circa 1900, enameled DAUM, NANCY, with Cross of Lorraine, good condition, fraying to covering of cord, 14-1/4" h. **$43,750**

Courtesy of Heritage Auctions

Legras Art Deco enameled and lighted vase, France, early 20th century, large yellow to clear Legras glass vase enamel-decorated in blue, white, green, and yellow and mounted as lamp with bulb inside on green-glazed terracotta pedestal, signed Legras in enamel on side of vase, good condition, 21-1/2" h. **$1,240**

Courtesy of Brunk Auctions

Royal Dux ceramic lamp of two dancers, circa 1920s, marked on underside, mint condition, 26" h. overall, figure approximately 13" h. **$210**

Courtesy of Morphy Auctions

Pair of Baccarat chandeliers, Baccarat, France, 20th century, 12-light crystal chandeliers with ceiling dome suspending beaded chains attached to 12 twisted and curved arms hung with shaped prisms, central twisted segmented standard terminating in floral pendant, 36" h., 30" dia................ **$10,000**

Courtesy of Heritage Auctions

LUXURY GOODS

ALTHOUGH THERE IS little question whether handbags are continuing their reign on the luxury accessories market, additional types of items and interested bidders in this high-end market also continue to grow.

In addition to the booming luxury handbag market, luxury accessories auctions also often feature luggage and trunks, dinner china, jewelry, watches, vintage clothing, and surfboards, rare vintage bicycles, and binoculars. For instance, Leslie Hindman Auctioneers hosts three luxury accessories and vintage fashion auctions each year, and while handbags are largely represented, so too are couture fashions from designers including Chanel, Christian Dior, Yves Saint Laurent, and Alexander McQueen, just to name a few.

This speaks to one of the most significant developments to come from the rise in luxury accessory auctions, the increase in collecting among women.

"Collectibles and collecting have traditionally been male-dominated pursuits," said Matt Rubinger, director of Heritage Auctions' Luxury Accessories category, as reported in *Warman's Antiques & Collectibles 2015*. "No one in the business was looking at these very high-quality pieces of enduring haute couture as having value beyond being arm candy. This assumption effectively dismissed half the potential population of collectors, that is, women."

In recent years, Heritage Auctions' has added luxury accessories to its list of record-setting categories. In fact, in 2014 Heritage Auctions reported more than $9.3 million in sales during luxury accessories auctions, up more than $1.6 million over its 2013 record. In September 2014, an Hermès Extraordinary Collection 30cm diamond matte Himalayan Nilo crocodile Birkin bag realized $185,000 at auction, which put it squarely in second place for the highest price paid for a handbag at auction. In June 2015, a new world record was set for the highest price paid for a handbag. A fuchsia Hermès Birkin handbag sold for $221,044 during an auction presented by Christie's. This topped the previous world record of $203,150 paid for a diamond Birkin in 2011, through Heritage Auctions.

As one may expect, brand name is said to play a part in the appeal of luxury accessories and goods. However, as Seung Yoon Rhee of the Hankuk Academy of Foreign Studies in South Korea discovered in "A Study of Why Luxury Goods Sell and their Effect on the Economy," it's not the only factor.

"Many luxury goods exhibit superior quality compared to goods from other brands," Rhee stated. "In these cases, luxury goods can be seen as worthwhile investments for people buying them."

Whatever the reason, based on the addition or expansion of existing luxury accessories departments within auction houses, the record-setting prices being paid at auction, and the evolving array of items being consigned, the appeal of luxury accessories is more than "skin deep."

Enamel and gold bracelet with full- and single-cut diamonds and pear-shaped rubies in 18k white and yellow gold, by Frascarolo, marked "MODELE," "FC," "MADE IN ITALY," very good condition, minor damage to enamel, 132.10 g., 7-1/4" x 7/8". $10,625

Courtesy of Heritage Auctions

LUXURY GOODS

GENERAL GOODS

Pair of Regency Wedgwood black basalt sphinxes, early 19th century, marked on bases, winged sphinxes seated in opposing stances, rectangular plinths, 9" h. **$3,750**

Courtesy of Neal Auction Co.

French luxury table stereo viewer, circa 1880, rootwood and ivory, for slides and photos measuring 3-1/2" x 7" with capacity for 50 pictures, with approximately 46 stereo views of Danzig and Baltic Sea, unmarked. **$12,914**

Courtesy of Auction Team Breker

Jaguar XK120 sports car, circa 1948, one of 12,000, restored, with silver finish on exterior, black canvas top, red English leather interior, said to be fastest production vehicle at time it was produced.......**$88,000**

Courtesy of Morphy Auctions

Pair of marble and gilt base urns, Russia, late 19th century, campana form, covered with mosaic of malachite, turned socles, square bases of gilt with green felt on undersides, very good condition................**$53,205**

Courtesy of Auctionata

Chanel limited edition natural burlwood surfboard, scarce model, in honey and chocolate burlwood pattern with Chanel CC logo on back, three plastic attachments for fins and ankle strap, black case, pristine condition, no signs of wear, 19" w. x 75" h. x 1" d. ...**$11,250**

Courtesy of Heritage Auctions

Cartier Thermos bottle, circa 1970s, primarily of 14k yellow and white gold and glass, bulbous body on round recessed foot with ornamental trim, filigree, ornate emblem on flask, marked "Cartier 14 KT" on bottom, good condition, minimal signs of wear, minor dent on lid, 754 g., 7-3/4" h. x 5-1/8". **$23,942**

Courtesy of Auctionata

"Three M's and one W II" gyratory stainless steel kinetic sculpture, George Warren Rickey, signed '87 Rickey, one of three, 8' 9" h. **$115,000**

Courtesy of Cottone Auctions

HANDBAGS/LUGGAGE/CARRYING CASES

◀ Nine-piece Cartier luggage set, circa 1990s, maroon suede and leather, gilt metal, three suitcases on rollers, two travel bags, one doctor's bag, one hand luggage suitcase, one attaché case and one beauty case, all cases stamped "Les Must de Cartier Paris," good condition, age-related signs of wear, 8" to 17". **$4,518**

Courtesy of Auctionata

Chanel beige lambskin leather camera bag with gold hardware throughout, originally designed to hold camera on trips, Chanel CC logo on front exterior, zip top closure, excellent condition, faint surface scratches to exterior, with Chanel literature, authenticity card and dustbag, 7" w. x 5" h. x 3" d. **$3,250**

Courtesy of Heritage Auctions

◀ Limited edition Louis Vuitton white and black monogram alligator and silk Linda Bag inspired by 1960s era, charm print on silk protected by crystal vinyl, handle of silk with gold chain link handle, gold-tone brass hardware and black alligator trim, interior of black leather, with dustbag and box, excellent condition, 10-1/2" w. x 8-1/2" h. x 3-1/5" d. **$3,500**

Courtesy of Heritage Auctions

Hermès Kiwi porosus crocodile clutch bag, Kelly cut, with palladium hardware, short top handle, interior in Kiwi Chevre leather, with slip pocket, pristine condition, original plastic still on hardware, with Hermès dustbag, care card, ribbon and box, 12" l. x 5" h. x 1" d. **$59,375**

Courtesy of Heritage Auctions

Hermès multicolored lizard and black Ardennes leather Kelly Nuages bag with palladium hardware, butterfly clasp and removable shoulder strap, excellent condition, scuffing toward base and interior, 12" w. x 9" h. x 4-1/2" d. **$12,500**

Courtesy of Heritage Auctions

Hermès amethyst and graphite crocodile Birkin bag, custom made, with gold hardware, graphite handles and arms, gold horseshoe symbol next to Hermès Paris stamp on front, with clochette, lock, keys, felt protector, exotic care card, small dustbag, and large dustbag, pristine condition, 14" w. x 10" h. x 7" d. **$68,750**

Courtesy of Heritage Auctions

Judith Leiber black crystal rose minaudière evening bag shaped like a rose, with push-lock closure, gold hardware, strap that can be tucked inside, coin purse, comb and mirror, very good to excellent condition, some missing crystals and scratches to hardware, 4-1/2" w. x 4" h. x 3-1/2" d........ **$1,000**

Courtesy of Heritage Auctions

Judith Leiber beaded crystal butterfly minaudière evening bag with Austrian crystals in blue, green and yellow, accented by gold with top closure, interior lined with metallic gold leather, with small double-sided mirror and gold comb with tassel, very good to excellent condition, missing coin purse, 6" w. x 3" h. x 1-1/2" d. **$2,750**

Courtesy of Heritage Auctions

Louis Vuitton travel trunk, early 20th century, wooden body covered with black leather, iron edges, corners and riveted flaps, beige linen lining on interior, four original leather grips, original label from Vuitton "Paris / Lille / Nice London" and blue label "Lille, 34 rue Faidherbe" on inside, manufacturer's name on wooden struts to sides and underside, 18-1/2" x 29" x 16-1/3"..........................**$2,104**

Courtesy of Auctionata

Louis Vuitton black Vuittonite travel trunk, circa early 20th century, black with red accent and beige strips on side, with stickers and name label with "Pierrpont" on both sides, good condition, markings and scratches on exterior and staining on interior canvas, vintage odor, 30" w. x 21" h. x 17" d. **$4,000**

Courtesy of Heritage Auctions

▲ Louis Vuitton classic monogram canvas hard-sided jewelry case with leather top handle, keys, clochette, S-lock closure, and leather and brown velvet interior with 13 different compartments, good to very good condition, scratches and markings to exterior, 14" w. x 10" h. x 2-1/2" d. $2,000

Courtesy of Heritage Auctions

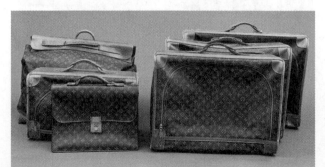

Six-piece Louis Vuitton monogram canvas luggage set, four soft-sided suitcases, steamer bag, and briefcase, largest suitcase 28" w., steamer bag 20" h., briefcase 15-1/2" w. **$2,750**

Courtesy of Neal Auction Co.

FASHION ACCESSORIES

Kieselstein Cord brown alligator belt and sterling silver alligator buckle with Kieselstein Cord dustbag, excellent condition, slight bend to belt from use, some wear to holes, 1-1/2" w. x 34" l. **$400**

Courtesy of Heritage Auctions

Katherine Bauman pill box fully beaded with gold-tone base and black and clear crystals in shape of champagne bottle top, spells out "Pop" in black crystals, thumb-down closure, gold fabric interior containing 14 extra crystals in plastic bag, excellent condition, some shifting of two crystals, small mark on one side of closure, with velvet pouch, 1" w. x 2" h. x 1" d. **$275**

Courtesy of Heritage Auctions

▶ Art Deco 18k yellow gold compact with compartments for lipstick, lighter, mirror, powder, watch, and comb set, with 66 rubies and 66 diamonds, eagle head touch mark on each piece, marked "Ostertag Paris Depose 39149," 289.9 g. **$19,200**

Courtesy of Nadeau's Auctions

Hermès palladium chain five-charm belt with iconic Hermès charms: lock, Kelly bag, Medor, link of chain d'Ancre, and Clous de Selle with Hermès Paris stamp, also with hook-eye closure and Hermès box, excellent condition, light surface scratching, 40" l. **$1,562**

Courtesy of Heritage Auctions

Hermès royal blue and navy "The Pony Express" silk pochette scarf by Kermit Oliver, excellent condition, 28" w. x 28" l. **$1,125**

Courtesy of Heritage Auctions

Two Hermès silk scarves: "Ex Libris" with four blue and green carriages, designed by Hugo Grygkan, white silk with slight toning, 34"; "Cheval Turc" with turbaned man tending to horse atop red background, designed by Christiane Vauzelles, good condition, 35". **$1,440**

Courtesy of Auctionata

MAPS & GLOBES

MAP COLLECTING IS slowly growing in visibility thanks to recent discoveries and sales of historically important maps. In 2010, a rare copy of George Washington's own map of Yorktown sold for more than $1.1 million. And a copy of "Theatrvm civitatvm et admirandorvm Italiae" (Theater of the Cities and Wonders of Italy), published in 1663 by the atlas maker Joan Blaeu of Amsterdam, was exhibited with much fanfare during the 2012 San Francisco Antiquarian Book Print and Paper Fair. It's asking price: $75,000.

Top of the market aside, map collecting remains a surprisingly affordable hobby when one considers most made in the early 19th century are hand-colored and represent the cutting edge scientific knowledge at the time. Most examples from the last 400 years are available for less than $500, and engravings depicting America or its states may be owned for less than $150. Larger maps are usually worth more to collectors.

Map of Mississippi River, "Les Costes aux Environs de la Riviere de Misisipi," Nicholas de Fer, 1705, in brass-inlaid wood frame, water damage to cloth mat, map in very good condition, sight 8-1/2" x 13"...................**$744**

Courtesy of Brunk Auctions

Lord of the Rings "A Map of Middle Earth" promotional poster, Ballantine, circa 1965, released in conjunction with 1965 Ballantine paperback book edition, with artwork by Barbara Remington (signing as "BRem"), excellent condition, sight 23-1/2" x 37", 25" x 39" framed with Plexiglas. **$335**

Courtesy of Heritage Auctions

Map of Italy, "Italia Cursoria Sev Tabula Geographica," Johann Baptista Homann (German, 1664-1724), published in 1720, double-page, hand-colored copper-engraved map, sight 20" h. x 23-1/2" w., framed 30" h. x 32-1/2" w. **$366**

Courtesy of Clars Auction Gallery, www.clars.com

Folk art double-hemisphere world map, American, 19th century, ink and watercolor on paper, hand-drawn and labeled continents, oceans, and countries, background with floral vines, eagles, and angels, in wood frame, toning, foxing, and tears, sight 21 3/4" x 29 1/2" **$100**

Courtesy of Cowan's Auctions

County map of New Jersey, J.H. Colton, New York, 1870, from "Colton's Map of the State of New Jersey," engraved, hand-colored in outline, framed, 19" x 13-1/4". **$126**

Courtesy of Leslie Hindman Auctioneers

Map of Virginia and Maryland, "Carte de la Virginie et du Maryland. Dressée sur la grand carte Angloise de Mrs. (Messieurs) Josué Fry et Pierre Jefferson, Par le Sr. Robert de Vaugondy, Geographe ordinaire du Rois. Avec Privilege," Robert de Vaugondy, 1755, hand-colored, engraved by E. Haussard, some toning, 18" x 24", 21" x 26-1/2" framed and glazed. **$1,353**

Courtesy of Cowan's Auctions

"L'Amerique Septentrionale," Amsterdam, Covens, Pieter and Cornelius Mortier, circa 1783, double-page engraved map hand-colored in outline, with hand-colored cartouche flanked by three figures, framed and matted, 10-1/4" x 14-1/2". **$410**

Courtesy of Leslie Hindman Auctioneers

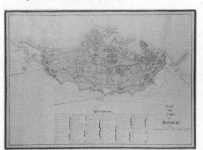

Two maps of Bombay (one shown), copper hand-painted engravings, 19th century, both unframed, 38" h. x 24" w. **$1,037**

Courtesy of Clars Auction Gallery, www.clars.com

"Official Centennial Map of Texas," Guy Cahoon, artist, Daughters of the Republic of Texas, Dallas: C.M. Burnett, 1934, color lithographic souvenir map commissioned by the Daughters of the Republic of Texas to commemorate Texas centennial, very good condition, minor wrinkling, fading and damp staining to map, minor wear to frame, glass cracked at top left corner, original paper backing peeling slightly, repaired at edges with clear tape, 25" x 34", 26" x 35" framed................................ **$500**

Courtesy of Heritage Auctions

"Anglia Regnum," circa 1606, Gerardus Mercator, cartographer (1512-1594), copper engraved map of Great Britain with hand-coloring, titled, double-leaf plate with descriptive text in Latin on verso, very good condition, minor toning and foxing to map, minor rubbing and edge wear to wooden frame, 16" x 21" framed........................ **$688**

Courtesy of Heritage Auctions

Map of Europe, hand-colored and engraved, marked "par le Robert de Vaugndy," sight 19" h. x 23" w., 25-7/8" h. x 29-1/2" w. framed.............. **$185**

Courtesy of Kaminski Auctions

Civil War era map, "New Military Map of the Border and Southern States," 1862, New York, H.H. Lloyd & Co., drawn by Edward S. Hall, engraved by Water & Son, hand-colored, 30-3/4" x 41" folded..... **$813**

Courtesy of Neal Auction Co.

Two terrestrial mahogany table globes, English, 20th century, lithograph-printed globe and cradle on four ring-turned legs with cross-stretcher support, ball feet, finely engraved brass meridian, globe marked "Malby Celestial and Terrestrial Globes 1860 / Manufactured and published under the superintendence of The Society for the Diffusion of Useful Knowledge," minor discoloration to paper on flat supports, globes 9" and 13" overall..................**$8,680**

Courtesy of Brunk Auctions

Terrestrial globe, circa 1870, made of brass, iron, wood, 12 printed paper gores laid on metal sphere, countries depicted in various colors, oceans in beige, analemma showing declination of sun placed in Pacific Ocean, full calibrated brass meridian ring and adjustment screw, brass hour circles at poles, walnut horizon band marked "Manufactured by Gilman Joslin Corrected to 1870" and signs of zodiac, calendar and equation of time table in green, salmon and brown within Greek key border, very good condition, losses on wood and discoloration on horizon band, light age checks in paper with no significant loss, 24" h. x 20" dia., globe 15" dia. **$1,370**

Courtesy of Louis J. Dianni, LLC Antiques Auctions

Rand McNally terrestrial globe on stand, dated 1909, 40" h. x 22" dia. (stand), globe 16" dia.......**$738**

Courtesy of Kaminski Auctions

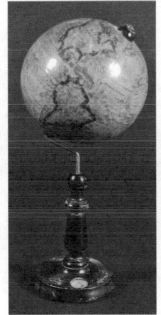

Miniature terrestrial table globe, circa 1900, made up of 12 color-printed gores and one polar calotte, equatorial graduated in degrees, no ecliptic shown, continents colored and outlined, oceans showing currents, on turned ebonized column and plinth, with inset compass, 9-1/2" h. x 4-1/2" dia..........................**$623**

Courtesy of Louis J. Dianni, LLC Antiques Auctions

Pair of Georgian library globes, circa 1833, by Smith, London, each made up of two sets of hand-colored finely engraved gores, engraved brass hour dials, brass meridian circle with graduated degrees, papered horizon rings with degrees of amplitude and azimuth, compass directions and houses of zodiac, celestial globe with constellations depicted by mythical figures and beasts, on Regency-style walnut stands, turned standard, down-curved legs with brass casters, 43-1/2" h., 18" dia. **$16,875**

Courtesy of Neal Auction Co.

MUSIC MEMORABILIA

THE STATE OF the hobby for those who collect music and related memorabilia is healthy. Before the economy went south in 2008, multiple buyers might be in the market for a pricey item, such as a fully signed photo of The Beatles. The resulting bidding battle could drive the price up to $10,000. These days, fewer people are looking for that type of item to begin with, and those who are interested likely would pay less for it, too. Instead, buyers are gravitating toward low- to mid-price lots that previously might not have been considered for auction. And the acts that buyers are interested in aren't necessarily your parents' favorites.

Artists from the late 1970s and 1980s, especially hard rock, heavy metal and pop acts, are poised to be the next generation of headlining acts for collectors. Guns N' Roses, Motley Crüe, Bon Jovi, U2, Prince and Madonna as prime examples.

And just as the desired artists are changing, so, too, are some of the items that are being collected. Concert posters are practically nonexistent because there isn't much of a need for them anymore. Also on the endangered species list: ticket stubs, printed magazines, handbills, and promotional materials.

On the other hand, T-shirts have come into their own. And those reports you've heard about the pending demise of vinyl records in the wake of digital formats? Don't believe them. Vinyl is far from dead. Of 60s artists, vinyl is a prime collectible, and collectors of '80s bands or artists are just as intrigued and as interested in vinyl as the previous generation.

One key piece of advice: Don't look at music memorabilia as an investment. Build a collection around your passion, be it punk music, concert posters, or all things Neil Diamond.

Here are some tips on collecting music memorabilia: Strive to acquire items that are in the best condition possible and keep them that way. Put a priority on provenance. Weigh quantity and rarity. Take advantage of opportunities geared toward collectors, such as Record Store Day. Refine the focus of your collection and don't try to collect everything. And think before you toss. Good-condition, once-common items that date back before World War II — like advertising posters, Coca-Cola bottles, 78 RPM records, and hand tools —are cherished by collectors today.

Floyd Rose Advantage six-string guitar signed in silver paint pen by all members of Bon Jovi, with original inspection sticker on pearlized pick guard and "Floyd Rose Advantage" label on body of guitar, 39" long. **$862**

Courtesy of Hakes Americana & Collectibles

Original Buddy Holly and the Crickets concert program, circa 1958, for a tour in the United Kingdom, signed by Holly on front and back cover in black ballpoint pen, signed by Crickets members on back cover, scarcely seen, signatures in excellent condition, some separation of pages and tearing, 8-1/2" x 10-1/2". **$1,000**

Courtesy of Gotta Have Rock and Roll

American Tour '81 program autographed by The Rolling Stones (Mick Jagger, Keith Richards, Ronnie Wood, Patti Hensen, Jerry Hall, Jo Wood and others), 12" x 12"................. **$896**

Courtesy of Julien's Auctions

Four velvet hats of varying styles and fabrics owned and stage worn by Ann Wilson of rock band Heart, from personal collection of Ann Wilson...... **$160**

Courtesy of Julien's Auctions

▲ Harmonica used by Bob Dylan and signed by him in black Sharpie pen, very good condition, with letter of provenance from Cesar Diaz, Dylan's long-time guitar amp technician....................... **$1,952**

Courtesy of Gotta Have Rock and Roll

▶ Pen, ink, and pencil on paper collection of humorous inside jokes between musicians Rod Stewart and Ronnie Wood, circa 1969, titled "Stewart & Wood's Glossary of Group Statements 1969 Edition No. 1 Volume One To Be Pronounced with a Northern Accent," signed "R.W." lower right of page, with black and white photograph of the two performing on stage, circa 1971. ....**$512**

Courtesy of Julien's Auctions

Pair of The Rolling Stones promotional Converse high-top, black canvas tennis shoes with red logo embroidery and original Converse box, marked men's size 12 on box, circa 1989........... **$448**

Courtesy of Julien's Auctions

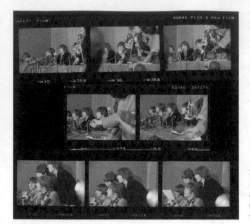

Eight black and white original negatives of Beatles at a press conference in New York in August 1965, with some images of all four Beatles...... **$993**

Courtesy of Omega Auctions

Signed menu from Onyx Jazz Club, 52nd Street, New York, "where Swing was born," which operated during Prohibition, circa 1937, published by Grinthal Press, cover with stiff Art Deco silver foil-type reflective paper, front with musical drawings and rear with page of facsimile "Signatures of the original Onyx Customers – July 27, 1930." **$246**

Courtesy of PBA Galleries Auctioneers & Appraisers

Handwritten scores for chart-topping hits "Chantilly Lace" and "Big Bopper's Wedding," both scored by J. P. Richardson (The Big Bopper), very fine condition, 9-1/2" x 12-1/2"............... **$687**

Courtesy of Heritage Auctions

Band uniform and signed photo of 1939 New York World's Fair Maestro Eugene LaBarre, cotton twill dress uniform, tailored with embroidered harp accent on jacket breast and American eagle braided epaulets on shoulders, brass buttons, slacks with stitched Smith-Gray tag, with 8" x 10-1/8" photo of LaBarre in uniform, signed "With Kindest Regards To My Good Friend, Mrs. Lillian Taylor. Sincerely, Capt. Eugene LaBarre – 8/3/41." **$172**

Courtesy of Hake's Americana & Collectibles

Four Elvis Presley concert tickets for shows on June 4, 1976 at The Omni in Los Angeles; April 24, 1977 at Chrisler Arena, Ann Arbor, Michigan, stub only with tears repaired with tape; May 21, 1977 at Freedom Hall, Louisville, Kentucky, unused complete ticket; and May 30 at Asheville Civic Center, Asheville, North Carolina, fair to very good condition. **$625**

Courtesy of Heritage Auctions

◄ Guitar owned by Eddie Van Halen, custom paint job with Van Halen's trademark "5150" red with white and black stripe pattern, first offered in 1998, oil finished hard rock maple neck and fingerboard with chrome tuners, excellent condition with light wear, 36-1/2" l.
.... **$696**

Courtesy of Hake's Americana & Collectibles

KISS lunch box and bottle with two different photo images of band, one of them in concert, King-Seely Thermos Co., circa 1977, with unused original King-Seeley bottle, sticker and insert sheet, near mint condition for both, trace of rim wear on lunchbox, bottle 6-1/2" h. **$569**

Courtesy of Hake's Americana & Collectibles

▶ Three pocket mirrors (one shown) with singer Arleen Whelan, circa 1920-1930s, one with Illinois dealer with record label "Her Bright Smile Haunts Me Still / Edward Johnson," second with Philadelphia dealer with record label "Aida-Celeste Aida-Enrico Caruso," third with "Arleen Whelan Gets Dreamy Eyed About Motorola Radio," excellent condition. **$115**

Courtesy of Hake's Americana & Collectibles

Cardboard window card for Nov. 10, 1956 concert performance in Pottstown, Pennsylvania of "The King of Swing Benny Goodman and his Orchestra," with black and white photo of Goodman playing clarinet, fine condition, signs of aging on edges of card and wear to tips of corners, 14" x 22-1/4".... **$487**

Courtesy of Hake's Americana & Collectibles

Album cover for Boston's self-titled debut album, released Aug. 25, 1976, with signatures of all founding and early band members in black felt tip pen, those of later members in blue felt tip pen, with inner sleeve and record, fine condition overall, signatures in excellent condition, rare, 12-1/4" x 12-1/4". **$379**

Courtesy of Hake's Americana & Collectibles

Glossy publicity photo of R.E.M. promoting 1996 "New Adventures In Hi-Fi" album, with all four members of band and their signatures in black felt tip pen, Peter Buck's signature in blue, scarce, 8" x 10". **$372**

Courtesy of Hake's Americana & Collectibles

Seven glossy handbills (four shown) with nature designs, hippies, and psychedelic text promoting concerts at Crystal Ballroom in Portland, Oregon, circa late 1960s, featured acts include The Buffalo Springfield, The Horsemen, The Redcoats, Warlocks, and The Weeds/Lollipop Shoppe, very good condition, tape staining along margins. **$498**

Courtesy of Hake's Americana & Collectibles

Sex Pistols "Never Mind the Bans, Sex Pistols Will Play" tour poster, circa 1977, Glitterbest LTD, general tour poster printed on white paper, design done in ransom note style with reproduction of actual ban letters, small tears at edges, small area of loss at top center, 11-3/4" x 16-1/2"; nine-date U.K. tour came on heels of a year of bad press for band. **$750**

Courtesy of Heritage Auctions

Three-dimensional Beatles Yellow Submarine model display, circa 1968, King Features-Subfilms, two opening hatches displaying Boob and Captain Fred, excellent condition as factory-sealed, some traces of aging under shrinkwrap, 6-1/2" x 9-1/2" x 3-1/2"; model gets wound and then glides through water. **$253**

Courtesy of Hake's Americana & Collectibles

Vintage Beatles apron made from layered paper material, black and white design of Beatles sketches, staffs with musical notes, and records "I Want to Hold Your Hand," "Not a Second Time," and "Hold Me Tight," very good condition, minor tears and some fraying, 30" x 16". **$625**

Courtesy of Heritage Auctions

Autograph album page signed in red ink "Respect – Otis Redding – To Carol," excellent condition, uneven left margin on page, 4-1/8" x 5"; Redding was best known for his song "Sittin' on the Dock of the Bay," the first posthumous number-one record on both Billboard Hot 100 and R&B charts. **$612**

Courtesy of Hake's Americana & Collectibles

"Electric" pants owned and worn by Liberace, circa 1960s, navy blue wool with white elastic suspenders, yellow stripes down legs, rhinestones, and electrical wiring hidden inside that allowed sides to light up, moth holes throughout, unknown if lighting feature still works. **$625**

Courtesy of Heritage Auctions

NATIVE AMERICAN ARTIFACTS

INTEREST IN NATIVE AMERICAN material cultural artifacts has been long-lived. In recent years it has become commonplace to have major sales of these artifacts by at least four major auction houses, in addition to the private trading, local auctions, and Internet sales of these items.

Other cultures have been fascinated with the material culture of Native Americans from the beginning of their contact with it. The majority of these valuable items are in repositories of museums, universities, and colleges, but many items that were traded to private citizens are now being sold to collectors of Native American material culture.

Native American artifacts are now acquired by collectors in the same fashion as any material cultural item. Individuals interested in antiques and collectibles find items at farm auction sales (an especially good place for farm family collections to be dispersed), yard sales, estate sales, specialized auctions, and from private collectors trading or selling items. The most wonderful of all sources is the Internet, especially online auction sales. There is no shortage of possibilities in finding items; it is merely deciding where to place one's energy and investment in adding to one's collection.

Native American artifacts are much more difficult to locate for a variety of reasons, including the following: scarcity of items; legal protection of items being traded; more vigorous collecting of artifacts by numerous international, national, state, regional, and local museums and historical societies; frailties of the items themselves, as most were made of organic materials; and a more limited distribution network through legitimate secondary sales.

However, it is still possible to find some types of Native American items through the traditional sources of online auctions, auction houses in local communities, antique stores and malls, flea markets, trading meetings, estate sales, and similar venues. The most likely items to find in these ways are items made of stone, chert, flint, obsidian, and copper. Most organic materials will not have survived the rigors of a marketplace unless they were recently released from some estate or collection and their value was unknown to the previous owner.

For more information on Native American collectibles, see *Warman's North American Indian Artifacts Identification and Price Guide* by Russell E. Lewis.

Acoma polychrome jar, circa 1900, clay, paint, pencil inscription on base "Ashfork Arizona," overall very good condition, surface with usual wear, loss to slip and abrasions on shoulder affecting painted design, 8-1/4" dia. **$1,000**

Courtesy of Heritage Auctions

Anasazi black on white bowl, circa 1100-1200 AD, clay, paint, 8" dia. **$750**

Courtesy of Heritage Auctions

Apache coiled storage jar, circa 1900, willow, devil's claw, 13" h. **$1,563**

Courtesy of Heritage Auctions

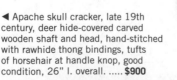

◄ Apache skull cracker, late 19th century, deer hide-covered carved wooden shaft and head, hand-stitched with rawhide thong bindings, tufts of horsehair at handle knop, good condition, 26" l. overall. **$900**

Courtesy of Thomaston Place Auction Galleries

Arapaho female doll, circa 1890, deer hide with blue trade wool beaded dress with red grosgrain ribbon border, leather belt, three-strand beaded necklace, ring earrings and high-top beaded moccasins, beaded features, braided real hair, minor losses, 16" h...**$1,500**

Courtesy of Thomaston Place Auction Galleries

Casas Grande polychrome jar, circa 1100-1200 AD, clay, paint, two stickers affixed to bottom, overall excellent condition, surface with minor abrasions and soiling, no apparent restoration, 9" dia.. **$1,750**

Courtesy of Heritage Auctions

Chippewa beaded bandolier bag with front slit, circa 1910-1920, parti-colored beadwork of flowers, translucent background on 5-1/4" w. strap, white background on 15" x 11-1/4" bag, loom-woven geometric pendant tabs with curly red Germantown yarn fringe, black cotton calico lining, blue wool edge binding, fine condition, never worn, 40" x 12" overall. **$700**

Courtesy of Thomaston Place Auction Galleries

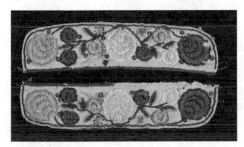

Chippewa cuffs, late 19th century, polychrome floral beadwork over white silk with scattered spangles, red stroud cloth backing, wine-colored silk binding, in display case, losses to fabric, beadwork largely intact, 11" x 2-3/4" each. **$250**

Courtesy of Thomaston Place Auction Galleries

Cree doeskin women's gauntlet gloves, circa 1880, beadwork trim and four-pointed star, three life lines on back of hand, embroidered polychrome vines, mountain sunrise on gauntlet, interior lined with flannel, remnants of pink silk ribbon edging, worn condition, 12" l. **$275**

Courtesy of Thomaston Place Auction Galleries

Choctaw iron trade knife in deer hide slinged sheath with white glass bead geometric decoration over blue and red wool, circa 1870, minor losses to beads and wool, signs of use and corrosion, shrinkage crack to handle, knife 13" l. overall, sheath and sling 28" l. overall, strap 2" w. **$4,000**

Courtesy of Thomaston Place Auction Galleries

◄ Hopi (Polacca) polychrome jar, circa 1880, clay, paint, stickers affixed to side, inscribed "From Moqui Pueblo Indians. N. W. of Jettyto Spring, Arizona," overall very good to excellent condition, surface with moderate wear, light soiling, pencil marks and crazing, 6-1/2" dia. **$625**

Courtesy of Heritage Auctions

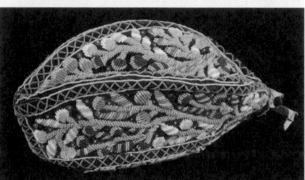

Iroquois beaded Glengarry cap on dark brown velvet base, 19th century, polychrome tree of life pattern with remnants of pink silk ribbon binding, cotton- and linen-lined interior, blue crisscross border, wear to binding and lining, beadwork intact, 11" x 4-1/4". **$650**

Courtesy of Thomaston Place Auction Galleries

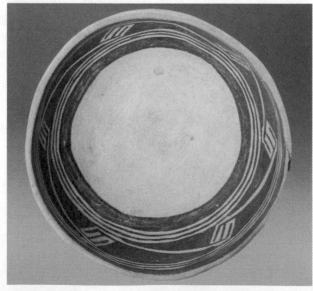

▲ Iroquois maple cane, early 19th century, carved with human head handle with one remaining inset bead eye and full-length body below, feathered cape, tapered and varnished shaft fully chip-carved with two entwined snakes carved of a piece with shaft, arrowhead form heads at top with fern fronds between, 32-1/2" l. **$950**

Courtesy of Thomaston Place Auction Galleries

◄ Kayenta black on white bowl, circa 1200 AD, clay, paint, overall good condition, loss to clay on exterior, light soiling, pencil marks and two stickers on bottom, no apparent restoration, 6-3/4" dia. **$938**

Courtesy of Heritage Auctions

Laguna polychrome storage jar, Arroh-ah-och, circa 1895, painted in red and black over white slip with four large-scale stepped elements, each enclosing diamond, all against hatched ground, surmounted by three bands of geometric designs, dark brown underbody, overall good condition, 13-1/2" dia....................$10,000

Courtesy of Heritage Auctions

▲ Lakota Sioux papoose carrier made from single pine plank and two cedar hoops, uppermost second generation replacement, top edge of plank carved and drilled, reverse scratch-carved with two birds kissing between stars, standing atop flowering vine, with "Yawaa" incised at spiral root (meaning esteem), arrow pointing down from word to dancing human figure with feather headdress, deer, fish, frog, and snake on right, in polychrome stain with green field, well used, repaired, 10" x 30" x 8"......................... $2,750

Courtesy of Thomaston Place Auction Galleries

Kiowa papoose carrier attributed to Tahdo, circa 1910, Oklahoma, lower half from blanket, attached by section of deer hide to beaded hood with red, blue, and green with gold over white geometric decoration, cotton chintz lining, deer hide ties, two picket boards brass-studded with crosses at top, good condition, beading intact, lower corner of one board cracked at lacing, 27-1/2" h. overall............ $1,000

Courtesy of Thomaston Place Auction Galleries

▲ Lakota Sioux woman's buckskin dress, early 20th century, fringed edging and long fringe with bead decoration, three flaps in front suspended from beaded strip, rows of money cowrie shells at strip and collar, some small holes, one small patch at shoulder, generally very good condition, 20" shoulder, 46" l., excluding fringe.......... $700

Courtesy of Thomaston Place Auction Galleries

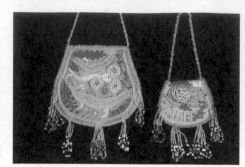

Two beaded bags: Mohawk, pink cotton with clear bead trim, handle, two mythical lake creatures on one side, captioned dog and deer on other, minor wear, 7" x 7-1/2", excluding loop fringe; Iroquois, marked "1909" with raised figure of rabbit, clear beaded edge and handle, remnants of red cloth at edges, exposed cardstock body, red polished cotton interior, 4" x 4-3/4", excluding loop fringe.............................**$650**

Courtesy of Thomaston Place Auction Galleries

Metis deerhide leggings, Quebec, Canada, polychrome floral faceted beadwork, different on both sides, white bead edging, tiny round brass button closure, densely spaced up one side, loss to white beaded edging, 9" x 6" tapering to 4-3/4".....................................**$300**

Courtesy of Thomaston Place Auction Galleries

Northwest Coast polychrome effigy bowl, 15-1/2" l. ..**$938**

Courtesy of Heritage Auctions

Northwest Coast polychrome plaited cedar bark mat, circa 1890, cedar, paint, 53" x 102"........... **$1,625**

Courtesy of Heritage Auctions

▲ Navajo four-medallion rug, early 20th century, very good condition, 27-1/2" x 48". **$900**

Courtesy of Thomaston Place Auction Galleries

◄ Two Northwest Coast plaited cedar bark mats, circa 1890, cedar, pigment, 45" x 75" and 52" x 89"...............**$438**

Courtesy of Heritage Auctions

Obijay incise-decorated birch bark creel with separate lid, leather thong handle, circa 1920, found in Maine, lid cupped, otherwise very good condition, 10-1/2" x 13" x 9". **$350**

Courtesy of Thomaston Place Auction Galleries

Ojibwa (Chippewa) child's pictorial vest, circa 1890, crossed U.S. flags and stars and with initials K.T. and H.W.S on two front buckskin panels and overall polychrome blossom decoration, later replaced cloth back, remnants of red edge binding and thong ties, unlined, wear from age and use, beadwork intact, 12" w. at shoulders, 12" l........ **$475**

Courtesy of Thomaston Place Auction Galleries

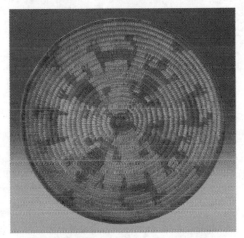

Three Plains knives with beaded hide sheaths, probably late 19th century, two with bone handles, one with wood handle, long use, 6-3/4" to 9-3/4" l. when sheathed.. **$250**

Courtesy of Heritage Auctions

Pima/Papago pictorial coiled tray, 11" dia.......**$188**

Courtesy of Heritage Auctions

◀ Plains pipe tomahawk, circa 1880-1915, beaded drop with all sinew sewn design with early glass seed trade beads, trade brass tacks, trade cloth, hand-cut long fringe, all on Indian tanned hide, tomahawk with forged iron head with pipe bowl and brass stud tacks, tomahawk 23-1/4" l. with 10-1/4" l. x 3-1/4" w. x 1-1/2" d. head with 13/16" bowl, beaded drop 24" l. overall x 4" w. **$750**

Courtesy of North American Auction Co.

◀ Western Plains tomahawk with pipe, circa 1870-1890, cast brass nickel-plated head with heart cutout, original wood shaft with steel tacks, lead seal, excellent condition, 18-3/4" l. **$550**

! top lot

Rare circa 1900 mask, most likely Tlingit, polychrome painted and carved wood with snake and warrior characters and applied wooden teeth, original as-found condition with untouched surface patina, missing four teeth, 20" x 22" x 11-1/2" d. Provenance: Acquired in 1908 and descended through consignor's family...........$95,000

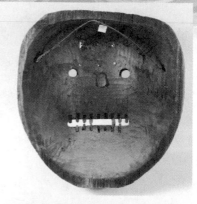

Salado polychrome bowl, circa 1150-1450 AD, clay, paint, 7-1/2" dia......**$813**

Courtesy of Heritage Auctions

San Juan red/buffware bowl, circa 1900, clay, paint, overall good condition, surface with some scuffs to red area and rim, pencil marks in basin and marks on exterior, small sticker affixed to bottom. 9" dia. **$500**

Courtesy of Heritage Auctions

Plateau twined cornhusk bag, circa 1900, woven of natural and dyed cornhusks, decorated with colored wool imbrication, each side with two confronting triangles, flanked top and bottom by pairs of smaller triangles, all overlying checkered ground, hide handles, overall excellent condition, 8 3/4" l., excluding handles. Provenance: Collected by Claus Elijah Andres (1869-1952), who broke and trained horses for Buffalo Bill Cody; through family by descent. **$750**

Courtesy of Heritage Auctions

Sioux War Club Plains (Sioux-Santee) gunstock war club, circa 1850, tiger maple with brass tacks, pierced ends, forged steel blade, very good condition, light scratches, age and use patina, 30-1/2" l. overall, 6" blade. **$2,700**

Courtesy of Thomaston Place Auction Galleries

Sioux fly wisk, circa 1860, painted hide handle, turkey feather fan and twisted leather thong cord with two glass beads, missing one feather, 21" l. ...**$275**

Courtesy of Thomaston Place Auction Galleries

ODDITIES

THESE COLLECTIBLES FALL in the "weird and wonderful" category of unusual items.

Cigar holder, steer horn forms holder for cigars with inset well for matches with striker, angry wood-carved Kodiak bear stands on horn with glass eyes, smaller horn positioned on front reads "Dexter Saloon, Nome A.T. 1900," base of white-veined black marble with egg and dart trim, raised on four disc and ball feet, 13-1/2" x 8-1/2" x 11" h. Wyatt Earp built Dexter Saloon in 1899 during the Alaska Territory Gold Rush and sold it in 1901..................**$2,000**

Courtesy of Omaha Auction Center

Victorian toleware poodle umbrella stand with dog on plush pillow with ribbon tied at neck with bell, 18-3/4" x 7-1/2" x 25".....................**$800**

Courtesy of Omaha Auction Center

Civil War-era hair wreath, twisted and looped with stylized flowers, signed in same manner, 8" x 5-1/4". **$75**

Courtesy of Omaha Auction Center

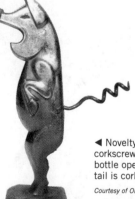

◄ Novelty bottle opener with corkscrew, pig's open mouth is bottle opener and tuck-a-way tail is corkscrew, 5" h. **$325**

Courtesy of Omaha Auction Center

▲ Trilobite fossil, Harpes perradiatus, Middle Devonian, Laatchana, Alnif, Morocco, 3" x 3-3/4" x 1". Trilobites are the quintessential fossils of the Paleozoic and were all extinct before the first dinosaur. . **$575**

Courtesy of Heritage Auctions

VISIT WWW.ANTIQUETRADER.COM

WWW.FACEBOOK.COM/ANTIQUETRADER

Peacock feathered Mardi Gras Venetian mask, with acrylic box, 32" h. x 36" w. x 6" d..........**$300**

Courtesy of Red Baron's Antiques

▶ Gadget sword cane with bird head handle and molded composition band, blade marked India, 22-1/2" h. **$75**

Courtesy of Omaha Auction Center

Unusual Chinese suit of armor, various sections composed of jade-like panels. **$384**

Courtesy of John Nicholson Auctioneers

Sculpture of duck, head and feet in silver-plate, body in natural coral, 6-1/2" h. **$30**

Courtesy of International Auction Gallery

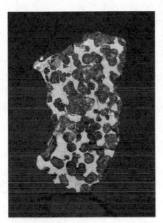

Rare meteorite: slice of Sterley Passasite, found in 1950 in Sterley, Texas, by farmer plowing his field, 3-1/2" x 2" x 0.11"................**$5,000**

Courtesy of Heritage Auctions

Eskimo stone oil lamp, circa 19th century, with unusual arch shape and ridge on one side, 10-1/2" l. x 5-5/8" w.............**$584**

Courtesy of Skinner Inc.; www.skinnerinc.com

Jerry Mahoney ventriloquist beanie cap, circa 1950s, Benay-Albee Novelty Co., painted molded thin plastic face with moveable mouth, on 100-percent recycled felt cap, 7" dia....................................**$20**

Courtesy of Morphy Auctions

Victorian cased taxidermy pigeon, possibly orange-breasted green pigeon of Sri Lanka or thick-billed green pigeon of Africa, 16" x 15". ..**$51**

Courtesy of Dickins Auctioneers, Ltd.

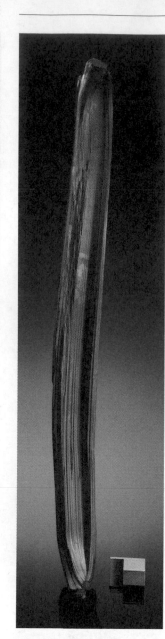

Gorham sterling salt and pepper shakers, grotesque head form with glass eyes, 1-1/2", 2.05 oz. **$1,300**

Courtesy of Briggs Auction, Inc., www.briggsauction.com

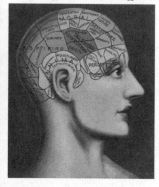

European school phrenology head study, 19th century, contained within ebonised frame, 8-1/4" x 7-1/2".........**$592**

Courtesy of Hannam's Auctioneers

German novelty tin toy of man at grindstone on circular base, circa 1900.........................**$550**

Courtesy of The RSL Auction Co.

Hematite "sword," Jackson Mine, Negaunee, Marquette Iron Range, Marquette County, Michigan, 14-1/2" x 1-1/4" x 1-1/4". Hematite is one of the main ores of iron mined for the steel industry and has been associated with human culture since prehistoric times. **$2,125**

Courtesy of Heritage Auctions

Automated bulldog, electric display with mouth that opens and closes as eyes roll from side to side, real animal hide tacked onto papier-mâché frame, access panel on side for mechanism, mascot for Drake, Georgia, 24" x 13" x 15-1/2" h.....................**$250**

Courtesy of Omaha Auction Center

Rare Sonneberg money-spinner, unusual squeaking figure, around 1850, about 5-1/2". **$1,776**

Courtesy of Ladenburger Spielzeugauktion GmbH

Liberty Bell lighter, all cast brass, 1926, 5" h.................**$60**

Courtesy of Milestone Auctions, www. milestoneauctions.com

Scarce set of roller skates made by famous gunmaker Winchester, all original with leather straps..**$20**

Courtesy of Milestone Auctions, www.milestoneauctions.com

Prisoner-of-war carved bone gaming box with sliding top revealing dominos, 19th century, border forming cribbage board, 8-1/2" w...... **$355**

Courtesy of Hamman's Auctioneers

Sculpted bronze bust of abstract, alien-like head on wooden base, artist unknown, circa 1960s, unmarked, approximately 13" h. without base x 13" l. x 6" w............ **$950**

Courtesy of Showplace Antique & Design Center

Spider web hanging lamp, three-sided wavy lobed form, caramel slag geometric spider web background with cast spelter downward-facing figural spiders on three convex sides with cutout eyes glowing through glass, open top with three chains holding single teardrop socket, signed on metal tag "B.M. Kasmark," mid-20th century, 15-1/2" dia. at widest point, shade 9" h. **$1,200**

Courtesy of Fontaines Auction Gallery

Wood relic from Chancellorsville battlefield containing lead minie ball, possibly Confederate two-ring Gardner, ball bent sideways with nose not deformed, ball and section of wood varnished for preservation and mounted on modern wood base, 8-3/4" h.....**$280**

Courtesy of Alexander Historical Auctions, LLC

PAPERWEIGHTS

ANTIQUE PAPERWEIGHTS MADE in the 19th century captured floral designs, reptiles and millefiori canes in very traditional Victorian styles encased in a solid sphere of clear crystal.

Artists of the 19th century generally produced paperweights in factory settings along with other decorative glass objects. Rarely signed by individual artists, most antique paperweights are attributed to a factory by motif, color palette, canes and shape. Little is known about individual artists who created the work.

In a 19th century society with fancy desks and paper, paperweights were functional objects of art. Flowers were a large part of Victorian society and both ladies and gentleman of the time were attracted to fauna and flora. Paperweights were considered fascinating objects of art and conversation pieces in Victorian homes.

Factories producing paperweights were primarily located in France, Italy, Czechoslovakia, America, and China. Factory-made paperweights often had similar motifs. Factories would also produce special pieces. These rare designs showcased fantastic capabilities and secret techniques only known to each factory. Today these special pieces bring staggering auction results.

In the mid-20th century there was a revival in modern paperweights. At first artists began creating updated versions using glass-working techniques of antique traditions. This revival began alongside the studio art glass movement in America. Individual glass artists opened homegrown studios in garages and basements. The pioneer and dean of the American paperweight revival was Charles Kaziun of Brockton, Massachusetts. Kaziun set new artistic standards and methods for creating paperweights at that time. He worked alone in his own small home studio creating the path that all subsequent contemporary paperweight artists followed.

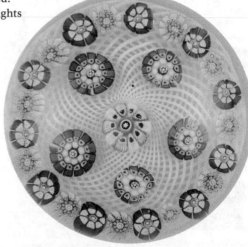

Contemporary artists making paperweights introduced several differences from the past: They worked alone or with an assistant in private home studios; concentrated only on paperweights; developed individual styles and methods of making the work; and always signed the artwork and often numbered editions.

Antique St. Louis patterned millefiori paperweight, central green and white cane cluster surrounded by five red, white, and blue canes, entire design surrounded by garland of blue, white, and chartreuse canes resting on spiral latticino ground, 2-5/8" dia. x 1-7/8" h. Provenance: Barry Schultheiss Collection **$590**

Courtesy of James D. Julia Auctioneers, Fairfield, Maine, www.jamesdjulia.com

VISIT WWW.ANTIQUETRADER.COM

WWW.FACEBOOK.COM/ANTIQUETRADER

Three vintage paperweights: Fin fish with rainbow body amid seaweed, 2-3/4"; cut and polished dome with millefiori, 2"; mini paperweight with millefiori florettes and spiral canes over mottled amber, 1-5/8", cut star beneath, all excellent condition. **$100**

Courtesy of Mark Mussio, Humler & Nolan

In the early years of collecting paperweights, few collectors knew much about paperweights and even less about how they were made. In 1955 Paul Jokelson, an avid antique paperweight collector and importer, founded the Paperweight Collectors Association. He promoted paperweights and created a forum for educating collectors and helping artists like Kaziun show and sell their new work. Jokelson published many early books on paperweights; other authors followed, creating a library of books on paperweights. The PCA has biannual paperweight conventions.

Today many artists all over the world are creating fine paperweights. The finest modern paperweights have made their way into private and museum art collections. The Bergstrom-Mahler Museum of Glass in Neenah, Wisconsin, houses one of the world's largest collections of paperweights in the United States. It's second only to the holdings of the Corning Museum of Glass in New York. Other institutions such as The Chicago Art Institute, Museum of Fine Arts in Boston, and The Currier Museum of Art in Manchester, New Hampshire, among others, also have modern paperweights on view.

Today's paperweight artists have stepped beyond the traditional form and are creating new works of contemporary art glass. They truly enjoy their work and continue to be motivated by their love of art.

Collectors love paperweights because, unlike other forms of art, collectors can hold them in their hands and be drawn into a fascinating miniature world.

Courtesy of James D. Julia Auctioneers, Fairfield, Maine, www.jamesdjulia.com, and Debbie Tarsitano Studios

Rookwood Z glaze paperweight made in 1904 for Elk's Club celebration, mat green glaze, marked with Rookwood symbol, date and shape 763 Z, small firing separation at elk's left antler, nick at base, rare, 4" dia.................................$180

Courtesy of Mark Mussio, Humler & Nolan

Rookwood sailing ship paperweight, William McDonald design, cast in 1946, high glaze chartreuse finish, impressed with Rookwood logo, date and shape 2792, fine overall crazing, restoration to prow, 3-7/8" h....................$100

Courtesy of Mark Mussio, Humler & Nolan

St. Louis double overlay mushroom paperweight, close pack millefiori surrounded by green over white double overlay, five side facets and one top facet, star cut base, signed "SL 1953" signature/date cane, 3" dia. x 2-1/4" h. Provenance: Barry Schultheiss Collection $373

Courtesy of James D. Julia Auctioneers, Fairfield, Maine, www.jamesdjulia.com

Rookwood bunny paperweight, designed by Louise Abel, cast in 1959, Wine Madder glaze, impressed with Rookwood logo, date and shape 6160, without crazing, fine original condition, 3-1/4" h. $200

Courtesy of Mark Mussio, Humler & Nolan

Baccarat mushroom paperweight, close concentric millefiori mushroom in red, yellow, white, and blue encased in red over white double overlay, six side facets and six fancy cut side flutes, star cut base, "1969" date cane contained within mushroom and signed on underside with acid-etched Baccarat insignia, 3" dia. x 2-1/4" h. Provenance: Barry Schultheiss Collection $531

Courtesy of James D. Julia Auctioneers, Fairfield, Maine, www.jamesdjulia.com

Baccarat paperweight, concentric millefiori mushroom in red, white, blue, and yellow encased with red-over-white double overlay cut with six side flutes and one top facet, signed "B 1970" signature/date cane, signed on base with Baccarat acid-etched insignia, 3" dia. x 2" h. Provenance: Barry Schultheiss Collection.........$590

Courtesy of James D. Julia Auctioneers, Fairfield, Maine, www.jamesdjulia.com

Rookwood open mouth frog figural paperweight, designed by Shirayamadani, cast in 1953, yellow glaze, impressed Rookwood symbol, date and shape 6007, lightly crazed, excellent original condition, 3" h...$225

Courtesy of Mark Mussio, Humler & Nolan

Baccarat millefiori mushroom paperweight in blue, rust and white, surrounded by blue over white double overlay, six side flutes and one top facet, signed "B 1970" signature/date cane, 3" dia. x 2" h. Provenance: Barry Schultheiss Collection............$460

Courtesy of James D. Julia Auctioneers, Fairfield, Maine, www.jamesdjulia.com

Baccarat mushroom paperweight, concentric millefiori in green, red, blue, and white encased in blue over white double overlay, five side facets and one top facet with "B 1972" signature/date cane, 2-7/8" dia. x 2-1/4" h. Provenance: Barry Schultheiss Collection $402

Courtesy of James D. Julia Auctioneers, Fairfield, Maine, www.jamesdjulia.com

St. Louis crown paperweight, red, green, blue, and yellow separated by white spiral latticino twists, central cane with "SL 1973" signature/date cane, 3" dia. x 2-1/2" h. Provenance: Barry Schultheiss Collection $472

Courtesy of James D. Julia Auctioneers, Fairfield, Maine, www.jamesdjulia.com

Five Continental clear glass paperweights with floral decorations, smallest signed Enleholt/1989, largest 3-1/2" dia..$31

Courtesy of Cowan's Auctions, Inc.

Orient & Flume paperweight by Ed Alexander in 1983, red strawberries, green foliage, and white flower over backdrop of metallic blue, engraved "Orient & Flume, E. Seaira" (aka Ed Alexander), date and other marks, millefiori flower with date and company monogram encased within, company paper label, excellent condition, 2-5/8" h. $110

Courtesy of Mark Mussio, Humler & Nolan

◄ Perthshire Magnum millefiori paperweight, central picture cane of horse and rider surrounded by six other picture silhouettes including rooster, duck, locomotive, insect, and two birds, with complex millefiori canes and latticino twists, translucent cranberry ground and signed "P 1995" signature/date cane, 12 side facets and one top facet, 4-1/4" dia. x 2-3/4" h. Provenance: Barry Schultheiss Collection $805

Courtesy of James D. Julia Auctioneers, Fairfield, Maine, www.jamesdjulia.com

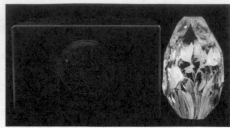

Orient & Flume Beyers Davis faceted paperweight, signed, lily-of-the-valley motif in original dust cover and box, approximately 4-1/2" h. x 3" dia. **$138**

Courtesy of J. Levine Auction & Appraisal LLC

Orient & Flume Sillars glass paperweight, signed by artist Sillars in swirled and floral pink/white pattern in original box, approximately 3" h. x 3-1/2" dia. **$109**

Courtesy of J. Levine Auction & Appraisal LLC

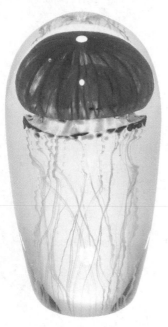

Cathy Richardson "ostrich egg" paperweight with wooded meadow in summertime, on banks of creek, engraved by artist with 2008 date, excellent condition, 5" h. **$100**

Courtesy of Mark Mussio, Humler & Nolan

Satava "Jellyfish" paperweight with Pacific Coast jelly with orange cap, engraved "Satava" and number 4035-10, excellent original condition, 5" h. **$225**

Courtesy of Mark Mussio, Humler & Nolan

Unsigned art glass paperweight with floral motif, approximately 2-1/4" h. x 2-3/4" dia. **$109**

Courtesy of J. Levine Auction & Appraisal LLC

PERFUME BOTTLES

ALTHOUGH THE HUMAN sense of smell isn't nearly as acute as that of many other mammals, we have long been affected by the odors in the world around us. Science has shown that scents or smells can directly affect our mood or behavior.

No one knows for certain when humans first rubbed themselves with plants or herbs to improve their appeal to other humans, usually of the opposite sex. However, it is clear that the use of unguents and scented materials was widely practiced as far back as Ancient Egypt.

Some of the first objects made of glass, in fact, were small cast vials used for storing such mixtures. By the age of the Roman Empire, scented waters and other mixtures were even more important and were widely available in small glass flasks or bottles. Since that time glass has been the material of choice for storing scented concoctions, and during the past 200 years some of the most exquisite glass objects produced were designed for that purpose.

It wasn't until around the middle of the 19th century that specialized bottles and vials were produced to hold commercially manufactured scents. Some aromatic mixtures were worn on special occasions, while many others were splashed on to help mask body odor. For centuries it had been common practice for "sophisticated" people to carry on their person a scented pouch or similar accoutrement, since daily bathing was unheard of and laundering methods were primitive.

Commercially produced and brand name perfumes and colognes have really only been common since the late 19th and early 20th centuries. The French started the ball rolling during the first half of the 19th century when D'Orsay and Guerlain began producing special scents. The first American entrepreneur to step into this field was Richard Hudnut, whose firm was established in 1880.

During the second half of the 19th century most scents carried simple labels and were sold in simple, fairly generic glass bottles. Only in the early 20th century did parfumeurs

Baccarat Christian Dior glass perfume bottle with stopper, red cut to clear faceted panels to stopper and body, gilt painted label reads Diorama, Christian Dior France, circa 1950, marks: BACCARAT, FRANCE, PARIS (acid-etched mark), surface scratches commensurate with age, stopper neck, mouth, and foot rim with chips, 7-1/4" h. including stopper. .... **$600-$900**

Courtesy of Heritage Auctions

Pair of 19th century enameled and gilt Bohemian opaline glass perfume bottles, excellent condition, 8-1/2" h. .... **$3,000-$4,000**

Courtesy of Fine Art Auctions, LLC

Pair of 19th century Bohemian perfume bottles, excellent condition, 12" h. .... **$2,000-$2,500**

Courtesy of Fine Art Auctions, LLC

Bohemian blue cut-to-clear glass perfume bottle with stopper, circa 1930, clear concave rectangles framed in blue ribbed webbing, surface scratches commensurate with age, 6-1/2" h. including stopper. .... **$300-$500**

Courtesy of Heritage Auctions

Bohemian red cut-to-clear perfume bottle with stopper, circa 1900, ovoid pattern bottle with floral formed stopper over low shoulder body with circular foot, surface scratches commensurate with age, stopper chipped at cleavage of scallop, small flea bites to mouth rim, 9" h. including stopper. ....**$300-$500**

Courtesy of Heritage Auctions

Continental 18k gold and cut glass lay-down perfume bottle with ruby stained foliates, first half 19th century, indistinguishable hallmarks on lid, 4-3/4" l. **$375**

Courtesy of Jackson's International Auctioneers & Appraisers

▶ Pair of English overlay glass floral perfume bottles with silver mounts, circa 1887, stamped silver hallmarks for Birmingham, maker's marks FE, surface scratches to silver and small missing flakes throughout bottles, 4-5/8" h.....**$3,000**

Courtesy of Heritage Auctions

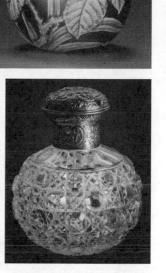

De Vilbiss art glass perfume bottle, full stopper, excellent condition, no damage, 7-1/2" h. **$350**

Courtesy of Morphy Auctions

Ruba Rombic green glass perfume bottle with satin finish, circa 1928, Consolidated Glass Co., Coraopolis, Pennsylvania, 4-3/4" h. x 3-3/4" w. x 1-3/4" d. **$1,900**

Courtesy of Neal Auction Co.

Antique English sterling silver and cut crystal perfume bottle, 1883 marks, 4 3/4" h. .... **$250-$300**

Courtesy of Fine Arts Auctions, LLC

introduce specially designed labels and bottles to hold their most popular perfumes. Coty, founded in 1904, was one of the first to do this, and they turned to Rene Lalique for a special bottle design around 1908. Other French firms, such as Bourjois (1903), Caron (1903), and D'Orsay (1904) were soon following this trend.

People collect two kinds of perfume bottles – decorative and commercial. Decorative bottles include any bottles sold empty and meant to be filled with your choice of scent. Commercial bottles are any that were sold filled with scent and usually carry the label of the perfume company.

The rules of value for perfume bottles are the same as for any other kind of glass – rarity, condition, age, and quality of glass.

The record price for a perfume bottle at auction is something over $310,000, and those little sample bottles of scent that we used to get for free at perfume counters in the 1960s can now bring as much as $300 or $400.

For more information on perfume bottles, see *Antique Trader Perfume Bottles Price Guide* by Kyle Husfloen.

▲ Tiffany & Co. silver and silver gilt two-
handled perfume bottle with screw-in cap
and floral acid-etched decoration, circa
1870-1875, marked TIFFANY & CO.,
STERLING SILVER, 2662 M 7862, 2" h. x
1" dia.. **$594**

Courtesy of Heritage Auctions

14k gold pill box with textured
finish and 14k gold perfume bottle with reeded finish,
very good overall condition, pill box 1-3/8" x 1",
perfume bottle 2-9/16" x 3/4"..............................**$1,000**

Courtesy of Heritage Auctions

Two antique glass perfume bottles, clear and frosted
glass, depicting flora and berries or grapes, circa
early 20th century, 9-3/4" h. $90

Courtesy of Midwest Auction Galleries

Antique cut crystal perfume bottle.................. $20

Courtesy of Omega Auction Corp.

▶ Pair of amethyst swirl perfume bottles, 6" h...... **$90**

Courtesy of Strawser Auctions

◀ Lalique Le Jade perfume bottle for Roger et Gallet, jade glass, molded ROGER ET GALLET PARIS, LE JADE, R. L. FRANCE, stopper and bottled etched 6251, flea bites to stopper and inner rim of bottle, 3-1/4" x 2-1/4".....**$2,500**

Courtesy of Rago Arts, www.ragoarts.com

German carved fluorite and rock crystal perfume bottle, Manfred Wild, Idar-Oberstein, Germany, carved frosted rock crystal flower top centrally accented with 18k yellow gold wirework stamen containing three cabochon cut rubies, collet of yellow gold, base formed from single amethyst crystal of variegated color ranging from translucent colorless quartz to transparent deep purple in fluted and flared design, 7cm h.....**$1,600**

Courtesy of Leslie Hindman Auctioneers

Lalique "les Sirenes" cut crystal perfume bottle with reticulated nude design, signed "Lalique France" to bottom rim and numbered 3550, original Lalique Paris Parfum sticker to base, 4-3/4" h. **$450**

Courtesy of Elite Decorative Arts

Steuben perfume bottle, gold iridescent shape #1455 melon-ribbed perfume with ball stopper and full dauber, allover red and blue highlights, signed Aurene 1455, no chips, cracks or repairs, 4-1/4" h............. **$450**

Courtesy of Omaha Auction Center

Vintage Murano perfume bottle paperweight with millefiori design from top to base, signed to base Murano 1968, 5-3/4" h. **$75**

Courtesy of Elite Decorative Arts

Large purple, blue, and clear glass perfume bottle, etched Murano Formia, 10-3/4" x 7-3/4..........**$170**

Courtesy of Vero Beach Auction

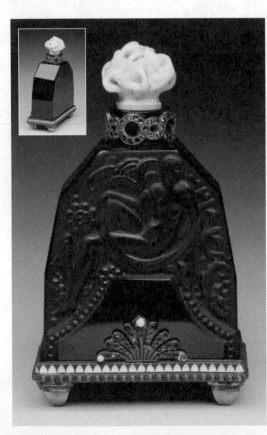

Large Shalimar French perfume bottle with contents, excellent condition, 15" h........**$700**

Courtesy of Morphy Auctions

◄ Onyx Art Deco glass perfume bottle with nude girl on front with metal holder, glass stopper, excellent condition, 4 -3/4" h.....**$1,200**

Courtesy of Morphy Auctions

Large Shalimar French perfume bottle, amber-colored container with amethyst-colored top, original stopper, excellent condition, no damage, 18" h. **$650**

Courtesy of Morphy Auctions

Lolita Lempicka store display perfume bottle, 10-1/2" h. ... **$125**

Courtesy of William J. Jenack Estate Appraisers & Auctioneers

Muller Fres French cameo glass perfume bottle, gray-colored satin glass overlaid with blue and cut with clematis vines and flowers, early 20th century, signed in cameo "Muller Fres Loneville," gilt mount stamped "Made in France," 7-1/2" h. **$425**

Courtesy of Jackson's International Auctioneers & Appraisers

Steuben glass perfume bottle, spherical form, flattened circular stopper, etched Steuben, numbered 5, overall good condition without repairs, hairline cracks to stopper and minor chip to top, moderate shelf wear, 4-1/2" h. overall. ... **$60**

Courtesy of Leslie Hindman Auctioneers

▲ Steuben blue Aurene perfume bottle and Whiting lady's purse, perfume bottle 7-3/4" h., purse 6-3/4" l. **$250**

Courtesy of Michaan's Auctions

Two vintage fancy glass perfume bottles with large stoppers frosted and cut to depict sunflowers, circa early to mid-20th century, 7-7/10" h. **$125**

Courtesy of Midwest Auction Galleries

Victorian-style silver filigree perfume bottle casket with hinged lid opening to fitted interior with nine open glass bottles, 2-1/4" h. x 6" w. **$400**

Courtesy of Leslie Hindman Auctioneers

Tiffany & Co. sterling silver perfume bottle with stopper designed by Elsa Peretti, sterling silver chain with silver balls, with pouch, 2" x 1-1/2". **$225**

Courtesy of Cowan's Auctions

▶ Louis Comfort Tiffany gold Favrile perfume bottle with rolled rim above iridescent bulbous body with trailing vine motif in green, terminating at tapered base, marked L.C. Tiffany Inc. Favrile 1052-387, later stopper, 5-3/4"h. x 4-1/2"w....................**$1,000-$1,500**

Courtesy of Clars Auction Gallery, www.clars.com

Lalique Art Nouveau perfume bottle with atomizer, excellent condition, 5-1/2" h......**$250**

Courtesy of Morphy Auctions

▶ Vintage Verre De Soir silver resist decorated perfume bottle, 5" h. **$40**

Courtesy of William J. Jenack Estate Appraisers & Auctioneers

top lot!

Lalique clear glass serpent perfume bottle with gray patina, circa 1920, molded Lalique, matching marks to stopper and bottle, good condition, fleabite to rim of bottle, 3-1/2" h. $6,250

PETROLIANA

DESPITE CHILLY TEMPS and snowfall the night before, auctioneer Tim Chapulis looked over a crowd some 300 bidders strong assembled in Plymouth, a town in west-central Connecticut. Another 1,000+ bidders were waiting patiently via the Internet in pursuit of the hottest collectibles on today's market: petroliana.

"It was the midst of winter and we had attendance records," said Chapulis, an auctioneer and owner of Tim's Auctions, Inc., with more than 36 years of experience. "Petroliana is one of the hottest markets – I think it's even surpassing gold and silver. This may be signaling a change away from what we were thought the meat-and-potatoes of an auction should be."

The "sell-to-the-walls" auction took place in January 2015 and disbursed the single-owner collection of the late Tim Donahue, whose collections were as broad in scope as they were impressive in quality. As the former owner of D&D Autoworks, Donahue displayed his impressive selection of petroliana and other gas station collectibles on a spacious property he called "Hooterville Farm" (after the fictional town in the hit 1960s TV shows "Petticoat Junction" and "Green Acres"). The long, winding driveway, lined with vintage street lamps, led to a house and an older three-bay barn containing the treasures. Donahue was a longtime customer and friend and Chapulis didn't charge the family his customary seller's commission.

In one case, a young man went paddle-to-paddle against bidders twice his age for a sign, perhaps as part of a new and rising hobby among younger buyers snapping up rough signs and trying to refurbish them, he said. "His mom was telling him to bid higher and he won!" Chapulis said. When the final bids were counted, Chapulis was shocked to see the crowd outspent Internet bidders. "That's the first time we've seen that in a long, long time, which is wonderful," he said. "It's great to see, honestly, because so many people have put some years into their collections and it's great to see young people taking to it. Let's face it – if you're in your 70s and 80s and have amassed a collection, you have to start making serious decisions on who's going to take over the collection. The smart sell when the market is up."

SIGNS, CANS, LIGHTS AND MORE

Petroliana differs from automobilia in that it specifically focuses on gasoline- and oil-related collectibles. The category is dominated by signs, but it can include posters, cans, premiums, lights, and service station items. Pieces are collected for display and a premium is placed on eye appeal and condition.

A relative newcomer to this category, Manifest Auctions of Greenville, South Carolina, launched full-scale auctions in July 2014 after several years as a respected dealer in American banknotes and coins. In early 2015 its winter auction featured a nice mix of decorative art and a selection of exemplary petroliana marked by a surprise: a rare Kelly Tires single-sided circular sign. The sign was well-known throughout the hobby and hammered for $86,250, against a $30,000 estimate.

"We knew about it and knew that it was really important," said Manning Garrett, owner of Manifest Auctions.

HOT SELLERS

Garrett and Chapulis both credit the explosive growth of the sign market to one pop culture phenomenon: the History channel's "American Pickers" TV show. "A lot of people watched that show and got interested," he said. "A lot of the public is finally aware that signs are interesting and that they've held their values over the last 10 years."

Signs enjoying the hottest demand are those measuring 30 to 42 inches, in near mint condition with interesting graphics and bright colors. "A sign that might have been $500 about 10 years ago can now sell for $3,000 to $4,000 today."

Although values are up across the country, demand seems hottest in Texas and Michigan – two hotspots responsible for feeding America's demand for oil and new automobiles in the first place, Garret said.

BEWARE FAKES & REPROS

Reproductions, fantasy pieces, and fakes have plagued petroliana collectors for decades. The relatively recent boon in the category has ushered in a new and diverse tidal wave of merchandise designed for fast profit, particularly porcelain signs. Brands such as Sinclair, Indian, Oilzum, and Mobilgas are actively sold on websites and at flea markets across the nation. These mass-produced signs are getting increasingly more difficult to distinguish from authentic, vintage survivors of the early 20th century. A few tips to keep in mind when purchasing petroliana signs:

Fakes, fantasy signs, and reproductions are flooding the market to meet rising collector demand. This fantasy Sinclair Pennsylvania Motor Oil sign, 12" w. x 15" h., is made of aluminum and sold for $10 at auction.

Courtesy of A Nice Gift For You, LiveAuctioneers

1. No two porcelain signs are ever truly identical. The original process used to make them was imperfect to begin with – each color layer of enamel was added and baked on in a special kiln at temperatures specific to each color. It's entirely natural that imperfections would occur, and authenticators now rely on these variations in much the same way as the FBI uses fingerprints.

2. Original signs are made of steel, not aluminum. A magnet will be attracted to an authentic sign.

3. Most circular signs are 28, 30, 42, or 48 inches in diameter. Look for telltale signs of use: scratches and deep chips around hang holes, even scratches around the perimeter from frames, rust on exposed steel in place of missing enamel.

For more advice on how to intelligently buy petroliana signs, check out *Picker's Pocket Guide – Signs: How to Pick Antiques Like a Pro* (Krause, 2014).

Dealer Billy Howard, owner of Flash Back Funtiques, says gas pumps – both original and refurbished – are brisk sellers at shows across the country. Collectors are looking for pumps from the 1950s with original glass globes in mint condition.

Courtesy of Eric Bradley

Silent Chief Motor Oil empty one-quart, round metal can with Indian and original paper label reading "Cream Sep. Motor Oil," by Security Oil Co., marked CCCO5-1, 5 -1/2" h......... **$1,400**

Courtesy of Morphy Auctions

Tiopet Motor Oil one-quart, round metal can, full, with Indian in full headdress graphics, top labeled Premium 20, "100% Pure Pennsylvania," 5 -1/2" h.. **$2,000**

Courtesy of Morphy Auctions

Sealed, empty Esso metal display motor oil can, "Esso Motor Oil – Happy Motoring," 4" dia., 5-1/2" h.; and Shell one-quart glass motor oil bottle embossed with Shell logo and "Shell-Penn Motor Oil," 2-3/4" x 14-3/8" **$125**

Courtesy of Morphy Auctions

Collector Tim Donahue loved gas pumps, and this Phillips 66 pump – in the desirable Harley-Davidson colors – sold for $2,214 at auction in early 2015.

Courtesy of Tim's, Inc. Auctions

Chrysler Plymouth dealer service sign, double-sided porcelain with pilgrim-style sailing ship, 18" w. x 22" h. **$1,053**

Courtesy of Manifest Auctions

Bell Gasoline Oils double-sided painted metal die-cut sign, bell shape in orange and blue, 48" w. x 48" h. **$1,989**

Courtesy of Manifest Auctions

Beth-O-Line Sinclair double-sided porcelain sign with original hanging bracket (Beth-O-Line Sinclair was sold by Sherwood Brothers, a Richfield/Sinclair jobber, from 1946-1964), rare, 8' h. x 4' w. **$1,287**

Courtesy of Manifest Auctions

More than 300 on-site bidders competed against thousands registered online to own a piece of the Tim Donahue collection of petroliana. On-site bidders won more lots, a result Tim's, Inc. Auctions hasn't seen in several years. At right, Iim Chapulis, auctioneer.

Courtesy of Tim's Auctions, Inc.

The late Tim Donahue, owner of D&D Autoworks of Plymouth, Connecticut, pursued pedal cars, telephone booths, and pinball machines, but petroliana was closest to his heart. In all, 499 lots were auctioned from Donahue's collection.

Courtesy of Tim's Auctions, Inc.

Oil cans, pressed glass globes in tin mounts..... **$175**

Courtesy of Fontaine's Auction Gallery

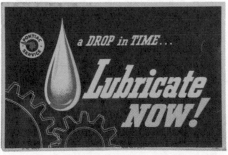

Poster, Pontiac "Lubricate Now!" service poster, 1956, 25-1/4" x 38"..................................... **$275**

Courtesy of Heritage Auctions

Conoco double-sided porcelain sign, die-cut upside-down triangle logo, marked "Manufactured in U.S.A. Veribrite Signs Chicago," 44" w. x 40" h. **$936**

Courtesy of Manifest Auctions

Dodge "Job Rated" Trucks Sales & Service sign, double-sided porcelain, gears logo with "Dodge Trucks" rounded typeface, marked "Walker & Co Detroit," 42" w. x 42" h... **$2,106**

Courtesy of Manifest Auctions

Pennzoil die-cut double-sided hanging sign, with "Sound Your Z" logo, 31" h. x 22" w....... **$438**

Courtesy of Manifest Auctions

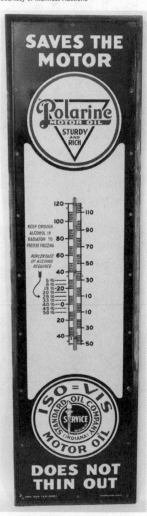

Magnolia Petroleium Company sign, double-sided porcelain, emblem of magnolia flower and leaves, 30" dia. **$1,111**

Courtesy of Manifest Auctions

Magnolia Gasoline meter lenses in metal body with seven-leaf logo design, 16-1/2" dia. . **$2,925**

Courtesy of Manifest Auctions

Plastic sign with embossed Firebird graphic, 12-1/4" w. x 14" h. **$117**

Courtesy of Manifest Auctions

Kelly Tires porcelain enamel sign with image of Kelly's "Lotta Miles" advertising woman, near mint condition, 42" dia. **$87,750**

Courtesy of Manifest Auctions

Polarine single-sided porcelain thermometer sign for Polarine Motor Oil and Iso-Vis Motor Oil, marked Veribrite Signs-Chicago, 18" w. x 6' h. **$2,106**

Courtesy of Manifest Auctions

Unity Oil Co. glass globes, Unity Oil Company – "Oh Boy What a Gas" tagline, circa 1920s, meter lenses, 15" dia................ **$4,972**

Courtesy of Manifest Auctions

Tombstone sign, double-sided porcelain, Quaker State Motor Oil, 26" h. x 30" w. **$292**

Courtesy of Manifest Auctions

Double-sided porcelain sign for Lion Gasoline with Lion Petroleum Products logo on red background, 42" h. **$3,300**

Courtesy of Manifest Auctions

Standard Oil Company (Indiana) Iso-Vis Motor Oil double-sided porcelain sign, 30" dia.......................... **$2,700**

Courtesy of Manifest Auctions

McColl-Frontenac Products sign with "red Indian" logo,....**$11,550**

Courtesy of Morphy Auctions

Sign for Spanish Sinclair Products (gasoline and motor oil), single-sided, porcelain layer with painted graphics, 48" dia............................. **$994**

Courtesy of Morphy Auctions

Standard Oil of Indiana "Clean Rest Rooms Award," 51" h. x 15" w. **$3,850**

Courtesy of Morphy Auctions

Saxon Motor Cars double-sided porcelain sign, marked Ohio Valley Enameling Co., Huntington, West Virginia, rare, 18" x 18". **$19,800**

Courtesy of Morphy Auctions

Texaco Motor Oil, double-sided porcelain curb sign, "Clean, Clear, Golden," "Property of the Texas Company" on cast iron base, 31" x 58" h. **$1,495**

Courtesy of Rich Penn Auctions

Sign, Goodyear Tires, circa 1930s, double-sided enamel, promoting "All Weather" tires, 34" h. **$1,125**

Courtesy of Heritage Auctions

Packard double-sided die-cut enamel service sign, 1970s reproduction, radiator shape, 39" h. x 27" w. **$750**

Courtesy of Heritage Auctions

Goodrich Tires sign, French, circa 1930s, artwork by Geo Ham, double-sided, 31-1/2" x 23-1/2". **$1,250**

Courtesy of Heritage Auctions

Advertising poster, British Petroleum, circa 1930s, BP Plus, 30" h. x 45" w. **$239**

Courtesy of Heritage Auctions

▶ Chrysler-Plymouth Approved Service double-sided porcelain die-cut sign, 42" w. x 44" h. **$4,620**

Courtesy of Morphy Auctions

POSTCARDS

IN THE FIRST HALF OF THE 20TH CENTURY, postcards were cheap, often one cent and rarely more than five cents on the racks. Worldwide exchanges were common, making it possible to gain huge variety without being rich.

Those days are gone forever, but collectors today are just as avid about their acquisitions. What postcards are bestsellers today? The people most likely to have the pulse of the hobby are dealers who offer thousands of cards to the public every year.

Ron Millard, longtime owner of Cherryland Auctions, and Mary L. Martin, known for running the largest store in the country devoted exclusively to postcards, have offered some insights into the current state of the market. Both dealers have taken a son into their business, a sure sign of the confidence they have in the future of postcard collecting.

Real photo postcards of the early 1900s are highly rated by both dealers. Martin, who sells at shows as well as through her store, reported that interest in rare real photos is "increasing faster than they can be bought."

Millard, whose Cherryland Auctions feature 1,800 lots closing every five weeks, indicated that real photos seem to be "holding steady with prices actually rising among the lower-end real photos as some people shy from paying the huge prices they have been bringing ... Children with toys and dolls have been increasing and also unidentified but interesting U.S. views."

Cherryland bidders have also been focused on "advertising cards, high-end art cards, Halloween, early political and baseball postcards." Movie stars, other famous people and transportation, especially autos and zeppelins, also do very well. Lower-priced cards with great potential for rising in value include linen restaurant advertising, "middle range" holidays, and World War I propaganda.

Millard also cited vintage chromes, especially advertising, is "really starting to take off with many now bringing $10 to $15. (These were $1 cards a few years ago.)"

At one time, foreign cards were largely ignored by collectors, but online sales have broadened the international market. In Millard's experience, "The sky is the limit on any China-related." Cherryland has had a huge influx of new bidders from Australia, and the number from Asia is also increasing.

Martin sees hometown views as the most popular category, with real photo social history, dressed animals, and Halloween also in high demand. She reported, "We see a lot of interest in military right now, and I don't believe it has really peaked yet." Social history from the 1950s and '60s also does well. She's encouraged by the number of new

Falstaff Lemp Beer mechanical Santa postcard, Falstaff Brewery, St. Louis, promotional item, circa 1931, calendar rotates, very good to excellent condition. **$324**

Courtesy of Morphy Auctions

Two lace-edged Santa postcards, one of Santa in purple coat atop donkey and one of Santa in green coat beside deer, both with toys for children, very good condition. $144

Courtesy of Morphy Auctions

Horizontal vintage holiday postcard of Santa Claus with attached trim hat and real hair beard, children and toys, very good condition..........$75

Courtesy of Morphy Auctions

Hold-to-light holiday postcard, artist-signed by Mailick, Santa in purple coat with Christ child in sleigh, very good to excellent condition. $180

Courtesy of Morphy Auctions

Twenty-nine postcards: 17 of Houston Carnival with images of floats and carnival displays; six "The Royal Horse Artillery" postcards with envelopes; and six "The French Army" postcards with envelopes, all manufactured by Tuck, very good to excellent condition. $144

Courtesy of Morphy Auctions

Six fantasy postcards of six different drinks with women in or by glasses, designed by Samuel Schmucher, published by Detroit Publishing Co., very good condition with album corner marks......$468

Courtesy of Morphy Auctions

Seldom-seen Halloween postcard of woman with masks and mask border, circa 1913, designed by Samuel Smucker, published by John Winsch, light cancel marks on two corners, very good condition.....$252

Courtesy of Morphy Auctions

Advertising trade postcard of "The Yellow Kid" cartoon character created by artist Richard Outcault (best known for Buster Brown character), promoting Dudley & Co., Providence, Rhode Island, early 20th century, good condition, some paper residue on back. **$288**

Courtesy of Morphy Auctions

and younger collectors at postcard shows.

Will anyone want your postcards when you're ready to sell? It's a valid question, and our two experts have good advice for anyone with a sizeable accumulation, say 500 or more postcards.

Auctions are one good option, both for direct purchases and consignments. Millard is always looking for quality postcards to offer collectors worldwide. His firm can handle collections of any size from small specialized to giant accumulations, and is willing to travel for large consignments. Active buying is a necessity for dealers to keep their customers supplied, which should reassure collectors that their cards will have a ready market. Contact Millard at CherrylandAuctions@charter.net or www.Cherrylandauctions.com.

Martin suggested that collectors go back to some of the dealers who sold them cards when they're ready to sell. Her firm is always willing to buy back good quality cards. She also sees reputable auction houses as a good avenue and strongly suggested, "They should never be sold as a very large group if they can be broken down into different subject matter or topics." Martin can be contacted at marymartinpostcards@gmail.com.

Both experts agree there's an active demand for quality collections. That would exclude postcards in poor condition, a caution for collectors expanding their holdings. Look for the best and pass up damaged and dirty cards.

Billions of postcards were produced in the last century on practically every topic imaginable. As collections become more specialized, new subjects are sure to attract attention. Many outstanding collections were put together with moderate expense by people who were among the first to recognize the value of a new collecting area.

As an example of an area yet to be fully explored, the photographers who made postcards possible haven't been widely collected in their own right. Many were anonymous, but some, like Bob Petley, famous for Western views as well as comic humor, have attracted collectors' attention. The Tucson Post Card Exchange Club has made a specialty of gathering and listing the output of its "favorite son." No doubt there are fresh, new specialties just waiting to be discovered.

Postcard collectors love history, appreciate fine art, enjoy humor, and above all, are imaginative. There's every indication that today's favorite topics will be joined by new and exciting ones in the future.

— Barbara Andrews

Real photo postcard of salesman with car advertising
Dr. Caldwell's Syrup Pepsin, postmarked Monticello,
Illinois, circa 1917, very good condition, moderate
corner bumps and creasing. $144

Courtesy of Morphy Auctions

Real photo postcard with group of children wearing
prohibition-themed pennants and hats, circa
early 20th century, unused, photographer William
Studio, Christopher, Illinois, excellent condition
with small tear along right-hand border...............$252

Courtesy of Morphy Auctions

Embossed Halloween postcard
with rare inset design of woman
in red cape, designed by Samuel
Schmucker, published by John
Winsch, slight half cancel, very
good condition, corner crease
lower left. **$468**

Courtesy of Morphy Auctions

Advertising postcard promoting
artist Louis Wain's Annual,
1905, collection of original
Louis Wain prints, mostly of
anthropomorphized cats, annuals
published from 1901 to 1915,
very good condition, slight crease
on lower right........................ **$540**

Courtesy of Morphy Auctions

Four Kewpie postcards
designed by Rose O'Neill,
published by Edward Gross
Co., early 20th century, part
of six-part series, Kewpie
Army, Kewpie Overshoes,
Kewpie Cook, and Kewpie
Careful of his voice, all
cancelled, two with stamps
removed from back, very good
to excellent condition, small
corner creases. **$216**

Courtesy of Morphy Auctions

Real photo postcard of Ty Cobb
at bat, rarely seen, published
by H.M. Taylor in Detroit,
cancelled July 27, 1908, very
good condition, minor corner
bumping and small nick on left
edge.............................. **$1,584**

Courtesy of Morphy Auctions

Postcard of Coca-Cola girl, circa 1909, designed by Hamilton King, seldom-seen, very good condition, crease on upper right corner, cancel stains and minor flaking on edges. **$1,008**

Courtesy of Morphy Auctions

Two scarce Keen Kutter advertising postcards, early-to-mid 20th century, one of Keen Kutter exhibit of tools and cutlery at Wichita Kansas Exposition, other with image of elephant with banner inviting people to visit Noland Jenkins & Wallace Hardware Store in Poplar Bluff, Mo., very good condition. **$216**

Courtesy of Morphy Auctions

Black and white movie theater advertising postcard, circa 1942, of Johnny Weismueller as Tarzan in "Tarzan's Secret Treasure" where he played opposite Maureen O'Sullivan, promotes showing at Grand Theatre in Independence, Iowa, very good to excellent condition. **$108**

Courtesy of Morphy Auctions

Three postcards with Art Nouveau women, two signed by Patella, excellent condition.. **$108**

Courtesy of Morphy Auctions

► St. Patrick's Day postcard of Irish castle and coastal landscape scene signed by Irish poet and Nobel Prize winner W.B. Yeats, with fountain pen ink signature and date of March 16, 1914, very good condition, light minor age wear........... **$550**

International Autograph Auctions, Ltd.

Postcard carried by Graf Zeppelin on first air mail flight from Rochester, New York, via Lakehurst, New Jersey, to Germany, with Rochester postmark and First Flight Air Mail stamp dated Oct. 28, 1928, Zeppelin cancel of Nov. 1, 1928, very good condition. **$36**

Courtesy of Morphy Auctions

Photo postcard of Fremont, Nebraska Fire Department and department's new engine built by Chemical Engine Co., postmarked 1912, excellent condition, minor corner bumps. **$72**

Courtesy of Morphy Auctions

Silk postcard of Palace of Mines and Metallurgy at Louisiana Purchase Exposition in St. Louis, circa 1904, scarce item, excellent condition. **$180**

Courtesy of Morphy Auctions

Real photo postcard of 1926 St. Louis Cardinals, National League and World Series champs that year, with inset photograph of Roger Hornsby, player-manager, with title "World's Coming Champions," card not cancelled, names of players and manager on back, excellent condition. **$1,152**

Courtesy of Morphy Auctions

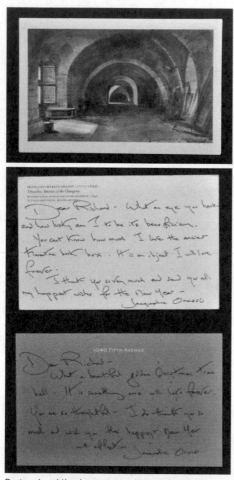

Hold-to-light postcard from 1904 Louisiana Purchase Exposition in St. Louis, Inside Inn (only hotel located within grounds of Expo), mailed Sept. 19, 1904, very good to excellent condition. **$180**

Courtesy of Morphy Auctions

Mechanical political campaign postcard of William Jennings Bryan and William Howard Taft in 1908 U.S. presidential election, wheels on card roll to depict candidates in motion with Taft in lead, minor corner fault. **$252**

Courtesy of Morphy Auctions

Postcard and thank you note written and sent by Jacqueline Kennedy Onassis to Richard Langham, who worked on several home decorating projects with Ms. Kennedy Onassis during a 10-year period in third and fourth quarters of 20th century. **$2,135**

Courtesy Palm Beach Modern Auctions

Novelty birch bark postcard, copyright 1907, very fine condition.... $15

Courtesy of Cherryland Postcard Auctions

Real photo postcard of Groucho Marx standing beside life-size Coca-Cola advertising cutout of Jean Harlow, typed greeting and signature on back reads "Merry Xmas to you all and the folks – Groucho Marx," mailed to "Mr. & Mrs. J W Adams Clifton Mass.," near mint condition.............. $420

Courtesy of Morphy Auctions

"A Lesson from the Grave" anti-drinking art by W.F. Miller, copyright 1907, divided back, monochrome. $10

Courtesy of Cherryland Postcard Auctions

Novelty hand-painted illusion postcard, turn reveals different face, Russian publisher on back, very fine condition........ $15

Courtesy of Cherryland Postcard Auctions

Golfing-related postcard advertising Chicken in the Rough Restaurant, Oklahoma City, Fantasy Rooster character on left, very fine condition........$15

Courtesy of Cherryland Postcard Auctions

Texas political postcard advertising Dr. Pepper with "Vote for Miss Walker – Sweetheart of Texas," unusual flat edge tape. **$25**

Courtesy of Cherryland Postcard Auctions

▲ Real photograph advertising Log Cabin Restaurant with "Freeland, Michigan" on back, wear to corner and edge, near fine to very fine condition. **$15**

Courtesy of Cherryland Postcard Auctions

▼ Artist-signed Philip Boileau, book reservation advertising National Cloak & Suit Co., New York Fashions, copyright 1910, written on front and creasing on corners... **$20**

Courtesy of Cherryland Postcard Auctions

Motor coach advertising Pickwick Observation-Buffet Motor Coaches, white background, monochrome, album marks on corner and some creasing, fine to very fine condition. **$25**

Courtesy of Cherryland Postcard Auctions

INSIDE INTEL
with
GEORGE HEESCHEN

The Southpaw Postcard Shop, *thesouthpaw.net*

WHAT'S HOT: First and foremost are things in excellent condition. State views and pre-World War I cards are selling well. People are collecting their hometowns, so big cities are harder to sell, but those from the smallest towns in any of the Southern states are selling very well.

TOP TIP: Every time a card gets handled it gets damaged. Keep them in a sleeve or in a binder. I store anything valued more than $3 in a 4ml polypropylene sleeve.

"The Queen of Diamonds" playing card image, Moffat Publishing, monochrome, divided back, corner creases, fine to very fine condition. **$25**

Courtesy of Cherryland Postcard Auctions

"Speed" carving of nurse, Dr. Niblack, copyright 1951, unusual color, near very fine condition. **$10**

Courtesy of Cherryland Postcard Auctions

POSTERS

A POSTER IS a large, usually printed placard, bill, or announcement, often illustrated, that is posted to advertise or publicize something. It can also be an artistic work, often a reproduction of an original painting or photograph, printed on a large sheet of paper.

Vintage posters are usually between 20 and 50 years old and must be original and not copies or newer reproductions.

The value of a vintage poster is determined by condition, popularity of the subject matter, rarity, artistic rendering, and the message it conveys.

MOVIE POSTERS

◀ "The Jackie Robinson Story" half sheet, 1950, 22" x 28". **$1,210**

Courtesy of Collect Auctions

Gulf promotional poster for "LeMans" starring Steve McQueen, 1971, McQueen with Porsche 917, poster only available through Gulf stations, 17" x 22".......................**$530**

Courtesy of Heritage Auctions

"The Maltese Falcon," Warner Brothers, R-1962, postwar release French Grande, very fine on linen, 47" x 63".............. **$14,340**

Courtesy of Heritage Auctions

"Niagra" three sheet, starring Marylyn Monroe, Joseph Cotton, and Jean Peters, 1953, linen mount, 81" x 41".......**$1,062**

Courtesy of Mosby & Co. Auctions

"Frankenstein" three sheet, Universal, 1931, Style C, professionally restored on linen, 41" x 78-1/2".............$358,500

Courtesy of Heritage Auctions

"Rogue of the Rio Grande" one sheet, Sono Art-World Wide Pictures, 1930, 27" x 41"....**$2,868**

Courtesy of Heritage Auctions

"Rear Window" one sheet, Paramount, 1954, restored, fine condition, on linen, 27-1/4" x 41"................. **$5,033**

Courtesy of Heritage Auctions

"Forbidden Planet" poster, MGM, 1956, fine/very fine condition, 40" x 60". **$6,573**

Courtesy of Heritage Auctions

"London After Midnight" one sheet, MGM, 1927, 27" x 41"....................**$478,000**

Courtesy of Heritage Auctions

"The Wizard of Oz" one sheet, MGM, 1939, Style D, fine+ condition, on linen, 27" x 41"....................**$65,725**

Courtesy of Heritage Auctions

▶ "Stagecoach" half sheet, United Artists, 1939, Style A, 22" x 28"........... **$14,340**

Courtesy of Heritage Auctions

MISCELLANEOUS POSTERS

Chang and Fakhong magic poster, horizontal one-sheet for "A Night in Tokio," mounted to foam core, 42-1/2" x 30".. **$384**

Courtesy of Mosby & Co. Auctions

Ted Kennedy for President poster, titled "To sail against the wind," pencil signed by artist, No. 37/200, 35 1/2" x 25"................................... **$142**

Courtesy of Mosby & Co. Auctions

Work incentive poster with Mather's typical humor-inspired art, 1923, with 41-1/2" x 28". **$250**

Courtesy of Mosby & Co. Auctions

Ventriloquist act poster for P. Carro, circa 1900, printed by Star Printing Office, mounted on linen, 36 1/4" x 27"... **$590**

Courtesy of Mosby & Co. Auctions

"A Tiny Boat" color lithographed Chinese classroom poster by Chen Baili, People's Educational Publishing House, 1959, 21" x 30"................ **$540**

Courtesy of Swann Galleries

Austin dealer eight sheet, 1939, printed by J. Howitt & Sons Limited, artwork by Millier, linen mounted, 121" x 161". **$708**

Courtesy of Mosby & Co. Auctions

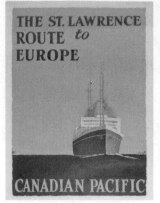

Canadian Pacific steamship poster, 1930s, used to promote St. Lawrence route to Europe, linen mounted, 36-1/4" x 24-1/4"...**$680**

Courtesy of Mosby & Co. Auctions

Poster of 101 Ranch Real Wild West Show performer Zack T. Miller, excellent condition, 44" x 31".......................**$1,680**

Courtesy of Morphy Auctions

"Exploring Space in a Rocket Ship" color lithographed Chinese poster by Zhang Ruiheng, Hebei People's Art Publishing House, 1963, 30" x 21".............**$1,440**

Courtesy of Swann Galleries

Russian wrestling poster, anonymous, 1955, 35-1/2" x 23-1/4". **$270**

Courtesy of Swann Galleries

Jugate poster titled "Socialist Candidates 1916," Benson and Kirkpatrick, 21" x 27-1/2"...**$1,250**

Courtesy of Heritage Auctions

Hamberg-Amerika Linie ship poster, 24" x 33"..............**$550**

Courtesy of Philip Weiss Auctions

Nenheit poster, linen backed, 35-1/2" x 50"....................**$100**

Courtesy of Philip Weiss Auctions

Original illustration art for Red Cross poster, Haskell Coffin, pastel on board, 37" x 28"..**$720**

Courtesy of Morphy Auctions

World War II GMC factory poster, No. GMC-44, linen mounted, 39-1/2" x 30". **$265**

Courtesy of Mosby & Co. Auctions

World War I Food Administration poster, artwork by Hendee, printed by Edwards & Deutsch, linen mounted, 28-1/2" x 21"........**$95**

Courtesy of Mosby & Co. Auctions

American Library Association World War I poster, artwork by Sheridan, printed by American Lithograph Co., linen mounted, 30" x 20"...........................**$225**

Courtesy of Mosby & Co. Auctions

War World II U.S. Marine Corps recruiting poster, "Want Action?" by James Montgomery Flagg, linen backed............**$300**

Courtesy of Philip Weiss Auctions

Old Gold large cardboard poster, artwork by Rolf Armstrong, good to very good condition, 51-1/2" x 38"....................**$210**

Courtesy of Morphy Auctions

World War II aircraft recognition poster, dated Nov. 1, 1942, for U.S Navy Patrol Bomber PBY-CATALINA, linen mounted, 21-1/4" x 14"....................**$130**

Courtesy of Mosby & Co. Auctions

Giant English Queen's Guard poster, printed by Creber Lithograph, Plymouth, linen mounted, 39-1/4" x 25".....**$354**

Courtesy of Mosby & Co. Auctions

Harley-Davidson poster for "New Stream-Line," 1925, excellent condition, 29" x 21-1/2"....................**$960**

Courtesy of Morphy Auctions

1895 reward poster offering $1,000 in conjunction with major train robbery using dynamite, 7-3/4" x 9"..............**$325**

Courtesy of Heritage Auctions

Monterey pop festival poster starring Jimi Hendrix and Janis Joplin, 1967, first printing poster, 12-1/4" x 21-1/2"... **$938**

Courtesy of Heritage Auctions

Thomas Dewey anti-Truman Klan poster, 1944, 28" x 41".. **$1,125**

Courtesy of Heritage Auctions

World War I poster, "Civilians / When We Go / Through This," The Jewish Welfare Board, Alco Gravure, Inc., 1918, artwork by Sidney H. Riesenberg (1885-1971), 22" x 33".............. **$575**

Courtesy of Heritage Auctions

Roberto Clemente *Sports Illustrated* poster, 1968, produced by Major League Posters and licensed to Renselaar Corp., 24" x 36"............................ **$120**

Courtesy of Collect Auctions

Eugene V. Debs poster, 1920, half-length portrait of five-time Socialist candidate for president, 18" x 24". In 1920 he ran for president from a jail cell in Atlanta and managed to get a million votes. **$1,063**

Courtesy of Heritage Auctions

Hopkins & Allen Arms Co. "Prairie Girl" poster, circa 1900, excellent condition, 26-1/2" x 11-1/2"........... **$2,700**

Courtesy of Morphy Auctions

◀ Bonnie and Clyde "Wanted" poster, 1934, issued by FBI, 8" x 8". **$157**

Courtesy of Collect Auctions

Andersonville Prison poster of atrocities that took place there, good condition, 24" x 30"............ **$840**

Courtesy of Morphy Auctions

Arthur Ashe "Wimbledon Champ" Coca-Cola poster, excellent condition, 24" x 36"............. **$570**

Courtesy of Morphy Auctions

Early Prince Albert poster with Chief Fights-the-Enemy, paper, excellent condition, 24 x 31"... **$1,140**

Courtesy of Morphy Auctions

U.S. Marines aviation recruitment poster, artwork by Howard Chandler Christy, 28" x 40". **$4,375**

Courtesy of Heritage Auctions

World War I U.S. Air Service recruiting poster, "Over There! / Skilled / Workers / On the ground / In the Air Service," artwork by Louis Fancher, 30" x 33-1/2"... **$470**

Courtesy of Heritage Auctions

QUILTS

EACH GENERATION MADE QUILTS, comforters, and coverlets, all intended to be used. Many were used into oblivion and rest in quilt heaven, but for myriad reasons, some have survived. Many of them remain because they were not used but stored, often forgotten, in trunks and linen cabinets.

A quilt is made up of three layers: the top, which can be a solid piece of fabric, appliquéd, pieced, or a combination; the back, which can be another solid piece of fabric or pieced; and the batting, the center layer, which can be cotton, wool, polyester, a blend of poly and cotton, or even silk. Many vintage quilts are batted with an old blanket or even another old, worn quilt.

The fabrics are usually cotton or wool or fine fancy fabrics like silk, velvet, satin, and taffeta. The layers of a true quilt are held together by the stitching – or quilting – that goes through all three layers and is usually worked in a design or pattern that enhances the piece overall.

Quilts made from a seemingly single solid piece of fabric are known as wholecloth quilts, or if they are white, as whitework quilts. Usually such quilts are constructed from two or more pieces of the same fabric joined to make up the necessary width. They are often quilted quite elaborately, and the seams virtually disappear within the decorative stitching. Most wholecloth quilts are solid-colored, but prints were also used. Whitework quilts were often made as bridal quilts and many were kept for "best," which means that they have survived in reasonable numbers.

Wholecloth quilts were among the earliest type of quilted bedcovers made in Britain, and the colonists brought examples with them according to inventory lists that exist from colonial times. American quiltmakers used the patterns early in the nation's history, and some were carried with settlers moving west across the Appalachians.

Appliqué quilts are made from shapes cut from fabric and applied, or appliquéd, to a background, usually solid-colored on vintage quilts, to make a design. Early appliqué quilts dating back to the 18th century were often worked in a technique called broderie perse, or Persian embroidery, in which printed motifs were cut from a piece of fabric, such as costly chintz, and applied to a plain, less-expensive background cloth.

Appliqué was popular in the 1800s, and there are thousands of examples, from exquisite, brightly colored

Patchwork linsey-woolsey quilt in Square in a Square pattern, early 19th century, possibly Pennsylvania Amish, two-section seamed mustard-colored backing, excellent condition with one small hole on front and several small holes on reverse, 62" x 72". **$450**

Courtesy of Hyde Park Country Auctions

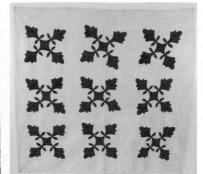

Appliqué quilt in Oak Leaves pattern, circa 1900, hand-sewn, red and white, cotton seed batting, fair condition with minor staining, 76" x 71". **$206**

Courtesy of A-1 Auction

Satin patchwork crib quilt in Rolling Block pattern, 20th century, green satin border with blue, green, and tan blocks, excellent condition, 37" x 47"... **$300**

Courtesy of Hyde Park Country Auctions

▲ Amish appliqué quilt in Rose Wreath pattern with "heart-in-hand" and floral quilting, 19th century, very good condition, fine stitching, approximately 9-11 stitches/inch, one L-shaped tear, slight fraying on edge, minor staining on dark green reverse, 71" x 76-1/2"..........................**$270**

Courtesy of Hyde Park Country Auctions

◄ Tennessee Ladies Auxiliary autograph or signature quilt, 1920s, pieced, hand-stitched rose-colored ground with 30 peach/gold-colored machine appliqué flowers, each petal and center embroidered with a name, some with town names as well, more than 450 in all, top signed "L.A. Society Unionville Tenn 1926-1927," fading overall, scattered staining, 86" x 77"..........**$1,353**

Courtesy of Case Antiques Auctions & Appraisals

Drunkard's Path pattern quilt in brown and white, late 19th century, scalloped border, possibly of homespun material, from early homestead in Salt Point, New York, small areas of staining on front and edges of back side, 80" x 92". $300

Courtesy of Hyde Park Country Auctions

Baltimore Album quilts made in and around Baltimore between circa 1840 and 1860, to elegant four-block quilts made later in the century. Many appliqué quilts are pictorial with floral designs the predominant motif. In the 20th century, appliqué again enjoyed an upswing, especially during the Colonial Revival period, and thousands were made from patterns or appliqué kits that were marketed and sold from 1900 through the 1950s.

Pieced or patchwork quilts are made by cutting fabric into shapes and sewing them together to make a larger piece of cloth. Patchwork became popular in the United States in the early 1800s. The patterns are usually geometric, and their effectiveness depends heavily on the contrast of not just the colors themselves, but of color value as well.

Colonial clothing was almost always made using cloth cut into squares or rectangles, but after the Revolutionary War, when fabric became more widely available, shaped garments were made, and these garments left scraps. Frugal housewives, especially among the westward-bound pioneers, began to use these cutoffs to put together blocks that could then be made into quilts. Patchwork quilts are by far the most numerous of all vintage-quilt categories, and the diversity of style, construction, and effect that can be found is a study all its own.

Dating a quilt is a tricky business unless the maker included the date on the finished item, and unfortunately for historians and collectors, few did. The value of a particular example is affected by its age, of course, and educating yourself about dating methods is invaluable. There are several aspects that can offer guidelines for establishing a date. These include fabrics, patterns, technique, borders, binding, batting, backing, quilting method, and colors and dyes.

In recent years many significant quilt collections have appeared in the halls of museums around the world, enticing both quilters and practitioners of art appreciation. One of the most noted collections to become a national exhibition in 2014 was the Pilgrim/Roy Collection. The selection of quilts included in the "Quilts and Color" exhibition, presented by the Museum of Fine Arts in Boston, was a mix of materials and designs, represented in nearly 60 distinct 19th and 20th century quilts.

For more information on quilts, see *Warman's Vintage Quilts Identification and Price Guide* by Maggi McCormick Gordon.

INSIDE INTEL
— *with* —
PAMELA GRAYSON

Owner, The Altered Muse,
thealteredmuse.blogspot.com

TOP TIP: Seek out conversation pieces and have all of your inventory priced. I find if it's not priced people will think it's too expensive. I read architectural and interior design magazines to understand what's up and coming. I read Veranda, Elle Décor and Architectural Digest. You have to take your business seriously and develop a trained eye.

Friendship/crazy quilt, circa 1937, silk, first prize winner at 1937 Topsfield Fair, with original blue ribbon and entry tag, 60" x 60". **$738**

Courtesy of Kaminski Auctions

Appliqué quilt in Rose Wreath pattern in red, green, white, and yellow with floral border, found in old farm in New Kingston, New York, very good condition, minor loss to yellow yard on perimeter flowers and some minor fraying on edges, 84" x 84". **$420**

Courtesy of Hyde Park Country Auctions

◄ Heavenly Stars variant pieced quilt, fourth quarter 19th century, yellow print eight-point stars with black print squares, rectangles, and diamonds, double-banded matching print border with zigzag-patterned hand stitching, excellent condition overall, some fading and possible restitching, 67" x 90"...................................... **$300**

Courtesy of Jeffrey S. Evans & Associates

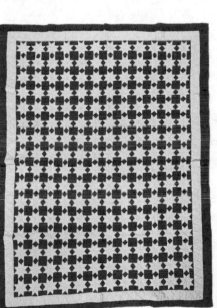

Printed chintz cotton fabric quilt in Ohio Star block pattern with matching printed floral border, early to mid-19th century, very good condition, soiling and staining on reverse, 71" x 94"............................ **$480**

Courtesy of Hyde Park Country Auctions

Primitive country calico quilt in Checkerboard pattern, circa 1900, nine-patch variation in red and yellow with zigzags, printed back, good condition, 78" x 81". **$177**

Courtesy of A-1 Auction

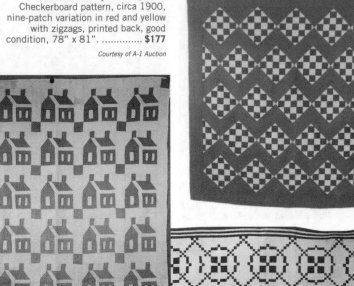

Schoolhouse cotton quilt, circa 1870, coastal Connecticut, blue and white, hand sewn, with sleeve for hanging, good condition, some toning throughout, 66" x 80".......................... **$632**

Courtesy of Thomaston Place Auction Galleries

▲ Geometric red and white patchwork quilt, 19th century, tight stitching, 8-10 stitches/inch, some losses, wear, light stains, and repairs, mostly to red fabric, 60" x 86". **$120**

Courtesy of Hyde Park Country Auctions

Blue and white printed quilt, 19th century, hand-sewn patches and hand quilting with Oriental garden houses, fruit, vegetables, leaves and vines, label attached from "Museum of American Folk Art, NY, NY – The New York Quilt Project 1988-1991 – display in 11-11-89," 88" x 62". **$1,320**

Courtesy of Hyde Park Country Auctions

Appliqué Princess Feather pattern quilt, late 19th century, red and green on white ground with feather border, diamond pattern throughout, initialed on reverse "A.A.F.," light fading and scattered losses to green fabric, minor spotting, 76-1/2" x 84".. **$1,240**

Courtesy of Case Antiques Auctions & Appraisals

Garden of Eden pieced hanging quilt bag, late 19th century, Rockingham County, Shenandoah Valley of Virginia, bag open at top, 30 3-1/8" sq. pattern blocks with various prints and solids, solid brown sashing with pink print blocks, red binding, straight-line hand quilting, 23" x 19".............. **$960**

Courtesy of Jeffrey S. Evans & Associates

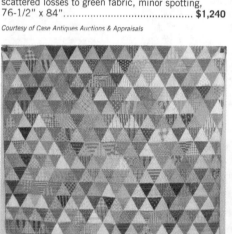

Patchwork quilt in earth tone colors, late 19th to early 20th century, two patches with fabric losses, one area with staining, 69" x 84". **$150**

Courtesy of Hyde Park Country Auctions

Pieced cotton album quilt, early 20th century, Johnson County, Tennessee, various colors on purple-printed ground, each square signed in center by maker along with their town of residence, fading to fabric, scattered losses to squares, 90-1/4" x 70"................................. **$465**

Courtesy of Case Antiques Auctions & Appraisals

◀ Pieced geometric block design quilt in navy, military green, evergreen, cream, yellow, carrot, spruce, salmon, carnation pink, and midnight blue, with tan border, 6' 8" x 6' 10". **$360**

Courtesy of Suane Merrill & Co.

top lot

Cotton summer quilt, 19th century, scalloped red binding over white field, diamond stitching overall with printed floral appliqués, white backing, minor wear on edges, 94" x 96"....................................$3,835

Patchwork quilt, late 19th century, mustard-colored sawtooth border and crocheted decorations with baskets, flowers, and teapots, good condition, 74" x 82". **$150**

Courtesy of Hyde Park Country Auctions

Silk, cotton, and velvet embroidered patchwork quilt, late 19th century, design created from tessellating triangles, multicolored with mix of pattern and solid blocks, reverse lined, 85" x 77"..............................**$721**

Courtesy of Dreweatts & Bloomsbury

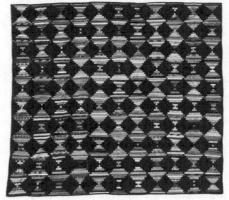

Log Cabin pattern quilt, late 19th century, mixed fabrics and colors, obverse of various silk pieces on black background, reverse of glazed blue sateen, wear consistent with age, 82" x 77". **$431**

Courtesy of Cordier Auctions & Appraisals

Lone Star pattern quilt, early 20th century, excellent condition, good-quality hand sewing, approximately eight stitches/inch, 71" x 89"............................. **$390**

Courtesy of Hyde Park Country Auctions

Appliqué and pieced quilt in Four Tulip pattern, mid-19th century, patriotic theme, 13 16" sq. blocks with solid red and green print outlined with red sashing, one with eagle and shield and figural Betty's lamp with crossed hammers, initials "G.A.", "V.M.W", "Z.A." stitched, other images of birds and grape cluster; heavy hand quilting and feathered bands; poor condition, significant deterioration to patterns and images, and discoloration and light staining, 76" x 77".................... **$360**

Courtesy of Jeffrey S. Evans & Associates

RECORDS

BEFORE YOU CAN determine a record's worth, you need to grade it. When visually grading records, use a direct light, such as a 100-watt desk lamp, to clearly show all defects. If you're dealing with a record that looks worse than it sounds, play grade it. You also need to assess the condition of each sleeve, cover, label, and insert. Think like the buyer as you set your grades. Records and covers always seem to look better when you're grading them to sell to someone else than when you're on the other side of the table, inspecting a record for purchase. If in doubt, go with the lower grade. And, if you have a still sealed record, subject it to as many of these same grading standards as you can without breaking the seal.

──────── Goldmine Grading ────────

MINT (M): Absolutely perfect. Mint never should be used as a grade unless more than one person agrees the item meets the criteria; few dealers or collectors use this term. There is no rule for calculating mint value; that is best negotiated between buyer and seller.
- Overall Appearance: Looks as if it just came off the manufacturing line.
- Record: Glossy, unmarred surface.
- Labels: Perfectly placed and free of writing, stickers, and spindle marks.
- Cover/Sleeve: Perfectly crisp and clean. Free of stains, discoloration, stickers, ring wear, dinged corners, sleeve splits, or writing.

NEAR MINT (NM) OR MINT MINUS (M-): Most dealers and collectors use NM/M- as their highest grade, implying that no record or sleeve is ever truly perfect. It's estimated that no more than 2% to 4% of all records remaining from the 1950s and 1960s truly meet near mint standards.

The Beatles, " John Lennon Roots" (Adam VIII 8018, 1975), NM; official name of compilation LP was "John Lennon Sings the Great Rock & Roll Hits," and "Roots" was the result; only a few thousand copies were produced before production halted. **$516**

Courtesy of Heritage Auctions

• Overall Appearance: Looks as if it were opened for the first time. Includes all original pieces, including inner sleeve, lyric sheets, inserts, cover, and record.

• Record: Shiny surface is free of visible defects and surface noise at playback. Records can retain NM condition after many plays provided the record has been stored, used, and handled carefully.

• Labels: Properly pressed and centered on the record. Free of markings.

• Cover/Sleeve: Free of creases, ring wear, cutout markings, and seam splits. Picture sleeves look as if no record was ever housed inside. Hint: If you remove a 45 from its picture sleeve and store it separately, you will reduce the potential for damage to the sleeve.

VERY GOOD PLUS (VG+) OR EXCELLENT (EX+): Minor condition issues keep these records from a NM grade. Most collectors who want to play their records will be happy with VG+ records.

• Overall Appearance: Shows slight signs of wear.

• Record: May have slight warping, scuffs or scratches, but none that affect the sound. Expect minor signs of handling, such as marks around the center hole, light ring wear, or discoloration.

• Labels: Free of writing, stickers, or major blemishes.

• Cover/Sleeve: Outer cover may have a cutout mark. Both covers and picture sleeves may have slight creasing, minor seam wear or a split less than 1" long along the bottom.

VERY GOOD (VG): VG records have more obvious flaws than records in better condition, but still offer a fine listening experience for the price.

• Overall Appearance: Shows signs of wear and handling, including visible groove wear, audible scratches and surface noise, ring wear, and seam splits.

• Record: Record lacks its original glossy finish and may show groove wear and scratches deep enough to feel with a fingernail. Expect some surface noise and audible scratches (especially during a song's introduction and ending), but not enough to overpower the music.

• Labels: May have minor writing, tape, or a sticker.

• Cover/Sleeve: Shows obvious signs of handling and wear, including dull or discolored images; ring wear; seam splits on one or more sides; writing or a price tag; bent corners; stains; or other problems. If the record has more than two of these problems, reduce its grade.

VERY GOOD MINUS (VG–), GOOD PLUS (G+) OR GOOD (G): A true G to VG- record still plays through without skipping, so it can serve as filler until something better comes along; you can always upgrade later. At most, these records sell for 10% to 15% of the near mint value.

• Overall Appearance: Shows considerable signs of handling, including visible groove wear, ring wear, seam splits, and damaged labels or covers.

• Record: The record plays through without skipping, but the surface sheen is almost gone, and the groove wear and surface noise is significant.

• Labels: Worn. Expect stains, heavy writing, and/or obvious damage from attempts to remove tape or stickers.

• Cover/Sleeve: Ring wear to the point of distraction; dinged and dog-eared edges; obvious seam splits; and heavy writing (such as radio station call letters or an owner's name).

FAIR (F) OR POOR (P): Only outrageously rare items ever sell for more than a few cents in this condition, if they sell at all. More likely, F or P records and covers will end up in the trash or be used to create clocks, journals, purses, jewelry, bowls, coasters or other art.

• Overall Appearance: Beat, trashed, and dull. Records may lack sleeves or covers.

• Record: Vinyl may be cracked, scratched, and/or warped to the point it skips.

• Labels: Expect stains, tears, soiling, marks, and damage, if the label is even there.

• Cover/Sleeve: Heavily damaged or absent.

LPS

Various artists, "The Wizard of Oz" (MGM E3464 ST, 1956), original cast "soundtrack," cover G+, vinyl VG, cover with tear to lower right portion, visible wear, corners rounded, tape strips near edges of front panel of album, vinyl album missing paper sleeve, some noticeable wear, especially to spindle, 3" scratch to side one, cover signed by Bert Lahr, Judy Garland, Billie Burke, Jack Haley, Margaret Hamilton, and Ray Bolger. **$800**

Courtesy of Quinn's Auction Galleries

Everly Brothers, "The Everly Brothers Greatest Hits" (Barnaby Records, 1974), VF, compilation double album, front of cover signed in blue felt tip pen by Phil Everly (1939-2014) and in black by Don Everly, light handling wear with some creases and corner tip wear, with inner sleeve, both records, and certificate of authenticity. **$185.50**

Courtesy of Hake's Americana & Collectibles

Dr. Timothy Leary, PH.D, "L.S.D" (Pixie Records, 1966), NM, sleeve yellowed at edges, vinyl LP in original sleeve; recorded at Leary's Millbrook estate; addresses effects of drug LSD. **$250**

Courtesy of PBA Galleries

George Thorogood & the Destroyers, "2120 South Michigan Avenue" (Capitol, 2011), EX, signed by George Thorogood, Jeff Simon, Billy Blough, Jim Suhler, and Buddy Leach during band's performance at Bethel Woods on Aug. 8, 2013...................**$45**

Courtesy of Online Sales Auctions

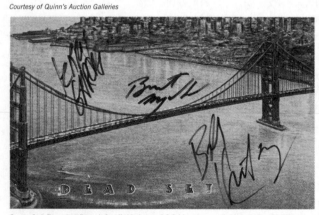

Grateful Dead, "Dead Set" (Arista, 1981), cover and records VG/EX-, double-disc vinyl with signatures from Jerry Garcia, Bill Kreutzmann, and Brent Mydland. **$938**

Courtesy of Heritage Auctions

◀ Elvis Presley, "You'll Never Walk Alone" (RCA Camden CDS 1088 Stereo, UK 1971), EX/NM; U.S. version was Elvis' first album release on RCA's new budget label Camden, with religious standards such as "Peace In the Valley," "I Believe," "It Is No Secret," and six others. **$150**

Courtesy of Heritage Auctions

Mötley Crüe, "Too Fast For Love" (Leathur, 1981), NM, sealed, second pressing, 4,000 copies. .... **$ 236**

Courtesy of Backstage Auctions, Inc.

Stevie Ray Vaughan and Double Trouble, "Couldn't Stand the Weather" (Epic FE 39304, 1984) no grade, signed on album cover "Stevie Ray Vaughan 89." **$1,024**

Courtesy of Julien's Auctions

Thelonius Monk, "Monk's Miracles," (Columbia Record Club exclusive #DS338), NM, first edition, Canadian compilation LP, light ring wear and edge marking on back only........................**$10**

Led Zeppelin, "Presence" (Swan Song SSK 59402, 1976), VG++, first U.K. pressing, light surface and shelf wear, one minor scuff, with original inner sleeve.......**$40**

Peter, Paul & Mary, "Peter, Paul and Mommy" (Warner Bros WS 1785), VG+, sealed original pressing from 1960s, gatefold cover with slight rack wear at corners. **$35**

Pink Floyd, "Atom Heart Mother " (Harvest SKAO 382, 1970) VG+, gatefold, cover with some wear to corners, seams and spine, no skips. **$35**

Bruce Springsteen, "Nebraska" (Columbia, 1982), VF, front cover signed in black felt tip pen by Springsteen, light handling wear with scattered creases and black ink color touch-ups, with inner lyrics and record and certificate of authenticity.......................**$387**

Courtesy of Hake's Americana & Collectibles

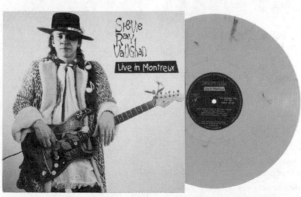

Stevie Ray Vaughan, "Live in Montreux" (The Swingin' Pig), NM, Green Vinyl LP, unauthorized live album recorded at Montreux Jazz Festival on July 15, 1985, record pressed in green swirl vinyl. **$213**

Courtesy of Heritage Auctions

PICTURE SLEEVES AND 45S

Elvis Presley, "Chante Avec" (France – RCA CF 513, 1976), book EX 7, record NM 8, Elvis Christmas stereo EP and booklet, orange label French release accompanied by booklet with words to "White Christmas," "Silent Night," "Blue Christmas," and "I Believe." **$53**

Courtesy of Heritage Auctions

Jimi Hendrix, "Lover Man" (Sterling Sound, circa 1967-1968), EX, stereo 45 rpm acetate, live version, with certificate of authenticity from Backstage Auctions, Inc., from Eddie Kramer collection. Hendrix recorded this song many times, including live versions on "Hendrix in the West" and "Live at Woodstock" and a studio version on "The Jimi Hendrix Experience" (2000). **$1,250**

Courtesy of Heritage Auctions

Dion and the Belmonts, "Every Little Thing I Do" / "A Lover's Prayer" (Laurie 3035, 1959), U.S., picture sleeve P/S, vinyl VG, light scratches, no gouges, will play through with light noise, cover VG+, no splits, some light creases, 7" 45 rpm............................. **$23**

Bobby Darin, "Rollin' River" / "Look For My True Love" / "Look For My Baby" (Atlantic Records, 1961), original test pressing with certificate of authenticity.......................... **$50**

Courtesy of Gotta Have Rock and Roll Auctions

Superman, "Magic Record Set #1" (Musette Records/ DC, 1947), VG, folder approximately 7-1/4" x 7-3/4" with two 45 rpm picture discs and illustrated storybook insert with "The Flying Train," discs with minor edge wear, appear playable, storybook cover with torn corner. **$47**

Courtesy of Heritage Auctions

Beach Boys "Surfin'" (X Records 301 and Candix 301, 1961 and 1962), Candix EX, X Records NM, rare pre-Capitol recordings, first single ever released by Beach Boys, originally released on Candix label as Candix 331 in November 1961, followed by X Records 301 in December 1961 and Candix in January 1962 as Candix 301........................ **$688**

Courtesy of Heritage Auctions

78S

Cecil Scott and His Orchestra, "Springfield Stomp" / "Bright Boy Blues" (Victor 38117, 1929) G+, 10" 78 rpm. **$255**

Bessie Smith, "Sweet Misstreater" / "Homeless Blues" (Columbia 14260, 1927), VG+, 10" 78 rpm. ... **$230**

Elvis Presley, "Shake, Rattle and Roll" / "Lawdy, Miss Clawdy" (RCA Victor 20-6642, 1956), VG-, VG+ generic sleeve, 10" 78 rpm. ... **$45**

PROMOS

Various artists, "Sgt. Pepper's Lonely Hearts Club Band" (RSO RS-2-4100, 1978), VG++, soundtrack promo, white center labels and two hype stickers on cover of gatefold sleeve, original inner sleeves, with poster, light ring wear. **$45**

Rolling Stones, promotional stereo LP (London, RSD-1, 1969), NM, approximately 200 copies produced, with 14 songs from various Stones albums from 1964-1969. .... **$1,375**

Courtesy of Heritage Auctions

Johnny Cash, "Johnny Cash Radio Special – A Believer Sings the Truth" (Cachet CL3-9001, 1979), promo double-LP, VG+, cover with corner creasing and 4" tape removal area along top front that removed some black color, original inner sleeves and KMO (Tacoma, Washington) radio sticker on front. **$29**

The Who, "Live At Leeds," promotional MCA Records vinyl record, EX+, slight jacket wear, signed by Roger Daltrey, Pete Townshend and John Entwistle, with professional display frame. **$80**

Courtesy of Great Estates Auctioneers & Appraisers

THE BEATLES

The Beatles, "Yellow Submarine," (1969), no grade, Paul McCartney signed on front of album sleeve in blue ink. **$1,600**

Courtesy of Julien's Auctions

The Beatles, "The Beatles' Story – A Narrative and Musical Biography of Beatlemania on 2 Long-Play Records" (Capitol 2222, 1964), mono, NM, sealed, price sticker still affixed to original shrink, interviews with group and fans, selections from recordings, photos.........................**$1,375**

Courtesy of Heritage Auctions

▶ The Beatles, "Can't Buy Me Love" b/w "You Can't Do That" (Capitol 5150, 1964), 45 rpm, VG+, record NM, U.S. picture sleeve ("East Coast Straight Cut" sleeves produced in limited numbers) with light trace of aging and small tan stains on front at lower left, back with small inked "2" on white background to left of Capitol logo......................... **$550**

Courtesy of Hake's Americana & Collectibles

The Beatles, "Yesterday and Today" (Capitol 2553, 1966), sealed, mono LP, NM (mild dents in corners), copy of group's ninth U.S. Capitol LPs. The group's U.K. releases contained more songs than the American releases, and this U.S. album was comprised mostly of "extra" cuts from the U.K. versions of "Help!," "Rubber Soul," and "Revolver." **$875**

Courtesy of Heritage Auctions

◀ The Beatles, "Love Me Do," 45 rpm record signed by Andy White (studio drummer for song), signed in mint silver ink, with 8" x 10" image signed by White, record with moderate wear. White drummed on the version of "Love Me Do" that was released in the United States, The Beatles' first U.S. hit. Ringo Starr drummed on the U.K. release. **$80**

Courtesy of Heritage Auctions

SALESMAN SAMPLES

DOOR-TO-DOOR SALESMEN MAY be a thing of the past, but salesman samples are a popular collectible of the present, sometimes drawing hefty sums at auction.

You don't have to look too far back in America's manufacturing and commerce history to see how salesmen and their samples transformed modern society. The practice largely came into play in the mid-to-late 19th century, according to Lisa Robinson of The San Lorenzo Valley Museum, in her report "A Brief History of Modern Miniatures." While it may have been visits from salesmen that first brought small business owners and consumers face-to-face with these miniature modern marvels, salesmen actually took a page out of the playbook of architects, engineers, and filmmakers when tapping into the small-scale samples. For years these other professions had used "scaled models to demonstrate or better understand the operation of full-size or large-scale devices," Robinson stated.

One of the people to discover the value of a sample early on was Arthur Vining Davis, general manager of the Aluminum Company of America (ALCOA), according to Walter A. Friedman, author of "Birth of a Salesman" (Harvard Business School website, http://bit.ly/ATCvr091714). It is said Davis worked with fabricators at the company's plant to create sample aluminum kitchen utensils, along with pots and pans, so a team of college students would have the samples to use in their door-to-door sales efforts.

The types of samples to show up most often at auctions in recent years include: farm machinery (plows, graders, wheat cleaners); stoves; barber chairs; washing machines; and items used by beverage companies to sell units into general stores (coolers and dispensing devices), among other items.

— *Antoinette Rahn*

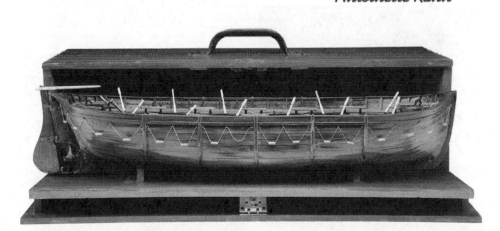

Wooden hand-propelled Fleming lifeboat with 24 seats, 12 levers and hand crank to show motion of levers, on pullout display board, part of original carrying case, related ephemera, 31" w. x 10" h. x 6-1/2" d. **$8,295**

Courtesy of James D. Julia Auctioneers, Fairfield, Maine, www.jamesdjulia.com

Glider rocker double patio seat, wooden model of slat patio chair in cream, green and orange with steel hardware and dual seats facing one another, affixed base of original case; near mint condition, case with wear and lifting to fabric covering in some spots, 8-3/4" w. x 20" l. x 9-1/2" h....... **$1,541**

Courtesy of James D. Julia Auctioneers, Fairfield, Maine, www.jamesdjulia.com

Four push mowers, two examples by C&C Manufacturing Co. of Newburgh, New York, with ribbed cast iron wheels, outside of wheels marked "NEW MODEL A 9," similar model with patent information dating it circa 1907-1909, and unmarked miniature push mower with older sickle bar, larger 36" l., smaller 9-1/2" l................ **$1,659**

Courtesy of James D. Julia Auctioneers, Fairfield, Maine, www.jamesdjulia.com

Patent models, grinder on thick wooden frame with large iron handle, iron chest of drawers with tin interior stenciled J. P. HAYES PHILA, barn pulley, and experimental running gear; overall good to very good condition, surface rust on running gear, largest 14" l. x 8" w. x 11" h...... **$972**

Courtesy of James D. Julia Auctioneers, Fairfield, Maine, www.jamesdjulia.com

Farm implement samples with primitive, elaborate reaper/cultivator in wood, iron and brass, walk-behind disc harrow with two hand levers, wooden hay loader, fertilizer or seed distributor, and partial model with two cast iron spoke wheels and brass levers; fair to good condition, largest 21" l. x 20" w. x 11" h.............. **$2,429**

Courtesy of James D. Julia Auctioneers, Fairfield, Maine, www.jamesdjulia.com

Five engines: Plastic gyroscopic Azimuth Reference Inertial System by Bendix Corp., metal-encased motor with large spoked flywheel, large cutaway model of single-piston engine, Rider-Ericsson single-piston steam engine, and static model business card holder of Baldor engine mounted to wooden base; overall near excellent condition, largest 20" l. x 10" h. x 7" d. **$830**

Courtesy of James D. Julia Auctioneers, Fairfield, Maine, www.jamesdjulia.com

Knife boxes, inlaid serpentine mahogany with decoration on lids and surrounded by inlaid banding at edges, lids hinged and open for storing sterling cutlery; near excellent condition, one hinge loose on one box, 3" h. **$1,481**

Courtesy of James D. Julia Auctioneers, Fairfield, Maine, www.jamesdjulia.com

Stransky-Light kit, circa 1920, travel box with leather gripped handle that holds lantern and salesman's notebook with detailed product information, 16" dia. molded ribbed glass dome and inverted egg-shaped dome below with brass tassel; excellent condition, box 10-1/2" w. x 10" d. x 14" h. **$363**

Courtesy of Fontaine's Auction Gallery

Sealtest Ice Cream Dairy Products electrified and illuminated Plexiglass sign with transformer in original carrying case and display, circa late 1950s-1960s; very good working condition, 24-1/2" w. x 4" h. x 18-1/2" d. **$889**

Courtesy of James D. Julia Auctioneers, Fairfield, Maine, www.jamesdjulia.com

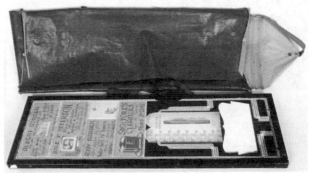

Wall mirror and thermometer, reverse painted and mirrored glass panel with black borders and red stenciling, four panels at top with various display advertisements over barometer and thermometer and mirrored panel at bottom, with leather salesman's carrying case with straps and buckles; good condition, 12-1/4" w. x 36-1/4" h. **$1,210**

Courtesy of Fontaine's Auction Gallery

Grain separator, elaborate all-wood model with funnel at top leading through hand-crank paddle and several graduated wire screens that shake to and fro with catching drawer below; with partial decal stating date of 1880; good to very good condition with minor chips and scratches, 18" l. x 14" h. x 11" w. **$474**

Courtesy of James D. Julia Auctioneers, Fairfield, Maine, www.jamesdjulia.com

Wood self-rake reaper in old red paint with white and black pinstripes and brass hardware, with delicate construction centering on wide trapezoidal bed stenciled "Walter A. Wood Self Rake Reaper, Hoosick Falls, N.Y." across it; used to grab recently cut hay before fluffing and churning it; near excellent condition, 18-1/2" w. x 17" d. x 10" h. **$11,850**

Courtesy of James D. Julia Auctioneers, Fairfield, Maine, www.jamesdjulia.com

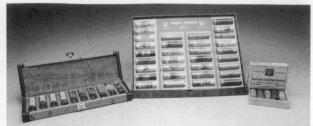

Oak sofa with bookcase top, 1890s style, original leather-type upholstery, unusual style; good condition, chip in upper right corner of bookcase frame, 12-1/4" w. x 6-3/4" d. x 12" h. **$715**

Courtesy of Omaha Auction Center

Antique French Provincial cabinetmaker's one-door armoire, circa 1900, with carved crest and floral decorated door, 11" w. x 7" d. x 18" h. **$363**

Courtesy of Bruhn's Auction Gallery, Inc.

Salesman samples in original boxes: 32 ornate paper shot shells, Rheinisch-Westfälischen Sprengstoff-Fabriken plastic hull shells, and Federal Cartridge Co. shotgun shell cutaways; all in very good condition, largest 14" l. **$330**

Courtesy of Morphy Auctions

Chair storage rack, 1908 patent date, no manufacturer information shown, wooden rack and 12 wooden chairs; excellent condition, 13" h. ...**$480**

Courtesy of Morphy Auctions

Brown & Bigelow sample playing card binder, circa 1950, leather binder with "Special Playing Card Department" and "Property of Brown & Bigelow St. Paul, Minn" stamped in gold on cover, with 54 pages of specialty advertising playing cards featuring universities, organizations, businesses, liquor and beer, soft drinks (Pepsi, Canada Dry), hotels; very good condition with some slight damage. **$184**

Courtesy of Potter & Potter Auctions

D.C. Curry grinder or Scheller sample, circa 1890s, original paint and hardware; good condition, repair to one side panel, other side with crack, 15" l. **$665**

Courtesy of Morphy Auctions

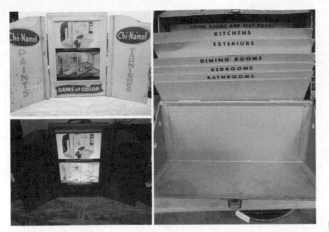

Chi Namel paint display, circa 1950, with metal case allowing salesman to show different slides of rooms that light up to demonstrate various paint options, with several slides in 1950s decorating styles. **$145**

Courtesy of Rockabilly Auction Co.

▲ Refrigerator in oak with nickel and brass trim, decal 60% and reads "KleenKold, Cobleskill, NY," all doors and latches functional, doors have one chipped corner on each, original patina, light to moderate wear, two small door latches appear to be replaced, 8-1/2" x 5" x 11-1/2".......... **$273**

Courtesy of Nette Auctions

Bagnall iron, brass, and tin fireplace insert with mantle, detailed design flanking opening to firebox, 9-3/4" w. x 11" h. **$246**

Courtesy of Pook & Pook, Inc.

Scarce folk art miniature toilet with flow blue markings by Puritas Co. of Cleveland, Ohio, high tank and pull chain mechanism; good condition, toilet 7" w. x 9" d. x 8" h., overall 14" w. x 17" d. x 34" h. with tank and display........................**$1,050**

Courtesy of Cedarburg Auction Co.

Heddon sample board, circa 1958, mounted on heavy Masonite backer board, display of four larger No. 9120 plastic Heddon Crazy Crawlers, five smaller No. 320 plastic Crazy Crawlers, and four No. 92052 prop plastic Dying Quivers, all baits unused and show various colors available for the year; baits and board unclean. **$290**

Courtesy of Crossroads Angling Auction

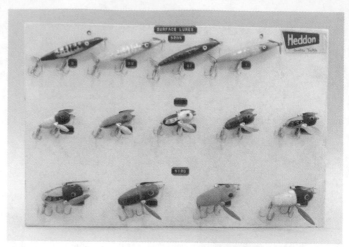

Kendall Refining Co. sample kit with black carrying case No. 60 with various vials and jars of lubes, crude oil, and grease, includes information on crude oil field in Bradford, Pennsylvania, and refining process chart; good condition, 16-3/4" w. x 5-1/4" d. x 15" h... **$180**

Courtesy of Morphy Auctions

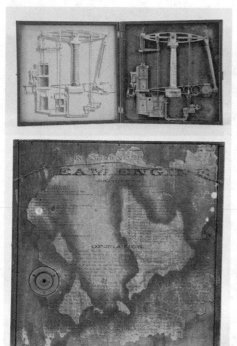

Cased working vertical steam engine, original case, working parts made of cast metal and steel, original label inside reads "Patent October 15th 1872," works stamped "Novelty MFG. Co. Boston, Mass," 70% of rear label remains and reads "Sectional Steam Engine," with key; good condition, missing crank and some wear, 12-1/2" w. x 2" d. x 12-1/2" h..................................... **$540**

Courtesy of Nest Egg Auctions

Burled veneered slant-front writing desk with brass hardware and large locking segmented lower drawer topped with flip-down leather top writing area with drawers and pigeonholes; very good to excellent condition with veneer chips, 19-1/4" w. x 12-1/2" d. x 10-1/2" h................................ **$355**

Courtesy of James D. Julia Auctioneers, Fairfield, Maine, www.jamesdjulia.com

Soda fountain, circa 1915-1925, complete with central onyx triple tap assembly and leaded shade, back of sample with stainless steel and marble work, true in scale and materials; very good-plus condition with normal wear overall, soiling and cracks in marble and wood, two collars remade, 36" l. **$12,000**

Courtesy of Morphy Auctions

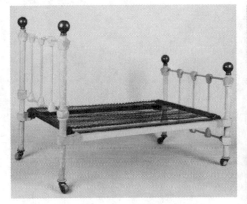

Painted iron bed, Art Bed Co., Chicago, on wooden wheels with box spring, brass balls on head, mattress rails marked "Art bed Co. Chicago," disassembles; good condition with original components and some paint wear, 28" w. x 18" d. x 22" h. **$546**

Courtesy of Morphy Auctions

Sickle bar mower, iron and wood model with large traction wheel connected to gear mechanism, when activated, puts sidebar blades in motion when pulled along floor; wooden tongue folds for storage within original wooden carrying case, accompanied by printer's block picturing similar sickle bar mower; very good condition overall, case 16" w. x 7-1/4" h................................. **$7,702**

Courtesy of James D. Julia Auctioneers, Fairfield, Maine, www.jamesdjulia.com

Above-ground swimming pool by Sears, model bolted down under plastic cover and labeled for Monte Designs, with original black leather case; discoloration to green grass material, some rusting of bolts and hardware, paint chips on wooden segments, scratches on plastic, open case 28-1/4" w. x 28-3/4" d. x 27" h............................**$258**

Courtesy of Cordier Auctions

Hires Munimaker dispenser, circa 1900, replicating full-size root beer dispenser of period; marble, glass, and nickel with zinc liner and coils inside; excellent condition, edge chips in marble, tarnish and staining. $84,000

COURTESY OF MORPHY AUCTIONS

▶ Scratch-built and authentically detailed wooden model of motorized bale harvester with adjustable conveyor, powered by associated electric motor, on oak stand; fine original condition, 34" w. x 59" h. x 11" d. **$750**

Courtesy of Heritage Auctions

Safe/vault, polished aluminum cubicle case stamped "12," four caster feet and exterior double-hinged door with four-handle turn lock and 72-hour time lock on reverse that appears to be reset by accompanying ratchet key, second double-hinge door with combination lock for added security on interior; near excellent condition, 12-1/4" w. x 11" d. x 14-1/2" h........ **$7,705**

Courtesy of James D. Julia Auctioneers, Fairfield, Maine, www.jamesdjulia.com

Paint-decorated cast iron safe by Geo. Zech, York, Pennsylvania, circa 1907, key lock mechanism with key in lock, hinged door, wooden interior with single vertical slot on one half and space for three drawers on other, single drawer remains, felt bottom on interior, 8" h. **$4,025**

Courtesy of Grogan & Co.

Tall case clock, inlaid walnut with works marked "Asprey & Son – 166 New Bond St. W," access to clockwork mechanism through door on back, front of case inlaid with central starburst and draping leaves and vines, bonnet inlaid with fleur-de-lis, brass spindle finial; very good to near excellent condition with functioning clock, 17" h....................... **$592**

Courtesy of James D. Julia Auctioneers, Fairfield, Maine, www.jamesdjulia.com

Chippendale chairs, circa 1920, six ribbon back mahogany chairs upholstered in pale blue stripe with rose stripes on gray silk; near excellent condition, 7-1/4" h. **$2,962**

Courtesy of James D. Julia Auctioneers, Fairfield, Maine, www.jamesdjulia.com

◀ Peerless Iceland ice cream maker, hand crank, circa early 20th century, Dana & Co., Cincinnati, with patented stationary dasher, claiming to take just three minutes to create ice cream, 7" h. **$360**

Courtesy of Pook & Pook, Inc.

Steel, iron and tin Great Majestic Junior stove, Majestic Mfg. Co., St. Louis, with Griswold "0" skillet, steel teakettle, and booklet, 33-1/2" h. x 22-3/4" w., 51" h. overall. **$4,320**

Courtesy of Pook & Pook, Inc.

Two furnace models, one aluminum and one painted tin, The Majestic Co., Huntington, Indiana, both marked "Holland," tin model marked "Holland 250A," with leather-covered carrying case; very good condition, wear to case, minor scratching, aluminum furnace 10" h., painted tin electric model 12" h....**$307**

Courtesy of Pook & Pook, Inc.

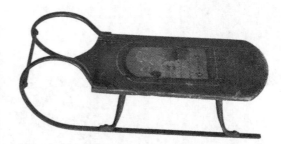

Early English sample bow-front tall chest, mahogany case with hand-cut dovetails on drawers, secondary wood is pine, circa 1835, 11" w. x 9" d. x 16" h. **$544**

Courtesy of Bruhn's Auction Gallery, Inc.

Wooden sled, paint decorated on seat with pond scene in panel on deep green background, with long metal runners with arched nose, original red paint on runners and original label reads "No. 5," repaired with replaced section of seat panel on right side, 6" w. x 14" l. x 5" h...**$211**

Courtesy of Fontaine's Auction Gallery

SCIENCE & TECHNOLOGY

IT'S THE TYPE OF PLACE where the question, "What is that?" is music to the ears.

The three-word question sparked hours of conversation and quite a few transactions at North America's largest and longest-running show devoted to antique scientific equipment and retro-technology, the Antique Science & Retro-Tech Show & Swap Meet in Dallas/Fort Worth. The annual event has a venerated reputation as a source for unusual discoveries, not to mention serving as the venue of the annual World Championship Slide Rule Competition. But at the 21st annual event, held in early 2015, organizers found something nearly as elusive as a Throughton & Simms geodetic theodolite: young collectors.

Photographer Ben D'Avanza hunted for objects to inspire his passion for machining, Triumph motorcycles, and vintage audio. He found a vintage microphone head that will look perfect incorporated in the interior design of his brother's new restaurant.

Casual shoppers like D'Avanza and a growing number of established collections returning to market are just a handful of the reasons why vintage science and technology is a growing segment of the hobby. Much like the objects themselves, collectors' passion for vintage technology can be diverse and intricate. And unlike some categories, vintage tech is still in the early stages of developing strong demand, leaving lots of fresh-to-market discoveries for the historic-minded tinkerer.

Retired software engineer Bob Patton started collecting handheld calculators roughly 25 years ago and has 350 unique models in his collection "but 569 have passed through my hands." He offered highlights from his collection priced from $10 to as much as $100. He sees the interest as rooted in a simpler time: "Any obsolete technology is just nostalgia and a curiosity in old technology," he said. "You can still find things that are valuable, you just need persistence and to look at garage sales, junk

Vintage tech collector Bill Stone showed off his two Wimshurst electrostatic generating machines invented in the 1880s. The devices employ rotating discs to generate an electric charge through contact with brushes on bars near the front and back of the discs. The charge is stored in the two Leyden jars and then converted to a spark between the two elevated electrodes.

Ben D'Avanza, left, buys a vintage microphone head from collector/vendor Lon Kelly at the Antique Science & Retro-Tech Show & Swap Meet in Dallas. The event marked its 21st year as the largest and longest-running show of its kind in North America. Attendance was strong at the 2015 event, with many young collectors buying and learning all day long.

Courtesy of Joaquin Andrew

stalls and antiques shops."

Among the collector's items for sale from Patton's inventory was a 1975 Inverton VIP 10 hand-held calculator from Germany. The arithmetic calculator has 10-digit precision and algebraic logic, six functions, 20 keys, and glowing red LED display. The asking price was $100 – a near 10,000% markup from Paton's purchase price. "I found it at an antique shop for 10 cents. The finds are still out there," he said.

These finds are not limited to low-run calculators. Science and technology is one of the broadest of all collecting categories and is generally thought to include fossils, fine minerals, medical and navigational devices, globes, and more. As it finds a new generation of collectors – one well-versed in technology from the beginning – the field is inclusive of artworks, computers, portable computing, documents and manuscripts, and oddities. Collections are limited only by budget and imagination. Early specialization based on passion helps the collector avoid fakes, new creations, and inflated prices.

The public's fervent fascination and curiosity with the scientific and technological mind seems especially boundless for pioneers such as Galileo Galilei, Albert Einstein, and Leonardo da Vinci. Visitors flock to exhibits featuring da Vinci's Codex Leicester, the most famous of the inventor's 30 surviving journals. Bill Gates, the founder of Microsoft and one of the world's richest individuals, purchased the Codex from Christie's for $30 million in 1994 and has placed the book on continual display around the world, most recently in the United States.

Letters and documents in Einstein's hand have a devoted collecting base as well. A letter referencing the persecution of the Jews in war-torn Europe sold for $12,500 at auction in late 2014, and a letter sent to Jewish philosopher Erik Gutkind, stating Einstein's belief that God does not exist, sold on eBay for more than $3 million in late 2012.

A 56-page composition notebook completed by Alan Turing, credited as a pioneer of computer science, was auctioned by Bonhams in early 2015 for $1,025,000. Material from Turing's accomplishments is rare, and the previously unknown and one-of-a-kind manuscript came to market just a year after the motion picture "The Imitation Game" made public his important role in cracking Nazi codes during World War II, which shortened the war by at least two years.

Thatcher's Calculating Instrument, circa 1880s, cylindrical slide rule, patented in 1881 by Edwin Thatcher Keuffel & Essex, New York, with mahogany base, 22" l. **$649**

Courtesy of Fairfield Auction

Arithmetic calculator, 1975, by Inverton, Germany, VIP 10m, hand-held, with 10-digit precision, algebraic logic, six functions, 20 keys, and glowing red LED display, 6" l. ... **$100**

Courtesy of Eric Bradley

Uyeda Camera Co. Star watch camera, circa 1912, Japan, with original chain, engraved "REGISTERED THE WATCH CAMERA S.C.W 49468" and "SILVEROID"; for taking circular images of 31mm in diameter on sheet film; this copy of Lancaster watch camera is one of the most rare Japanese cameras. **$30,700**

Courtesy of Westlicht Photographica Auction

Noon Cannon sundial, circa late 19th century, French, signed "Darreny London a Paris 969," components with stamped fondeur mark of cockerel and initials H.D., two latitude ACS supporting burning glass, oxidized copper base plate mounted with compass, universal bubble level, uninscribed crescent dial and acorn center securing bolt, circular base with three adjustable screws and urn-shaped decoration, 10 3/4" h. **$2,400**

Courtesy of Capo Auction NYC

Sundial, 19th century, marble plinth base engraved with sundial, gnomon set for 49 ° 29', tapering cannon barrel mounted on twin supports, burning glass with two shaped arms to twin supports (sun beam at noon ignites powder in cannon to sound top of hour), 9" dia. **$800**

Courtesy of Capo Auction NYC

Scale, brass weights, 18-1/2" w... **$125**

Courtesy of Capo Auction NYC

Sextant, early 20th century, brass arc signed "Kelvin Bottomley & Baird Ltd., Glasgow, No 1692," with 6-1/2" radius, sighting tube, seven shades, two mirrors and rosewood handle, in original wood carrying case.............. **$300**

Courtesy of Capo Auction NYC

Telescope, late 18th century, signed Adams, London on vernier arm of 5-7/8" vertical circle with silvered scales, 21" l. telescope with short draw-tube focusing 1-3/4" objective glass, axis with graduated bubble level located on twin trunnions with vertical circle twin supports and securing arm, stand with three adjustable supports, 18-5/8" h........ **$2,100**

Courtesy of Capo Auction NYC

Goniometer, late 19th century, signed on stand "Societe genevoise Instruments Physique & Mecanique Geneve," prismatic sighting tube mounted on limb with counterbalance and vertical circle with engraved silvered scale, vernier and magnifier, axis with adjustable specimen holding arm adjusted by tangent screw with micrometer fine motion scale with vernier, circuit stage with silvered scale and adjustable ground glass hemispherical table, with center light source tube and adjustable plano-concave mirror, Y-shaped base with tapering pillar stand with various objectives, additional telescope with iris diaphragm and other items in fitted fruitwood case, 15-1/4" h............... **$9,500**

Courtesy of Capo Auction NYC

Western Electric National Cash Register telephone, circa 1890s, counter, rare, 11" h. x 7-1/2" w. x 8-1/2" d. **$187**

Courtesy of Concept Art Gallery, LiveAuctioneers.com

Binoculars, circa 1914-17, U.S. Navy, "Big Eye" ship's bridge binoculars, polished steel with brass lens shields and adjustments, marked "A21 BU 321-5-1 USN," 58" h. x 37" d. **$15,000**

Courtesy of Heritage Auctions

Chicago copper oil can candlestick telephone, copper base and shaft, nickel-plated head, unmarked but possibly Montgomery Ward, Chicago telephone satisfy receiver cap, 11" h. **$125**

Courtesy of Morphy Auctions

Binoculars, circa 1940-45, U.S. Navy "Big Eye" bridge binoculars, marked "A21 BU 321-5-1 USN," hinged lens covers, elevation controls, focus adjustments and traversing mechanism, 55" h. x 36-1/5" d. **$9,375**

Courtesy of Heritage Auctions

Telephone, "The Motograph," 1877, patented on July 30, 1877, by Thomas A. Edison, with carbon-button microphone and electromotograph (chalk) receiver with revolving drum of chalk and small crank, ornate cast iron housing, lower cover replaced, only two examples known to exist. After Edison came in second in the race to patent the telephone in America, he tried to establish footing in the English market in competition with Bell's patent. However, after only two years, Bell's system met with success in England as well, while Edison's invention failed commercially. **$40,000**

Courtesy of Auction Team Breker

Telephone, 1893-1894, No. 1 Speaking Tube desk set, Western Electric, Alexander Graham Bell's first upright desktop telephone model, hard rubber marked transmitter face designed specifically for Speaking Tube use and Code No. 129 unipolar low resistance watch case receiver with matching serial numbers, potbelly base, rare, 13" h. **$31,000**

Courtesy of Morphy Auctions

Telephone, 1898, Manhattan Electrical Supply Co., Inc., forked switch hook and outside terminal long pole receiver, Manhattan seal on front of transmitter and single button in base, re-nickled, 12-1/2" h. $15,000

Courtesy of Morphy Auctions

Telephone, 1903, Automatic Electric Co. Strowger set, one of the first desk telephones manufactured by Automatic Electric Co., finger wheel designed, forked spear hook with rounded bulbous ends, back plate reproduction, rare, 12" h. $9,500

Courtesy of Morphy Auctions

Telephone, 1895-1899, Public Telephone Co., Shaver style "g," Dolphin, no buzzer on back, rare, 11-1/2" h. $6,500

Courtesy of Morphy Auctions

top lot

Telephone, circa 1890-1895, American Bell No. 2 Speaking Tube desk set, early Bell desk stand, with high-resistance lettered White Solid Back six-digit beveled edge transmitter code No. 225, code No. 129 unipolar low resistance receiver, rare, 13" h..$42,000

In 1892, one year before Alexander Graham Bell's original patent expired, he introduced the first upright desktop telephone in America, available in two styles. Model No. 1 was a potbelly style and No. 2 was a swirl base. No. 1 and No. 2 supported a speaking tube transmitter. Since the first telephones were heavy wooden wall telephones, and since Bell's fundamental patents for the telephone were expiring in 1893 and 1894, opening the door to competition, Bell was motivated to keep a competitive edge by introducing newer, better telephones. The upright desktop telephone was introduced for the first time with these Bell speaking tubes in 1892. By 1894, all serious competitors were building candlesticks to compete and were rolling them out as Bell's second patent expired.

COURTESY OF MORPHY AUCTIONS

Bergeon bench tool and miscellaneous watchmaker's tools, 20th century, two large bezel checks, miscellaneous lathes chucks, burrs and cutters. **$312**

Courtesy of Heritage Auctions

Calculator cane, circa 1900, Otis King slide rule calculator system, enamel numbers, metal ferrule, and malacca wood, 36-1/2" l. **$4,687**

Courtesy of Heritage Auctions

Pike microscope, circa 1860, brass, three-foot base, engraved Pike / Maker / 518 Broadway / New York / No. 1172 / screw adjustable focus, single eye and nose piece, missing reflecting mirror, 16-1/5" h. **$437**

Courtesy of Concept Art Gallery, LiveAuctioneers.com

Microscope, 1876, by J. Zentmayer, Philadelphia, brass body with iron three-branch foot, adjustable focus, single eye and nose piece, 11-1/2" h. **$187**

Courtesy of Concept Art Gallery, LiveAuctioneers.com

Keuffel & Esser land surveyor's transit, 1919, brass with black lacquer finish, in fitted dovetailed wood case with 11" telescope, plumb bob, adjusting knobs, etc., serial # 40336. .... **$281**

Courtesy of Concept Art Gallery, LiveAuctioneers.com

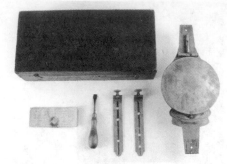

Compass, 19th century, Edmund Draper (Philadelphia, 1805-1882), plane, round silvered dial engraved with Draper's shaded seven-point star and "Edmund Draper/Philad'a 459/Warranted," spirit levels and base socket far Jacob's Staff and contained fitted, case, 6-1/4". **$625**

Courtesy of Concept Art Gallery, LiveAuctioneers.com

"Station" music box, Switzerland, circa 1890, coin-activated, attributed to Henri Vidoudez of St. Croix, No. 13909, with four six-air cylinders, nickel-plated Mermod-type movement with crank-wind double-spring motor driving cylinder and gear for candy dispenser, six dancing dolls and additional band members. **$38,000**

Courtesy of Auction Team Breker

Snuff music box, early 19th century, silver and silver-gilt, Swiss two-air cylinder movement, sectional comb of 63 teeth (complete) in groups of three, micro-mosaic lid, 2-1/4" w. x 3-1/2" l. **$24,000**

Courtesy of Auction Team Breker

Music box, circa 1870, No. 19579, playing six airs accompanied by two combs of 80 teeth in total (complete) and optional central 17-note organ for bird whistle, Gamme No. 75, with flat-topped winding lever, compensated governor, automaton bird, "A. Rivenc & Co., Manufacturers, Geneva" 25" w. **$24,000**

Courtesy of Auction Team Breker

Golf club disguised as walking stick, circa 1880, sterling head and nickel ferrule, coconut wood shaft, hiding cigarette and match holder; referred to as "Sunday sticks" or "Sabbath sticks," these devices were golf enthusiasts' answer to the Church of Scotland's discouraging golfing on Sundays............................**$684**

Courtesy of Louis J. Dianni, LLC

Theodolite, circa 1890, German, made by Hildebrand, Freiberg i./S., double telescope transit theodolite, original oxidized and lacquered brass, oculars with micrometers, two striding levels, four telescopic magnifiers, two swing-adjustable reflector mirrors, silver scales, length of telescopes: 18-1/10" l., 15-3/4" l., 19-3/4" h. overall **$17,000**

Courtesy of Auction Team Breker

Theodolite, circa 1890, made by Starke & Kammerer, signed "Wien, Nr. 367," original lacquered and oxidized brass, silver scales and verniers, three magnifiers, two microscopic magnifiers with micrometers, one level, one striking level, telescope with rack-and-pinion focusing, 15-3/4" h. **$0,000**

Courtesy of Auction Team Breker

Hand-carved oak mannequin, 19th century, fully articulated, peg construction, mounted on stand, pen mark PC-36006 Maurice on finger, rare, 5-1/4' h. **$15,730**

Courtesy of Austin Auction Gallery

Tellurium, circa 1880, by Jan Fekl of Prague, with lunarium, working demonstration model to demonstrate orbit of earth and moon around sun (represented by candle), signed on earth globe "Zemekoule Vydal. J. Felkl syn Roztoky u Praha," bronzed cast-metal and lacquered brass, 2-1/2" plaster globe with 12 lithographed gores, compass showing houses of zodiac, sun as candle with brass reflector, hand-crank-operated, 60-3/4" l. **$12,000**

Courtesy of Auction Team Breker

Sea quadrant No. 13 by George Adams the elder, rosewood, brass, and boxwood with original lacquer, mica window, scale graduated 0-90 and 90-0 degrees, dated "11 Nov 1751" and signed "Invented and made by Geo. Adams at Tycho Brahe's Head in Fleet Street, London," 17-1/4 l. index arm and 4" l. telescope. **$24,250**

Courtesy of Auction Team Breker

Octant, circa 1760, by Jan Cornelius von Voer, German, serial No. 226, frame and index arm with engraved acanthus ornamentation and figure of stylized girl with basket of flowers in center, transversal scale 0° to 90°, radius 8", sight vane with one pinhole and two index shades, rare and important. **$5,900**

Courtesy of Auction Team Breker

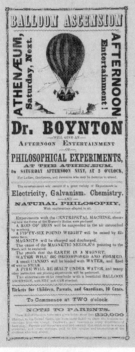

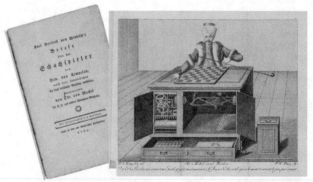

Pamphlet, "Briefe über den Schachspieler des Hrn. von Kempelen," by Karl Gottlieb von Windisch, 58 pages with three folded copper plates, published in 1783, eye-witness recollection on working performance of automaton known as "Turk" developed by Wolfgang von Kempelen (1734-1804), who claimed invention was able to play human opponent at chess; device was a mechanical illusion that allowed human chess master to operate machine from inside..... **$4,700**

Courtesy of Auction Team Breker

James H. Cafferty (American, 1819-1869), "Portrait of Robert Fulton, 1852," oil on panel, 23" x 19-1/4." Fulton (1765-1815) was an American inventor and mechanical engineer. His work resulted in advancements to shipping canal systems, modern aqueducts, milling technology, dredging equipment, submersibles, and torpedoes. **$11,350**

Courtesy of Heritage Auctions

Broadside, circa 1880, advertising balloon ascension and various other scientific experiments, 5-1/2" w. x 12" h. **$59**

Courtesy of Heritage Auctions

Color lithograph prints, English, first quarter 20th century: Comical interpretation of fast-developing technological advancements pertaining to locomotion, including flight, automobiles, and "robotic legs"; and documenting changes that technology and scientific enquiry bring to outdated English law and quack doctor practices; each 15-1/2" x 19-1/2".............. **$250**

Courtesy of Heritage Auctions

Fossil tooth, Megalodon shark, Carcharocles megalodon, Miocene, Morgan River, South Carolina, North America, 3.56" l. **$500**

Courtesy of Heritage Auctions

Wooly mammoth hair, Mammuthus primigenius, Pleistocene, Tarantian stage, Yakutia, Eastern Siberia, 2-1/4" x 8-1/4"................. **$593**

Courtesy of Heritage Auctions

Fossil skull, Einiosaurus, Einiosaurus procurvicornis, Upper Cretaceous, Two Medicine Formation, Montana, North America, ceratopsian dinosaur, forward-curving nasal horn, two horns retaining on frill, rare 5' l. **$31,250**

Courtesy of Heritage Auctions

SILVER

STERLING SILVER (standard silver) is an alloy made of silver and copper and is harder than pure silver. It is used in the creation of sterling silver flatware – silverware – as well as tea services, trays, salvers, goblets, water and wine pitchers, candlesticks and centerpieces. Coin silver is slightly less pure than sterling.

The value of silver has seen steady growth since the first indications of the Great Recession in late 2008. From a low of $8.92 in November 2008, silver prices topped out at $48.48 in May 2011 and hit a plateau between $25 and $35 in late 2012 and early 2013. Silver prices are so high that in some cases the auction value of an antique or collectible silver object is nearly identical to the prices paid for scrap silver. This presents a quandary for newly inherited silver and a looming threat for unique works produced by craftsmen: High melt prices threaten objects whose designs enhance its value among collectors or institutions.

"For those of us dedicated to the world of antiques and art, the idea of scrapping is difficult to take, but we know that it is an option for people looking to generate income from unwanted objects," said Skinner Auctioneers, Inc. CEO Karen Keane on the Skinner blog. "But with all things being equal, before making that decision, we encourage investigating selling your silver at auction rather than melting it down."

This is but one reason why it's important to take a piece of silver to an auction house for inspection before you consider a dealer or scrap metal buyer. A seller should know both the spot silver price as well as the historical or decorative price in order to make the best decisions. Some dealers do not deal in silver weight and couldn't care less about current spot silver prices.

In addition to relatively high silver melt values, older silver objects suffer another threat. American dealers often lament that young buyers are turned off by the thought of owning silver. It's seen as a high-maintenance object. What they may not know is that fine silver of some quality

Silver and mixed metals hand-hammered tea caddy with applied holly sprig with copper berries on tapering conical body, Gorham, Providence, Rhode Island, circa 1881, applied cast mouse-form finial to lid, monogrammed DEF to bottom, originally retailed by J.E. Caldwell & Co., Philadelphia, marks: (lion-anchor-G), STERLING, 135, J. E. CALDWELL & CO., N, pin dents to beveled lip, dent to lid, surface scratches commensurate with age, 4-3/8" h., 5.92 troy oz. **$2,125**

Courtesy of Heritage Auctions

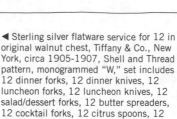

◄ Sterling silver flatware service for 12 in original walnut chest, Tiffany & Co., New York, circa 1905-1907, Shell and Thread pattern, monogrammed "W," set includes 12 dinner forks, 12 dinner knives, 12 luncheon forks, 12 luncheon knives, 12 salad/dessert forks, 12 butter spreaders, 12 cocktail forks, 12 citrus spoons, 12 bouillon spoons, 12 teaspoons, 12 gumbo spoons, 12 cream soup/dessert spoons, 12 iced-tea spoons, 12 demitasse spoons, four tablespoons, one tomato server, one sugar spoon, one gravy ladle, one sauce ladle, two vegetable serving spoons, two buffet forks, one meat fork, one cheese slicer, one pastry server, one two-piece roast carving set, one two-piece steak carving set, approximately 250 troy oz. total............. **$2,524**

Courtesy of Bonhams

◄ Renaissance Revival sterling silver pitcher, Gorham, 1890, polished body with chased and hammered scrolling acanthus, 7-1/2" h., together with tongs by Towle Silversmiths, 21.83 troy oz. **$450**

Courtesy of Clars Auction Gallery, www.clars.com

▲ Hammered silver bowl, Erik Magnussen, Denmark/Germany, circa 1925, signed with impressed manufacturer's mark to underside "Sterling Germany Handmade Erik Magnussen," with touchmarks, 2-1/4" h., 10-1/2" dia..................... **$1,905**

Courtesy of Wright Auctions & Appraisers

◄ Continental silver oblong serving tray, likely Austrian, 831 grams. ...**$424**

Courtesy of A.H. Wilkens Antiques & Appraisals

Sterling silver petal-edge bowl, Richard Dimes, 10" dia., 23 troy oz......**$360**

Courtesy of Sandwich Auction House

SILVER

Nine sterling silver items, China, 20th century: Two bristled cloth brushes, two bristled hair brushes, mirror, shoehorn, handled straightener, and handled hook, all with iris and crane designs, marks to some, to 9-3/8" h. and to 6-1/4" w.; cube box with hinged cover with single dragon and flaming pearl stretching along four sides and another on cover top, signed "Shang bao cheng jiyu sheng," 2-1/4" x 3-1/2" x 3-1/8", all in repoussé on chased ground. **$1,000**

Courtesy of Skinner, Inc.; www.skinnerinc.com

English three-piece sterling silver tea service: Creamer, sugar bowl, and covered teapot, Charles Lias, London, 1838, fully hallmarked, teapot with small damage to handle and missing tip on lid, 45 troy oz. **$1,050**

Courtesy of Arus Auctions

Sterling silver coffeepot in Francis I pattern, Reed & Barton, 1907, 10" h., 32.38 troy oz................................. **$900**

Courtesy of Clars Auction Gallery, www.clars.com

actually improves in value if it's used rather than stored.

What silver objects are likely to increase in value? High-quality silver objects from American name-brand makers, such as Gorham, Tiffany, Towle, Stieff, and Reed & Barton, remain desirable and represent a solid purchase. Functional pieces will survive longer than those that are purely decorative.

There exist a number of excellent resources on the topic of sterling silver. The most famous continues to be *Discovering Hallmarks on English Silver* by John Bly. This 1968 book was re-released in 2008 by Shire Publishing and remains the mainstay for English hallmarks. Flatware is well covered in *Warman's Sterling Silver Flatware,* 2nd edition, by Phil Dreis. However, a 21st century generation of resources is available on tablets and tablet personal computers: Dealer Steve Freeman developed a free app for iPad users offering a free library of hundreds of images of English silver maker's marks. The SilverMakers app was released in 2012 and offers an easy way to find marks based on the object's intended use, marks, and even silver content.

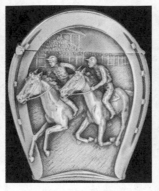

Pitcher with chased repoussé woodland scene on stippled ground with house to front and chapel to verso, Baltimore Silversmiths Mfg. Co., Baltimore, circa 1903, monogrammed AB to underside, marks: B, (lion's head), S, STERLING 925/1000 FINE, 1150, surface scratches commensurate with age, 8" x 8-1/4" x 6", 22.55 troy oz. **$3,000**

Courtesy of Heritage Auctions

Horseshoe-form match safe with repoussé horse and jockey scene to front, Battin, Newark, New Jersey, circa 1898, opening to hidden photo to interior, with original photo, horse hoof motif to reverse, match strike to bottom, marks: PAT. MARCH 1898, (trident-B), STERLING 258, bent bevel to hidden photo panel, scratch to front, surface scratches commensurate with age, 2-3/8" h., 1.54 troy oz. **$531**

Courtesy of Heritage Auctions

Oval shell-form card tray with undulating rim and repoussé figure of standing female, Unger Brothers, Newark, New Jersey, circa 1900, marks: UB (interlaced), STERLING, 925, FINE, 0543, slight surface scratches commensurate with age, 3/4" x 3-1/4" x 5-3/4", 1.50 troy oz. **$200**

Courtesy of Heritage Auctions

Silver and silver gilt two-handled punch bowl, Willhelm Ludwig, Hanau, Germany, circa 1935, 10-sided bowl with two cast handles, chased repoussé scrolling leaves to shoulder, raised on conforming spreading foot, silver gilt interior, marks: 925, STERLING, HANDARBEIT, (shield), surface scratches commensurate with age, 8" h. x 15-3/4" w., 53 troy oz. **$1,250**

Courtesy of Heritage Auctions

Covered sugar bowl with swan finial over bulbous-form repoussé body with double handles, S. Kirk & Son, Baltimore, circa 1925-1932, cinched base and circular foot, monogrammed to lower front, marks: S. KIRK & SON, INC., Sterling, 925/1000, 273, surface scratches commensurate with age, 5-3/4" x 6-3/4" x 5-1/2", 17.60 troy oz. **$438**

Courtesy of Heritage Auctions

top lot

Silver and cut-glass ewer with silver-mounted rim, Gorham, Providence, Rhode Island, circa 1875, everted spout and flowering vines on stippled chased repoussé ground, silver C-scroll handle mounted at rim and terminating at silver band to body, monogrammed to interior of silver mount, marks: (lion-anchor-G), S1118, STERLING, chips to raised crosscut motif near base and foot rim, scratches commensurate with age, 14" x 8-1/2" x 4-1/2"...................$10,000

Silver and silver gilt covered tureen and ladle, Elsa Peretti for Tiffany & Co., Italy, circa 1984, with silver gilt interior, ladle in Padova pattern, marks: TIFFANY & CO., ELSA PERETTI, 925, ITALY, 12; T. & CO., STERLING, PERETTI, ITALY, 1984, general surface wear indicative of use, 7-1/2" h., 12" dia., 98.16 troy oz................... **$3,750**

Courtesy of Heritage Auctions

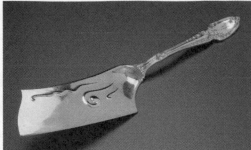

Broom Corn pattern silver and silver gilt ice cream slice with shaped silver gilt blade, Tiffany & Co., New York, designed 1890, handle with meandering vine, terminal end monogrammed U, marks: TIFFANY & CO., STERLING, PAT 1890, M, rub to gilt finish on raised swirl on blade and verso where item rests, slight surface scratches commensurate with age, 12-3/8" l., 6.40 troy oz... **$375**

Courtesy of Heritage Auctions

Georgian sterling silver weighted candleholders, I & T.S. Sheffield, 1840, each with scalloped base, fluted standard surrounded by floral repoussé, 11-3/4" h. **$950**

Courtesy of Clars Auction Gallery, www.clars.com

Sterling silver menorah masoret, center shamos, 15" h. x 12" w., 17.25 troy oz..............................**$400**

Courtesy of Elite Decorative Arts

Large vintage floral chased covered bowl, marked sterling to base, 10" w. x 6-1/2" h., 37.6 troy oz............**$500**

Courtesy of Elite Decorative Arts

Center bowl with turn-over rim decorated with alternating floral cartouches and rectangular chased panels with garland band to edge, American, circa 1920, marks: STERLING, 6321, 16IN., pin dents and surface scratches commensurate with age, small vertical crack to rim, 4" h., 16" dia., 46.75 troy oz. **$1,000**

Courtesy of Heritage Auctions

Chilly pattern silver chamber stick with two repoussé putti near fire and C-scroll handle, Unger Brothers, Newark, New Jersey, circa 1910, marks: UB (interlaced), STERLING, 925, slightly bent "teeth" at top of bobeche, surface scratches commensurate with age, 1-3/4" h. x 2-3/4" dia., 0.75 troy oz. **$438**

Courtesy of Heritage Auctions

▲ Cake stand with gadrooned edge, raised on circular foot, Reed & Barton, Taunton, Massachusetts, circa 1900, monogrammed JEG to central field, marks: (eagle-R-lion), STERLING, 383, REED & BARTON, surface scratches commensurate with age and some pitting to front near monogram and to verso, 2" h. x 10-3/4" dia., 19.55 troy oz. **$406**

Courtesy of Heritage Auctions

◄ Audrey Hepburn sterling silver Tiffany & Co. cup related to "Breakfast at Tiffany's," Paramount, 1961, mug form with handle on right, inside lining with gold wash, front engraved "Audrey Hepburn / Breakfast at Tiffany's / 1961," bottom engraved "Paramount" and stamped "Tiffany & Co. / Makers / Sterling Silver / 25088," most likely given to star by director or producer of film, good condition with minor scratches and dings, 3-1/3" h. **$5,625**

Courtesy of Heritage Auctions

Georgian sterling silver repoussé water pitcher, Phillip Rundell, London, 1821, hinged cover surmounted with sculpted flower finial, bulbous body with hammered band with polished scrolling floral acanthus above arrow fluting, set on circular base with stylized details, 8-1/2" h., 29.17 troy oz... **$1,900**

Courtesy of Clars Auction Gallery, www.clars.com

Sterling silver vase, Redlich & Co., New York, 1895-1946, polished trumpet form set with flared collar and stylized bell-shaped base with pierced rosette-accented trellis and rocaille reserves, 14-3/4" h., 12.90 troy oz. **$500**

Courtesy of Clars Auction Gallery, www.clars.com

English sterling cream jug, London, circa 1765, with repoussé and chased exterior, trefid pad feet, with London hallmark and date mark and hallmark of cross-shaped cartouche with maker's mark AJNS, 4" h., 2.46 troy oz.... **$250**

Courtesy of Cowan's Auctions

Art Deco lidded waste bowl, Italian, mid-20th century, by Pradella Ilario for Tiffany & Co., bulb form with zigzag pattern with shell and spiral feet, underside impressed with maker and retailer's marks, 7-1/2" h., 22.5 troy oz. **$1,000**

Courtesy of Cowan's Auctions

Punchbowl with gadrooned foot and rim and lion head mounts, Tuttle Silversmiths, Boston, 1963-1969, marked sterling with hallmarks for Tuttle Silversmiths and 1963-1969 date mark, 6-1/4" h., 11" dia., 59.379 troy oz. **$850**

Courtesy of Cowan's Auctions

Pierced fruit basket with floral motif and fruit swags, German, 20th century, oblong shape with scalloped rim raised on oblong foot, marked Sterling 925 fine Germany, illegible monogram on bottom, 5" h. x 11-3/4" w. x 8" d., 26.73 troy oz............. **$550**

Courtesy of Cowan's Auctions

SILVER

Seven-piece service for 12 with 21 additional utensils (105 total pieces), sterling silver, stainless steel, and plastic, signed with impressed manufacturer's mark to each element: Reed & Barton Sterling, Italy/USA, 1958. ....**$11,250**

Courtesy of Wright Auctions & Appraisers

Persian 84 teapot hand done with images of sultans and women playing musical instruments, elongated spout, 10" h., 20 troy oz............... **$450**

Courtesy of Elite Decorative Arts

Chinese sterling silver vases with scene of warriors among mountains in relief, two dragon handles, 7-1/2" h., 14.75 troy oz............................... **$4,600**

Courtesy of Elite Decorative Arts

Plymouth pattern teakettle on stand with warmer, Gorham, Providence, Rhode Island, 46.12 troy oz. **$850**

Courtesy of Clars Auction Gallery, www.clars.com

Silver two-handled vegetable tureen and cover, Gorham Mfg. Co., Providence, Rhode Island, 1907, oval, sides chased with rocaille and scrolling foliage, both sides with rococo cartouches enclosing applied monograms LN and RN, conforming loop handles, lobed domed cover chased to match with scroll finial, underside of dish with inscription dated "February 7th 1909," marked on base, numbered A6403 with date symbol for 1907, lid marked sterling and numbered 32 F, 11-7/8" l., 32 troy oz... **$950**

Courtesy of Leslie Hindman Auctioneers

Russian/Polish sterling silver candlesticks with floral repoussé, Shmul Szkarlat (1866-1904), made in Poland, "84" mark dated 1889, assayer's mark of OC, 12" h. **$600**

Courtesy of Elite Decorative Arts

▶ Compote with grapes, Georg Jensen, early 20th century, shallow flared bowl above spiraled stem and circular foot, other side with pendant grape clusters and meandering vine, signed with old "GJ" mark, 10-1/2" h., 10" dia., 38.35 troy oz....................... **$3,800**

Courtesy of Elite Decorative Arts

Silver Torah crown, American, second half 20th century, in style of William B. Meyer, lower band pierced with Hebrew inscription translated, "It is a tree of life to them that hold fast to it, and everyone that upholds it is happy/blessed," scrolled ribs spaced by cast symbols of 12 tribes with names within stylized leaves, top mounted with tablets, lower band stamped STERLING, 12-1/4" h., 63 troy oz...... **$3,200**

Courtesy of Leslie Hindman Auctioneers

Sterling silver pedestal water pitcher, mounted with loop handle, raised on circular base, Revere Silversmiths, 10-1/2" h., 20.82 troy oz. **$425**

Courtesy of Clars Auction Gallery, www.clars.com

Heavy sterling silver covered ice bucket, English, Lionel Alfred Crichton, early to mid-20th century, with applied handles of putti with rosebud finial handle, floral decorated bucket, signed to base, 12" h. with cover, 15" dia., 85 troy oz....**$2,500**

Courtesy of Elite Decorative Arts

Silversmithing in America goes back to the early 17th century in Boston and New York and the early 18th century in Philadelphia. Boston artisans were influenced by English styles, New Yorkers by Dutch. American manufacturers began to switch to the sterling standard about the time of the U.S. Civil War.

Repoussé chocolate pot, American, Davis & Galt, late 19th century, all-over repoussé decoration of flowers and scrolling leaves with gooseneck spout and hinged lid with ball finial, underside marked Sterling / 2 with shielded fleur-de-lis maker's mark and Isbell & Co. retailer's mark, underside monogrammed, 7-1/2" h., 10.78 troy oz. **$500**

Courtesy of Cowan's Auctions

◀ Birmingham sterling inkwell, British, Liberty and Co., early 1920s, round, lidded, with wooden underside, incised motifs, "Lion passant" sterling and year mark to interior of lid, maker's mark, city mark, year mark, and numbers to bottom rim, 4" dia., 3-1/4" h............**$50**

Courtesy of Cowan's Auctions

SOUVENIRS

COLLECTIBLE SOUVENIRS ARE so much more than refrigerator magnets and generic t-shirts.

Inspired by the lure of the open road and the mystique of a foreign city, the souvenir is an age-old collectible that touches the heart of collecting itself, and the category is extremely diverse, colorful, and increasingly popular.

Soldiers during World War I and II used the only paper they had at hand, namely foreign currency, to collect signatures of fellow soldiers in their unit or famous political leaders they met during the war. Bills were taped or fastened together in a strip now referred to as "short snorters." The short snorter is also a nickname of a person who crossed the ocean in an airplane, and those who did signed their names on dollar bills. If a soldier is unable to produce this "certificate," then he must buy everyone in the vicinity a small drink, or snort of liquor. These souvenirs are hot collectibles now and can range in price from as

Souvenirs relating to Gen. Douglas MacArthur, plaque, bookend, bust, ceramic hat, bank, pocketknife, pinbacks, and various period collectibles. **$286**

Courtesy of Heritage Auctions

VISIT WWW.ANTIQUETRADER.COM

WWW.FACEBOOK.COM/ANTIQUETRADER

low as $30 to as much as $4,000 if the short snorter has signatures from U.S. presidents, astronauts, or entertainers.

On the homefront, citizens occupied their time collecting souvenirs relating to Gen. Douglas MacArthur and various patriotic items urging Americans to "Remember Pearl Harbor" and "Keep 'em Flying." Busts, plaques, banners, mugs, charms, and pins are highly sought after. Sports souvenirs flourished during the 1940s as pennants, programs, and premiums ranged from the practical to the downright ridiculous. Baseball great Joe DiMaggio's Restaurant based in San Francisco created odd souvenir lamps made of seashells that are now worth $300.

CROSSOVER APPEAL

By their very nature, these items are pursued by history buffs as well as those who seek unusual souvenirs. Tokens, plates, teacups, and books are just a few of the souvenir items that appeal to more than one collecting group. Major mass culture events of the 20th century, such as various World's Fairs, Charles Lindberg's flight, and the Apollo 11 moon landing generated huge demand for mementos, not to mention gift shops for every tourist location across the county. The heyday of American tourism and the good ol' fashioned road trip (1920-1960) stuffed car trunks full of keepsakes from Maine to Hawaii.

One of the most ubiquitous souvenirs ever mass-produced are sterling silver spoons. Created during the mid-19th century, original retail prices of collectible spoons were inexpensive, but the sentimental nature encouraged travelers to save them by the millions. Most sterling spoons are worth less than $50 on today's market, with the top of the market settling at $300. Silver-plated spoons – those often used for state spoons or made by Rogers Bros. - sell for $1 or less. When spoons do appear at auction or in a shop, they are most often sold in a set.

Souvenirs were in demand long before the 20th century. Upper class European young men, from the late 1660s to the mid-1800s, often embarked on a Grand Tour as a rite of passage. The traditional tour was deemed necessary for noblemen and impresarios to experience other cultures, music, and exotic customs. It was important for these gentlemen to tour antiquity collections and amass a respectable amount for their estates. The market for coins, paintings, medals, and replicas of ancient works of art exploded during this time and are now an important segment of the fine and decorative art market, with values generally starting at $1,000. A circa 1885 Parisian gilt bronze box with eglomisé panels depicting famous Grand Tour locations such as Opera, the Madeleine, L' Arc de Triomphe, Notre Dame, and Luxembourg Palace is valued at more than $2,000, and a pair of Italian marble Grand Tour souvenirs depicting fluted Corinthian columns, inscribed TEMPLUM CASTORIS ET POLLICIS and TEMPLUM VESPASIANI, sold for $7,500 at auction in 2013.

Souvenirs weren't only reserved for the ruling class. Promoters in Victorian Europe gifted young middle class debutantes with gilded dance ball souvenirs to be affixed to dance cards. The little charms were often stamped with a date and were popular from the 1870s to 1900, although they are still made today. These charms are popular collectibles and now trade for $100 to $500.

DIFFERENCE BETWEEN SOUVENIRS AND RELICS

There is a stark difference between objects we call souvenirs and relics, although both serve to memorialize important events, locations, and people. Souvenirs are generally mass-produced objects designed chiefly for tourists. Relics, on the other hand, are objects with a stronger tie to the subject itself. A relic of the Battle of Gettysburg might be a Civil War minnie ball embedded in a chuck of fence post or tree bark left over from the conflict; a Gettysburg souvenir might be a pottery stein depicting artists' scenes and memorial buildings relating to the battle, once available in a gift shop. Both are valued at roughly $200 each.

Deep collecting interest remains for both, with prices particularly on the rise for those objects that have some age or show some quirky appeal – a pair of painted wood clogs decorated with painted U.S. and Netherlands flags and designed to hang on the wall. The oddity commemorates the strong relationship between The Netherlands, the United States, and the United Nations and is valued at $180.

MINIATURE BUILDINGS

The Souvenir Building Collectors Society, a club for those who collect souvenir buildings, has more than 200 members and celebrated its 20th anniversary in 2014. The three-dimensional miniature versions of famous or notable buildings can still be found in gift centers, but vintage versions can sell for as much as $220 if rare, taller than 10 inches, or made from precious metals. Replica miniature banks were popular premiums during the mid-20th century, and skyscrapers remain popular collectibles. One of the most valuable souvenir buildings ever made celebrates the Exposition Universelle held in Paris in 1900. A marvelous lithographed image of the great building is glued on finely cut wood blocks and features both exterior and interior views. It sold for $1,600 in 2007 and would likely bring more if offered in today's market.

Group of 38 travel charms from America and United Kingdom, 9-18k, 55.4 dwt. **$1,500**

Courtesy of Rago Arts, www.ragoarts.com

Lighter, 1912, after design by Marconi, with impressed English hallmarks, circular stone base, and fitted leather case reading Souvenir of the International Radiotelegraphic Conference, London, 1912 From Marconi's Wireless Telegraph Company Ltd., 3-3/4" h. **$930**

Courtesy of Leslie Hindman Auctioneers

Carved wood mirror frame, naval theme, painted with U.S. flag and naval ensign of Republic of China, most likely from U.S. Marine occupation of city of Tientsin during the 1912 Chinese Revolution, as ensign was only in use for two years, rare, 13" h. x 8-1/2" w. **$413**

Courtesy of Thomaston Place Auctions

Statue of elderly man walking, inscribed on stand in black letters (Hebrew) "Souvenir from the 14th Zionist Congress in Vienna 1925," maker's emblem Goldscheider, made in Austria, missing cane, 8" h. **$1,476**

Courtesy of Kadem Auction House

Fan, wooden bat-formed, marked "Pittsburg Pirates" on one side, other side marked, "The fan's fan," patented November 1908, handle with whistle, light cardboard blades with pictures of championship team members, rare, 12-1/2" w. x 10-1/2" l.................. **$2,100**

Courtesy of Mosby & Co. Auctions

Pill box, circa late 18th/ early 19th century, English, porcelain and enamel box marked "A Present from Windsor," 1-3/4" l. **$125**

Courtesy of Leslie Hindman Auctioneers

Four medals, Christopher Columbus Exhibition, circa 1892-1893, by Augustus St. Gaudens, two souvenirs, larger 3" dia................................. **$275**

Courtesy of Rago Arts, www.ragoarts.com

Satchel Paige souvenir pennant, circa 1948, originally purchased at Cleveland Stadium around time of Cleveland Indians' 1948 World Championship season, original tassels, rare, 28" l. **$1,314**

Courtesy of Heritage Auctions

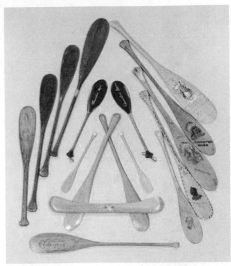

Canoe paddles, set of 14, nine decorated with Native Americans and place names including Montana, Maine, Massachusetts, New York, New Jersey, with souvenir wall sign with three paddles in relief arranged as triangle, "Old Town" decal, various 17-1/2" to 22-1/2" l......................... **$1,800**

Courtesy of Brunk Auctions

Green Bay Packers porcelain ashtray and shot glass, circa 1960s, 1967 World Championship, 7" glass ashtray, 3" "Hedy" shot glass............. **$167**

Courtesy of Heritage Auctions

Cup souvenir commemorating 200th stage performance of "The Wizard of Oz" in 1903. .... **$4,300**

Courtesy of Philip Weiss Auctions

Letter openers, 116 different openers collected between circa 1900 and 1939, including Shikudo, Japanese and European ivory and bronze, sterling, carved wood, micromosaic, souvenir, advertising and whaling, various lengths. **$3,000**

Courtesy of Rago Arts, www.ragoarts.com

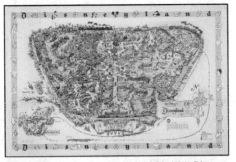

Disneyland souvenir map/poster, 1961, Walt Disney, 30" x 44-1/2"..**$84**

Courtesy of Heritage Auctions

Jacksons Victory Tour souvenir concert program, 1984, Don King/Joseph & Katherine Productions, 32 pages, 11" x 14"..**$15**

Courtesy of Heritage Auctions

Russian Army tourist souvenir fur hat, late 20th century, small, quilted interior with Russian army insignia. **$26**

Courtesy of Heritage Auctions

Plate with portrait of George Washington in center, gold gilt at edges and handles, souvenir issue for 1876 centennial, 9" dia. **$334**

Courtesy of Heritage Auctions

Bristol glass vase, pre-1850, souvenir of "Capitol of the U.S. Washington," 9-1/4" h. **$1,075**

Courtesy of Heritage Auctions

Queen Victoria commemorative travel perfume vial, circa 1887, Royal Worcester, ivory porcelain with medallions on both faces, marks: stamped signature in gilt, 2" h. **$1,075**

Courtesy of Heritage Auctions

Spoons, 91 examples of various origins and designs, set in five frames, 5" l. **$2,750**

Courtesy of Leslie Hindman Auctioneers

Roman-style oxidized bronze cistern model, Grand Tour souvenir, 19th century, 5-1/2" w. x 12-1/2" l. x 4" d. **$1,625**

Courtesy of Heritage Auctions

Chicago Century of Progress bottle, 1934, dark brown glass, one side reads "1934 A CENTURY OF PROGRESS CHICAGO" against scrolled and foliate border, bottle's lip and corked stopper of sterling silver, 10" h. **$119**

Courtesy of Heritage Auctions

Elvis Presley souvenir ballpoint pen, 1972, RCA, text reads "Elvis Now 1972 Now," 6" l. $18
Courtesy of Heritage Auctions

Eight figural examples of macerated currency (shredded and chopped U.S. bills), various forms: pitchers, cat in boot, Washington Monument, top hat, and shoes. $231
Courtesy of Heritage Auctions

Match safe, circa 1895, maker unknown but American, figural form of Daniel Boone, souvenir of 29th National Encampment of Grand Army of The Republic in Louisville, Kentucky, stamped to front and reverse GAR (in logo), 29TH NATL. ENCPT, LOUISVILLE, DANIEL BOONE, hinged lid, match strike to bottom, 2-7/8" h., 3 oz.........$500

Courtesy of Heritage Auctions

Sourvenir wooden box marking opening of Erie Canal, 1825, dated Oct. 26, 1825, labels read "THIS BOX was made of a piece of wood, brought from Erie in the first Canal Boat / THE SENECA CHIEF," 2" dia. $388
Courtesy of Heritage Auctions

Sesquicentennial souvenir lamp, 1926, Liberty Bell shade mounted on swinging yoke, base reads "Souvenir The Sesqui-Centennial International Exposition 1776 Philadelphia 1926 150 Years of American Independence," rare, 7" h... $593

Courtesy of Heritage Auctions

Gold nugget souvenir token, circa 1900, from Wm. Haferkorn cigar store in Everett, Washington, likely made to promote Haferkorn's cigar store at Alaska Yukon Pacific Exposition in 1909, rare. $3,500
Courtesy of Hollabird-Kagin Americana

Tea caddy and butter spreader, circa 1900, souvenirs from Salem, Massachusetts, marking Salem witch trials, mark of Daniel Low on spreader, tea caddy spoon maker unknown, 5-3/4" l. **$870**

Courtesy of Heritage Auctions

Sterling silver spoons with cactus motif, circa 1900, Shreve & Co., San Francisco, marks: SHREVE & CO., 4-1/2" l., 1.55 troy oz. **$137**

Courtesy of Heritage Auctions

Wooden shoes from Harry S. Truman administration, "President Truman + Koningin Juliana Souvenir 1949," U.S. and Belgium flags and artist's rendering of United Nations headquarters building, 3-1/5" w. x 9" l. **$180**

Courtesy of Heritage Auctions

Scarf, 1936, souvenir of the Berlin Summer Olympics, silk, 30" sq. **$197**

Courtesy of Heritage Auctions

Two sterling silver souvenir spoons, circa 1900, Native American motif, Paye & Baker Manufacturing Co., North Attleboro, Massachusetts and George W. Shiebler & Co., New York, marks: P&B (in hearts), (winged S), 6-1/8" l., 2.01 troy oz. **$64**

Courtesy of Heritage Auctions

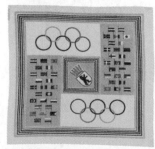

1903 G$1 Louisiana Purchase souvenir spoon with McKinley gold dollar, scene of Festival Hall and Cascades in bowl, embedded McKinley commemorative gold dollar, 5-1/2" l. **$1,175**

Courtesy of Heritage Auctions

SPORTS

PEOPLE HAVE BEEN saving sports-related equipment since the inception of sports. Some of it was passed down from generation to generation for reuse; the rest was stored in closets, attics, and basements.

Two key trends brought collectors' attention to sports collectibles. First, decorators began using old sports items, particularly in restaurant décor. Second, collectors began to discover the thrill of owning the "real" thing.

There are collectible items representing nearly every sport, but baseball memorabilia is probably the most well-known segment. The "national pastime" has millions of fans, with enthusiastic collectors seeking out items associated with players such as Babe Ruth, Lou Gehrig, and others who became legends in their own lifetimes. Although baseball cards, issued as advertising premiums for bubble gum and other products, seem to dominate the field, there are numerous other items available.

Sports collectibles are more accessible than ever before because of online auctions and several auction houses that dedicate themselves to that segment of the hobby. Provenance is extremely important when investing in high-ticket sports collectibles. Being able to know the history of the object may greatly enhance the value, with a premium paid for items secured from the player or directly from his/her estate.

White Spalding game-worn cleats signed by Terry Bradshaw, Pro Football Hall of Famer and former Pittsburgh Steelers quarterback, 1980s, Bradshaw's faded uniform number 12 written on heel of each shoe, MEARS, JSA authentication. ...**$1,185**

Courtesy of Goldin Auctions

USC Trojans 1962 football national championship trophy, 32" h. Provenance: Newport Sports Museum Collection. ... **$11,990**

Courtesy of SCP Auctions

Unopened 1975 Topps Football cello box containing 24 packs of football cards, as presented from Topps when it was delivered in 1975. .... **$2,719**

Courtesy of Collect Auctions

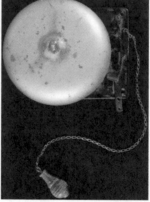

Thurman Munson signed 1976 Topps baseball card, authenticated and slabbed Authentic by PSA/DNA. The former catcher was an MVP and Rookie of the Year with the New York Yankees. Munson signatures are rare because the former MVP died in a plane crash in 1979 at the age of 32. .... **$1,655**

Courtesy of Collect Auctions

Official program for the "Ice Bowl," 1967 NFL championship game with Green Bay Packers vs. Dallas Cowboys at Lambeau Field in Green Bay, Wisconsin, on Dec. 31, 1967. ....**$562**

Courtesy of Collect Auctions

Vintage boxing ring bell, circa 1930s, all pieces believed to be original with original chain link "rope" affixed to well-worn wooden handle. **$86**

Courtesy of Collect Auctions

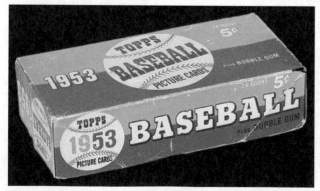

Five-cent display box for 1953 Topps baseball cards, which originally housed 24 nickel packs..**$840**

Courtesy of Robert Edward Auctions

Rare 1907 Joe McGinnity flipbook produced as part of a series by Winthrop Moving Picture Postcard Co., allowing viewer to see Joe "Iron Man" McGinnity's pitching motion in action, 2-1/4" x 4". **$720**

Courtesy of Robert Edward Auctions

Rare CDV of Alexander Joy Cartwright, a "Founding Father" of baseball, circa 1865, photographer's credit "H. L. Chase, Honolulu, H. I." on reverse, 2-1/2" x 4". ... **$3,600**

Courtesy of Robert Edward Auctions

1886 McLoughlin Bros. Game of Base-Ball with all 10 painted metal baseball figures, box 17-1/4" x 9-1/2" x 1-3/4".. **$3,000**

Courtesy of Robert Edward Auctions

Ty Cobb photo in PSA/DNA slab labeled Type I; photo from 1944 from Acme Newspictures, dated July 22, original caption affixed to back and identifies scene as an opening ceremony preceding Pacific Coast All-Star Game, 8" x 10"......................**$60**

Courtesy of Collect Auctions

Cap Anson ginger beer bottle, circa 1900, 7" h. The legend of Anson's ginger beer includes the story that Anson was storing the inventory of full bottles in his basement when the bottles exploded, ending the business.................................**$720**

Courtesy of Robert Edward Auctions

New York Yankees locker room chair, circa 1920s, with ball club's 50th anniversary plaque affixed to front of backrest, obtained during 1973 renovation, 16" x 13" x 30-1/2"...............**$960**

Courtesy of Robert Edward Auctions

1912 King of Clubs sheet music with full-length photo of Ty Cobb, written by William Brede and published by Will Rossiter, Chicago, 10-1/2" x 14".........**$960**

Courtesy of Robert Edward Auctions

top lot

Joe DiMaggio game-used and signed New York Yankees home flannel jersey from 1942, one of the oldest authenticated DiMaggio jerseys known and only known surviving DiMaggio jersey from 1942 Wartime Season, with MEARS grade of A6. DiMaggio's "5" was stripped off and replaced with a "4" sometime after the 1942 World Series. The "5" present on the jersey today is a replacement. $169,400

1961-1963 Houston Colt .45s blue-uniform bobble head, rare variation of white jersey bobble head.................................. **$540**

Courtesy of Robert Edward Auctions

"Luke Appling" folk art baseball hand-painted by former Minor League umpire George Sosnak (1922-1992), signed by Appling, LOA from James Spence/JSA... **$3,900**

Courtesy of Robert Edward Auctions

Ty Cobb signed check, made out to "cash" on June 29, 1946, from First National Bank of Nevada, JSA LOA certification. **$968**

Courtesy of Goldin Auctions

Duke Snider "Look All National League" presentation 14K gold Cyma men's wristwatch, 1953, with hand-written letter of provenance from Snider and PSA/DNA; *Look Magazine* selected him to its All-National League Team, and the watch was given to The Duke in recognition of that honor. . **$2,489**

Courtesy of Goldin Auctions

Cincinnati Royals (NBA) rare promotional lighter, circa 1960s, one side with team's logo and name, opposite side with club's home arena, Cincinnati Gardens. **$120**

Courtesy of Robert Edward Auctions

SPORTS

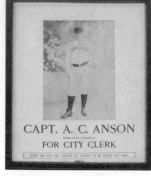

Program for 1995 funeral of New York Yankees great Mickey Mantle, who died on Aug. 13 at Baylor University Medical Center with funeral service at Lovers Lane United Methodist Church in Dallas two days later, 8-1/2" x 5-1/2".. **$267**

Courtesy of Goldin Auctions

Advertisement for Baseball Hall of Famer Cap Anson's campaign for Chicago city clerk, 9" x 11"; he won the election but his tenure was full of missteps and his political career ended a few years later. **$770**

Courtesy of Goldin Auctions

Canton Bulldogs vintage pennant, 23" l...................................... **$207**

Courtesy of Goldin Auctions

Walter Payton canvas street banner, 1999, once hung above streets of Chicago, 3' x 8'. **$1,007**

Courtesy of Goldin Auctions

Bob Feller 1950s "Steamball" time-lapse original photo by Frank Bauman for *Look Magazine*, PSA/DNA Type I photo, 7" x 9". **$242**

Courtesy of Goldin Auctions

Catcher's mask, circa 1890, rare style often referred to as "spider" mask with ornate cage held together with hooks and wires, and extended area of cage to protect chin and throat. **$484**

Courtesy of Goldin Auctions

Michael Jordan Caesar Rfo limited edition plaque, edition number 195/500, 12-1/2" dia., mounted to 15" x 18" wooden plaque. **$533**

Courtesy of Goldin Auctions

Danica Patrick 2012 Daytona 500 Sprint Cup debut race fender from her No. 10 Go-Daddy car, first female to race in Daytona 500, Feb. 27, 2012, 31" x 34"............**$1,896**

Courtesy of Goldin Auctions

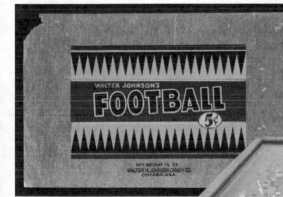

◀ 1930s Walter H. Johnson Candy Co. "Football" uncirculated wrapper, 5" x 7-7/8".........................**$359**

Courtesy of Legendary Auctions

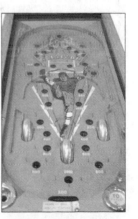

1933 Genco Gridiron football coin-op machine, classic pinball style but without flippers, 42" x 38" x 17". **$299**

Courtesy of Legendary Auctions

Muhammad Ali Effenbee doll, 1986, "Great Moments in Sports" series, 18" h. **$212**

Courtesy of Goldin Auctions

Lou Gehrig Huskies cereal advertising sign, 1930s, reinforced with 1/4" cardboard backing, 20" w. x 29" h...... **$837**

Courtesy of Legendary Auctions

Napoleon Lajoie Cleveland Leader watch fob scorer, circa 1909, issued by the *Cleveland Leader*, reverse engineered as hand-held scoring device with dials for "VISITORS," "HOME CLUB," and "INNINGS." **$896**

Courtesy of Legendary Auctions

Vince Lombardi 1961 *Los Angeles Times* "Coach of the Year" National Sports Award, 5-1/4" h., medallion 2 -7/8".................**$5,378**

Courtesy of Legendary Auctions

Babe Ruth Mutoscope machine, 1930s, fitted with 2001 reproduction (by American Pict-O-Graph Co.) of 1935 reel titled "Babe Ruth – All American," 45-1/2" h.......................... **$2,032**

Courtesy of Legendary Auctions

1908 Rose postcard, George Stovall, Cleveland, dated April 23, 1909, 3-1/2" x 5-1/2".. **$508**

Courtesy of Legendary Auctions

Admission pass for "Cleveland Base Ball Club" from 1890s, bottom with stamping from Cleveland Spiders owner Frank D. H. Robison, 2-1/2" x 4".. **$239**

Courtesy of Legendary Auctions

Former Chicago Bulls star Scottie Pippen 1994 All-Star Game MVP award, 10" h. **$8,963**

Courtesy of Legendary Auctions

NFL World Championship press pin, 1947, Comiskey Park, where Chicago Cardinals defeated Philadelphia Eagles 28-21. .... **$269**

Courtesy of Legendary Auctions

New York Giants silk scarf, 1950s, with illustration of Polo grounds in center, Giants logo and New York City skyline, 32" x 32".......... **$149**

Courtesy of Legendary Auctions

1924 New York Giants world tour game-worn cap from Giants' and Chicago White Sox's five-month goodwill tour of Europe to promote baseball................ **$2,578**

Courtesy of SCP Auctions

▼ Muhammad Ali vs. George Foreman unused full ticket for Sept. 25, 1974 bout in Kinshasa, Zaire; boxing match actually took place Oct. 30. ..**$940**

Courtesy of SCP Auctions

▲ Duke Snider signed Brooklyn Dodgers equipment bag, 1950s, 24" l. x 18" w., PSA/DNA authentication. Provenance: Delbert Mickel Collection. **$3,194**

Courtesy of SCP Auctions

Hillerich & Bradsby metal revolving bat rack, 1960s, 4' h. Provenance: Bill Riddell Collection. **$1,319**

Courtesy of SCP Auctions

top lot

Lyle Alzado 1983 Los Angeles Raiders Super Bowl XVLL championship ring, 14K gold, size 15.5, 46g. Raiders beat Washington Redskins 38-9; Alzado died of brain cancer in 1992 at age 43. .... $80,750

COURTESY OF SCP AUCTIONS

Warren Spahn Milwaukee Braves game-worn jacket, 1950s, Wilson size 46 tag sewn in collar and Spahn's uniform number "21" tag sewn inside front tail...$10,367

Courtesy of SCP Auctions

Harlem Globetrotters satin warm-up suit, 1950s, items belonged to Joshua "Josh" Grider, with "Grider - 34 - 31 - R No. 38" sewn into waistline. $1,517

Courtesy of SCP Auctions

STAR WARS
action figures

Editor's Note: In his new book, *The Ultimate Guide to Vintage Star Wars Action Figures, 1977-1985,* Mark Bellomo explores the popular franchise's back stories and the universe of playthings it has spawned. This introduction takes a look at the inaugural Kenner "Star Wars" toy promotion and illustrates the first 12 Kenner "Star Wars" figures. For more information on the book, visit www.krausebooks.com.

• • •

"STAR WARS EPISODE IV: A New Hope" (1977) – the epic space opera that launched one of the premiere media franchises in history – opened in theaters on May 25, 1977, with a budget of $11 million.

Although the profound, lasting influence of the "Star Wars" franchise on the collective consciousness of Generation X (and nearly every generation since) may never be accurately assessed, Episode IV's runaway success at the box office certainly took the many hard-working people who were involved in "A New Hope's" production by surprise.

Not even toy companies believed in the property. When Lucas originally shopped around the license to produce toys, none of the major buyers pursued the film. Only Kenner Toys – a subsidiary of the Fortune 500 food-processing company, General Mills, Inc. (i.e., part of the company's toy division) – bit on the license. This is why the large capital, cursive "G" that represented a General Mills brand was emblazoned on every Star Wars toy's proof-of-purchase seal.

However, following the film's premiere, "Star Wars" was a bona fide hit with moviegoers. Lines of fans who viewed the film for the third, fourth, or fifth time wrapped around city blocks. Phrases such as "lightsaber," "The Force," and "Death Star" entered the American lexicon, and "Star Wars" reaped worldwide, lifetime box office receipts of more than three-quarters of a billion dollars.

But in spite of the runaway success of "Star Wars," the aforementioned production delay didn't just affect the release of the movie. Kenner Toys – now the film's license holder fortunate enough to produce action figures based on the film's characters – faced a similar delay in getting its own products to retail. Before the movie hit theaters, Kenner severely underestimated consumer demand for "Star Wars" merchandise, and did not develop an action figure line quickly enough for a fourth quarter Christmastime 1977 release on store shelves (since it takes time to craft toys and action figures), so one of the company's executives, Bernard Loomis, a man responsible

R2-D2: MOC: "Star Wars" 12B: **$285,** 20/21B: **$190;** "Empire Strikes Back": **$80;** MLC: darker "Early Bird" dome: **$35-$38,** standard color dome: **$12**

Chewbacca: MOC: "Star Wars" 12B: **$375+,** 20/21B: **$215;** "Empire Strikes Back": **$100;** "Return of the Jedi": **$80;** "Power of the Force": **$115;** MLC: standard crossbow: **$16,** iridescent early issue crossbow: **$30-$35**

Luke Skywalker (standard lightsaber above left, telescoping lightsaber above right): MOC: "Star Wars" 12B: **$650+,** 20/21B: **$325;** "Empire Strikes Back" brown hair: **$250,** blond hair: **$225;** "Return of the Jedi": **$210;** MLC: standard lightsaber, blond hair: **$21,** standard lightsaber, brown hair: **$50-$60+,** double-telescoping lightsaber: **$225-$325+,** depending on condition

Princess Leia Organa (shown on "Star Wars" card): MOC: "Star Wars" 12B: **$325+,** 20/21B: **$215;** "Empire Strikes Back": **$175;** "Return of the Jedi": **$300;** MLC: $25

Obi-Wan Kenobi: MOC: "Star Wars" 12B: $325, 20/21B: **$175;** "Empire Strikes Back": **$65+;** "Return of the Jedi": **$120;** "Power of the Force": **$150;** MLC: standard lightsaber, white hair: **$20,** standard lightsaber, gray hair: **$20,** double-telescoping lightsaber: **$325-$375+,** depending on condition

Darth Vader: MOC: "Star Wars" 12B: **$575-$650+,** 20/21B: **$325;** "Empire Strikes Back": **$150;** "Return of the Jedi": **$120;** "Power of the Force": **$210;** MLC: standard lightsaber: **$18,** with soft head variation: **$25-$32,** double-telescoping lightsaber: **$325-$375++,** depending on condition

for some of the most important decisions in the toy industry for many decades, made a stunning decision – to afford kids and collectors the mere promise of action figures to come. Kenner's postponement yielded collectors their very first "Star Wars"-related product; not of action figures or poseable creatures or deluxe playsets, mind you, but a sort of chipboard place holder to placate rabid fans until toy factories finished production on the first assortment of the original 12 "Star Wars" action figures, which hit retail shelves in 1978.

THE EARLY BIRD PACKAGE

Since Kenner had initially underestimated demand for "Star Wars" product, it had nothing ready for the Christmas season of 1977. Thankfully, Kenner concocted a revolutionary idea – the Early Bird Certificate Package – selling American children the promise of figurines.

Kenner limited sales to 500,000 units, and the two million figures in the Gift Certificate Program promoted the sale of a whopping 40 million figures the following year.

Solicited at retail "for a limited time only – not to be sold after Dec. 31, 1977," the "Star Wars" Early Bird Certificate Package, essentially a slapdash gift set comprised entirely of color-printed paper and chipboard, was sold for $7.99 at finer retail outlets and department stores across America. Before submitting the redemption certificate to Kenner, here is what this Early Bird Kit (the set's nickname from collectors) contained:

- Early Bird Certificate (coupon) "good for 4 authentically detailed Star Wars Action Figures" – can be separated into "coupon" and "receipt"
- Colorful display stand with "Star Wars" (characters) picture
- Star Wars Space Club membership card signed by Luke Skywalker
- "Star Wars" stickers, four: "May the Force Be With You," C-3PO, R2-D2, "Star Wars" logo
- Proof-of-purchase coupon
- "After Tearing Off at Perforations" directions

The set's chipboard-comprised colorful display stand featured painted portrayals of the first 12 "Star Wars" characters, the same painted representations found on the original "Star Wars" 12-back [12B] action figure packages, and it could be folded to construct a display stand for the first 12 figures. The base "stage" of the stand had 12 oval-shaped holes that could be punched out so that when your four "Star Wars" figures arrived via the mail, you would

Original Early Bird Certificate Package Envelope: MISP: **$2,650-$2,800+**; MIP (with all paperwork): **$385-$425+**; Early Bird Certificate Coupon (on its own): MLC: **$235-$255+**; Early Bird Certificate Package Colorful Display Stand (on its own): MLC: **$75-$100+.** Boxed Early Bird figures and foot pegs (all sealed in baggies) with plastic tray and paperwork: MISP: **$2,650-$2,900+**; MIB: **$1,350-$1,650+**

also receive a set of 12 white action figure foot pegs to encourage you to buy the remaining eight of the 12 initial figures.

After you sent the Early Bird Certificate to Kenner for redemption, you would receive the following in the mail, far earlier than originally stated. Kenner shipped every figure by March 1978. [MIBaggie means "Mint In Sealed (translucent) Baggie."]

- White rectangular mailer box (from Maple Plain, Minnesota)
- Artoo-Detoo action figure, MIBaggie (stamped "MADE IN HONG KONG" in black lettering)
- Chewbacca action figure, MIBaggie (stamped "MADE IN HONG KONG" in black lettering)
- Luke Skywalker action figure, MIBaggie (stamped "MADE IN HONG KONG" in black lettering)
- Princess Leia action figure, MIBaggie (stamped "MADE IN HONG KONG" in black lettering)
- 12 white foot pegs/plastic holders to attach figures to the already-purchased stand, MIBaggie
- White, fragile, vaccu-formed plastic figure holder tray
- "Early Bird Set Premium Offer of Collector Stand" paper redemption slip / "Welcome to the Exciting World of Star Wars!" form (also shows how to use foot pegs)
- 1977 "Star Wars" catalog
- White paper insert (no printing)

The baggies containing the four Early Bird figures could be either taped or heat-sealed. If taped, on almost every found sample, the tape has become a bit yellowed and brittle, so be careful handling samples.

Regardless of how the bags were sealed, there are four different types of stamped plastic baggies: 1.) Baggie horizontally stamped "MADE IN HONG KONG" in small white letters (roughly waist or chest high to the figure in question), stamped either on the front or back of the baggie, since these figures were quickly placed into the baggies. 2.) Baggie with "MADE IN HONG KONG" stamped in small black letters running horizontally. 3.) Occasionally, a baggie with "MADE IN HONG KONG" in small black lettering again, yet running vertically (usually only on the Chewbacca baggie), and running the length of the entire baggie. 4.) Very rarely, a baggie may be stamped – usually on the backside – with the "Kenner" logo in blue lettering (usually only on the R2-D2 baggie). The final figureless baggie, the sealed baggie containing the 12 white foot pegs for the Early Bird Display Stand, has no lettering and is never taped shut – it is heat-sealed.

It should also be noted that the earliest versions of the Luke Skywalker action figure in this set sometimes included a "double-telescoping" lightsaber. This is a very rare and hard-to-find accessory and causes the value of this already rare set to jump in price by $400 to $500 or more. Since it is difficult to determine an average price for this set, an estimated value of $4,500-$5,000 has been established by using value averages from full mint, sealed sets (all pieces and parts MISP).

Pricing Key: MOC (mint on card), MLC (mint, loose, and complete), MISB (mint in sealed box), MIB (mint in box), MISP (mint in sealed package); 12B (12 characters listed on card back), 20/21B (20 or 21 characters listed on card back).

— *Mark Bellomo*

Han Solo: MOC: "Star Wars" 12B, small head: **$750**, large head: **$550**; 20/21B, small head: **$440**, large head: **$450**; "Empire Strikes Back" small head: **$300**, large head: **$245**; "Return of the Jedi": **$175**; MLC: small head version: **$25**, large head version: **$20**

C-3PO: MOC: "Star Wars" 12B: **$315**, 20/21B: **$225**; "Empire Strikes Back": **$150-$165**; "Power of the Force": **$100**; MLC: **$15-$20**, depending on condition of chrome

Stormtrooper: MOC: "Star Wars" 12B: **$375**, 20/21B: **$275**; "Empire Strikes Back": **$175-$190**; "Return of the Jedi": **$120**; "Power of the Force": **$215**; MLC: **$15-$20**, depending on condition of white plastic

Jawa: MOC: "Star Wars" 12B, vinyl cape: **$2,750-$3,000+**, cloth cape: **$210-$225**; 20/21B: **$125-$140**; "Empire Strikes Back": **$65-$75**; "Return of the Jedi": **$80-$100**; "Power of the Force": **$115-$135**; MLC: vinyl cape: **$275-$350+**, cloth cape, very light stitching: **$25-$32**, cloth cape, standard: **$12-$16**

Star Destroyer Commander: MOC: "Star Wars" 12B: **$425-$450**, 20/21B: **$215-$235**; "Empire Strikes Back": **$125-$150**; "Return of the Jedi": **$65-$70**; MLC: **$12-$15**

Sand Person/Tusken Raider: MOC: "Star Wars" 12B: **$225**, 20/21B: **$135**; "Empire Strikes Back": **$95**; "Return of the Jedi" standard: **$65**, hollow cheek tubes: **$135-$150+**; MLC: hollow cheek tubes: **$65**, standard release: **$15**

767

TOOLS

TOOL COLLECTING IS nearly as old as tools themselves. Certainly it was not long after Stone Age man used his first stone tool that he started watching for that special rock or piece of bone. Soon he would have been putting tools away just for the right time or project. The first tool collector was born!

Since earliest man started collecting tools just for the right time or project, many other reasons to collect have evolved. As man created one tool, he could then use that tool to make an even better tool.

Very quickly toolmakers became extremely skilled at their craft, and that created a new collecting area – collecting the works of the very best makers. In time toolmakers realized that tools were being purchased on the bases of the quality of workmanship alone. With this realization an even more advanced collector was born as toolmakers began making top-of-the-line tools from special materials with fine detailing and engraving. These exquisite tools were never intended for use but were to be enjoyed and collected. Many of the finest tools were of such quality that they are considered works of art.

So many tools exist in today's world that many tool collectors focus on one special category. Some of the most popular categories to collect fall into the general areas of: function, craft or trade, personal connection, company or brand, patents, and investments.

For more information on tools, see *Antique Trader Tools Price Guide* by Clarence Blanchard.

◄ Carved walnut tool carrier, early 19th century, 11" h. x 31-1/2" w. **$246**

Courtesy of Pook & Pook, Inc.

Chandler & Barber maple adjustable work bench, Boston, metal label, 33" h. x 42" l. x 24" d. **$790**

Courtesy of Skinner, Inc.; www.skinnerinc.com

Walt Disney Mickey Mouse toy tool chest marked "Walt Disney Enterprises," 11-1/2" l. **$180**

Courtesy of Morphy Auctions

Antique jade tool, China,
8-1/4" l. **$303**

Courtesy of Essex Auction and Estate Services

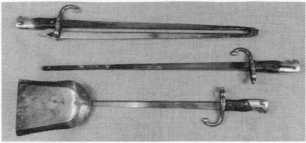

Three French bayonets converted into fireplace tools,
19th century. **$154**

Courtesy of Pook & Pook, Inc.

Painted pine tool chest, late
19th century, original yellow-
grained surface, 19-3/4" h. x
34" w. **$370**

Courtesy of Pook & Pook, Inc.

▲ Thos. Ibbotson & Co
woodworking plane, 18" l... **$170**

Courtesy of Ewbank's

◄ Antique wooden
machinist tool cabinet, eight
drawers of varying size, each
lined with felt, 9" x 20-1/2"
x 12-1/2" h................... **$100**

Courtesy of North American Auction Co.

Primitive pleating tool by T.
Leavitt, Boston. **$70**

Courtesy of Hamilton's Auction Gallery

Ten sewing tools, ivory sewing
clamp, carved ivory and ivory-
type needle, thimble and
thread cases, one umbrella
with 1851 World Expo "Crystal
Palace" Stanhope in handle,
4-1/2" l. **$420**

Courtesy of Rich Penn Auctions

▶ Native American ice hatchet/ice pick, stamped
"George Washington's Warranted Cast Steel Empire
Port Forge Co.," 14-3/4" l. **$150**

Courtesy of Rich Penn Auctions

Early farrier's tools, 19th to early 20th century, seven period tools including rasp, tongs, and others, mounted for carrying on horse, embossed mark on leather "US Fifth Cav-Lt.," 19" l. **$420**

Courtesy of Morphy Auctions

Tool possibly used to smash beer and whiskey kegs during Prohibition, 20" l. **$90**

Courtesy of Morphy Auctions

Countertop cardboard stand-up tool display filled with Mephisto tools, 12-3/8" l. **$120**

Courtesy of Morphy Auctions

Templeton cheese cutter in display case, manufactured by Computing Scale Co. of Dayton, Ohio, marked "Dunn Mfg. By The Anderson Tool Co.," plate on cutter marked "The Computing Scale Co. Dayton, OH Pat. 1543 circa 1902," 12" x 22-1/2" x 27-1/2"..... **$270**

Courtesy of Morphy Auctions

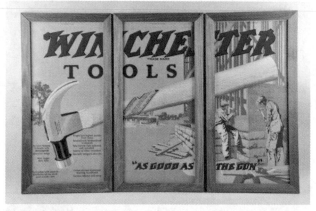

Winchester Tools three-panel framed poster, two-sided, each panel 43-1/4" x 21-3/4"... **$600**

Courtesy of Morphy Auctions

Two wrought iron hearth tools: Gridiron with shaped handle and heart cut-out, and toaster with arch supports, both in good condition, 20-1/4" and 15". **$60**

Courtesy of Conestoga Auction Co.

Early miter trimmer on wood base, 24" x 9" x 4". **$72**

Courtesy of Concord Auction Center

INSIDE INTEL

with

LYNN DOWD

Lifelong tool collector and owner of Dowd Antique & Vintage Tools, *dowdstools.com*

BEST ADVICE: There seem to be three schools of thought when it comes to cleaning tools. Some people like to make the tool look brand new; some like to remove just the surface rust; and some like to keep them as dirty and rusty as they found [them]. I'm in the middle camp: I remove the loose surface rust and use a nice paste wax to preserve the patina and prevent future rust.

HOT OR NOT: Pre-World War II Stanley tools, especially in the original box, are still good sellers. Tools seem to have regional popularity – what sells well in one area may have less appeal in other parts of the country and vice versa. I do well with woodworking hand planes as many collectors who are in denial will buy them "to use," and there is a strong market for good used hand planes, as well as other woodworking tools. More ornate and unusual tools of the 18th and 19th century, especially tools with a limited production run and in excellent condition, have a strong following.

American Stanley 604 woodworking plane, circa 1911, 9" base with "No 604, Bedrock" on front and "Made in USA, U.S patent Apr-19-10," 9-1/2" l. **$110**

Courtesy of Dickins Auctioneers

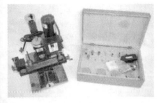

Sherline 5400 clock gear cutter and tools, used, working machine with box of assorted parts and accessories. **$775**

Courtesy of Tom Harris Auctions

Tooled brass bed warmer, 19th century, English, hardwood handle, 32" x 14" x 7". **$61**

Courtesy of Flannery's Auction & Estate Services

Brass and steel rounding-up tool, Switzerland, last half 19th century, used for final shaping of watch wheel teeth, 15-1/2" l................ **$800**

Courtesy of Skinner, Inc.; www.skinnerinc.com

▲ Two woodworking tools: Folding carpenter ruler and "keyhole" hand saw, once owned and used by Thomas McCauley, carpenter and cabinetmaker at Harland and Wolff Shipyard in Belfast, Ireland, during construction of famous Titanic and Olympic ships. **$1,800**

Courtesy of RR Auction

Child-size workbench with 14 woodworking tools, including marking gauges, brass-clad rulers, bevels, and spoke shaves, bench 23" x 26" x 16"................................. **$1,020**

Courtesy of Brunk Auctions

Vibrator tool by E. Luthy-Hirt, Bienne, serial No. 6201, used to test balances and springs for accuracy, 4-3/8" h.............. **$220**

Courtesy of Tom Harris Auctions

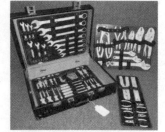

Salesman sample tool display carrying case with printed panels for tools, 19" w. x 15" l. x 6" d................................. **$129**

Courtesy of Meissner's Auction Service

J. Stoll-inscribed woodworking plane, 19th century, "Otto Tool Co. 96" stamped on one end...**$110**

Courtesy of DuMouchelles

K & D staking set, walnut case, case 6" x 7". **$81**

Courtesy of Tom Harris Auctions

▶ Trio of billiard tools: Cue shaft re-surfacer, cue cutter, and tenon cutter, circa late 1800s. **$96**

Courtesy of Rich Penn Auctions

Millers Falls tools block plane, No. 1, with original box. **$25**

Courtesy of Skinner, Inc.; www.skinnerinc.com

Antique J. B. Mast Co. cast iron stamping tool, case bolts to work table, turn wood handle to move dial from letter to letter, 10" x 16"..............................**$84**

Courtesy of Tom Harris Auctions

Framed sign for "Buffalo Forge Co. Forges, Blowers and Blacksmith Tools," colored lithograph on trimmed and laminated paper, 25" x 14-1/2". **$300**

Courtesy of Rich Penn Auctions

Buddy L toy tool chest and tools, wooden chest with original label inside lid, original decoration on outside lid, contents: Buddy L padlock, pliers, saw, and apron, other unrelated tools, nails, and project instructions, case 6-1/2" x 23" x 11-1/2"....... **$330**

Courtesy of Tom Harris Auctions

Brass and cast metal De Paris punch tool, mounts to workbench, turn handle and punch comes down to fitted hole, 6" x 4"........................**$60**

Courtesy of Tom Harris Auctions

John Deere chain splitter, embossed "John Deere" on handle, cast iron with original green paint, three slots for different sized chain, 4-1/2" x 8-1/2"...............................**$48**

Courtesy of Rich Penn Auctions

Slanted glass-front walnut tool display cabinet marked "Union Tool Company, Machinist's Tools of Quality, Orange, Mass., U.S.A.," with metal nameplate and assortment of machinists tools, 24" x 15"................. **$325**

Courtesy of Rich Penn Auctions

Two laboratory tools: 1901 London Clinometer by Stanley London, with polished wood box with brass ID and edging on hinged box top, intact paper label on bottom of box; and microscope, unmarked but complete with swivel magnifying glass in wood box................ **$120**

Courtesy of Rich Penn Auctions

Native American rifleman's small American bag axe with original handle, 15-1/4" l.....................**$210**

Courtesy of Rich Penn Auctions

Billiards level for pool tables, walnut, Stanley Rule & Level Co., New Britain, Connecticut, patented September 1869, 3" h. x 27" l........................**$60**

Courtesy of Rich Penn Auctions

TOYS

IN HIS *PICKER'S POCKET GUIDE: TOYS,* author Eric Bradley says no other hobby touches collectors, and people in general, quite like toys.

Bradley, also the editor of the annual *Antique Trader Antiques & Collectibles Price Guide,* says the people who collect vintage toys are those who are simply revisiting their first collection. In some cases, they never left it. That's the thing about toy collecting: You can find amazing examples in abundant supply from any time period – especially your own.

Sales data shows you'll have lots of company in your toy collecting hobby, but also lots of competition for finer examples. The collectible toy business is one of the largest in both the retail market and the secondary market, and is also perhaps one of the first types of established collecting genres ever defined. It's interesting to note that FAO Schwarz, founded in 1862 as America's first toy store, launched its "Toy Bazaar" antique toy department in the early 1960s to meet collector demand. Toy collecting is an old and venerated hobby, he said.

No figures are kept for the number of vintage collectible toys sold every year, but Bradley said the number sold at auction is growing. At any given time, more than five million toys are for sale or taking bids on eBay. LiveAuctioneers, one of the world's largest auction-hosting websites, shows an estimated half-million toys were sold by brick and mortar auction houses at auction during the last 16 years. In many cases, these sales have set new records as collections finally come to market after decades in private hands, he said.

Among these private collections, Bradley said few reached the size, scope, and value of that owned by Donald Kaufman, whose family founded Kay Bee Toys in 1922, and who decided in 2009 to sell his collection. Kaufman felt collectors would care for the toys better than any museum ever could. It took four auctions to sell the great Kaufman collection of automotive toys for a record $12.1 million. The collection stands as the most valuable of its kind in history.

You don't need to spend $12 million on toys to have an amazing collection. But it certainly helps to bring a fraction of the passion Kaufman brought to his hobby. You probably have a few toys hanging around the house, and it's never been easier to find unusual examples. Adding to them can become addictive, especially when you find ones you had as a kid ... or the ones you always wanted.

Bradley said toy collecting allows for an infinite number of specialized collecting variations. Want cast iron cars made between 1930 and 1940? You could start with the Hubley Manufacturing Co. and collect by size. Only want dolls that were first introduced as paper dolls in the early 1950s? Betsy McCall is your gal. Have an affinity for pre-war metal squirt guns made in Michigan? Versions made by All Metal Products Co., better known as Wyandotte Toys, can be found for $20 on up, depending on condition. With toys,

Snow White Dopey limited edition ceramic pull toy by Brenda White Original Art #1/1, hand-painted and handcrafted, glazed, signed by artist, 14" x 18"..............**$1,434**

Courtesy of Heritage Auctions

1950s Wolverine Coca-Cola tin toy truck, 12" l...**$240**

Courtesy of Morphy Auctions

Cast iron hansom cab drawn by one horse, original driver in rear, no passenger, original horse but possibly not to this toy, 11" l..........................**$210**

Courtesy of Morphy Auctions

Marklin die-cast toy with original box, missing wheel, missing one soldier, with spare tire, 5" l. **$225**

Courtesy of Morphy Auctions

Cast iron large Hubley Royal Circus Wagon, missing animal, driver possibly not original to toy, two horses in front, toy repainted, 16" l.................**$150**

Courtesy of Morphy Auctions

Marx tin litho battery-operated Nutty Mads toy, car with graphics all around, missing one hubcap, remainder of hubcaps with graphics, 9" l.........**$150**

Courtesy of Morphy Auctions

Marx Donald Duck the Skier toy with original box, plastic Donald, tin skis, one ski pole missing, with original wind-up key, 11" h............................**$180**

Courtesy of Morphy Auctions

DC superhero-related memorabilia group (DC, 1960s-1990s): 1985 Batman Pez dispenser, 1966 General Electric Batman/Robin reversible cardboard mask, two circa 1966 Batman coloring books, 1966 "Batman" TV series soundtrack album, 1966 jigsaw puzzle inspired by cover of Detective Comics #259, Superman jigsaw puzzle, 1960s Comic Book Heroes record album, buttons, stickers, toys, and more......................**$74**

Courtesy of Heritage Auctions

your collection can be as specialized or as general as you want it to be.

Bradley said toy values are chiefly influenced by demand, rarity, and condition, but there are other factors as well: authenticity, exposure, provenance, quality, and, most importantly, condition.

Authenticity is black or white. There are no gray areas with authenticity: Either the toy is right or it is wrong. It is either authentic or it is a fake.

Exposure influences demand for a work and brings prestige to its owner. When Steve Geppi, the president and CEO of Diamond Comic Distributors, paid $200,000 for the world's most valuable action figure – the first handcrafted prototype of the 1963 G.I. JOE® action figure – the sale made international news and earned a Guinness World Record. Exposure is crucial for building collector demand around a single piece or an entire category.

Provenance explains an established history of ownership. Once a vintage toy has entered the secondary market it develops a provenance. A famous owner can add 15 percent or more to the value of a toy, but there are exceptions and this changes dramatically depending on who owned the toy in the past. When Leonardo DiCaprio sold part of his action figure collection at Morphy Auctions in 2006, values were stronger than expected, thanks to his famous name.

Quality may be a subjective criterion; however, a well-constructed toy is hard to find and fewer still survive for decades or even centuries. The more time you spend looking at quality toys, the easier it is to recognize good craftsmanship when you see it.

Condition is of the utmost importance in today's collector market. The most valuable items are in original condition with minimal restoration or alterations. This "best or nothing" approach to condition has probably been the most influential change in the hobby during the last decade. Values of toys in mid-range to low condition have fallen while values of rare toys in top condition often skyrocket beyond all expectations.

Set of Peanuts characters: Soft rubber squeaker toy Snoopy with long nose, dated 1958, approximately 7-1/2" h., and hard rubber Charlie Brown, 1960s, no date, 9" h. **$95**

Courtesy of Heritage Auctions

Two carved and painted wooden horse pull toys, America, second half 19th century, larger painted red/brown horse on blue platform with wooden wheels, smaller painted black horse, 14" h. and 9-1/2" h., respectively.................................... **$338**

Courtesy of Skinner Inc.; www.skinnerinc.com

Horse pull toy, two brown horses with manes and black canvas accents on wheeled wooden platform, 13-1/2" h. x 12-1/2" w. x 8-3/4" d. **$738**

Courtesy of Skinner Inc.; www.skinnerinc.com

Carved wood patriotic eagle push toy, 20th century, eagle perched atop wheeled base with flapping wing mechanism, 20-1/4" h. x 22" w. x 31" d. **$3,321**

Courtesy of Skinner Inc.; www.skinnerinc.com

◄ Badge premium, Superman, 1949, Fo-Lee Gum Corp., Philadelphia, die-cut shield badge with classic enamel paint image of Superman from waist up breaking chest chains with his name in text at bottom coming out of circular border with enamel paint stars surrounded by brass luster burst design, 1-5/8" h. **$4,807**

Courtesy of Hake's Americana & Collectibles

▲ Ring premium of Clarabell the Clown character from "Howdy Doody," one of five known to exist, issued circa 1950 by Palmolive, with two images of Clarabell with elaborate collar and brass loop to hold battery with same maker's name "Brownie Mfg. Co." and "Pat. No. 2,516,180." **$4,174**

Courtesy of Hake's Americana & Collectibles

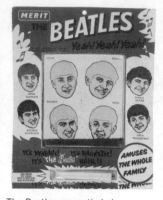

The Beatles magnetic hair game with wand by Merit (UK NEMS, 1964), heavyweight card with hairless images of Beatles inside hard plastic cover full of black magnetic shavings that can be moved into place using "magnetic pencil," 8" x 10-1/2". **$938**

Courtesy of Heritage Auctions

Kingsbury blue-painted pressed steel Parcel Delivery van, circa 1920s, with mesh sides, red disc wheels, white rubber tires stamped "Kingsbury Toys Pat'd," clockwork mechanism, and polychrome-painted driver, 10" l. **$615**

Courtesy of Skinner Inc.; www.skinnerinc.com

◄ Lionel prewar O gauge 2226W tender... **$2,400**

Courtesy of Stout Auctions

Large collection of toy figures, primarily World War I soldiers and nurses, along with cowboys, knights, Revolutionary War soldiers, 19th century uniformed figures, cannons, and other items........... **$984**

Courtesy of Skinner Inc., www.skinnerinc.com

June Bug limited edition ceramic pull toy by Brenda White Original Art #1/1, one-of-a-kind hand-painted and handcrafted, glazed ceramic toy, signed by artist, 14" x 16"; June Bug is in 1932 Walt Disney Silly Symphony short titled "Bugs in Love." **$956**

Courtesy of Heritage Auctions

Strauss tin lithographed wind-up Santee Claus toy with Santa Claus in holly-covered and genre scene-decorated sleigh pulled by two reindeer with jingle bells, with partial original box, 11" l............. **$800**

Courtesy of Skinner Inc.; www.skinnerinc.com

Lone Ranger tin-over-cardboard target practice board used with rubber-tipped suction-cup spring-loaded dart toy gun, with original box, 6" w. x 27" h. **$42**

Courtesy of Heritage Auctions

Six vintage mohair teddy bears and toys, no labels or tags, including Steiff-type standing bear cub and "bear boy" of child in teddy bear outfit, 5" to 20" h. **$2,460**

Courtesy of Skinner Inc.; www.skinnerinc.com

Two cast iron toy cap guns, America, late 19th century, Lightning Express and Sambo, 5" and 4-1/2" l.............**$492**

Courtesy of Skinner Inc.; www.skinnerinc.com

Painted sheet and cast iron Hill Climber fire pumper toy, Germany, late 19th century, painted white overall with gold water reservoir, green striping, light blue running boards, and cast iron driver painted blue with red helmet, paint loss, dirty overall, 7" h. x 14-1/4" l. **$431**

Courtesy of Skinner Inc.; www.skinnerinc.com

◀ Home video game console, Coleco Vision, 1982, with accessories and Donkey Kong cartridge game, mint in box condition. ....**$300-$500**

Courtesy of eBay

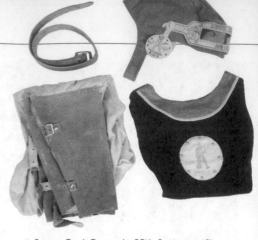

▲ Scarce Buck Rogers in 25th Century outfit, marked John Dille Co., 1934, by Sackman Bros., New York City, size 10, with rare original box, 14-1/4" l. $3,300

Courtesy of Morphy Auctions

Iron Man action figure, 1974, MEGO, type 1, original box with 25¢ price tag, mint in box condition, 8" h. .... $200-$250

Courtesy of Hake's Americana & Collectibles

▶ Nintendo Game Boy released in 1989 with monochromatic body and stereo sound, early versions trade for **$10-$50**, depending on accessories.

Courtesy of Nintendo

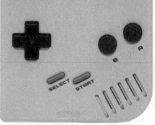

▲ Space toys, circa 1930s: Flash Gordon rocket ship, Flash with ray gun in open cockpit, and Tom Corbett rocket ship, both toys create rocket sound and a flint in rear causes sparks to fly out, 12" l. .... **$592 set**

Courtesy of James D. Julia Auctioneers, Fairfield, Maine, www.jamesdjulia.com

◀ Carved and painted articulated dancing man toy, America, late 19th century, painted facial features and red boots, "dances" on platform, 7" h., platform 9-1/2" l. .. **$1,046**

Courtesy of Skinner Inc.; www.skinnerinc.com

▲ Locomotive, Schoenner, Germany, Gauge 5, early boxed set, mostly nickeled overall, red painted spoke wheels, together with tin coach with steps and bench seating, 7" l. **$2,778**

Courtesy of Stout Auctions

WATCHES

COLLECTING TIMEPIECES IS not a new fad, but one enjoyed by men and women, the young and old alike. Essentially, there is something for everyone. Whether you collect by maker, by style, or by the type of movement, you can find watches to fit any budget.

Most everyone has a watch. They were given as graduation gifts from high school or college, something that was handed down to you from a family member, or potentially a gift received from a company you work for. By collecting watches, not only do you have a fun collectible, but one that also has function.

Over the last 100+ years, millions of watches have been produced. Some were made for the masses, others made in very small quantities for a select few. There are dealers that specialize in watches, but timepieces can also be found at flea markets, garage sales, auctions, on the Internet, and at antique shops. Collecting creates an opportunity for you to have a watch for every occasion. You can have a watch to wear to work, one when out on the town, another one to use while participating in sports, and finally, an everyday watch.

The values placed on the watches illustrated in this section are market value, representing what they have recently sold for privately or at auction. Values can fluctuate due to numerous variables. How a watch is sold, where it is sold, and its condition all play a big role in the value. The Internet has helped collectors identify watches worn by their favorite celebrities, worn on the moon, in a car race, in their favorite action film, etc.

One of the not-so-positive aspects of Internet collecting is the sheer volume of reproductions out there posing as authentic watches. They turn up everywhere, with links to professionally designed websites offering the best of the best for a discount, or up for bid on an Internet auction. You must keep in mind the old saying, "If it looks too good to be true, it probably is."

For more information on watches, see *Warman's Watches Field Guide* by Reyne Haines.

Swiss massive 18k rose gold minute repeating hunters case pocket watch, circa 1900; case: 18k rose gold, four body, 59mm, plain back, front with ornate applied overlay monogram, gold cuvette, gold slide for repeat; dial: white enamel, black Arabic numerals, outer minute track with five minute numerals, gold Louis XV hands, sub seconds; movement: nickel bridge movement with straight line lever escapement, bi-metallic compensated balance with Breguet spring, 27 jewels, wolf's tooth winding, jeweled to hammers; cuvette signed "Medaille D' Or Paris 1900, Repetition Minutes, Premier Qualite, Fabricado Expresamente Para Nicolas G. Grezzi." **$5,625**

Courtesy of Heritage Auctions

Nathaniel Barrow pocket watch, circa 1690, tortoiseshell outer case, circa 1800, tulip and baluster pillars, blued steel work, early 19th century white dial, single hand, spring barrel pierced and engraved, verge escapement, bell strikes on hour............... **$1,900**

Courtesy of Cowan's Auctions

▶ Rockford gold 21 jewel railroad grade 18 size hunters case pocket watch, circa 1904; case: 14k gold, four body, gold cuvette, 18 size, 55mm, vermicelli on rim, outer edge with circle motifs, large flowers and leaves, dog's head on back cover at center; dial: double-sunk enamel, Arabic hour numerals, red five minutes, sub seconds, blue spade hands; movement: No. 542860, nickel full plate, 21 jewels, adjusted, recessed balance wheel, gold lettering, marked RG (railroad grade), checkerboard and wavy line damaskeening; signed Rockford RG and 805 grade number on movement. **$1,688**

Courtesy of Heritage Auctions

◀ Early E. Howard Series 3 pocket watch; case: ore silver, "N" size, single hinged plain back; dial: enamel, Roman, spade hands; movement: 15 jewel, gilt, 3/4 plate, Mershon's Paten April 26, 1859, number 8101; signed: E. Howard & Co. Boston, two scratches on crystal, re-case shows some wear, movement running. **$425**

Courtesy of Heritage Auctions

▶ Jean Étienne Piot Geneva multicolor gold and turquoise verge fusee pocket watch, circa 1795; case: 18k gold, engine-turned, 40mm, bezel and back with raised multicolor flowers and leaves, turquoise stones around edges and central raised bird and torch medallion; dial: engine-turned gold, Roman chapters, blued steel Breguet moon hands; movement: gilt full plate, No. 9348, cylindrical pillars, verge, pierced and engraved two-footed balance cock, silver disc regulator, polished steel end cap on balance.......... **$1,000**

Courtesy of Heritage Auctions

Cortebert wristwatch, circa 1950s; case: 18k rose gold, three body, fluted lugs, 36mm; dial: silver, rose Arabic numerals and feuille hands, sub seconds; movement: caliber 677, rose finish, 17 jewels, manual wind, straight line lever escapement. **$813**

Courtesy of Heritage Auctions

Hamilton Piping Rock 14k gold wristwatch, circa 1937; case: 14k yellow gold, three body, 41mm x 28mm, hinged lugs, black enameled bezel with gold Roman numerals; dial: silver, black minute track, blued steel epee hands; movement: grade 979-Г, No. 2921026, 19 jewels, adjusted, straight line damaskeening; triple signed Hamilton....**$1,063**

Courtesy of Heritage Auctions

Haas Neveux & Cie Rare tri-color gold jump hour wristwatch, circa 1925; case: two body, hinged white gold back, wire lugs, 26mm, Art Deco rose, yellow, and white gold design on front cover, apertures for hours and minutes; dial: white discs with black Arabic numerals; movement: No. 71168, nickel bridge, straight line lever escapement, bi-metallic componented balance, 18 jewels, stamped twice with Geneva quality hallmarks; lizard band, movement and case signed Haas Neveux Cie. **$5,000**

Courtesy of Heritage Auctions

Hamilton Pacer electric wristwatch, circa 1957; case: white and yellow gold-filled, two body, 45mm x 32mm; dial: black, applied gold arrow markers and Arabic numerals, gold Dauphine hands; movement: grade 500, electric, adjusted; leather band, signed Hamilton, with original box showing retail tag of $110. .... **$1,188**

Courtesy of Heritage Auctions

Minerva Large "Regulateur" wristwatch, circa 1915; case: .800 silver, double-hinged back, striped design on back with initial crest, 49.5mm, gilt finish on edges; dial: black with hand-painted yellow minute track and five minute numerals, offset seconds at nine, hour dial at top, painted silver hands with red tips; movement: gilt, three-finger bridge, straight line lever escapement, 15 jewels; leather band, signed Minerva on dial, "Remontoir" on cuvette............**$1,063**

Courtesy of Heritage Auctions

LeCoultre wristwatch, circa 1940s; case: 14k rose gold, two body, 40mm x 20mm, curved back, sloping hooded lugs; dial: rose, applied gold dart indexes, outer minute track, sub seconds, gold Dauphine hands; movement: No. 137164, rectangular, rhodium finish, 17 jewels, straight line lever, monometallic balance with gold screws; lizard band, triple signed LeCoultre..............$1,375

Courtesy of Heritage Auctions

Omega gold wristwatch, triple calendar with moon phases, circa 1950s; case: 14k yellow gold, three body, 35mm, snap back, down-turned teardrop lugs; dial: silver, applied gold dart and baton indexes, gold Dauphine hands, outer blue date numerals, sub seconds, apertures for days of week, months and moon phase; movement: caliber 381, rose finish, 3/4 plate, 17 jewels, straight line lever escapement, shock absorber; band: Omega signed leather with plated stainless buckle; all signed Omega, with original guarantee of origin papers, service transport case.......$3,750

Courtesy of Heritage Auctions

Patek Philippe Ref. 2589 fine yellow gold wristwatch, circa 1959; case: No. 2602168, three body, 18k yellow gold, inscribed snap on back, 33mm, curved downturned lugs; dial: golden, applied yellow gold bar indexes, pointed gold baton hands; movement: No. 781260, caliber 23-300, rhodium finish, straight line lever escapement, 18 jewels, Gyromax balance adjusted to heat, cold, isochronism and five positions, stamped twice with Geneva quality hallmark; triple signed Patek Philippe Geneve...$6,250

Courtesy of Heritage Auctions

Patek Philippe Ref. 2507/1 gold wristwatch, circa 1951; case: No. 672301, three body, 18k yellow gold, curved lugs; dial: silver, applied gold indexes and numerals, subsidiary seconds, gold baton hands; movement: No. 957261, rhodium finish, fausses cotes decoration, 18 jewels, Geneva quality hallmark, lever escapement, monometallic balance adjusted for heat, cold, isochronism and five positions, micrometric regulator; lizard band; triple signed Patek Philippe, case back engraved "Wa. Sheaffer II, Fort Madison IA," personal watch of founder's grandson and former president and chairman of Sheaffer Pen Co...$4,063

Courtesy of Heritage Auctions

Patek Philippe & Co. vintage wristwatch, circa 1940; case: 18k rose gold, No. 507215, two body, curved back, 36mm x 20mm; dial: silver, applied rose gold Roman numerals and bar markers, sub seconds, black minute track, pointed rose gold batons; movement: No. 834221, rectangular, stamped twice with Geneva quality hallmarks, 18 jewels, adjusted to heat, cold, isochronism and five positions, straight line lever, micrometric regulator; lizard band, triple signed Patek Philippe & Co. Geneve. $4,063

Courtesy of Heritage Auctions

Rolex Ref. 5512 steel oyster perpetual submariner wristwatch, circa 1967; case: No. 1888611, three body, stainless steel, 40mm, bi-directional rotating bezel, screw back; dial: black luminous indexes and steel skeleton hands, white minute marks; movement: caliber 1570, rhodium finish, 26 jewels, straight line lever, adjusted five positions and temperature; band: 4/69, stainless steel, fold-over links, deployant clasp with flip lock; all signed Rolex. **$6,250**

Courtesy of Heritage Auctions

1972 Rolex Super Bowl VI Championship gold wristwatch presented to Dallas Cowboys football player Bob Lilly, oyster perpetual day date with diamond-studded bezel and hour markers, engraved "Super Bowl VI, R.L." on reverse with Zale jeweler's logo, with handwritten letter of provenance from Lilly. **$10,158**

Courtesy of Heritage Auctions

Rolex rare two-tone gold Prince Brancard wristwatch, circa 1930; case: No. 22604, two body, 14k gold, yellow gold curved back, white gold flared sides, raised white gold ribs between lugs, 44mm x 23mm; dial: rose and white, blue batons, golden Arabic numerals, black minute track; movement: Extra Prima, 15 jewels, Observatory Quality, timed six positions for all climates, lateral lever escapement, bi-metallic compensated balance; triple signed Rolex. **$4,688**

Courtesy of Heritage Auctions

FAR LEFT Rolex rare Ref. 3716 "Empire" yellow gold automatic wristwatch, circa 1943; case: 18k yellow gold, two body, 32mm, screw down back and oyster crown, long straight down-turned lugs, wide bezel; dial: silver, painted Roman numerals and line markers, sub seconds, blued steel baton hands; movement: nickel finish, 19 jewels, straight line lever escapement, monometallic balance, automatic, No. 98052; band: black alligator, plated buckle; triple signed Rolex.....**$8,438**

Courtesy of Heritage Auctions

LEFT Rolex Ref. 3777 wristwatch, circa 1940; case: No. 54619, two body, 18k rose gold, 37mm x 26mm, tapered lugs; dial: two-tone rose, black Roman numerals, sub seconds, black baton hands; movement: chronometer, 18 jewels, timed six positions, ultra prima, manual wind, straight line lever escapement; triple signed Rolex. **$2,000**

Courtesy of Heritage Auctions

WATCHES

Universal Geneve gold Tri-Compax, circa 1940s; case: 14k gold, three body, concave lugs, inclined bezel, snap on back, 35mm, rectangular push buttons; dial: silver, applied gold baton indexes, gold Dauphine hands, apertures for date, days and months, moon phase at 12, subsidiary dials for seconds, 30 minute and 12 hour registers; movement: caliber 481, nickel finish, straight line lever escapement, 17 jewels, monometallic balance, index regulator; triple signed Universal Geneve... **$2,750**

Courtesy of Heritage Auctions

Vacheron Constantin early gold wristwatch, circa 1918; case: three body, 18k yellow gold, 31mm, No. 232401, straight teardrop-shaped lugs; dial: silver, radial luminous Arabic numerals, black minute track, sub seconds, luminous skeleton hands; movement: No. 378398, gilt finish, straight line lever escapement, 16 jewels, five adjustments; crocodile band; dial and movement signed Vacheron & Constantin Geneve. **$1,625**

Courtesy of Heritage Auctions

Women's Patek Philippe platinum, enamel and diamond wristwatch for Tiffany & Co., circa 1912; case: No. 270460, three body, platinum back with engraving, 24mm, platinum center, gold bezel with blue guilloche enamel, hinged pierced lug frames with rose-cut diamonds; dial: white enamel, Arabic numerals, blue spade hands; movement: No. 161861, nickel bridge, 18 jewels, eight adjustments, straight line lever escapement; band: 14k white gold expansion links, 6" to 6-1/4", case and movement signed Patek Philippe & Co., dial signed Tiffany........................**$9,375**

Courtesy of Heritage Auctions

▼ Waltham early sterling American wristwatch, circa 1915; case: sterling, cushion shape with down-turned lugs, 32mm, back engraved "Chaplain L. D. Williams, Cleveland O. USA"; dial: enamel, Arabic with red fives, skeleton spade hands; movement: nickel, 3/4 plate, 7 jewels.............. **$194**

Courtesy of Heritage Auctions

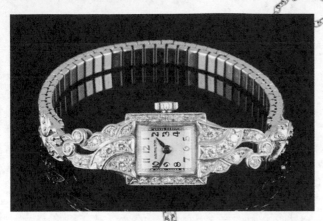

Women's platinum Hamilton watch, circa 1940s, approximately .55 troy oz., 10 DWT TW, excluding movement................................... **$700**

Courtesy of Kaminski Auctions

Women's Vulcain 14k yellow gold watch with six diamonds on either side of the face, circa 1930s, estimated .25CTW, approximately 1.4 oz. **$650**

Courtesy of Kaminski Auctions

Women's Royce lavalier pendant watch, 14k yellow gold, 17 jewels, 11.3 dwt., excellent working condition................. **$225**

Courtesy of Morphy Auctions

▶ Longines gold and enamel pendant watch with chain, circa 1910; case: 28mm, three body, 14k gold, blue and white enameled rim and bezel, back with guilloche blue and silver enameled sunray and swirl motif, with matching gold, pearl and enamel 25" neck chain; dial: golden, black Arabic numerals, black minute track, moon hands; movement: nickel bridge, 15 jewels, adjusted three positions, straight line lever escapement................................ **$813**

Courtesy of Heritage Auctions

▲ Women's Rolex white gold and diamond wristwatch, circa 1950s; case: 14k white gold, 15mm, diamond set lugs; dial: silver, faceted baton indexes, black baton hands; movement: caliber 1400, 18 jewels, manual wind; triple signed Rolex... **$1,000**

Courtesy of Heritage Auctions

top lot

Art Deco Patek Philippe enamel and diamond lapel watch, circa 1925; case: black Japanese enamel motif, green enamel, small jade cabochon, accented by rose-cut diamonds, black stone crown, 18k yellow gold platinum trim, inside marked PP&C Geneva seal, #300426, Swiss quality gold mark; dial: stamped Patek Philippe, silvered, black Arabic numerals (refinished); movement: Patek Philippe 18 jewel manual wind, #200426, eight adjustments; 3" l., signed on movement, case and dial Patek Philippe..$30,000

WORLD WAR II COLLECTIBLES

DURING THE SEVEN decades since the end of World War II, veterans, collectors, and nostalgia-seekers have eagerly bought, sold, and traded the "spoils of war." Actually, souvenir collecting began as soon as troops set foot on foreign soil. Whether Tommies from Great Britain, Doughboys from the United States, or Fritzies from Germany, soldiers eagerly looked for trinkets and remembrances that would guarantee their place in the historic events that unfolded before them. Helmets, medals, firearms, field gear, daggers, and other pieces of war material filled parcels and duffel bags on the way back home.

As soon as hostilities ended in 1945, the populations of defeated Germany and Japan quickly realized they could make money selling souvenirs to the occupation forces. The flow of war material increased. Values became well established.

Over the years these values have remained proportionally consistent, and though values have increased dramatically, demand has not dropped off a bit. In fact, World War II collecting is the largest segment of the militaria hobby.

Surprisingly, the values of items have been a closely guarded secret. Unfortunately, the hobby has relied on paying veterans and their families far less than a military relic is worth with the hope of selling later for a substantial profit. This attitude has given the hobby a bad reputation.

The advent of the Internet, though, significantly leveled the playing field for sellers and buyers. No longer does a person have to blindly offer a relic for sale to a collector or dealer. Simply logging onto one of several Internet auctions will give the uninitiated an idea of value.

But a little information can be dangerous. The value of military items resides in variation. Whether it is a difference in manufacturing technique, material, or markings, the nuances of an item will determine the true value. Don't expect 20 minutes on the Internet – or even glancing through this section – to teach you these nuances. Collectors are a devoted bunch. They have spent years and hundreds, if not thousands, of dollars to establish the knowledge base that enables them to navigate through the hobby.

For more information on World War II collectibles, see *Warman's World War II Collectibles,* 3rd edition, by John Adams-Graf.

Japanese Army tanker's jacket. ... **$375-$425**
Courtesy of AdvanceGuardMilitaria.com

CLOTHING

British RAF No 8 Group Pathfinder Force flying officer uniform, air gunner. ....**$425-$495**

Courtesy of AdvanceGuardMilitaria.com

German Waffenrock for captain of Panzer Grenadiers. ....**$2,500-$3,000**

Courtesy of Hermann-Historica.de

German Luftwaffe leather trousers for fighter pilots. ....**$3,500-$5,000**

Courtesy of Hermann-Historica.de

U.S. AAF 5th Air Force officer's embroidered M41 field jacket. ....**$1,400-$1,600**

Courtesy of AdvanceGuardMilitaria.com

USMC baseball uniform...**$300-$365**

Courtesy of AdvanceGuardMilitaria.com

U.S. navy blue denim "dungarees" trousers. .**$245-$325**

Courtesy of AdvanceGuardMilitaria.com

HEADGEAR

British RAF commissioned
officers of air rank visor cap.
..................................$225-$265

Courtesy of AdvanceGuardMilitaria.com

German M40 helmet
camouflaged with sand-colored
paint. **$5,000**

Courtesy of Hermann-Historica.de

German Army M18 double-decal helmet. **$2,000**

Courtesy of Hermann-Historica.de

"Blitzkrieg" 1940 pilot's
helmet and goggles.....**$385-$465**

Courtesy of AdvanceGuardMilitaria.com

▲ German SS camouflage
cover for steel helmet, oak leaf
pattern. .... **$4,000-$5,000**

Courtesy of Hermann-Historica.de

▶ Japanese Naval Landing Force
helmet, cover and net. **$1,600**

Courtesy of HistoryHunter.com

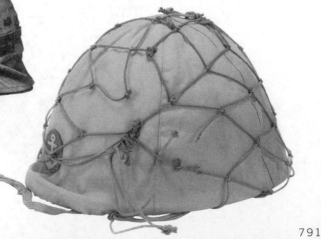

German Waffen SS
officer's visor cap,
Cavalry............ **$16,000-$19,000**

Courtesy of HistoryHunter.com

German glider pilot's protective
helmet................. **$4,000-$5,000**

Courtesy of Hermann-Historica.de

Italian Divisional General's visor
cap. .... **$1,100-$1,450**

Courtesy of Hermann-Historica.de

RAF flying helmet,
Type D. ....**$300-$350**

Courtesy of AdvanceGuardMilitaria.com

Soviet Model 1922 budenovka,
Summer Pattern. ....**$465-$600**

Courtesy of AdvanceGuardMilitaria.com

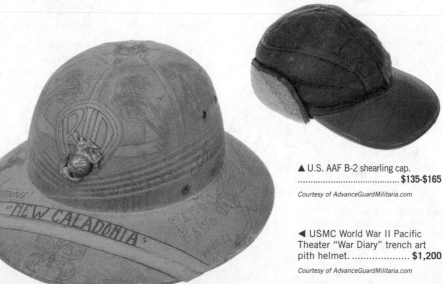

▲ U.S. AAF B-2 shearling cap.
.... **$135-$165**

Courtesy of AdvanceGuardMilitaria.com

◄ USMC World War II Pacific
Theater "War Diary" trench art
pith helmet. **$1,200**

Courtesy of AdvanceGuardMilitaria.com

ACCOUTREMENTS

British early war gas mask...**$100-$130**

Courtesy of AdvanceGuardMilitaria.com

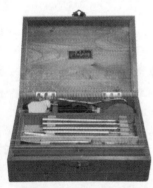

Japanese dental kit captured on Guadalcanal. **$1,075**

Courtesy of Heritage Auctions

Japanese Navy pilot's goggles with "Man" maker's logo.
...................................**$300-$345**

Courtesy of AdvanceGuardMilitaria.com

German Wehrmacht 18-liter drinking water backpack container. ....**$100-$135**

Courtesy of AdvanceGuardMilitaria.com

German field radio "Feldfu. b1." ....**$950-$1,200**

U.S. submachine gun ammunition magazine carrier with shoulder strap. ....**$125-$145**

Courtesy of AdvanceGuardMilitaria.com

▶ USMC camouflage shelter half. ....**$265-$325**

Courtesy of AdvanceGuardMilitaria.com

German Custom Services officer's brocade belt. .... **$1,500-$2,500**

German Kriegsmarine sextant.
.... **$950-$1,200**

USAAF 5th Air Force NCO's painted B-4 suitcase...........**$185**

Courtesy of AdvanceGuardMilitaria.com

SPECIAL CONTRIBUTORS
AND ADVISORS

The following collectors, dealers, sellers, and researchers have supported the **Antique Trader Antiques & Collectibles Price Guide** with their pricing and contacts for nearly 30 years. Many continue to serve as a valuable resource to the entire collecting hobby, while others have passed away. We honor all contributors past and present as their hard work and passion lives on through this book.

Andre Ammelounx

Mannie Banner

Ellen Bercovici

Sandra Bondhus

James R. and Carol S. Boshears

Bobbie Zucker Bryson

Emmett Butler

Dana Cain

Linda D. Carannante

David Chartier

Les and Irene Cohen

Amphora Collectors International

Marion Cohen

Neva Colbert

Marie Compton

Susan N. Cox

Caroline Torem-Craig

Leonard Davis

Bev Dieringer

Janice Dodson

Del E. Domke

Debby DuBay

Susan Eberman

Joan M. George

Roselyn Gerson

William A. and Donna J. Gray

Pam Green

Linda Guffey

Carl Heck

Alma Hillman

K. Robert and Bonne L. Hohl

Ellen R. Hill

Joan Hull

Hull Pottery Association

Louise Irvine

Helen and Bob Jones

Mary Ann Johnston

Donald-Brian Johnson

Dorothy Kamm

Edwin E. Kellogg

Madeleine Kirsh

Vivian Kromer

Curt Leiser

Gene Loveland

Mary McCaslin

Pat Moore

Reg G. Morris

Craig Nissen

Joan C. Oates

Margaret Payne

Gail Peck

John Petzold

Dr. Leslie Piña

Joseph Porcelli

Arlene Rabin

John Rader, Sr.

Betty June Wymer

LuAnn Riggs

Tim and Jamie Saloff

Federico Santi

Peggy Sebek

Steve Stone

Phillip Sullivan

Mark and Ellen Supnick

Tim Trapani

Jim Trautman

Elaine Westover

Kathryn Wiese

Laurie Williams

Nancy Wolfe

CONTRIBUTORS BY SUBJECT

Advertising Items: Kristine Manty

Barbie: Steve Evans

Bottles: Michael Polak

Clocks: Kristine Manty/Donald-Brian Johnson

Coins and Currency: Eric Bradley/Arlyn G. Sieber

Country Store: Donald-Brian Johnson/
Antoinette Rahn

Disney Collectibles: Tom Bartsch

Fine Art: Eric Bradley

Hunting and Fishing Collectibles: Eric Bradley

Kitchenwares (vintage): Chriss Swaney

Electric Lighting: Joseph Porcelli/Tom Bartsch

Early Lighting: Donald-Brian Johnson

Luxury Goods: Antoinette Rahn

Records: Pat Prince

Salesman Samples: Antoinette Rahn

Souvenirs and Travel Collectibles: Eric Bradley

Sports: Tom Bartsch

Vintage Clothing: Nancy Wolfe and
Madeleine Kirsh

World War II: John Adams-Graf

CERAMICS

Amphora-Teplitz: Les and Irene Cohen

Belleek (American): Peggy Sebek

Belleek (Irish): Del Domke

Blue & White Pottery: Steve Stone

Buffalo Pottery: Phillip Sullivan

Doulton/Royal Doulton: Reg Morris, Louise Irvine
and Ed Pascoe

Fulper Pottery: Karen Knapstein

Gouda: Antoinette Rahn

Haeger: Donald-Brian Johnson

Ironstone: General - Bev Dieringer; Tea Leaf –
The Tea Leaf Club International

Limoges: Karen Knapstein

Majolica: Michael Strawser

McCoy: Craig Nissen

Mettlach: Andre Ammelounx

Overbeck: Karen Knapstein

Red Wing: Gail Peck

R.S. Prussia: Mary McCaslin

Satsuma: Melody Amsel-Arieli

Stoneware and Spongeware: Bruce and
Vicki Waasdorp

Sumida Gawa: Karen Knapstein

Zsolnay: Federico Santi/John Gacher

GLASS

Animals: Helen and Bob Jones

Carnival Glass: Jim and Jan Seeck

Crackle Glass: Donald-Brian Johnson

Depression Glass: Ellen Schroy

Fenton: Helen and Bob Jones/Mark F. Moran

Fire King: Karen Knapstein

Higgins Glass: Donald-Brian Johnson

Opalescent Glass: James Measell

Phoenix Glass: Helen and Bob Jones

Sugar Shakers: Scott Beale/Karen Knapstein

Wall Pocket Vases: Bobbie Zucker Bryson

PRICING, IDENTIFICATIONS, AND IMAGES PROVIDED BY:

LIVE AUCTION PROVIDERS

AuctionZip
113 West Pitt St., Suite C
Bedford, PA 15522
(814) 623-5059
www.auctionzip.com

Artfact, LLC
38 Everett St., Suite 101
Allston, MA 02134
(617) 746-9800
www.artfact.com

LiveAuctioneers, LLC
2nd Floor
220 12th Ave.
New York, NY 10001
www.liveauctioneers.com

AUCTION HOUSES

A-1 Auction
2042 N Rio Grande Ave., Suite E
Orlando, FL 32804
(407) 839-0004
http://www.a-1auction.net/

Allard Auctions, Inc.
P.O. Box 1030
St. Ignatius, MT 59865
(406) 745-0500
(800) 314-0343
www.allardauctions.com

American Bottle Auctions
2523 J St., Suite 203
Sacramento, CA 95816
(800) 806-7722
americanbottle.com

American Pottery Auction
Vicki and Bruce Waasdorp
P.O. Box 434
Clarence, NY 14031
(716) 759-2361
www.antiques-stoneware.com

Antique Helper Auction House
2764 East 55th Pl.
Indianapolis, IN 46220
(317) 251-5635
www.antiquehelper.com

Apple Tree Auction Center
1616 West Church St.
Newark, OH 43055-1540
(740) 344-4282
www.appletreeauction.com

Artingstall & Hind Auctioneers
9312 Civic Center Dr., #104
Beverly Hills, CA 90210
(310) 424-5288
www.artingstall.com

Arus Auctions
(617) 669-6170
www.arusauctions.com

ATM Antiques & Auctions, LLC
811 SE US Hwy. 19
Crystal River, FL 34429
(352) 795-2061
(800) 542-3877
www.charliefudge.com

Auction Team Breker
Otto-Hahn-Str. 10
50997 Köln (Godorf), Germany
02236 384340
www.breker.com

Backstage Auctions
448 W. 19th St., Ste. 163
Houston, TX 77008
(713) 862-1200
www.backstageauctions.com

Belhorn Auctions, LLC
2746 Wynnerock Ct.
Hilliard, OH 43026
(614) 921-9441
auctions@belhorn.com
www.belhorn.com
www.potterymarketplace.com

Bertoia Auctions
2141 DeMarco Dr.
Vineland, NJ 08360
(856) 692-1881
www.bertoiaauctions.com

Bonhams
7601 W. Sunset Blvd.
Los Angeles, CA 90046
(323) 850-7500
www.bonhams.com

Brunk Auctions
P.O. Box 2135
Asheville, NC 28802
(828) 254-6846
www.brunkauctions.com

Briggs Auction, Inc.
1347 Naamans Creek Rd.
Garnet Valley, PA 19060
(610) 566-3138 (Office)
(610) 485-0412 (Showroom)
www.briggsauction.com

Bunte Auction Services and Appraisals
755 Church Rd.
Elgin, IL 60123
(847) 214-8423
www.bunteauction.com

Butterscotch Auction Gallery
608 Old Post Rd.
Bedford, NY 10506
(914) 764-4609
www.butterscotchauction.com

Capo Auction
3601 Queens Blvd.
Long Island City, NY 11101
(718) 433-3710
www.capoauctionnyc.com

Charles Miller Ltd.
Suite 6 Imperial Studios
3/11 Imperial Rd.
London, England
SW6 2AG
+44 (0) (207) 806-5530
www.charlesmillerltd.com

Charlton Hall Auctioneers
912 Gervais St.
Columbia, SC 29201
www.charltonhallauctions.com

Cherryland Postcard Auctions
Ronald & Alec Millard
P.O. Box 427
Frankfort, MI 49635
(231) 352-9758
CherrylandPostcards.com

Christie's New York
20 Rockefeller Plaza
New York, NY 10020
www.christies.com

Cincinnati Art Galleries
225 East Sixth St.
Cincinnati, OH 45202
www.cincinnatiartgalleries.com

Clars Auction Gallery
5644 Telegraph Ave.
Oakland, CA 94609
(510) 428-0100
www.clars.com

The Coeur d'Alene Art Auction
8836 North Hess St., Suite B
Hayden, ID 83835
(208) 772-9009
www.cdaartauction.com

John W. Coker, Ltd.
1511 W. Hwy. 11E
New Market, TN 37820
(865) 475-5163
www.antiquesonline.com

Collect Auctions
(888) 463-3063
collectauctions.com

Conestoga Auction Co.
768 Graystone Rd.
Manheim, PA 17545
(717) 898-7284
www.conestogaauction.com

Constantine & Pletcher
1321 Freeport Rd.
Cheswick, PA 15024
(724) 275-7190
Fax: (724) 275-7191
www.cpauction.info

Copake Auction, Inc.
266 Route 7A
Copake, NY 12516
(518) 329-1142
www.copakeauction.com

Cordier Auctions
1500 Paxton St.
Harrisburg, PA 17104
(717) 731-8662
www.cordierantiques.com

Cowan's Auctions
6270 Este Ave.
Cincinnati, OH 45232
(513) 871-1670
www.cowanauctions.com

CRN Auctions, Inc.
57 Bay State Rd.
Cambridge, MA 02138
(617) 661-9582
www.crnauctions.com

Dargate Auction Galleries
326 Munson Ave.
McKees Rocks, PA 15136
(412) 771-8700
Fax: (412) 771-8779
www.dargate.com

Rachel Davis Fine Arts
1301 West 79th St.
Cleveland, OH 44102
(216) 939-1190
www.racheldavisfinearts.com

Decoys Unlimited, Inc.
P.O. Box 206
2320 Main St.
West Barnstable, MA 02668-0206
(508) 362-2766
decoysunlimited.net

DGW Auctioneers & Appraisers
760 Kifer Rd.
Sunnyvale, CA 94086
www.dgwauctioneers.com

Dickins Auctioneers Ltd.
Calvert Rd.
Middle Claydon
Buckingham, England
MK18 2EZ
+44 (129) 671-4434
www.dickinsauctioneers.com

Doyle New York
175 E. 87th St.
New York, NY 10128
(212) 427-2730
www.doylenewyork.com

**Dreweatts &
Bloomsbury Auctions**
24 Maddox St.
London, England W1S 1PP
+44 (207) 495-9494
www.dreweatts.com/

Elite Decorative Arts
1034 Gateway Blvd., #108
Boynton Beach, FL 33426
(561) 200-0893
www.eliteauction.com

Fine Arts Auctions, LLC
324 S. Beverly Dr., #175
Beverly Hills, CA 90212
(310) 990-2150
www.fineartauctionllc.com

Fontaines Auction Gallery
1485 W. Housatonic St.
Pittsfield, MA 01210
www.fontainesauction.net

Forsythes' Auctions, LLC
P.O. Box 188
Russellville, OH 45168
(937) 377-3700
www.forsythesauctions.com

Fox Auctions
P.O. Box 4069
Vallejo, CA 94590
(631) 553-3841
Fax: (707) 643-3000
www.foxauctionsonline.com

Frasher's Doll Auction
2323 S. Mecklin Sch. Rd.
Oak Grove, MO 64075
(816) 625-3786

J. Garrett Auctioneers, Ltd.
1411 Slocum St.
Dallas, TX 75207
(214) 683-6855
www.jgarrettauctioneers.com

Garth's Arts & Antiques
P.O. Box 369
Delaware, OH 43015
(740) 362-4771
www.garths.com

Glass Works Auctions
Box 180
East Greenville, PA 18041
(215) 679-5849
www.glswrk-auction.com

The Golf Auction
209 State St.
Oldsmar, FL 34677
(813) 340-6179
thegolfauction.com

**Great Gatsby's Antiques
and Auctions**
5180 Peachtree Industrial Blvd.
Atlanta, GA 30341
(770) 457-1903
www.greatgatsbys.com

Grogan & Co.
22 Harris St.
Dedham, MA 02026
(781) 461-9500
www.groganco.com

Guyette & Deeter
24718 Beverly Rd.
St. Michaels, MD 21663
(410) 745-0485
Fax: (410) 745-0487
www.guyetteandschmidt.com

GWS Auctions, LLC
41841 Beacon Hill # E
Palm Desert, CA 92211
(760) 610-4175
www.gwsauctions.com

**Ken Farmer Auctions
and Appraisals**
105 Harrison St.
Radford, VA 24141
(540) 639-0939
www.kfauctions.com

**Hake's Americana
& Collectibles**
P.O. Box 12001
York, PA 17402
(717) 434-1600
www.hakes.com

**Hamilton's Antique &
Estate Auctions, Inc.**
505 Puyallup Ave.
Tacoma, WA 98421
(253) 534-4445
www.joe-frank.com

Norman Heckler & Co.
79 Bradford Corner Rd.
Woodstock Valley, CT 06282
www.hecklerauction.com

Heritage Auctions
3500 Maple Ave.
Dallas, TX 75219-3941
(800) 872-6467
www.ha.com

Hess Fine Auctions
1131 4th St. N.
St. Petersburg, FL 33701
(727) 896-0622
www.hessfineauctions.com

Hewlett's Antique Auctions
PO Box 87
13286 Jefferson St.
Le Grand, CA 95333
(209) 389-4542
Fax: (209) 389-0730
http://www.hewlettsauctions.com

Holabird-Kagin Americana
3555 Airway Dr., #308
Reno, NV 89511
(775) 852-8822
www.holabirdamericana.com

Homestead Auctions
3200 Greenwich Rd.
Norton, OH 44203
(330) 807-1445
www.homesteadauction.net

**Bill Hood & Sons Art
& Antique Auctions**
2925 S. Federal Hwy.
Delray Beach, FL 33483
(561) 278-8996
www.hoodauction.com

Humler & Nolan
The Auctions at Rookwood
225 E. Sixth St., 4th Floor
Cincinnati, OH 45202
(513) 381-2041
Fax: (513) 381-2038
www.humlernolan.com

iGavel Auctions
229 E. 120th St.
New York, NY 10035
(212) 289-5588
www.igavelauctions.com

Ivy Auctions
22391 Hwy. 76 E.
Laurens, SC 29360
(864) 682-2750
www.ivyauctions.com

**Jackson's International
Auctioneers & Appraisers**
2229 Lincoln St.
Cedar Falls, IA 50613
jacksonsauction.com

James D. Julia, Inc.
P.O. Box 830
203 Skowhegan Rd.
Fairfield, ME 04937
(207) 453-7125
jamesdjulia.com

Jeffrey S. Evans & Associates
2177 Green Valley Ln.
Mount Crawford, VA 22841
(540) 434-3939
www.jeffreysevans.com

John Moran Auctioneers
735 West Woodbury Rd.
Altadena, CA 91001
(626) 793-1833
www.johnmoran.com

Julien's Auctions
9665 Wilshire Blvd., Suite 150
Beverly Hills, CA 90210
(310) 836-1818
www.juliensauctions.com

Kaminski Auctions
564 Cabot St.
Beverly, MA 01915
(978) 927-2223
Fax: (978) 927-2228
www.kaminskiauctions.com/

Kennedy Auctions Service
160 West Court Ave.
Selmer, TN 38375
(731) 645-5001
www.kennedysauction.com

Lang's Sporting Collectibles
663 Pleasant Valley Rd.
Waterville, NY 13480
(315) 841-4623
www.langsauction.com

Legend Numismatics
P.O. Box 9
Lincroft, NJ 07738
(800) 743-2646
www.legendcoin.com

Legendary Auctions
17542 Chicago Ave.
Lansing, IL 60438
(708) 889-9380
www.legendaryauctions.com

Los Angeles Modern Auctions
16145 Hart St.
Van Nuys, CA 91406
(323) 904-1950
www.lamodern.com

Leslie Hindman Auctioneers
1338 West Lake St.
Chicago, IL 60607
(312) 280-1212
www.lesliehindman.com

**Louis J. Dianni,
LLC Antiques Auctions**
May 1-Oct. 15:
982 Main St., Suite 175
Fishkill, NY 12524
Oct. 20-April 15:
1304 SW 160th Ave., Suite 228A
Sunrise, FL 33326
https://louisjdianni.com

Love of the Game Auctions
P.O. Box 157
Great Meadows, NJ 07838
loveofthegameauctions.com

Manitou Auctions
205 Styer Dairy Rd.
Reidsville, NC 27320
(336) 349-6577
www.manitou-auctions.com

Manor Auctions
2415 N. Monroe St.
Tallahassee, FL 32303
(850) 523-3787
Fax: (850) 523-3786
www.manorauctions.com

Mark Mattox Auctioneer & Real Estate Broker, Inc.
3740 Maysville Rd.
Carlisle, KY 40311
(859) 289-5720
http://mattoxauctions.com/auctions/

Martin J. Donnelly Antique Tools
5523 County Rd. 8
Avoca, NY 14809
(607) 566-2617
www.mjdtools.com

Matt Maring Auction Co.
P.O. Box 37
Kenyon, MN 55946
(507) 789-5227
www.maringauction.com

Material Culture
4700 Wissahickon Ave.
Philadelphia, PA 19144
(215) 849-8030
www.materialculture.com

Matthews Auctions
111 South Oak St.
Nokomis, IL 62075-1337
(215) 563-8880
www.matthewsauctions.com

McLaren Auction Service
21507 Highway 99E
Aurora, OR 97002
(503) 678-2441
www.mclarenauction.com

McMasters-Harris Auction Co.
P.O. Box 755
Cambridge, OH 43725
www.mcmastersharris.com

Michaan's Auctions
2751 Todd St.
Alameda, CA 94501
(510) 740-0220
www.michaans.com

Midwest Auction Galleries
925 North Lapeer Rd.
Oxford, MI 48371
(877) 236-8181 or (248) 236-8100
Fax: (248) 236-8396
www.midwestauctioninc.com

Mile High Card Co.
7200 S. Alton Way, Suite A230
Centennial, CO 80112
(303) 840-2784
www.milehighcardco.com

Milestone Auctions
3860 Ben Hur Ave., Unit 8
Willoughby, OH 44094
(440) 527-8060
www.milestoneauctions.com

Dan Morphy Auctions
2000 N. Reading Rd.
Denver, PA 17517
(717) 335-3435
morphyauctions.com

Mohawk Arms, Inc.
P.O. Box 157
Bouckville, NY 13310
(315) 893-7888
www.militaryrelics.com

Mosby & Co. Auctions
5714-A Industry Ln.
Frederick, MD 21704
(240) 629-8139
www.mosbyauctions.com

Neal Auction Co.
4038 Magazine St.
New Orleans, LA 70115
(504) 899-5329
www.nealauctions.com

Nest Egg Auctions
30 Research Pkwy.
Meriden, CT 06450
(203) 630-1400
www.nesteggauctions.com

New Orleans Auction Gallery
1330 St. Charles Ave.
New Orleans, LA 70130
www.neworleansauction.com

Nico Auctions
4023 Kennett Pike, Suite 248
Greenville, DE 19807
(888) 390-0201
www.nicoauctions.com

Noel Barrett Antiques & Auctions, Ltd.
P.O. Box 300
Carversville, PA 18913
(215) 297 5109
www.noelbarrett.com

North American Auction Co.
78 Wildcat Way
Bozeman, MT 59718
(800) 686-4216
www.northamerican
auctioncompany.com

Northeast Auctions
93 Pleasant St.
Portsmouth, NH 03801
(603) 433-8400
Fax: (603) 433-0415
www.northeastauctions.com

O'Gallerie: Fine Arts, Antiques and Estate Auctions
228 Northeast 7th Ave.
Portland, OR 97232-2909
(503) 238-0202
www.ogallerie.com

Omaha Auction Center
7531 Dodge St.
Omaha, NE 68114
(402) 397-9575
www.omahaauctioncenter.com

Omega Auction Corp.
1669 W. 39th Pl.
Hialeah, FL 33012
(786) 444-4997
www.omegaauctioncorp.com

Pacific Galleries Auction House and Antique Mall
241 South Lander St.
Seattle, WA 98134
(206) 441-9990
Fax: (206) 448-9677
www.pacgal.com

Past Tyme Pleasures
39 California Ave., Suite 105
Pleasanton, CA 94566
www.pasttyme1.com

PBA Galleries
133 Kearny St., 4th Floor
San Francisco, CA 94108
(415) 989-2665
www.pbagalleries.com

Phoebus Auction Gallery
18 East Mellen St.
Hampton, VA 23663
(757) 722-9210
www.phoebusauction.com

Pioneer Auction Gallery
14650 SE Arista Dr.
Portland, OR 97267
(503) 496-0303
www.pioneerantiqueauction.com

Pook & Pook, Inc.
463 East Lancaster Ave.
Downingtown, PA 19335
(610) 269-4040
www.pookandpook.com

Potter & Potter Auctions
3759 N. Ravenswood Ave., #121
Chicago, IL 60613
(773) 472-1442
www.potterauctions.com

Premier Auction Galleries
12587 Chillicothe Rd.
Chesterland, OH 44026
(440) 688-4203
Fax: (440) 688-4202
www.pag4u.com

Don Presley Auction
1319 West Katella Ave.
Orange County, CA 92867
(714) 633-2437
www.donpresley.com

Preston Hall Gallery
2201 Main St., Suite #820
Dallas, TX 75201
(214) 718-8624
www.prestonhallgallery.com

Profiles in History
26901 Agoura Rd., Suite 150
Calabasas Hills, CA 91301
(310) 859-7701
www.profilesinhistory.com

Purcell Auction Gallery
2156 Husband Rd.
Paducah, KY 42003
(270) 444-7599
www.purcellauction.com/

Quinn's Auction Galleries
360 S. Washington St.
Falls Church, VA 22046
(703) 532-5632
www.quinnsauction.com

Rago Arts & Auction Center
333 N. Main St.
Lambertville, NJ 08530
(609) 397-9374
www.ragoarts.com

Red Baron's Antiques
8655 Roswell Rd.
Atlanta, GA 30350
(770) 640-4604
www.rbantiques.com

Richard Opfer Auctioneering, Inc.
1919 Greenspring Dr.
Lutherville-Timonium, MD 21093
(410) 252-5035
www.opferauction.com

Rich Penn Auctions
P.O. Box 1355
Waterloo, IA 50704
(319) 291-6688
www.richpennauctions.com

RM Auctions
One Classic Car Dr.
Blenheium, Ontario
N0P 1A0 Canada
+1 (519) 352-4575
www.rmauctions.com

Robert Edward Auctions
P.O. Box 7256
Watchung, NJ 07069
(908) 226-9900
www.robertedwardauctions.com

Rock Island Auction Co.
7819 42 St. West
Rock Island, IL 61201
(800) 238-8022
www.rockislandauction.com

Roland Auction NY
80 E 11th St.
New York, NY 10003
(212) 260-2000
www.rolandauctions.com

RR Auction
5 Route 101A, Suite 5
Amherst, NH 03031
(603) 732-4280
www.rrauction.com

Saco River Auction Co.
2 Main St.
Biddeford, ME 04005
(207) 602-1504
www.sacoriverauction.com

Scheerer McCulloch Auctioneers
515 E Paulding Rd
Fort Wayne, IN 46816
(260) 441-8636
www.smauctioneers.com

SCP Auctions, Inc.
32451 Golden Lantern, Suite 308
Laguna Niguel, CA 92677
(949) 831-3700
www.SCPauctions.com

Seeck Auction Co.
Jim and Jan Seeck
P.O. Box 377
Mason City, IA 50402
www.seeckauction.com

SeriousToyz
1 Baltic Pl.
Croton on Hudson, NY 10520
(866) 653-8699
www.serioustoyz.com

Showtime Auction Service
22619 Monterey Dr.
Woodhaven, MI 48183-2269
(734) 676-9703
www.showtimeauctions.com

Skinner, Inc.
357 Main St.
Boston, MA 01740
(617) 350-5400
www.skinnerinc.com

Sloans & Kenyon Auctioneers and Appraisers
7034 Wisconsin Ave.
Chevy Chase, MD 20815
(301) 634-2330
www.sloansandkenyon.com

Sotheby's New York
1334 York Ave.
New York, NY 10021
(212) 606-7000
www.sothebys.com

Specialists of the South, Inc.
544 E. Sixth St.
Panama City, FL 32401
(850) 785-2577
www.specialistsofthesouth.com

Stanley Gibbons
399 Strand
London
WC2R 0LX
England
+44 (0)207 836 8444
www.stanleygibbons.com

Carl W. Stinson, Inc.
293 Haverhill St.
Reading, MA 01867
(617) 834-3819
www.stinsonauctions.com

Stefek's Auctioneers & Appraisers
18450 Mack Ave.
Grosse Pointe Farms, MI 48236
(313) 881-1800
www.stefeksltd.com

Stephenson's Auctioneers & Appraisers
1005 Industrial Blvd.
Southampton, PA 18966
(215) 322-6182
www.stephensonsauction.com

Stevens Auction Co.
301 North Meridian St.
Aberdeen, MS 39730-2613
(662) 369-2200
www.stevensauction.com

Strawser Majolica Auctions
P.O. Box 332
Wolcottville, IN 46795
www.strawserauctions.com

Sullivan & Son Auction, LLC
1995 E. County Rd. 650
Carthage, IL 62321
(217) 743-5200
www.sullivanandsonauction.com

Swann Auction Galleries
104 E 25th St., # 6
New York, NY 10010-2999
(212) 254-4710
www.swanngalleries.com

Teel Auction Services
619 FM 2330
Montabla, TX 75853
(903) 724-4079
www.teelauctionservices.com

Theriault's – The Doll Masters
P.O. Box 151
Annapolis, MD 21404
(800) 638-0422
www.theriaults.com

Thomaston Place Auction Galleries
51 Atlantic Hwy.
Thomaston, ME 04861
(207) 354-8141
www.thomastonauction.com

John Toomey Gallery
818 North Blvd.
Oak Park, IL 60301
(708) 383-5234
http://johntoomeygallery.com

Tory Hill Auction Co.
5301 Hillsborough St.
Raleigh, NC 27606
(919) 858-0327
www.toryhillauctions.com

Tradewinds Antiques & Auctions
24 Magnolia Ave.
Manchester-by-the-Sea, MA 01944
(978) 526-4085
www.tradewindsantiques.com

Treadway Gallery, Inc.
2029 Madison Rd.
Cincinnati, OH 45208
www.treadwaygallery.com

Turkey Creek Auctions, Inc.
13939 N. Hwy. 441
Citra, FL 32113
(352) 622-4611
(800) 648-7523
www.antiqueauctionsfl.com

Vero Beach Auction
492 Old Dixie Hwy.
Vero Beach, FL 32962
(772) 978-5955
Fax: (772) 978-5954
www.verobeachauction.com

Victorian Casino Antiques Auction
4520 Arville St., #1
Las Vegas, NV 89103
(702) 382-2466
www.vcaauction.com

Weiderseim Associates, Inc.
PO Box 470
Chester Springs, PA 19425
(610) 827-1910
www.wiederseim.com

Philip Weiss Auctions
74 Merrick Rd.
Lynbrook, NY 11563
(516) 594-0731
www.weissauctions.com

William J. Jenack Estate Appraisers & Auctioneers
62 Kings Highway Bypass
Chester, NY 10918
(877) 282-8503
www.jenack.com

Witherell's Art & Antiques
300 20th St.
Sacramento, CA 95811
(916) 446-6490
witherells.com

Woodbury Auction, LLC
50 Main St. N.
Woodbury, CT 06798
(203) 266-0323
www.woodburyauction.com

Woody Auction
317 S. Forrest St.
Douglass, KS 67039
(316) 747-2694
www.woodyauction.com

Wright
1440 W. Hubbard St.
Chicago, IL 60642
(312) 563-0020
www.wright20.com

Zurko Promotions
115 E. Division St.
Shawano, WI 54166
www.zurkopromotions.com

INDEX